Lecture Notes in Computer Science 1494

Edited by G. Goos, J. Hartmanis and J. van Leeuwen

Springer

Berlin
Heidelberg
New York
Barcelona
Hong Kong
London
Milan
Paris
Singapore
Tokyo

Grzegorz Rozenberg   Frits Vaandrager (Eds.)

Lectures on Embedded Systems

European Educational Forum
School on Embedded Systems
Veldhoven, The Netherlands
November 25-29, 1996

Springer

Series Editors

Gerhard Goos, Karlsruhe University, Germany
Juris Hartmanis, Cornell University, NY, USA
Jan van Leeuwen, Utrecht University, The Netherlands

Volume Editors

Grzegorz Rozenberg
Leiden University, Department of Computer Science
P.O. Box 9512, 2300 RA Leiden, The Netherlands
E-mail: rozenber@wi.leidenuniv.nl

Frits W. Vaandrager
University of Nijmegen, Computing Science Institute
P.O. Box 9010, 6500 GL Nijmegen, The Netherlands
E-mail: Frits.Vaandrager@cs.kun.nl

Cataloging-in-Publication data applied for

Die Deutsche Bibliothek - CIP-Einheitsaufnahme

Lectures on embedded systems / European Educational Forum
School on Embedded Systems, Veldhoven, The Netherlands,
November 25 - 29, 1996. Grzegorz Rozenberg ; Frits Vaandrager
(ed.). - Berlin ; Heidelberg ; New York ; Barcelona ; Budapest ; Hong
Kong ; London ; Milan ; Paris ; Singapore ; Tokyo : Springer, 1998
   (Lecture notes in computer science ; Vol. 1494)
   ISBN 3-540-65193-4

CR Subject Classification (1998): D.4.7, C.3, D.2, J.7, C.1.M, F.3

ISSN 0302-9743
ISBN 3-540-65193-4 Springer-Verlag Berlin Heidelberg New York

© Springer-Verlag Berlin Heidelberg 1998
Printed in Germany

Typesetting: Camera-ready by author
SPIN 10638897   06/3142 – 5 4 3 2 1 0   Printed on acid-free paper

Preface

Embedded systems are computer systems that form an integral part of a larger system like a production cell, a controller for a home heating system, a television set, or an airplane. The term "embedded systems" encompasses thus a broad class of systems, ranging from simple microcontrollers to large and complex multiprocessors and distributed systems. In general engineering terms, embedded systems are used for the control of industrial or physical processes. Sensors continuously gather information from the environment. The service of the embedded system is to process this information and to signal the actuators in accordance with the mechanisms of the controlled process. This means that one can design and reason about embedded systems only if one takes the behavior of their environment into account. In computer science terms, embedded systems are distributed reactive systems. Typically, embedded systems have to react to stimuli from their environment in real-time. This can be highly nontrivial in situations where a lot of signal processing must be carried out on the inputs in order to compute the outputs (e.g., multimedia applications). Consequently, real-time issues often play a major role in the design and analysis of embedded systems.

This volume is based on the lectures presented at the School on Embedded Systems which took place in Veldhoven, The Netherlands, in the period November 25–29, 1996.

The School was the first event organized by the European Educational Forum (EEF) which is a joint initiative of three interuniversity research schools: BRICS (Basic Research In Computer Science) in Denmark, IPA (Institute for Programming research and Algorithmics) in The Netherlands, and TUCS (TUrku centre for Computer Science) in Finland. Altogether, EEF involves 14 universities in Denmark, The Netherlands, and Finland. The common denominator of BRICS, IPA, and TUCS is the training of Ph.D. students and young researchers. The mission of EEF is to organize educational training activities covering a broad spectrum of basic research and its applications directed at this audience.

Apart from papers based on the lectures presented at the School, some other papers have also been included in this volume. In this way, we hope to give a broad and well balanced picture of current research in embedded systems. The material from the School presented in this volume was prepared after the School, so that it also reflects the discussions that took place.

We are grateful to the contributors to this volume for their effort, and to the participants at the School for their enthusiastic and active participation. We also thank the members of the Program Committee for putting together such an interesting program. The members of the Program Committee were: Ralph Back, Ed Brinksma, Dieter Hammer, Kim Larsen, Mogens Nielsen, Kaisa Sere, and Frits Vaandrager (chair).

Finally, we are very much indebted to the management team of IPA, Jos Baeten, Alda Bouten, and Herman Geuvers, for organizing such a successful meeting.

February 1998

G. Rozenberg
F.W. Vaandrager

Table of Contents

Industrial Perspective

Introduction

Frits Vaandrager

Computing Science Institute, University of Nijmegen
P.O. Box 9010, 6500 GL Nijmegen, The Netherlands
fvaan@cs.kun.nl

With the decrease in the size and price of computing elements, more and more computers are used within real-world technical applications such as in avionics, process control, robotics, telecommunications and consumer products. The software within such applications is called "embedded" since it determines to a large extent the functionality of the product; the software and the rest of the product have no meaning without each other. Characteristics of these applications are:

- Complex interaction with environment. One can only design and reason about embedded systems if one takes the behavior of their environment into account. Frequently this environment is highly nondeterministic and intrinsically continuous. Moreover the rate at which input signals arrive is often enormous and signal processing and information filtering become key issues.
- High dependability requirements. Besides functional constraints many other aspects play a role in the design of embedded systems: timeliness, fault tolerance, availability, security, safety, etc.

In recent years there has been a dramatic growth of the number of embedded applications and of the size and complexity of the software used in these applications. For many products in the area of consumer electronics the amount of code is doubling every two years. As a result, for instance, a high-end television today contains about 1.4M of software and a GSM phone 2M of software. The number of microprocessors that we encounter daily in our lives has increased from 2 in 1985 to 50 in 1995. In 1994, a group of experts estimated that the number of software engineers who design and write embedded software will increase from 2 million in 1994 to 10 million in 2004. Indeed, embedded software is the fastest increasing area of information technology, with the exception of the "intermittent programming" by non-software professionals.

The construction of large real-time embedded computer systems is one of the most challenging tasks facing the computer science community, if not the engineering community as a whole, and raises important questions to both science and technology in areas such as extended product lifecycle, product families, interaction with the environment, productivity, and dependability. The objective of the School on Embedded Systems was to give young researchers a good feeling for the practical problems that arise during the construction of embedded systems, and an overview of some important methods and techniques that may help to address these problems. Amongst the lecturers at the School there was agreement that there are many architectural and algorithmic problems in the area of embedded systems that have well documented optimal or correct solutions, notably in the areas of real-time computing, distributed computing, and fault-tolerant computing. However, only a small subset of these solutions have so far translated into commercial, off-the-shelf products or operational computer-base systems. We already have plenty of theoretical results, what we need now is making these work in large-scale applications.

Formal Models and Analysis Within Computer Science enormous progress has been made during the last decade in the area of formal models that support analysis of embedded systems. A hierarchy of three (types of) models, each extending its predecessor, has been developed:

- *Reactive system* models that capture the *qualitative* temporal precedence aspect of time. These models can only identify that one event precedes another but not by how much.
- *Real-time system* models that capture the *metric* aspect of time in a reactive system. These models can measure the time elapsing between two events.
- *Hybrid system* models that allow the inclusion of *continuous* components in a reactive real-time system. Such continuous components may cause continuous change in the values of some state variables according to some physical or control law.

Building on their earlier work on reactive system models, *Kesten, Manna and Pnueli* give a detailed exposition of a state-of-the-art computational model for real-time and hybrid systems (the "clocked transition system (CTS) model"). They discuss requirement specification and system description languages based on this model, and proof rules by which valid properties of systems can be verified, showing that systems satisfy their specifications. *Branicky* studies real-world hybrid control systems from the perspective of Control Theory and introduces a mathematical model of them. Based on this model stability properties of hybrid systems can be analyzed, and optimal hybrid control systems can be synthesized. *Yovine* presents a survey of the different algorithms, data-structures and tools that have been proposed in the literature to solve reachability questions for real-time systems.

Real-time Systems One of the fundamental problems in real-time research is to devise accurate yet tractable models for real-time tasks. *Chen, Mok and Baruah* try to organize different models and their feasibility difficulties into a uniformed structure. Their paper covers probably the most general Liu&Layland-type real-time scheduling model to-date.

Traditional approaches to the design and implementation of real-time embedded applications transfer timing requirements into machine dependent operations using low level programming languages, such as Assembly or C. This approach reduces the modularity and reusability of software components. In order to address these difficulties, *Ren and Agha* develop a high-level language approach (the "RTsynchronizer") to support a stronger separation of design concerns.

Development and Engineering In his important contribution, *Le Lann* argues that system engineering rather than software engineering currently is the weakest (i.e., least rigorous) of all those engineering disciplines covered by what the IEEE Computer Society refers to as the Engineering of Computer-Based Systems. He introduces some basic principles that underlie proof-based system engineering, a discipline which serves to avoid system engineering faults. An analysis of the Ariane 5 Flight 501 failure serves to illustrate how proof-based system engineering also helps in diagnosing causes of failures.

In traditional design methodologies, the system designer typically develops the application in a sequential paradigm almost to completion before addressing issues of parallelism and mapping to a heterogeneous architecture. As the architectural complexity of these applications increase (which is often the case for embedded applications) this process becomes too costly since implementation must be started anew after the design. *Bhatt and Shackleton* present a new methodology and toolset aimed at addressing this problem and at improving the system development process for high-performance embedded applications.

Van den Hoogenhof examines some important techniques and constructions used in the mainstream object-oriented software engineering methodologies, and elaborates on their common properties and weaknesses in practical use. He concludes that the maturity of methodologies is only partially reflected by their properties. Perhaps the main problem is the attitude of software engineers who reflect their failures on the methodologies rather than taking the full responsibility themselves. *Kuusela* presents an overview of OCTOPUS, a software development method for embedded real-time systems that has been developed and is used by Nokia.

Case Studies This volume includes three case studies in which formal methods are applied in the development of realistic embedded applications. *Ravn, Eriksen, Holdgaard and Rischel* use Duration Calculus to develop a multi-threaded, multiprocessor control program for a robot. *Kars* uses the SPIN tool set and Z to formally specify and analyze a storm barrier control system. Finally, *Douglas, Harel and Trakhtenbrot* describe the use of statecharts for the specification of a cardiac pacemaker.

Industrial Perspective In his contribution, *Bourgonjon* discusses some impressive statistics that illustrate the increasing use of embedded software in electronic consumer products. *Van Rietschote* presents Telecommunication Applications as the largest, most complex embedded software applications in the world today, and discusses what Computer Science research could do for enabling programming large and complex embedded systems. *Veltmaat* describes the realistic side of embedded software development at ICT Automatisering, one of the largest embedded software development companies in the Netherlands, and discusses rules of conduct and possible ways to improve the cooperation between the software industry and the scientific community.

Verification of Clocked and Hybrid Systems[*]

Yonit Kesten[†]   Zohar Manna[‡]   Amir Pnueli[†]

Abstract. This paper presents a new computational model for real-time systems, called the *clocked transition system* (CTS) model. The CTS model is a development of our previous *timed transition* model, where some of the changes are inspired by the model of *timed automata*. The new model leads to a simpler style of temporal specification and verification, requiring no extension of the temporal language. We present verification rules for proving safety properties (including time-bounded response properties) of clocked transition systems, and separate rules for proving (time-unbounded) response properties. All rules are associated with verification diagrams. The verification of *response* properties requires adjustments of the proof rules developed for untimed systems, reflecting the fact that progress in the real time systems is ensured by the progress of time and not by fairness. The style of the verification rules is very close to the verification style of untimed systems which allows the (re)use of verification methods and tools, developed for untimed reactive systems, for proving all interesting properties of real-time systems.

We conclude with the presentation of a branching-time based approach for verifying that an arbitrary given CTS is *non-zeno*.

Finally, we present an extension of the model and the invariance proof rule for hybrid systems.

Table of Contents

---

[*] This research was supported in part by the National Science Foundation under grant CCR-95-27927, the Defense Advanced Research Projects Agency under NASA grant NAG2-892, ARO under grant DAAH04-95-1-0317, ARO under MURI grant DAAH04-96-1-0341, by Army contract DABT63-96-C-0096 (DARPA), by a basic research grant from the Israeli Academy of Sciences, and by the European Community ESPRIT Basic Research Action Project 6021 (REACT).   Preliminary versions of some parts of this paper appeared in [KMP95] and [MP95a].

[†] Department of Computer Science, Weizmann Institute, Rehovot, Israel, e-mail: `amir@wisdom.weizmann.ac.il`

[‡] Department of Computer Science, Stanford University, Stanford, CA 94305, e-mail: `manna@cs.stanford.edu`

1 Introduction

A formal framework for specifying and verifying temporal properties of reactive systems often contains the following components:

- A *computational model* defining the set of behaviors (computations) that are to be associated with systems in the considered model.
- A *requirement specification* language for specifying properties of systems within the model. The languages we have considered in our previous work are all variants of temporal logic extended to deal with various aspects specific to the considered model, such as real-time and continuously changing variables.
- A *system description* language for describing systems within the model. We frequently use both a textual programming language and appropriate extensions of the graphical language of statecharts [Har87] to present systems.
- A set of *proof rules* by which valid properties of systems can be verified, showing that the systems satisfy their specifications.
- A set of *algorithmic methods* enabling a fully automatic verification of decidable subclasses of the verification problem such as the verification of finite-state systems (*model checking*).

In [MP93a], we considered a hierarchy of three models, each extending its predecessor, as follows:

- A *reactive systems* model that captures the *qualitative* (non-quantitative) temporal precedence aspect of time. This model can only identify that one event precedes another but not by how much.
- A *real-time systems* model that captures the *metric* aspect of time in a reactive system. This model can measure the time elapsing between two events.
- A *hybrid systems* model that allows the inclusion of *continuous* components in a reactive real-time system. Such continuous components may cause continuous change in the values of some state variables according to some physical or control law.

The computational model proposed for reactive systems is that of a *fair transition system* (FTS) [MP91b].

The approach to real time presented in [MP93a] and [HMP94] is based on the computational model of *timed transition systems* (TTS) in which time itself is not explicitly represented but is reflected in a time stamp affixed to each state in a computation of a TTS.

In this paper we present a new computational model for real-time systems: *clocked transition system* (CTS). This model represents time by a set of clocks (timers) which increase uniformly whenever time progresses, but can be set to arbitrary values by system (program) transitions. The CTS model can be viewed as a natural first-order extension of the timed automata model [AD94].

It is easy and natural to stipulate that one of the clocks T is never reset. In this case, T represents the *master clock* measuring real time from the beginning of the computation. This immediately yields the possibility of specifying timing properties of systems by unextended temporal logic, which may refer to any of the system variables, including the master clock T.

Consider, for example, the following two important timed properties:

- *Bounded response*: Every p should be followed by an occurrence of a q, not later than d time units.
- *Minimal separation*: No q can occur earlier than d time units after an occurrence of p.

Within the CTS computational model, these two yardstick properties can be specified by the following (unextended) temporal formulas:

- Bounded response: $p \,\wedge\, (T = t_0) \quad \Rightarrow \quad \Diamond(q \,\wedge\, T \leq t_0 + d)$.
- Minimal separation: $p \,\wedge\, (T = t_0) \quad \Rightarrow \quad \Box(T < t_0 + d \,\rightarrow\, \neg q)$.

The new computational model has several advantages over previous models such as the model of *timed transition systems* (TTS, see [HMP94]).

The first advantage of the new model, as shown above, is that it leads to a more natural style of specification, explicitly referring to clocks, which are just another kind of system variables, instead of introducing special new constructs, such as the *bounded temporal operators* proposed in *metric temporal logic* (MTL) (see [KVdR83], [KdR85], and [Koy90]) or the *age function* proposed in [MP93a].

A second advantage of the CTS model is that we can reuse many of the methods and tools developed for verifying untimed reactive systems (e.g. [MP95b]) for verifying real-time systems under the CTS model. The move from TTS to CTS brings us closer to the approach proposed in [AL94], which also recommends handling real time with a minimal extension of the reactive-systems formalism.

The model of Clocked Transition Systems, as presented in this paper, has been successfully implemented in the *Stanford Temporal Verifier* support system STeP[BBC+95]. We refer the reader to the paper [BMSU97] which uses clocked transition systems to model and verify the generalized railroad crossing benchmark problem.

A model similar to the CTS model presented here was introduced in [AH94], and proof rules for establishing response properties for this model were presented in [HK94]. However, the response verification rules presented there for the general case were based on consideration of the region graph associated with timed automata which, in many cases, becomes very big. Our approach to response verification, while considering the general case, does not refer to the region graph and can be viewed as a natural modification of the response rules for untimed fair transition systems, except that the notion of fairness is replaced by the guaranteed progress of time.

We refer the reader to [AH89], [Ost90], [AL94], and the survey in [AH92], for additional logics, models, and approaches to the verification of real-time systems. In the process algebra school, some of the representative approaches to real time are [NSY92], [MT90], and many others are listed in [Sif91].

The paper is organized as follows. In Section 2, we present the real-time computational model of *clocked transition systems* (CTS). In Section 3, we show how programs augmented with timing bounds for the execution of statements can be represented as clocked transition systems. In Section 4, we present rules and verification diagrams for verifying safety properties of CTS's. In Section 5, we present rules and verification diagrams for establishing response properties of clocked transition systems. In Section 6, we present an approach to verifying that a given CTS is non-zeno. Finally, in Section 7, we present the extension of the CTS model to deal with general hybrid systems. This yields an extended model to which we refer as a *phase transition system*. A proof rule for verifying safety properties of hybrid systems is introduced and illustrated.

A part of an ongoing research has implemented support for phase transition systems in STeP, and has used it to successfully (and actually without too much user interaction) verify a few of the HyTech examples [HHWT95].

Preliminary versions of some parts of this paper appeared in [MP95a] and [KMP96].

2 Real-Time Systems

We now introduce a computational model for real-time systems.

2.1 Computational Model: Clocked Transition System

Real-time systems are modeled as *clocked transition systems* (CTS). A clocked transition system $\Phi = \langle V, \Theta, \mathcal{T}, \Pi \rangle$ consists of:

- V : A finite set of *system variables*. The set $V = D \cup C$ is partitioned into $D = \{u_1, \ldots, u_n\}$ the set of *discrete variables* and $C = \{c_1, \ldots, c_k\}$ the set of *clocks*. Clocks always have the type *real*. The discrete variables can be of any type. We introduce a special clock $T \in C$, representing the *master clock*, as one of the system variables.
- Θ : The *initial condition*. A satisfiable assertion characterizing the initial states. It is required that

$$\Theta \quad \rightarrow \quad T = 0,$$

  i.e., $T = 0$ at all initial states.
- $\mathcal{T}$: A finite set of *transitions*. Each transition $\tau \in \mathcal{T}$ is a function

$$\tau : \Sigma \mapsto 2^{\Sigma},$$

  mapping each state $s \in \Sigma$ into a (possibly empty) set of τ-*successor* states $\tau(s) \subseteq \Sigma$.

  The function associated with a transition τ is represented by an assertion $\rho_\tau(V, V')$, called the *transition relation*, which relates a state $s \in \Sigma$ to its τ-successor $s' \in \tau(s)$ by referring to both unprimed and primed versions of the system variables. An unprimed version of a system variable refers to its value in s, while a primed version of the same variable refers to its value in s'. For example, the assertion $x' = x + 1$ states that the value of x in s' is greater by 1 than its value in s.

  For every $\tau \in \mathcal{T}$, it is required that

$$\rho_\tau \quad \rightarrow \quad T' = T,$$

  i.e., the master clock is modified by no transition.
- Π : The *time-progress condition*. An assertion over V. The assertion is used to specify a global restriction over the progress of time.

Extended Transitions

Let $\Phi : \langle V, \Theta, \mathcal{T}, \Pi \rangle$ be a clocked transition system. We define the set of *extended transitions* $\mathcal{T}_T$ associated with Φ as follows:

$$\mathcal{T}_T = \mathcal{T} \cup \{tick\}.$$

Transition *tick* is a special transition intended to represent the passage of time. Its transition relation is given by:

$$\rho_{tick}: \quad \exists \Delta.\, \Omega(\Delta) \,\wedge\, D' = D \,\wedge\, C' = C + \Delta,$$

where $\Omega(\Delta)$ is given by

$$\Omega(\Delta): \quad \Delta > 0 \ \wedge \ \forall t \in [0, \Delta). \ \Pi(D, C + t).$$

Let $D = \{u_1, \ldots, u_m\}$ be the set of discrete variables of Φ and $C = \{c_1, \ldots, c_k\}$ be the set of its clocks. Then, the expression $C' = C + \Delta$ is an abbreviation for

$$c_1' = c_1 + \Delta \ \wedge \ \cdots \ \wedge \ c_k' = c_k + \Delta,$$

and $\Pi(D, C + t)$ is an abbreviation for $\Pi(u_1, \ldots, u_m, c_1 + t, \ldots, c_k + t)$.

Runs and Computations

Let $\Phi : \langle V, \Theta, \mathcal{T}, \Pi \rangle$ be a clocked transition system. A *run* of Φ is a finite or infinite sequence of states $\sigma : s_0, s_1, \ldots$ satisfying:

- *Initiation*: $s_0 \models \Theta$
- *Consecution*: For each $j \in [0, |\sigma|)$ $s_{j+1} \in \tau(s_j)$, for some $\tau \in \mathcal{T}_T$.

A state is called (Φ-)*accessible* if it appears in a run of Φ.

A *computation* of Φ is an infinite run satisfying:

- *Time Divergence:* The sequence $s_0[T], s_1[T], \ldots$ grows beyond any bound. That is, as i increases, the value of T at s_i increases beyond any bound.

A Frequently Occurring Case

In many cases, the time-progress condition Π has the following special form

$$\Pi: \quad \bigwedge_{i \in I} (p_i \to c_i < E_i),$$

where I is some finite index set and, for each $i \in I$, the assertion p_i and the real-valued expression E_i do not depend on the clocks, and $c_i \in C$ is some clock. This is, for example, the form of the time-progress condition for any CTS representing a real-time program. For such cases, the time-increment limiting formula $\Omega(\Delta)$ can be significantly simplified and assumes the following form:

$$\Omega(\Delta): \quad \Delta > 0 \ \wedge \ \bigwedge_{i \in I} (p_i \to c_i + \Delta \leq E_i)$$

Note, in particular, that this simpler form does not use quantifications over t.

Non-Zeno Systems

A CTS is defined to be *non-zeno* if every finite run can be extended into a computation (see [AL94], [Hen92]). An equivalent formulation is that Φ is non-zeno if it satisfies

A finite sequence σ is a run of Φ iff σ is a prefix of some computation of Φ.

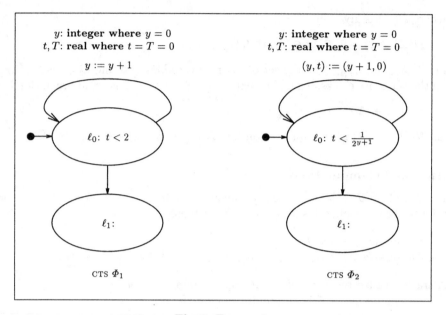

Fig. 1. Two CTS's.

A consequence of Φ being non-zeno is that a state s is Φ-accessible iff it appears in some computation of Φ.

Example 1.   Consider the CTS's Φ_1 and Φ_2 presented in Fig 1. In Fig 2, we present these two CTS's in textual form. The predicate $pres(y, t, T)$ is an abbreviation for the assertion

$$pres(y, t, T): \quad y' = y \ \wedge \ t' = t \ \wedge \ T' = T,$$

stating that y, t, and T, are preserved by the transition.

It is not difficult to establish that both Φ_1 and Φ_2 are non-zeno CTS's. This is because, from any accessible state, we can always move to state ℓ_1 from which we can continue to take infinitely many time steps with increment 1.

The *tick* transitions for these two CTS's are given by

$$\rho^1_{tick}: \exists \Delta > 0. \, pres(\pi, y) \wedge (t', T') = (t + \Delta, T + \Delta) \wedge (\pi = 0 \rightarrow t + \Delta \leq 2)$$
$$\rho^2_{tick}: \exists \Delta > 0. \, pres(\pi, y) \wedge (t', T') = (t + \Delta, T + \Delta) \wedge (\pi = 0 \rightarrow t + \Delta \leq \tfrac{1}{2^y+1}).$$

$V: \underbrace{\{\pi\colon \{0,1\}; y\colon \mathbf{integer}\}}_{D} \cup \underbrace{\{t,T\colon \mathbf{real}\}}_{C}$	$V: \underbrace{\{\pi\colon \{0,1\}; y\colon \mathbf{integer}\}}_{D} \cup \underbrace{\{t,T\colon \mathbf{real}\}}_{C}$
$\Theta: \pi = y = t = T = 0$	$\Theta: \pi = y = t = T = 0$
$\mathcal{T}: \{\tau_0, \tau_1\}$ with transition relations	$\mathcal{T}: \{\tau_0, \tau_1\}$ with transition relations
$\quad \tau_0: \pi = \pi' = 0 \wedge y' = y+1$	$\quad \tau_0: \pi = \pi' = t' = 0 \wedge y' = y+1$
$\quad\quad\quad\quad\quad\quad\quad \wedge pres(t,T)$	$\quad\quad\quad\quad\quad\quad\quad \wedge pres(T)$
$\quad \tau_1: \pi = 0 \wedge \pi' = 1 \wedge pres(y,t,T)$	$\quad \tau_1: \pi = 0 \wedge \pi' = 1 \wedge pres(y,t,T)$
$\Pi: \pi = 0 \rightarrow t < 2$	$\Pi: \pi = 0 \rightarrow t < \frac{1}{2^y+1}$
CTS Φ_1	CTS Φ_2

Fig. 2. The two CTS's in textual form.

Following is a computation of CTS Φ_1:

$$\langle \pi\colon 0\,,\, y\colon 0\,,\, t\colon 0\,,\, T\colon 0 \rangle \xrightarrow{tick(1)} \langle \pi\colon 0\,,\, y\colon 0\,,\, t\colon 1\,,\, T\colon 1 \rangle \xrightarrow{\tau_0},$$
$$\langle \pi\colon 0\,,\, y\colon 1\,,\, t\colon 1\,,\, T\colon 1 \rangle \xrightarrow{\tau_0} \langle \pi\colon 0\,,\, y\colon 2\,,\, t\colon 1\,,\, T\colon 1 \rangle \xrightarrow{tick(1)}$$
$$\langle \pi\colon 0\,,\, y\colon 2\,,\, t\colon 2\,,\, T\colon 2 \rangle \xrightarrow{\tau_0} \langle \pi\colon 0\,,\, y\colon 3\,,\, t\colon 2\,,\, T\colon 2 \rangle \xrightarrow{\tau_0},$$
$$\langle \pi\colon 0\,,\, y\colon 4\,,\, t\colon 2\,,\, T\colon 2 \rangle \xrightarrow{\tau_1} \langle \pi\colon 1\,,\, y\colon 4\,,\, t\colon 2\,,\, T\colon 2 \rangle \xrightarrow{tick(1)}$$
$$\langle \pi\colon 1\,,\, y\colon 4\,,\, t\colon 3\,,\, T\colon 3 \rangle \xrightarrow{tick(1)} \langle \pi\colon 1\,,\, y\colon 4\,,\, t\colon 4\,,\, T\colon 4 \rangle \xrightarrow{tick(1)}$$
$$\cdots$$

Note that to be a computation, time must grow beyond any bounds. Since, at location ℓ_0 of CTS time cannot grow beyond 2, any computation of Φ_1 must eventually move to location ℓ_1, where time can grow beyond any bounds. ⌐

3 Programs as Clocked Transition Systems

In this section we show how to represent real-time programs as clocked transition systems.

In [MP91b], we introduced a simple programming language SPL. Here we consider a subset of the language, restricting our attention to the following statements:

skip, assignment, await, noncritical, critical, conditional, concatenation, selection, while, and *block.*

Not including the *cooperation* statement has the effect that parallelism is allowed only at the top level of the program. That is, a program is a parallel composition of processes, each of which is sequential.

We refer the reader to Chapter 0 of [MP95b] for the construction of a fair transition system $\mathcal{F}_P$ corresponding to an SPL program P. This construction introduces an explicit control variable π which ranges over sets of locations. System

$\mathcal{F}_P$ associates a single transition with each *executable* statement, which includes all statements except *concatenation*, *selection*, and *block*. Here, we deviate from the construction of [MP95b] in the transitions associated with the *await* and the *noncritical* statements. Instead, we associate with each statement of the form

$\ell:$ **await** $c;$ $\widehat{\ell}:$

a transition τ_ℓ, whose transition relation ρ_ℓ is given by

$$\rho_\ell: \quad \ell \in \pi \wedge \begin{pmatrix} c \wedge \pi' = \pi - \{\ell\} \cup \{\widehat{\ell}\} \\ \vee \\ \neg c \wedge \pi' = \pi \end{pmatrix} \wedge pres(V - \{\pi\}).$$

The reason for this change is that the new definition makes the *await* transition enabled once control reaches ℓ. Therefore, within a time lying between L and U, it will be taken. When taken, control either moves from ℓ to $\widehat{\ell}$ (if c is true) or remains in place. In any case, the clock associated with this statement will be reset. In the old transition relation associated with the *await* statement, the transition was disabled as long as c is false. Consequently, if c is false for more than U time units, time cannot advance beyond U and the transition cannot be taken. This would have caused the whole system to deadlock while blocking the progress of time.

With each statement of the form

$\ell:$ **noncritical** $;$ $\widehat{\ell}:$

we associate a transition τ_ℓ, whose transition relation ρ_ℓ is given by

$$\rho_\ell: \quad \ell \in \pi \wedge \left(\pi' = \pi - \{\ell\} \cup \{\widehat{\ell}\} \vee \pi' = \pi \right) \wedge pres(V - \{\pi\}).$$

This modified transition relation allows a process to remain forever in its non-critical section even when we impose the uniform upper bound u_s on the execution of all statements.

For all other statements (excluding the *await* statement), we follow [MP95b] in the association of transitions with executable statements.

Another difference from [MP95b] is that we only associate transitions with the executable statements and do not standardly include the idling transition τ_I.

Let P be an SPL program. To obtain a real-time program, we associate with each S, an executable statement of P, a pair of values $[l_s, u_s]$, called the *lower* and *upper* bounds of S. These values, satisfying $0 \leq l_s \leq u_s \leq \infty$, are intended to provide a lower and upper bound on the length of time the statement can be enabled without being taken. We refer to a program with an assignment of time bounds as an SPL_T program, and view it as a real-time program.

Note that assigning time bounds to each executable statement of P is equivalent to assigning time bounds $[l_\tau, u_\tau]$ to each transition τ associated with an executable statement.

For locations ℓ_i, ℓ_j, and ℓ_k, we denote:

$$at\_\ell_i \quad : \ell_i \in \pi$$
$$at\_\ell_{j,k} : at\_\ell_j \vee at\_\ell_k$$

3.1 The CTS corresponding to an SPL$_T$ program

Let P be an SPL$_T$ program. That is, an SPL program with time bounds $[l_\tau, u_\tau]$ associated with each transition $\tau \in \mathcal{T}_P - \{\tau_I\}$. We will show how to construct a CTS Φ_P corresponding to the SPL$_T$ program P.

As a first step, we construct the FTS $\mathcal{F}_P : \langle V, \Theta, \mathcal{T}, \mathcal{J}, \mathcal{C} \rangle$ corresponding to program P. Note that if program P uses only the statements in the previously presented subset, then we can take $\mathcal{J} = \mathcal{T} - \{\tau_I\}$ and $\mathcal{C} = \emptyset$. Assume that program P is a parallel composition of m processes. That is, P has the form

$$\text{declarations;} \quad P_1 \parallel \cdots \parallel P_m,$$

where each P_i is a (sequential) statement, called a *process*.

The CTS corresponding to P is given by $\Phi_P : \langle \widetilde{V}, \widetilde{\Theta}, \widetilde{\mathcal{T}}, \Pi \rangle$, where

- *System Variables:* $\widetilde{V} = V \cup \{t_1, \ldots, t_m, T\}$.
  Thus, $\widetilde{V}$ consists of the system variables of $\mathcal{F}_P$, to which we add $m+1$ clocks, one clock t_i for each process P_i, $i = 1, \ldots, m$, plus the master clock T.
- *Initial Condition:* $\widetilde{\Theta}$: $\Theta \wedge t_1 = \cdots = t_m = T = 0$.
- *Transitions:* $\widetilde{\mathcal{T}} : \{\widetilde{\tau} \mid \tau \in \mathcal{T} - \{\tau_I\}\}$.
  Let $\tau \in \mathcal{T} - \{\tau_I\}$ be a transition corresponding to an executable statement in process P_i. The transition relation for transition $\widetilde{\tau}$ is given by:

  $$\widetilde{\rho_\tau}: \quad \rho_\tau \wedge t_i \geq l_\tau \wedge t_i' = 0 \wedge pres(t_1, \ldots, t_{i-1}, t_{i+1}, \ldots, t_m, T).$$

  Thus, the transition can be taken only when t_i, the clock corresponding to process P_i, is not below l_τ, the lower bound associated with τ. When taken, the transition resets clock t_i to 0.
- *Time-progress condition Π:* For each executable statement

  $$\ell : S$$

  in process P_i, Π includes the conjunct

  $$\ell \in \pi \quad \rightarrow \quad t_i < u_s,$$

  where u_s is the upper bound associated with statement S. This ensures that control cannot wait at location ℓ for more than u_s without the transition associated with S (or another transition causing control to move away from ℓ) being taken.

Note that the lower bounds of statements are added as constraints to transitions, while the upper bounds are added as constraints to the time-progress condition Π.

Example 2. Figure 3 presents a simple program consisting of two processes communicating by the shared variable x.

To make it an SPL$_T$ program, we uniformly associate each of its executable statements with the time bounds $[3, 5]$. The CTS $\Phi_{\text{ANY-Y}_{[3,5]}}$ associated with ANY-Y$_{[3,5]}$ is defined as follows:

$$\boxed{\begin{array}{c} x, y: \textbf{ integer where } x = y = 0 \\[2mm] \begin{bmatrix} \ell_0 : \textbf{while } x = 0 \textbf{ do} \\ \quad \ell_1 : \ y := y + 1 \\ \ell_2 : \end{bmatrix} \quad \Big\| \quad \begin{bmatrix} m_0 : x := 1 \\ m_1 : \end{bmatrix} \\[3mm] -\ \ P_1\ \ - \qquad\qquad -\ \ P_2\ \ - \end{array}}$$

Fig. 3. Program ANY-Y.

- *System Variables:* $V = \{\pi, x, y, t_1, t_2, T\}$. In addition to the control variable π and data variables x and y, the system variables also include clock t_1, measuring delays in process P_1, clock t_2, measuring delays in process P_2, and the master clock T, measuring time from the beginning of the computation.
- *Initial Condition:*

$$\Theta : \quad \pi = \{\ell_0, m_0\} \wedge x = y = 0 \wedge t_1 = t_2 = T = 0.$$

- *Transitions:* $\mathcal{T} : \{\ell_0, \ell_1, m_0\}$ with transition relations:

$$\rho_{\ell_0} : \ \ell_0 \in \pi \ \wedge \begin{pmatrix} x = 0 \ \wedge \ \pi' = \pi - \{\ell_0\} \cup \{\ell_1\} \\ \vee \\ x \neq 0 \ \wedge \ \pi' = \pi - \{\ell_0\} \cup \{\ell_2\} \end{pmatrix} \wedge t_1 \geq 3 \wedge t_1' = 0$$
$$\wedge \ pres(\{x, y, t_2, T\})$$

$$\rho_{\ell_1} : \ \ell_1 \in \pi \wedge \pi' = \pi - \{\ell_1\} \cup \{\ell_0\} \wedge y' = y + 1 \wedge t_1 \geq 3 \wedge t_1' = 0$$
$$\wedge \ pres(\{x, t_2, T\})$$

$$\rho_{m_0} : m_0 \in \pi \wedge \pi' = \pi - \{m_0\} \cup \{m_1\} \wedge x' = 1 \wedge t_2 \geq 3 \wedge t_2' = 0$$
$$\wedge \ pres(\{y, t_1, T\}).$$

- *Time-progress condition:*

$$\Pi : \quad (at\_\ell_{0,1} \ \rightarrow \ t_1 < 5) \wedge (at\_m_0 \ \rightarrow \ t_2 < 5)$$

The *tick* transition relation for this system is given by

$$\rho_{tick}: \quad \exists \Delta > 0. \ pres(\pi, x, y) \ \wedge \ (t_1', t_2', T') = (t_1 + \Delta, t_2 + \Delta, T + \Delta) \ \wedge$$
$$(at\_\ell_{0,1} \ \rightarrow \ t_1 + \Delta \leq 5) \wedge (at\_m_0 \ \rightarrow \ t_2 + \Delta \leq 5) \quad \lrcorner$$

3.2 Specification Language

To specify properties of reactive systems, we use the language of temporal logic, as presented in [MP91b]. Here, we only use the following:

- *State formulas* (*assertions*) - any first-order formula, possibly including at_ℓ expressions

- $\Box\, p$ — Always p, where p is an assertion. We refer to such a formula as an *invariance formula*.
- $p \Rightarrow (q\,\mathcal{W}\,r)$ — p entails q waiting for r, where p, q, and r are assertions. We refer to such a formula as a *waiting-for formula*.
- $p \Rightarrow \Diamond\, r$ — p entails eventually r, where p and r are assertions. We refer to such a formula as a *response formula*.

For a state s and assertion p, we write $s \models p$ to indicate that p holds (is true) over s. Let $\sigma : s_0, s_1 \ldots$ be an infinite sequence of states, to which we refer as a *model*. For an assertion p, we say that $j \geq 0$, is a *p-position* if $s_j \models p$. Satisfaction of (the three considered) temporal formulas over a model σ is defined as follows:

- A model σ satisfies the invariance formula $\Box\, p$, written $\sigma \models \Box\, p$, if all positions within σ are p-positions.
- A model σ satisfies the waiting-for formula $p \Rightarrow (q\,\mathcal{W}\,r)$, written $\sigma \models p \Rightarrow (q\,\mathcal{W}\,r)$, if every p-position i within σ initiates an interval of positions, all of which satisfy q. This continuous-q interval can either extend to infinity or terminate in an r-position which is not in the interval. That is,

$$\sigma[i] \models p \text{ implies } \sigma[j] \models q \text{ for all } j \geq i, \text{ or}$$
$$\sigma[k] \models r \text{ for some } k \geq i \text{ and } \sigma[j] \models q \text{ for all } j, i \leq j < k.$$

- A model σ satisfies the response formula $p \Rightarrow \Diamond\, r$, written $\sigma \models p \Rightarrow \Diamond\, r$, if every p-position i within σ is followed by an r-position $j \geq i$.

A temporal formula φ is said to be *valid over* CTS Φ (or *Φ-valid*) if $\sigma \models \varphi$ for every computation σ of Φ. We write $\Phi \models \varphi$ to indicate this fact. An assertion p is called *Φ-state valid* if it holds at every Φ-accessible state. We write $\Phi \Vvdash p$ to indicate that assertion p is Φ-state valid.

In the case that CTS Φ is derived from an SPL$_T$ program P, we use the terms *P-valid*, *P-state valid*, and *P-accessible* as synonymous to Φ_P-valid, Φ_P-state valid, and Φ_P-accessible. We also write $P \models \varphi$ and $P \Vvdash p$ to denote $\Phi_P \models \varphi$ and $\Phi_P \Vvdash p$, respectively.

4   Verifying Safety Properties of Clocked Transition Systems

In this section, we present methods for verifying safety properties of clocked transitions systems.

4.1   The Invariance Rule

As is explained in [MP91b], the properties expressible by temporal logic can be arranged in a hierarchy that identifies different classes of properties according to the form of formulas expressing them.

Here we consider *invariance* properties, namely, properties that can be expressed by the formula $\Box\, p$, for some assertion p.

The Accessibility Rule

As a preliminary step, we introduce a rule that establishes the Φ-state validity of an assertion p. This is rule ACC, presented in Fig. 4.

For assertions φ and p,

      A1. $\varphi \rightarrow p$

      A2. $\Theta \rightarrow \varphi$

      A3. $\rho_\tau \wedge \varphi \rightarrow \varphi'$ for every $\tau \in \mathcal{T}_T$

         $\Phi \models p$

Fig. 4. Rule ACC (Φ-state validity of assertion p).

The rule uses an auxiliary assertion φ. Premise A1 of rule ACC requires that the auxiliary assertion φ implies assertion p, whose Φ-state validity we wish to prove. Premise A2 of the rule requires that Θ, the initial condition of P, implies the auxiliary assertion φ. Premise A3 requires that all transitions in $\mathcal{T}_T^\Phi$ (extended transitions of Φ) preserve φ. Premises A2 and A3 state that φ holds at the initial state of every run and that it propagates from any state to its τ-successor, for every transition $\tau \in \mathcal{T}_T$ of the system. Thus, every state in each run of Φ satisfies φ. Due to the implication A1, every such state also satisfies p. It follows that p holds on every accessible state of system Φ and, therefore, assertion p is Φ-state valid.

Rule INV

Assume that we have shown that assertion p is Φ-state valid, i.e., every accessible state of Φ satisfies p. Since all states appearing in a computation are accessible (every computation is a run), all states in every computation satisfy p. It follows that every computation of Φ satisfies $\square\, p$. Thus, we may use the premises of rule ACC to establish that the temporal formula $\square\, p$ is Φ-valid. Consequently, we propose rule INV, presented in Fig. 5, as the main tool for verifying invariance properties of a CTS Φ.

Example 3. We use rule INV to establish the invariance of the assertion

    p: $at\_\ell_{0,1} \vee at\_m_1$

over program ANY-Y$_{[3,5]}$ (Fig. 3). This assertion claims that, at every state in the execution of program ANY-Y$_{[3,5]}$, either control of process P_1 is at ℓ_0 or ℓ_1, or control of P_2 is at m_1. In particular, it implies that if P_1 is at ℓ_2 then P_2 has already arrived in m_1.

For assertions φ and p,

      I1. $\varphi \rightarrow p$

      I2. $\Theta \rightarrow \varphi$

      I3. $\rho_\tau \wedge \varphi \rightarrow \varphi'$ for every $\tau \in \mathcal{T}_T$

      $\Phi \models \Box p$

Fig. 5. Rule INV (invariance) applied to CTS Φ.

We apply rule INV to this choice of p, taking

φ: $(x = 0 \wedge at\_\ell_{0,1}) \vee at\_m_1$

as the auxiliary assertion.

Premise I1 assumes the form

$$\underbrace{(x = 0 \wedge at\_\ell_{0,1}) \vee at\_m_1}_{\varphi} \quad \rightarrow \quad \underbrace{at\_\ell_{0,1} \vee at\_m_1}_{p},$$

which is obviously valid.

Premise I2 assumes the form

$$\underbrace{\pi = \{\ell_0, m_0\} \wedge x = 0 \wedge \cdots}_{\Theta} \quad \rightarrow \quad \underbrace{(x = 0 \wedge at\_\ell_{0,1}) \vee \cdots}_{\varphi}$$

which is obviously valid.

Premise I3 has to be checked for each $\tau \in \{\ell_0, \ell_1, m_0, tick\}$. For example, premise I3 for ℓ_0 assumes the form

$$\left(\begin{array}{l} \cdots \wedge \underbrace{\left(\begin{array}{c} x = 0 \wedge \pi' = \pi - \{\ell_0\} \cup \{\ell_1\} \\ \vee \\ x \neq 0 \wedge \pi' = \pi - \{\ell_0\} \cup \{\ell_2\} \end{array} \right) \wedge x' = x \wedge \cdots}_{\rho_{\ell_0}} \\ \wedge \quad \underbrace{(x = 0 \wedge (\ell_0 \in \pi \vee \ell_1 \in \pi)) \vee m_1 \in \pi}_{\varphi} \end{array} \right) \rightarrow$$

$$\underbrace{\left(x' = 0 \wedge (\ell_0 \in \pi' \vee \ell_1 \in \pi') \right) \vee m_1 \in \pi'}_{\varphi'}.$$

It is not difficult to see that this implication is valid.

This establishes the P-validity of the invariant $\Box p$, i.e.,

$$P \models \Box(at\_\ell_{0,1} \vee at\_m_1). \quad \blacksquare$$

Invariance Verification Diagrams

An effective way of presenting the verification of an invariance property by rule INV is provided by the graphical formalism of *verification diagrams* [MP94]. An (invariance) verification diagram is a directed labeled graph, constructed as follows:

- *Nodes* in the graph are labeled by assertions $\varphi_1, \ldots, \varphi_m$. We will often refer to a node by the assertion labeling it.
- *Edges* in the graph represent transitions between assertions. Each edge departs from one node, connects to another, and is labeled by the name of a transition in the program. We refer to an edge labeled by τ as a τ-*edge*.
- Some of the nodes are designated as *initial nodes*. They are annotated by an entry arrow ↘.

For example, in Fig. 6 we present a verification diagram for program ANY-Y$_{[3,5]}$.

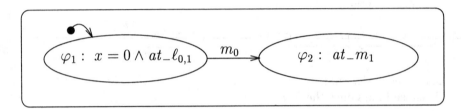

Fig. 6. Verification Diagram D_1

Verification Conditions for Diagrams

To facilitate the expression of verification conditions, we introduce the abbreviation

$$\{p\}\tau\{q\} \qquad \text{standing for} \qquad \rho_\tau \wedge p \;\rightarrow\; q',$$

for assertions p and q and transition τ.

With each verification diagram, we associate the following *verification conditions*:

- Let φ_1 be the (single) initial node in the diagram. The verification condition corresponding to premise I2 of rule INV is given by

$$\Theta \;\rightarrow\; \varphi_1.$$

- Let φ be a node in the graph, τ be a transition in the program, and let $\varphi_1, \ldots, \varphi_k$ be the nodes reached by τ-edges departing from φ. The case that no τ-edges depart from φ, i.e., $k = 0$, is also included. The verification condition associated with φ and τ (corresponding to premise I3) is given by

$$\{\varphi\}\,\tau\,\{\varphi \vee \varphi_1 \vee \ldots \vee \varphi_k\}$$

For example, the verification conditions associated with diagram D_1 (Fig. 6), are:

I2: $\qquad\qquad\qquad \Theta \rightarrow x = 0 \wedge at\_\ell_{0,1}$

I3 for φ_1 and ℓ_0 : $\qquad \{x = 0 \wedge at\_\ell_{0,1}\}\,\ell_0\,\{x = 0 \wedge at\_\ell_{0,1}\}$

I3 for φ_1 and ℓ_1 : $\qquad \{x = 0 \wedge at\_\ell_{0,1}\}\,\ell_1\,\{x = 0 \wedge at\_\ell_{0,1}\}$

I3 for φ_1 and m_0 : $\qquad \{x = 0 \wedge at\_\ell_{0,1}\}\,m_0\,\{(x = 0 \wedge at\_\ell_{0,1}) \vee at\_m_1\}$

I3 for φ_1 and $tick$: $\qquad \{x = 0 \wedge at\_\ell_{0,1}\}\,tick\,\{x = 0 \wedge at\_\ell_{0,1}\}$

I3 for φ_2 and ℓ_0 : $\qquad \{at\_m_1\}\,\ell_0\,\{at\_m_1\}$

I3 for φ_2 and ℓ_1 : $\qquad \{at\_m_1\}\,\ell_1\,\{at\_m_1\}$

I3 for φ_2 and m_0 : $\qquad \{at\_m_1\}\,m_0\,\{at\_m_1\}$

I3 for φ_2 and $tick$: $\qquad \{at\_m_1\}\,tick\,\{at\_m_1\}$

We say that a verification diagram is *valid* if all the verification conditions associated with the diagram are valid.

Let D_P be a verification diagram associated with a program P. Let $\varphi_1, \ldots, \varphi_m$ be the assertions labeling the nodes of D_P.

Claim 1 *If the verification diagram D_P is valid, then*

$$P \models \Box \bigvee_{i=1}^{m} \varphi_i$$

If, in addition, $\varphi_i \rightarrow p$ for every $i = 1, \ldots, m$, then

$$P \models \Box\, p.$$

For example, all the verification conditions associated with diagram D_1 are valid and the verification diagram D_1 establishes

$$\text{ANY-Y} \models (at\_\ell_{0,1} \vee at\_m_1) \tag{1}$$

Encapsulation Conventions

There are several encapsulation conventions that improve the presentation and readability of verification diagrams. We extend the notion of a directed graph into a structured directed graph by allowing *compound nodes* that may encapsulate other nodes, and edges that may depart or arrive at compound nodes. A node that does not encapsulate other nodes is called a *basic node*.

We use the following conventions:

- *Labels of compound nodes*: A diagram containing a compound node n, labeled by an assertion φ and encapsulating nodes $n_1, \ldots, n_k$ with assertions $\varphi_1, \ldots, \varphi_k$, is equivalent to a diagram in which n is unlabeled and nodes $n_1, \ldots, n_k$ are labeled by $\varphi_1 \wedge \varphi$, ..., and $\varphi_k \wedge \varphi$.
- *Edges entering and exiting compound nodes*: A diagram containing an edge e connecting node A to a compound node n encapsulating nodes $n_1, \ldots, n_k$ is equivalent to a diagram in which there is an edge connecting A to each n_i, $i = 1, \ldots, k$, with the same label as e. Similarly, an edge e connecting the compound node n to node B is the same as having a separate edge connecting each n_i, $i = 1, \ldots, k$, to B with the same label as e.

With these conventions we can draw a more detailed verification diagram establishing (1), as shown in Fig. 7.

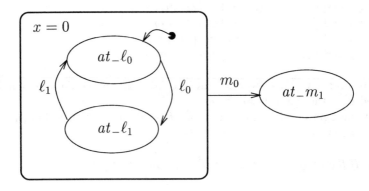

Fig. 7. A more detailed diagram, using encapsulation conventions

In the diagram of Fig. 7, the single assertion $x = 0 \wedge at\_\ell_{0,1}$, has been broken into the two sub-cases: $x = 0 \wedge at\_\ell_0$ and $x = 0 \wedge at\_\ell_1$, explicitly displaying the fact that transitions ℓ_0 and ℓ_1 cause the system to move between these two sub-cases.

Example 4. We use rule INV to prove that program ANY-Y$_{[3,5]}$ terminates within 15 time units, as specified by the following invariance formula:

$$\Box (T \leq 15 \vee (at\_\ell_2 \wedge at\_m_1))$$

This formula claims that every accessible state in which the program has not terminated yet (i.e., $at\_\ell_2 \wedge at\_m_1$ does not hold), can only be observed when the master clock T has not yet passed 15. It follows that any state observed later than $T = 15$ must be a termination state.

The proof is presented by the invariance diagram in Fig. 8.

The assertions are indexed in descending order from φ_3 on top to φ_0 at bottom in order to keep compatibility with the chain diagrams introduced in Section 5.

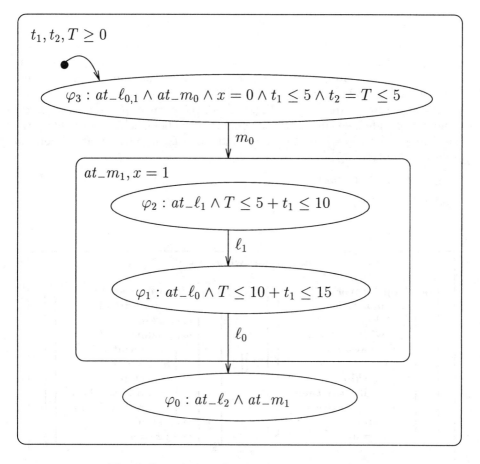

Fig. 8. Termination of ANY-Y within 15 time units.

Note that no edge in the diagram is labeled by the *tick* transition. This implies that all verification conditions involving the *tick* transition are of the form $\{\varphi_i\}\ tick\ \{\varphi_i\}$ claiming that the *tick* transition preserves each of the assertions appearing in the diagram.

As an example, consider the verification condition claiming that assertion φ_2: $at\_\ell_1 \wedge T \le 5 + t_1 \le 10$ is preserved by the *tick* transition.

$$\underbrace{at\_\ell_1 \wedge T \le 5 + t_1 \le 10}_{\varphi_2} \quad \wedge$$

$$\underbrace{\Delta > 0 \wedge \pi' = \pi \wedge T' = T + \Delta \wedge t_1' = t_1 + \Delta \wedge (at\_\ell_1 \rightarrow t_1 + \Delta \le 5) \wedge \cdots}_{\rho_{tick}}$$

$$\rightarrow \quad \underbrace{at'\_\ell_1 \wedge T' \le 5 + t_1' \le 10}_{\varphi_2'}$$

It is not difficult to see that this implication is state-valid. ◢

Example 5. As a second example, we present a mutual-exclusion algorithm, due to M. Fischer, which functions properly only due to the timing constraints associated with the statements. Similar proofs to the one we will present here are given in [SBM92], [AL94], and [MMP92].

The algorithm is presented in Fig. 9 under the name of program MUTEX. By assigning all statements in MUTEX the uniform time bounds $[L, U]$, we obtain the timed program MUTEX$_{[L,U]}$. Assuming that $2L > U$, we prove that the mutual exclusion property

$$\Box \, \neg(at\_\ell_8 \, \wedge \, at\_m_8)$$

is valid for MUTEX$_{[L,U]}$.

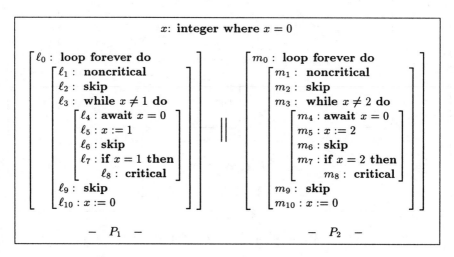

Fig. 9. Program MUTEX, implementing Fischer's protocol.

Let us explain informally why mutual exclusion for program MUTEX is guaranteed and the role of the *skip* statements at ℓ_6 and m_6. Assume a violation of mutual exclusion in which process P_1 entered its critical section (location ℓ_8) first and, while P_1 is still there, process P_2 enters m_8. When P_1 entered ℓ_8, x was 1. For P_2 to enter m_8 later, it was necessary for it to set x to 2 first, which can only be done at m_5. Since after P_1 set x to 1 at ℓ_5, P_2 cannot pass the test for $x = 0$ at m_4, the only possibility is that P_2 kept waiting at m_5 while P_1 executed ℓ_6 and the test at ℓ_7. This must have taken P_1 at least $2L$, since L is the lower bound for execution of a statement. However, P_2 cannot wait at m_5 for as long as $2L$ because $2L > U$ and no process can delay the execution of a statement for more than U. It follows that the described scenario in which P_2 keeps waiting at m_5 until P_1 enters ℓ_8 is impossible. The role of the *skip* statement at ℓ_6 is therefore to introduce an additional delay of at least L time units.

The *skip* statements at ℓ_9 and m_9 are necessary to guarantee the response properties of this algorithm, and we will discuss them in the next section. The *skip* statements at ℓ_2 and m_2 represent exits out of the noncritical sections (at ℓ_1 and m_1, respectively) and intentions to enter the critical sections.

A formal proof that the assertion $\neg(at\_\ell_8 \land at\_m_8)$ is an invariant of program MUTEX is presented by the invariance diagram of Fig. 10.

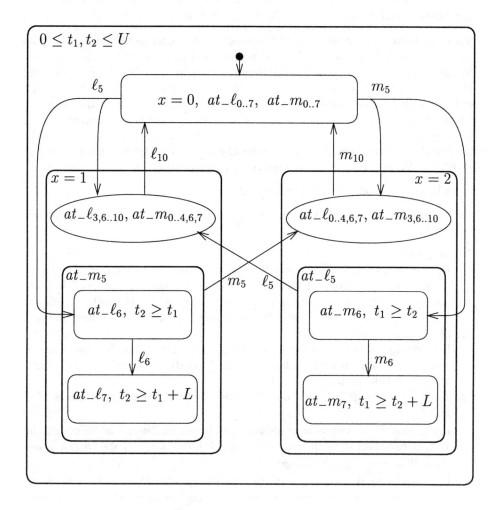

Fig. 10. Mutual exclusion for program MUTEX.

All verification conditions associated with this diagram, have been verified automatically (with no user intervention) by the STeP verifier [BBC+95], using the axiom $2L > U$.

This concludes the proof of mutual exclusion for program MUTEX. ◢

Completeness of Rule INV

Rule INV is complete for verifying invariances of clocked transition systems. This is stated by the following claim.

Claim 2 *If formula $\Box p$ is valid over non-zeno* CTS Φ, *then there exists an assertion φ such that premises I1-I3 of rule* INV *are state-valid.*

Justification The basic idea of the proof is the construction of an assertion acc_Φ that holds in a state s iff s is Φ-accessible, i.e., appears in some run of Φ. We then show that if $\Box p$ is Φ-valid, then the premises of rule INV are state-valid (implying that they are also Φ-state valid) when taking acc_Φ for φ. Since we are only proving *relative* completeness, it is enough to show validity of the premises, assuming an oracle that provides proofs or otherwise verifies all generally valid assertions.

For the construction of acc_Φ, we refer the reader to [MP91a] or Chapter 2 of [MP95b]. Assume that we have constructed an assertion acc_Φ such that

$$s \models acc_\Phi \qquad \text{iff} \qquad s \text{ is a } \Phi\text{-accessible state.}$$

We show that acc_Φ, when substituted for φ, validates the three premises of rule INV.

I1. $acc_\Phi \rightarrow p$

By our assumption that $\Box p$ is Φ-valid, it follows that each state appearing in some computation satisfies p. As Φ is non-zeno, every accessible state appears in some computation and, hence, every accessible state satisfies p. Since acc_Φ characterizes precisely the accessible states, the premise follows.

I2. $\Theta \rightarrow acc_\Phi$

It is obvious that every state satisfying Θ is initial and is, therefore, Φ-accessible. Consequently, such a state must satisfy acc_Φ, which characterizes all Φ-accessible states.

I3. $\rho_\tau(U, \widetilde{U}) \wedge acc_\Phi(U) \quad \rightarrow \quad acc_\Phi(\widetilde{U})$, for each $\tau \in \mathcal{T}$ and every values of U and $\widetilde{U}$.

Let U and $\widetilde{U}$ be two lists of values, which can be viewed as values of the system variables V, such that both $\rho_\tau(U, \widetilde{U})$ and $acc_\Phi(U)$ are true. We will show that $acc_\Phi(\widetilde{U})$ is also true.

Let s and $\widetilde{s}$ be two arbitrary states such that $s[V] = U$ and $\widetilde{s}[V] = \widetilde{U}$. Since $acc_\Phi(U) = \text{T}$, we have that $s \models acc_\Phi$. By the meaning of acc_Φ, it follows that s is Φ-accessible. From $\rho_\tau(U, \widetilde{U}) = \text{T}$, it follows that $\langle s, \widetilde{s} \rangle \models \rho_\tau(V, V')$ and, therefore, that $\widetilde{s}$ is a τ-successor of s. Since s is accessible, it follows that also $\widetilde{s}$ is accessible and, hence $\widetilde{s} \models acc_\Phi$, leading to $acc_\Phi(\widetilde{U}) = \text{T}$

This concludes the proof of completeness of rule INV. ◢

The following example demonstrates that the assumption that Φ is non-zeno is essential to the completeness of the rule.

Example 6. Consider the CTS Φ_3 which is presented graphically in Fig. 11 and textually in Fig. 12.

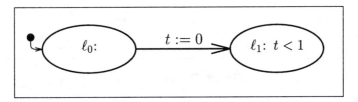

Fig. 11. CTS Φ_3.

Clearly, CTS Φ_3 is a possibly-zeno system because, once a run enters location ℓ_1, time is bounded and cannot diverge. Thus, a run entering location ℓ_1 cannot be extended into a computation of Φ_3. A result of the fact that no computation of Φ_3 ever enters location ℓ_1 is that the invariance formula $\Box\,at\_\ell_0$ is Φ_3-valid. However, examination of the arguments for the soundness of rule INV shows

$$
\begin{array}{l}
V:\ \{\pi\colon\{0,1\};\,t,T\colon\mathbf{real}\}\\
\Theta\colon\ \pi = t = T = 0\\
T\colon\ \{\tau_{01}\}\text{ with transition relation}\\
\quad\ \tau_{01}\colon\ \pi = 0 \wedge \pi' = 1 \wedge t' = 0 \wedge T' = T\\
\Pi\colon\ \pi = 1 \rightarrow t < 1
\end{array}
$$

Fig. 12. CTS Φ_3 in textual form.

that any assertion p, whose invariance is proven by rule INV, must hold on all accessible states. The state $\langle\pi\colon 1\rangle$ is accessible for CTS Φ_3 but does not satisfy at_ℓ_0. Therefore, the Φ_3-validity of $\Box\,at\_\ell_0$ cannot be proven by rule INV. ⌟

4.2 Verifying Waiting-for Formulas

The invariance formula $\Box\,q$ states that q holds continuously from the beginning of the computation to infinity. In comparison, the waiting-for formula

$$p \quad\Rightarrow\quad q\,\mathcal{W}\,r$$

also states the continuous holding of q but only for an interval that is initiated by an occurrence of p and may be terminated by an occurrence of r. Such formulas are useful for expressing timing properties, where time is measured since an occurrence of an event, rather than from the beginning of a computation.

$$x, y: \textbf{ integer where } x = y = 0$$

$$\begin{bmatrix} \ell_0 : \textbf{ loop forever do} \\ \quad \begin{bmatrix} \ell_1 : \textbf{while } x = 0 \textbf{ do} \\ \quad \begin{bmatrix} \ell_2 : \ y := y + 1 \\ \ell_3 : x := 0 \end{bmatrix} \end{bmatrix} \end{bmatrix} \quad \| \quad \begin{bmatrix} m_0 : \textbf{ loop forever do} \\ \quad \begin{bmatrix} m_1 : x := 1 \\ m_2 : \textbf{await } x = 0 \end{bmatrix} \end{bmatrix}$$

$$- \quad P_1 \quad - \qquad\qquad\qquad - \quad P_2 \quad -$$

Fig. 13. Program CYCLIC.

Example 7.   Consider program CYCLIC, presented in Fig. 13. This program can be viewed as a generalization of program ANY-Y, in which the basic interaction between processes P_1 and P_2 is embedded within an endless loop.

Since program CYCLIC never terminates, a relevant time-related property is that from any state in which we observe P_1 at ℓ_1 and P_2 at m_1, P_1 will reach location ℓ_3 within at most 15 time units.

This property can be stated by the following waiting-for formula:

$$at\_\ell_1 \wedge at\_m_1 \wedge x = 0 \wedge T = a \quad \Rightarrow \quad (T \leq a + 15)\,\mathcal{W}\,at\_\ell_3.$$

This formulas uses a rigid variable a to record the time at the initial observation state. It claims that from the time we observe a state satisfying $at\_\ell_1 \wedge at\_m_1 \wedge x = 0$, time will not progress by more than 15 units before we observe P_1 at ℓ_3.

To facilitate the expression of such properties, we introduce the abbreviation

$$T_a \quad = \quad T - a.$$

With this abbreviation we can write the property of "reaching ℓ_3 within 15 time units" as

$$at\_\ell_1 \wedge at\_m_1 \wedge x = 0 \wedge T_a = 0 \quad \Rightarrow \quad (T_a \leq 15)\,\mathcal{W}\,at\_\ell_3.$$

The T_a abbreviation allows us to view T_a as a special timer, reset at the initial point of observation. ⌐

A Waiting-for Rule

To establish the P-validity of a waiting-for formula, we may use rule WAIT, presented in Fig. 14.

Waiting Diagrams

Proofs by rule WAIT can be succinctly represented by special verification diagrams to which we refer as *waiting diagrams*.

A waiting diagram is a directed labeled graph constructed as follows:

For assertions p, q, φ, and r,

> U1. $\varphi \;\rightarrow\; q$
>
> U2. $p \;\rightarrow\; r \vee \varphi$
>
> U3. $\rho_\tau \wedge \varphi \;\rightarrow\; r' \vee \varphi'$ for every $\tau \in \mathcal{T}_T$

$$P \;\models\; p \Rightarrow q\,\mathcal{W}\,r$$

Fig. 14. Rule WAIT (waiting-for) applied to CTS P.

- *Nodes* in the graph are labeled by assertions $\varphi_0, \ldots, \varphi_m$. We will often refer to a node by the assertion labeling it.

  The node labeled by φ_0 is called the *terminal node* and is graphically identified by being drawn with bold-face boundaries.

- *Edges* in the graph represent transitions between assertions. Each edge is labeled by the name of a transition in the program. We refer to an edge labeled by τ as a τ-*edge*. No edges depart form the terminal node.

- Some of the nodes are designated as *initial nodes*. They are annotated by an entry arrow.

Verification Conditions Implied by a Waiting Diagram

Consider a nonterminal node labeled by assertion φ. Let $\tau \in \mathcal{T}_T$ be a transition and let $\varphi_1, \ldots, \varphi_k$, $k \geq 0$, be the successors of φ by edges labeled with τ (possibly including φ itself). With each such node and transition, we associate the following verification condition:

$$\{\varphi\} \; \tau \; \{\varphi \vee \varphi_1 \vee \cdots \vee \varphi_k\}.$$

In particular, if $k = 0$ (i.e., φ has no τ-successors), the associated verification condition is

$$\{\varphi\} \; \tau \; \{\varphi\}.$$

Valid Waiting Diagrams

A waiting diagram is said to be *valid over* CTS P (*P-valid* for short) if all the verification conditions associated with the diagram are P-state valid.

The consequences of having a valid chain diagram are stated in the following claim:

Claim 3 *If D is a P-valid waiting diagram with nodes $\varphi_0, \ldots, \varphi_m$, then*

$$P \models \bigvee_{j=0}^{m} \varphi_j \;\Rightarrow\; (\bigvee_{j=0}^{m} \varphi_j) \mathcal{W} \varphi_0$$

If, in addition, $\varphi_0 = r$,

$$\text{U1:} \quad \bigvee_{j=0}^{m} \varphi_j \;\rightarrow\; q, \qquad \text{and} \qquad \text{U2:} \quad p \;\rightarrow\; \bigvee_{j=1}^{m} \varphi_j,$$

then we can conclude:

$$P \models p \;\Rightarrow\; q \, \mathcal{W} \, r.$$

Justification   We observe first that the verification conditions associated with a waiting diagram imply premise U3 of rule WAIT, when we take φ to be $\varphi_1 \vee \cdots \vee \varphi_m$ and r to be φ_0.

If we further take $p = \varphi_0 \vee \cdots \vee \varphi_m$ and $q = \varphi_1 \vee \cdots \vee \varphi_m$, we find that premises U1 and U2 hold trivially. This yields the first part of the claim.

The second part of the claim considers different p and q but explicitly requires that premises U1 and U2 are P-valid. The conclusion follows by rule WAIT. ◢

Example 8.   In Fig. 15, we present a waiting diagram that establishes the property

$$at\_\ell_1 \wedge at\_m_1 \wedge x = 0 \wedge T_a = 0 \quad \Rightarrow \quad (T_a \leq 15) \, \mathcal{W} \, at\_\ell_3$$

for program CYCLIC$_{[3,5]}$. ◢

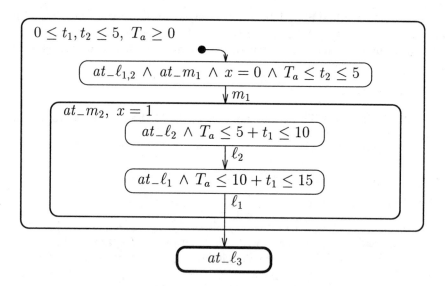

Fig. 15. A waiting diagram, establishing the formula
$$at\_\ell_1 \wedge at\_m_1 \wedge x = 0 \wedge T_a = 0 \quad \Rightarrow \quad (T_a \leq 15) \, \mathcal{W} \, at\_\ell_3$$

5 Verifying Response Properties of Clocked Transition Systems

In this section, we present methods for verifying response properties of clocked transitions systems.

5.1 The Clock-Bounded Chain Rule

The basic rule for proving response properties of clocked transition systems is the *clock-bounded chain rule* (rule CB-CHAIN) presented in Fig. 16. The rule uses auxiliary assertions $\varphi_1, \ldots, \varphi_m$ and refers to assertion q also as φ_0. With each assertion φ_i we associate one of the clocks $c_i \in C$, to which we refer as the *helpful clock*, and a real-valued upper bound b_i. The intention is that while remaining in states satisfying φ_i, the clock c_i is bounded by b_i. Since time in a computation grows beyond any bound, this will imply that we cannot continually stay at a φ_i-state for too long.

For assertions p, q, and $\varphi_0 = q, \varphi_1, \ldots, \varphi_m$,
clocks $c_1, \ldots, c_m \in C$, and
real constants $b_1, \ldots, b_m \in \mathsf{R}$,

C1. $\quad p \;\rightarrow\; \bigvee_{j=0}^{m} \varphi_j$

The following two premises hold for $i = 1, \ldots, m$

C2. $\quad \rho_\tau \wedge \varphi_i \;\rightarrow\; (\varphi_i' \wedge c_i' \geq c_i) \vee \bigvee_{j<i} \varphi_j'$

$\qquad\qquad\qquad\qquad$ for every $\tau \in \mathcal{T}_T$

C3. $\quad \varphi_i \;\rightarrow\; c_i \leq b_i$

$\qquad\qquad p \;\Rightarrow\; \Diamond\, q$

Fig. 16. Rule CB-CHAIN (clock-bounded chain rule for response).

Premise C1 requires that every p-position satisfies one of $\varphi_0 = q, \varphi_1, \ldots, \varphi_m$.

Premise C2 requires that every τ-successor (for any $\tau \in \mathcal{T}_T$) of a φ_i-state s is a φ_j-state for some $j \leq i$. In the case that the successor state satisfies φ_i, it is required that the transition does not decrease the value of c_i.

Premise C3 requires that assertion φ_i implies that c_i is bounded by the constant b_i.

The following claim states the soundness of the rule:

Claim 4 *Rule* CB-CHAIN *is sound for proving that a response formula is Φ-valid.*

Justification: Assume that the premises of the rule are Φ-valid, and let σ be a computation of Φ. We will show that σ satisfies the rule's consequence

$$p \Rightarrow \Diamond q,$$

i.e., every p position in σ is followed by a q-position.

Assume that p holds at position k and no later position $i \geq k$ satisfies q. By C1 some φ_j must hold at position k. Let j_k denote the minimal index such that φ_{j_k} holds at k. Obviously $j_k > 0$ by our assumption that q never occurs beyond position k.

By C2, state s_{k+1} must satisfy φ_j for some j, $0 < j \leq j_k$. Let j_{k+1} denote the minimal such index. Continuing in this manner we obtain that every position i beyond k satisfies some φ_{j_i}, where $j_i > 0$ and

$$j_k \geq j_{k+1} \geq j_{k+2} \geq \cdots .$$

Since we cannot have an infinite non-increasing sequence of natural numbers which decreases infinitely many times, there must exist a position $r \geq k$ such that

$$j_r = j_{r+1} = j_{r+2} = \cdots .$$

Denote the value of this eventually-stable assertion index by $u = j_r$.

Consider the value of the clock c_u at states s_i, $i \geq r$. By C2, the value of c_u never decreases. Also, whenever a *tick* transition with increment Δ is taken, c_u increases (as do all clocks) by Δ. It follows that the master clock T cannot increase by more than $b_u - s_r[c_u]$ from its value at state s_r. This contradicts the fact that σ is a computation in which the master clock increases beyond all bounds.

We conclude that our assumption of the existence of a p-position not followed by any q-position is false. Consequently, if the premises of the rule hold then every p-position must be followed by a q-position, establishing the consequence of the rule. ◢

Example 9. We illustrate the use of rule CB-CHAIN to prove the termination of program ANY-Y$_{[3,5]}$, which can be stated by the response formula

$$at\_\ell_0 \wedge at\_m_0 \wedge x = t_1 = t_2 = T = 0 \quad \Rightarrow \quad \Diamond(at\_\ell_2 \wedge at\_m_1).$$

To apply rule CB-CHAIN, we identify $at\_\ell_0 \wedge at\_m_0 \wedge x = t_1 = t_2 = T = 0$ as p and $at\_\ell_2 \wedge at\_m_1$ as q. The auxiliary assertions, helpful clocks, and bounds are presented in the following table:

φ_0: $at\_\ell_2 \wedge at\_m_1$	$-$	$-$
φ_1: $at\_\ell_0 \wedge at\_m_1 \wedge x = 1 \wedge t_1 \leq 5$	c_1: t_1	b_1: 5
φ_2: $at\_\ell_1 \wedge at\_m_1 \wedge x = 1 \wedge t_1 \leq 5$	c_2: t_1	b_2: 5
φ_3: $at\_\ell_{0,1} \wedge at\_m_0 \wedge x = 0 \wedge t_1 \leq 5 \wedge t_2 \leq 5$	c_3: t_2	b_3: 5

We check the premises of rule CB-CHAIN for this selection of auxiliary assertions, helpful clocks, and bounds.

- Premise C1 assumes the form

$$\underbrace{at\_\ell_0 \wedge at\_m_0 \wedge x = t_1 = t_2 = T = 0}_{p} \rightarrow$$

$$\cdots \vee \underbrace{at\_\ell_{0,1} \wedge at\_m_0 \wedge x = 0 \wedge t_1 \leq 5 \wedge t_2 \leq 5,}_{\varphi_3}$$

which is obviously state valid.
- Premise C2 has to be checked for each $i = 1, \ldots, m$ and each $\tau \in \mathcal{T}_T$. We present only a few representative cases.
Premise C2 for φ_3 and transition m_0 assumes the form

$$\underbrace{\pi' = \pi - \{m_0\} \cup \{m_1\} \wedge x' = 1 \wedge t_1' = t_1 \wedge \cdots}_{\rho_{m_0}} \wedge \underbrace{at\_\ell_{0,1} \wedge t_1 \leq 5 \wedge \cdots}_{\varphi_3}$$

$$\rightarrow \left(\begin{array}{c} \cdots \\ \vee \quad \underbrace{at'\_\ell_0 \wedge at'\_m_1 \wedge x' = 1 \wedge t_1' \leq 5}_{\varphi_1'} \\ \vee \quad \underbrace{at'\_\ell_1 \wedge at'\_m_1 \wedge x' = 1 \wedge t_1' \leq 5}_{\varphi_2'} \end{array} \right),$$

which is obviously state valid.
Premise C2 for φ_2 and the *tick* transition assumes the form

$$\underbrace{\Delta > 0 \wedge \pi' = \pi \wedge x' = x \wedge t_1' = t_1 + \Delta \wedge (at\_\ell_{0,1} \rightarrow t_1 + \Delta \leq 5) \wedge \cdots}_{\rho_{tick}}$$

$$\wedge \underbrace{at\_\ell_1 \wedge at\_m_1 \wedge x = 1 \wedge t_1 \leq 5}_{\varphi_2} \rightarrow$$

$$\underbrace{at'\_\ell_1 \wedge at'\_m_1 \wedge x' = 1 \wedge t_1' \leq 5}_{\varphi_2'} \wedge \underbrace{t_1 \leq t_1'}_{c_2 \leq c_2'},$$

which is obviously state valid.
- Premise C3 is trivially valid, since each φ_i, $i = 1, \ldots, 3$ includes $c_i \leq b_i$ as a conjunct.

This analysis indicates that all premises of rule CB-CHAIN are state valid. It follows that the response formula

$$at\_\ell_0 \wedge at\_m_0 \wedge x = t_1 = t_2 = 0 \quad \Rightarrow \quad \Diamond(at\_\ell_2 \wedge at\_m_2)$$

is valid over program ANY-Y$_{[3,5]}$. ◢

5.2 Clock-Bounded Chain Diagrams

The main ingredients of a proof by rule CB-CHAIN can be conveniently and effectively presented by a special type of verification diagrams that summarize the auxiliary assertions with their helpful clocks and bounds, and display the possible transitions between the assertions.

We define a *clock bounded chain diagram* (*chain diagram* for short) to be a directed labeled graph constructed as follows:

- *Nodes* in the graph are labeled by assertions. One node is designated as a *terminal node* and is graphically identified by being drawn with bold-face boundaries. This node is labeled by an assertion φ_0.

  All other nodes are labeled by a pair of assertions: ϕ_i and β_i, for $i = 1, \ldots, m$. The assertion β_i has the form $c_i \leq b_i$, where $c_i \in C$ is a clock and b_i is a real constant. We refer to the conjunction $\phi_i \wedge \beta_i$ as φ_i, and say that the node is labeled by the (combined) assertion φ_i.

  We often refer to nodes by the assertion φ_i labeling them.

- *Edges* in the graph represent transitions between assertions. Each edge connects one assertion to another and is labeled by one or more transitions. An edge can connect node φ_i to node φ_j only if $i \geq j$. This imposes the restriction that the graph of a chain diagram is weakly acyclic, i.e., the only cycles in the graph consist of a node connected to itself.

Verification Conditions Implied by a Chain Diagram

Consider a nonterminal node labeled by assertion φ: $\phi \wedge \beta$ where the clock-bound assertion is β: $c \leq b$. Let $\tau \in \mathcal{T}_T$ be a transition and let $\varphi_1, \ldots, \varphi_k$, $k \geq 0$, be the successors of φ by edges labeled with τ (possibly including φ itself). With each such node and transition, we associate the following verification condition:

$$\rho_\tau \wedge \varphi \;\longrightarrow\; (\varphi' \wedge c' \geq c) \vee \varphi'_1 \vee \cdots \vee \varphi'_k.$$

In particular, if $k = 0$ (i.e., φ has no τ-successors), the associated verification condition is

$$\rho_\tau \wedge \varphi \;\longrightarrow\; \varphi' \wedge c' \geq c.$$

Valid Chain Diagrams

A chain diagram is said to be *valid over* CTS Φ (Φ-*valid* for short) if all the verification conditions associated with the diagram are Φ-state valid.

The consequences of having a valid chain diagram are stated in the following claim:

Claim 5 *If D is a Φ-valid chain diagram with nodes $\varphi_0, \ldots, \varphi_m$, then*

$$\Phi \;\models\; \left(\bigvee_{j=0}^{m} \varphi_j \right) \Rightarrow \Diamond \varphi_0$$

If, in addition, $\varphi_0 = q$ and

$$\text{C1:} \quad p \;\longrightarrow\; \bigvee_{j=0}^{m} \varphi_j,$$

then we can conclude:

$$\Phi \models p \Rightarrow \Diamond q.$$

The claim follows from the observation that the verification conditions associated with a chain diagram precisely correspond to premise C2 of rule CB-CHAIN. Premise C1 is trivially satisfied for the first part of the claim, where we take p to be $\bigvee_{j=0}^{m} \varphi_j$. It is explicitly provided in the second part of the claim. Premise C3 is trivially satisfied by having β_i: $c_i \leq b_i$ as an explicit conjunct of $\varphi_i = \phi_i \wedge \beta_i$.

Example 10. In Fig. 17, we present a chain diagram for proving that

$$at\_\ell_0 \wedge at\_m_0 \wedge x = t_1 = t_2 = T = 0 \quad \Rightarrow \quad \Diamond(at\_\ell_2 \wedge at\_m_1)$$

is valid over program ANY-Y$_{[3,5]}$.

Note the use of encapsulation in labeling the compound node by the common clock bound B: $t_1 \leq 5$, which is factored out of nodes φ_1 and φ_2. We also remove the index from the β assertion labeling a node and write β instead of β_i. ◢

5.3 Winning a Race

We introduce an additional graph-structuring convention which leads to more economic and comprehensible verification diagrams. Similar to the previously introduced encapsulation conventions, this one is also inspired by the Statechart language [Har87].

A *conjunctive compound node* is a compound node which contains two sets of encapsulated nodes: $\{\phi_1, \ldots, \phi_m\}$ and $\{\psi_1, \ldots, \psi_n\}$. The two sets are separated by a dashed line. Edges may connect nodes within each of the sets, and external nodes to nodes in each of the sets. No edge may connect a ϕ-node to a ψ-node. We also allow a multi-source edge such as the edge connecting nodes ϕ_2 and ψ_2 to the external node χ.

In Fig. 18, we present a graph with a conjunctive compound node.

Any diagram containing conjunctive nodes can be expanded into an equivalent flat diagram, to which we refer as the *expanded diagram*, as follows:

- For each $i \in \{1, \ldots, m\}$ and $j \in \{1, \ldots, n\}$, the expanded diagram contains a node, labeled by the conjunction $\phi_i \wedge \psi_j$.
- For each τ-labeled edge connecting ϕ_a to ϕ_b, there are τ-labeled edges connecting expanded node $\phi_a \wedge \psi_j$ to $\phi_b \wedge \psi_j$ for all $j \in \{1, \ldots, n\}$.
- For each τ-labeled edge connecting ψ_c to ψ_d, there are τ-labeled edges connecting expanded node $\phi_i \wedge \psi_c$ to $\phi_i \wedge \psi_d$ for all $i \in \{1, \ldots, m\}$.
- For each τ-labeled edge connecting ϕ_a to external node χ, there are τ-labeled edges connecting expanded node $\phi_a \wedge \psi_j$ to χ for all $j \in \{1, \ldots, n\}$.
- For each τ-labeled edge connecting ψ_c to external node χ, there are τ-labeled edges connecting expanded node $\phi_i \wedge \psi_c$ to χ for all $i \in \{1, \ldots, m\}$.
- For each τ-labeled multi-source edge connecting nodes ϕ_a and ψ_c to external node χ, there exists a τ-labeled edge connecting expanded node $\phi_a \wedge \psi_c$ to node χ.

In Fig. 19, we present the flat diagram equivalent to the diagram of Fig. 18.

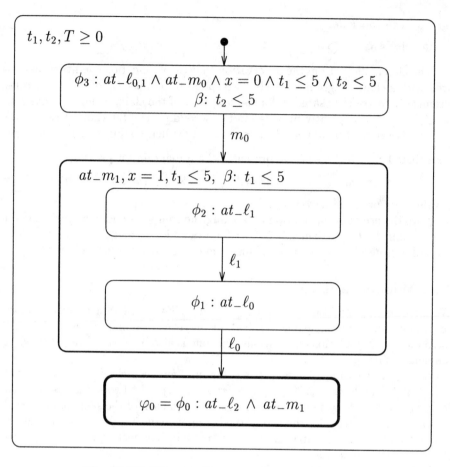

Fig. 17. Verifying termination of program ANY-Y$_{[3,5]}$.

Analyzing Races between Processes

Conjunctive nodes are particularly helpful for proving that one process always wins in a race against a competing process. Consider the trivial program RACE presented in Fig. 20.

As in the case of program MUTEX$_{[L,U]}$, we assign to all statements of program RACE time bounds $[L, U]$, stipulating that $2L > U$. It is clear that when this program is run, process P_1 will terminate before P_2 does. This is because P_1 must terminate within $2U$ time units, while P_2 must take at least $4L > 2U$ time units to terminate. How do we formally prove this property which can be stated by the response formula

$$at\_\ell_0 \wedge at\_m_0 \wedge t_1 = t_2 = T = 0 \quad \Rightarrow \quad \Diamond(at\_\ell_2 \wedge at\_m_{0..3})\ ?$$

In Fig. 21, we present a chain diagram which proves this property.

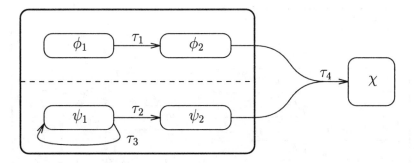

Fig. 18. A conjunctive compound node.

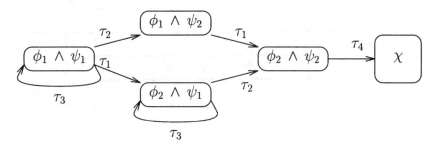

Fig. 19. An expanded equivalent to the conjunctive diagram.

A central argument in the validation of this diagram is that transition m_3 is disabled on all nodes within the conjunctive compound node. Transition m_3 can be enabled only on an at_m_3-state and only when $t_2 \geq L$. Combining the assertion attached to the at_m_3-node with $t_2 \geq L$, we obtain $T \geq 4L > 2U$. However, all assertions on the left-hand side of the conjunctive node imply $T \leq 2U$. This shows that m_3 is disabled on all states covered by the conjunctive node, and the only exit is via ℓ_1.

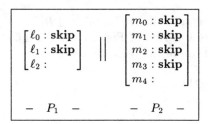

Fig. 20. Program RACE.

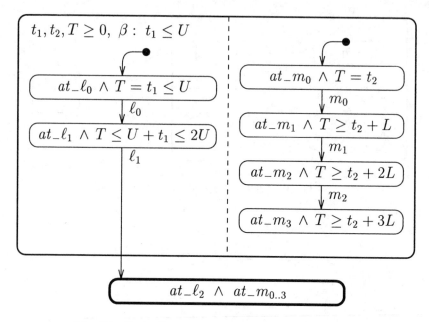

Fig. 21. Chain diagram proving that P_1 wins the race.

This establishes the property

$$at\_\ell_0 \wedge at\_m_0 \wedge t_1 = t_2 = T = 0 \quad \Rightarrow \quad \Diamond(at\_\ell_2 \wedge at\_m_{0..3}).$$

5.4 Proving Accessibility for Program MUTEX$_{[L,U]}$

As a more ambitious example, we prove for program MUTEX$_{[L,U]}$ (Fig. 9) the property of accessibility which can be stated (for process P_1) by the response formula

$$at\_\ell_2 \quad \Rightarrow \quad \Diamond at\_\ell_8.$$

A similar formula states accessibility for process P_2.

From the invariance diagram of Fig. 10, we can infer the following five invariants, which we will use in the response proof:

$$
\begin{aligned}
\chi_0: &\quad \Box(x \in \{0,1,2\}) \\
\chi_1: &\quad at\_\ell_{0..2,4,5} \quad \Rightarrow \quad x \neq 1 \\
\chi_2: &\quad at\_m_{0..2,4,5} \quad \Rightarrow \quad x \neq 2 \\
\chi_3: &\quad at\_\ell_4 \quad \Rightarrow \quad x = 0 \vee (at\_m_{6..10} \wedge x = 2) \\
\chi_4: &\quad at\_\ell_{6,7} \wedge x = 1 \quad \Rightarrow \quad at\_m_{0..7}
\end{aligned}
$$

The accessibility formula is proved in several steps, verifying separately the following response formulas:

ψ_1: $at\_\ell_2 \quad \Rightarrow \quad \Diamond\, at\_\ell_4$

ψ_2: $at\_\ell_4 \wedge x = 0 \quad \Rightarrow$
$$\Diamond\big(at\_\ell_8 \;\vee\; (at\_\ell_{4,6,7} \wedge at\_m_6 \wedge x = 2 \wedge t_2 = 0)\big)$$

ψ_3: $at\_\ell_{4,6,7} \wedge at\_m_6 \wedge x = 2 \wedge t_2 = 0 \quad \Rightarrow$
$$\Diamond\big(at\_\ell_4 \wedge at\_m_0 \wedge x = 0 \wedge t_2 = 0\big)$$

ψ_4: $at\_\ell_4 \wedge at\_m_{6..10} \wedge x = 2 \quad \Rightarrow$
$$\Diamond\big(at\_\ell_4 \wedge at\_m_0 \wedge x = 0 \wedge t_2 = 0\big)$$

ψ_5: $at\_\ell_4 \wedge at\_m_0 \wedge x = 0 \wedge t_2 = 0 \quad \Rightarrow$
$$\Diamond\big(at\_\ell_6 \wedge at\_m_{0..4} \wedge x = 1\big)$$

ψ_6: $at\_\ell_6 \wedge at\_m_{0..4} \wedge x = 1 \quad \Rightarrow \quad \Diamond\, at\_\ell_8$

It is not difficult to see that response formulas ψ_1–ψ_6 lead to the accessibility property.

We proceed to prove each of the response formulas.

Proving ψ_1: $at\_\ell_2 \;\Rightarrow\; \Diamond\, at\_\ell_4$

Formula ψ_1 states that, starting at ℓ_2, process P_2 is guaranteed to reach ℓ_4. Statement ℓ_2 is unconditional and is guaranteed to terminate within U time units. By X_1, when we enter ℓ_3 from ℓ_2, x is different from 1, and will remain so as long as we stay at ℓ_3 (ℓ_5 is the only statement that can set x to 1). Consequently, within U time units, P_1 will proceed to ℓ_4.

The formal proof of ψ_1 is provided by the chain diagram of Fig. 22

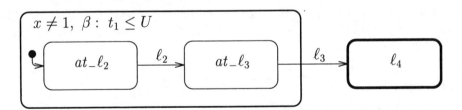

Fig. 22. Chain diagram for ψ_1: $at\_\ell_2 \;\Rightarrow\; \Diamond\, at\_\ell_4$.

Proving ψ_2

Response formula ψ_2 is given by

$$at\_\ell_4 \wedge x = 0 \quad \Rightarrow \quad \Diamond\big(at\_\ell_8 \;\vee\; (at\_\ell_{4,6,7} \wedge at\_m_6 \wedge x = 2 \wedge t_2 = 0)\big).$$

It states that, starting at location ℓ_4 with $x = 0$, process P_1 will either reach the critical section (at ℓ_8), or be overtaken by process P_2 just entering location m_6

(and hence $t_2 = 0$), while setting x to 2. In the latter case, P_1 will be overtaken at one of the locations ℓ_4, ℓ_6, or ℓ_7.

The formal proof of ψ_2 is presented by the chain diagram of Fig. 23.

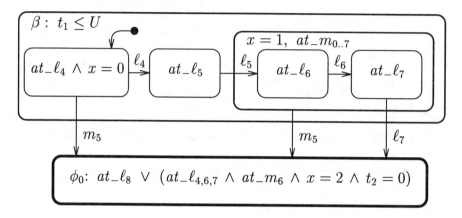

Fig. 23. Chain diagram for the formula
$$\psi_2: \; at\_\ell_4 \wedge x = 0 \;\; \Rightarrow \;\; \Diamond\big(at\_\ell_8 \vee (at\_\ell_{4,6,7} \wedge at\_m_6 \wedge x = 2 \wedge t_2 = 0)\big).$$

The diagram follows the progress of process P_1 from ℓ_4 with $x = 0$. While P_1 is at ℓ_4, P_2 may execute statement m_5 and set x to 2, which reaches the goal ϕ_0. If this does not happen, P_1 proceeds to ℓ_5 and then to ℓ_6, setting x to 1. Here, we use invariant χ_4 to infer that when P_1 moves from ℓ_5 to ℓ_6, setting x to 1, process P_2 can only be at locations $\ell_0, \ldots, \ell_7$. From this point on, either P_2 will perform m_5, leading again to ϕ_0, or P_2 will perform ℓ_7 moving to ℓ_8, which is also a goal state.

Proving ψ_3

Response formula ψ_3 is given by

$$at\_\ell_{4,6,7} \wedge at\_m_6 \wedge x = 2 \wedge t_2 = 0 \;\; \Rightarrow \;\; \Diamond(at\_\ell_4 \wedge at\_m_0 \wedge x = 0 \wedge t_2 = 0).$$

The formula states that, once P_1 has been overtaken by P_2, it will return to location ℓ_4 *before* P_2 exits its critical section and returns to m_0, setting x back to 0. The fact that, being denied entry to ℓ_8, process P_1 must eventually return to ℓ_3 and proceed to ℓ_4 is obvious. Less obvious is the fact that when P_2 performs m_{10} on its exit from the critical section, P_1 is already at $\ell 4$. This result from the number of statements that each process has to execute until they reach ℓ_4 and m_0, respectively, and from the assumption $U < 2L$ which guarantees that P_1 completes the execution of a single statement before P_2 can complete the execution of two statements.

The worst case for P_1 is if it is overtaken at ℓ_6. To reach ℓ_4 it must execute 3 statements: ℓ_6, ℓ_7, and ℓ_3. It will take P_1 at most $3U$ to do so. To reach location m_0 from its initial location at m_6, P_2 has to execute at least 6 statements: m_6, m_7, m_8, m_3, m_9, and m_{10}. It will take P_2 at least $6L$ to reach m_0. Since $3U < 6L$, P_1 will get to ℓ_3 first.

The precise analysis of this race between P_1 and P_2 is presented by the chain diagram of Fig. 24

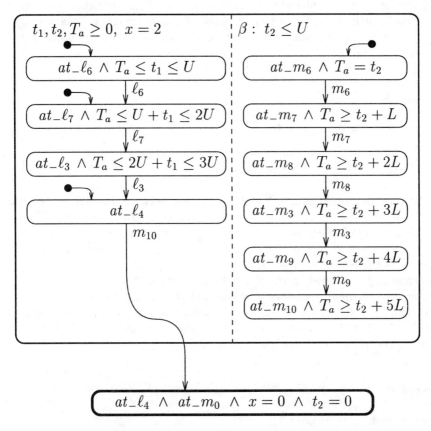

Fig. 24. Chain diagram for the formula

$$\psi_3: \quad at\_\ell_{4,6,7} \wedge at\_m_6 \wedge x = 2 \wedge t_2 = 0 \wedge T_a = 0 \quad \Rightarrow$$
$$\Diamond(at\_\ell_4 \wedge at\_m_0 \wedge x = 0 \wedge t_2 = 0).$$

Note that m_{10} is enabled only at states in which P_1 is at ℓ_4. This is because at all other P_1-locations, $T_a \leq 3U < 6L$. For m_10 to be enabled, T_a must be at least $6L$.

Proving ψ_4

Response formula ψ_4 is given by

$$at\_\ell_4 \wedge at\_m_{6..10} \wedge x = 2 \quad \Rightarrow \quad \Diamond(at\_\ell_4 \wedge at\_m_0 \wedge x = 0 \wedge t_2 = 0).$$

The formula states that, starting with P_1 at ℓ_4, $x = 2$, and P_2 somewhere within $\{m_6, \ldots, m_{10}\}$, we are guaranteed to reach a state in which P_1 is still at ℓ_4 but P_2 has just moved to m_0 (hence $t_2 = x = 0$). This property relies on the progress of P_2 through $\{m_6, \ldots, m_{10}\}$ to m_0 while $x = 2$ and P_1 cannot change the value of x, being stuck at ℓ_4. For a formal proof of this property, we can use again the diagram of Fig. 24, where the initial nodes are within the compound node labeled by at_ℓ_4.

Proving ψ_5

Response formula ψ_5 is given by

$$at\_\ell_4 \wedge at\_m_0 \wedge x = 0 \wedge t_2 = 0 \quad \Rightarrow \quad \Diamond(at\_\ell_6 \wedge at\_m_{0..4} \wedge x = 1).$$

The formula considers another possible race between P_1 and P_2, starting with P_1 at ℓ_4 and P_2 just arriving to m_0. Formula ψ_5 states that P_1 will reach ℓ_6 (with $x = 1$) before P_2 reaches m_5. Note that from a state satisfying $at\_\ell_6 \wedge at\_m_{0..4} \wedge x = 1$ the entry of P_1 to its critical section is guaranteed, since P_2 cannot pass the test at m_4 and interfere with P_1's progress.

Formula ψ_5 is verified by the chain diagram of Fig. 25.

A simple informal argument explains why P_1 is sure to win this race. To move from ℓ_4 to ℓ_6, P_1 has to execute 2 statements: ℓ_4 and ℓ_5, which takes at most $2U$. In that time, P_2 cannot complete the execution of the 5 statements m_0–m_4 necessary to reach m_5, since $5L > 2U$.

Proving ψ_6

Response formula ψ_6 is given by

$$\psi_6: \quad at\_\ell_6 \wedge at\_m_{0..4} \wedge x = 1 \quad \Rightarrow \quad \Diamond at\_\ell_8.$$

This formula states that, once P_1 reached ℓ_6 while P_2 is still confined within the range $\{m_0, \ldots, m_4\}$, entry of P_1 to ℓ_8 is guaranteed. The proof presented in the diagram of Fig. 26 simply traces the progress of P_1 from ℓ_6 to ℓ_8, while x keeps its value of 1.

This concludes the proof of accessibility for program MUTEX$_{[L,U]}$.

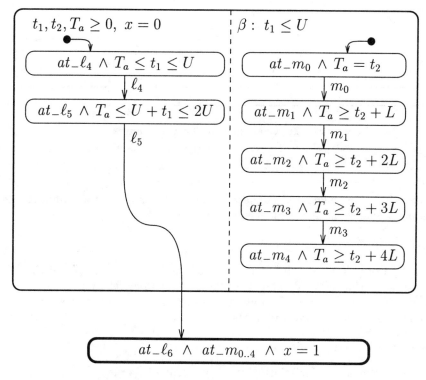

Fig. 25. Chain diagram for the formula

ψ_5: $at\_\ell_4 \wedge at\_m_0 \wedge x = 0 \wedge t_2 = 0 \wedge T_a = 0 \quad \Rightarrow \quad \Diamond(at\_\ell_6 \wedge at\_m_{0..4} \wedge x = 1)$.

5.5 Clock-Bounded Well-Founded Rule

Rule CB-CHAIN is adequate for proving response properties in which a q state is achieved in a number of significant steps which is a priori bounded. For example, in verifying termination of program ANY-Y$_{[3,5]}$, there were 3 helpful steps leading to termination. These are represented in the chain diagram of Fig. 17 by the edges entering nodes ϕ_2–ϕ_0.

In many cases, the number of helpful steps needed to reach the goal q cannot be bounded a priori. For these cases we need a stronger rule, based on well-founded ordering.

Well-founded Domains

We define a *well-founded domain* $(\mathcal{A}, \succ)$ to consist of a set $\mathcal{A}$ and a *well-founded order* relation $\succ$ on $\mathcal{A}$. A binary relation $\succ$ is called an *order* if it is

- transitive: $a \succ b$ and $b \succ c$ imply $a \succ c$, and
- irreflexive: $a \succ a$ for no $a \in \mathcal{A}$.

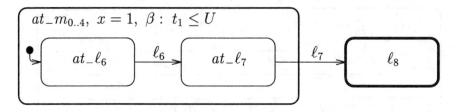

Fig. 26. Chain diagram for the formula
$$\psi_6: \quad at\_\ell_6 \wedge at\_m_{0..4} \wedge x = 1 \quad \Rightarrow \quad \Diamond at\_\ell_8.$$

The relation $\succ$ is called *well-founded* if there does not exist an infinitely descending sequence $a_0, a_1, \ldots$ of elements of $\mathcal{A}$ such that

$$a_0 \; \succ \; a_1 \; \succ \; \cdots \; .$$

A typical example of a well-founded domain is $(\mathrm{N}, >)$, where N are the natural numbers (including 0) and $>$ is the greater-than relation. Clearly, $>$ is well-founded over the natural numbers, because there cannot exist an infinitely descending sequence of natural numbers

$$n_0 \; > \; n_1 \; > \; n_2 \; > \; \ldots \; .$$

For $\succ$, an arbitrary order relation on $\mathcal{A}$, we define its *reflexive extension* $\succeq$ to hold between $a, a' \in \mathcal{A}$ if either $a \succ a'$ or $a = a'$.

Lexicographic Tuples

Another frequently used well-founded domain is $(\mathrm{N}^k, \succ)$, where N^k is the set of k-tuples of natural numbers. The order $\succ$ is defined by

$$(n_1, \ldots, n_k) \; \succ \; (m_1, \ldots, m_k) \quad \text{iff} \quad \begin{aligned} &n_1 = m_1, \; \ldots, \; n_{i-1} = m_{i-1}, \; n_i > m_i \\ &\text{for some } i, \; 1 \leq i \leq k. \end{aligned}$$

For example, for $k = 3$

$$(7, \, 2, \, 1) \; \succ \; (7, \, 0, \, 45).$$

It is easy to show that the domain $(\mathrm{N}^k, \succ)$ is well-founded.

It is possible to make lexicographic comparisons between tuples of integers of different lengths. The convention is that the relation holding between $(a_1, \ldots, a_i)$ and $(b_1, \ldots, b_k)$ for $i < k$ is determined by lexicographically comparing $(a_1, \ldots, a_i, 0, \ldots, 0)$ to $(b_1, \ldots, b_i, b_{i+1}, \ldots, b_k)$. That is, we pad the shorter tuple by zeros on the right until it assumes the length of the longer tuple.

According to this definition, $(0, 2) \succ 0$, since $(0, 2) \succ (0, 0)$. In a similar way, $1 \succ (0, 2)$.

5.6 Rule CB-WELL

In Fig. 27, we present the *clock-bounded well-founded response rule* (rule CB-WELL) for proving response properties of clocked transition systems. The rule uses auxiliary assertions $\varphi_1, \ldots, \varphi_m$ and refers to assertion q also as φ_0. With each assertion φ_i, $i > 0$, we associate one of the clocks $c_i \in C$, to which we refer as the *helpful clock*, and an upper bound B_i, which is a real-valued expression. Also required are a well-founded domain $(\mathcal{A}, \succ)$, and ranking functions $\delta_i \colon \Sigma \mapsto \mathcal{A}$, $i = 1, \ldots, m$, mapping states of the system to elements of $\mathcal{A}$. The ranking functions measure progress of the computation towards the goal q.

For assertions p, q, and $\varphi_0 = q, \varphi_1, \ldots, \varphi_m$,
clocks $c_1, \ldots, c_m \in C$,
real expressions $B_1, \ldots, B_m \in \mathsf{R}$,
a well-founded domain $(\mathcal{A}, \succ)$, and
ranking functions $\delta_1, \ldots, \delta_m \colon \Sigma \mapsto \mathcal{A}$,

W1. $\quad p \;\rightarrow\; \displaystyle\bigvee_{j=0}^{m} \varphi_j$

The following two premises hold for $i = 1, \ldots, m$

W2. $\quad \rho_\tau \wedge \varphi_i \;\rightarrow\; \displaystyle\bigvee_{j=0}^{m} (\varphi_j' \wedge \delta_i \succ \delta_j') \;\vee$
$$(\varphi_i' \wedge \delta_i' = \delta_i \wedge c_i \leq c_i' \wedge B_i' \leq B_i)$$

$$\text{for every } \tau \in \mathcal{T}_T$$

W3. $\quad \varphi_i \;\rightarrow\; c_i \leq B_i$

$$p \;\Rightarrow\; \Diamond\, q$$

Fig. 27. Rule CB-WELL (clock-bounded well-founded rule for response).

Premise W1 requires that every p-position satisfies one of $\varphi_0 = q, \varphi_1, \ldots, \varphi_m$.

Premise W2 requires that every τ-successor (for any $\tau \in \mathcal{T}_T$) of a φ_i-state s is a φ_j-state for some j, with a rank δ_j' not exceeding δ_i. In the case that the successor state satisfies φ_i, it is allowed that $\delta_i' = \delta_i$ but is required that the transition does not decrease the value of c_i or increase the value of B_i. In all other cases it is required that $\delta_j' \prec \delta_i$, i.e., that the rank strictly decreases.

Premise W3 requires that assertion φ_i implies that c_i is bounded by the constant B_i.

The following claim states the soundness of the rule:

Claim 6 *Rule CB-WELL is sound for proving that a response formula is Φ-valid.*

Justification: Assume that the premises of the rule are Φ-valid, and let σ be a computation of Φ. We will show that σ satisfies the rule's consequence

$$p \Rightarrow \Diamond q.$$

Assume that p holds at position k and no later position $i \geq k$ satisfies q. By W1 some φ_j must hold at position k. Let $u_k \in \mathcal{A}$ be the minimal rank of state s_k, i.e. the minimal value of $\delta_j(s_k)$ among all φ_j which hold at s_k. Let j_k be the smallest index such that φ_{j_k} holds at s_k and $u_k = \delta_{j_k}(s_k)$.

By W2, state s_{k+1} must satisfy φ_j for some $j > 0$, implying that s_{k+1} has a defined rank u_{k+1}. Premise W2 requires that $u_{k+1} \preceq u_k$.

Proceeding in this manner we obtain that every position i beyond k has a rank u_i, such that

$$u_k \succeq u_{k+1} \succeq u_{k+2} \succeq \cdots .$$

Since $\mathcal{A}$ is well-founded, there must exist a position $r \geq k$ such that

$$u_r = u_{r+1} = u_{r+2} = \cdots .$$

Denote the value of this eventually-stable rank by $u = u_r$, and let $j_r > 0$ be the index of the assertion such that $\delta_{j_r}(s_r) = u$.

Consider the value of the clock c_{j_r} at states s_i, $i \geq r$. Since the rank never decreases beyond r, the value of c_{j_r} never decreases and the value of B_{j_r} never increases beyond that position. Also, whenever a *tick* transition with increment Δ is taken, c_{j_r} increases (as do all clocks) by Δ. It follows that the master clock T cannot increase by more than $B_{j_r}(s_r) - s_r[c_{j_r}]$ from its value at state s_r. This contradicts the fact that σ is a computation in which the master clock increases beyond all bounds.

We conclude that our assumption of the existence of a p-position not followed by any q-position is false. Consequently, if the premises of the rule hold then every p-position must be followed by a q-position, establishing the consequence of the rule. ◢

Claim 7 *Rule* CB-WELL *is complete for proving that a response formula is valid over a non-zeno system Φ.*

Justification (A sketch): The meaning of this claim is that if the response formula $p \Rightarrow \Diamond q$ is valid over the non-zeno system Φ, then there exist constructs as required by rule CB-WELL, such that all premises of the rule are Φ-state valid.

An execution segment σ is called *q-free* if no state in σ satisfies q. A state s' is said to be a *$\neg q$-follower* of state s if there is a q-free Φ-execution segment leading from s to s'. We follow the techniques of [MP91a] and take for (a single) φ the assertion $pending_q$, constructed in such a way that

$$s \models pending_q \qquad \text{iff} \qquad s \text{ is a } \neg q\text{-follower of a } \Phi\text{-accessible } p\text{-state.}$$

We define a binary relation $\sqsupset$ such that $s \sqsupset s'$ if s satisfies $pending_q$, s' is a $\neg q$-follower of s, and $s'[T] \geq s[T] + 1$. Obviously, $\sqsupset$ is well-founded, because an infinite sequence $s_0 \sqsupset s_1 \sqsupset s_2 \sqsupset \cdots$ would lead to a computation violating $p \Rightarrow \Diamond q$.

Based on a transcendentally inductive construction, we can define a ranking function $\delta \colon \Sigma \mapsto \mathcal{O}rd$, mapping states into the ordinals, such that

O1. If s' is a $\neg q$-follower of the $pending_q$-state s, then $\delta(s) \geq \delta(s')$.
O2. If $s \sqsupset s'$, where s is a $pending_q$-state, then $\delta(s) > \delta(s')$.

Given a pending state s, let $B(s)$ denote the supremum of all values $s'[T]$ where s' is a $\neg q$-follower of s and $\delta(s') = \delta(s)$. Due to property O2, this supremum exists and is bounded by $s[T] + 1$. It can now be shown that all premises of rule CB-WELL hold for the choice of $m = 1$, $\varphi_1 = pending_q$, $c_1 = T$, $B_1 = B(s)$, $(\mathcal{A}, \succ) = (\mathcal{O}rd, >)$, and $\delta_1 = \delta$ as defined above. ▪

The following example illustrates an application of rule CB-WELL.

Example 11. Consider program UP-DOWN presented in Fig. 28.

$$x, y\colon \textbf{integer where } x = y = 0$$

$$\left[\begin{array}{l} \ell_0 : \textbf{while } x = 0 \textbf{ do} \\ \quad \ell_1 : \; y := y + 1 \\ \ell_2 : \textbf{while } y > 0 \textbf{ do} \\ \quad \ell_3 : \; y := y - 1 \\ \ell_4 : \end{array}\right] \quad \Big\| \quad \left[\begin{array}{l} m_0 : x := 1 \\ m_1 : \end{array}\right]$$

$$- \; P_1 \; - \qquad\qquad - \; P_2 \; -$$

Fig. 28. Program UP-DOWN.

This program can be viewed as a generalization of program ANY-Y in which, after terminating the while loop at ℓ_0, ℓ_1, process P_1 proceeds to perform a second while loop at ℓ_2, ℓ_3, decrementing y until it reaches 0.

Assume, we assign the uniform time bounds $[L, U]$ to all executable statements of program UP-DOWN, where our only information about L and U is given by

$$0 \leq L < U < \infty.$$

We use rule CB-WELL to verify that program UP-DOWN terminates. This property can be expressed by the response formula

$$\underbrace{at_\ell_0 \wedge at_m_0 \wedge x = y = t_1 = t_2 = T = 0}_{p} \quad \Rightarrow \quad \Diamond(\underbrace{at_\ell_4 \wedge at_m_1}_{q}).$$

As the well-founded domain, we take $(N^2, \succ)$, i.e., the domain of lexicographic pairs. As time bounds, we use $B_i: U$ for all $i = 1, \ldots, 5$. The auxiliary assertions, helpful clocks, and ranking functions are given by the following table:

$$
\begin{array}{lll}
\varphi_0: \ at\_\ell_4 \wedge at\_m_1 & & \delta_0: \ 0 \\
\varphi_1: \ at\_\ell_3 \wedge at\_m_1 \wedge x = 1 \wedge y > 0 \wedge t_1 \leq U & c_1: \ t_1 & \delta_1: \ (1, 2y) \\
\varphi_2: \ at\_\ell_2 \wedge at\_m_1 \wedge x = 1 \wedge y \geq 0 \wedge t_1 \leq U & c_2: \ t_1 & \delta_2: \ (1, 2y + 1) \\
\varphi_3: \ at\_\ell_0 \wedge at\_m_1 \wedge x = 1 \wedge y \geq 0 \wedge t_1 \leq U & c_3: \ t_1 & \delta_3: \ 2 \\
\varphi_4: \ at\_\ell_1 \wedge at\_m_1 \wedge x = 1 \wedge y \geq 0 \wedge t_1 \leq U & c_4: \ t_1 & \delta_4: \ 3 \\
\varphi_5: \ at\_\ell_{0,1} \wedge at\_m_0 \wedge x = 0 \wedge y \geq 0 \wedge t_1 \leq U \wedge t_2 \leq U & & \\
& c_5: \ t_2 & \delta_5: \ 4
\end{array}
$$

We consider two instances of premise W2: transition ℓ_2 taken from φ_2 and transition ℓ_3 taken from φ_1.

For the case of φ_2, premise W2 assumes the form

$$
\underbrace{\begin{pmatrix} y > 0 \wedge move(\ell_2, \ell_3) \\ \vee \\ y \leq 0 \wedge move(\ell_2, \ell_4) \end{pmatrix}}_{\rho_{\ell_2}} \wedge \ pres(V - \{\pi\}) \wedge \underbrace{at\_m_1 \wedge x = 1 \wedge y \geq 0 \wedge t_1 \leq U}_{\varphi_2}
$$

$$
\rightarrow
$$

$$
\cdots \vee \begin{pmatrix} \underbrace{at'\_\ell_3 \wedge at'\_m_1 \wedge x' = 1 \wedge y' > 0 \wedge t_1' \leq U}_{\varphi_1'} \wedge \underbrace{(1, 2y + 1) \succ (1, 2y)}_{\delta_2 \succ \delta_1'} \\ \vee \\ \underbrace{at'\_\ell_4 \wedge at'\_m_1}_{\varphi_0'} \wedge \underbrace{(1, 2y + 1) \succ 0}_{\delta_2 \succ \delta_0'} \end{pmatrix}
$$

The implication uses the abbreviation

$$
move\,\ell_i, \ell_j: \quad \ell_i \in \pi \wedge \pi' = (\pi - \{\ell_i\}) \cup \{\ell_j\}.
$$

Note that $move(\ell_i, \ell_j)$ implies at'_ℓ_j and $at'\_m_1 = at\_m_1$. Since ρ_{ℓ_2} implies $y' = y$, the implication is obviously valid. In particular, due to

$$
(1, 2y + 1) \succ (1, 2y) \quad \text{and} \quad (1, 2y + 1) \succ 0.
$$

Premise W2 for φ_1 and transition ℓ_3 assumes the form

$$
\underbrace{move(\ell_3, \ell_2) \wedge y' = y - 1 \wedge pres(x, t_1, t_2, T)}_{\rho_{\ell_3}} \wedge
$$

$$
\underbrace{at\_\ell_3 \wedge at\_m_1 \wedge x = 1 \wedge y > 0 \wedge t_1 \leq U}_{\varphi_1} \ \rightarrow
$$

$$
\cdots \vee \begin{pmatrix} \underbrace{at'\_\ell_2 \wedge at'\_m_1 \wedge x' = 1 \wedge y' \geq 0 \wedge t_1' \leq U}_{\varphi_2'} \wedge \underbrace{(1, 2y) \succ (1, 2y' + 1)}_{\delta_1 \succ \delta_2'} \end{pmatrix}
$$

Since ρ_{ℓ_3} implies $y' = y - 1$, it is easy to verify that $y > 0$ implies $y' \geq 0$ and

$$(1, 2y' + 1) = (1, 2(y - 1) + 1) = (1, 2y - 1) \prec (1, 2y).$$

This establishes that the response property

$$at\_\ell_0 \wedge at\_m_0 \wedge x = y = t_1 = t_2 = T = 0 \quad \Rightarrow \quad \Diamond(at\_\ell_4 \wedge at\_m_1).$$

is valid over program UP-DOWN. ⌐

5.7 Ranked Diagrams

The main ingredients of a proof by rule CB-WELL can be conveniently and effectively presented by a special type of verification diagrams that summarize the auxiliary assertions, their helpful clocks and bounds, and their ranking functions, and display the possible transitions between the assertions.

We define a *ranked diagram* to be a directed labeled graph constructed as follows:

- *Nodes* in the graph are labeled by assertions. Each node is labeled by a pair of assertions: ϕ_i and β_i, for $i = 0, \ldots, m$, and a ranking function δ_i. The assertion β_i has the form $c_i \leq B_i$, where $c_i \in C$ is a clock and B_i is a real-valued expression. We refer to the conjunction $\phi_i \wedge \beta_i$ as φ_i, and say that the node is labeled by the (combined) assertion φ_i. We often refer to nodes by the assertion φ_i labeling them.

  The node labeled by φ_0 is called the *terminal node* and is graphically identified by being drawn with bold-face boundaries.

- *Edges* in the graph represent transitions between assertions. Each edge connects one assertion to another and is labeled by one or more transitions.

Verification Conditions Implied by a Ranked Diagram

Consider a nonterminal node labeled by assertion φ: $\phi \wedge \beta$ where the clock-bound assertion is β: $c \leq B$ and the ranking function is δ. Let $\tau \in \mathcal{T}_T$ be a transition and let $\varphi_1, \ldots, \varphi_k$, $k \geq 0$, be the successors of φ by edges labeled with τ (possibly including φ itself). With each such node and transition, we associate the following verification condition:

$$\rho_\tau \wedge \varphi \quad \rightarrow \quad (\varphi' \wedge \delta' = \delta \wedge c \leq c' \leq B' \leq B) \vee (\varphi' \wedge \delta \succ \delta') \vee$$
$$(\varphi_1' \wedge \delta \succ \delta_1') \vee \cdots \vee (\varphi_k' \wedge \delta \succ \delta_k').$$

In particular, if $k = 0$ (i.e., φ has no τ-successors), the associated verification condition is

$$\rho_\tau \wedge \varphi \quad \rightarrow \quad (\varphi' \wedge \delta' = \delta \wedge c \leq c' \leq B' \leq B) \vee (\varphi' \wedge \delta \succ \delta').$$

Valid Ranked Diagrams

A ranked diagram is said to be *valid over* CTS Φ (*Φ-valid* for short) if all the verification conditions associated with the diagram are Φ-state valid.

The consequences of having a valid ranked diagram are stated in the following claim:

Claim 8 *If D is a Φ-valid ranked diagram with nodes $\varphi_0, \ldots, \varphi_m$, then*

$$\Phi \models \bigvee_{j=0}^{m} \varphi_j \;\Rightarrow\; \Diamond \varphi_0$$

If, in addition, $\varphi_0 = q$ and

$$W1: \quad p \;\rightarrow\; \bigvee_{j=0}^{m} \varphi_j,$$

then we can conclude:

$$\Phi \models p \;\Rightarrow\; \Diamond q.$$

Example 12. In Fig. 29, we present a ranked diagram which establishes that the response property

$$at\_\ell_0 \wedge at\_m_0 \wedge x = y = t_1 = t_2 = T = 0 \;\Rightarrow\; \Diamond(at\_\ell_4 \wedge at\_m_1).$$

is valid over program UP-DOWN.

Observe that the β assertions for nodes ϕ_1-ϕ_4 appear at the head of the compound nodes containing these nodes, as part of the encapsulation conventions.

◢

5.8 From Waiting-for to Response Properties

In many useful cases, we can infer response formulas from a waiting-for formula of a particular form.

Rule W→R, presented in Fig. 30, supports the inference of a response formula from a waiting-for formula of a special form. The rule refers to a *rigid expression* B, which is an expression that does not change its value from one state to the next.

Justification: Assume that the waiting-for premise is Φ-valid. Consider a Φ-computation σ, and a p-position $j \geq 0$ in σ. By the waiting-for formula, j initiates an interval, all of whose positions satisfy $q \wedge T_a \leq B$, which either extends to infinity or is terminated by an r-position. Since σ is a computation, T must grow beyond all values and cannot remain bounded by the constant value of B at all positions. It follows that j must be followed by an r-position.

◢

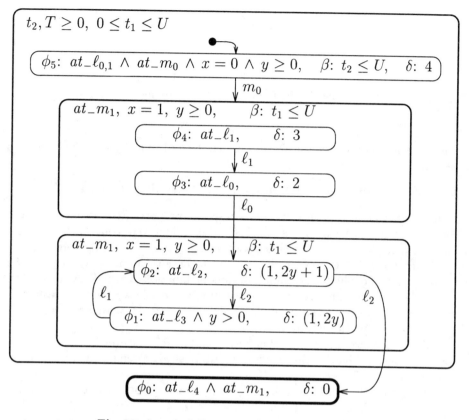

Fig. 29. A ranked diagram, establishing the formula
$$at\_\ell_0 \wedge at\_m_0 \wedge x = y = t_1 = t_2 = T = 0 \quad \Rightarrow \quad \Diamond(at\_\ell_4 \wedge at\_m_1)$$

Example 13.   Consider the SPL$_T$ program UP-DOWN$_{[1,5]}$, which is program UP-DOWN with time bounds [1,5] uniformly assigned to all executable statements.

We use rule W→R to verify that the response formula

$$at\_\ell_0 \wedge at\_m_0 \wedge x = y = T_a = 0 \quad \Rightarrow \quad \Diamond(at\_\ell_4 \wedge at\_m_1 \wedge T_a \le 50)$$

is valid over program UP-DOWN$_{[1,5]}$.

In Fig. 31, we present a waiting diagram which establishes the UP-DOWN$_{[1,5]}$-validity of the waiting-for formula

$$at\_\ell_0 \wedge at\_m_0 \wedge x = y = T_a = 0 \quad \Rightarrow \quad (T_a \le 50)\,\mathcal{W}\,(at\_\ell_4 \wedge T_a \le 50)$$

Note that the assertion describing the initial state does not specify initial values for either t_1 or t_2. To show that the waiting diagram is valid, we rely on the following invariant:

$$\Box\big((at\_\ell_0 \;\rightarrow\; 0 \le t_1 \le 5) \wedge (at\_m_0 \;\rightarrow\; 0 \le t_2 \le 5)\big).$$

> For assertions p, q, and r, and rigid expression B,
>
> $$\frac{p \quad \Rightarrow \quad (q \wedge T_a \leq B) \, \mathcal{W} \, r}{p \quad \Rightarrow \quad \Diamond \, r}$$

Fig. 30. Rule W→R (from waiting-for to response formulas).

This invariant can be separately established, using the methods of Section 4. ◢

5.9 Are Rules CB-CHAIN and CB-WELL Really Necessary?

Rule W→R enables the derivation of a response property from a timed waiting-for property, which can be established using rule WAIT. Rule WAIT (and its equivalent formulation in terms of waiting diagrams) is, in principle, simpler than either rule CB-CHAIN or rule CB-WELL, because it does not require the identification of explicit time bounds or ranking functions as auxiliary constructs.

In view of this, a naturally rising question is why do we need the response-specific rules CB-CHAIN and CB-WELL. Isn't rule W→R adequate for establishing all response properties of interest?

We provide two answers to this question. The first answer is that there are some response properties that cannot be established through timed waiting-for properties.

To support this point, consider again program UP-DOWN but with general (uniform) time bounds, $[L, U]$, such that $0 \leq L \leq U < \infty$. For all cases that $L > 0$, we can essentially repeat the analysis done in Example 13, and establish the waiting-for formula

$$at\_\ell_0 \wedge at\_m_0 \wedge x = y = T_a = 0 \quad \Rightarrow \quad (T_a \leq B) \, \mathcal{W} \, (at\_\ell_4 \wedge T_a \leq B),$$

where

$$B = (6 + 2 \left\lfloor \frac{U}{2L} \right\rfloor) U.$$

Applying rule W→R to this formula, one can infer the response formula

$$at\_\ell_0 \wedge at\_m_0 \wedge x = y = T_a = 0 \quad \Rightarrow \quad \Diamond(at\_\ell_4 \wedge T_a \leq B),$$

guaranteeing termination within B time units.

One can see that as L gets closer to 0, the bound on termination time gets larger. It is therefore not surprising that when $L = 0$, there is no bound on the time it takes the program to terminate. Yet, all computations of this program eventually lead to the termination state at_ℓ_4. Thus, termination of program UP-DOWN in the case of $L = 0$ is a response property that cannot be verified using rule W→R. On the other hand, in Example 11, we established termination of UP-DOWN, using rule CB-WELL, in a proof that is valid for all $L \geq 0$. This

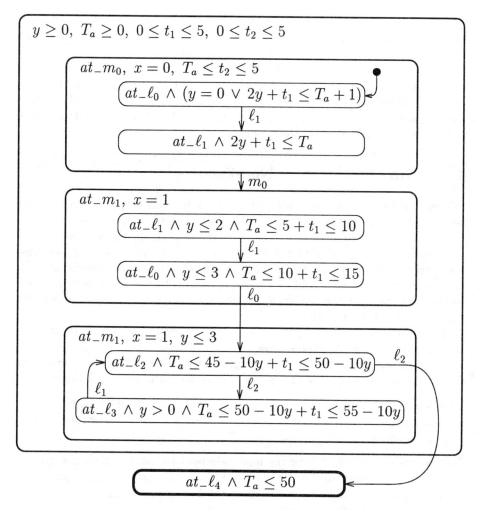

Fig. 31. A waiting diagram, establishing the formula

$$at\_\ell_0 \wedge at\_m_0 \wedge x = y = T_a = 0 \quad \Rightarrow \quad (T_a \leq 50) \, \mathcal{W} \, (at\_\ell_4 \wedge T_a \leq 50)$$

illustrates the case of a response property that cannot be proven by rule W→R, but is provable by rule CB-WELL.

As the second answer justifying the introduction of rule CB-WELL, we propose to compare the verification diagram of Fig. 29 with that of Fig. 31, both establishing termination of UP-DOWN for the time bounds [1, 5] (Fig. 29 actually established it for general [L, U]). It is obvious that diagram 31 requires a much more detailed analysis of the precise time interval which we can spend at each of the diagram nodes. In comparison, the diagram of Fig. 29 said very little about these time intervals. The only timing information included in this diagram was that the time spent at each of the nodes is bounded by U. Thus, when we need or are ready to conduct a very precise analysis of the time intervals spent at each node, it makes sense to use waiting diagrams and rule W→R. If, on the other hand, we are content with less quantitative analysis, and are only interested in the qualitative fact that *eventually q* will occur (which is the essence of the ◇ temporal operator), we may use rule CB-WELL or rule CB-CHAIN. These rules may be conceptually more complicated than rule WAIT, but their application calls for a simpler analysis of the program.

6 Proving that a CTS is Non-Zeno

It is by now a widely accepted notion that the only interesting real-time systems are those which obey the non-zeno restriction. One of the reasons is that, since we only consider time-divergent runs as computations, a possibly-zeno system may contain components that will never be accessed in a computation. In some sense, these components are redundant to the description of the system and their inclusion is superfluous and often confusing and misleading. Non-zeno systems, on the other hand, contain no such redundancy, since every accessible state also appears in some computation.

In view of the significance of the non-zeno restriction, it is important to be able to verify that an arbitrary given CTS is non-zeno.

In many cases, there are simple sufficient conditions which guarantee that the system is non-zeno. One of the most important cases is the following:

Claim 9 *Let P be an* SPL$_T$ *program in which the upper bound assigned to each executable statement is a positive constant. Then Φ_P, the* CTS *corresponding to P, is a non-zeno system.*

Justification Let $U_m > 0$ be the minimal upper bound. Consider a finite run $r: s_0, \ldots, s_k$. We wish to show that r can be extended into a computation.

The recipe for extending r considers the last reached state $s\ (= s_k)$ and decides to apply the next transition as follows:

- If the *tick* transition is enabled on s, take the *tick* transition with increment $\Delta > 0$, which is the maximal $\Delta \leq 1$ satisfying $s \models \Omega(\Delta)$.
- If the *tick* transition is disabled on s, it must be blocked by one of the processes, say P_i, whose clock t_i has reached the upper bound of some transition τ of P_i which is currently enabled. In this case, take this ripe transition τ.

It is not difficult to check that an accessible state in a clocked transition systems derived from a program with positive upper bounds always has at least one extended transition enabled on it. Thus, the described recipe produces an infinite run. This observation hinges on the revised transition relation we associated with the *wait* statement.

It only remains to check that the infinite run produced by this recipe is time-divergent and, hence, is a computation. By considering the different possibilities, we observe that two cases are possible.

In one case, we eventually reach a state s such that $s \models \Omega(\Delta)$, for every $\Delta > 0$. In this case, once we reach this s, we continue to take *tick* steps with $\Delta = 1$.

In the remaining case, for every reached state s_i, there exists a limit Δ_i such that $s_i \models \Omega(\Delta)$ for no $\Delta > \Delta_i$. In this case, our construction must take infinitely many untimed transitions, i.e., transitions $\tau \neq$ *tick*. Note that each such transition resets one of the clocks to 0. It follows that the construction of the infinite run causes at least one of the clocks, say t_i, to be reset to 0 infinitely many times. It is not difficult to see that between two consecutive resets of clock t_i, time must progress by at least U_m. It follows that time has progressed infinitely many times by the amount $U_m > 0$ and, therefore, the run is time-divergent. ⏹

6.1 A Rule for Establishing Non-Zenoness

While Claim 9 settles the question of non-zenoness for many useful cases, there are additional cases which require different methods. The claim was established for the simpler case that the upper bounds assigned to transitions were positive constants. It can easily be generalized to state-dependent upper bounds which are bounded from below by a positive constant. However, this still does not cover all possible cases. For example, CTS Φ_4 presented in Fig. 32, is a non-zeno system, even though, the upper bounds of the transition connecting ℓ_0 to itself have no lower bound.

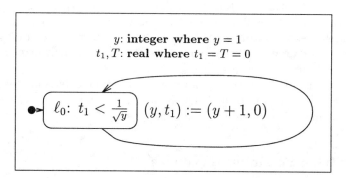

Fig. 32. A non-zeno CTS Φ_4 with upper bounds tending to 0.

The general strategy we propose for proving that a given CTS Φ is non-zeno is summarized in rule NONZ, presented in Fig. 33.

The rule uses an auxiliary assertion φ. Premise N1 requires that φ is Φ-state valid, and can be proven using rule ACC.

Premise N2 belongs to the realm of branching-time temporal logic, which is different from the linear-time temporal framework we have been consistently

For assertion φ,

  N1. $\quad \Phi \models \varphi$

  N2. $\quad \Phi \models AG(\varphi \wedge T_a = 0 \quad \rightarrow \quad EF(T_a \geq 1))$

  _____

  $\quad \Phi$ is non-zeno

Fig. 33. Rule NONZ (Φ is a non-zeno CTS).

using in this paper. It has long been observed that the property of being non-zeno cannot be formulated in linear-time TL and needs branching-time TL for its precise formulation. In a recent paper ([Lam95]), Lamport makes this observation but suggests a method by which properties such as non-zenoness can still be verified in a linear framework. We prefer to use the branching-time logic CTL([EC82]) for formulating the required property, as in premise N2, and present a single proof rule which is adequate to establish CTL formulas such as the one presented in N2. A deductive system for verifying the main CTL properties appeared in [BAMP83]. A more comprehensive deductive system for CTL was recently proposed in [FG95].

Premise N2 states that, from every φ-state s, it is possible to trace a computation segment in which time increases by at least 1 from its value at s. We use the constant a to represent the global time at s.

Justification By premise N1, all Φ-reachable states satisfy the assertion φ. Let s be an arbitrary reachable Φ-state. By N1, it satisfies φ. By N2, we can construct a computations segment from s to another state s_1, such that $s_1[T] \geq s[T] + 1$. Applying premise N2 to s_1, we are guaranteed of a computations segment leading from s_1 to some state s_2, such that $s_2[T] \geq s_1[T] + 1$.

Proceeding in this manner, we can construct a time-divergent run, starting at s. It follows that any finite run, such as the one leading to s, can be extended to a computation. We conclude that Φ is non-zeno. ∎

6.2 Verifying Possibility Formulas

A *possibility formula* is a CTL formula of the form

$$AG(p \rightarrow EFq),$$

for assertions p and q. Without entering into the individual meaning of the CTL temporal operators AG and EF, we say that the possibility formula $AG(p \rightarrow EFq)$ is *valid over* CTS Φ (Φ-*valid*) if

For every accessible p-state s, there exists a run segment $s = s_1, \ldots, s_k$ leading from s to a q-state s_k.

We write

$$\Phi \models AG(p \; \rightarrow \; EFq)$$

to indicate that the possibility formula $AG(p \rightarrow EFq)$ is Φ-valid.

In Fig. 34, we present rule POSS which is sound and complete for proving the Φ-validity of a possibility formula.

For assertions p, q, and $\varphi_0 = q, \varphi_1, \ldots, \varphi_m$,
transitions $\tau_1, \ldots, \tau_m \in T_T$,
functions $Next_1, \ldots, Next_m \colon \Sigma \mapsto \Sigma$,
a well-founded domain $(\mathcal{A}, \succ)$, and
ranking functions $\delta_0, \ldots, \delta_m \colon \Sigma \mapsto \mathcal{A}$,

G1. $\quad p \; \rightarrow \; \bigvee_{j=0}^{m} \varphi_j$

The following premise holds for $i = 1, \ldots, m$

G2. $\quad \varphi_i \wedge V' = Next_i \quad \rightarrow \quad \rho_{\tau_i} \wedge \bigvee_{j=0}^{m} (\varphi_j' \wedge \delta_i \succ \delta_j')$

$$\Phi \models AG(p \; \rightarrow \; EFq)$$

Fig. 34. Rule G-POSS (Φ validity of a possibility formula).

The rule requires finding auxiliary assertions φ_i, functions $Next_i \colon \Sigma \mapsto \Sigma$, and transitions τ_i, $i = 1, \ldots, m$, a well-founded domain $(\mathcal{A}, \succ)$, and ranking functions $\delta_i \colon S \mapsto \mathcal{A}$. Each assertion φ_i is associated with the transition τ_i that is helpful at positions satisfying φ_i, with a function $Next_i$ that selects a successor state, and with its own ranking function δ_i. We have presented the successor-selection functions $Next_i$ as mapping states to states but, in fact, they map $s[V]$, i.e., the values of the system variables in state s, to $s'[V]$, the values of the system variables in a successor state s'.

Premise G1 requires that every p-position satisfies one of $\varphi_0, \ldots, \varphi_m$.

Premise G2 considers a φ_i-state s and a state $\tilde{s}$ such that $\tilde{s}[V] = s[V'] = Next_i$, for some $i = 1, \ldots, m$. The premise requires that $\tilde{s}$ is a τ_i-successor of s which satisfies φ_j, for some $j = 0, \ldots, m$ and has a rank lower than that of s.

Justification Let s be a p-state. We will show that there exists a run segment $s = s_1, \ldots, s_k$ which leads from s to a q-state. By premise G1, $s = s_1$ must satisfy φ_j, for some $j = 0, \ldots, m$. Let j_1 be the minimal j such that $s \models \varphi_j$. If $j_1 = 0$, we are done, since s_1 satisfies $\varphi_0 = q$.

Otherwise, $j_1 > 0$ and let $u_1 = \delta_{j_1}(s_1)$. Let s_2 be any state such that $s_2[V] = Next_{j_1}(s_1[V])$. By premise G2, s_2 is a τ_{j_1}-successor of s_1, satisfies φ_{j_2} for some

$j_2 \in \{0, \ldots, m\}$, and a rank $u_2 = \delta_{j_2}(s_2) \prec u_1$. If $j_2 = 0$, we are done. Otherwise, we take s_3 to be some $Next_{j_2}$-selected successor of s_2, and so on.

This construction can terminate when we reach some k such that $j_k = 0$. If it does not terminate, we generate an infinite descending sequence

$$u_1 \succ u_2 \succ \cdots.$$

This is impossible due to the well-foundedness of $\mathcal{A}$. We conclude that the construction must terminate in a state s_k satisfying $\varphi_0 = q$. ◢

Example 14. We illustrate the application of rule G-POSS for proving that the possibility formula

$$AG\big(\underbrace{at\_\ell_{0,1} \wedge T_a = 0}_{p} \quad \rightarrow \quad EF(\underbrace{T_a \geq 1}_{q})\big)$$

is valid over CTS Φ_5, presented in Fig. 35.

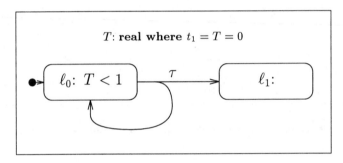

Fig. 35. A non-zeno CTS Φ_5.

Observe that transition τ, the only transition in Φ_5, has two successors. One satisfying at_ℓ_0 and the other satisfying at_ℓ_1.

To apply rule G-POSS, we take $(\mathbb{N}, >)$ (the domain of the natural numbers) as the well-founded domain. The auxiliary assertions, helpful transitions, successor-selection functions, and ranking functions are given by the following table:

$$
\begin{array}{llll}
\varphi_0\colon T_a \geq 1 & \tau_0\colon tick & Next_0\colon (\pi'\colon 1,\ T'\colon T+1) & \delta_0\colon 0 \\
\varphi_1\colon at\_\ell_1 \wedge T_a \geq 0 & \tau_1\colon tick & Next_1\colon (\pi'\colon 1,\ T'\colon T+1) & \delta_1\colon 1 \\
\varphi_2\colon at\_\ell_0 \wedge T_a \geq 0 & \tau_2\colon \tau & Next_2\colon (\pi'\colon 1,\ T'\colon T) & \delta_2\colon 2
\end{array}
$$

This choice of constructs, corresponds to a strategy of constructing a run segment in which time will progress by at least 1. According to this strategy, if we are at ℓ_0, we choose to take transition τ and choose a τ-successor state satisfying at_ℓ_1. If we are at ℓ_1, we choose to take the *tick* transition with time increment 1.

It is not difficult to check that all premises of rule G-POSS are satisfied by this choice of constructs.

It follows that the possibility formula

$$AG\big(at\_\ell_{0,1} \wedge T_a = 0 \quad \rightarrow \quad EF(T_a \geq 1)\big)$$

is Φ_5-valid. ⏌

Systems with Deterministic Transitions

Rule G-POSS is very general and can be shown to be complete for proving possibility properties of all clocked transition systems. However, there is a big family of systems which can be handled by a rule which call for identification of simpler constructs.

A transition τ of a CTS is called *deterministic* if all the τ-successors of an accessible state assign the same values to the system variables. That is, if we restrict our attention to the values of the system variables, each accessible state has at most one τ-successor. We say that a CTS Φ is *transition-deterministic* (Φ is a TD-CTS for short) if all of its (untimed) transitions are deterministic. All the systems we have presented in this paper, excluding Φ_5, are transition-deterministic.

Consider a TD-CTS Φ. Assume that we wish to construct the successor-selection function $Next_i$ corresponding to assertion φ_i, where $\tau_i \neq tick$. Since τ_i is deterministic, $Next_i$ is uniquely determined, and its explicit specification is redundant. The situation is different with the *tick* transition, which may have (uncountably) many successors, each corresponding to a different value of the time increment Δ. However, once we specify the value of Δ, the successor of a *tick* transition is also uniquely determined up to differences in non-system variables.

Thus, instead of specifying a complete successor function, specifying the values of all system variables in the successor state, it is sufficient to specify the time increment Δ_i associated with the successor. For uniformity, we specify values of Δ_i also for untimed transitions, but then we ensure that $\Delta_i = 0$.

This leads to rule POSS (Fig. 36) which is adequate for proving possibility properties of every TD-CTS. Rule POSS has more premises than rule G-POSS but it requires the identification of simpler constructs, and the premises are easier to verify.

Note that rule POSS splits premise G2 of rule G-POSS into two premises. Premise P2 guarantees that the (unique) successor of a φ_i-state corresponding to the identification of the helpful transition τ_i and the time increment Δ_i (if it exists), satisfies some φ_j with a lower rank. Premise P3 guarantees that each φ_i-state does have a successor corresponding to τ_i and Δ_i. The premise is split into the case of the *tick* transition (sub-premise P3t) and the case of all other untimed transitions (sub-premise P3n). Sub-premise P3t requires that φ_i implies $\Omega(\Delta_i)$, the enabling condition of transition *tick*, with the specified Δ_i. Sub-premise P3n requires that $\Delta_i = 0$ and that φ_i implies the enableness of τ_i.

For assertions p, q, and $\varphi_0 = q, \varphi_1, \ldots, \varphi_m$,
transitions $\tau_1, \ldots, \tau_m \in T_T$,
time increments $\Delta_1, \ldots, \Delta_m \geq 0$,
a well-founded domain $(\mathcal{A}, \succ)$, and
ranking functions $\delta_0, \ldots, \delta_m \colon \Sigma \mapsto \mathcal{A}$,

P1. $\quad p \quad \rightarrow \quad \displaystyle\bigvee_{j=0}^{m} \varphi_j$

The following premises hold for $i = 1, \ldots, m$

P2. $\quad \rho_{\tau_i} \wedge T' = T + \Delta_i \wedge \varphi_i \quad \rightarrow \quad \displaystyle\bigvee_{j=0}^{m} (\varphi_j' \wedge \delta_i \succ \delta_j')$

P3. If $\tau_i = tick$ then
$\quad$ P3t. $\quad \varphi_i \quad \rightarrow \quad \Omega(\Delta_i)$
$\quad$ Otherwise
$\quad$ P3n. $\quad \varphi_i \quad \rightarrow \quad \Delta_i = 0 \wedge En(\tau_i)$

$\Phi \models AG(p \quad \rightarrow \quad EFq)$

Fig. 36. Rule POSS (Φ validity of a possibility formula).

Example 15. We illustrate the use of rule POSS for proving that the possibility formula

$$AG(\underbrace{at\_\ell_0 \wedge 1 \leq y = u \wedge 0 \leq t_1 \leq \frac{1}{\sqrt{y}} \wedge T_a = 0}_{p} \quad \rightarrow \quad EF(\underbrace{T_a \geq 1}_{q}))$$

is valid over CTS Φ_4, where u is an auxiliary rigid variable (retaining the same value over all states) recording the value of y at the state described by $at\_\ell_0 \wedge 1 \leq y \wedge 0 \leq t_1 \leq \frac{1}{\sqrt{y}} \wedge T_a = 0$.

Note that CTS Φ_4 has a single untimed transition, to which we refer as τ_{00}.

As the well-founded domain, we take $(\mathbb{N}^2, \succ)$, the domain of lexicographic pairs. The auxiliary assertions, helpful transitions, time increments, and ranking functions are given by the following table:

φ_0: $T_a \geq 1$ τ_0: τ_{00} Δ_0: 0 δ_0: 0

φ_1: $at\_\ell_0 \wedge 1 \leq u \leq y \leq 2u+1 \wedge t_1 = 0 \wedge \frac{y-u-1}{\sqrt{2u+1}} \leq T_a < 1$

τ_1: $tick$ Δ_1: $\frac{1}{\sqrt{y}}$ δ_1: $(|2u+1-y|, 2)$

φ_2: $at\_\ell_0 \wedge 1 \leq u \leq y \leq 2u+1 \wedge t_1 = \frac{1}{\sqrt{y}} \wedge \frac{y-u}{\sqrt{2u+1}} \leq T_a < 1$

τ_2: τ_{00} Δ_2: 0 δ_2: $(|2u+1-y|, 1)$

φ_3: $at\_\ell_0 \wedge 1 \leq u \leq y \leq 2u+1 \wedge 0 < t_1 < \frac{1}{\sqrt{y}} \wedge 0 \leq T_a < 1$

τ_3: $tick$ Δ_3: $\frac{1}{\sqrt{y}} - t_1$ δ_3: $2u+2$

The idea behind this selection is the following. Starting in a state at which $y = u \geq 1$ and $0 < t_1 < \frac{1}{\sqrt{y}}$ (described by assertion φ_3), we first step time with an increment $\frac{1}{\sqrt{y}} - t_1$, this will get us to a state in which $t_1 = \frac{1}{\sqrt{y}}$ (described by φ_2). From this point on, we alternate between taking untimed transition τ_{00} which increments y by 1 but preserves time, and taking transition $tick$, which increments time by $\frac{1}{\sqrt{y}}$ but preserves the value of y. We repeat this couple of steps at most $u+1$ times, letting y increase from u to $2u+1$. Since the time step in each round is decreasing, the total time increase is not less than $u+1$ times the last time increment which is $\frac{1}{\sqrt{2u+1}}$. Thus the total time increase is not less than

$$\frac{u+1}{\sqrt{2u+1}} \geq 1,$$

where the inequality holds for every $u \geq 1$.

This informal argument can be formalized by checking that all premises of rule POSS are state valid for the specified selection of the auxiliary assertions, helpful transitions, time increments, and well-founded ranking.

This establishes that the possibility formula

$$AG(at\_\ell_0 \wedge 1 \leq y = u \wedge 0 \leq t_1 \leq \frac{1}{\sqrt{y}} \wedge T_a = 0 \quad \rightarrow \quad EF(T_a \geq 1))$$

is valid over CTS Φ_4. ⌐

6.3 Possibility Diagrams

Proofs according to rule POSS can be succinctly represented by *possibility diagrams*.

A possibility diagram is a directed labeled graph constructed as follows:

- *Nodes* in the graph are labeled by assertions $\varphi_0, \ldots, \varphi_m$. We will often refer to a node by the assertion labeling it. In addition to the assertion, each node is also labeled by a ranking function δ.

  The node labeled by φ_0 is called the *terminal node* and is graphically identified by being drawn with bold-face boundaries.

- *Edges* in the graph represent transitions between assertions. Each edge is labeled by the name of an untimed transition in the program or by a label of the form $tick(\Delta)$. We refer to an edge labeled by τ (including the case that $\tau = tick$) as a τ-*edge*. All edges departing from the same node must have the same label. Every non-terminal node must have an edge departing from it. No edges depart form the terminal node.
- Some of the nodes are designated as *initial nodes*. They are annotated by an entry arrow.

Verification Conditions Implied by a Possibility Diagram

Consider a nonterminal node labeled by assertion φ and ranking function δ. Let $\varphi_1, \ldots, \varphi_k$, $k > 0$, be the successors of φ by edges departing from φ (possibly including φ itself). With each such node, we associate the following verification condition:

- If the label of all edges departing from φ is $tick(\Delta)$, then we require the following verification conditions to hold:

P2. $\quad \rho_{tick} \wedge T' = T + \Delta \wedge \varphi \quad \rightarrow \quad (\varphi_1' \wedge \delta \succ \delta_1') \vee \cdots \vee (\varphi_k' \wedge \delta \succ \delta_k')$
P3t. $\quad \varphi \quad \rightarrow \quad \Omega(\Delta)$

- If the label of all edges departing from φ is $\tau \neq tick$, then we require the following verification conditions to hold:

P2. $\quad \rho_\tau \wedge T' = T \wedge \varphi \quad \rightarrow \quad (\varphi_1' \wedge \delta \succ \delta_1') \wedge \cdots \wedge (\varphi_k' \wedge \delta \succ \delta_k')$
P3n. $\quad \varphi \quad \rightarrow \quad En(\tau)$

Valid Possibility Diagrams

A possibility diagram is said to be *valid over* CTS Φ (Φ-*valid* for short) if all the verification conditions associated with the diagram are P-state valid.

The consequences of having a valid possibility diagram are stated in the following claim:

Claim 10 *If D is a Φ-valid possibility diagram with nodes $\varphi_0, \ldots, \varphi_m$, then*

$$\Phi \models AG(\bigvee_{j=0}^{m} \varphi_j \quad \rightarrow \quad EF\varphi_0)$$

If, in addition, $\varphi_0 = q$, and

$$p \quad \rightarrow \quad \bigvee_{j=0}^{m} \varphi_j,$$

then we can conclude:

$$\Phi \models AG(p \quad \rightarrow \quad EFq).$$

Example 16. In Fig. 37, we present a possibility diagram that establishes the possibility property

$$AG(at\_\ell_0 \land 1 \leq y = u \land 0 \leq t_1 \leq \frac{1}{\sqrt{y}} \land T_a = 0 \quad \rightarrow \quad EF(T_a \geq 1))$$

for system Φ_4. ◢

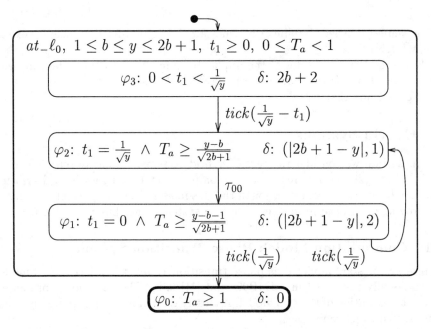

Fig. 37. A possibility diagram, establishing the formula
$$AG(at\_\ell_0 \land 1 \leq y = u \land 0 \leq t_1 \leq \frac{1}{\sqrt{y}} \land T_a = 0 \quad \rightarrow \quad EF(T_a \geq 1))$$

6.4 Proving that Φ_4 is Non-Zeno

We conclude this discussion by applying rule NONZ to show that CTS Φ_4 is non-zeno.

As the assertion φ required by rule NONZ, we take

$$\varphi: \quad at\_\ell_0 \land y \geq 1 \land 0 \leq t_1 \leq \frac{1}{\sqrt{y}}.$$

It is not difficult to show by rule ACC that φ is Φ_4-state valid. This establishes premise N1 of rule NONZ.

For premise N2 of NONZ, we have to verify the possibility formula

$$AG(at\_\ell_0 \land y \geq 1 \land 0 \leq t_1 \leq \frac{1}{\sqrt{y}} \land T_a = 0 \quad \rightarrow \quad EF(T_a \geq 1)). \tag{2}$$

Example 15 establishes the possibility formula

$$AG(at\_\ell_0 \wedge y \geq 1 \wedge 0 \leq t_1 \leq \frac{1}{\sqrt{y}} \wedge y = u \wedge T_a = 0 \quad \rightarrow \quad EF(T_a \geq 1)),$$

to which we may apply existential quantification over the rigid variable u to obtain

$$AG(\exists u: \left(at\_\ell_0 \wedge y \geq 1 \wedge 0 \leq t_1 \leq \tfrac{1}{\sqrt{y}} \wedge y = u \wedge T_a = 0 \right) \quad \rightarrow \\ EF(T_a \geq 1)), \quad (3)$$

using well-established simplification rules for rigid quantification (see, for example [MP91b]).

Since the left-hand sides of the implications in (2) and (3) can be shown to be equivalent, it follows that the formula (2) is Φ_4-valid.

We conclude that CTS Φ_4 is non-zeno.

7 Hybrid Systems

In this section we consider the case of hybrid systems. Similar to our treatment of real-time systems, we present first a computational model for hybrid systems that can be viewed as an extension of the CTS model. Then we present rule INV-H for proving invariance properties of hybrid systems, and illustrate its use.

7.1 Computation Model: Phase Transition System

Hybrid systems are modeled as phase transition systems (PTS). The PTS model was originally presented in [MMP92] and [MP93b]. The PTS model presented here is an extension of the CTS model. A closely related model for hybrid systems is presented in [NOSY93].

A *phase transition system* (PTS) $\Phi = \langle V, \Theta, \mathcal{T}, \mathcal{A}, \Pi \rangle$ consists of:

- $V = \{u_1, ..., u_n\}$: A finite set of *system variables*. The set $V = D \cup I$ is partitioned into D the set of *discrete variables* and I the set of *integrators*. Integrators always have the type *real*. The discrete variables can be of any type. We introduce a special integrator $T \in I$ representing the *master clock*.
- Θ : The *initial condition*. A satisfiable assertion characterizing the initial states. It is required that

$$\Theta \quad \rightarrow \quad T = 0.$$

- $\mathcal{T}$: A finite set of *transitions*. Each transition $\tau \in \mathcal{T}$ is a function

$$\tau : \Sigma \mapsto 2^{\Sigma},$$

mapping each state $s \in \Sigma$ into a (possibly empty) set of τ-*successor* states $\tau(s) \subseteq \Sigma$. As before, the successor function for τ is defined by a transition relation $\rho_\tau(V, V')$, which may refer to V and modify $V - \{T\}$. For every $\tau \in \mathcal{T}$, it is required that

$$\rho_\tau \quad \rightarrow \quad T' = T.$$

- $\mathcal{A}$: A finite set of *activities*. Each activity $\alpha \in \mathcal{A}$ is represented by an *activity relation*:

$$p_\alpha \;\to\; I(t) = F^\alpha(V^0, t)$$

where p_α is a predicate over D called the *activation condition* of α. Activity α is said to be *active* in state s if its activation condition p_α holds on s. If p_α is *true*, it may be omitted.

Let $I = \{x_1, \ldots, x_m = T\}$ be the integrators of the system. The vector equality $I(t) = F^\alpha(V^0, t)$ is an abbreviation for the following set of individual equalities:

$$x_i(t) = F_i^\alpha(V^0, t), \quad \text{for each } i = 1, \ldots, m,$$

which define the evolution of the integrators throughout a phase of continuous change according to the activity α. The argument V^0 represents the initial values of all the system variables at the beginning of the phase. For every $\alpha \in \mathcal{A}$ it is required that

$$F_i^\alpha(V^0, 0) = x_i^0, \quad \text{for every } i = 1, \ldots, m$$
$$F_T^\alpha(V^0, t) = F_m^\alpha(V^0, t) = T^0 + t.$$

That is, $F_i^\alpha(V^0, 0)$ agrees with the initial value of x_i, and the effect of evolution of length t on the master clock (integrator x_m) is to add t to T.

It is required that the activation conditions associated with the different activities be exhaustive and exclusive, i.e., exactly one of them holds on any state.

- Π : The *time-progress condition*, is an assertion over V. The assertion is used to specify a global restriction over the progress of time.

The enableness of a transition τ can be expressed by the formula

$$En(\tau) : \quad (\exists V')\rho_\tau(V, V'),$$

which is true in s iff s has some τ-successor. The enabling condition of a transition τ can always be written as $\delta \wedge \kappa$, where δ is the largest sub-formula that does not depend on integrators. We call κ the *integrator component* of the enabling condition, and denote it by $En_I(\tau)$.

In descriptions of concrete hybrid systems, the evolution functions $F^\alpha(V^0, t)$ are often presented by sets of ordinary differential equations of the form $\dot{x}_j = g_j^\alpha(V)$ for $j = 1, \ldots, m$. In such cases, the evolution functions $F^\alpha(V^0, t)$ can be obtained as solutions of the differential equations. It is straightforward to extend the model to also cover non-deterministic evolutions. In such cases, we may represent the evolution functions as solutions of differential inclusions.

Example 17. Consider the hybrid system Φ_1 presented in figure 38.

Fig. 38. A hybrid system Φ_1.

This system can be modeled by the following PTS:

$V = I : \{x, T\}$
$\Theta :$ $x = 1 \wedge T = 0$
$\mathcal{T} :$ $\{\tau\}$ where $\rho_\tau : x = -1 \wedge x' = 1 \wedge T' = T$
$\mathcal{A} :$ $\{\alpha\}$ with activity relation (omitting the α subscript and superscript)
     $\underbrace{true}_{p} \to \underbrace{x = x^0 - t}_{F(x^0, t)}$
$\Pi :$ $x \geq -1$

The behavior of this system is (informally) presented in Fig. 39. ◢

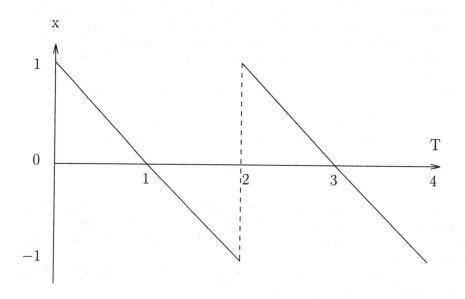

Fig. 39. Behavior of PTS Φ_1.

Extended Transitions

Let $\Phi : \langle V, \Theta, \mathcal{T}, \mathcal{A}, \Pi \rangle$ be a phase transition system. We define the set of *extended transitions* $\mathcal{T}_H$ associated with Φ as follows:

$$\mathcal{T}_H = \mathcal{T} \cup \mathcal{T}_\Phi, \quad \text{where} \quad \mathcal{T}_\Phi = \{\tau_\alpha \mid \alpha \in \mathcal{A}\}.$$

For each $\alpha \in \mathcal{A}$, the transition relation of τ_α is given by

$$\rho_{\tau_\alpha}: \quad \exists \Delta > 0 \quad \begin{pmatrix} D' = D \wedge p_\alpha \wedge I' = F^\alpha(V, \Delta) \\ \wedge \\ \forall t \in [0, \Delta). \ \Pi(D, F^\alpha(V, t)) \end{pmatrix}.$$

The transition relation ρ_{τ_α} characterizes possible values of the system variables at the beginning and end of an α-phase, where $V = (D, I)$ denotes the values at the beginning of the phase and $V' = (D', I')$ denotes their values at the end of the phase. The formula assumes a positive time increment Δ which will be the length of the phase. It then states that the values of the discrete variables are preserved ($D' = D$), the activation condition p_α currently holds, the values of the integrators at the end of the phase are given by $F^\alpha(V, \Delta)$, and the time-progress condition Π holds for all intermediate time points within the phase, i.e., for all t, $0 \leq t < \Delta$.

Runs and Computations

A *run* of a phase transition system $\Phi : \langle V, \Theta, \mathcal{T}, \mathcal{A}, \Pi \rangle$ is an infinite sequence of states $\sigma : s_0, s_1, \ldots$ satisfying:

- *Initiation:* $\quad s_0 \models \Theta$
- *Consecution:* For each $j = 0, 1, \ldots$, $s_{j+1} \in \tau(s_j)$, for some $\tau \in \mathcal{T}_H$.

A *computation* of a PTS is a run satisfying:

- *Time Divergence:* The sequence $s_0[T], s_1[T], \ldots$ grows beyond any bound.

Non-Zeno Systems

As in the case of the CTS model, we restrict our attention to non-zeno PTS's. These are systems for which any prefix of a run can be extended to a computation.

System Description by Hybrid Statecharts

Hybrid systems can be conveniently described by an extension of statecharts [Har87] called *hybrid statecharts*. The main extension is

- States may be labeled by (unconditional) differential equations. The implication is that the activity associated with the differential equation is active precisely when the state it labels is active.

We illustrate this form of description by the example of *Cat and Mouse* taken from [MMP92]. At time $T = 0$, a mouse starts running from a certain position on the floor in a straight line towards a hole in the wall, which is at a distance X_0 from the initial position. The mouse runs at a constant velocity v_m. After a delay of Δ time units, a cat is released at the same initial position and chases the mouse at velocity v_c along the same path. Will the cat catch the mouse, or will the mouse find sanctuary while the cat crashes against the wall?

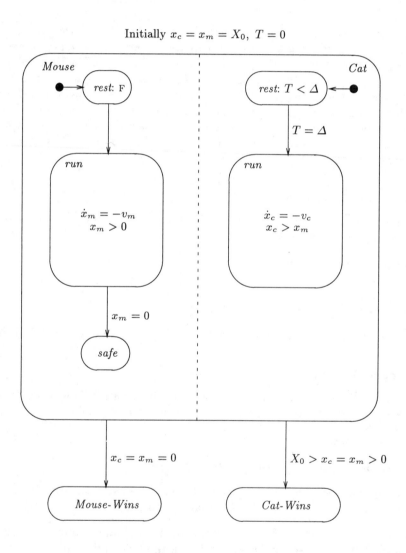

Fig. 40. Specification of Cat and Mouse.

The statechart in Fig. 40 describes the possible scenarios. This statechart (and the underlying phase transition system) uses the integrators x_m and x_c, measuring the distance of the mouse and the cat, respectively, from the wall. The waiting time of the cat before it starts running is measured by the master clock T. The statechart refers to the constants $X_0, v_m, v_c,$ and Δ.

A behavior of the system starts with states $M.rest$ and $C.rest$ active, variables x_m and x_c set to the initial value X_0, and the master clock T set to 0. The mouse proceeds immediately to the state of running, in which its variable x_m changes continuously according to the equation $\dot{x}_m = -v_m$. The cat waits for a delay of Δ before entering its running state, using the master clock T to measure this delay. There are two possible termination scenarios. If the event $x_m = 0$ happens first, the mouse reaches sanctuary and moves to state $safe$, where it waits for the cat to reach the wall. As soon as this happens, detectable by the condition $x_c = x_m = 0$ becoming true, the system moves to state $Mouse\text{-}Wins$. The other possibility is that the event $X_0 > x_c = x_m > 0$ occurs first, which means that the cat overtook the mouse before the mouse reached sanctuary. In this case they both stop running and the system moves to state $Cat\text{-}Wins$. The compound conditions $x_c = x_m = 0$ and $X_0 > x_c = x_m > 0$ stand for the conjunctions $x_c = x_m \wedge x_m = 0$ and $X_0 > x_c \wedge x_c = x_m \wedge x_m > 0$, respectively.

The statechart representation of the Cat and Mouse illustrates the typical interleaving between continuous activities and discrete state changes which, in this example, only involve changes of control.

The Underlying Phase Transition System

Following the graphical representation, we identify the phase transition system underlying the picture of Fig. 40. We refer to states in the diagram that do not enclose other states as *basic states*.

- *System Variables:* $V = D \cup I$, where $D: \{\pi\}$ and $I: \{x_c, x_m, T\}$. Variable π is a control variable whose value is the set of basic states of the statechart which are currently active.
- *Initial Condition:* Given by

$$\Theta: \quad \pi = \{M.rest, C.rest\} \wedge x_c = x_m = X_0 \wedge T = 0.$$

- *Transitions:* Listed together with the transition relations associated with them.

$$M.rest\text{-}run : M.rest \in \pi \wedge \pi' = \pi - \{M.rest\} \cup \{M.run\}$$
$$C.rest\text{-}run : C.rest \in \pi \wedge T = \Delta \wedge \pi' = \pi - \{C.rest\} \cup \{C.run\}$$
$$M.run\text{-}safe : M.run \in \pi \wedge x_m = 0 \wedge \pi' = \pi - \{M.run\} \cup \{M.safe\}$$
$$M.win : (Active \cap \pi) \neq \phi \wedge x_c = x_m = 0 \wedge \pi' = \{Mouse\text{-}Wins\}$$
$$C.win : (Active \cap \pi) \neq \phi \wedge X_0 > x_c = x_m > 0 \wedge \pi' = \{Cat\text{-}Wins\},$$

where the set $Active$ stands for the set of basic states

$$Active: \quad \{M.rest, M.run, M.safe, C.rest, C.run\}.$$

- *Activities:* It is possible to group all the activities into a single activity, given by:

$$\alpha: \quad x_m = x_m^0 - (at\_M.run)\cdot v_m t \,\wedge\, x_c = x_c^0 - (at\_C.run)\cdot v_c t \,\wedge\, T = T^0 + t.$$

In this representation, we used arithmetization of control expressions by which $at\_M.run$ equals 1 whenever $M.run \in \pi$ and equals 0 at all other instances. A less compact representation lists four activities corresponding to the four cases of: cat and mouse both resting, cat rests and mouse runs, cat runs and mouse is safe, cat and mouse both running.

- *Time Progress Condition:* Given by

$$\Pi : \begin{pmatrix} M.rest \notin \pi \,\wedge\, (C.rest \in \pi \,\rightarrow\, T < \Delta) \,\wedge \\ (M.run \in \pi \,\rightarrow\, x_m > 0) \,\wedge\, (C.run \in \pi \,\rightarrow\, x_c > x_m) \end{pmatrix}$$

7.2 Verifying Invariance Properties over PTS

Invariance properties of hybrid systems can be verified by rule INV-H, presented in Fig. 41.

For assertions φ and p,

I1. $\varphi \,\rightarrow\, p$

I2. $\Theta \,\rightarrow\, \varphi$

I3. $\rho_\tau \,\wedge\, \varphi \,\rightarrow\, \varphi'$ for every $\tau \in \mathcal{T}_H$

$$\Phi \models \Box\, p$$

Fig. 41. Rule INV-H (invariance) applied to PTS Φ.

Rule INV-H is sound and (relatively) complete for proving all invariance properties of non-zeno PTS's.

Note that rule INV-H is identical to rule INV, except that we use $\mathcal{T}_H$ as the set of extended transitions. Consequently, we can adopt the notations of invariance diagrams for the concise representation of invariance proofs over PTS's.

Verifying a Property of the Cat and Mouse System

Consider the property that, under the assumptions

$$X_0,\ v_c,\ v_m,\ \Delta > 0, \qquad \frac{X_0}{v_m} < \Delta + \frac{X_0}{v_c} \tag{4}$$

all computations of the Cat and Mouse system satisfy

$$\Box\big(x_c = x_m \,\rightarrow\, x_c = X_0 \vee x_m = 0\big).$$

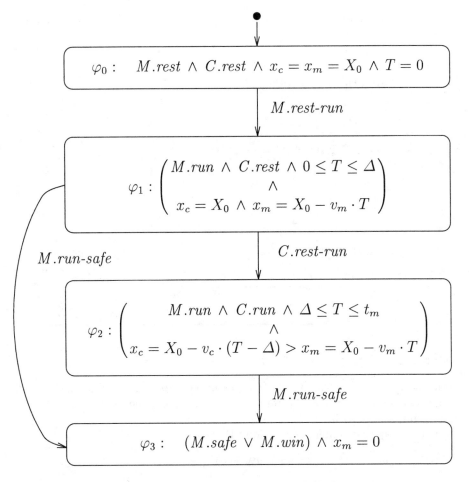

Fig. 42. A hybrid invariance proof diagram.

This invariant guarantees that the cat can never win.

In Fig. 42, we present a verification diagram for this invariance property. In this diagram we use control assertions indicating that certain basic states are contained in π. For example, $C.run$ stands for $Cat.run \in \pi$. We also use t_m for $\frac{X_0}{v_m}$, the time it takes the mouse to run the distance X_0.

It is not difficult to verify that the diagram is valid, including the preservation of all assertions under the single activity-induced transition τ_α.

The part that requires some attention is showing that the φ_2 conjunct

$$x_c = X_0 - v_c \cdot (T - \Delta) \quad > \quad x_m = X_0 - v_m \cdot T$$

is maintained until transition $M.run\text{-}safe$ becomes enabled, that is, as long as x_m is nonnegative. Obviously, $x_m \geq 0$ implies $T \leq t_m$. To show that the conjunct is maintained, it is sufficient to show $v_c \cdot (T - \Delta) < v_m \cdot T$ which is equivalent to

$$\frac{v_m}{v_c} > 1 - \frac{\Delta}{T} \tag{5}$$

From inequality (4), we can obtain

$$\frac{v_m}{v_c} > 1 - \Delta \cdot \frac{v_m}{X_0}$$

which, using the definition of $t_m = \dfrac{X_0}{v_m}$, gives

$$\frac{v_m}{v_c} > 1 - \frac{\Delta}{t_m}. \tag{6}$$

Since $T \leq t_m$, we have $1 - \dfrac{\Delta}{t_m} \geq 1 - \dfrac{\Delta}{T}$ establishing (5).

It remains to show that

$$\underbrace{M.rest \,\wedge\, C.rest \,\wedge\, x_c = x_m = X_0 \,\wedge\, y = 0 \,\wedge T = 0}_{\Theta} \;\;\rightarrow$$

$$\underbrace{M.rest \,\wedge\, C.rest \,\wedge\, x_c = x_m = X_0 \,\wedge\, y = T = 0}_{\varphi_0} \tag{7}$$

$$\varphi_0 \,\vee\, \cdots \,\vee\, \varphi_3 \rightarrow \Big(x_c = x_m \;\rightarrow\; x_c = X_0 \,\vee\, x_m = 0 \Big). \tag{8}$$

Implication (7) is obviously valid. To check implication (8), we observe that both φ_0 and φ_1 imply $x_c = X_0$, φ_2 implies $x_c > x_m$ (using the assumption $\Delta > 0$), and φ_3 implies $x_m = 0$.

This shows that under assumption (4), property

$$\Box(x_c = x_m \;\;\rightarrow\;\; x_c = X_0 \,\vee\, x_m = 0)$$

is valid for the Cat and Mouse system.

8 Conclusions

In this paper we have presented the real-time model of clocked transition system (CTS). This model can be viewed as an extension of the timed automata model [AD94]. In addition to algorithmic verification of finite-state systems, the CTS model can also support deductive verification. We presented verification rules for invariance properties which are identical to the invariance verification rules of fair transition systems [MP95b]. For response properties, we presented rules similar to the CHAIN and W-RESP rules of fair transition systems [MP91a]. The main differences between the timed and the untimed versions of these rules is that the timed version does not use the concept of a helpful transition but replaces it with the concept of a *helpful clock*, whose boundedness and the fact that it is not reset while its associated assertion holds, implies that we can stay in states that satisfy this assertion only for a bounded time, and must move elsewhere.

We proceeded with the presentation of an approach for verifying that an arbitrary CTS satisfies the non-zeno restriction. We use branching-time TL (CTL) to formulate the non-zeno property, and give a single proof rule to establish the CTL formula.

We concluded with an extension of the CTS model to hybrid systems, and presentation of a rule for verifying safety properties of such systems.

As previously mentioned, the model of Clocked Transition Systems and its verification rules have been successfully implemented in the STeP system [BBC+95]. Many of the examples presented in this paper have been verified within STeP. Implementation of the Hybrid Systems extension is under way.

Acknowledgment

We gratefully acknowledge the careful reading and critical comments of previous versions of this paper by Oded Maler and Tomás Uribe. Nikolaj Bjørner implemented the clocked transition system model and its verification rules within STeP. Special thanks are due to Henny Sipma for a thorough examination of the current (and previous) versions, the detection and correction of some subtle errors, and the STeP mechanical verification of some of the more difficult examples.

References

[AD94]   R. Alur and D.L. Dill. A theory of timed automata. *Theor. Comp. Sci.*, 126:183–235, 1994.

[AH89]   R. Alur and T.A. Henzinger. A really temporal logic. In *Proc. 30th IEEE Symp. Found. of Comp. Sci.*, pages 164–169, 1989.

[AH92]   R. Alur and T. Henzinger. Logics and models of real time: A survey. In J.W. de Bakker, C. Huizing, W.P. de Roever, and G. Rozenberg, editors, *Proceedings of the REX Workshop "Real-Time: Theory in Practice"*, volume 600 of *Lect. Notes in Comp. Sci.*, pages 74–106. Springer-Verlag, 1992.

[AH94]   R. Alur and T.A. Henzinger. Real-time system = discrete system + clock variables. In T. Rus and C. Rattray, editors, *Theories and Experiences for Real-time System Development*, AMAST Series in Computing 2, pages 1–29. World Scientific, 1994.

[AL94]   M. Abadi and L. Lamport. An old-fashioned recipe for real time. *ACM Trans. Prog. Lang. Sys.*, 16(5):1543–1571, 1994.

[BAMP83] M. Ben-Ari, Z. Manna, and A. Pnueli. The temporal logic of branching time. *Acta Informatica*, 20:207–226, 1983.

[BBC+95] N. Bjørner, I.A. Browne, E. Chang, M. Colón, A. Kapur, Z. Manna, H.B. Sipma, and T.E. Uribe. STeP: The Stanford Temporal Prover, User's Manual. Technical Report STAN-CS-TR-95-1562, Computer Science Department, Stanford University, November 1995.

[BMSU97] N.S. Bjørner, Z. Manna, H.B. Sipma, and T.E. Uribe. Deductive verification of real-time systems using STeP. In *4th Intl. AMAST Workshop on Real-Time Systems*, volume 1231 of *Lect. Notes in Comp. Sci.*, pages 22–43. Springer-Verlag, May 1997.

[EC82]   E.A. Emerson and E.M. Clarke. Using branching time temporal logic to synthesize synchronization skeletons. *Sci. Comp. Prog.*, 2:241–266, 1982.

[FG95]   L. Fix and O. Grumberg. Verificaiton of temporal properties. to appear in *Logic and Computation*, 1995.

[Har87]   D. Harel. Statecharts: A visual formalism for complex systems. *Sci. Comp. Prog.*, 8:231–274, 1987.

[Hen92]   T.A. Henzinger. Sooner is safer than later. *Info. Proc. Lett.*, 43(3):135–142, 1992.

[HHWT95]   T.A. Henzinger, P.-H. Ho, and H. Wong-Toi. A user guide to HYTECH. In *Proceedings of the Workshop on Tools and Algorithms for the Construction and Analysis of Systems (TACAS)*, Aarhus, Denmark, 1995. To appear.

[HK94]   T.A. Henzinger and P.W. Kopke. Verification methods for the divergent runs of clock systems. In H. Langmaack, W.-P. de Roever, and J. Vytopil, editors, *FTRTFT 94: Formal Techniques in Real-time and Fault-tolerant Systems*, Lecture Notes in Computer Science 863, pages 351–372. Springer-Verlag, 1994.

[HMP94]   T. Henzinger, Z. Manna, and A. Pnueli. Temporal proof methodologies for timed transition systems. *Inf. and Comp.*, 112(2):273–337, 1994.

[KdR85]   R. Koymans and W.-P. de Roever. Examples of a real-time temporal logic specifications. In B.D. Denvir, W.T. Harwood, M.I. Jackson, and M.J. Wray, editors, *The Analysis of Concurrent Systems*, volume 207 of *Lect. Notes in Comp. Sci.*, pages 231–252. Springer-Verlag, 1985.

[KMP96]   Y. Kesten, Z. Manna, and A. Pnueli. Verifying clocked transition systems. In R. Alur, T.A. Henzinger, and E.D. Sontag, editors, *Hybrid Systems III*, volume 1066 of *Lect. Notes in Comp. Sci.*, pages 13–40. Springer-Verlag, 1996.

[Koy90]   R. Koymans. Specifying real-time properties with metric temporal logic. *Real-time Systems*, 2(4):255–299, 1990.

[KVdR83]   R. Koymans, J. Vytopyl, and W.-P. de Roever. Real-time programming and asynchronous message passing. In *Proc. 2nd ACM Symp. Princ. of Dist. Comp.*, pages 187–197, 1983.

[Lam95]   L. Lamport. Proving possibiity properties. Technical Report 137, Digital Equipment Corporation, Systems Research Center, Palo Alto, July 1995.

[MMP92]   O. Maler, Z. Manna, and A. Pnueli. From timed to hybrid systems. In J.W. de Bakker, C. Huizing, W.P. de Roever, and G. Rozenberg, editors, *Proceedings of the REX Workshop "Real-Time: Theory in Practice"*, volume 600 of *Lect. Notes in Comp. Sci.*, pages 447–484. Springer-Verlag, 1992.

[MP91a]   Z. Manna and A. Pnueli. Completing the temporal picture. *Theor. Comp. Sci.*, 83(1):97–130, 1991.

[MP91b]   Z. Manna and A. Pnueli. *The Temporal Logic of Reactive and Concurrent Systems: Specification*. Springer-Verlag, New York, 1991.

[MP93a]   Z. Manna and A. Pnueli. Models for reactivity. *Acta Informatica*, 30:609–678, 1993.

[MP93b]   Z. Manna and A. Pnueli. Verifying hybrid systems. In R.L. Grossman, A. Nerode, A. Ravn, and H. Rischel, editors, *Hybrid Systems*, volume 736 of *Lect. Notes in Comp. Sci.*, pages 4–35. Springer-Verlag, 1993.

[MP94]   Z. Manna and A. Pnueli. Temporal verification diagrams. In T. Ito and A. R. Meyer, editors, *Theoretical Aspects of Computer Software*, volume 789 of *Lect. Notes in Comp. Sci.*, pages 726–765. Springer-Verlag, 1994.

[MP95a]   Z. Manna and A. Pnueli. Clocked transition systems. In *Logic and Software Workshop*, August 1995. Beijing, China.

[MP95b]   Z. Manna and A. Pnueli. *Temporal Verification of Reactive Systems: Safety*. Springer-Verlag, New York, 1995.

[MT90]   F. Moller and C. Tofts. A temporal calculus of communicating systems. In J.C.M. Baeten and J.W. Klop, editors, *Proceedings of Concur'90*, volume 458 of *Lect. Notes in Comp. Sci.*, pages 401–415. Springer-Verlag, 1990.

[NOSY93]   X. Nicollin, A. Olivero, J. Sifakis, and S. Yovine. An approach to the description and analysis of hybrid systems. In R.L. Grossman, A. Nerode, A. Ravn, and H. Rischel, editors, *Hybrid Systems*, volume 736 of *Lect. Notes in Comp. Sci.*, pages 149–178. Springer-Verlag, 1993.

[NSY92]   X. Nicollin, J. Sifakis, and S. Yovine. From ATP to timed graphs and hybrid systems. In J.W. de Bakker, C. Huizing, W.P. de Roever, and G. Rozenberg, editors, *Proceedings of the REX Workshop "Real-Time: Theory in Practice"*, volume 600 of *Lect. Notes in Comp. Sci.*, pages 549–572. Springer-Verlag, 1992.

[Ost90]   J.S. Ostroff. *Temporal Logic of Real-Time Systems*. Advanced Software Development Series. Research Studies Press (John Wiley & Sons), Taunton, England, 1990.

[SBM92]   F. B. Schneider, B. Bloom, and K. Marzullo. Putting time into proof outlines. In J.W. de Bakker, C. Huizing, W.P. de Roever, and G. Rozenberg, editors, *Proceedings of the REX Workshop "Real-Time: Theory in Practice"*, volume 600 of *Lect. Notes in Comp. Sci.*, pages 618–639. Springer-Verlag, 1992.

[Sif91]   J. Sifakis. An overview and synthesis on timed process algebra. In K.G. Larsen and A. Skou, editors, *3rd Computer Aided Verification Workshop*, volume 575 of *Lect. Notes in Comp. Sci.*, pages 376–398. Springer-Verlag, 1991.

Analyzing and Synthesizing Hybrid Control Systems

Michael S. Branicky

Dept. of Electrical Engineering and Applied Physics
Case Western Reserve University
10900 Euclid Avenue, Cleveland, OH 44106-7221 USA

Abstract. Embedded systems possess a hybrid structure, combining
continuous-variable dynamics and logical decision-making. We study such
real-world hybrid control systems and introduce a mathematical model
of them. Then, we develop tools for analyzing their stability. Finally, we
review the theory of optimal hybrid control and present algorithms for
synthesizing optimal hybrid control systems.

1 Introduction

Embedded microcontrollers allow incorporating complex decision-making into
even the simplest device control loops. They typically issue continuous-variable
controls and perform logical checks that determine the mode—and hence the
control algorithms—the continuous-variable device is operating under at any
given moment. A "hybrid control system," mixing discrete and continuous worlds
is the result. They are the focus of this paper. See Figure 1.

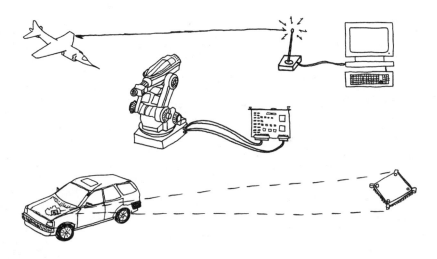

Fig. 1. Rendition of the two worlds (analog and digital) comprising hybrid control
systems.

Simply speaking, a hybrid control system is one that combines both discrete and continuous inputs, outputs, state variables, and dynamical equations. See Figure 2. We will see that examples of such systems abound, and they are growing in importance every day. These range from on-off thermostats in our homes through programmable logic controllers (PLCs) in our factories to mode-switched flight control in our skies.

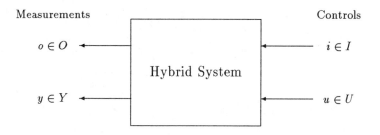

Fig. 2. Hybrid control system (I/O model).

In the case of embedded systems, as foreshadowed above, hybrid control systems arise due to the interaction of microcontrollers and the physical devices they control. Here, the microcontroller and its program live in the discrete world of symbols, registers, and interrupts. They may be modeled as fin e state machines, with inputs and outputs belonging to finite alphabets. On the other hand, the physical devices under control live in the analog world of position, velocity, temperature, pressure, etc. They are most naturally described by differential equations, with states, inputs, and outputs taking values in Euclidean spaces. See Figure 3. In some cases, the physical device itself might also possesses hybrid dynamics. Consider the hopping robot in Figure 6(a). The differential equations governing its continuous states switch among different modes or *phases* whenever those variables satisfy certain relationships (e.g., when the hopper's height above the ground becomes zero). In Figure 6(b), the associated controller tries to track these phase transitions and implements different feedback strategies depending upon the detected phase.

In the case of complex embedded systems, there are typically many control subsystems with many control modes for each subsystem. The control subsystems that are active and the modes that are enforced at any given time is usually determined by a group of interacting computer programs (cf. threads). The collection of these computer programs is a complex dynamical system in its own right and may be modeled as a network of finite state machines, Petri nets, etc. Further, the "transitions" of these programs are not entirely independent of the physical system under control; many depend on the logical truth of statements concerning the continuous values of the physical variables. Also, since the logical state of the computer program determines which control mode is in use, the evolution of states of the physical system is likewise influenced by the values

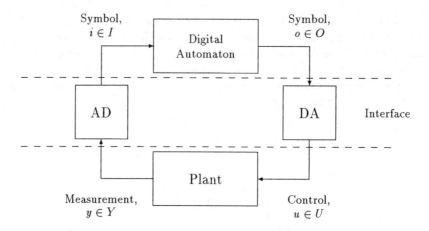

Fig. 3. Hybrid control system (closed-loop).

of these logical variables. In real-world systems, this interaction is complicated by the fact that there is not a strict dichotomy between discrete and continuous components. The entire system may be made up of subsystems accurately modeled as discrete, continuous, or hybrid.

The goal of the *field* of hybrid systems is to create an engineering science to deal rigorously with the mixed analog-digital systems talked about above. Herein, I hope to give a brief introduction to this field, largely based on my own work. The concentration is on analyzing and synthesizing hybrid control systems, but we will begin at the beginning.

The chapter is organized as follows. We have already given an intuitive definition of hybrid control systems and mentioned some examples in passing. Section 2 tries to fix ideas by examining a slew of real-world systems combining both continuous and discrete states, dynamics, and controls. In Section 3, we introduce a mathematical model of such hybrid control systems. The model captures the significant phenomena found in the example systems, encompasses previously posed hybrid systems models, yet possesses enough structure to allow rigorous posing and solution of analysis and control problems, building on existing control theory tools and intuition. Section 4 provides an introduction to analyzing hybrid control systems, concentrating on their stability analysis using "multiple Lyapunov functions." Sections 5 and 6 turn to performing optimal hybrid control. The sections review theory and outline synthesis algorithms, respectively. The latter ends with solving a small example that illustrates the control design process.

Below, we use standard notation, including $\mathbf{R}$, $\mathbf{R}_+$, $\mathbf{Z}$, $\mathbf{Z}_+$, and $\mathbf{N}$ for the reals, nonnegative reals, integers, nonnegative integers, and natural numbers, respectively. Other notation is introduced as it is needed. I have tried to keep the exposition self-contained, but refer the reader to [11] for clarification and further references.

2 Hybrid Control Systems All Around Us

Real-world applications areas of hybrid control systems include switching circuits (e.g., relays and power electronics with state-dependent circuit switching), motion control (disk drives, transmissions, stepper motors, position encoders, etc.), robotics (constrained robots, flexible manufacturing, interacting agents), automated highway systems (with platoons of automated vehicles and interaction of engine/vehicle dynamics with communication protocols and high-level goals), and aerospace (mode-switched flight, vehicle management systems, air traffic control). Below, we examine some of these in more detail.

Switching Circuits. Perhaps the most mundane example of a hybrid control system arises from the hysteresis present in most thermostats. There, the multivalued hysteresis curve yields a discrete state on which the overall dynamics depends. More specifically, we may model a thermostatically-controlled room as follows

$$\dot{x} = f(x, H(x), u). \tag{1}$$

The function f denotes dynamics of temperature about some desired temperature, T_d. It depends on the value of $x = T - T_d$ (where T is the current room temperature), whether the furnace is switched On or Off (denoted by the function H), and some auxiliary control signal u (e.g., the fuel burn rate). A typical H is depicted in Figure 4. Such a controller can be depicted as a finite state machine (see Figure 5). Thus, Equation (1) is a differential equation for room temperature that depends on the discrete state of the thermostat's finite state machine.

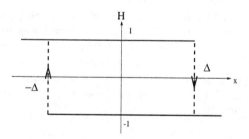

Fig. 4. Hysteresis function, H.

Motion Control. A computer disk drive receives external **Read** commands and symbolic inputs of disk sectors and locations; it outputs symbols corresponding to the bytes read. It may also receive symbolic commands like **Reinitialize** and transmit symbolic outputs like **ReadError**. The action of the drive, however, is also governed by the physics of its disk, spindle, disk arm, and motors. Their dynamical behavior may be captured well by differential (or difference) equations.

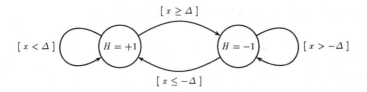

Fig. 5. Finite automaton associated with hysteresis function.

An automobile transmission system takes the continuous inputs of accelerator position and engine RPM and the discrete input of gear position and translates them into motion of the vehicle. Suppose one is designing a cruise control system that accelerates and decelerates under different profiles. The desired profile is chosen depending on sensor readings (continuous reading of elevation, discrete coding of road condition, etc.). In such a case, we are to design a control system with both continuous and discrete states and controls.

Constrained Physical Systems. A ball bouncing in an enclosed room is a hybrid system. Upon impact with the sides of the box, the component of its velocity normal to the impact surface is immediately reset (to close approximation), perhaps taking into account a coefficient of restitution.

Interesting examples of hybrid control systems are constrained robotic systems. In particular, recall Raibert's hopping robot in Figure 6 (also see [37]). The dynamics of these devices are governed by gravity, as well as the forces generated by passive and active (pneumatic) springs. The dynamics change abruptly at certain event times, and fall into distinct phases: Flight, Compression, Thrust, and Decompression. See Figure 6(a). In fact, Raibert has built controllers for these machines that embed a finite state machine that transitions according to these detected phases. For instance, the transition from Flight to Compression occurs when touchdown is detected; that from Decompression to Flight upon liftoff. Thus, finite state machines and differential equations naturally interact in such devices and their controllers.

Inventory Management. In a simple inventory management model [5], there are a "discrete" set of restocking times $\theta_1 < \theta_2 < \cdots$ and associated order amounts $\alpha_1, \alpha_2, \ldots$. The equations governing the stock at any given moment are

$$\dot{y}(t) = -\mu(t) + \sum_i \delta(t - \theta_1)\alpha_i$$

where μ represents degradation or utilization dynamics and δ is the Dirac delta function.

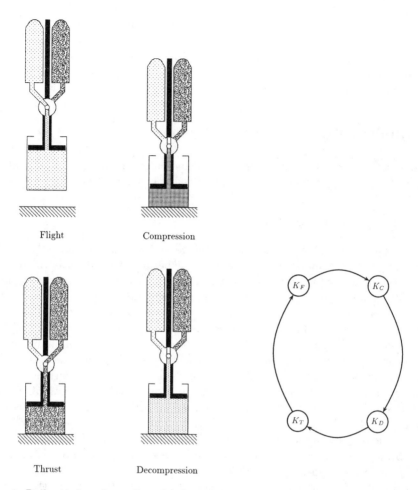

Flight   Compression

Thrust   Decompression

Fig. 6. Raibert's hopping robot: (a) dynamic phases (reproduced from [3]), (b) finite state controller.

AHS and Flight Control. A more complicated example of a hybrid system arises in the control structures for so-called automated highway systems (AHS) [32, 44]. The basic goal of one such system is to increase highway throughput by means of a technique known as *platooning*. A platoon is a group of between, say, one and twenty vehicles traveling closely together in a highway lane at high speeds. To ensure safety—and proper formation and dissolution of structured platoons from the "free agents" of single vehicles—requires a bit of control effort! Protocols for basic maneuvers such as Merge, Split, and ChangeLane have been proposed in terms of finite state machines. More conventional controllers govern the engines and brakes of individual vehicles. Clearly, the system is hybrid, with each vehicle having a state determined by:

- continuous variables, such as velocity, engine RPM, distance to car ahead;
- the finite states of its protocol-enacting state machines.

Flight controllers are also organized around the idea of modes. For example, one might easily imagine different control schemes for Take-Off, Ascend, Cruise, Descend, and Land. More complex is a whole flight vehicle management system which coordinates flight in these different regimes, while also planning flight paths considering air traffic, weather, fuel economy, and passenger comfort.

3 Modeling Hybrid Control Systems

In this section we classify the significant phenomena found in the examples above and give a mathematical model for hybrid control systems.

3.1 Background and Motivation

Hybrid systems involve both continuous-valued and discrete variables. Their evolution is given by equations of motion that generally depend on both. In turn these equations contain mixtures of logic, discrete-valued or *digital* dynamics, and continuous-variable or *analog* dynamics. The continuous dynamics of such systems may be continuous-time, discrete-time, or mixed (sampled-data), but is generally given by differential equations. The discrete-variable dynamics of hybrid systems is generally governed by a *digital automaton*, or input-output transition system with a countable number of states. The continuous and discrete dynamics interact at "event" or "trigger" times when the continuous state hits certain prescribed sets in the continuous state space. See Figure 3. *Hybrid control systems* are control systems that involve both continuous and discrete dynamics and continuous and discrete controls. The continuous dynamics of such a system is usually modeled by a controlled vector field or difference equation. Its hybrid nature is expressed by a dependence on some discrete phenomena, The result is a system as in Figure 2.

In this chapter, our focus is on the case of hybrid systems where the continuous dynamics is modeled by a differential equation[1]

$$\dot{x}(t) = \xi(t), \qquad t \geq 0. \tag{2}$$

Here, $x(t)$ is the *continuous component* of the state, taking values in some subset of a Euclidean space. $\xi(t)$ is a *controlled vector field* that generally depends on $x(t)$, the *continuous component* $u(t)$ of the control policy, and the aforementioned discrete phenomena. We have classified the discrete phenomena generally considered into four types [15], each of which was illustrated in the real-world examples in the last section:

1. *autonomous switching*, where the vector field $\xi(\cdot)$ changes discontinuously when the state $x(\cdot)$ hits certain "boundaries" (as in the hysteresis example);
2. *autonomous impulses*, where $x(\cdot)$ jumps discontinuously on hitting prescribed regions of the state space (as for the bouncing ball and hopping robot);

---

[1] Please refer to [11] for background, references, and details.

3. *controlled switching*, where $\xi(\cdot)$ changes abruptly in response to a control command (as in the gears of an automobile transmission); and

4. *controlled impulses*, where $x(\cdot)$ changes discontinuously in response to a control command (as in the case of inventory management).

3.2 A Mathematical Model

We now introduce a mathematical model of hybrid control systems that is general enough to

- cover the significant, identified phenomena found in real-world examples and
- encompass other reasonable models,

but is specific enough

- to build on previous insight and results and
- to be able to derive new theory.

The Foundation: Dynamical Systems. The notion of dynamical system has a long history as an important conceptual tool in science and engineering [29, 41]. Examples of dynamical systems abound, including autonomous ODEs, autonomous difference equations, finite automata, pushdown automata, Turing machines, Petri nets, etc. We have chosen the rich notion of dynamical system as the foundation of our formulation of controlled hybrid dynamical systems, which we build up in steps below.

A dynamical system is simply a rule specifying how the states of a system evolve over time. Formally, a *dynamical system* [39] is a system

$$\Sigma = [X, \Gamma, \phi],$$

where X is an arbitrary topological space, the *state space* of Σ; here we primarily consider X a subset of n-dimensional Euclidean space, $\mathbf{R}^n$ for some $n \in \mathbf{N}$. Time is represented by the *transition semigroup* Γ, which is a topological semigroup with identity. Here, we consider $\Gamma = \mathbf{R}_+$ for continuous time and $\Gamma = \mathbf{Z}_+$ for discrete-time systems (each under addition with identity element 0). The *extended transition map* $\phi : X \times \Gamma \to X$ is a continuous function satisfying the following:

1. *Identity*. For all $x \in X$, $\phi(x, 0) = x$.
2. *Semigroup*. For all $x \in X$ and arbitrary g_1, g_2 in Γ,

$$\phi(\phi(x, g_1), g_2) = \phi(x, g_1 + g_2).$$

3. *Continuity*. ϕ is continuous in both arguments simultaneously, i.e., for any neighborhood W of the point $\phi(x, g)$ there exist neighborhoods U and V of the point x and the element g respectively such that $\phi(U, V) \subset W$.

We will also denote by dynamical system the system

$$\Sigma = [X, \Gamma, f],$$

where X and Γ are as above, but the *transition function* f is the *generator* of the extended transition function ϕ. Here, we primarily restrict our attention to the case where the transition map is given by vector fields: $\dot{x}(t) = f(x(t))$.

Example 1. Recall a linear continuous-time system, $\dot{x}(t) = Ax(t)$, has $\phi(x, t) = e^{At}x$. This model is also *time-invariant*, because A is not a function of t. ◇

Example 2. A discrete-time system has time represented by $\mathbf{Z}_+$. Its transition or "next-step" function is

$$x(k+1) = f(x(k)), k \in \mathbf{Z}_+.$$

Again, the system is time-invariant, since f does not explicitly depend on k. Its extended transition function is given by iterates of this local rule

$$\phi(x, k) = f^k(x) \equiv \underbrace{f(\cdots f(f(x)) \cdots)}_{k \text{ times}}.$$

In this case, $f(\cdot) \equiv \phi(\cdot, 1)$. A linear discrete-time system, $x(k+1) = Ax(k)$, has $\phi(x, k) = A^k x$. ◇

Example 3. An *inputless finite automaton* is one whose input alphabet is empty, i.e., one whose transition function depends solely on its state. Its state space may be taken as $Q = \{1, \ldots, N\}$ for some $N \in \mathbf{N}$; its transition semigroup is $\mathbf{Z}_+$. Its transition function is some $\delta : Q \to Q$, and its extended transition function is $\phi(q, k) = \delta^k(q)$. ◇

Figure 7 shows a collection of dynamical systems and sample trajectories. For each state space, X_i, we have added a special subset, A_i of "final" states, at which the dynamics halts (cf. halting states of Turing machines).

On to Hybrid: HDS. Briefly, a hybrid dynamical system is an indexed collection of dynamical systems along with some map for "jumping" among them (switching dynamical system and/or resetting the state). This jumping occurs whenever the state satisfies certain conditions, given by its membership in a specified subset of the state space. Hence, the entire system can be thought of as a sequential patching together of dynamical systems with initial and final states, the jumps performing a reset to a (generally different) initial state of a (generally different) dynamical system whenever a final state is reached. See Figure 8.

Formally, a *hybrid dynamical system (HDS)*[2] is a system $H_c = [Q, \Sigma, \mathbf{A}, \mathbf{G}]$, with constituent parts as follows.

---

[2] For specificity, we now switch to the primary case of dynamical system mentioned above: continuous-time systems in $\mathbf{R}^n$ given by vector fields. A more general framework, encompassing *GHDS (General HDS)*, appears in [11]. In the parlance of that document, we are restricting ourselves to continuous-time-uniform, c-Euclidean-uniform, d-countable GHDS.

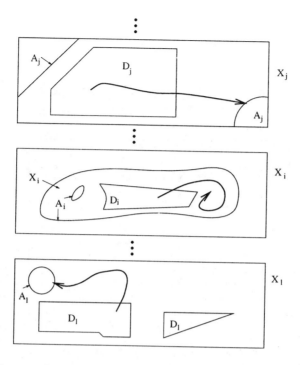

Fig. 7. A collection of dynamical systems with final states.

- Q, isomorphic to a subset of $\mathbf{N}$ is the countable set of *index* or *discrete states*.
- $\Sigma = \{\Sigma_q\}_{q \in Q}$ is the collection of dynamical systems, where each

$$\Sigma_q = [X_q, \mathbf{R}_+, f_q]$$

  is a dynamical system. Here, the $X_q \subset \mathbf{R}^{d_q}$, $d_q \in \mathbf{N}$, are the *continuous state spaces* and the vector fields $f_q : X_q \to \mathbf{R}^{d_q}$ represent the *continuous dynamics*.
- $\mathbf{A} = \{A_q\}_{q \in Q}$, $A_q \subset X_q$ for each $q \in Q$, is the collection of *autonomous jump sets*.
- $\mathbf{G} = \{G_q\}_{q \in Q}$, where $G_q : A_q \to S$ are the *autonomous jump transition maps*, said to represent the *discrete dynamics*.

Thus, $S = \bigcup_{q \in Q} X_q \times \{q\}$ is the *hybrid state space* of H. For convenience, we use the following shorthand. $S_q = X_q \times \{q\}$, and $A = \bigcup_{q \in Q} A_q \times \{q\}$ is *the* autonomous jump set. $G : A \to S$ is *the* autonomous jump transition map, constructed componentwise in the obvious way. The *jump destination sets* $\mathbf{D} = \{D_q\}_{q \in Q}$ are given by $D_q = \pi_1[G(A) \cap S_q]$, where π_i is projection onto the ith coordinate. The *switching* or *transition manifolds*, $M_{q,p} \subset A_q$ are given by $M_{q,p} = G_q^{-1}(D_p, p)$, i.e., the set of states from which transitions from index q to index p can occur.

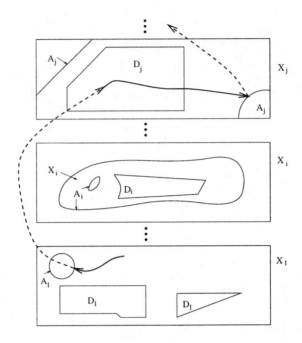

Fig. 8. Example hybrid dynamical system.

The dynamics of the HDS H are as follows.[3] The system is assumed to start in some hybrid state in $S \backslash A$, say $s_0 = (x_0, q_0)$. It evolves according to $\phi_{q_0}(x_0, \cdot)$ (or, equivalently, $\dot{x} = f_{q_0}(x)$) until the state enters—if ever—A_{q_0} at the point $s_1^- = (x_1^-, q_0)$. At this time it is instantly transferred according to transition map to $G_{q_0}(x_1^-) = (x_1, q_1) \equiv s_1$, from which the process continues.

We now collect some notes about HDS:

- *Dynamical Systems.* First, note that in the case $|Q| = 1$ and $A = \emptyset$ we recover all differential equations.
- *Transition Delays.* It is possible to model the fact that autonomous jumps may not be instantaneous by simply adding an *autonomous jump delay map*, $\Delta_a : A \times V \to \mathbf{R}_+$. This map associates a (possibly zero) delay to each autonomous jump. Thus, a jump begins at some time, τ, and is completed at some later time time $\Gamma \geq \tau$. This concept is useful as jumps may be introduced to represent an aggregate set of relatively fast, transitory dynamics. Also, some commands include a finite delay from issuance to completion. An example is closing a hydraulic valve.
- *Changing State Space and Overlaps.* The state space may change. This is useful in modeling component failures or changes in dynamical description based on autonomous—and later, controlled—events which change it. Examples include the collision of two inelastic particles or an aircraft mode

---

[3] For the process described to be well defined, it is sufficient that for all q, A_q is closed, $D_q \cap A_q = \emptyset$, and f_q is Lipschitz continuous. See [11] for details.

transition that changes variables to be controlled [31]. We allow the X_q to overlap and the inclusion of multiple copies of the same space. This may be used, for example, to take into account : overlapping local coordinate systems on a manifold [3]. It was also used in the hysteresis example.

- *Hybrid Systems.* The case of HDS with $|Q|$ finite is a coupling of finite automata and differential equations and includes many previously posed hybrid systems models [1, 3, 20, 33, 42, 47], systems with impulse effect [4], and hybrid automata [23]. For more details, refer to [11].

Adding Control: CHDS. We now add to the above the ability to make decisions, that is, to control the process by choosing among sets of possible actions at various times. For example, consider the controlled vector field

$$\dot{x}(t) = f(x(t), u(t)), \qquad u(t) \in U \subset \mathbf{R}^m,$$

which gives rise to a *controlled dynamical system*

$$\Sigma = [X, \Gamma, f, U], \qquad (\text{or } \Sigma = [X, \Gamma, \phi, U]),$$

where U is the set of inputs.

Example 4. A controlled continuous-time [resp. discrete-time] linear system has transition function

$$\dot{x}(t) = Ax(t) + Bu(t), \qquad [\text{resp. } x(k+1) = Ax(k) + Bu(k)].$$

An *finite automaton* adds a finite input alphabet, $I = \{i_1, \ldots, i_m\}$, to the inputless finite automaton described above. Its transition function is some $\delta : Q \times I \to Q$. $\diamond$

Allowing decisions at jump points and in the choice of whether to jump or not, we arrive at the notion of a *controlled* HDS. Formally, a *controlled hybrid dynamical system* (*CHDS*) is a system $H_c = [Q, \Sigma, \mathbf{A}, \mathbf{G}, \mathbf{C}, \mathbf{F}]$, with constituent parts as above, except as follows.

- $\Sigma = \{\Sigma_q\}_{q \in Q}$ is now a collection of *controlled* dynamical systems, where each

$$\Sigma_q = [X_q, \mathbf{R}_+, f_q, U_q].$$

Here, the controlled vector fields $f_q : X_q \times U_q \to \mathbf{R}^{d_q}$ represent the (controlled) *continuous dynamics*. $U_q \subset \mathbf{R}^{m_q}$ are the *continuous control spaces*, with $m_q \in \mathbf{N}$.
- $\mathbf{G} = \{G_q\}_{q \in Q}$, where $G_q : A_q \times V_q \to S$ are the *autonomous jump transition maps*, now modulated by the *discrete decision sets* V_q.
- $\mathbf{C} = \{C_q\}_{q \in Q}$, $C_q \subset X_q$, is the collection of *controlled jump sets*.
- $\mathbf{F} = \{F_q\}_{q \in Q}$, where $F_q : C_q \to 2^S$, is the collection of set-valued *controlled jump destination maps*.

Again, $S = \bigcup_{q \in Q} X_q \times \{q\}$ is the hybrid state space of H_c. As before, we introduce some shorthand beyond that defined for HDS above. We let $C = \bigcup_{q \in Q} C_q \times \{q\}$; we let $F : C \to 2^S$ denote *the* set-valued map composed in the obvious way from the set-valued maps F_q. Below, we will only deal with the case where the control and decision spaces are uniform: $U_q = U$, $V_q = V$, each for all q. Hence, $G : A \times V \to S$ may be defined from its constituents.

The dynamics of H_c are as follows. The system is assumed to start in some hybrid state in $S \backslash A$, say $s_0 = (x_0, q_0)$. It evolves according to $\phi_{q_0}(\cdot, \cdot, u)$ (equivalently, $\dot{x} = f_{q_0}(x, u)$) until the state enters—if ever—either A_{q_0} or C_{q_0} at the point $s_1^- = (x_1^-, q_0)$. If it enters A_{q_0}, then it *must* be transferred according to transition map $G_{q_0}(x_1^-, v)$ for some chosen $v \in V_{q_0}$. If it enters C_{q_0}, then we *may* choose to jump and, if so, we may choose the destination to be any point in $F_{q_0}(x_1^-)$. In either case, we arrive at a point $s_1 = (x_1, q_1)$ from which the process continues. See Figure 9.

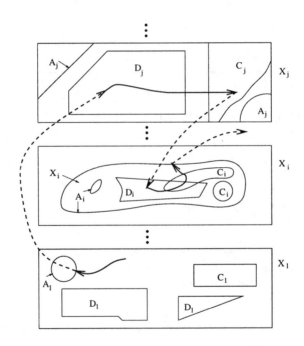

Fig. 9. Example dynamics of controlled hybrid dynamical system.

A CHDS can be pictured as an automaton as in Figure 10. There, each node is a constituent dynamical system, with the index the name of the node. Each edge represents a possible transition between constituent systems, labeled by the appropriate condition for the transition's being "enabled" and the update of the continuous state (cf. [25]). The notation ![condition] denotes that the transition *must* be taken when enabled. The notation ?[condition] denotes an enabled transition that *may* be taken on command; ":∈" means reassignment to some value in the given set.

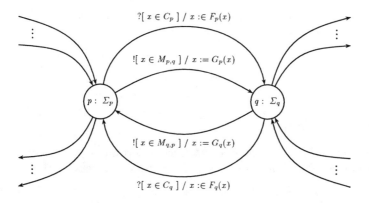

Fig. 10. Automaton representation of CHDS.

Notes.

- *Refinements.* Systems with state-output or edge-output are easily added. A *controlled jump delay map*, Δ_c, may be added like Δ_a above.
- *Nondeterminism and Disturbances.* Nondeterminism in transitions may be taken care of by partitioning ?[condition] into those which are controlled and uncontrolled (cf. [27]). Disturbances (and other forms of nondeterminism) may likewise be modeled by partitioning U, V, and C into portions that are under the influence of the controller or nature respectively.
- *Jump Equivalence.* We could, but do not for pedagogical reasons, combine autonomous and controlled jumps by defining a set-valued *autonomous* jump map $G' : A \cup C \to 2^S$ by

$$G'(s) = \begin{cases} G(s, V), & s \in A, \\ F(s) \cup \{s\}, & s \in C. \end{cases}$$

Example 5 (Controlled Hysteresis). Consider again the hysteresis example of Equation (1), but changing coordinates to $x = T - T_d$ and adding a control: For specificity, consider a system with control, namely, $f \equiv H(x) + u$.

For specificity, consider a system with control, namely, $f \equiv H(x) + u$. It can be modeled as follows. The state space is $X = \{X_{-1}, X_1\}$, with $X_{-1} = [-\Delta, \infty)$ and $X_1 = (-\infty, \Delta]$. The continuous dynamics is given by

$$f_{-1} = u - 1,$$
$$f_1 = u + 1.$$

The discrete dynamics is governed by the autonomous jump sets A_{-1} and A_1 and their associated transitions, which are, respectively,

$$(-\Delta, -1) \mapsto (-\Delta, +1),$$
$$(+\Delta, +1) \mapsto (+\Delta, -1).$$

$\diamond$

3.3 Classifying Hybrid Systems

A hybrid dynamical system may be classified according to the discrete dynamic phenomena that it exhibits as follows (cf. our previous classification).

- *Autonomous-switching.* The autonomous jump map $G \equiv \nu$ is the identity in its continuous component, i.e., $\nu : A \to S$ has $\nu(x, q) = (x, q')$.
- *Autonomous-impulse.* $G \equiv J$ is the identity in its discrete component.
- *Controlled-switching.* The controlled jump map F is the identity in its continuous component, i.e., $F(x, q) \subset \{x\} \times Q$.
- *Controlled-impulse.* F is the identity in its discrete component.

To end this section, we give explicit representations of the different classes of hybrid systems arising from the definitions above. A (continuous-time) *autonomous-switched hybrid system* may be defined as follows:

$$\dot{x}(t) = f(x(t), q(t)),$$
$$q^+(t) = \nu(x(t), q(t)),$$

(3)

where $x(t) \in \mathbf{R}^n$, $q(t) \in Q \simeq \{1, \ldots, N\}$. Here, $f(\cdot, q) : \mathbf{R}^n \to \mathbf{R}^n$, $q \in Q$, each globally Lipschitz continuous, is the *continuous dynamics* of Equation (3);[4] and $\nu : \mathbf{R}^n \times Q \to Q$ is the *finite dynamics* of Equation (3). Here, the notation t^- indicates that the finite state is piecewise continuous from the right. Thus, starting at $[x_0, i]$, the continuous state trajectory $x(\cdot)$ evolves according to $\dot{x} = f(x, i)$. If $x(\cdot)$ hits some $(\nu(\cdot, i))^{-1}(j)$ at time t_1, then the state becomes $[x(t_1), j]$, from which the process continues. Clearly, this is an instantiation of autonomous switching. Switchings that are a fixed function of time may be taken care of by adding another state dimension, as usual. An example is the differential automata of Tavernini [42].

Note. The notation t^- may used to indicate that the finite state is piecewise continuous from the right: $q(t) = \nu(x(t), q(t^-))$. Likewise, $q(t^+) = \nu(x(t), q(t))$ denotes it is piecewise-continuous from the left. To avoid making the distinction here, we have used Sontag's more evocative discrete-time transition notation, where $q^+(t)$ is used to denote the "successor" of $q(t)$ [41]. Its "predecessor" is denoted $q^-(t)$. This notation makes sense since no matter which convention is used for $q(t)$'s piecewise continuity, we still have $q^+(t) = q(t^+)$.

By a *c-controlled autonomous-switching hybrid system* we have in mind a system of the form:

$$\dot{x}(t) = f(x(t), q(t), u(t)),$$
$$q^+(t) = \nu(x(t), q(t), u(t)),$$

(4)

---

[4] Note: these maps are equivalent to our previous $f_q(\cdot)$.

where everything is as above except that $u(t) \in \mathbf{R}^m$, with f and ν modified appropriately. An example is Witsenhausen's hybrid system model [47].

An *autonomous-impulse hybrid system* is a system

$$
\begin{aligned}
\dot{x}(t) &= f(x(t)), & x(t) \notin M \\
x^+(t) &= J(x(t)), & x(t) \in M
\end{aligned}
\tag{5}
$$

where $x(t) \in \mathbf{R}^n$, and $J : \mathbf{R}^n \to \mathbf{R}^n$. Examples include autonomous systems with impulse effect [4].

Finally, a hybrid system with autonomous switching and autonomous impulses (i.e., the full power of autonomous jumps) is just a combination of those discussed above:

$$
\begin{aligned}
\dot{x}(t) &= f(x(t), q(t)), \\
x^+(t) &= J(x(t)), \\
q^+(t) &= \nu(x(t), q(t)),
\end{aligned}
$$

where $x(t) \in \mathbf{R}^n$ and $q(t) \in Q \subset \mathbf{N}$. Examples include the hybrid model of [3].

Likewise, we can define discrete-time autonomous and controlled hybrid systems by replacing the ODEs above with difference equations. In this case, Equation (3) represents a simplified view of some of the models in [20]. Also, adding controls—both discrete and continuous—is straightforward. Finally, non-uniform continuous state spaces, i.e., $x(t) \in X_{q(t)}$, may be added with little change in the foregoing.

4 Analyzing Hybrid Control Systems

In this section, we present some general background on stability analysis, and then work on the stability analysis of hybrid control systems. Specifically, we review *multiple Lyapunov functions* as a tool for analyzing Lyapunov stability. Other stability notions and other analysis tools are discussed in the subsection Going Further.

4.1 Background and Motivation

Suppose we are given a dynamical system in $\mathbf{R}^n$ specified by a differential [resp. difference] equation:

$$
\Sigma : \quad \dot{x}(t) = f(x(t)) \qquad [\text{resp. } x(t+1) = f(x(t))].
\tag{6}
$$

An important concept when analyzing such systems is stability. We give a taste of stability theory below and refer the reader to the excellent introduction in [29] for further details and more advanced references. See also [26, 46, 45].

Stability means that small changes in operating conditions, such as differences in initial data, lead to small changes in behavior. Specifically, let $x(t)$ and $z(t)$ be solutions of Σ when the initial conditions are x_0 and z_0, respectively. Further, let $\|\cdot\|$ denote the Euclidean distance between vectors, $\|z - x\| = [\sum_{i=1}^{n} (z_i - x_i)^2]^{1/2}$.

Definition 1 (Lyapunov Stability of Solution). A solution $x(t)$ of Σ is *Lyapunov stable* if for any $\epsilon > 0$, there exists a $\delta(\epsilon) > 0$ such that all solutions of Σ with $\|z_0 - x_0\| < \delta$ are such that $\|z(t) - x(t)\| < \epsilon$ for all $t > 0$. $\qquad \triangle$

An *equilibrium point* of Σ is one which remains unchanged under the dynamics, namely a point $\overline{x}$ where $f(\overline{x}) = 0$ [resp. $f(\overline{x}) = \overline{x}$]. Since the equilibrium point $\overline{x}$ is a particular kind of solution (namely, one where $x(t) \equiv \overline{x}$ for all t), we may talk of the Lyapunov stability of equilibrium points. Instead of simply repeating the definition for this specific case, though, it is convenient to introduce some new notation. Let $B(\overline{x}, R)$ denote the ball of radius R about $\overline{x}$, that is, all the points y in the state space such that $\|\overline{x} - y\| < R$.

Definition 2 (Lyapunov Stability of Equilibrium Point). An equilibrium point $\overline{x}$ of Σ is *Lyapunov stable* if for any $R > 0$, there exists an r, $0 < r < R$, such that if z_0 is inside $B(\overline{x}, r)$, then $z(t)$ is inside $B(\overline{x}, R)$ for all $t > 0$. $\qquad \triangle$

For an illustration of the concept, see Figure 11, which depicts two stable trajectories in continuous time. Other notions are defined in terms of this primitive concept. For instance, an equilibrium point is *asymptotically stable* if it is stable and there is a $A > 0$ such that if the system is initiated inside $B(\overline{x}, A)$ the trajectory is attracted to $\overline{x}$ as time increases; it is exponentially stable if it is attracted to $\overline{x}$ at an exponential rate, i.e., $\|x(t) - \overline{x}\| \leq ce^{-\mu t}$, $c, \mu > 0$; it is *globally asymptotically stable* if A may be taken arbitrarily large; it is *unstable* if it is not stable.

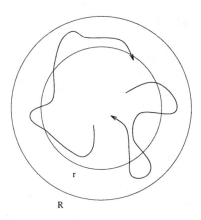

Fig. 11. Lyapunov stability.

Besides introducing the notion of stability above, Lyapunov devised two methods for testing the stability of an equilibrium point, which have come to be known as (1) Lyapunov's indirect method, and (2) Lyapunov's direct method. The indirect method involves examining the stability of a linearized version of the function f. Specifically, one examines the *Jacobian matrix*, the $n \times n$ matrix of first derivatives of f with respect to x, evaluated at the equilibrium point:

$$
F = \begin{bmatrix}
\frac{\partial f_1}{\partial x_1} & \frac{\partial f_1}{\partial x_2} & \cdots & \frac{\partial f_1}{\partial x_n} \\
\frac{\partial f_2}{\partial x_1} & \frac{\partial f_2}{\partial x_2} & \cdots & \frac{\partial f_2}{\partial x_n} \\
\vdots & \vdots & \ddots & \vdots \\
\frac{\partial f_n}{\partial x_1} & \frac{\partial f_n}{\partial x_2} & \cdots & \frac{\partial f_n}{\partial x_n}
\end{bmatrix}_{x=\overline{x}}
$$

To first order near the equilibrium point,

$$
f(\overline{x} + y) \approx f(\overline{x}) + Fy = Fy, \qquad [\text{resp. } \overline{x} + Fy]
$$

so that

$$
\dot{y}(t) = Fy(t) \qquad [\text{resp. } y(t+1) = Fy(t)] \tag{7}
$$

gives a linear approximation of the perturbations to the solution of Σ near $\overline{x}$. In some cases, the stability properties of the system in Σ can be inferred from those of the linear system in Equation (7). In particular, if all the eigenvalues of F have strictly negative real parts [resp. magnitude strictly less than one], then $\overline{x}$ is an asymptotically stable equilibrium point of Σ. If any eigenvalue has a positive real part [resp. magnitude greater than one], it is unstable. If all have non-positive real parts but some have zero real parts [resp. have magnitude less than or equal to one but some have unity magnitude], then nothing can be concluded about stability from this indirect method alone.

Lyapunov's other, direct method for verifying stability works directly with the nonlinear system rather than its linearized version. The basic idea is to seek a type of "energy function" that "decreases along trajectories of the system." Next, we make these notions precise. Suppose that $\overline{x}$ is an equilibrium point of a given dynamic system.

Definition 3 (Lyapunov Function). A *candidate Lyapunov function* for the system Σ and the equilibrium point $\overline{x}$ is a real-valued function V, which is defined over a region Ω of the state space that contains $\overline{x}$, and satisfies the two requirements:

- *Continuity.* V is continuous and, in the case of a continuous-time system, V has continuous partial derivatives.
- *Positive Definiteness.* $V(x)$ has a unique minimum at $\overline{x}$ with respect to all other points in Ω. Without loss of generality, we henceforth assume $V(\overline{x}) = 0$.

A *Lyapunov function* for the system Σ and the equilibrium point $\overline{x}$ is a candidate Lyapunov function V which also satisfies the requirement:

- *Non-increasing.* Along any trajectory of the system contained in Ω the value of V never increases. That is, for a continuous-time system, the function

$\dot{V}(x) = \nabla V(x)f(x) \leq 0$ for all x in Ω;[5] for a discrete-time system, the function $\Delta V(x) = V(f(x)) - V(x) \leq 0$ for all x in Ω. $\triangle$

With these definitions, we may state the following important theorem (see [29], or our Theorem 8 in the case $N = 1$, for continuous- and discrete-time proofs).

Theorem 4 (Lyapunov Theorem). *If there exists a Lyapunov function $V(x)$ in the region $B(\overline{x}, R)$, $R > 0$, then the equilibrium point $\overline{x}$ is Lyapunov stable.*

Summarizing, to use Lyapunov's direct method (in continuous time, for example) you

1. Pick Lyapunov function candidate V
2. Compute $\dot{V}$ [resp. ΔV]
3. Draw conclusions about the system Σ in Equation (6).

See Figure 12. Also, some important things to note are

- Engineering insight is used to pick V, e.g., in mechanical and electrical problems, V can often be chosen as the total (kinetic plus potential) energy of the system.
- The above Lyapunov theorem has a converse, but its sufficiency form stated above is often useful as a design tool (e.g., in adaptive control, where one chooses a candidate Lyapunov function and then a parameter update rule that will result in its being non-increasing over trajectories [40]).

Given the above, whole books may be written—and many have—on the qualitative theory of dynamical systems, extending to theorems on asymptotic stability and instability, global and uniform versions, etc. For one example,

Theorem 5 [29]. *Suppose V is a Lyapunov function for a dynamic system and an equilibrium point $\overline{x}$. Suppose in addition that*

- *V is defined on the entire state space.*
- *$\dot{V}(x) < 0$ [resp. $\Delta V(x) < 0$] for all $x \neq \overline{x}$.*
- *$V(x)$ goes to infinity as $\|x - \overline{x}\|$ goes to infinity.*

Then $\overline{x}$ is globally asymptotically stable.

---

[5] $\nabla V(x)$ is the *gradient vector*

$$\left[\frac{\partial V(x)}{\partial x_1}, \frac{\partial V(x)}{\partial x_2}, \ldots, \frac{\partial V(x)}{\partial x_n}\right].$$

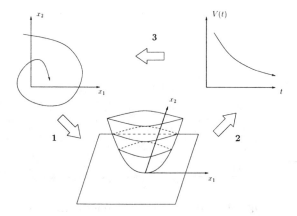

Fig. 12. Lyapunov's direct method.

4.2 Why a Different Theory for Hybrid Systems?

Imagine now that we want to analyze the (Lyapunov) stability of (an equilibrium point of) a hybrid system. Why is a different theory needed for hybrid systems? The reason is that stability of a hybrid system depends on (1) the dynamics of its constituent parts, and (2) the transition map, or "switching rules."

Example 6. Consider $f_i(x) = A_i x$ where

$$A_1 = \begin{bmatrix} -1 & 10 \\ -100 & -1 \end{bmatrix}, \qquad A_2 = \begin{bmatrix} -1 & 100 \\ -10 & -1 \end{bmatrix}.$$

Then one may check that each system $\dot{x} = f_i(x)$ is globally exponentially stable for $i = 1, 2$. See Figures 13 and 14, which plot one second of trajectories for f_1 and f_2 starting from $(1, 0)$, $(0, 1)$, respectively. Hence, the trivial switching rules "always use f_i," $i = 1, 2$, are stable. Another switching rule that is stable is one which uses f_2 in the second and fourth quadrants and f_1 in the first and third quadrants. ◇

However, it is easy to combine the above two globally asymptotically stable systems with a switching scheme that sends all trajectories to infinity:

Example 7. The switched system using f_1 in the second and fourth quadrants and f_2 in the first and third quadrants is unstable. See Figure 15, which plots one second of the trajectory starting from $(10^{-6}, 10^{-6})$. ◇

Such examples appear to be classical [2]. A similar example, producing a stable system by appropriately switching between two unstable ones appears in [43].

The bottom line: even if we have Lyapunov functions for each system f_i individually, we need to impose restrictions on switching to guarantee stability.

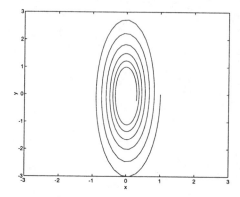

Fig. 13. Trajectory of f_1. Motion is clockwise.

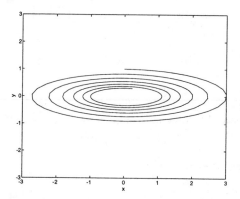

Fig. 14. Trajectory of f_2. Motion is clockwise.

4.3   Stability via Multiple Lyapunov Functions

In this section, we discuss Lyapunov stability of switched and hybrid systems via *multiple Lyapunov functions* (*MLF*). In particular, we impose restrictions on switching sufficient to guarantee stability. We will make rigorous the following "theorem":

Theorem 6 (Multiple Lyapunov Method). *Given N dynamical systems, Σ_1, ..., Σ_N, each with equilibrium point $\bar{x}$, and N candidate Lyapunov functions, $V_1, \ldots, V_N$.*

If V_i decreases when Σ_i is active and

$$V_i \left(\begin{array}{c} \text{time when } \Sigma_i \\ \text{switched in} \end{array} \right) \leq V_i \left(\begin{array}{c} \text{last time } \Sigma_i \\ \text{switched in} \end{array} \right)$$

for all $i = 1, \ldots, N$, then the hybrid system is Lyapunov stable.

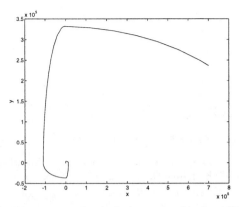

Fig. 15. Trajectory of switched system. Motion is clockwise.

For simplicity, we restrict ourselves to the case of autonomous switching, that is, we assume there are no discontinuous jumps of the continuous state. To further simplify the problem, we suppress the finite dynamics, which is equivalent to considering the following case:

$$\Sigma_i : \quad \dot{x}(t) = f_i(x(t)), \quad [\text{resp. } x(t+1) = f_i(x(t))], \quad i \in Q \simeq \{1, \ldots, N\}, \quad (8)$$

where $x(t) \in \mathbf{R}^n$, each f_i is continuous, and i is chosen according to some switching scheme. However, in the case of continuous-time systems, we add the following *switching rules*, the second of which could be specified in terms of restrictions on the function ν:

- Each f_i is Lipschitz continuous.
- The i's are picked in such a way that there are finite switches in finite time.

Finally, we assume that the equilibrium point is the origin, which is without loss of generality after a change of coordinates. Accordingly, we let $S(r)$, $B(r)$, and $\overline{B}(r)$ represent the sphere, ball, and closed ball of Euclidean radius r about the origin in $\mathbf{R}^n$, respectively.

Below, we deal with systems as in Equation (8), which switch among vector fields [resp. difference equations] over time or regions of state-space. One can associate with such a system the following (*anchored*) *switching sequence*, indexed by an initial state, x_0:

$$S = x_0; \ (i_0, t_0), (i_1, t_1), \ldots, (i_N, t_N), \ldots. \quad (9)$$

The sequence may or may not be infinite. In the finite case, we may take $t_{N+1} = \infty$, with all further definitions and results holding. However, we present in the sequel only in the infinite case to ease notation. The switching sequence, along with Equation (8), completely describes the trajectory of the system according to the following rule: (i_k, t_k) means that the system evolves according to $\dot{x}(t) = f_{i_k}(x(t), t)$ for $t_k \leq t < t_{k+1}$. We denote this trajectory by $x_S(\cdot)$. Throughout, we assume that the switching sequence is *minimal* in the sense that $i_j \neq i_{j+1}$, $j \in \mathbf{Z}_+$.

We can take projections of this sequence onto its first and second coordinates, yielding the sequence of indices,

$$\pi_1(S) = x_0; \ i_0, i_1, \ldots, i_N, \ldots,$$

and the sequence of switching times,

$$\pi_2(S) = x_0; \ t_0, t_1, \ldots, t_N, \ldots,$$

respectively. Suppose S is a switching sequence as in Equation (9). We denote by $S|i$ the endpoints of the times that system i is active in both the continuous- and discrete-time cases. The *interval completion* $\mathcal{I}(T)$ of a strictly increasing sequence of times $T = t_0, t_1, \ldots, t_N, \ldots$, is the set

$$\bigcup_{j \in \mathbf{Z}_+} [t_{2j}, t_{2j+1}].$$

Hence, $\mathcal{I}(S|i)$ is the set of times that the ith system is active (up to a set of measure zero in the continuous-time case). Finally, let $\mathcal{E}(T)$ denote the *even sequence* of T: $t_0, t_2, t_4, \ldots$.

Note that by previous conventions, we assume a candidate Lyapunov function has $V(0) = 0$.

Definition 7 (Lyapunov-like). Given a strictly increasing sequence of times T in $\mathbf{R}$ [resp. $\mathbf{Z}$], we say that V is *Lyapunov-like* for function f and trajectory $x(\cdot)$ over T if

- $\dot{V}(x(t)) \leq 0$ [resp. $V(x(t+1)) \leq V(x(t))$] for all $t \in \mathcal{I}(T)$,
- V is monotonically nonincreasing on $\mathcal{E}(T)$.   △

The second condition ensures that energy function V is not increasing at each time it is "switched in."

Theorem 8 (Multiple Lyapunov Functions). *Suppose we have candidate Lyapunov functions V_i, $i = 1, \ldots, N$, and vector fields $\dot{x} = f_i(x)$ [resp. difference equations $x(t+1) = f_i(x(t))$] with $f_i(0) = 0$, for all i. Let S be the set of all switching sequences associated with the system.*

If for each $S \in \mathcal{S}$ we have that for all i, V_i is Lyapunov-like for f_i and $x_S(\cdot)$ over $S|i$, then the system is stable in the sense of Lyapunov.

Proof. In each case, we do the proofs only for $N = 2$.

- *Continuous-time:* Let $R > 0$ be arbitrary. Let $m_i(\alpha)$ denote the minimum value of V_i on $S(\alpha)$. Pick $r_i < R$ such that in $B(r_i)$ we have $V_i < m_i(R)$. This choice is possible via the continuity of V_i. Let $r = \min(r_i)$. With this choice, if we start in $B(r)$, either vector field alone will stay within $B(R)$. Now, pick $\rho_i < r$ such that in $B(\rho_i)$ we have $V_i < m_i(r)$. Set $\rho = \min(\rho_i)$. Thus, if we start in $B(\rho)$, either vector field alone will stay in $B(r)$. Therefore, whenever the other is first switched on we have $V_i(x(t_1)) < m_i(R)$, so that we will stay within $B(R)$. See Figures 16 and 17.

– *Discrete-time:* Let $R > 0$ be arbitrary. Let $m_i(\alpha, \beta)$ denote the minimum value of V_i on the closed annulus $\overline{B}(\beta) - B(\alpha)$. Pick $R_0 < R$ so that none of the f_i can jump out of $B(R)$ in one step. Pick $r_i < R_0$ such that in $B(r_i)$ we have $V_i < m_i(R_0, R)$. This choice is possible via the continuity of V_i. Let $r = \min(r_i)$. With this choice, if we start in $B(r)$, either equation alone will stay within $B(R)$.

Pick $r_0 < r$ so that none of the f_i can jump out of $B(r)$ in one step. Now, pick $\rho_i < r_0$ such that in $B(\rho_i)$ we have $V_i < m_i(r_0, r)$. Set $\rho = \min(\rho_i)$. Thus, if we start in $B(\rho)$, either equation alone will stay in $B(r_0)$, and hence $B(r)$. Therefore, whenever the other is first switched on we have $V_i(x(t_1)) < m_i(R_0, R)$, so that we will stay within $B(R_0)$, and hence $B(R)$.

The proofs for general N require N sets of concentric circles constructed as the two were in each case above. □

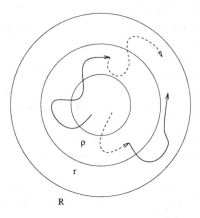

Fig. 16. Multiple Lyapunov stability, $N = 2$.

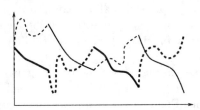

Fig. 17. Multiple Lyapunov Stability. Lyapunov function values versus time.

Some remarks are in order:

- The case $N = 1$ is the usual theorem for Lyapunov stability [29]. Also, compare Figures 11 and 16, both of which depict the continuous-time case. Also, compare Figures 12 and 17 which depict a Lyapunov function (upper right) and multiple Lyapunov functions over time, respectively.
- The theorem also holds if the f_i are time-varying.
- It is easy to see that the theorem does not hold if $N = \infty$, and we leave it to the reader to construct examples.
- It is not hard to generalize our MLF theory to the case of different equilibria, which is generally the case in hybrid systems. For example, under a Lyapunov-like switching rule, after all controllers have been switched in at level α_i, the set $\bigcup_i V_i^{-1}(\alpha_i)$ is invariant.
- It is not hard to extend the presented theorems to consider variations such as (1) relaxing *the first part* of our Lyapunov-like definition by allowing the Lyapunov functions to increase in each active region if the gain from "switch in" to "switch out" is given by a positive definite function [48], or, more provocatively, (2) allowing increases over energy V_i at its switching times with a similar constraint from initial value to final limit.
- The result above generalizes some theorems in the literature, including [35] (see below) and [34]. In the latter, Pavlidis concludes stability of differential equations containing impulses by introducing a positive definite function which decreases during the occurrence of an impulse and remains constant or decreases during the "free motion" of the system. Hence, it is a special case of our results.
- The stabilization strategies proposed in [30], e.g., choosing at each time the minimum of several Lyapunov functions, clearly satisfies our switching condition.
- Sliding modes may be taken care by defining each sliding mode and its associated sliding dynamics as an additional system to which we can switch. We then merely check the conditions as before.
- In proving stability, we can use more Lyapunov functions than constituent systems (see [36] for an example where this is necessary) by simply introducing new discrete sub-states with the same continuous dynamics but different Lyapunov functions.
- When the dynamics are piecewise affine, computational tests may be used to compute appropriate switching conditions ([35]; eigenvalue analysis) or to find Multiple Lyapunov functions that prove stability ([28]; LMIs).

Example 8. Pick any line through the origin. Going back to Example 7 and choosing to use f_1 above the line and f_2 below it, the resulting system is globally asymptotically stable. See Figure 18, which plots one second of a trajectory for the switched system starting from $(1, 1)$. While stability may be clear from the figure, we can prove it using our theorem. The reason is that each system is an asymptotically stable linear system and hence diminishes $V_i = x^T P_i x$ for some $P_i > 0$ [29]. However, since switchings occur on a line through the origin, we are assured that on switches to system i, V_i is at a lower energy than when it was last switched out. Why? Assume we switch from f_i to f_j at the point y. At that point, $V_i(y) = y^T P_i y$ and $V_j(y) = y^T P_j y$. At the next switch point, z, we go from f_j to f_i. There, since V_j is Lyapunov-like for f_j, we have

$$V_j(z) = z^T P_j z < y^T P_j y = V_j(y). \tag{10}$$

However, since the switching line is the origin, $z = \alpha y$. Further, from Equation (10), we know that $\alpha^2 < 1$. Thus, we have that

$$V_i(z) = z^T P_i z = \alpha^2 y^T P_i y < y^T P_i y = V_i(y),$$

which satisfies our theorem. ◇

Example 9. Consider the following system, inspired from one in [36]: $\dot{x}(t) = A_i(t)x(t)$ with

$$A_1 = \begin{bmatrix} -1 & -100 \\ 10 & -1 \end{bmatrix}, \qquad A_2 = \begin{bmatrix} 1 & 10 \\ -100 & 1 \end{bmatrix}.$$

with the switching rule that we go from system i to j on hitting the sets $c_{i,j}^T x(t) = 0$ *in the second and fourth quadrants* where

$$c_{1,2} = [4, 3], \qquad c_{2,1} = [3, 4].$$

An example trajectory is shown in Figure 19. There, the dynamics alternate between going counterclockwise along a short, fat ellipse and then clockwise along a tall, skinny one.

It is clear that the conic switching region (1) is attractive, (2) leads to a hybrid system, and (3) admits no single Lyapunov function (depending only on the continuous state) that can be used to show stability (because the system's trajectories intersects themselves).

However, it is also easy to see that energy is decreasing at switching times (just consider the switching lines through the origin and note we get closer). Multiple Lyapunov functions showing this may be computed using LMIs which encode the conditions of our theorem above [28]. ◇

It is possible to use different conditions on the V_i to ensure stability. For instance, consider the following

Definition 9 (Sequence Nonincreasing). If there are candidate Lyapunov functions V_i corresponding to f_i for all i, we say they satisfy the *sequence nonincreasing condition* for a trajectory $x(\cdot)$ if $V_{i_{j+1}}(x(t_{j+1})) < V_{i_j}(x(t_j))$. △

This is a stronger notion than the Lyapunov-like condition used above.

Now, consider the case where the index set is an arbitrary compact set:

$$\dot{x} = f(x, \lambda), \qquad \lambda \in K, \text{ compact.} \tag{11}$$

Here, $x \in \mathbf{R}^n$ and f is globally Lipschitz in x, continuous in λ. For brevity, we only consider the continuous-time case. Again, we assume finite switches in finite time. As above, we may define a switching sequence

$$S = x_0; \ (\lambda_0, t_0), (\lambda_1, t_1), \ldots, (\lambda_N, t_N), \ldots$$

with its associated projection sequences.

Theorem 10 [10]. *Suppose we have candidate Lyapunov functions $V_\lambda \equiv V(\cdot, \lambda)$ and vector fields as in Equation (11) with $f(0, \lambda) = 0$, for each $\lambda \in K$. Also, $V : \mathbf{R}^n \times K \to \mathbf{R}_+$ is continuous. Let $\mathcal{S}$ be the set of all switching sequences associated with the system.*

If for each $S \in \mathcal{S}$ we have that for all λ, V_λ is Lyapunov-like function for f_λ and $x_S(\cdot)$ over $S|\lambda$, and the V_λ satisfy the sequence nonincreasing condition for $x_S(\cdot)$, then the system is stable in the sense of Lyapunov.

This theorem is a different generalization of the aforementioned theorems of [34, 35], but its proof is deleted since it contains more advanced analysis.

4.4 Going Further

The MLF stability results above are sufficiency conditions on the continuous dynamics and switching. We do not consider this a drawback since Lyapunov theory is almost always used in its sufficiency form; also, the use of such conditions in *design* of provably stable control laws is an important area of future research (cf. our previous mention of using Lyapunov's Theorem to design stable adaptive control laws). Also, we saw it is not hard to generalize our MLF theory to the case of different equilibria, which is generally the case in hybrid systems. For example, under a Lyapunov-like switching rule, after all controllers have been switched in at level α_i, the set $\bigcup_i V_i^{-1}(\alpha_i)$ is invariant. This work, then, represents the rudiments of a stability theory of hybrid systems. Indeed, the sufficiently motivated reader may write whole books by using the above ideas to examine asymptotic stability, instability, global and uniform versions, etc. for hybrid systems. We also discussed the case where $\{1, \ldots, N\}$ in Equation (8) is replaced by an arbitrary compact set. The reader interested in stability is directed to [10], which introduced MLFs but also addresses ultimate boundedness of trajectories (Lagrange stability) using tests inspired by iterated function systems, or IFS.

We have also studied other analysis questions and tools. In general, such analysis questions are undecidable since even differential equations in $\mathbf{R}^3$ can simulate arbitrary Turing machines [12]. Topological issues arising in hybrid systems, such as how to define continuity when finite alphabets impact the dynamics, are discussed in [7]. Other analysis tools besides MLFs and IFS have been developed. These include comparison theorems to infer properties of hybrid systems from ones established by analyzing "continuations" of them, in which the discontinuous logic is smoothed by allowing intermediate values [9]. They also include extensions of Bendixson's theorem (used for detecting limit cycles in the plane) to systems possessing less stringent continuity requirements on the vector field. This represents a move toward hybrid systems, namely through the study of their "continuations." These latter tools, plus MLFs, are illustrated in [8, 10, 13].

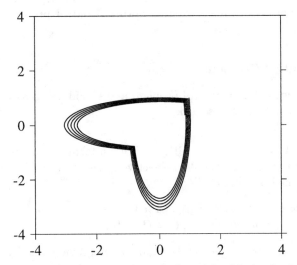

Fig. 18. Switching on a line through the origin. Motion is clockwise.

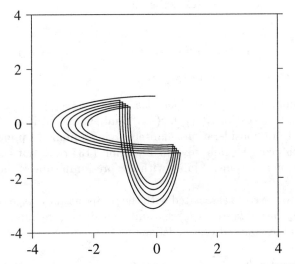

Fig. 19. A switching system requiring hybrid states and MLFs. Motion is counter-clockwise.

5 Theory of Optimal Hybrid Control Systems

In this section, we define an optimal hybrid control problem and review some theoretical results, including an existence result for optimal controls and a set of inequalities (called "generalized quasi-variational inequalities," or GQVIs) that the value function associated with this optimal control problem must satisfy [14, 15, 11, 17].

5.1 The Control Problem

In this section, we define a control problem and elucidate all assumptions used in deriving the results in the sequel.

Problem. First, we consider a CHDS with uniform continuous control and discrete decision spaces, U and $\mathcal{V}$, respectively. Next, we add transition delay maps as mentioned in notes earlier:

- autonomous transition delay $\Delta_a : A \times V \to \mathbf{R}_+$.
- controlled transition delay $\Delta_c : C \times D \to \mathbf{R}_+$.

Let $a > 0$ be a *discount factor*. We add to our previous model the following known maps:

- running cost $k : S \times U \to \mathbf{R}_+$.
- transition cost $c_a : A \times \mathcal{V} \to \mathbf{R}_+$.
- impulse cost $c_c : C \times D \to \mathbf{R}_+$, satisfying

$$c_c(s_1, s_2) \geq c_0 > 0, \tag{12}$$

$$c_c(s_1, s_2) < c_c(s_1, s_3) + e^{-a\Delta_c(s_1, s_3)} c_c(s_3, s_2), \tag{13}$$

for all $s_1 \in C$, $s_2 \in F(s_1) \cap F(s_3)$, and $z \in F(s_1)$.

Thus, autonomous jumps are done at a cost of $c_a(s(\tau_j), v_j)$ paid at time τ_j; impulsive jumps at a cost of $c_c(s(\tau_j), x(\Gamma_j))$ paid at time τ_j. Note that Equation (12) rules out from consideration infinitely many impulsive jumps in a finite interval—lest the cost be infinite; adn Equation (13) rules out the merging of post-jump time of an impulsive jump with the pre-jump time of the next impulsive jump.

In addition to the costs associated with the jumps as above, the controller also incurs a *running cost* of $k(s(t), u(t))$ per unit time during the intervals $[\Gamma_{j-1}, \tau_j)$, $j \in \mathbf{N}$. The total discounted cost is defined as

$$\int_{\mathbf{T}} e^{-at} k(s(t), u(t))\, dt + \sum_i e^{-a\sigma_i} c_a(s(\sigma_i), v_i) + \sum_i e^{-a\zeta_i} c_c(s(\zeta_i), s(\zeta_i')), \tag{14}$$

where $\mathbf{T} = \mathbf{R}_+ \backslash (\bigcup_i [\tau_i, \Gamma_i))$, $\{\sigma_i\}$ (resp. $\{\zeta_i\}$) are the successive pre-jump times for autonomous (resp. impulsive) jumps and ζ_j' is the post-jump time for the jth impulsive jump. The *decision* or *control* variables over which Equation (14) is to be minimized are the continuous control $u(\cdot)$, the discrete control $\{v_i\}$ exercised at the pre-jump times of autonomous jumps, the pre-jump times $\{\zeta_i\}$ of impulsive jumps, and the associated *destinations* $\{s(\zeta_i')\}$.

The dynamics of the control system is much the same as for CHDS above, except that the delay maps give rise to a sequence of *pre-jump times* $\{\tau_i\}$ and another sequence of *post-jump times* $\{\Gamma_i\}$ satisfying $0 = \Gamma_0 \leq \tau_1 < \Gamma_1 < \tau_2 < \Gamma_2 < \cdots \leq \infty$. On each interval $[\Gamma_{j-1}, \tau_j)$ with non-empty interior, $x(\cdot)$ evolves according to $\dot{x}(t) = f_i(x(t), u(t))$ in some X_i, $i \in \mathbf{Z}_+$. At the next pre-jump time (say, τ_j) it jumps to some $D_k \in X_k$ according to one of the following two possibilities:

1. $x(\tau_j) \in A_i$, in which case it *must* jump to $(x(\Gamma_j), k) = G_i(x(\tau_j), v_j) \in D$ at time $\Gamma_j = \tau_j + \Delta_a(x(\tau_j), i, v_j)$, $v_j \in V$ being a control input. We call this phenomenon an autonomous jump.
2. $x(\tau_j) \in C_i$ and the controller *chooses* to—it does not have to—move the trajectory discontinuously to $(x(\Gamma_j), k) \in D$ at time $\Gamma_j = \tau_j + \Delta_c(x(\tau_j), i, x(\Gamma_j))$. We call this a controlled (or impulsive) jump.

See Figure 9.

Thus, the *admissible control actions* available are

- the *continuous controls* $u(\cdot)$, exercised in each constituent regime,
- the *discrete controls* $\{v_i\}$ exercised at the pre-jump times of autonomous jumps (which occur on hitting the set A),
- the pre-jump or *intervention times* $\{\zeta_i\}$ and associated *destinations* $\{x(\zeta_i')\}$ of the controlled jumps.

Assumptions. Throughout the sequel, we make use of the following further assumptions on our abstract model, which are collected here for clarity and convenience.

For each $i \in \mathbf{N}$, the following hold: X_i is the closure of a connected open subset of Euclidean space $\mathbf{R}^{d_i}$, $d_i \in \mathbf{N}$, with Lipschitz boundary ∂X_i. $A_i, C_i, D_i \subset X_i$ are closed. In addition, ∂A_i is Lipschitz and contains ∂X_i.

The maps G, Δ_a, Δ_c, c_a, c_c, and k are bounded uniformly continuous. The vector fields f_i, $i \in \mathbf{N}$, are bounded (uniformly in i), uniformly Lipschitz continuous in the first argument, uniformly equicontinuous with respect to the rest. U, V are compact metric spaces. Below, $u(\cdot)$ is a U-valued control process, assumed to be measurable.

All the above are fairly mild assumptions. The following are more technical assumptions. They may be traded for others as discussed in [11]. However, in the sequel we construct examples pointing out the necessity of such assumptions or ones like them.

Assumption 1 $d(A_i, C_i) > 0$ *and* $\inf_{i \in \mathbf{N}} d(A_i, D_i) > 0$, d *being the appropriate Euclidean distance.*

Assumption 2 *Each* D_i *is bounded and for each* i, *there exists an integer* $N(i) < \infty$ *such that for* $x \in C_i$, $y \in D_j$, $j > N(i)$, $c_c(x, y) > \sup_z J(z)$. *(J is the cost-to-go function, defined below.)*

Assumption 3 *For each i, ∂A_i is an oriented C^1-manifold without boundary and at each point x on ∂A_i, $f_i(x, u)$ is "transversal" to ∂A_i for all choices of u. By this we require that (i) the flow lines be transversal in the usual sense[6] and (ii) the vector field does not vanish on ∂A_i.*

Assumption 4 *Same as Assumption 3 but with C_i replacing A_i.*

5.2   Theoretical Results

Let $V(s)$ denote the infimum of Equation (14) over all choices of $u(\cdot), \{v_i\}, \{\zeta_i\}, \{s(\zeta_i')\}$ when $s(0) = s$. We have

Theorem 11. *A finite optimal cost exists for any initial condition.*

Corollary 12. *There are only finitely many autonomous jumps in finite time.*

In [17], we use the framework of relaxed control of [49]. This framework is well-known in the control literature, so we do not give full details here. It suffices to say that this framework replaces the set of controls U' with the set of probability distributions over those controls $U = \mathcal{P}(U')$, as a means to "convexify" the control space. We say a control is *precise* if it is deterministic i.e., has all its probability at a single point in U'.

Example 10 (PWM). For comparison, one may think of the more familiar case of *pulse-width modulation* (PWM). With an "ideal PWM," one replaces 0 and 1 outputs with the whole range of outputs $[0, 1]$ by suitable modulation of the duty cycle. It remains to check that a "real PWM" can achieve such a task closely enough. This is indeed the case. Although the control signal p, $0 < p < 1$ (a relaxed control with p probability on 1 and $1 - p$ probability on 0), cannot be output exactly, it can be approximated by keeping the output at 1 for ph time units every h seconds. As h goes to zero, the approximation becomes arbitrarily good. ◇

In the relaxed control framework, we have shown

Theorem 13. *An optimal trajectory exists for any initial condition.*

Theorem 14. *Under Assumptions 2–4, for every $\epsilon > 0$ an ϵ-optimal control policy exists wherein $u(\cdot)$ is precise.*

Let $V(s)$ denote the optimal cost corresponding to initial data $s(0) = s$. Then in dynamic programming parlance, $s \mapsto V(s)$ defines the "value function" for our control problem. Finally, let

$$F(s, u) \equiv \langle \nabla_x V(s), f_q(x, u) \rangle - aV(s) + k(s, u).$$

---

[6] Transversality implies that ∂A_i is $(d_i - 1)$-dimensional.

In [17], we proposed the following system of *generalized quasi-variational inequalities* (*GQVIs*) $V(\cdot)$ is expected to satisfy, which are formally derived in [17]. For $s \in S$,

$$\min_u F(s, u) \leq 0. \tag{15}$$

On A,

$$V(s) \leq \min_v \left\{ c_a(s, v) + e^{-a\Delta_a(s,v)} V(G(s, v)) \right\}. \tag{16}$$

On C,

$$V(s) \leq \min_{s' \in D} \left\{ c_c(s, s') + e^{-a\Delta_c(s,s')} V(s') \right\}, \tag{17}$$

$$\left(V(s) - \min_{s' \in D} \left\{ c_c(s, s') + e^{-a\Delta_c(s,s')} V(s') \right\} \right) \cdot (\min_u F(s, u)) = 0. \tag{18}$$

Equation (18) states that at least one of Equations (15) and (17) must be an equality on C. Equations (15)–(18) generalize the traditional quasi-variational inequalities encountered in impulse control [5]. We do not address the issue of well-posedness of Equations (15)–(18).

6   Synthesizing Hybrid Control Systems

In this section, we outline several approaches for computing the solutions to the GQVIs that we saw arise in optimal hybrid control problems above. The algorithms presented can be viewed as generalizations to the case of hybrid control systems of dynamic programming (see [6] for an introduction and references). In each case, the underlying feedback controls can be subsequently computed. An illustrative example is worked out to fix ideas.

6.1   Hybrid Dynamic Programming

The starting point for our algorithms is the "hybrid" Bellman Equation:

$$V(s) = \min_{a \in \mathcal{A}} \left\{ g(s, a) + V(s'(s, a)) \right\} \tag{19}$$

where $\mathcal{A}$ is a generalized set of actions. The three classes of actions available in our hybrid systems framework at each x are

- **Continuous Controls**: $u \in U$.
- **Controlled Jumps**, choosing source and destination (if $x \in C$).
- **Autonomous Jumps**, possibly modulated by discrete controls $\mathcal{V}$ (if $x \in A$).

To solve on a computer, we (discretize the continuous state and controls and) compute for $x \in S_j$ the minimum of the following three quantities:

$$\min_u \left\{ \int_0^\delta k(s(t), u) \, dt + V \left(x + \int_0^\delta f_q(x(t), u) \, dt, q \right) \right\},$$

$$\min_{s' \in D} \left\{ c_c(s, s') + e^{-a\Delta_c(s,s')} V(s') \right\}$$

$$\min_{v \in \mathcal{V}} \left\{ c_a(s, v) + e^{-a\Delta_a(s,v)} V(G(s, v)) \right\}$$

with several caveats. First, we make sure that we do not hit A in our computation of the first quantity. (Briefly, if we do, we replace dt by $\sigma_{1_u} - t$.) Second, the last two quantities are not taken into account if $x \notin C$ or $x \notin A$, respectively.

Value and Policy Iteration. The resulting system may be solved via value or policy iteration. So far, we have concentrated on value iteration (solved via relaxation) and call the resulting algorithm "Generalized Value Iteration."

More specifically, the algorithm is as follows:

1. Discretize the state space into $\mathcal{S}$ and set of continuous controls into $\mathcal{U}$.
2. For each $s \in \mathcal{S}$, guess a value for $V(s)$, e.g., zero.
3. For each $s \in \mathcal{S}$, compute the minimum of the three quantities described above, subject to the caveats. The first minimum is taken with respect to $u \in \mathcal{U}$ with the cost-to-go a weighted sum of the costs-to-g o of nearest neighbors. Set $V(s)$ equal to that minimum. Repeat until convergence.

We do not go into theoretical results here, but only note that the theoretical framework of [21] is very general, allowing, e.g., piecewise Lipschitz continuous dynamics.

Linear Programming. Linear programming has been used to solve for the value function associated with optimal control of Markov decision processes [38]. Here we use it to solve hybrid control problems.

Again assume we have discretized the state space into $\mathcal{S}$ and the set of continuous controls into $\mathcal{U}$ (yielding $|\mathcal{A}|$ finite). Consider the right-hand side of Equation (19) as an operator, T, on functions V. Arguing as in [38, Lemma 6.21, p. 151], monotonicity of T and $V^* = TV^*$, imply that V^* may be obtained by solving

Maximize V subject to $TV \geq V$.

However, since maximizing $V(s)$ for each $s \in \mathcal{S}$ also maximizes $\sum V(s)$, the problem reduces to

Maximize $\sum V(s)$ subject to
$\min_{a \in \mathcal{A}} \{g(s, a) + V(s'(s, a))\} \geq V(s)$, for all $s \in \mathcal{S}$.

Alternatively, we can write this as

Maximize $\sum V(s)$ subject to
$\{g(s, a) + V(s'(s, a))\} \geq V(s)$, for all $a \in \mathcal{A}$ and $s \in \mathcal{S}$.

This is just a linear program and may be solved by standard techniques. The problem is that these linear programs may be large. If $|\mathcal{S}| = N$, and $|\mathcal{A}| = M$, then we have N variables and MN constraints. The advantage is that the matrix of constraints is sparse. Briefly, this is since the row corresponding to (s, a) only has non-zero weights for the nearest neighbors of the state $s'(s, a)$.

6.2 Solving an Example

Here, we give an example problem in our framework and summarize its solution by the three methods discussed above. We now consider a hybrid control example which combines continuous control with the phenomenon of autonomous switching.

Example 11. Recall the control system with hysteresis of Example 5. s a control problem we consider minimizing

$$J = \int_0^\infty \frac{1}{2}(qx^2 + u^2)e^{-at}dt \equiv \int_0^\infty k(s, u)e^{-at}dt \qquad (20)$$

Let $s = (x, H(x))$. We first solve for $V(s)$, and then for u. By symmetry, we expect $V(-\Delta, 1) = V(\Delta, -1)$. From the GQVIs, we expect V to satisfy

$$\min_u \{-aV(s) + V_x(s) \cdot f_{H(x)}(x, u) + k(s, u)\} = 0,$$
$$V(\Delta, 1) = c + V(\Delta, -1), \qquad (21)$$
$$V(-\Delta, -1) = c + V(-\Delta, 1),$$

where $H(x)$ takes on the values ± 1 and c represents the cost associated with the autonomous-switchings. ◇

We have solved these equations numerically for the case $c = 0$, $a = 1$, $\Delta = 0.1$. For future comparison, we computed these directly using a boundary-value algorithm. This was straightforward for our example due to its one-dimensional constituent state spaces (see [11] for more details). The resulting control u, plotted against x (for $H(x) = 1$) and q, is shown in Figure 20. As the state is increasingly penalized, the control action increases in such a way to "invert" the hysteresis function H.

To get an idea of the dynamics we plot the state and control over time for several values of q in Figures 21 and 22, respectively. As the penalty on the state increases, the control acts in such a manner as to keep the state closer to zero for successively larger fractions of each "cycle." Concomitantly, we see how the controls begin to try to "invert" the hysteresis, as we just mentioned.

Next, we compare the solutions found above with those computed by the generalized value iteration and linear programming algorithms outlined above. In Figure 23 we plot the optimal control again, but this time we compare those previously shown (which were computed using the boundary-value algorithm mentioned above) with those obtained using generalized value iteration arising from the Bellman equation described above. While the surfaces do look similar, we also plot several "slices" for better comparison. Up to the discretization used in the value iteration algorithm, the plots are seen to agree.

Next, we compare the optimal costs computed by linear programming with those computed with value iteration for successively tighter convergence criteria. See Figure 24. Note that the value iteration solutions are converging to those found via linear programming. Both algorithms used the same discretization and the same computer resources (Matlab on a Sparc5 after data initialization using a C program). In this case, the wall time to compute *each curve shown* was about equal. Thus for this problem linear programming yielded more than a factor of four speed-up.

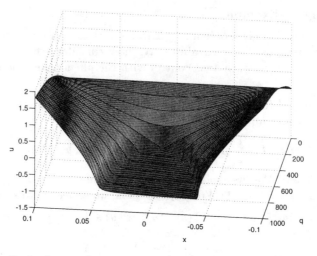

Fig. 20. Optimal control u versus x and q, for the case $a = 1$, $c = 0$, $\Delta = 0.1$.

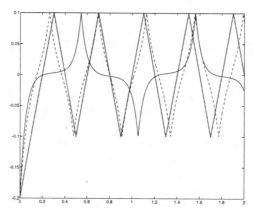

Fig. 21. Comparison of x versus time, under different values of q. Solid, $q = 400$; dashed, $q = 200$; dotted, $q = 0$.

6.3 Going Further

Here, we introduced several algorithms for synthesizing optimal hybrid control systems by solving the associated GQVIs. These included several for solving hybrid dynamic programs, including value iteration and linear programming. For more details on the algorithms, the reader is referred to [19, 17]. Besides other examples, these include a whole different algorithmic approach: iterative algorithms inspired by those for piecewise-deterministic processes [22].

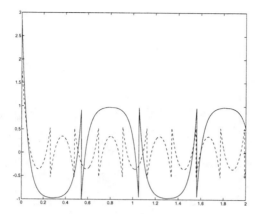

Fig. 22. Comparison of u versus time, under different values of q. Solid, $q = 400$; dashed, $q = 200$; when $q = 0$, u is identically zero (not plotted)

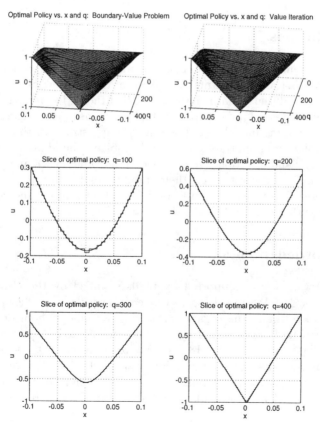

Fig. 23. Comparison of policies computed by boundary-value and value iteration. Slices show details. Smooth, boundary-value; staircase, value iteration

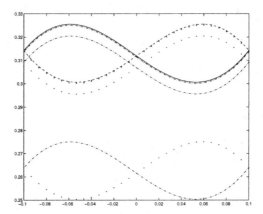

Fig. 24. Cost-to-go for hysteresis example versus state ($H(x) = 1, -1$ superimposed). Plot shows the convergence of value iteration solutions (dash-dot and dotted lines) to that found by linear programming (solid and dashed).

7 Conclusions

Embedded systems are hybrid control systems, combining continuous-variable dynamics and logical decision-making. We examined a slew of such real-world systems and introduced a mathematical model of them. The model captures the significant phenomena found in the example systems, encompasses previously posed hybrid systems models, yet possesses enough structure to allow rigorous posing and solution of analysis and control problems, building on existing control theory tools and intuition. We provided an introduction to analyzing hybrid control systems, concentrating on their stability analysis using "multiple Lyapunov functions." We then turned to optimal hybrid control, and covered both theory and synthesis algorithms.

8 Acknowledgments

During this work I was supported by funds supplied by the Case School of Engineering at Case Western Reserve University, which are greatly appreciated. I would also like thank the organizers of the November School on Embedded Systems, particularly Frits Vaandrager, for inviting me to be a part of the School and this special volume. Figures 18 and 19 were produced by the simulation tool Omsim, from Lund Institute of Technology, using hybrid systems macros written by the author. See [18] for details. Figures 13–15 and 20–24 were produced using Matlab. Finally, I would like to thank the anonymous reviewers for their comments.

References

1. Panos J. Antsaklis, James A. Stiver, and Michael D. Lemmon. Hybrid system modeling and autonomous control systems. In Grossman et al. [24], pages 366–392.

2. Karl J. Åström. Course notes on nonlinear systems. Lund Institute of Technology, 1968.

3. Allen Back, John Guckenheimer, and Mark Myers. A dynamical simulation facility for hybrid systems. In Grossman et al. [24], pages 255–267.

4. Dimitur D. Bainov and Pavel S. Simeonov. *Systems with Impulse Effect*. Ellis Horwood, Chichester, England, 1989.

5. Alain Bensoussan and Jacques-Louis Lions. *Impulse Control and Quasi-Variational Inequalities*. Gauthier-Villars, Paris, 1984.

6. Dmitri P. Bertsekas. *Dynamic Programming : Deterministic and Stochastic Models*. Prentice Hall, Englewood Cliffs, NJ, 1987.

7. Michael S. Branicky. Topology of hybrid systems. In *Proc. IEEE Conf. Decision and Control*, pages 2309–2314, San Antonio, December 1993.

8. Michael S. Branicky. Analyzing continuous switching systems: Theory and examples. In *Proc. American Control Conf.*, pages 3110–3114, Baltimore, June 1994.

9. Michael S. Branicky. Continuity of ODE solutions. *Applied Mathematics Letters*, 7(5):57–60, 1994.

10. Michael S. Branicky. Stability of switched and hybrid systems. In *Proc. IEEE Conf. Decision and Control*, pages 3498–3503, Lake Buena Vista, FL, December 1994.

11. Michael S. Branicky. *Studies in Hybrid Systems: Modeling, Analysis, and Control*. PhD thesis, Massachusetts Institute of Technology, Dept. of Electrical Engineering and Computer Science, June 1995.

12. Michael S. Branicky. Universal computation and other capabilities of hybrid and continuous dynamical systems. *Theoretical Computer Science*, 138(1):67–100, 1995.

13. Michael S. Branicky. Multiple Lyapunov functions and other analysis tools for switched and hybrid systems. *IEEE Transactions on Automatic Control*, April 1998. In press.

14. Michael S. Branicky, Vivek Borkar, and Sanjoy K. Mitter. A unified framework for hybrid control. Technical Report LIDS-P-2239, Laboratory for Information and Decision Systems, Massachusetts Institute of Technology, April 1994. Extended abstract in [16]. Summary and examples in [15].

15. Michael S. Branicky, Vivek S. Borkar, and Sanjoy K. Mitter. A unified framework for hybrid control. In *Proc. IEEE Conf. Decision and Control*, pages 4228–4234, Lake Buena Vista, FL, December 1994.

16. Michael S. Branicky, Vivek S. Borkar, and Sanjoy K. Mitter. A unified framework for hybrid control. In G. Cohen and J-P. Quadrat, editors, *Proceedings 11th INRIA International Conference on the Analysis and Optimization of Systems*, volume 199 of *Lecture Notes in Control and Information Sciences*, pages 352–358, New York, 1994. Springer-Verlag. Extended Abstract.

17. Michael S. Branicky, Vivek S. Borkar, and Sanjoy K. Mitter. A unified framework for hybird control: Model and optimal control theory. *IEEE Transactions on Automatic Control*, pages 31–45, January 1998.

18. Michael S. Branicky and Sven Erik Mattsson. Simulation of hybrid systems. In Panos J. Antsaklis, Wolf Kohn, Anil Nerode, and Shankar Sastry, editors, *Hybrid*

Systems IV, volume 1273 of *Lecture Notes in Computer Science*, pages 31–56. Springer-Verlag, New York, 1997.

19. Michael S. Branicky and Sanjoy K. Mitter. Algorithms for optimal hybrid control. In *Proc. IEEE Conf. Decision and Control*, New Orleans, December 1995. 2661–2666.

20. Roger W. Brockett. Hybrid models for motion control systems. In H. L. Trentelman and J. C. Willems, editors, *Essays in Control: Perspectives in the Theory and its Applications*, pages 29–53. Birkhäuser, Boston, 1993.

21. Chee-Seng Chow and John N. Tsitsiklis. An optimal one-way multigrid algorithm for discrete-time stochastic control. *IEEE Trans. Automatic Control*, 36(8):898–914, 1991.

22. O. L. V. Costa and M. H. A. Davis. Impulse control of piecewise deterministic processes. *Math. Control Signals Syst.*, 2:187–206, 1989.

23. Akash Deshpande. *Control of Hybrid Systems*. PhD thesis, University of California at Berkeley, Dept. of Electrical Engineering and Computer Science, 1994.

24. Robert L. Grossman, Anil Nerode, Anders P. Ravn, and Hans Rischel, editors. *Hybrid Systems*, volume 736 of *Lecture Notes in Computer Science*. Springer-Verlag, New York, 1993.

25. David Harel. Statecharts: A visual formalism for complex systems. *Science of Computer Programming*, 8:231–274, 1987.

26. Morris W. Hirsch and Stephen Smale. *Differential Equations, Dynamical Systems, and Linear Algebra*. Academic Press, San Diego, 1974.

27. Yu-Chi Ho, editor. *Discrete Event Dynamic Systems: Analyzing Complexity and Performance in the Modern World*. IEEE Press, Piscataway, NJ, 1992.

28. Mikael Johansson and Anders Rantzer. Computation of piecewise quadratic Lyapunov functions for hybrid systems. Internal Report TFRT–7549, Department of Automatic Control, Lund Institute of Technology, June 1996. Submitted for journal publication.

29. David G. Luenberger. *Introduction to Dynamic Systems: Theory, Models, and Applications*. Wiley, New York, 1979.

30. Jorgen Malmborg, Bo Bernhardsson, and Karl J. Åström. A stabilizing switching scheme for multi-controller systems. In *Proc. IFAC World Congress*, page to appear, San Francisco, July 1996.

31. George Meyer. Design of flight vehicle management systems. In *Proc. IEEE Conf. Decision and Control*, Lake Buena Vista, FL, December 1994. Plenary Lecture.

32. Sanjoy K. Mitter and Shankar Sastry. 6.291; Special Topics: Intelligent Control. Course Notes, Department of Electrical Engineering and Computer Science, Massachusetts Institute of Technology, Fall 1992.

33. Anil Nerode and Wolf Kohn. Models for hybrid systems: Automata, topologies, stability. In Grossman et al. [24], pages 317–356.

34. Theodosios Pavlidis. Stability of systems described by differential equations containing impulses. *IEEE Trans. Automatic Control*, 12(1):43–45, 1967.

35. Philippos Peleties and Raymond DeCarlo. Asymptotic stability of m-switched systems using Lyapunov-like functions. In *Proc. American Control Conf.*, pages 1679–1684, Boston, June 1991.

36. Stefan Pettersson and Bengt Lennartson. Modelling, analysis, and synthesis of hybrid systems. In *Preprints of the Reglermöte*, Lulea, Sweden, June 1996.

37. Marc H. Raibert. *Legged Robots that Balance*. MIT Press, Cambridge, MA, 1986.

38. Sheldon M. Ross. *Applied Probability Models with Optimization Applications*. Dover, New York, 1992.

39. Konstantin S. Sibirsky. *Introduction to Topological Dynamics*. Noordhoff International Publishing, Leyden, The Netherlands, 1975. Translated by Leo F. Boron.

40. Jean-Jacques E. Slotine and Weiping Li. *Applied Nonlinear Control*. Prentice-Hall, Englewood Cliffs, NJ, 1991.

41. Eduardo D. Sontag. *Mathematical Control Theory: Deterministic Finite Dimensional Systems*, volume 6 of *Texts in Applied Mathematics*. Springer-Verlag, New York, 1990.

42. Lucio Tavernini. Differential automata and their discrete simulators. *Nonlinear Analysis, Theory, Methods, and Applications*, 11(6):665–683, 1987.

43. Vadim I. Utkin. Variable structure systems with sliding modes. *IEEE Trans. Automatic Control*, 22(2):212–222, 1977.

44. Pravin P. Varaiya. Smart cars on smart roads: Problems of control. *IEEE Trans. Automatic Control*, 38(2):195–207, February 1993.

45. Mathukumalli Vidyasagar. *Nonlinear Systems Analysis*. Prentice-Hall, Englewood Cliffs, NJ, 1978. Also: 2nd Edition, 1993.

46. Jacques Leopold Willems. *Stability Theory of Dynamical Systems*. Nelson, London, 1970.

47. Hans S. Witsenhausen. A class of hybrid-state continuous-time dynamic systems. *IEEE Trans. Automatic Control*, 11(2):161–167, 1966.

48. Hui Ye, Anthony N. Michel, and Ling Hou. Stability theory for hybrid dynamical systems. In *Proc. IEEE Conf. Decision and Control*, pages 2679–2684, New Orleans, December 1995.

49. Laurence Chisolm Young. *Lectures on the Calculus of Variations and Optimal Control Theory*. Chelsea, New York, 2nd edition, 1980.

Model Checking Timed Automata

Sergio Yovine * **

VERIMAG
Centre Equation
2, Av. de Vignate
38610 Gières, France

Abstract. The theory of *timed automata* provides a formal framework to model and to verify the correct functioning of *real-time* systems. Among the different verification problems that have been investigated within this theory, the so-called *reachability* problem has been the most throughly studied. This problem is stated as follows. Given two states of the system, is there an execution starting at one of them that reaches the other? The first reason for studying such problem is that *safety* properties can expressed as the non-reachability of a set of states where the system is consider to show an *incorrect* or *unsafe* functioning. Second, the algorithms developed for analyzing other classes of properties are essentially based on the algorithms developed for solving the reachability question. In this paper we survey the different algorithms, data-structures and tools that have been proposed in the literature to solve this problem.

1 Introduction

The theory of *timed automata* provides a formal framework to model and to analyze the behavior of *real-time* systems, that is, of systems whose correct functioning is subject to and must ensure the respect of strict timing constraints such as execution times, response times, tasks' periods, communication delays and so on.

Timed automata have been first proposed in [5] as an extension of the automata-theoretic approach to the modeling of real-time systems. Since then, the theory of timed automata has been an intensive field of research in computer science. With the aim of demonstrating that the ultimate goal of the theoretical achievements is to apply them to solve real-life problems, the work on the theory of timed automata has been consistently accompanied by the development of tools.

1.1 Timed automata

A timed automaton is a finite-state machine equipped with a set of *clocks*. Clocks are piece-wise continuous real-valued functions of time that precisely record the

---

* Sergio.Yovine@imag.fr. http://www.imag.fr/VERIMAG/PEOPLE/Sergio.Yovine
** Currently visiting California PATH, University of California at Berkeley, Richmond Field Station Bldg. 452, 1301 S. 46th St, Richmond CA 94804.

time elapsed between events. All clocks are synchronized, that is, they all advance at the same pace. More precisely, all clocks have the same derivative with respect to time, which is assumed to be by definition equal to one. Discontinuities may occur when a transition is taken. In this case, clocks are allowed to be reset to a new value which becomes the initial value of the next continuous phase. Transitions are associated with a *guard* which is a predicate over the clocks. The guard determines when a transition can be taken. The behavior of a clock as a function of time is illustrated in Figure 1. Timed automata are formally presented in Section 2.

1.2 Algorithmic verification

The constraints imposed on the clocks model the timing constraints the real-time system is subject to. Analyzing the behavior of the timed automaton consists in verifying whether it satisfies the timing properties it is supposed to ensure. Such properties are generically called *requirements*. Assuming that we have a formal way of expressing the requirements, we can state the *verification problem* as follows. Given a timed automaton A, a requirement R and a *satisfaction relation* $\models$, does $A \models R$ hold?

Researchers focused their work on the development of algorithmic methods for solving this problem, mainly along the lines of the so-called *model checking* approach. This approach consists in providing an algorithm that answers yes or no for every instance of a class of verification questions. Such a class of problems is obtained by fixing the formalism to express the requirements and the satisfaction relation. Some examples of classes of verification problems are the following: requirements are also expressed as timed automata and the satisfaction relation corresponds to bisimulation equivalence [18, 35, 42, 44], or requirements are expressed as formulas of a logic and the satisfaction relation is "being a model of" [6, 4, 31, 13]. [1]

1.3 Reachability

Many different instances of the verification question have been studied in the literature. In this paper we survey the different algorithms and data-structures that have been proposed in the seek for efficiency. For the sake of simplicity, we focus our attention on algorithms for solving the so-called *reachability problem*. This problem is stated as follows. Given two states of the system, is there an execution starting at one of them that reaches the other?

The first reason for studying such algorithms is that they allow us to check for *safety* properties, which are expressed as the non-reachability of a set of states where the system is consider to show an *incorrect* or *unsafe* functioning.

---

[1] As a matter of fact, it was this last class of problems that gave the name to the approach. Today, however, the term "model checking" is used as a synonym for "algorithmic verification", in contrast to "theorem proving" which is used to mean "deductive verification". [43]

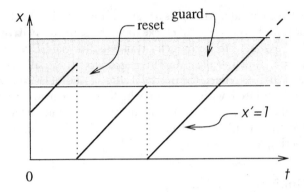

Fig. 1. A clock (x) is a piece-wise continuous function of time (t).

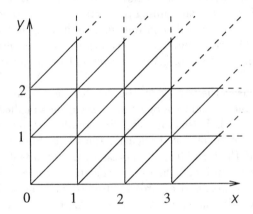

Fig. 2. Partition of the space of clock valuations into regions.

Second, the algorithms developed for analyzing other classes of properties are essentially based on the same techniques and data-structures.

1.4   Algorithms

Verification algorithms can be viewed as algorithms that *search* for particular states among all the possible states of the system. States are related by a *transition relation* that specifies how to move from one state to another. That is, the state-space of a system is structured as a graph. Conceptually, the search can be performed in either of two ways: *forwards* or *backwards*. Forward search consists in traversing the state-space by moving from one state to its successors. The backward search analyzes the graph by exploring the predecessors of a state.

The state-space of a timed automaton is clearly infinite since clocks are variables that range over the set of real numbers. A very important observation in [5] is that the space of clock valuations, which is indeed dense, can be partitioned into a finite set of classes which are given the name of *clock regions*. The important property of the partition is that the verification question has the same answer for all the clock valuations in a region. [2] This technique is studied in Section 3.

Algorithms directly based on the explicit construction of such a partition are however unlikely to perform efficiently in practice. The main reason for this is that the size of the partition, that is, the number of regions, is an exponential function of the number of clocks and of the constants against which the clocks are compared to. [3] Thus, different techniques have been proposed in order to overcome this problem.

Another approach consists in *discretizing* the space of clock valuations and the flow of time in such a way that at least one *representative* of every clock region belongs to the discretized space. Though this approach could suffer of the same exponential blow-up of the number of representatives, which is at least as large as the number of regions, its main advantage is the possibility of using well-known data-structures and algorithms that have been developed for the analysis of purely discrete systems. This approach is briefly discussed in Section 4.

An important corollary that follows from the results in [5] is that sets of regions can be characterized as conjunctions and disjunctions of linear inequalities over the clocks. Thus, a question that naturally arises is the following. Is it possible to analyze a timed automaton without explicitly and a-priori constructing the partition into regions, but rather by symbolically manipulating the inequalities? This problem has been explored in [31] in a more general verification problem than reachability, namely the verification of properties stated in the temporal logic called TCTL. Section 5 discusses the application of the techniques developed in [31] to solve the reachability problem. The verification question for TCTL is described in Appendix A.

The fourth and last approach over-viewed in this paper consists in finding a partition of the state-space that has two properties. First, it is *coarser*, and hence it has fewer classes, than the partition into regions. Second, for all the states in the same class, the verification question has the same answer. This approach is explained in Section 6.

---

[2] In [5] this partition is constructed to solve the so-called *emptiness* problem. Given an initial state, is there at least one infinite execution starting from this state? Indeed, later developments showed that the partitioning of the space into regions is a fundamental property of timed automata: all the proofs of decidability and complexity of the verification problems considered in the literature rely on the construction of such a partition. One such proof for instance is the one provided in [4] concerning the question whether a timed automaton satisfies a specification given as a formula of the temporal logic TCTL.

[3] This complexity is an intrinsic problem of equipping automata with clocks, and it has to be added to the well-known problem of the combinatorial explosion regarding the analysis of automata.

1.5 Data structures and tools

A consequence of the results in [4, 31] is that convex sets of regions can be represented as conjunctions of inequalities involving only one clock or the difference between two of them. This observation lead to the study of a data-structure called Difference Bound Matrices (DBM) [23].[4]

The key idea behind the use of DBM's as a data-structure for encoding the space of clock valuations is to have a compact representation of sets of adjacent regions. However, a set containing regions that are apart from each other cannot be efficiently represented. Instead, a different approach consists in representing each region by one or more representative clock valuations. In this case, the partition is viewed as a finite set of points whose characteristic function can be encoded using Binary Decision Diagrams (BDD) [16]. Such an encoding leads to a compact representation of a sparse sets of regions.

These two data-structures and the tools that used them are discussed in Section 7.

2 Timed automata

2.1 Clocks

Hereinafter, $\mathbb{N}$ denotes the set of natural numbers, $\mathbb{Z}$ denotes the set of integer numbers, $\mathbb{R}$ denotes the set of real numbers and $\mathbb{R}^+$ denotes the set of non-negative real numbers.

Let $\mathcal{X}$ be a finite set of variables called *clocks*. A *clock valuation* is a function that assigns a non-negative real number to every clock. The set of valuations of $\mathcal{X}$, denoted $\mathcal{V}_\mathcal{X}$, is the set $[\mathcal{X} \overset{tot}{\to} \mathbb{R}^+]$ of total functions from $\mathcal{X}$ to $\mathbb{R}^+$.

Let $v \in \mathcal{V}_\mathcal{X}$ and $\delta \in \mathbb{R}^+$. We denote by $v + \delta$ the clock valuation that maps each clock $x \in \mathcal{X}$ to the value $v(x) + \delta$.

Let $\mathcal{X}^*$ be the set $\mathcal{X} \cup \{0\}$. An *assignment* is a function that maps every clock into another clock or 0. The set of assignments over $\mathcal{X}$, denoted $\Gamma_\mathcal{X}$, is the set $[\mathcal{X} \overset{tot}{\to} \mathcal{X}^*]$.

Let $v \in \mathcal{V}_\mathcal{X}$ and $\gamma \in \Gamma_\mathcal{X}$. We denote by $v[\gamma]$ the clock valuation such that for all $x \in \mathcal{X}$,

$$v[\gamma](x) = \begin{cases} v(\gamma(x)) & \text{if } \gamma(x) \in \mathcal{X}, \\ 0 & \text{otherwise.} \end{cases}$$

2.2 Clock constraints

The set $\Psi_\mathcal{X}$ of *clock constraints* over the set of clocks $\mathcal{X}$ is defined by the following grammar:

$$\psi ::= x \prec c \mid x - x' \prec c \mid \psi \wedge \psi \mid \neg\psi$$

---

[4] As a matter of fact, DBM's were already used for the analysis of Timed Petri Nets in [38], though their use for analyzing timed automata required the development of new algorithms [46, 39, 2].

where $x, x' \in \mathcal{X}$, $\prec \in \{<, \leq\}$ and $c \in \mathbb{Z}$.

Clock constraints are evaluated over clock valuations. A valuation $v \in \mathcal{V}_{\mathcal{X}}$ is said to *satisfy* the clock constraint $\psi \in \Psi_{\mathcal{X}}$, denoted $v \models \psi$, if

$$
\begin{aligned}
v &\models x \prec c && \text{iff } v(x) \prec c \\
v &\models x - x' \prec c && \text{iff } v(x) - v(x') \prec c \\
v &\models \psi \wedge \psi' && \text{iff } v \models \psi \quad \text{and} \quad v \models \psi' \\
v &\models \neg \psi && \text{iff } v \not\models \psi
\end{aligned}
$$

We denote by $\llbracket \psi \rrbracket$ the set of valuations that satisfy ψ, that is,

$$
\llbracket \psi \rrbracket = \{ v \in \mathcal{V}_{\mathcal{X}} \mid v \models \psi \}.
$$

We denote by $\psi[x/x']$ the clock constraint obtained by replacing each occurrence of x in ψ by x'. Throughout the text we use typical abbreviations such as $x \geq c$ for $\neg(x < c)$, $x = c$ for $x \leq c \wedge x \geq c$, and so forth.

2.3 Timed automata

A *timed automaton* $\mathbf{A}$ is a tuple $\langle \mathcal{S}, \mathcal{X}, \Sigma, \mathcal{E}, I \rangle$ where:

1. $\mathcal{S}$ is a finite set of *locations*.
2. $\mathcal{X}$ is a finite set of *clocks*.
3. Σ is a finite set of *labels*.
4. $\mathcal{E}$ is a finite set of *edges*. Each edge e is a tuple $(s, \sigma, \psi, \gamma, s')$ where
   (a) $s \in \mathcal{S}$ is the *source*,
   (b) $s' \in \mathcal{S}$ is the *target*,
   (c) $\sigma \in \Sigma$ is the *label*,
   (d) $\psi \in \Psi_{\mathcal{X}}$ is the *enabling condition*, and
   (e) $\gamma \in \Gamma_{\mathcal{X}}$ is the *assignment*.
5. $I \in [\mathcal{S} \overset{tot}{\to} \Psi_{\mathcal{X}}]$. We refer to $I(s)$ as the *invariant* of s.

Example 1. Figure 3 shows a timed automaton with three locations: Idle, HPM and LPM; and two clocks: h and r. This timed automaton models the behavior of a FDDI's sender station [32]. In location Idle, the station is waiting for the token. The arrival of the token is model by the transition labeled GT. Clock r counts the time elapsed since the last reception of the token. Each time the token is received, r is reset to 0 and h is assigned the value of r. All the assignments are executed in parallel, that is, the order in which the list of assignments is given is meaningless. In location HPM, the station is sending high-priority messages. This phase can last at most 2 time units. This timing constraint is modeled by the invariant condition $r \leq 2$. The station terminates the transmission either because 2 time units have elapsed or because it has no more high-priority messages to send. If more than 100 time units have elapsed since the previous reception of the token, the station goes back to location Idle, otherwise, it goes to location LPM where it can send low-priority messages while the value of the clock h is less than 100. When the station has no more low-priority messages to send, it releases the token. □

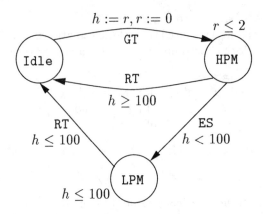

Fig. 3. Timed automaton of a FDDI's sender station.

2.4 States and transitions

The meaning of **A** is an infinite *transition system* $\langle Q, \rightarrow \rangle$ where Q is the set of *states* and $\rightarrow$ is the *transition relation*. A *state* of **A** is given by a location and a valuation of the clocks. At any state, **A** can move along one of the outgoing edges or it can remain in the location while time passes. In the first case, the transition results in a new state whose location is the target location of the edge and the valuation is modified according to the assignment. Such a transition is called a *discrete* transition, and may only happen when the valuation satisfies the enabling condition of the edge. Idling in a location during some time results in the values of the clocks to be updated by the amount of time elapsed. Such transitions are called *timed* transitions. While remaining in a given location, **A** must respect the corresponding invariant condition.

Formally, $\langle Q, \rightarrow \rangle$ is defined as follows:

1. $Q = \{(s, v) \in \mathcal{S} \times V_{\mathcal{X}} \mid v \models I(s)\}$.
2. The transition relation $\rightarrow \subseteq Q \times (\Sigma \cup \mathbf{R}^+) \times Q$ is defined by the following rules:

(a) Discrete transitions:

$$\frac{(s, \sigma, \psi, \gamma, s') \in \mathcal{E} \quad v \models \psi \quad v[\gamma] \models I(s')}{(s, v) \overset{\sigma}{\rightarrow} (s', v[\gamma])} \tag{1}$$

State $(s', v[\gamma])$ is said to be a *discrete successor* of (s, v), and conversely, the latter is said to be a *discrete predecessor* of the former.

(b) Timed transitions:

$$\frac{\delta \in \mathbf{R}^+ \quad \forall \delta' \in \mathbf{R}^+. \; \delta' \leq \delta \Rightarrow (s, v + \delta') \models I(s)}{(s, v) \overset{\delta}{\rightarrow} (s, v + \delta)} \tag{2}$$

State $(s, v + \delta)$ is said to be a *time successor* of (s, v), and conversely, the latter is said to be a *time predecessor* of the former.

We denote by $q + \delta$ the state $(s, v + \delta)$ and by $q[\gamma]$ the state $(s, v[\gamma])$.

2.5 Executions

An *execution* or *run* r of $\mathbf{A}$ is an infinite sequence of states and transitions:

$$r = q_0 \xrightarrow{\ell_0} q_1 \xrightarrow{\ell_1} \cdots$$

where for all $i \in \mathbb{N}$, $q_i \in \mathcal{Q}$ and $\ell_i \in (\Sigma \cup \mathbf{R}^+)$. We denote by $\mathcal{R}_{\mathbf{A}}(q)$ the set of runs starting at $q \in \mathcal{Q}$ and by $\mathcal{R}_{\mathbf{A}} = \bigcup_{q \in \mathcal{Q}} \mathcal{R}_{\mathbf{A}}(q)$ the set of runs of $\mathbf{A}$.

For $r \in \mathcal{R}_{\mathbf{A}}$ and $i \in \mathbb{N}$, we define $\Delta_r(i)$ to be the time elapsed from state q_0 to state q_i. $\Delta_r(i)$ is inductively defined as follows:

$$\Delta_r(0) = 0$$

$$\Delta_r(i+1) = \Delta_r(i) + \begin{cases} 0 & \text{if } \ell_i \in \Sigma, \\ \ell_i & \text{otherwise.} \end{cases}$$

A run $r \in \mathcal{R}_{\mathbf{A}}$ is said to be *time-divergent* if $\lim_{i \to \infty} \Delta_r(i) = \infty$. We denote by $\mathcal{R}_{\mathbf{A}}^{\infty}(q)$ the set of time-divergent runs starting at $q \in \mathcal{Q}$ and by $\mathcal{R}_{\mathbf{A}}^{\infty} = \bigcup_{q \in \mathcal{Q}} \mathcal{R}_{\mathbf{A}}^{\infty}(q)$ the set of time-divergent runs of $\mathbf{A}$.

A state q' is *reachable* from state q if it belongs to some run starting at q. We define $\mathsf{Reach}_{\mathbf{A}}(q)$ to be the set of states reachable from q. That is,

$$\mathsf{Reach}_{\mathbf{A}}(q) = \{q' \in \mathcal{Q} \mid \exists r = q_0 \xrightarrow{\ell_0} q_1 \xrightarrow{\ell_1} \cdots \in \mathcal{R}_{\mathbf{A}}(q), \exists i \in \mathbb{N}. \ q_i = q'\}.$$

We define $\mathsf{Reach}_{\mathbf{A}}^{\infty}(q)$ to be the set of states reachable from q along some time-divergent run. That is,

$$\mathsf{Reach}_{\mathbf{A}}^{\infty}(q) = \{q' \in \mathcal{Q} \mid \exists r = q_0 \xrightarrow{\ell_0} q_1 \xrightarrow{\ell_1} \cdots \in \mathcal{R}_{\mathbf{A}}^{\infty}(q), \exists i \in \mathbb{N}. \ q_i = q'\}.$$

$\mathbf{A}$ is said to be *Non-Zeno* or *well-timed* if for all states $q \in \mathcal{Q}$, $\mathsf{Reach}_{\mathbf{A}}^{\infty}(q) \neq \emptyset$. That is, every state can let time progress without bound.

Property 1. If $\mathbf{A}$ is *Non-Zeno*, $q' \in \mathsf{Reach}_{\mathbf{A}}^{\infty}(q)$ iff $q' \in \mathsf{Reach}_{\mathbf{A}}(q)$, for all $q, q' \in \mathcal{Q}$. □

Given a state $q \in \mathcal{Q}$, we are interested in computing the sets of states $\mathsf{Reach}_{\mathbf{A}}(q)$ and $\mathsf{Reach}_{\mathbf{A}}^{\infty}(q)$. The rest of this paper explains different approaches to compute that sets. In order to simplify the notation, we shall omit the subscript $\mathbf{A}$ from now on.

3 Analysis using the region graph

In this section we show how to compute the set of states reachable from a state $q \in \mathcal{Q}$ by *partitioning* the space of clock valuations.

3.1 Region equivalence

Let $\hat{\Psi} \subseteq \Psi_{\mathcal{X}}$ be a *non-empty* set of clock constraints over $\mathcal{X}$. Let $C \in \mathbb{N}$ be the smallest constant which is greater than or equal to the absolute value $|c|$ of every constant $c \in \mathbb{Z}$ appearing in a clock constraint in $\hat{\Psi}$.

We define $\simeq_{\hat{\Psi}} \subseteq V_{\mathcal{X}} \times V_{\mathcal{X}}$ to be the largest *reflexive* and *symmetric* relation such that $v \simeq_{\hat{\Psi}} v'$ iff for all $x, y \in \mathcal{X}$, the following three conditions hold:

1. $v(x) > C$ implies $v'(x) > C$,
2. if $v(x) \leq C$ then
   (a) $\lfloor v(x) \rfloor = \lfloor v'(x) \rfloor$, and
   (b) $\vartheta(v(x)) = 0$ implies $\vartheta(v'(x)) = 0$,
   where $\lfloor \cdot \rfloor : \mathbf{R}^+ \to \mathbb{N}$ and $\vartheta(\cdot) : \mathbf{R}^+ \to [0, 1)$, such that for $\delta \in \mathbf{R}^+$, $\lfloor \delta \rfloor$ is the integer part of δ, and $\vartheta(\delta)$ is its fractional part.
3. for all clock constraints in $\hat{\Psi}$ of the form $x - y \prec c$, $v \models x - y \prec c$ implies $v' \models x - y \prec c$.

Property 2. It is not difficult to prove that $\simeq_{\hat{\Psi}}$ is an *equivalence* relation with a finite number of classes.

$\simeq_{\hat{\Psi}}$ is called the *region* equivalence for the set of clock constraints $\hat{\Psi}$. We denote by $[v]$ the equivalence class (or region) of v.

Example 2. Figure 2 illustrates the region equivalence for two clocks x and y with $C = 3$. □

The region equivalence has the following properties.

Property 3. Every region can be characterized by a clock constraint. □

Property 4. Let $v \simeq_{\hat{\Psi}} v'$. For every $\psi \in \hat{\Psi}$, $v \models \psi$ iff $v' \models \psi$. □

Property 5. Let $\hat{\Psi}$ be the set of all clock constraints appearing in $\mathbf{A}$, and let $v \simeq_{\hat{\Psi}} v'$.

1. For all $\gamma \in \Gamma_{\mathcal{X}}$, $v[\gamma] \simeq_{\hat{\Psi}} v'[\gamma]$.
2. For all $\delta \in \mathbf{R}^+$, there exists $\delta' \in \mathbf{R}^+$, such that $v + \delta \simeq_{\hat{\Psi}} v' + \delta'$.

We say that the region equivalence $\simeq_{\hat{\Psi}}$ is *stable* with respect to the assignments and the flow of time. □

Example 3. Figure 4 illustrates the above property. Consider the region defined by the clock constraint $2 < x < 3 \wedge 1 < y < 2 \wedge x - y < 1$. Let v be any clock valuation in this region.

a. Consider the assignment $y := 0$. The clock valuation $v[y := 0]$ belongs to the region $2 < x < 3 \wedge y = 0$.

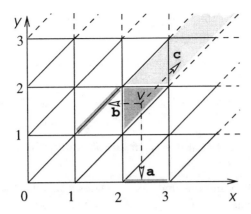

Fig. 4. Properties of the region equivalence.

b. Consider the assignment $x := y$. The clock valuation $v[x := y]$ belongs to the region $1 < x < 2 \land 1 < y < 2 \land x = y$.

c. Each time successor of v belongs to some of the regions crossed by a straight line drawn in the direction of the arrow.

□

Property 6. Let ρ be a region such that for all v such that $[v] = \rho$, $v(x) > C$ for all $x \in \mathcal{X}$. Clearly, $[v + \delta] = \rho$ for all $\delta \in \mathbf{R}^+$. Such a region is said to be *unbounded* because the values of the clocks may grow without bound. □

Property 7. The number of regions is of the order of $n! \cdot 2^n \cdot C^n$, where n is the number of clocks. [5] □

3.2 Region graph

Let $(\mathcal{Q}, \rightarrow)$ be the transition system of $\mathbf{A}$. We extend the region equivalence $\simeq_{\hat{\psi}}$ to the states of $\mathcal{Q}$ as follows. Two states $q = (s, v)$ and $q' = (s', v')$ are *region-equivalent*, denoted $q \simeq_{\hat{\psi}} q'$, iff $s = s'$ and $v \simeq_{\hat{\psi}} v'$. We denote by $[q]$ the equivalence class of q.

The region equivalence over states has the following properties.

---

[5] In [5] the region equivalence is defined by taking for each clock $x \in \mathcal{X}$ the smallest constant $C_x \in \mathbf{N}$ greater than or equal to the absolute value of every constant $c \in \mathbf{Z}$ appearing in a constraint of the form $x \prec c$ or $x - y \prec c$. That definition generates a smaller number of classes, namely $n! \cdot 2^n \cdot \Pi_{x \in \mathcal{X}} C_x$. However it is not correct in the presence of assignments of the form $x := y$. It is not difficult to find an example that violates item (1) in Property 5. Nevertheless, it is straightforward to modify our definition of the region equivalence so a constant C_x is associated with every clock $x \in \mathcal{X}$ in order to get a smaller number of regions.

Property 8. Let $\hat{\Psi}_{\mathbf{A}}$ be the set of all clock constraints appearing in $\mathbf{A}$, and let $q_1 \simeq_{\hat{\psi}} q_2$.

1. For all $\sigma \in \Sigma$, whenever $q_1 \xrightarrow{\sigma} q_1'$ for some q_1', there exists q_2' such that $q_2 \xrightarrow{\sigma} q_2'$ and $q_2 \simeq_{\hat{\psi}} q_2'$.

2. For all $\delta \in \mathbf{R}^+$, whenever $q_1 \xrightarrow{\delta} q_1'$ for some q_1', there exists q_2' and $\delta' \in \mathbf{R}^+$ such that $q_2 \xrightarrow{\delta'} q_2'$ and $q_2 \simeq_{\hat{\psi}} q_2'$.

The region equivalence over states is said to be *stable* with respect to the transition relation $\rightarrow \subseteq Q \times (\Sigma \cup \mathbf{R}^+) \times Q$. $\qquad \square$

The above property implies that, for all region-equivalent states q_1 and q_2, if some state q_1' is reachable from q_1, a region-equivalent state q_2' is reachable from q_2.

Let $\hat{\Psi} \subseteq \Psi_{\mathcal{X}}$ be a set of clock constraints, $\hat{\Psi}_{\mathbf{A}}$ be the set of clock constraints of $\mathbf{A}$, and $\simeq$ be the region equivalence defined over $\hat{\Psi} \cup \hat{\Psi}_{\mathbf{A}}$. Let $\tau \notin \Sigma$ and $\Sigma_\tau = \Sigma \cup \{\tau\}$.

The *region graph* $\mathsf{RG}(\mathbf{A}, \hat{\Psi})$ is the transition system $(Q_\simeq, \rightarrow)$, where:

1. $Q_\simeq = \{[q] \mid q \in Q\}$.
2. $\rightarrow \subseteq Q_\simeq \times \Sigma_\tau \times Q_\simeq$ is such that:
   (a) for all $\sigma \in \Sigma$ and for all $\rho, \rho' \in Q_\simeq$, $\rho \xrightarrow{\sigma} \rho'$ iff there exists $q, q' \in Q$ such that $\rho = [q]$, $\rho' = [q']$, and $q \xrightarrow{\sigma} q'$.
   (b) for all $\rho, \rho' \in Q_\simeq$, $\rho \xrightarrow{\tau} \rho'$ iff
      i. $\rho = \rho'$ is an unbounded region, or
      ii. $\rho \neq \rho'$ and there exists $q \in Q$ and $\delta \in \mathbf{R}^+$ such that $q \xrightarrow{\delta} q'$, and $\rho = [q]$, $\rho' = [q+\delta]$, and for all $\delta' \in \mathbf{R}^+$, if $\delta' \leq \delta$ then $[q+\delta']$ is either ρ or ρ'.

Notice that only unbounded regions have self-loops labeled by τ. Thus, these loops represent the divergence of time at a location.

We define $\mathsf{Reach}(\rho)$ to be the set of regions reachable from the region ρ:

$$\mathsf{Reach}(\rho) = \{\rho' \mid \rho \rightarrow^* \rho'\}$$

where $\rightarrow^*$ is the reflexive and transitive closure of $\rightarrow$.

We denote by $\langle q \rangle$ any clock constraint $\psi \in \Psi$ such that $q \models \psi$, and for all $\psi' \in \Psi$, if $q \models \psi'$ then ψ implies ψ'. That is, $\langle q \rangle$ is the *tightest* (modulo logical equivalence) clock constraint that characterizes the values of the clocks in q. Now, the question whether the state q' is reachable from the state q can be answered as follows.

Property 9. Let $\mathbf{A}$ be a timed automaton, $q, q' \in Q$, and let $\mathsf{RG}(\mathbf{A}, \{\langle q \rangle, \langle q' \rangle\})$ be the corresponding region graph. Then,

$$q' \in \mathsf{Reach}(q) \text{ iff } [q'] \in \mathsf{Reach}([q]).$$

Notice that the constraints $\langle q \rangle$ and $\langle q' \rangle$ characterize exactly the equivalence classes $[q]$ and $[q']$, respectively. $\qquad \square$

Property 9 says that the reachability problem for q and q' has the same answer for all the states which are region-equivalent to them.

Property 10. Because of Property 1, if $\mathbf{A}$ is *Non-Zeno*, Property 9 also holds for reachability along time-divergent executions. That is, for all $q, q' \in \mathcal{Q}$,

$$q' \in \mathsf{Reach}^{\infty}(q) \text{ iff } [q'] \in \mathsf{Reach}([q]).$$

$\square$

3.3 Region-graph based algorithms

The last property says that verifying whether q' is reachable from q is decidable. Indeed, it is possible to find the answer to such question by traversing the region graph. There are basically two ways of doing so.

Forward traversal. This method consists in starting from $[q]$ and visiting the set of its successors and the successors of those and so on, until all the reachable regions have been visited. In other words, it consists in constructing the sequence of sets of regions $F_0 \subseteq F_1 \subseteq \cdots$, such that

$$F_0 = [q]$$
$$F_{i+1} = F_i \cup \mathsf{Suc}(F_i)$$

where $\mathsf{Suc}(F_i) = \{\rho \mid \exists \rho_i \in F_i.\ \rho_i \to \rho\}$.

Property 11. For all $q, q' \in \mathcal{Q}$, $[q'] \in \mathsf{Reach}([q])$ iff $[q'] \in \bigcup_{i \geq 0} F_i$. $\square$

Backward traversal. This method consists in starting from $[q']$ and visiting the set of its predecessors and the predecessors of those and so on, until all the regions from which is possible to reach $[q']$ have been visited. It consists then in constructing the sequence of sets of regions $B_0 \subseteq B_1 \subseteq \cdots$, such that

$$B_0 = [q']$$
$$B_{i+1} = B_i \cup \mathsf{Pre}(B_i)$$

where $\mathsf{Pre}(B_i) = \{\rho \mid \exists \rho_i \in B_i.\ \rho \to \rho_i\}$.

Property 12. For all $q, q' \in \mathcal{Q}$, $[q'] \in \mathsf{Reach}([q])$ iff $[q] \in \bigcup_{i \geq 0} B_i$. $\square$

4 Analysis using representatives

Let $\mathcal{X} = \{x_1, \cdots, x_n\}$. Each region of the region graph can be represented by associating with every clock $x \in \mathcal{X}$, either a constant $c \in \{0, \cdots, C_x\}$, an interval $(c - 1, c)$ with $c \in \{1, \cdots, C_x\}$, or the interval (C_x, ∞), and an ordering $x_{i_1} \#_{i_1} \cdots \#_{i_n} x_{i_n}$, with $\# \in \{<, \leq, =\}$, that encodes the ordering of the fractional parts. Instead, another approach consists in representing a region by one or more appropriately chosen representative states.

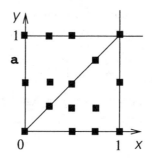

Fig. 5. Each region is represented by a finite set of representatives.

4.1 Transition system of representatives

Let $\mathcal{D}$ be a finite subset of $\mathcal{Q}$ such that for all regions $\rho \in \mathcal{Q}_{\simeq}$, $\rho \cap \mathcal{D} \neq \emptyset$. We denote by d the elements of $\mathcal{D}$ and by $\mathsf{rep}(\rho) = \rho \cap \mathcal{D}$ the set of representatives of ρ.

Let $(\mathcal{D}, \to)$ be any transition system such that the transition relation $\to \subseteq \mathcal{D} \times \Sigma_\tau \times \mathcal{D}$ satisfies the following conditions:

1. for all $d, d' \in \mathcal{D}$ and for all $\lambda \in \Sigma_\tau$, if $d \overset{\lambda}{\to} d'$ then $[d] \overset{\lambda}{\to} [d']$;
2. for all $\rho, \rho' \in \mathcal{Q}_{\simeq}$ and for all $\lambda \in \Sigma_\tau$, if $\rho \overset{\lambda}{\to} \rho'$ then for all $d \in \mathsf{rep}(\rho)$ there exists $d' \in \mathsf{rep}(\rho')$ such that $d \overset{\lambda}{\to} d'$.

Condition 1. ensures that every transition of $(\mathcal{D}, \to)$ corresponds to some transition of the region graph $(\mathcal{Q}_{\simeq}, \to)$. Condition 2. states that all the transitions of the region graph are represented in $(\mathcal{D}, \to)$ and, moreover, that each representative can perform all the transitions that can be performed by the corresponding region.

Remark 4. Notice that in the definition above, d' need not be a (time or discrete) successor of d. $\qquad\square$

4.2 Algorithms

The question whether a region ρ' is reachable from a region ρ can be answered by traversing $(\mathcal{D}, \to)$ either forwards or backwards.

Forward traversal. This method consists in computing the sequence of sets of representatives $F_0 \subseteq F_1 \subseteq \cdots$, such that

$$F_0 = \mathsf{rep}(\rho)$$
$$F_{i+1} = F_i \cup \mathsf{Suc}(F_i)$$

where $\mathsf{Suc}(F_i) = \{d \mid \exists d_i \in F_i.\ d_i \to d\}$.

Property 13. $\rho' \in \mathsf{Reach}(\rho)$ iff $\mathsf{rep}(\rho') \cap \bigcup_{i \geq 0} F_i \neq \emptyset$.

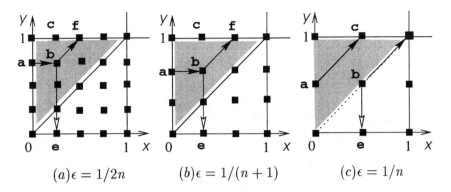

$$(a)\epsilon = 1/2n \qquad (b)\epsilon = 1/(n+1) \qquad (c)\epsilon = 1/n$$

Fig. 6. Different discretizations of the space of clock valuations for $n = 2$.

Backward traversal. This method consists in computing the sequence of sets of representatives $B_0 \subseteq B_1 \subseteq \cdots$, such that

$$B_0 = \mathsf{rep}(\rho')$$
$$B_{i+1} = B_i \cup \mathsf{Pre}(B_i)$$

where $\mathsf{Pre}(B_i) = \{d \mid \exists d_i \in B_i.\ d \to d_i\}$.

Property 14. $\rho' \in \mathsf{Reach}(\rho)$ iff $\mathsf{rep}(\rho) \subseteq \bigcup_{i \geq 0} B_i$.

4.3 Representation schemes

In practice, the set of representatives of a region is obtained by *discretizing* the space of clock valuations as follows. Let ϵ be a rational constant such that $0 < \epsilon < 1$. Then, for every region ρ which is not unbounded, the set of its representatives is defined as follows:

$$\mathsf{rep}(\rho) = \{(s,v) \in \rho \mid \forall x \in \mathcal{X}, \exists k_x \in \mathbb{N}.\ \vartheta(v(x)) = k_x \cdot \epsilon\}$$

Unbounded regions can be represented by a single representative. Figure 6 shows three examples of discretization schemes.

Figures 6(a) and 6(b) illustrate the representatives obtained with $\epsilon = (1/2n)$ and $\epsilon = 1/(n+1)$ where n is the number of clocks [27]. For such discretizations, a discrete transitions $d \xrightarrow{\sigma} d'$ between two representatives $d, d' \in \mathcal{D}$ can be obtained by applying the semantic rule for discrete transitions given in Section 2.4. For instance, the discrete successor of b by a transition that resets y is e. However, in general, the time successor of a representative d cannot be obtained by simply adding ϵ to the values of the clocks. For instance, the time successor of a is not c as we could imagine, but b. Letting c be a time successor of a would violate condition 1. in the definition of $(\mathcal{D}, \to)$ which requires any representative d of a region ρ to have a (timed) transition to a representative d' of region ρ' only if

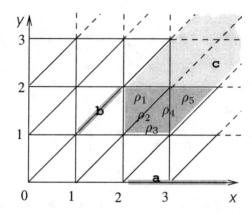

Fig. 7. Representation of sets of regions as clock constraints.

ρ has a (timed) transition to ρ'. In the example, the region $0 < y < 1 \wedge x = 0$ (represented by **a**) does not have a time transition to the region $0 < x < 1 \wedge y = 1$ (represented by **c**), but to the region $0 < y < 1 \wedge 0 < x < y$ (represented by **b**).

In [9, 15] a simpler discretization has been proposed based on the following observation. The special class of timed automata where all the clock constraints are of the form $x \geq c$ or $x < c$, admits a slightly simpler and coarser region graph [30], in which, for instance, the two regions $0 < y < 1 \wedge x = 0$ and $0 < y < 1 \wedge 0 < x < y$ are collapsed into a single region $0 < y < 1 \wedge 0 \leq x < y$ which has a timed transition to region $0 < x < 1 \wedge y = 1$. For these automata, a discretization with $\epsilon = 1/n$, where the passage of time is simply the addition of ϵ to all the clocks, is sufficient. In Figure 6(c), **a** (a representative of the region $0 < y < 1 \wedge 0 \leq x < y$) has a timed transition to **c** (a representative of region $0 < x < 1 \wedge y = 1$).

5 Analysis using clock constraints

Let F be the set of regions $\bigcup_{i \geq 0} F_i$ computed by the forward traversal algorithm explained in Section 3. Then F can be symbolically represented as a disjoint union of the form $\biguplus_{s \in \mathcal{S}} F_s$, where F_s is the clock constraint that characterizes the set of regions that belong to F whose location is equal to s. The same observation holds for B. Indeed, such characterization can be computed without a-priori constructing the region graph.

5.1 Forward computation of clock constraints

Let $s \in \mathcal{S}$, $\psi_s \in \Psi_{\mathcal{X}}$ and $e = (s, \psi, \sigma, \gamma, s') \in \mathcal{E}$. We denote by $\mathsf{Suc}_e(\psi_s)$ the predicate over $\mathcal{X}$ that characterizes the set of clock valuations that are reachable from the clock valuations in ψ_s when the timed automaton executes the discrete transition corresponding to the edge e. That is,

$$v \models \mathsf{Suc}_e(\psi_s) \text{ iff } \exists v' \in \mathcal{Q}. \ v = v'[\gamma] \wedge v' \models (\psi_s \wedge \psi).$$

Property 15. $\mathsf{Suc}_e(\psi_s) \in \Psi_{\mathcal{X}}$. □

Example 5. Consider again the example illustrated in Figure 7. Recall that ψ is the clock constraint $1 < y < 2 \wedge 2 < x \wedge x - y < 2$.

a. The result of executing the transition resetting x to 0 is computed as follows.

$$
\begin{aligned}
\mathsf{Suc}_a(\psi_s) &= \\
&= \exists x', y'. \ \psi_s[x/x', y/y'] \wedge y = 0 \wedge x = x' \\
&= \exists x', y'. \ 1 < y' < 2 \wedge 2 < x' \wedge x' - y' < 2 \wedge y = 0 \wedge x = x' \\
&= \exists y'. \ 1 < y' < 2 \wedge 2 < x \wedge x - y' < 2 \wedge y = 0 \\
&= 2 < x \wedge x < 4 \wedge y = 0
\end{aligned}
$$

Since the upper bound of 4 is greater than the constant $C = 3$, we can eliminate the clock constraint $x < 4$ and obtain: $\mathsf{Suc}_a(\psi_s) = 2 < x \wedge y = 0$.

b. Now, consider the assignment $x := y$.

$$
\begin{aligned}
\mathsf{Suc}_b(\psi_s) &= \\
&= \exists x', y'. \ \psi_s[x/x', y/y'] \wedge y = y' \wedge x = y' \\
&= \exists x', y'. \ 1 < y' < 2 \wedge 2 < x' \wedge x' - y' < 2 \wedge y = y' \wedge x = y' \\
&= \exists x'. \ 1 < y < 2 \wedge 2 < x' \wedge x' - y < 2 \wedge x = y \\
&= 1 < y < 2 \wedge 0 < y \wedge x = y \\
&= 1 < y < 2 \wedge x = y
\end{aligned}
$$

□

In other words, to compute $\mathsf{Suc}_e(\psi_s)$ is equivalent to visit all the regions that are e-successors of the regions in ψ_s, but without having to explicitly represent each one of them.

Let $s \in \mathcal{S}$ and $\psi_s \in \Psi_{\mathcal{X}}$. We denote by $\mathsf{Suc}_\tau(\psi_s)$ the predicate over $\mathcal{X}$ that characterizes the set of clock valuations that are reachable from the clock valuations in ψ_s when the timed automaton lets time pass at s. That is,

$$v \models \mathsf{Suc}_\tau(\psi_s) \text{ iff } \exists \delta \in \mathbf{R}^+. \ v - \delta \models \psi_s \wedge \forall \delta' \in \mathbf{R}^+. \ \delta' \le \delta \Rightarrow v - \delta' \models I(s).$$

Property 16. $\mathsf{Suc}_\tau(\psi_s) \in \Psi_{\mathcal{X}}$. □

Example 6. Consider again the example illustrated in Figure 7. Case c corresponds to letting time pass at the location. For simplicity, we assume here that the invariant condition is true.

$$\mathsf{Suc}_\tau(\psi_s) =$$
$$= \exists \delta \in \mathbf{R}^+.\ \psi_s\,[x/x - \delta,\, y/y - \delta]$$
$$= \exists \delta \in \mathbf{R}^+.\ 1 < y - \delta < 2 \wedge 2 < x - \delta \wedge (x - \delta) - (y - \delta) < 2$$
$$= \exists \delta \in \mathbf{R}^+.\ 1 < y - \delta < 2 \wedge 2 < x - \delta \wedge x - y < 2 \wedge$$
$$= 1 < y \wedge 2 < x \wedge y - x < 0 \wedge x - y < 2$$

$\square$

Notice that $\mathsf{Suc}_\tau(\psi_s)$ characterizes the set of the regions that contains the regions characterized by ψ_s and the regions reachable from them by taking only τ-transitions.

Now, we can solve the reachability problem by computing the sequence of sets of clock constraints $F_0, F_1, \cdots$ as follows:

$$F_0 = \langle q \rangle$$

$$F_{i+1} = \biguplus_{s \in \mathcal{S}} \left(\mathsf{Suc}_\tau(F_{i,s}) \ \uplus \ \biguplus_{e \in \mathcal{E}} \mathsf{Suc}_e(F_{i,s}) \right)$$

Notice that $F_{i,s}$ implies $F_{i+1,s}$ for all $i \geq 0$ and $s \in \mathcal{S}$.

Property 17. Let $F = \bigcup_{i \geq 0} F_i$, $q = (s, v)$, and $q' = (s', v')$. $[q'] \in \mathsf{Reach}([q])$ iff $\langle q' \rangle$ implies $F_{s'}$.

$\square$

5.2 Backward computation of clock constraints

Let $s \in \mathcal{S}$, $\psi_s \in \Psi_\mathcal{X}$ and $e = (s', \psi, \sigma, \gamma, s) \in \mathcal{E}$. We denote by $\mathsf{Pre}_e(\psi_s)$ the predicate over $\mathcal{X}$ that characterizes the set of clock valuations that can reach a clock valuation in ψ_s when the timed automaton executes the discrete transition corresponding to the edge e. That is,

$$v \models \mathsf{Pre}_e(\psi_s) \text{ iff } v \models \psi \wedge v[\gamma] \models \psi_s$$

Property 18. $\mathsf{Pre}_e(\psi_s) \in \Psi_\mathcal{X}$.

$\square$

Example 7. Consider the example illustrated in Figure 8. Let ψ_s be the clock constraint $0 \leq y < 2 \wedge 1 < x < 2$.

a. Suppose that the edge we are considering has a guard ψ given by the constraint $y > x + 1$. The predecessors of ψ_s with respect to the transition that resets y to 0 are computed as follows.

$$\mathsf{Pre}_a(\psi_s) = \psi_s\,[y/0] \wedge \psi$$
$$= 0 \leq 0 < 2 \wedge 1 < x < 2 \wedge y > x + 1$$
$$= 1 < x < 2 \wedge y > x + 1$$

b. Now, consider the assignment $x := y$ and suppose that the edge has a guard ψ given by the constraint $x > y + 1$.

$$\begin{aligned}
\mathsf{Pre}_b(\psi_s) &= \psi_s[x/y] \wedge \psi \\
&= 0 \leq y < 2 \wedge 1 < y < 2 \wedge x > y + 1 \\
&= 1 < y < 2 \wedge x > y + 1
\end{aligned}$$

$\square$

Again, to compute $\mathsf{Pre}_e(\psi_s)$ is equivalent to visit all the regions that are e-predecessors of the regions in ψ_s, but without having to explicitly represent each one of them.

Let $s \in \mathcal{S}$ and $\psi_s \in \Psi_{\mathcal{X}}$. We denote by $\mathsf{Pre}_\tau(\psi_s)$ the predicate over $\mathcal{X}$ that characterizes the set of clock valuations that can reach a clock valuation in ψ_s when the timed automaton lets time elapse at location s.

$$v \models \mathsf{Pre}_\tau(\psi_s) \text{ iff } \exists \delta \in \mathbf{R}^+.\ v + \delta \models \psi_s \wedge \forall \delta' \in \mathbf{R}^+.\ \delta' \leq \delta \Rightarrow v + \delta' \models I(s).$$

Property 19. $\mathsf{Pre}_\tau(\psi_s) \in \Psi_{\mathcal{X}}$. $\qquad\qquad\square$

Example 8. Consider again the example illustrated in Figure 8. Case **c** corresponds to letting time pass at the location.

$$\begin{aligned}
\mathsf{Pre}_\tau(\psi_s) &= \exists \delta \in \mathbf{R}^+.\ \psi_s[x/x + \delta, y/y + \delta] \\
&= \exists \delta \in \mathbf{R}^+.\ 0 \leq y + \delta < 2 \wedge 1 < x + \delta < 2 \\
&= 0 \leq y < 2 \wedge 0 \leq x < 2 \wedge y - x < 1 \wedge x - y < 2
\end{aligned}$$

$\square$

That is, $\mathsf{Pre}_\tau(\psi_s)$ characterizes the set of regions that contains the regions characterized by ψ_s and all the regions that can reach one of them by taking only τ-transitions of the region graph.

Now, we can solve the reachability problem by computing the sequence of sets of clock constraints $B_0, B_1, \cdots$ as follows:

$$B_0 = \langle q' \rangle$$

$$B_{i+1} = \biguplus_{s \in \mathcal{S}} \left(\mathsf{Pre}_\tau(B_{i,s}) \uplus \biguplus_{e \in \mathcal{E}} \mathsf{Pre}_e(B_{i,s}) \right)$$

Notice that $B_{i,s}$ implies $B_{i+1,s}$ for all $i \geq 0$ and $s \in \mathcal{S}$.

Property 20. Let $B = \bigcup_{i \geq 0} B_i$, $q = (s, v)$, and $q' = (s', v')$. $[q'] \in \mathsf{Reach}([q])$ iff $\langle q \rangle$ implies B_s. $\qquad\qquad\square$

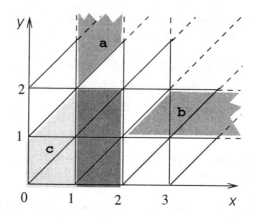

Fig. 8. Computing predecessors.

6 Analysis using bisimulation equivalences

Recall that the region graph is the quotient of the transition system of a timed automaton with respect to the region equivalence. Another way of trying to cope with the complexity of building the region graph consists in finding an equivalence relation that yields a quotient graph which is smaller than the region graph. If the former satisfies the same properties as the latter, it can be used for verification purposes. In this section we define one such equivalence and provide an algorithm to efficiently construct the quotient graph.

6.1 Time-abstracting equivalence

A *time-abstracting bisimulation* is a *symmetric* binary relation $\mathcal{B} \subseteq \mathcal{Q} \times \mathcal{Q}$ between states such that for all $q_1, q_2 \in \mathcal{Q}$, $(q_1, q_2) \in \mathcal{B}$, if

1. For all $\sigma \in \Sigma$, whenever $q_1 \overset{\sigma}{\to} q_1'$ for some q_1', there exists q_2' such that $q_2 \overset{\sigma}{\to} q_2'$ and $(q_2, q_2') \in \mathcal{B}$.
2. For all $\delta \in \mathbf{R}^+$, whenever $q_1 \overset{\delta}{\to} q_1'$ for some q_1', there exists q_2' and $\delta' \in \mathbf{R}^+$ such that $q_2 \overset{\delta'}{\to} q_2'$ and $(q_2, q_2') \in \mathcal{B}$.

The *time-abstracting equivalence*, denoted $\approx$, is the the largest time-abstracting bisimulation. Notice that the region equivalence is a time-abstracting bisimulation. However, it is not necessarily the largest such bisimulation.

Example 9. Consider, for instance, a location s whose invariant condition is *true*. Suppose that s has only two outgoing transitions labeled α and β, such that:

1. they both have the same guard, namely $2 < x < 3 \wedge 1 < y < 2$,
2. α resets the value of y to 0 (i.e., the assignment is $y := 0$),

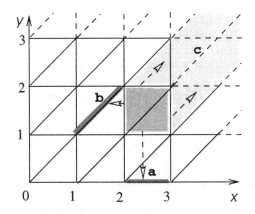

Fig. 9. Example of time-abstracting bisimulation.

3. β resets the value of x to the value of y (i.e., the assignment is $x := y$).

All the states of the form (s, v) such that v satisfies the guard are time-abstracting equivalent. This fact is graphically depicted in Figure 9. Consider two states (s_1, v_1) and (s_2, v_2) such that, for $i = 1, 2$, $2 < v_i(x) < 3 \wedge 1 < v_i(y) < 2$. Let (s_i^α, v_i^α), be an α-successor of (s_i, v_i), for $i = 1, 2$. Then, clearly, $v_i^\alpha(y) = 0 \wedge 2 < v_i^\alpha(x) < 3$. That is, (s_1^α, v_1^α) and (s_2^α, v_2^α) belong to the region (**a**) and they are therefore time-abstracting equivalent. The same happens with the β-successors. For $i = 1, 2$, (s_i^β, v_i^β) are such that $1 < v_i^\beta(x) = v_i^\beta(y) < 2$ and they are therefore time-abstracting equivalent because they belong to the region (**b**). Finally, the set of time successors is characterized by the clock constraint $3 \le x \wedge x - y < 2 \vee 2 \le y < x$ (**c**). The states that satisfy this constraint are also time-abstracting equivalent because (1) none of them can execute neither α not β, and (2) all their time successors are also in (**c**). $\qquad\square$

6.2 Coarsest partition

The largest time-abstracting bisimulation is an equivalence relation. Thus, computing such a bisimulation consists in constructing a partition of the state-space. Let B and C two sets of regions. We define the following operators:

$$\mathsf{Pre}_\sigma[B](C) = \{\rho \in B \mid \exists \rho' \in C. \ \rho \xrightarrow{\sigma} \rho'\}$$
$$\mathsf{Pre}_\tau[B](C) = \{\rho_0 \mid \exists \rho_n \in C, n \ge 1. \ \rho_0 \xrightarrow{\tau} \cdots \xrightarrow{\tau} \rho_n \wedge \forall 0 \le i < n. \ \rho_i \in B\}$$

Let Ω be a partition of $\mathcal{Q}$ such that every $B \in \Omega$ is a set of regions. The quotient of $(\mathcal{Q}, \rightarrow)$ with respect to Ω is transition system $(\Omega, \rightarrow)$, such that for all $B, C \in \Omega$, and for all $\ell \in \mathcal{L} = \Sigma \cup \{\tau\}$,

$$B \xrightarrow{\ell} C \text{ iff } \mathsf{Pre}_\ell[B](C) \ne \emptyset.$$

We write $B \to C$ if $B \overset{\ell}{\to} C$ for some ℓ. B is *stable* with respect to C if for all $\ell \in \mathcal{L}$, $\mathsf{Pre}_\ell[B](C)$ is either B or empty. B is stable with respect to Ω if it is stable with respect to all $C \in \Omega$. Ω is stable if all $B \in \Omega$ are stable with respect to Ω. We define $\mathsf{Suc}_\Omega(B) = \{C \in \Omega \mid B \to C\}$ and $\mathsf{Pre}_\Omega(B) = \{C \in \Omega \mid C \to B\}$.

Property 21. Let $\Omega_\approx$ be the partition induced by $\approx$. Clearly, $\Omega_\approx$ is stable.

The quotient of $(\mathcal{Q}, \to)$ with respect to the time-abstracting equivalence is the quotient of $(\mathcal{Q}, \to)$ with respect to the coarsest partition Ω which is stable.

6.3 Computing the coarsest partition

Several algorithms have been proposed in the literature to compute the coarsest partition which is stable with respect to a transition relation [36, 12]. Here we adapt the generic algorithm developed in [12] in order to construct the partition $\Omega_\approx$. The algorithm is illustrated in Figure 10.

$$
\begin{array}{ll}
\Omega := \Omega_0; & (0) \\
Acc := \{B \in \Omega \mid B \cap Init \neq \emptyset\}; & (1) \\
Sta := \emptyset; & (2) \\
\textbf{while } \exists B \in Acc \setminus Sta & (3) \\
\quad C_B := \mathsf{Split}(B, \Omega) & (4) \\
\quad \textbf{if } (C_B = \{B\}) & (5) \\
\quad \textbf{then} & (6) \\
\quad\quad Sta := Sta \cup \{B\}; & (7) \\
\quad\quad Acc := Acc \cup \mathsf{Suc}_\Omega(B); & (8) \\
\quad \textbf{else} & (9) \\
\quad\quad Acc := Acc \setminus \{B\}; & (10) \\
\quad\quad \Omega := (\Omega \setminus \{B\}) \cup C_B; & (11) \\
\quad\quad Sta := Sta \setminus \mathsf{Pre}_\Omega(B); & (12) \\
\quad\quad \textbf{if } B \cap Init \neq \emptyset & (13) \\
\quad\quad \textbf{then} & (14) \\
\quad\quad\quad Acc := Acc \cup \{C \in C_B \mid C \cap Init \neq \emptyset\}; & (15) \\
\textbf{end} & (16)
\end{array}
$$

Fig. 10. Algorithm for computing the coarsest partition.

The algorithm constructs the coarsest stable partition containing only classes that are reachable from a given set *Init* of initial regions. Ω is the current partition. *Acc* is the set of reachable classes, that is, those classes containing at least one reachable region. $Sta \subseteq Acc$ is the set of stable reachable classes. $\mathsf{Split}(B, \Omega)$ refines the class B by choosing a class C with respect to which B is potentially unstable, and then computing $C_B = \{B_1, B_2\}$ with $B_1 = \mathsf{Pre}_\ell[B](C)$

and $B_2 = B \setminus \mathsf{Pre}_\ell[B](C)$ for some $\ell \in \mathcal{L}$. If indeed $B_i \neq \emptyset$, for $i = 1, 2$, B is *effectively* split (11-12), its predecessors become unstable (13), and the elements of C_B that contain an initial region are added to Acc (14-15). If $C_B = \{B\}$, i.e., $B_1 = \emptyset$ or $B_2 = \emptyset$, then B is both stable (7) and reachable, so its successor classes in Ω are added to the set of reachable classes (8). [6]

For better understanding how the algorithm works, we have explained it as if the region-graph had been constructed before. However, in order for the algorithm to be useful, it should be implemented without a-priori constructing the region-graph. This can be done following a clock-constrained based approach [42]. The operator $\mathsf{Pre}_\ell[B](C)$ can be defined as we defined the operator $\mathsf{Pre}_\ell(C)$ in Section 5. As a matter of fact, $\mathsf{Pre}_\ell[B](C)$ is defined in Appendix A since it is needed for verification of TCTL.

7 Data-structures

In this section we present two data-structures used by the implementations of the algorithms presented in the previous sections.

7.1 Difference Bound Matrices

Let $\mathcal{X} = \{x_1, \cdots, x_n\}$, and let $\Lambda \subseteq \Psi_\mathcal{X}$ be the set of clock constraints over $\mathcal{X}$ defined by conjunctions of constraints of the form $x_i \prec c$, $c \prec x_i$ and $x_i - x_j \prec c$ with $c \in \mathbb{Z}$. Let x_0 be a clock whose value is always 0, that is, its value does not increase with time as the values of the other clocks. Then, the constraints in Λ can be uniformly represented as bounds on the difference between two clock values, where for $x_i \in \mathcal{X}$, $x_i \prec c$ is expressed as $x_i - x_0 \prec c$, and $c \prec x_i$ as $x_0 - x_i \prec -c$.

Such constraints can be then encoded as a $(n+1) \times (n+1)$ square matrix D whose indices range over the interval $[0, \cdots, n]$ and whose elements belong to $\mathbb{Z}_\infty \times \{<, \leq\}$, where $\mathbb{Z}_\infty = \mathbb{Z} \cup \{\infty\}$. The first column of D encodes the upper bounds of the clocks. That is, if $x_i - x_0 \prec c$ appears in the constraint, then D_{i0} is the pair $(c, \prec)$, otherwise it is $(\infty, <)$ which says that the value of clock x_i is unbounded. The first row of D encodes the lower bounds of the clocks. If $x_0 - x_i \prec -c$ appears in the constraint, D_{0i} is $(-c, \prec)$, otherwise it is $(0, \leq)$ because clocks can only take positive values. The element D_{ij} for $i, j > 0$, is the pair $(c, \prec)$ which encodes the constraint $x_i - x_j \prec c$. If a constraint on the difference between x_i and x_j does not appear in the conjunction, the element D_{ij} is set to $(\infty, <)$.

---

[6] This algorithm constructs the *minimal* finite transition system which is equivalent to the region-graph upto time-abstracting bisimulation. Another different approach consists in minimizing the timed automaton itself, rather than its model, in order to obtain an equivalent timed automaton which is minimal upto a stronger notion of bisimulation. This subject has been explored in [40]. A more practical point of view is adopted in [22], also explained in Appendix B.

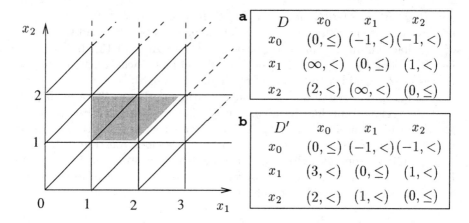

Fig. 11. Representation of convex sets of regions by DBM's.

Example 10. Let Λ be the clock constraint $1 < y < 2 \wedge 1 < x \wedge x - y < 2$. Figure 11a shows its matrix representation. □

Remark 11. Every region can be characterized by a clock constraint, and therefore be represented by a DBM.

As a matter of fact, many different DBM's represent the same clock constraint. This is because some of the bounds may not be *tight* enough.

Example 12. Consider again the clock constraint depicted in Figure 11. The matrix **b** is an equivalent encoding of the clock constraint obtained by setting the upper bound of x_1 to be $(3, <)$ and the difference $x_2 - x_1$ to be $(1, <)$. Notice that this two constraints are implied by the others.

However, given a clock constraint in Λ, there exists a *canonical* representative. Such a representative exists because pairs $(c, \prec) \in \mathbb{Z}_\infty \times \{<, \leq\}$, called *bounds*, can be ordered. This induces a natural ordering of the matrices. Bounds are ordered as follows. We take $<$ to be strictly less than $\leq$, and then for all $(c, \prec), (c', \prec') \in \mathbb{Z}_\infty \times \{<, \leq\}$, $(c, \prec) \leq (c', \prec')$ iff $c < c'$ or $c = c'$ and $\prec \leq \prec'$. Now, $D \leq D'$ iff for all $0 \leq i, j \leq n$, $D_{ij} \leq D'_{ij}$.

Example 13. Consider the two matrices in Figure 11. Notice that $D' \leq D$.

For every clock constraint $\psi \in \Lambda$, there exists a unique matrix C_ψ that encodes ψ and such that, for every other matrix D that also encodes ψ, $C_\psi \leq D$. The matrix C_ψ is called the canonical representative of ψ. The matrix C_ψ can be obtained from any matrix D that encodes ψ, by applying to D the Floyd-Warshall [1] algorithm [23, 46, 39]. For any matrix D that encodes ψ we denote by $\mathsf{cf}(D)$ the canonical representative C_ψ. Having a canonical representative gives us a simple method for checking whether two matrices represent the same constraint: D and D' encode the same constraint iff $\mathsf{cf}(D) = \mathsf{cf}(D')$.

Example 14. In Figure 11, $D' = \mathsf{cf}(D)$.

Encoding convex timing constraints by DBM's requires then $\mathcal{O}(n^2)$ memory space, where n is the number of clocks. Several algorithms have been proposed to reduce the memory space needed [22, 33]. The algorithm proposed in [22] is explained in Appendix B.

The verification algorithms require basically six operations to be implemented over matrices: conjunction, time successors, reset successors, time predecessors, reset predecessors and disjunction. These operations are implemented as follows.

Conjunction. Given D and D', $D \wedge D'$ is such that for all $0 \leq i, j \leq n$, $(D \wedge D')_{i,j} = \min(D_{ij}, D'_{ij})$.

Time successors. As time elapses, clock differences remain the same, since all clocks increase at the same rate. Lower bounds do not change either since there are no decreasing clocks. Upper bounds have to be pushed to infinity, since an arbitrary period of time may pass. Thus, for a canonical representative D, $\mathsf{Suc}_\tau(D)$ is such that:

$$\mathsf{Suc}_\tau(D)_{ij} = \begin{cases} (\infty, <) & \text{if } j = 0, \\ D_{ij} & \text{otherwise.} \end{cases}$$

Reset successors. First notice that resetting a clock to 0 is the same as setting its value to the value of x_0, that is, $\gamma(x_i) = 0$ is the same as $\gamma(x_i) = x_0$. Now, when we set the value of x_i to the value of x_j, x_i and x_j become equal and all the constraints on x_j become also constraints on x_i. Having this in mind, the matrix characterizing the set of reset-predecessors of D by reset γ consists in just copying some rows and columns. That is, the matrix $D' = \mathsf{Suc}_\gamma(D)$ is such that for all $0 \leq i, j \leq n$, if $\gamma(x_i) = x_j$ then $\mathsf{row}_i(D') = \mathsf{row}_j(D)$ and $\mathsf{col}_i(D') = \mathsf{col}_j(D)$. [7]

Time predecessors. To compute the time predecessors we just need to push the lower bounds to 0, provided that the matrix is in canonical form. Thus, for a canonical representative D, $\mathsf{Pre}_\tau(D)$ is such that:

$$\mathsf{Pre}_\tau(D)_{ij} = \begin{cases} (0, \leq) & \text{if } i = 0, \\ D_{ij} & \text{otherwise.} \end{cases}$$

Reset predecessors. Recall that the constraint characterizing the set of predecessors is obtained by substituting each clock x_i by $\gamma(x_i)$. Now suppose that we have two constraints $x_k - x_l < c_{kl}$ and $x_r - x_s < c_{rs}$ and we substitute x_k and x_r by x_i, and x_l and x_s by x_j. Then, we obtain the constraints $x_i - x_j < c_{kl}$ and $x_i - x_j < c_{rs}$ which are in conjunction, and so $x_i - x_j < \min(c_{kl}, c_{rs})$. Thus, the matrix $D' = \mathsf{Pre}_\gamma(D)$ is such that for all $0 \leq i \leq n$, $D'_{ij} = \min\{D_{kl} \mid \gamma(x_k) = x_i \wedge \gamma(x_l) = x_j\}$.

---

[7] Recall that $\gamma(\cdot)$ is a total function.

Disjunction. Clearly, the disjunction of two DBM's is not necessarily a DBM. That is, Λ is not closed under disjunction, or in other words, the disjunction of two constraints in Λ is not convex. Usually, the disjunction of D and D' is represented as the set $\{D, D'\}$. Thus, a lot of computational work is needed in order to determine whether two sets of DBM's represent the same constraint.

It may turn out, for example, that a set of DBM's can be replaced by a single DBM. The tool KRONOS, for instance, use some heuristics to check whether the union of two DBM's is indeed a DBM. Such heuristics are applied when the number of DBM's stored in memory becomes greater than some threshold. However, checking whether a set of more than two DBM's can be represented as a DBM is computationally expensive.

7.2 Symbolic Graphs

One solution adopted in some of the verification tools to overcome the problem of the non-convexity of the union of DBM's, consists in structuring the set of reachable states as a graph rather than as a union of DBM's. The main difference between this graph and the region graph is that its nodes are pairs $(s, D) \in \mathcal{S} \times \Lambda$, instead of regions. This graph is called *forward-simulation* graph or *backward-simulation* graph, according to which method is used to construct it.

Let q and q' be two states. To verify whether $q' \in \mathsf{Reach}(q)$, the forward-simulation graph is the pair (N, E) constructed as follows:

1. $\mathsf{Suc}_\tau(\langle q \rangle) \in N$.
2. For every $(s, D) \in N$, and for every $e = (s, \sigma, \psi, \gamma, s') \in \mathcal{E}$, if $D' = \mathsf{Suc}_\tau(\mathsf{Suc}_e(D)) \neq \emptyset$, then $(s', D') \in N$ and $e \in E$.

The backward-simulation graph is the pair (N, E) constructed as follows:

1. $\mathsf{Pre}_\tau(\langle q' \rangle) \in N$.
2. For every $(s, D) \in N$, and for every $e = (s', \sigma, \psi, \gamma, s) \in \mathcal{E}$, if $D' = \mathsf{Pre}_\tau(\mathsf{Pre}_e(D)) \neq \emptyset$, then $(s', D') \in N$ and $e \in E$.

These graphs can be constructed using a depth-first or a breadth-first techniques indistinctly. For instance, the algorithm for constructing the forward-simulation graph using a breadth-first technique is illustrated in Figure 12.

These algorithms only store matrices in canonical form and only one copy of each matrix is stored, making the test whether a node already exists very simple indeed. The major drawback of these algorithms is that they can introduce a lot of redundancy, in the sense that the same region can belong to many nodes of the graph. The number of nodes of the graph can be reduced by testing whether the matrix of the newly constructed node is *included in*, instead of *equal to*, an already existing node.

Besides, they do not need to be entirely constructed, that is, their construction can be stopped as soon as a node is found to intersect $\langle q' \rangle$, in the case of the forward-simulation graph, or $\langle q \rangle$ in the other case.

```
M := Sucτ(⟨q⟩);
N := ∅;
while M ≠ ∅ do
  let M = (s, D) · M';
  N := N ∪ {(s, D)};
  M := M';
  for all e = (s, σ, ψ, γ, s') ∈ ℰ do
    if (D' = Sucτ(Suce(D)) ≠ ∅) & (s', D') ∉ N ∪ M
    then M := M · (s', D')
  end
end
```

Fig. 12. Forward-simulation graph using a breadth-first technique.

7.3 Decision Diagrams

Other data-structures that have been proposed are based on the so-called *Binary Decision Diagrams*. BDD's, first introduced in [16], are efficient canonical representations of a formulas of propositional logic. BDD's have been successfully used in verification, especially in the analysis of digital circuits [17,37].

The first idea consists in encoding the regions and the transition relation defined by the region graph using BDD's, based on the fact that the region graph is just a finite graph. This approach is followed in [8].

BDD's are also used by the algorithms based on the discretization of the state-space. For instance, when $\epsilon = 1/n$, such algorithms can be efficiently implemented using the so-called *Numeric Decision Diagrams* [9]. The idea behind NDD's is very simple. Suppose that each clock can take values in the range $[0, k)$, and consider a discretization of time such that the possible clock values are $K = \{0, \ldots, k - 1\}$. Each clock can be treated as a bounded integer variable and any of its possible values can be encoded in binary using $\log k$ bits. Consequently, any subset of K^n can be viewed as a subset of $\{0, 1\}^{n \log k}$ and represented by a BDD over $n \log k$ boolean variables. Given a fixed variable ordering, this representation is canonical. All the operations described for DBM's can be simply implemented as operations on BDD's.

7.4 Tools

A lot of tools have been developed based on the algorithms and data-structures described in this paper. It is not the purpose of this paper to review each of them in detail. The reader is referred to the bibliography and to the web pages (whenever available) for a more detailed information about the tools.

- COSPAN [28] has been extended in several different ways to deal with timing [20,8,7].

- EPSILON [19][8] and REAL TIME EXPLORER [44] are two tools based on the notions of bisimulation and refinement.
- KRONOS[9] implements the model-checking algorithm for TCTL described in Appendix A, the backward and forward reachability algorithms using DBM's [21,14] and NDD's [15], and the algorithm for computing the coarsest partition modulo the timed-abstracting bisimulation [42]. This last algorithm allows using the tool ALDEBARAN [26] [10] to check for different kinds of bisimulation equivalences. KRONOS also implements an on-the-fly verification algorithm for checking automata-emptiness (i.e., the existence of a divergent run) and liveness properties [14].
- RT-SPIN [41] extends the on-the-fly, depth-first, forward verification algorithm of SPIN[11] using DBM's for encoding timing constraints.
- UPPAAL[12] implements forward and backward reachability algorithms based on DBM's [34,11,29] that allow checking for safety properties.
- VERITI [45,24] implement a reachability algorithm that uses data-structures that combine both BDD's and DBM's to check for safety properties. The tool also implements an algorithm that computes the coarsest partition modulo the timed-abstracting equivalence [3,2].

8 Concluding remarks

In this paper we have over-viewed four different techniques for analyzing properties of real-time systems specified as timed automata. For the sake of simplicity, we have only discussed how these techniques are used to solve the so-called reachability problem. Other verification problems can also be solved by adapting these four basic procedures. As an example, we discuss in Appendix A how the region-graph and clock-constraint based algorithms can be used to solve the model-checking problem for TCTL. Furthermore, it is worthy to mention here that the question whether a timed automaton is *Non-Zeno* cannot be rephrased in terms of whether some state reaches another state, and therefore it cannot be answered by the reachability algorithms described so far. This issue is also discussed in Appendix A.

The algorithms we have studied always terminate with a yes or no answer for the reachability problem. As we have already mentioned in the introduction, the complexity of this problem is exponential on the number of clocks and in the encoding of the constants[13]. Even though these algorithms and the data-structures they used have been designed to try to avoid that complexity in practice, the state-space to be explored for a given system could anyway exceed the memory capabilities.

---

[8] http://www.cs.auc.dk/general/FS/epsilon-dir/folder.html

[9] http://www.imag.fr/VERIMAG/PEOPLE/Sergio.Yovine

[10] http://www.imag.fr/VERIMAG/DIST_SYS/aldebaran-english.html

[11] http://netlib.bell-labs.com/netlib/spin/whatispin.html

[12] http://www.docs.uu.se/docs/rtmv/uppaal/index.shtml

[13] It is indeed PSPACE-complete [5].

To overcome this problem, some of the algorithms described in this paper have been modified in such a way that they do no longer analyze the exact set of reachable states but an over- or under-approximated one. These algorithms rely on the fact that even if the state-space is larger, its representation is more compact, that is, it requires less memory space.

One such algorithm is the one described in [10] where the state-space is over-approximated by replacing the disjunction operator of clock constraints by the convex hull of them, that is, by the smallest convex clock constraint that contains the disjunction of them. This technique, combined with a BDD-based encoding of the state-space, permit a very compact representation of the set of reachable states. This method allows us to partially solve the verification question for safety properties. That is, the property is satisfied if the algorithm does not find an unsafe state in the larger space, however, if such a state is indeed found, we cannot immediately conclude that the system does not satisfy the property because that particular state may not belong to the exact set of reachable states.

This problem is solved in [24]. There, both under- and over-approximations of the set of reachable states are maintained. Basically, the algorithm iterates and repeatedly changes from one approximating set to the other according to the results obtained in the previous iteration. At each iteration, the approximations are made more accurate, and therefore, eventually become equal to the set of reachable states. This algorithm gives an exact answer to the problem, and it takes advantage of the compact representation of the approximated state-spaces. However, it might end up by constructing the exact state-space before being able to verify the property, in which case, it will perform worst (in both time and space) than the exact algorithms because of the additional computations and memory required to finally construct the set of reachable states.

References

1. A.V. Aho, J. E. Hopcroft and J. D. Ullman. *The design and analysis of computer algorithms*, Addison-Wesley, 1974.
2. A. Alur, C. Courcoubetis, D. Dill, N. Halbwachs, and H. Wong-Toi. An implementation of three algorithms for timing verification based on automata emptiness. In *Proc. 13th IEEE Real-Time Systems Symposium*. IEEE Computer Society Press, 1992.
3. A. Alur, C. Courcoubetis, D. Dill, N. Halbwachs, and H. Wong-Toi. Minimization of timed transition systems. In W.R. Cleaveland, editor, *CONCUR 92: Theories of Concurrency*, pages 340–354. Lecture Notes in Computer Science 630, Springer-Verlag, 1992.
4. R. Alur, C. Courcoubetis, and D. Dill. Model-checking for real-time systems. In *Proc. 5th Symp. on Logics in Computer Science*, pages 414–425. IEEE Computer Society Press, 1990. See also "Model checking in dense real time", *Information and Computation*, 104(1):2–34, 1993.
5. R. Alur and D. Dill. Automata for modeling real-time systems. In *Proc. 17th ICALP*, pages 322–335. Lecture Notes in Computer Science 443, Springer-Verlag, 1990. See also "A theory of timed automata", *Theoretical Computer Science*, 126:183–235, 1994.

6. R. Alur and T. Henzinger. Logics and models of real-time: a survey. In *Proc. REX Workshop "Real-Time: Theory in Practice"*, the Netherlands, June 1991. Lecture Notes in Computer Science 600, Springer-Verlag.

7. R. Alur, A. Itai, R. Kurshan, and M. Yannakakis. Timing verification by successive approximation. In *Proc. 4th Workshop on Computer-Aided Verification*. Lecture Notes in Computer Science 663, Springer-Verlag, 1992. Also in *Information and Computation*, 118(1):142–157, 1995.

8. R. Alur and R.P. Kurshan. Timing analysis in COSPAN. In T.A. Henzinger R. Alur and E. Sontag, editors, *Hybrid Systems III*, pages 220–231. LNCS 1066, Springer-Verlag, 1996.

9. E. Asarin, M. Bozga, A. Kerbrat, O. Maler, A. Pnueli, and A. Rasse. Data-structures for the verification of timed automata. In O. Maler, editor, *Proc. HART'97*, pages 346–360. LNCS 1201, Springer-Verlag, 1997.

10. F. Balarin. Approximate reachability analysis of timed automata. In *Proc. 1996 IEEE Real-Time Systems Symposium, RTSS'96*, Washington, DC, USA, December 1996. IEEE Computer Society Press.

11. J. Bengtsson, W. Griffioen, K. Kristorffersen, K. Larsen, F. Larsson, P. Pettersson, and Wang Yi. Verification of an audio protocol with bus using Uppaal. In *Proc. 8th Conference Computer-Aided Verification, CAV'96*, pages 244–256, Rutgers, NJ, July 1996. Lecture Notes in Computer Science 1102, Springer-Verlag.

12. A. Bouajjani, J.C. Fernandez, N. Halbwachs, P. Raymond, and C. Ratel. Minimal state graph generation. *Science of Computer Programming*, 18:247–269, 1992.

13. A. Bouajjani, Y. Lakhnech, and S. Yovine. Model checking for extended timed temporal logics. In *Proc. 4th Intl. Symp. Formal Techniques in Real-Time and Fault-Tolerant Systems, FTRTFT'96*, Uppsala, Sweden, September 1996.

14. A. Bouajjani, S. Tripakis, and S. Yovine. On-the-fly symbolic model-checking for real-time systems. In *Proc. 18th IEEE Real-Time Systems Symposium, RTSS'97*, San Francisco, USA, December 1997. IEEE Computer Society Press.

15. M. Bozga, O. Maler, A. Pnueli, and S. Yovine. Some progress in the symbolic verification of timed automata. In *Proc. 1997 Computer-Aided Verification, CAV'97*, Israel, June 1997. to appear in LNCS, Springer-Verlag.

16. R.E. Bryant. Graph-based algorithms for boolean function manipulation. *IEEE Transactions on Computers*, 35(8):677–692, 1986.

17. J.B. Burch, E.M. Clarke, D.Dill, L.J. Hwang, and K.L. McMillan. Symbolic model checking: 10^{20} states and beyond. In *Proc. 5th Symp. on Logics in Computer Science*, pages 428–439. IEEE Computer Society Press, 1990.

18. K. Čerāns. Decidability of bisimulation equivalences for parallel timer processes. In *Proc. 4th Workshop on Computer-Aided Verification*. Lecture Notes in Computer Science 663, Springer-Verlag, 1992.

19. K. Cerans, J. C. Godskesen, and K. G. Larsen. Timed modal specifications - theory and tools. In C. Courcoubetis, editor, *Proc. 5th Computer-Aided Verification*, pages 253–267. LNCS 697, Springer-Verlag, June 1993.

20. C. Courcoubetis, D. Dill, M. Chatzaki, and P. Tsounakis. Verification with real-time COSPAN. In *Proc. 4th Workshop on Computer-Aided Verification*. Lecture Notes in Computer Science 663, Springer-Verlag, 1992.

21. C. Daws and S. Yovine. Two examples of verification of multirate timed automata with KRONOS. In *Proc. 1995 IEEE Real-Time Systems Symposium, RTSS'95*, Pisa, Italy, December 1995. IEEE Computer Society Press.

22. C. Daws and S. Yovine. Reducing the number of clock variables of timed automata. In *Proc. 1996 IEEE Real-Time Systems Symposium, RTSS'96*, Washington, DC, USA, December 1996. IEEE Computer Society Press.

23. D. Dill. Timing assumptions and verification of finite-state concurrent systems. In J. Sifakis, editor, *Proc. 1st Workshop on Computer-Aided Verification*, France, 1989. Lecture Notes in Computer Science 407, Springer-Verlag.

24. D. L. Dill and H. Wong-Toi. Verification of real-time systems by successive over and under approximation. In Pierre Wolper, editor, *Proceedings of the Seventh Conference on Computer-Aided Verification, CAV'95*, Lecture Notes in Computer Science 939, pages 409–422, Liege, Belgium, 1995. Springer-Verlag.

25. E.A. Emerson and E. Clarke. Design and synthesis of synchronization skeletons using branching-time temporal logic. In *Proc. Workshop on Logic of Programs*. Lecture Notes in Computer Science 131, Springer-Verlag, 1981.

26. J.C. Fernandez and L. Mounier. On the fly verification of behavioural equivalences and preorders. In *Proc. CAV'91*. LNCS 757, Springer-Verlag, 1991.

27. A. Göllü, A. Puri, and P. Varaiya. Discretization of timed automata. In *Proc. 33rd CDC*, 1994.

28. Z. Har'El and R. Kurshan. Automatic verification of coordinating systems. In J. Sifakis, editor, *Proc. 1st Workshop on Computer-Aided Verification*. Lecture Notes in Computer Science 407, Springer-Verlag, 1989.

29. K. Havelund, A. Skou, K. G. Larsen, and K. Lund. Formal modelling and analysis of an audio/video protocol: an industrial case study using uppaal. In *Proc. 18th IEEE Real-Time Systems Symposium, RTSS'95*, San Francisco, California, USA, December 1997. IEEE Computer Society Press.

30. T.A. Henzinger, Z. Manna, and A. Pnueli. What good are digital clocks? In *Proc. REX Workshop "Real-Time: Theory in Practice"*, New York, 1992. Springer-Verlag.

31. T.A. Henzinger, X. Nicollin, J. Sifakis, and S. Yovine. Symbolic model-checking for real-time systems. In *Proc. 7th Symp. on Logics in Computer Science*, pages 394–406. IEEE Computer Society Press, 1992. Also in *Information and Computation*, 111(2):193–244, 1994.

32. R. Jain. *FDDI handbook: high-speed networking using fiber and other media.* Addison-Wesley, 1994.

33. K. G. Larsen, F. Larsson, P. Pettersson, and Wang Yi. Efficient verification of real-time systems: compact data structure and state-space reduction. In *Proc. 18th IEEE Real-Time Systems Symposium, RTSS'95*, San Francisco, California, USA, December 1997. IEEE Computer Society Press.

34. K. G. Larsen, P. Petterson, and Wang Yi. Compositional and symbolic model-checking of real-time systems. In *Proc. 1995 IEEE Real-Time Systems Symposium, RTSS'95*, Pisa, Italy, December 1995. IEEE Computer Society Press.

35. K. G. Larsen and Y. Wang. Timed abstracted bisimulation: implicit specification and decidability. In *Proc. MFPS'93*, 1993.

36. D. Lee and M. Yannakakis. Online minimization of transition systems. In *ACM Symp. on Theory of Computing*. ACM Press, 1992.

37. K.L. McMillan. *Symbolic model-checking: an approach to the state-explosion problem.* Kluwer, 1993.

38. M. Measche and B. Berthomieu. Time petri-nets for analyzing and verifying time dependent communication protocols. In H. Rudin and C.H. West, editors, *Protocol Specification, Testing and Verification, III*. IFIP, North-Holland, 1983.

39. A. Olivero. Modélisation et analyse de systèmes temporisés et hybrides. Thèse, Institut National Polytechnique de Grenoble, Grenoble, France, September 1994.

40. J.G. Springintveld and F.W. Vaandrager. Minimizable timed automata. In B. Jonsson and J. Parrow, editors, *Proc. FTRTFT'96*, Uppsala, Sweden, 1996. LNCS 1135, 130–147, Springer-Verlag.

41. S. Tripakis and C. Courcoubetis. Extending promela and spin for real time. In *TACAS'96*, Passau, Germany, 1996. Lecture Notes in Computer Science 1055, Springer-Verlag.

42. S. Tripakis and S. Yovine. Analysis of timed systems based on time–abstracting bisimulations. In *Proc. 8th Conference Computer-Aided Verification, CAV'96*, pages 232–243, Rutgers, NJ, July 1996. Lecture Notes in Computer Science 1102, Springer-Verlag.

43. VERIMAG. School on Methods and Tools for the Verification of Infinite-State Systems. `http://www.imag.fr/VERIMAG`. Grenoble, France, March 1997.

44. C. Weise and D. Lenzkes. Efficient scaling invariant checking of timed bisimulation. In *STACS'97*. Springer-Verlag, 1997.

45. Howard Wong-Toi and David L. Dill. Approximations for verifying timing properties. In Teo Rus and Charles Rattray, editors, *Theories and Experiences for Real-Time System Development (Proceedings First AMAST Workshop on Real-Time System Development)*, chapter 7, pages 177–204. World Scientific Publishing, 1994.

46. S. Yovine. Méthodes et outils pour la vérification symbolique de systèmes temporisés. Thèse, Institut National Polytechnique de Grenoble, Grenoble, France, May 1993.

A   The logic TCTL

In the previous sections we have studied the so-called reachability problem. In this section we define the temporal logic TCTL and explain how to check whether a timed automaton satisfies a formula of the logic. TCTL is an extension of the temporal logic CTL [25].

A.1   Syntax

Let **A** be a timed automaton with set of clocks $\mathcal{X}$ and set of atomic propositions Π, and let $\mathcal{Z}$ be a set of clocks disjoint with $\mathcal{X}$, that is, $\mathcal{Z} \cap \mathcal{X} = \emptyset$. The set $\Phi_{\mathcal{X},\mathcal{Z},\Pi}$ of formulas of TCTL are defined by the following grammar:

$$\varphi ::= \psi \mid \pi \mid z.\varphi \mid \neg\varphi \mid \varphi_1 \vee \varphi_2 \mid \varphi_1 \exists \mathcal{U} \varphi_2 \mid \varphi_1 \forall \mathcal{U} \varphi_2$$

where $\psi \in \Psi_{\mathcal{X} \cup \mathcal{Z}}$, $\pi \in \Pi$, and $z \in \mathcal{Z}$.

Let $\varphi \in \Phi_{\mathcal{X},\mathcal{Z},\Pi}$. We define $\mathsf{free}(\varphi)$ to be the set of *free* clocks of φ. $\mathsf{free}(\varphi)$ is inductively defined as follows:

$$
\begin{aligned}
\mathsf{free}(\psi) &= \mathsf{clk}(\psi) \\
\mathsf{free}(\pi) &= \emptyset \\
\mathsf{free}(z.\varphi) &= \mathsf{free}(\varphi) \setminus \{z\} \\
\mathsf{free}(\neg\varphi) &= \mathsf{free}(\varphi) \\
\mathsf{free}(\varphi_1 \vee \varphi_2) &= \mathsf{free}(\varphi_1) \cup \mathsf{free}(\varphi_2) \\
\mathsf{free}(\varphi_1 \exists \mathcal{U} \varphi_2) &= \mathsf{free}(\varphi_1) \cup \mathsf{free}(\varphi_2) \\
\mathsf{free}(\varphi_1 \forall \mathcal{U} \varphi_2) &= \mathsf{free}(\varphi_1) \cup \mathsf{free}(\varphi_2)
\end{aligned}
$$

We say that φ is *closed* if $\mathsf{free}(\varphi) \subseteq \mathcal{X}$, that is, every occurrence of a clock $z \in \mathcal{Z}$ is under the scope of a "$z.$" operator. Table 1 shows some typical abbreviations and their intuitive meaning.

Abbrev.	Formula	Explanation
$\exists\Diamond\varphi$	$true\,\exists\mathcal{U}\varphi$	a state satisfying φ is reachable
$\forall\Box\varphi$	$\neg\exists\Diamond\neg\varphi$	φ holds along all executions
$\forall\Diamond\varphi$	$true\,\forall\mathcal{U}\varphi$	all executions lead to a state satisfying φ
$\exists\Box\varphi$	$\neg\forall\Diamond\neg\varphi$	there is an execution along which φ holds everywhere
$\exists\Diamond_{\leq c}\varphi$	$z.\exists\Diamond(\varphi \wedge z \leq c)$	φ is reachable within a time less than or equal to c
$\forall\Diamond_{\leq c}\varphi$	$z.\forall\Diamond(\varphi \wedge z \leq c)$	all executions lead to φ in at most c time units

Table 1. Typical abbreviations and their meaning.

Example 15. Consider the FDDI system depicted in Figure 3. Some properties that we would like the system to satisfy are the following.

1. At any state, each station *eventually* has time to send low-priority messages. This property can be expressed in TCTL as follows:

$$(\mathtt{Idle_1} \wedge h_1 = 0 \wedge r_1 = 0) \Rightarrow \forall\Box\forall\Diamond\mathtt{LPM_1}.$$

2. After having released the token, the station *eventually* gets the token in a time less than or equal to 104:

$$\mathtt{Idle_1} \Rightarrow \forall\Diamond_{\leq 104}\mathtt{HPM_1}.$$

$\Box$

A.2 Semantics

In order to give the formal semantics of TCTL we need to introduce some definitions and notation.

A *position* p of a run $r \in \mathcal{R}_\mathbf{A}$ is a pair $(i,\delta) \in \mathbb{N} \times \mathbf{R}^+$ such that $\delta = 0$ if $\ell_i \in \Sigma$, otherwise $\delta = \ell_i$. We denote by $\mathcal{P}_r$ the set of positions of r. For a given $i \geq 0$, the set of positions of the form (i,δ) characterizes the set of states through which the run r passes while time flows from state q_i to state q_{i+1}. We define $\Xi(i,\delta)$ to be the state $(s_i, v_i + \delta)$. We define a total order $\ll$ on $\mathcal{P}_r$ as follows:

$$(i,\delta) \ll (j,\delta') \text{ iff } i < j \vee (i = j \wedge \delta \leq \delta').$$

The formulas of $\Phi_{\mathcal{X},\mathcal{Z},\Pi}$ are interpreted over *extended states*. An extended state is a triplet (s,v,ζ) such that $(s,v) \in \mathcal{Q}$ is a state of $\mathbf{A}$, and $\zeta \in [\mathcal{Z} \overset{tot}{\to} \mathbf{R}^+]$ is a valuation of the clocks in $\mathcal{Z}$. We define $v + \zeta$ to be the following valuation:

$$(v + \zeta)(y) = \begin{cases} v(y) \text{ if } y \in \mathcal{X}, \\ \zeta(y) \text{ if } y \in \mathcal{Z}. \end{cases}$$

Let $\varphi \in \Phi_{\mathcal{X}, \mathcal{Z}, \Pi}$ be a closed formula. An extended state (s, v, ζ) *satisfies the* formula φ, denoted $(s, v, \zeta) \models \varphi$, if

$$
\begin{aligned}
(s, v, \zeta) &\models \psi && \text{iff } v + \zeta \models \psi \\
(s, v, \zeta) &\models \pi && \text{iff } \pi \in P(s) \\
(s, v, \zeta) &\models z.\varphi && \text{iff } (s, v, \zeta[z/0]) \models \varphi \\
(s, v, \zeta) &\models \neg\varphi && \text{iff } (s, v, \zeta) \not\models \varphi \\
(s, v, \zeta) &\models \varphi_1 \vee \varphi_2 && \text{iff } (s, v, \zeta) \models \varphi_1 \text{ or } (s, v, \zeta) \models \varphi_2 \\
(s, v, \zeta) &\models \varphi_1 \exists \mathcal{U} \varphi_2 && \text{iff } \exists r \in \mathcal{R}^\infty(s, v).\exists p \in \mathcal{P}(r). \\
& && \quad (\Xi(p), \zeta + \Delta(p)) \models \varphi_2 \\
& && \quad \wedge \\
& && \quad \forall p' \ll p. \ (\Xi(p'), \zeta + \Delta(p')) \models \varphi_1 \vee \varphi_2 \\
(s, v, \zeta) &\models \varphi_1 \forall \mathcal{U} \varphi_2 && \text{iff } \forall r \in \mathcal{R}^\infty(s, v).\exists p \in \mathcal{P}(r). \\
& && \quad (\Xi(p), \zeta + \Delta(p)) \models \varphi_2 \\
& && \quad \wedge \\
& && \quad \forall p' \ll p. \ (\Xi(p'), \zeta + \Delta(p')) \models \varphi_1 \vee \varphi_2
\end{aligned}
$$

A state (s, v) satisfies φ if the extended state (s, v, ζ) satisfies φ where ζ is such that $\zeta(z) = 0$ for all $z \in \mathcal{Z}$. The set of states that satisfy the formula φ, denoted $[\![\varphi]\!]$, is called the *characteristic set* of φ. $\mathbf{A}$ satisfies φ, denoted $\mathbf{A} \models \varphi$, if all the states of $\mathbf{A}$ satisfy φ.

A.3   Region-graph based algorithm

Given a timed automaton $\mathbf{A}$ and a TCTL-formula φ, we are interested in checking whether $\mathbf{A}$ satisfies φ. Let $\hat{\Psi}$ be the set of sub-formulas of φ that belong to Ψ. The region graph $\mathrm{RG}(\mathbf{A}, \hat{\Psi})$ can be used to solve the problem.

Let $[\varphi]$ to be the set of regions defined as follows.

$$
\begin{aligned}
[\psi] &= \{[(s, v, \zeta)] \mid v + \zeta \models \psi\} \\
[\pi] &= \{[(s, v, \zeta)] \mid \pi \in P(s)\} \\
[z.\varphi] &= \{[(s, v, \zeta)] \mid [(s, v, \zeta[z/0])] \in [\varphi]\} \\
[\neg\varphi] &= \mathcal{Q}_{\sim} \setminus [\varphi] \\
[\varphi_1 \vee \varphi_2] &= [\varphi_1] \cup [\varphi_2] \\
[\varphi_1 \exists \mathcal{U} \varphi_2] &= EU([\varphi_1], [\varphi_2]) \\
[\varphi_1 \forall \mathcal{U} \varphi_2] &= AU([\varphi_1], [\varphi_2])
\end{aligned}
$$

where $EU(R_1, R_2) = \bigcup_{i \geq 0} E_i$ such that

$$
E_0 = R_2
$$
$$
E_{i+1} = E_i \cup R_1 \cap \mathsf{Pre}(E_i)
$$

and $AU(R_1, R_2) = \bigcup_{i \geq 0} A_i$ such that

$$
A_0 = R_2
$$
$$
A_{i+1} = E_i \cup R_1 \cap \mathsf{Pre}(E_i) \cap \widetilde{\mathsf{Pre}}(E_i)
$$

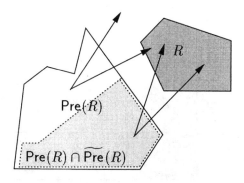

Fig. 13. Pre(R) and $\widetilde{\text{Pre}}(R)$.

where $\widetilde{\text{Pre}}(E_i) = \mathcal{Q}_\sim \setminus \text{Pre}(\mathcal{Q}_\sim \setminus E_i)$. That is, a region belongs to $\widetilde{\text{Pre}}(E_i)$ if all its successors belong to E_i. Thus, $\text{Pre}(E_i) \cap \widetilde{\text{Pre}}(E_i)$ characterizes all the regions that have a successor that belongs to E_i and all its successors belong to E_i. This prevents considering regions that do not have any successors. See Figure 13.

Property 22. Let **A** be a *Non-Zeno* timed automaton. A region ρ belongs to $EU(R_1, R_2)$ if there is a sequence of regions and transitions starting at ρ that reaches a region in R_2 such that all the intermediate regions belong to R_1:

$$EU(R_1, R_2) = \{\rho_0 \mid \exists \rho_0 \to \rho_1 \cdots . \exists n \in \mathbb{N}. \ \rho_n \in R_2 \wedge \forall i \le n.\rho_i \in R_1 \cup R_2\}.$$

That is, $EU([\varphi_1], [\varphi_2])$ characterizes the set of states of **A** that satisfy the formula $\varphi_1 \exists \mathcal{U} \varphi_2$. *Non-Zenoness* ensures that the sequence of states and transitions is indeed a time-divergent execution. □

Property 23. Let **A** be a *Non-Zeno* timed automaton. A region ρ belongs to $AU(R_1, R_2)$ if every sequence of regions and transitions starting at ρ reaches a region in R_2 and all the intermediate regions belong to R_1:

$$AU(R_1, R_2) = \{\rho_0 \mid \forall \rho_0 \to \rho_1 \cdots . \exists n \in \mathbb{N}. \ \rho_n \in R_2 \wedge \forall i \le n.\rho_i \in R_1 \cup R_2\}.$$

That is, $AU([\varphi_1], [\varphi_2])$ characterizes the set of states that satisfy the formula $\varphi_1 \forall \mathcal{U} \varphi_2$. This holds because in the region graph there are no self-loops labeled τ other than the ones at unbounded regions, and also because *Non-Zenoness* ensures that every region has at least one successor.

Property 24. If **A** is *Non-Zeno*, $q \models \varphi$ iff $[q] \in [\varphi]$.

A.4 Clock-constraint based algorithm

Let **A** be a *Non-Zeno* timed automaton and φ a formula of TCTL. We present here an algorithm that constructs a disjoint union of clock constraints $\biguplus_{s \in \mathcal{S}} \psi_s$,

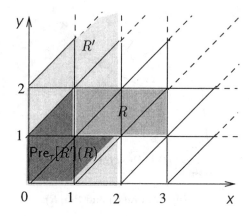

Fig. 14. Conditional timed predecessors.

denoted $((\varphi))$, that characterizes $[\![\varphi]\!]$ without explicitly building a-priori the region graph.

For formulas φ not containing the temporal operators $\exists\mathcal{U}$ and $\forall\mathcal{U}$, $((\varphi))$ is defined as follows.

$$
\begin{aligned}
((\psi)) &= \biguplus_{s\in\mathcal{S}} I(s) \wedge \psi \\
((\pi)) &= \biguplus_{s\in\mathcal{S},\pi\in P(s)} I(s) \\
((z.\varphi)) &= \biguplus_{s\in\mathcal{S}} I(s) \wedge ((\varphi))_s[z/0] \\
((\neg\varphi)) &= \biguplus_{s\in\mathcal{S}} I(s) \wedge \neg((\varphi))_s \\
((\varphi_1 \vee \varphi_2)) &= ((\varphi_1)) \cup ((\varphi_2))
\end{aligned}
$$

where $((\varphi))_s$ is the clock constraint corresponding to s in $((\varphi))$.

Now, let $s \in \mathcal{S}$ and $\psi', \psi_s \in \Psi_{\mathcal{X}}$. We denote by $\mathsf{Pre}_\tau[\psi'](\psi_s)$ the predicate over $\mathcal{X}$ that characterizes the set of clock valuations that can reach a clock valuation in ψ_s when the timed automaton lets time elapse at location s such that all the clock valuations in between satisfy either ψ' or ψ_s.

$$v \models \mathsf{Pre}_\tau[\psi'](\psi_s) \text{ iff } \exists\delta \in \mathbf{R}^+.$$

$$v + \delta \models \psi_s$$

$$\wedge$$

$$\forall\delta' \in \mathbf{R}^+.\ \delta' \leq \delta \Rightarrow v + \delta' \models I(s) \wedge \psi'.$$

That is, $\mathsf{Pre}_\tau[\psi'](\psi_s)$ characterizes the set of regions that contains the regions characterized by ψ_s and all the regions characterized by ψ' that can reach them by taking only τ-transitions (Figure 14).

Property 25. $\mathsf{Pre}_\tau[\psi'](\psi_s) \in \Psi_{\mathcal{X}}$. □

The algorithm for constructing $((\varphi_1\exists\mathcal{U}\varphi_2))$ is very similar to the one based on the region graph. That is,

$$((\varphi_1\exists\mathcal{U}\varphi_2)) = EU(((\varphi_1)), ((\varphi_2)))$$

where $EU(R_1, R_2) = \bigcup_{i \geq 0} E_i$ such that

$$E_0 = R_2$$

$$E_{i+1} = \biguplus_{s \in \mathcal{S}} \left(\mathsf{Pre}_\tau[R_{1,s}](E_{i,s}) \ \uplus \ \biguplus_{e \in \mathcal{E}} \mathsf{Pre}_e(E_{i,s}) \right)$$

The algorithm for computing $((\varphi_1 \forall \mathcal{U} \varphi_2))$ is however different to the one based on the region graph. For the sake of simplicity, we only explain here the algorithm for computing $((\forall \Diamond \varphi))$. The full algorithm is given in [31]. The algorithm relies on the following observation. The set of states that *eventually* reach a state in a set of regions, say A_0, can be iteratively approximated by computing the sequence of sets of regions $A_0 \subseteq A_1 \subseteq \cdots$ where $A_{i+1} = \forall \Diamond_{\leq c} A_i$. Figure 15 illustrates this observation. Now, the characteristic set of $\forall \Diamond \varphi$ is

$$((\forall \Diamond \varphi)) = AD(((\varphi)))$$

where $AD(R) = \bigcup_{i \geq 0} A_i$ such that

$$A_0 = R$$

$$A_{i+1} = A_i \uplus ((\forall \Diamond_{\leq c} A_i))$$

where $c \in \mathbb{N}$ is any constant such that $c \geq 1$.

It remains now to give the algorithm to compute $((\forall \Diamond_{\leq c} A_i))$. This algorithm is based on the following property.

Property 26. If $\mathbf{A}$ *Non-Zeno*, $\forall \Diamond_{\leq c} \varphi$ is equivalent to $\neg z.(\neg \varphi \exists \mathcal{U} z > c)$. □

That is, all executions reach a state satisfying φ within a time less than or equal to c iff no execution continuously satisfy $\neg \varphi$ for a time greater than c. Thus,

$$((\forall \Diamond_{\leq c} \varphi)) = ((\neg z.(\neg \varphi \exists \mathcal{U} z > c))).$$

A.5 Verifying the Non-Zenoness hypothesis

The two algorithms proposed above to verify whether a timed automaton $\mathbf{A}$ satisfies a TCTL-formula φ rely on the hypothesis that $\mathbf{A}$ is in fact a *Non-Zeno* timed automaton. But how do we check if $\mathbf{A}$ is indeed *Non-Zeno*?.

Recall that $\mathbf{A}$ is *Non-Zeno* if every state has a time-divergent execution starting at it. The following property has been proven in [31].

Property 27. $\mathbf{A}$ is *Non-Zeno* iff for all states $q \in \mathcal{Q}$, $q \models \exists \Diamond_{=1} true$.

In other words, verifying the *Non-Zenoness* hypothesis amounts to checking whether all the states of $\mathbf{A}$ can let time progress by 1.

Now, if $\mathbf{A}$ turns to be a *Zeno* timed automaton, we can compute the largest set of *Non-Zeno* states as $NZ = \bigcap_{i \geq 0} NZ_i$, where:

$$NZ_0 = true$$

$$NZ_{i+1} = NZ_i \cap ((\exists \Diamond_{=1} NZ_i))$$

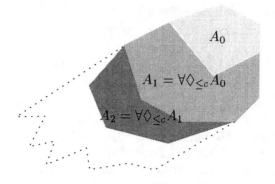

Fig. 15. Computing $\forall \Diamond A_0$.

From **A**, we can construct the *Non-Zeno* timed automaton $\mathbf{A}_{NZ}$ containing all the *Non-Zeno* states of **A** by taking the invariant condition of each location $s \in \mathcal{S}$ to be NZ_s.

B   Reduction of the number of clocks

Recall that the complexity of analyzing timed automata is exponential on the number of clocks. In this section we present two algorithms that can be used to reduce the number of clock variables of a timed automaton. These algorithms have been developed in [22].

B.1   Equivalence

Let **A** be a timed automaton and $(\mathcal{Q}, \rightarrow)$ its transition system.

A *timed bisimulation* $\mathcal{B} \subseteq \mathcal{Q} \times \mathcal{Q}$ is a *symmetric* binary relation between states such that for all $q_1, q_2 \in \mathcal{Q}$, $(q_1, q_2) \in \mathcal{B}$, if for all $\ell \in \Sigma \cup \mathbf{R}^+$,

1. if $q_1 \xrightarrow{\ell} q_1'$ for some q_1', there exists q_2' such that $q_2 \xrightarrow{\ell} q_2'$ and $(q_1', q_2') \in \mathcal{B}$.

The *timed equivalence*, denoted $\sim$, is the the largest timed bisimulation.

B.2   Renaming

Given a timed automaton **A** over a set of clocks $\mathcal{X}$, our aim is to find a set of clocks $\mathcal{Z}$ smaller than $\mathcal{X}$, such that appropriately renaming conditions and assignments of **A** with clocks in $\mathcal{Z}$ we obtain an equivalent behavior.

Let $\mathcal{X}$ and $\mathcal{Z}$ be two disjoint sets of clocks, **A** be a timed automaton over $\mathcal{X}$, and $\Re$ be a family of partial functions $\Re_s$ from $\mathcal{X}$ to $\mathcal{Z}$. We denote $\Re(\mathbf{A})$ the timed automaton obtained from **A** by replacing clocks in $\mathcal{X}$ by clocks in $\mathcal{Z}$ in all conditions and assignments as follows. For all $s \in \mathcal{S}$,

1. $\Re(I(s)) \in \Psi_{\mathcal{Z}}$ is obtained by replacing every $x \in \mathcal{X}$ by $\Re_s(x)$ in $I(s)$, and
2. for every $e = (s, \sigma, \psi, \gamma, s) \in \mathcal{E}$, $\Re(e) = (s, \sigma, \Re(\psi), \Re(\gamma), s')$ is such that,
   (a) $\Re(\psi) \in \Psi_{\mathcal{Z}}$ is obtained by replacing every $x \in \mathcal{X}$ by $\Re_s(x)$ in ψ,
   (b) $\Re(\gamma)$ is the assignment $\gamma' \in \Gamma_{\mathcal{Z}}$ such that $\gamma' \circ \Re_{s'} = \Re_s \circ \gamma$, where $\circ$ denotes the composition of functions.

For $\Re(\mathbf{A})$ to be well defined we need to require that for all $s \in \mathcal{S}$,

1. $\Re_s(x)$ is defined for all $x \in \mathsf{clk}(I(s))$, and
2. for all $e = (s, \sigma, \psi, \gamma, s') \in \mathcal{E}$,
   (a) $\Re_s(x)$ is defined for all $x \in \mathsf{clk}(\psi)$, and
   (b) $\Re_{s'}(x) = \Re_{s'}(y)$ then $\Re_s(\gamma(x)) = \Re_s(\gamma(y))$.

The aim is to find a set of clocks $\mathcal{Z}$ with $\mathsf{card}(\mathcal{Z}) \leq \mathsf{card}(\mathcal{X})$ and clock renaming $\Re$ from $\mathcal{X}$ to $\mathcal{Z}$ such that $\Re(\mathbf{A})$ is bisimilar to $\mathbf{A}$. This notion of reduction is global, that is, $\mathsf{card}(\mathcal{Z})$ of clocks are globally required to model the same behavior. However, it may happen that not all the clocks are always necessary. More formally, it may be the case that $\Re_s$ is such that every state (s, v) is bisimilar to $(s, \hat{v})$, where $\hat{v} \in V_{\Re_s(\mathcal{X})}$, is such that $\hat{v}(z) = v(x)$, for $z = \Re_s(x)$. Therefore, only $\mathsf{card}(\Re_s(\mathcal{X}))$ of clocks are locally needed at location s to model the same behavior.

B.3 Activity

The first algorithm is based on the notion of *activity* of a clock. Intuitively, a clock is *active* at some location if its value at the location may influence the future evolution of the system. This may happen whenever the clock appears in the invariant condition of the location, it is tested in the condition of some of the outgoing edges, or an active clock takes its value when moving through an outgoing edge.

For $\psi \in \Psi_{\mathcal{X}}$ we write $\mathsf{clk}(\psi)$ to denote the set of clocks that appear in ψ. $\mathsf{clk}(\psi)$ is inductively defined as follows:

$$
\begin{aligned}
\mathsf{clk}(x \prec c) &= \{x\} \\
\mathsf{clk}(x - x' \prec c) &= \{x, x'\} \\
\mathsf{clk}(\psi \wedge \psi') &= \mathsf{clk}(\psi) \cup \mathsf{clk}(\psi') \\
\mathsf{clk}(\neg\psi) &= \mathsf{clk}(\psi)
\end{aligned}
$$

We define the function act that associates with each location $s \in \mathcal{S}$ the set $\mathsf{act}(s) \subseteq \mathcal{X}$ of active clocks at s as follows. For all $s \in \mathcal{S}$, $\mathsf{act}(s) = \bigcup_{i \geq 0} \mathsf{act}_i(s)$, where:

$$
\mathsf{act}_0(s) = \mathsf{clk}(I(s)) \cup \bigcup_{(s, \sigma, \psi, \gamma, s') \in \mathcal{E}} \mathsf{clk}(\psi)
$$

$$
\mathsf{act}_{i+1}(s) = \mathsf{act}_i(s) \cup \bigcup_{(s, \sigma, \psi, \gamma, s') \in \mathcal{E}} \gamma(\mathsf{act}_i(s'))
$$

where $\gamma(X) \subseteq \mathcal{X}$ is such that, $y \in \gamma(X)$ iff there exists $x \in \mathcal{X}$ such that $\gamma(x) = y$.

Notice that the definition of $\mathsf{act}_{i+1}(s)$ says that if a clock x is active in s', and there is an edge with an assignment γ such that $\gamma(x) = y$, then y is active in s, since in fact, the value of x in s' is the value of y in s.

Property 28. Let $s \in \mathcal{S}$ and $v, v' \in \mathcal{V}_{\mathcal{X}}$, with $v(x) = v'(x)$ for all $x \in \mathsf{act}(s)$. Then, $(s, v) \sim (s, v')$.

Property 29. Let $\Re$ be any renaming such that for all $s \in \mathcal{S}$, $\Re_s$ is an injective function defined for all $x \in \mathsf{act}(s)$. Then, $\mathbf{A} \sim \Re(\mathbf{A})$.

B.4 Equality

The second algorithm is based on the notion of *equality* between clocks. Intuitively, two clocks $x, y \in \mathcal{X}$ are equal in $s \in \mathcal{S}$ if they have the same value in that location for every run, that is, if for every reachable state (s, v) we have that $v(x) = v(y)$. In this case, only one of the clocks is necessary to determine the behavior of the system at the location.

We define the equality relation such that two clocks are equal in a location if they are set by the assignment of every incoming edge either both to 0 or to clocks that are themselves equal in the source location.

Let $R \subseteq \mathcal{X} \times \mathcal{X}$. We denote R^* the relation $R \cup \{(0,0)\}$. Let γ be an assignment. We denote $\gamma(R)$ the set of pairs $(x, y) \in \mathcal{X} \times \mathcal{X}$ such that $(\gamma(x), \gamma(y)) \in R^*$. Now we formally define the equality relation equ to be the family of relations such that for all $s \in \mathcal{S}$, $\mathsf{equ}(s) = \bigcup_{i \geq 0} \mathsf{equ}_i(s)$, where:

$$\mathsf{equ}_0(s) = \mathcal{X} \times \mathcal{X}$$
$$\mathsf{equ}_{i+1}(s) = \mathsf{equ}_i(s) \cap \bigcap_{(s',\sigma,\psi,\gamma,s) \in \mathcal{E}} \gamma(\mathsf{equ}_i(s'))$$

That is, the algorithm starts by assuming that all clocks are equal everywhere. The definition of $\mathsf{equ}_{i+1}(s)$ says that if two clocks x and y are equal in s, and they both get assigned the values of two clocks x' and y' that are equal in s' or they are both reset to 0 when taking a transition from s' to s, then they remain equal. However, if x' and y' are not equal in s', or one of them is reset but not the other, then the pair (x, y) is removed from the relation associated with s.

Property 30. For all $s \in \mathcal{S}$, $\mathsf{equ}(s)$ is an equivalence relation.

Property 31. Let $\Re$ be any renaming such that for all $s \in \mathcal{S}$, $\Re_s$ is a total function such that for all $x, y \in \mathcal{X}$, $\Re_s(x) = \Re_s(y)$ iff $(x, y) \in \mathsf{equ}(s)$. Then, $\mathbf{A} \sim \Re(\mathbf{A})$.

On Modeling Real-Time Task Systems

Deji Chen[1], Aloysius Mok[1] and Sanjoy Baruah[2]

[1] Department of Computer Sciences
University of Texas at Austin
Austin, TX 78712, USA
{*cdj, mok*}@cs.utexas.edu
[2] Department of Computer Science
The University of Vermont
Burlington, VT 05405, USA
sanjoy@cs.uvm.edu

Abstract. The basic problem in real-time research is how to model a real-time application. In this paper we look at the modeling itself. A real-time task is defined as a sequence of execution requirements with deadlines. The feasibility difficulties of different models are analysed. It turns out generalizing the conventional model does not increase the complextiy level of feasibility testing while it gives us more flexibility to model real-time problems. Adding start time to a task model increases the chance of feasibility but at the same time raises the complexity level into co-NP-complete in the strong sense.

1 Introduction

One of the fundamental problems in real-time research is to devise accurate yet tractable mathematical models for real-time tasks. Liu & Layland introduced the basic periodic model in 1973 [13]. Since then, there have been many variations of it. Mok relaxed it with the sporadic model [14]. Leung & Whitehead considered the periodic model with starting time [12]. Mok & Chen later considered the variation of execution time and proposed a multiframe model [15]. Baruah et. al. further introduced generalized multiframe model [1]. The scheduling of different models has also been extensively analyzed in other literatures [4, 6, 10, 11, 17, 18]. In this paper, we take a look at the modeling itself and try to organize different models and their feasibility difficulties into a uniformed structure. Some of the work in above literature are recited or reproduced to make this chapter a self-contained unit.

There is yet another type of models in which the parameters of each task depend on how they are scheduled. Harbour et. al. introduced a two-level(task-subtask) model [9] where the real-time requirement of a subtask depends on how the previous subtask is scheduled; Han et. al. introduced the distance constrained real-time task where the finishing times of consecutive jobs must not be separated larger than a minimum time [8]. In this work we will concentrate on independent task models where the parameters of a task does not depend on how it is scheduled.

154

To begin with, we introduce a list of symbols which will be further defined and used throughout the paper.

J a real-time job
T a real-time task
S a real-time system
a the starting time of a real-time task
C the execution time of a job
D the deadline of a job relative to its request time
P period or the separation time of two consecutive jobs
n number of tasks in a system
N number of jobs in a repeat of a task
C a list of N job execution times
D a list of N job deadlines
P a list of N job separation times
$\eta_i(t_1, t_2)$ the sum of all execution times of T_i's jobs that both request and have deadline within (t_1, t_2).
$\eta_i(t)$ the maximum of all $\eta_i(t_1, t_2)$ where $t_2 - t_1 = t$.

We will also make use of the following example to illustrate the mathematics in the paper. Figure 1 depicts a legal execution of the robot in the example.

Example 1. Let's consider a robot assembling a product on an assembly line. First it has to collect parts, which takes 1 time unit and must be finished within 2 time units. 3 time units later the parts are placed on the assembly line. Within 2 time units the robot has to assemble the parts, which takes exactly 2 time units. After that the robot uses 5 time units to inspect the product. This can be finished in 8 time units. 3 time units after inspection starts the robot starts a one-time-unit bookkeeping which must be done in 5 time units. Finally, 4 time units after the bookkeeping starts, the robot is ready for the next round.

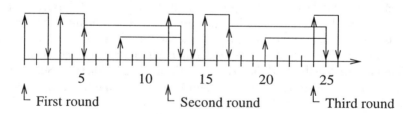

Fig. 1. an Instance of the Robot

We will only look at scheduling a real-time system on single processor. The analysis will be the same for multi-processors if tasks can not migrate among processors, and the assignment of tasks to processors is predetermined (the problem of determining such an assignment will not be addressed in this paper).

This chapter is organized as follows. The next section starts with the general task model and leads to what is going to be addressed in the paper. Section 3 talks about asynchronous models. Section 4 talks about synchronous models. Sections 5 and 6 are about special reduced models. Section 5 is about models with implicit deadlines; and section 6 is about 0-phased synchronous models. Finally section 7 concludes the chapter.

2 Real-time Systems

In this section, we start with what a real-time system is and its properties. Then we look into different possible aspects of it and lead our focus to the system of independent tasks of infinite jobs.

Definition 2.

- a real-time job $J = (C, D)$ defines a basic request for execution. When such a request is made, C time units of processor time must be allocated to this job over the next D time units. C is called the *execution requirement*, and D the *(relative) deadline* of the job.
- a real-time task $T = (J_0, J_1, \ldots)$ is a sequence of real-time jobs that are semantically related. For any $0 \leq i < j$, the request time of J_i is no later than the request time of J_j. In addition, different models place different restrictions upon the permissible request times of the jobs of a particular task. An *instance* of a task is a sequence of jobs satisfying the restrictions asociated with the task.
- a real-time system $S = \{T_1, T_2, \ldots, T_n\}$ is a set of real-time tasks that constitutes a complete system of real-time application. An instance of a real-time system is a sequence of jobs such that all the jobs of each task T_i satisfy the restrictions associated with T_i.
- If for any possible instance of a real-time system there is a schedule such that every job in the system meets the deadline, we say the system is *feasible*.

Example 3. The robot in Example 1 is a real-time task with a repetition of four jobs: the preparation job $J_0 = (1, 2)$, the assembly job $J_1 = (2, 2)$, the inspection job $J_2 = (5, 8)$, and the bookkeeping job $J_3 = (1, 5)$.

Note that Definition 2 is a general one. It encompasses all real-time task models proposed so far. The Liu & Layland model [13] represents a subset of real-time systems where all jobs within a task are the same and are separated by the deadline; the multiframe model [15] represents a subset of real-time systems where jobs within a task repeat after a while and are also separated by the deadline; in the two-level model [9], the job request time depends on the previous job finish time. As we go through this paper, conclusions drawn for more general models can be applied to less general ones.

A job can be looked as a task with only one job; a task can be looked as a system with only one task; a job can also be looked as a system with only one

one-job task. A multi-task system can be looked as a one-task system where all jobs in multi-tasks are considered related and they are part of a big task. Last, a system can also be viewed as a collection of jobs. Defining three levels of job, task, and system is for the convenience of our analysis. This is also the normal way the real-time community models real-time applications.

In the following, a real-time job(or task, system) will be simply called a job(or task, system) if there is no confusion.

It has been shown that the ED(The job with the Earliest Deadline has the highest priority, ties are broken arbitrarily) priority assignment is optimal for scheduling a real-time system [7].

Theorem 4 ([7]). *The ED algorithm is optimal in that if there exists any algorithm that can achieve scheduling of a task system on a single processor, then ED algorithm will also achieve scheduling.*

Definition 5.

- For an instance of a task T_i and two time points t_1, t_2, define $\eta_i(t_1, t_2) = \Sigma_{(a_j \geq t_1) \wedge (a_j + D_j \leq t_2)} C_j$, where $J_j = (C_j, D_j)$ is a job of T_i, J_j starts at a_j.
- For a task T_i, define $\eta_i(t) = \max_{t_2 - t_1 = t} \eta_i(t_1, t_2)$.

$\eta_i(t_1, t_2)$ is the sum of all execution times of the jobs that arrive after t_1 and have deadlines before t_2.

Theorem 6. *A task system S is infeasible iff there exists an instance of S and a pair (t_1, t_2) such that $\Sigma_{i=1}^{n} \eta_i(t_1, t_2) > (t_2 - t_1)$.*

Proof. If for some instance and some t_1, t_2 we have $\Sigma_{i=1}^{n} \eta_i(t_1, t_2) > (t_2 - t_1)$, at least one job within (t_1, t_2) will miss deadline, so S is infeasible.

If S is infeasible, there is some instance where some deadline is missed by ED assignment, Let t_2 denote the first time a deadline is missed. Let t_1 denote the latest time-instant prior to t_2 such that all jobs that arrived prior to t_1 and have deadlines at or before t_2 have completed execution in this ED-schedule (if no such t_1 exists, set t_1 equal to zero). Since ED is used we know all jobs executed within (t_1, t_2) have deadline no later than t_2. Since a deadline is missed at t_2, it follows that $\Sigma_{i=1}^{n} \eta_i(t_1, t_2) > (t_2 - t_1)$. □

A task can have a finite or an infinite number of jobs. In the following only the infinite case is considered. A system of real-time requirement usually runs continuously and can be modeled more accurately with infinite tasks. On the other hand, a finite task can be treated as an infinite one by simply repeating the finite part. If the infinite one can be scheduled, so can the finite one. But not vice versa.

For infinite tasks, in actual systems it usually turns out that the job requirements will repeat eventually. This leads to the revised task definition.

Definition 7. a task $T = (\boldsymbol{C}, \boldsymbol{D}) = ((C_0, C_1, \ldots, C_{N-1}), (D_0, D_1, \ldots, D_{N-1}))$ is an infinite sequence of jobs that are semantically related. $N > 0$ is called the length of the task. The i'th $(i \geq 0)$ job has the execution time $C_{i \bmod N}$ and deadline $D_{i \bmod N}$. For any $0 \leq i < j$, the request time of the i'th job is no later than the request time of the j'th job.

Example 8. The robot in Example 1 can also be modeled as a task $T = \{(1, 2, 5, 1), (2, 2, 8, 5)\}$.

The normal conventional periodic or sporadic task model is a special case of above model with $N = 1$.

Remember in our definition the execution time and deadline of each job is fixed. The only variant is the starting time of the jobs. As we stated in the beginning, we only consider independent task models, where the starting time of each job is independent of the execution of other jobs. In theory, job interdependent cases such as task communication can be modified into independent cases [14].

We can imagine independence model as two separate parts, the task independently generating jobs and the environment where the jobs are executed. The task receives no feedback from the executing environment.

The job starting time can be classified into two categories, the starting time of the whole task a, and the separation time between starting times of two consecutive jobs P. Depending on whether a and/or P are fixed or not, we have four types of tasks.

asynchronous sporadic task: a can take on any value; for any two consecutive jobs J_i and J_{i+1} where $i \geq 0$, there is a minimum separation time $P_{i \bmod N}$; i.e., the request time of J_{i+1} must be no earlier than that of J_i plus $P_{i \bmod N}$.

synchronous sporadic task: a is fixed; for any two consecutive jobs J_i and J_{i+1} where $i \geq 0$, there is a minimum separation time $P_{i \bmod N}$.

asynchronous non-sporadic task: a can take on any value; the request time difference of any two consecutive jobs J_i and J_{i+1} is exactly $P_{i \bmod N}$, where $i \geq 0$.

synchronous non-sporadic task: a is fixed; the request time difference of any two consecutive jobs J_i and J_{i+1} is exactly $P_{i \bmod N}$, where $i \geq 0$.

Note we use the term "synchronous" differently from [12] where synchronous means all tasks start at time 0 and asynchronous means tasks have different starting time.

We shall correspond a synchronous task with an asynchronous task if they are identical except the starting time; we shall correspond a sporadic task with a nonsporadic task if the minimum separation time of the former equals the separation time of the latter and all others are identical. We shall call a synchronous task system to be a system consisting solely of synchronous tasks; we shall call a synchronous sporadic task system to be a system consisting solely of synchronous sporadic tasks, etc.

Theorem 9. *If an asynchronous task system is feasible, then its corresponding synchronous system is also feasible.*

Proof. If the corresponding synchronous sporadic task system is infeasible, its infeasible instance is exactly an instance of the asynchronous task system, which is thus infeasible. $\square$

Theorem 10. *A synchronous sporadic task system is feasible iff the corresponding asynchronous sporadic system is.*

Proof. If an asynchronous sporadic task system is feasible, according to Theorem 9, so is its corresponding synchronous sporadic system.

If an asynchronous sporadic task system is infeasible, there must be an instance R of it when at some time point t_0 a job misses deadline when scheduled according to ED. Let $L_i = a_i + \sum_{j=0}^{N_i-1} P_j$, and $L = \max_{i=1}^{n} L_i$. We construct an instance of the corresponding synchronous sporadic system such that for a task T, its first N jobs request at the minimum separation time and $\forall i \geq N$, J_i requests at time $L + t$ if J_{i-N} of the asynchronous task requests at time t in R. This is a legitimate instance and its suffix after time L is identical to R. Thus a deadline will be missed at time $L + t_0$ by ED if there is no deadline missing prior to that. So the synchronous sporadic task system is infeasible. $\square$

Theorem 11. *An asynchronous sporadic task system is feasible iff the corresponding asynchronous non-sporadic system is.*

Proof. If an asynchronous non-sporadic task system is infeasible, there must be an instance of it when at some time point a job misses deadline by ED. This instance is certainly an instance of its corresponding asynchronous sporadic system, which is hence also infeasible.

If an asynchronous sporadic task system is infeasible, according to Theorem 6, there must be an instance of it and two values t_1, t_2 such that $\sum \eta(t_1, t_2) > t_2 - t_1$. For every task T locate its first job request J after t_1. Now rearrange the requests of T such that all jobs before J are moved toward J until minimum separation time, and all jobs after J are moved toward J until minimum separation time. This will only increase $\eta(t_1, t_2)$ if it ever changes. So we have $\Sigma \eta(t_1, t_2) > t_2 - t_1$ for the new instance. It is easy to see the new instance is also an instance of the asynchronous non-sporadic system, which is hence infeasible. $\square$

Theorem 10 simply says adding starting time to a sporadic task system makes no difference as far as feasibility is concerned. Sporadic task is more general than non-sporadic task, but the difficulties are the same as far as feasibility is concerned according to Theorem 11. For the remainder of this paper, we will primarily discuss two types of task models: *synchronous models*, which means synchronous non-sporadic models, and *asynchronous models*, which covers the other three models. And unless otherwise specified, we will assume non-sporadic task systems during proofs.

3 Asynchronous Real-time Systems

An asynchronous task can be represented as a triple $(\boldsymbol{C}, \boldsymbol{D}, \boldsymbol{P})$ where $\boldsymbol{C} = (C_0, C_1, \ldots, C_{N-1})$ is a list of execution requirements, $\boldsymbol{D} = (D_0, D_1, \ldots, D_{N-1})$ is a list of relative deadlines, and $\boldsymbol{P} = (P_0, P_1, \ldots, P_{N-1})$ is a list of (minimum) separation times.

Example 12. The robot in Example 1 can also be modeled as a task $T = ((1, 2, 5, 1), (2, 2, 8, 5), (3, 2, 3, 4))$.

In an asynchronous system, the task can start at any time. So a job of one task can coincide with any job in any other task. The CPU intensive part of a task can happen at the same time with other tasks' CPU intensive parts.

Theorem 13. *An asynchronous task system S is infeasible iff*
$\exists t > 0, \sum_{i=1}^{n} \eta_i(t) > t.$

Proof. If S is infeasible, there exists an instance and t_1, t_2 when $\sum_{i=1}^{n} \eta_i(t_1, t_2) > t_2 - t_1$. Let $t = t_2 - t_1$, we have $\sum_{i=1}^{n} \eta_i(t) \geq \sum_{i=1}^{n} \eta_i(t_1, t_2) > t_2 - t_1 = t$.

Suppose that $\sum_{i=1}^{n} \eta_i(t') > t'$. For every task T_i there is an instance R_i and $t_{i,1}, t_{i,2}$ with $t_{i,2} - t_{i,1} = t'$, $\eta_i(t_{i,1}, t_{i,2}) = \eta(t')$. Let $t_1^m = \max_{i=1}^{n} t_{i,1}$. Now we construct an instance of S. Consider a new instance obtained by delaying, for each task T, the arrival-times of all the jobs in instance R_i by $t_1^m - t_{i,1}$ time units. For this new instance, $\sum_{i=1}^{n} \eta_i(t_1^m, (t_1^m + t')) = \sum_{i=1}^{n} \eta_i(t') > t' = (t_1^m + t) - t_1^m$. According to Theorem 6, S is infeasible. $\qquad\square$

In task model $(\boldsymbol{C}, \boldsymbol{D}, \boldsymbol{P})$, if $\boldsymbol{C} = (C, C, \ldots, C)$, we rewrite the model as $(C, \boldsymbol{D}, \boldsymbol{P})$. The same applies to D and P. We thus have 8 different models for asynchronous task: (C, D, P), $(\boldsymbol{C}, D, P)$, $(C, \boldsymbol{D}, P)$, $(C, D, \boldsymbol{P})$, $(\boldsymbol{C}, \boldsymbol{D}, P)$, $(\boldsymbol{C}, D, \boldsymbol{P})$, $(C, \boldsymbol{D}, \boldsymbol{P})$, and $(\boldsymbol{C}, \boldsymbol{D}, \boldsymbol{P})$.

The model (C, D, P) is the conventional sporadic task model. The associated feasibility problem is known to be in co-NP. No polynomial-time algorithms have yet been devised; however, there exist pseudo-polynomial algorithms [3, 16] for the feasibility testing of systems of such tasks, provided the total utilization factor of the system is bounded by a constant $c < 1$. The model $(\boldsymbol{C}, \boldsymbol{D}, \boldsymbol{P})$ is called generalized multiframe model in [1].

For the feasibility analysis of model (C, D, P), we need only consider the instance when all tasks start at time 0 and request at the minimum separation time. This is because $\eta(t) = \eta(0, t)$ and the above instance is the worst from time 0. The $\eta(t)$ for other models may not necessarily equal $\eta(0, t)$ or $\eta(t_0, t)$ for some constant t_0. For the robot Example 12, $\eta(2) = \eta(3, 5) = 2$, $\eta(5) = \eta(0, 5) = 3$. The issue therefore is to compute the function $\eta(t)$ for task model $(\boldsymbol{C}, \boldsymbol{D}, \boldsymbol{P})$. Observe that for any t, there is always a t' such that $\eta(t) = \eta(t', t' + t)$ and t' is the request time of a certain job. Since the jobs repeat every N times, we have the following equations. ($\eta^i(t)$ is the case when we calculate execution time starting with the arrival of job J_i.)

$$\eta(t) = \max_{i=0}^{N-1} \eta^i(t) \tag{1}$$

$$\eta^i(t) = \sum_{j=0}^{N-1} \left(C_{(i+j) \bmod N} \times \left\lfloor \frac{\max(0, t - \sum_{k=i}^{i+j-1} P_{k \bmod N} - D_{(i+j) \bmod N})}{P_{\text{sum}}} \right\rfloor \right) \tag{2}$$

where $P_{\text{sum}} = \sum_{i=0}^{N-1} P_i$, $C_{\text{sum}} = \sum_{i=0}^{N-1} C_i$, and $D_{\max} = \max_{i=0}^{N-1} D_i$.

Lemma 14.

- $\eta(t + mP_{\text{sum}}) = \eta(t) + mC_{\text{sum}}$, where $D_{\max} \le t < D_{\max} + P_{\text{sum}}$ and $m > 0$.
- $\eta(t)$ is a monotonic nondecreasing step-function of t
- Let $\mathcal{N}$ to be number of steps of $\eta(t)$ in $(0, D_{\max} + P_{\text{sum}})$, then $\mathcal{N} = \mathcal{O}(N * (N + N * \frac{D_{\max}}{P_{\text{sum}}}))$.
- The complexity of calculating $\eta(t)$ in $(0, D_{\max} + P_{\text{sum}})$ is $\mathcal{O}(N * (N + N * \frac{D_{\max}}{P_{\text{sum}}}) * \log(N + N * \frac{D_{\max}}{P_{\text{sum}}})$

Proof.

- for $D_{\max} \le t < D_{\max} + P_{\text{sum}}$ and $m > 0$, we have,

$$\eta^i(t + mP_{\text{sum}})$$

$$= \sum_{j=0}^{N-1} \left(C_{(i+j) \bmod N} \times \left\lfloor \frac{\max(0, (t + mP_{\text{sum}}) - \sum_{k=i}^{i+j-1} P_{k \bmod N} - D_{(i+j) \bmod N})}{P_{\text{sum}}} \right\rfloor \right)$$

$$= \sum_{j=0}^{N-1} \left(C_{(i+j) \bmod N} \times \left\lfloor \left(m + \frac{\max(0, t - \sum_{k=i}^{i+j-1} P_{k \bmod N} - D_{(i+j) \bmod N})}{P_{\text{sum}}} \right) \right\rfloor \right)$$

$$= \sum_{j=0}^{N-1} \left((C_{(i+j) \bmod N} \times m) + \eta^i(t) \right)$$

$$= C_{\text{sum}} \times m + \eta^i(t)$$

So, we have

$$\eta(t + mP_{\text{sum}}) = \max_{i=0}^{N-1} \eta^i(t + mP_{\text{sum}})$$

$$= \max_{i=0}^{N-1} (\eta^i(t) + mC_{\text{sum}})$$

$$= \max_{i=0}^{N-1} \eta^i(t) + mC_{\text{sum}}$$

$$= \eta(t) + mC_{\text{sum}}$$

- $\eta^i(t)$ is monotonic non-decreasing and, increases only when a deadline is hit and the increase equals the execution time of the job whose deadline is hit. Hence $\eta(t) = \max_{i=0}^{N-1} \eta^i(t)$ is also a monotonic non-decreasing step function of t.
- The number of steps of $\eta^i(t)$ in $(0, D_{\max} + P_{\text{sum}})$ is the number of deadlines hit, which is $\mathcal{O}(N + N * \frac{D_{\max}}{P_{\text{sum}}})$. So $\mathcal{N} = \mathcal{O}(N * (N + N * \frac{D_{\max}}{P_{\text{sum}}}))$
- The complexity of calculating $\eta^i(t)$ in $(0, D_{\max} + P_{\text{sum}})$ is $\mathcal{O}((N + N * \frac{D_{\max}}{P_{\text{sum}}}) * \log(N + N * \frac{D_{\max}}{P_{\text{sum}}})$, so is $\mathcal{O}(N * (N + N * \frac{D_{\max}}{P_{\text{sum}}}) * \log(N + N * \frac{D_{\max}}{P_{\text{sum}}})$ for $\eta(t)$.
  □

For any task of model $(\boldsymbol{C}, \boldsymbol{D}, \boldsymbol{P})$, we can get its stepwise $\eta(t)$ within $(0, D_{\max} + P_{\text{sum}})$ in polynomial time and we know the pattern repeats after $D_{\max} + P_{\text{sum}}$.

Example 15. The $\eta(t)$ for the robot task is a stepwise function. Its part between $(0, D_{\max} + P_{\text{sum}} = 20)$ is shown as the bold outer contour in Fig. 2.

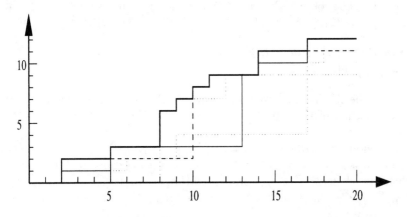

Fig. 2. $\eta(t)$ of the Robot

Theorem 16. *The feasibility problem of task set of model $(\boldsymbol{C}, \boldsymbol{D}, \boldsymbol{P})$ is in co-NP.*

Proof. We can guess a t and calculate $\sum_i^n \eta_i(t)$ in polynomial time and find it is larger than t and hence the set is infeasible according to Theorem 13. □

Definition 17. A task satisfies the *localized Monotonic Absolute Deadline (l-MAD)* property if its i'th job has a deadline no later than that of its $(i + 1)$'th job, $i \geq 0$.

l-MAD is a reasonable property as semantically related jobs in a task always follow a sequence. (Also note tasks of models (C, D, P),$(\boldsymbol{C}, D, P)$, $(C, D, \boldsymbol{P})$, and $(\boldsymbol{C}, D, \boldsymbol{P})$, are all l-MAD.) Next we will transform a special l-MAD task of model $(\boldsymbol{C}, \boldsymbol{D}, \boldsymbol{P})$ into a set of (C, D, P) tasks.

Algorithm 1.

  (01) $\Upsilon = \emptyset$
  (02) for $i:=1$ to $\mathcal{N}$
  (03)   *begin*
  (04)   *t_i:=the i'th step in the step function;*
  (05)   *if $\eta(t_i) > 0$ then*
  (06)   *begin*
  (07) $C := \eta(t_i)$;
  (08) $D := t_i$;
  (09) $P := P_{\text{sum}}$;
  (10) $\Upsilon := \Upsilon + \{(C, D, P)\}$;
  (11)   *Substract C from $\eta(t)$ for all $t > t_i$*
  (12)   *end*
  (13)   *end*

Example 18. The robot task is l-MAD, and can be transformed to task set $\{(2, 2, 12), (1, 5, 12), (3, 8, 12), (1, 9, 12), (1, 10, 12), (1, 11, 12)\}$ with Algorithm 1.

Lemma 19. *In Algorithm 1, $\sum_{(C_i, D_i, P_i) \in \Upsilon} C_i = C_{\text{sum}}$, and $\forall t > 0$; $\sum_{(C_i, D_i, P_i) \in \Upsilon} \eta_i(t) = \eta(t)$.*

Proof. Let the $\mathcal{N}$'th step happen at time $t_{\mathcal{N}}$. Because of l-MAD property, at time $t_{\mathcal{N}}$ each job of the repeat only occurs once. So we have $C_{\text{sum}} = \eta(t_{\mathcal{N}}) = \sum_{C_i, D_i, P_i) \in \Upsilon} C_i$.

It is obvious from Algorithm 1 that $\sum_{(C_i, D_i, P_i) \in \Upsilon} \eta_i(t) = \eta(t)$ for $t < D_{\max} + P_{\text{sum}}$. Let $D_{\max} \leq t < D_{\max} + P_{\text{sum}}$ and $m > 0$. Because of the property of the task model (C, D, P), $\sum_{(C_i, D_i, P_i) \in \Upsilon} \eta_i(t + mP_{\text{sum}}) = \sum_{(C_i, D_i, P_i) \in \Upsilon} \eta_i(t) + \sum_{(C_i, D_i, P_i) \in \Upsilon} C_i$. On the other hand, $\eta(t + mP_{\text{sum}}) = \eta(t) + mC_{\text{sum}}$ according to Lemma 14. So we have $\forall t > 0$; $\sum_{(C_i, D_i, P_i) \in \Upsilon} \eta_i(t) = \eta(t)$. $\square$

Theorem 20 follows from Theorem 13.

Theorem 20. *A system of tasks of l-MAD model (C, D, P) is feasible iff $\bigcup \Upsilon$ — the transformed system of sporadic tasks—is feasible.*

Thus, we have reduced the problem of determining feasibility of a set of (C, D, P) tasks to the problem of determining feasibility of a set of "regular" sporadic tasks. This reduction consists of calculate $\eta(t)$ for $t < D_{\max} + P_{\text{sum}}$, followed by a call of Algorithm 1. The complexity is $\mathcal{O}(N * (N + N * \frac{D_{\max}}{P_{\text{sum}}}) * \log(N + N * \frac{D_{\max}}{P_{\text{sum}}}))$

The problem of determining feasibility of a system of sporadic tasks has been previously studied [2]. The major result is that the sporadic task system can be tested for feasibility in pseudo-polynomial time if the total utilization factor is less than a constant $c < 1$. As a consequence, we conclude that a l-MAD task system of model (C, D, P) can be tested for feasibility in pseudo-polynomial time when the density $\sum \frac{C_{\text{sum}}}{P_{\text{sum}}}$ is a priori bounded from above by some constant $c < 1$.

Since all other models are special cases of model (C, D, P), we have the following theorem.

Theorem 21. *The feasibility problem of a task system of any one of above 8 models is in co-NP. There is pseudo-polynomial algorithm for the testing if it is l-MAD and the density is a priori bounded from above by some constant $c < 1$.*

As is also shown in [1], we can not test feasibility of model (C, D, P) system by simply simulating the system from time 0 at minimum separation time. The reason for that is this instance may not generate the "critical" value for $\sum \eta(t)$ — the one that would cause the system to fail the feasibility test.

4 Synchronous Real-Time Systems

In the previous section we have assumed that a task may start execution at any time. Now we turn our attention to synchronous tasks, where each task has one more parameter—the starting time a. In this case the system has only one possible instance. A synchronous system can be viewed as one instance of the corresponding asynchronous system. Thus, the synchronous system is feasible if the non-synchronous system is. However, the converse may not hold, since the CPU intensive execution of all tasks $\eta(t)$ may not coincide in the synchronous case. In other words, a synchronous system may be feasible even when the corresponding asynchronous system is infeasible. However, determining feasibility for synchronous systems turns out to be harder than for asynchronous systems.

Similar to asynchronous task, a synchronous task can be represented as a tuple (a, C, D, P) where a is the task starting time, and P is a list of separation times. The i'th job starts at time $t = a + \lfloor \frac{i}{N} \rfloor \cdot P_{\text{sum}} + \Sigma_{j=0}^{(i \bmod N)-1} P_j$, has execution time $C_{i \bmod N}$, and must be finished before $t + D_{i \bmod N}$, where $i \geq 0$.

In task model (a, C, D, P), if $C = (C, C, \ldots, C)$, we rewrite the model as (a, C, D, P). the same applies to D and P. We thus have 8 different models for synchronous task: (a, C, D, P), (a, C, D, P), (a, C, D, P), (a, C, D, P), (a, C, D, P), (a, C, D, P), (a, C, D, P), and (a, C, D, P).

The model (a, C, D, P) is called "asynchronous" periodic model in [12] and its feasibility problem is shown to be co-NP-complete in the strong sense [3].

Theorem 22. *The feasibility problem of a task system of any one of above 8 models is co-NP-complete in the strong sense.*

Proof. A task T of model (a, C, D, P) is equivalent to a set $\{T_0, T_1, \ldots, T_{N-1}\}$ of N tasks of model (a, C, D, P) where $T_i = (a + \Sigma_{j=0}^{i-1} P_j, C_i, D_i, \Sigma_{j=1}^{N} P_j)$. So a system of model (a, C, D, P) can be reduced polynomially into a system of model (a, C, D, P). In the mean time, all other models can be reduced to (a, C, D, P)

model in polynomial time. So all 8 models have the same complexity for feasibility testing. As the feasibility problem of model (a, C, D, P) is co-NP-complete in the strong sense, so is it for all the 8 models. □

Example 23. To model robot task as a synchronous one, let's say it starts at time 0. We have $(a, \boldsymbol{C}, \boldsymbol{D}, \boldsymbol{P})$ model $(0, (1, 2, 5, 1), (2, 2, 8, 5), (3, 2, 3, 4))$. It can be further decoupled into four (a, C, D, P) model tasks $\{(0, 1, 2, 12), (3, 2, 2, 12), (5, 5, 8, 12), (8, 1, 5, 12)\}$.

Table 1 lists the 16 models we addressed so far in this and the previous section. The first row represents conventional task models where the execution time, deadline, and (minimum) separation time(or period) are constant within each task. We have shown that generalizing conventional model does not increase the complexity of feasibility testing whereas the generalization gives us more flexibility to model real-time applications.

Table 1. Task Models

(C, D, P)	(a, C, D, P)
$(\boldsymbol{C}, D, P)$	$(a, \boldsymbol{C}, D, P)$
$(C, \boldsymbol{D}, P)$	$(a, C, \boldsymbol{D}, P)$
$(C, D, \boldsymbol{P})$	$(a, C, D, \boldsymbol{P})$
$(\boldsymbol{C}, \boldsymbol{D}, P)$	$(a, \boldsymbol{C}, \boldsymbol{D}, P)$
$(\boldsymbol{C}, D, \boldsymbol{P})$	$(a, \boldsymbol{C}, D, \boldsymbol{P})$
$(C, \boldsymbol{D}, \boldsymbol{P})$	$(a, C, \boldsymbol{D}, \boldsymbol{P})$
$(\boldsymbol{C}, \boldsymbol{D}, \boldsymbol{P})$	$(a, \boldsymbol{C}, \boldsymbol{D}, \boldsymbol{P})$

5 Deadline Implicit Systems

We have shown that the feasibility problem of $(a, \boldsymbol{C}, \boldsymbol{D}, \boldsymbol{P})$ is co-NP-complete in the strong sense, and there exist pseudo-polynomial time algorithms for testingthe feasibility of $(\boldsymbol{C}, \boldsymbol{D}, \boldsymbol{P})$. The next question would be if there is simplified models that are less complex for feasibility testing. Unfortunately, as we have seen, reducing $\boldsymbol{C}$ to C, $\boldsymbol{D}$ to D, or $\boldsymbol{P}$ to P does not help.

There is yet another type of model — the *implicit deadline models* — in which the deadline of a job is assumed to be equal to the (minimum) separation time. Once again, we can define 8 such models: (C, P), $(\boldsymbol{C}, P)$, $(C, \boldsymbol{P})$, and $(\boldsymbol{C}, \boldsymbol{P})$ for asynchronous models and (a, C, P), $(a, \boldsymbol{C}, P)$, $(a, C, \boldsymbol{P})$, and $(a, \boldsymbol{C}, \boldsymbol{P})$ for synchronous models. We have the following theorems.

Theorem 24 (Liu73). *A system of model* (C, P) *or* (a, C, P) *is feasible iff* $\Sigma(\frac{C}{P}) \leq 1$.

The complexity of the algorithm from Theorem 24 is $\mathcal{O}(n)$.

Theorem 25. *Feasibility-analysis for a task system in the models* (C, P), $(C, \boldsymbol{P})$, *and* $(\boldsymbol{C}, \boldsymbol{P})$ *is in co-NP. There is a pseudo-polynomial algorithm for feasibility-testing, if the utilization factor is bounded from above by a constant* $c < 1$.

Proof. All three models can be polynomially reduced to l-MAD $(\boldsymbol{C}, \boldsymbol{D}, \boldsymbol{P})$ that is in co-NP and there is pseudo-polynomial algorithm for feasibility testing if the utilization factor is less than a constant $c < 1$. ☐

The model $(\boldsymbol{C}, P)$ is called multiframe model [15], and [5] suggests its feasibility testing might be simpler than that of model (C, D, P).

To prove the hardness of the synchronous deadline-implicit models, we will make use of the properties of the *simultaneous congruences problem*, which is defined as follows:

Definition 26 (The Simultaneous Congruences Problem (SCP)).

Given $A = \{(r_1, b_1), (r_2, b_2), \ldots, (r_n, b_n)\} \subset N \times N$ and an integer s,
Determine whether there is an $A' \subseteq A$ of s pairs and a natural number x such that, for every $(r_i, b_i) \in A'$, $x \equiv r_i \bmod b_i$.

It has been shown [3] that this problem is NP-complete in the strong sense.

Theorem 27. *The feasibility problem of a task system of* $(a, \boldsymbol{C}, P), (a, C, \boldsymbol{P})$, *or* $(a, \boldsymbol{C}, \boldsymbol{P})$ *is co-NP-complete in the strong sense.*

Proof. First of all, all models are special cases of model $(a, \boldsymbol{C}, \boldsymbol{D}, \boldsymbol{P})$, which is in co-NP for feasibility testing. So they are in co-NP as well. We next prove they are all co-NP hard.

$(a, \boldsymbol{C}, P)$: We reduce SCP to $(a, \boldsymbol{C}, P)$ with the following method.
$$f(< \{(r_1, b_1), (r_2, b_2), \ldots, (r_n, b_n)\}, s >) = \{T_1, T_2, \ldots, T_n\}$$
$$a_i = (s - 1)r_i$$
$$\boldsymbol{C} = (1, \overbrace{0, 0, \ldots, 0}^{b_i - 1})$$
$$P_i = s - 1$$
This reduction is not, in general, a polynomial-time one; furthermore, f may be of size exponential to the size of the SCP problem. However, if all the numbers in SCP are restricted to be polynomial in n, then both the time-complexity of the transformation, and the size of the transformed instance, are polynomial in the size of the input instance.

Observe that the length N_i of task T_i is equal to b_i for each i, and that the only jobs generated by task T_i that have a non-zero computation requirement are exactly the jobs J_{i,kb_i}, for all non-negative integers k. Furthermore, all tasks have the same period — $s - 1$. Hence, for f to be infeasible, it is necessary that at least s jobs J_{i,kb_i} — those with non-zero execution requirements — have their arrival times coincide; since all the jobs have a relative deadline of $s - 1$, it is also sufficient that s such jobs arrive simultaneously. We now show that s jobs J_{i,kb_i} have their arrival times coincide if and only if

SCP has a solution. Suppose that the arrival times of jobs J_{i,k,b_i} and $J_{j,k_j b_j}$ coincide — i.e., $a(J_{i,k_i b_i}) = a(F_{j,k_j b_j})$:

$$
\begin{aligned}
&a(J_{i,k_i b_i}) = a(J_{j,k_j b_j}) \\
\equiv \quad & a_i + k_i b_i \cdot (s - 1) = a_j + k_j b_j \cdot (s - 1) \\
\equiv \quad & (s - 1)r_i + (s - 1)k_i b_i = (s - 1)r_j + (s - 1)k_j b_j \\
\equiv \quad & r_i + k_i b_i = r_j + k_j p_j
\end{aligned}
$$

Hence we have: in above transformation, instance SCP has a solution iff f is infeasible. So (a, C, P) feasibility is at least co-NP-hard in the strong sense.

$(a, C, \boldsymbol{P})$: We reduce SCP to $(a, C, \boldsymbol{P})$ with the following method.

$f(< \{(r_1, b_1), (r_2, b_2), \ldots, (r_n, b_n)\}, s >) = \{T_1, T_2, \ldots, T_n\}$

$a_i = 4n(s - 1)r_i$

$C_i = 1$

$\boldsymbol{P} = (s - 1, (4nb_i - 1)(s - 1))$

The transformation is linear.

We see that if s tasks have their first-period-frame request simultaneously, then after $s - 1$ one of them will miss deadline, that results in task set infeasible. We now show that if that never happen, that is, If there are no s tasks having their first-period-frame requested simultaneously, then the task set is feasible.

Let's use the following scheduling policy:

- first-period-frames have arbitrary priority over one another
- any first-period-frame has higher priority over any second-period frame
- second-period frames are scheduled by EDA, and ties are arbitrarily broken
- any frame missing deadline is discarded at its deadline time point

Since there are at most $s - 1$ first-period-frames request at the same time in which they all are scheduled within $s - 1$ time length. So all first-period-frames are scheduled within deadlines. Let's consider only those second-period frames.

We assume $s > 1$ since $s = 1$ is a trivial case. For any second-period frame invocation of task T_i at time t with period $(4nb_i - 1)(s - 1)$. Let's consider the time period $(t, t + 3n)$. Because deadline missing frames are discarded immediately, we know there are at most three requests for any task in $(t, t + 3n)$, so there are totally at most $n * 3$ execution units requested in $(t, t + 3n)$ per task. So T finishes no later than $t + 3n \leq (4nb_i - 1)(s - 1)$. So any second-period frame does not miss deadline. So the task set is feasible.

The k_ith occurrence of task T_i's first-period-frame starts at $t_i^{k_i} = a_i + k_i * \Sigma p_i = 4n(s - 1)r_i + k_i((s - 1) + (4nb_i - 1)(s - 1)) = 4n(s - 1)(r_i + k_i b_i))$. So if $t_i^{k_i} = t_j^{k_j}$, we have $r_i + k_i b_i = r_i + k_i b_i = x$.

If there is a subset of size s in SCP with x, then each task transformed from an element of that subset will have a first-period-frame requested at time $4n(s - 1)x$, so the task set is infeasible; if the task set is infeasible, then there must be s tasks have their first-period-frame request at the same time

t, then the original pairs in SCP of the s tasks are a legitimate subset with $x = t/(4n(s-1))$, so we have a solution to SCP.

Hence we have: in above transformation, instance SCP has a solution iff f is infeasible. So $(a, C, \boldsymbol{P})$ feasibility is at least co-NP-hard in the strong sense.

$(a, \boldsymbol{C}, \boldsymbol{P})$: We can reduce either model $(a, \boldsymbol{C}, P)$ or $(a, C, \boldsymbol{P})$ into model $(a, \boldsymbol{C}, \boldsymbol{P})$ in linear time. So model $(a, \boldsymbol{C}, \boldsymbol{P})$ is is at least the same hard for feasibility testing, i.e., co-NP-hard in the strong sense. □

Note adding starting time to task models will always get the feasibility testing into co-NP-complete in the strong sense except the simplest one (a, C, P).

6 0-phased Synchronous Systems

Of many synchronous models, there is a special one where all tasks have start time 0. These include 12 models: $(0, C. P)$, $(0, \boldsymbol{C}, P)$, $(0, C, \boldsymbol{P})$, $(0, \boldsymbol{C}, \boldsymbol{P})$, $(0, C, D, P)$, $(0, \boldsymbol{C}, D, P)$, $(0, C, \boldsymbol{D}, P)$, $(0, C, D, \boldsymbol{P})$, $(0, \boldsymbol{C}, \boldsymbol{D}, P)$, $(0, \boldsymbol{C}, D, \boldsymbol{P})$, $(0, C, \boldsymbol{D}, \boldsymbol{P})$, and $(0, \boldsymbol{C}, \boldsymbol{D}, \boldsymbol{P})$. We call them 0-phased synchronous models. In this section, we will see if their feasibility problems are like general synchronous model to be co-NP-complete in the strong sense.

Definition 28. A 0-phase task is called AM(Accumulatively Monotonic) if $\forall t > 0, \eta(t) = \eta(0, t)$.

Theorem 29. *A system S of AM 0-phased model is feasible iff its corresponding asynchronous system S' is.*

Proof. If S' is feasible, so is S according to Theorem 9.

If S' is infeasible, there exists t such that $\Sigma\eta(t) > t$ for S'. So for S we have $\Sigma\eta(0, t) > t - 0$. So S is infeasible. □

Corollary 30. *There is a pseudo-polynomial algorithm for testing the feasibility of system of task model $(0, C, D, P)$ if the utilization factor is less than a constant $c < 1$.*

A 0-phased synchronous system is the worst running cases of its corresponding asynchronous system if every task in the system is AM. If such worst running cases is feasible, so shoud be the corresponding asynchronous system. This is why we can test conventional periodic system (C, P) and (C, D, P) by testing only the case when all tasks start at 0. This is also why people often make no difference between models (C, P) and $(0, C, P)$, or between models (C, D, P) and $(0, C, D, P)$. For models other than these, we could not simply test the running case when all tasks start at 0 because they may not be AM and the running case may not be the worst one. This shows the model generalizations is not trivial [1, 15]

The AM property can be generalized such that the initial time is not 0 as we did in [5, 15].

7 Conclusion

Table 2. Complete Task Models

(C,P)	(C,D,P)	$(0,C,P)$	$(0,C,D,P)$	(a,C,P)	(a,C,D,P)
$(\boldsymbol{C},P)$	$(\boldsymbol{C},D,P)$	$(0,\boldsymbol{C},P)$	$(0,\boldsymbol{C},D,P)$	$(a,\boldsymbol{C},P)$	$(a,\boldsymbol{C},D,P)$
$(\boldsymbol{C},P)$	$(\boldsymbol{C},\boldsymbol{D},P)$	$(0,\boldsymbol{C},P)$	$(0,\boldsymbol{C},\boldsymbol{D},P)$	$(a,\boldsymbol{C},P)$	$(a,C,\boldsymbol{D},P)$
$(\boldsymbol{C},\boldsymbol{P})$	$(\boldsymbol{C},\boldsymbol{D},\boldsymbol{P})$	$(0,\boldsymbol{C},\boldsymbol{P})$	$(0,\boldsymbol{C},\boldsymbol{D},\boldsymbol{P})$	$(a,\boldsymbol{C},\boldsymbol{P})$	$(a,C,D,\boldsymbol{P})$
	$(\boldsymbol{C},\boldsymbol{D},P)$		$(0,\boldsymbol{C},\boldsymbol{D},P)$		$(a,\boldsymbol{C},\boldsymbol{D},P)$
	$(\boldsymbol{C},\boldsymbol{D},P)$		$(0,\boldsymbol{C},\boldsymbol{D},P)$		$(a,\boldsymbol{C},\boldsymbol{D},P)$
	$(C,\boldsymbol{D},P)$		$(0,C,\boldsymbol{D},P)$		$(a,C,\boldsymbol{D},P)$
	$(\boldsymbol{C},\boldsymbol{D},\boldsymbol{P})$		$(0,\boldsymbol{C},\boldsymbol{D},\boldsymbol{P})$		$(a,\boldsymbol{C},\boldsymbol{D},\boldsymbol{P})$

In this chapter we have investigated different models for real-time applications. They are listed in Table 2. Some normal names for those models are:

- (C,P), $(0,C,P)$: Liu & Layland Model
- $(\boldsymbol{C},P)$, $(0,\boldsymbol{C},P)$: Multiframe Model
- (C,D,P): Sporadic Model
- $(\boldsymbol{C},\boldsymbol{D},\boldsymbol{P})$: gmf(Generalized MultiFrame) Model
- $(a,\boldsymbol{C},P)$: Synchronous Multiframe Model
- (a,C,D,P): (A)synchronous Periodic Model

Among all models, the feasibility of only three models (C,P), $(0,C,P)$, and (a,C,P) can be decided by checking if $U \leq 1$.

All task models in the first four columns except (C,P) and $(0,C,P)$ can be tested with a pseudo-polynomial algorithm if l-MAD and the utilization factor is less than a constant $c < 1$. They are all in co-NP. However, no one knows if they are co-NP-complete. $(\boldsymbol{C},P)$ looks simpler than (C,D,P) as suggested by [5].

All task models in the sixth column are co-NP-complete in the strong sense.

In the fifth column, (a,C,P) has linear complexity. $(a,\boldsymbol{C},P)$, $(a,\boldsymbol{C},\boldsymbol{P})$, and $(a,C,\boldsymbol{P})$ are all co-NP-complete in the strong sense.

The synchronousness increases the chance of feasibility but also increases the complexity of checking. One possible solution is to use corresponding asynchronous models to false-negatively test feasibility.

References

1. Baruah, S.K., Chen, D., Gorinsky, S., Mok, A.K.: Generalized Multiframe Tasks. To appear in Real-Time Systems Journal
2. Baruah, S.K., Howell, R.R., Rosier, L.E.: Feasibility Problems for Recurring Tasks on One Processor. Theoretical Computer Science. **118(1)** (1993) 3–20
3. Baruah, S.K., Mok, A.K., Rosier, L.E.: Preemptively Scheduling Hard-Real-Time Sporadic Tasks on One Processor IEEE Real-Time Systems Symposium. December (1991)

4. Burns, A., Wellings, A.J.: Dual Priority Assignment: A Practical Method for Increasing Processor Utilization. Fifth Euromicro Workshop on Real-Time Systems. Oulu. (1993) 48–55

5. Chen, D., Baruah, S.K., Mok, A.K., Gorinsky, S.: Synchronous Multiframe Tasks. To be submitted. (1997)

6. Chetto, H., Chetto, M.: Some Results of the Earliest Deadline Scheduling Algorithm. IEEE Transactions on Software Engineering. 15(10) (1989)

7. Dertouzos, M.: Control Robotics: The Procedural Control of Physical Processes. Proceedings of the IFIP Congress. (1974) 807–813

8. Han, C.C., Lin, K.J.: Scheduling Distance-constraint Real-time Tasks. IEEE Real-Time Systems Symposium. December (1992) 814–826

9. Harbour, M.G., Klein, M.H., Lehoczky, J.P.: Timing Analysis for Fixed-Priority Scheduling of Hard Real-Time Systems. IEEE Transaction on Software Engineering. 20(1) (1994) 13–28

10. Lehoczky, J.P.: Fixed Priority Scheduling of Periodic Task Sets with Arbitrary Deadlines. IEEE Real-Time Systems Symposium. December (1990)

11. Lehoczky, J.P., Sha, L., Ding, Y.: The Rate Monotonic Scheduling Algorithm - Exact Characterization and Average Case Behavior. IEEE Real-Time Systems Symposium. December (1989)

12. Leung, J.Y.T., Whitehead, J.: On the Complexity of Fixed-Priority Scheduling of Periodic, Real-Time Tasks. Performance Evaluation. 2 (1982) 237–250

13. Liu, C.L., Layland, J.W.: Scheduling Algorithms for Multiprogramming in a Hard-Real-Time Environment. Journal of ACM. 20(1) (1973)

14. Mok, A.K.: Fundamental Design Problems of Distributed Systems for the Hard-Real-Time Environment. Ph.D. thesis. MIT. (1983)

15. Mok, A.K., Chen, D.: A Multiframe Model for Real-Time Tasks. IEEE Real-Time Systems Symposium. December (1996)

16. Ripoll, I., Crespo, A., Mok, A.K.: Improvement in Feasibility Testing for Real-Time Tasks. Real-Time Systems. 11 (1996) 19–39

17. Sha, L., Goodenough, J.B.: Real-Time Scheduling Theory and Ada. IEEE Computer. 23(4) (1990) 53–62

18. Sprunt, B., Sha, L., Lehoczky, J.P.: Aperiodic Task Scheduling for Hard Real-Time Systems. Real-Time Systems: The International Journal of Time-Critical Computing Systems. 1 (1989) 27–60

A Modular Approach for Programming Embedded Systems *

Shangping Ren and Gul A. Agha

Department of Computer Science
1304 W. Springfield Avenue
University of Illinois at Urbana-Champaign
Urbana, IL 61801, USA
{ren | agha}@cs.uiuc.edu
WWW home page: http://www-osl.cs.uiuc.edu

Abstract. A real-time system not only must generate correct results, it must generate those results *on time*. In embedded systems, these results include control signals, actuator reactions, etc. Traditional approaches to the design and implementation of real-time embedded applications first transfer timing requirements into machine dependent operations using low level programming languages, such as Assembly or C. By intermixing functional behavior with timing behavior, low-level programming languages reduce the modularity and reusability of software components. For example, it is difficult to incrementally modify either existing application code to meet new functionality requirements, or the scheduling to meet changing hardware or network requirements. In order to address these difficulties, we develop a high-level language approach to support a stronger separation of design concerns. We use *actors* as a formal model of computation in an embedded system and separate timing requirements from the actors' functional behavior. A new language construct, called RTsynchronizer, is introduced to express timing requirements. Our approach provides a formal basis for a component-based compositional software development methodology for distributed real-time and embedded systems.

Keywords

Actors, real-time systems, concurrency, distributed systems, embedded systems, scheduling, object-oriented programming

---

* The research described has been made possible in part by support from the Office of Naval Research (ONR contract numbers N00014-90-J-1899 and N00014-93-1-0273), by an Incentives for Excellence Award from the Digital Equipment Corporation Faculty Program, by Hitachi, by the National Science Foundation (NSF CCR 93-12495, NSF CCR-9523253 and NSF CCR-9619522); and by the Air Force Office of Scientific Research (AF DC 5-36128). The authors would like to thank Brian Nielsen, Daniel Sturman, Mark Astley, Nadeem Jamali, WooYoung Kim, Prasannaa Thati, James Waldby and other members of the Open Systems Laboratory who have provided helpful suggestions and discussion.

1 Introduction

A key reason for the success of object-oriented programming is that it provides a mechanism for separating *what* an object does (its abstraction or interface) from *how* it does it (its implementation or representation). Such separation can allow different objects with the same interface to be substituted for one another, thus promoting modularity and re-use. However, in sequential object-oriented programming, *when* actions are done is part of the representation of an object: an object calls procedures (or methods) in another object and waits for the actions of that call to terminate. In other words, sequential programming fixes the temporal order of events between objects. By contrast , the order of events between different objects may not be fixed in concurrent programming – such events are only partially ordered.

Embedded systems are inherently *asynchronous* and *distributed*. For example, in air traffic control systems, control towers at ground and control panels on planes operate concurrently and these two types of components are physically distributed. As such, *concurrency* is inherent in embedded systems. Distributed computing provides information and resource sharing among different applications and it can be used to ensure greater reliability and availability [41].

We model concurrent systems using *actors*. In its abstract form, the Actor model is a model of message passing between autonomous concurrent objects. The model is very general; actors may uniformly represent processes, controllers, cpu's, memory, sensors, actuators, etc. and the model may be used to represent the interaction between such entities. As in sequential object systems, one can substitute an actor for another if it has the same interface (message-passing or input-output) behavior. However, in the Actor model, each concurrent object (or actor) is asynchronous and carries out its activity potentially in parallel with another actor. Instead of waiting for the results of calling a procedure in another actor, an actor may proceed in parallel, if it chooses to. Thus control in actor systems is distributed between different actors, as many actors may be executing potentially in parallel. The maximum parallelism in an actor system is limited only by the number of actors in the system; the parallelism available in an actor system depends on the number of actors that have a message to process at a given time. Both actors and messages may be dynamically created.

The processing of a message by an actor is defined as an *event*. Events at an actor are linearly ordered; events between actors form a partial order corresponding to the relation between the event causing a message to be sent and the event corresponding to the receipt of the message. A message sent will be asynchronously delivered after some arbitrary but finite time. The temporal order of actions in an actor system is limited only by causal relations in a computation. There is no unique global order of events in an actor system, and no corresponding global clock.

Embedded systems pose a number of problems for the standard actor model, as we have defined above. First, real-time requirements are typically expressed in terms of a global clock which is assumed to be unique and shared between different actors. Second, in a concurrent system with real-time constraints, *when* events are carried out is critical. Often there is a timing constraint between two different events in a system, e.g. a reaction event must happen within a certain fixed time interval after another event has occurred. Such constraints imply that events in a real-time actor system cannot simply be modeled as asynchronous events.

An important concern is the impact of real-time constraints on the program development methodology. As in the sequential object model, the separation of the interface of an actor from its representation allows modular decomposition of the state of a system and the re-use of its components. However, if real-time constraints are expressed in terms of the representation of individual actors rather than their interface, actors cannot be substituted based on their common interface. In particular, if a pairwise real-time constraint is decomposed in terms of individual actor behavior, the code for such actors cannot be reused except in the context of a similarly constrained pairwise interaction.

Another way to understand the requirements of modular real-time programming is as follows. Real-time constraints involve *how long* some actions take; it is a concern that is orthogonal to how the action is computed. In order to preserve modularity in system software, we want to express *how long* in terms of *what* rather than in terms of *how*.

Embedded systems typically use low level programming languages, such as Assembly and C. The timing constraints intermix with the functional requirements. Using low level programming languages limits the reusability of both the functional code as well as the timing constraint specification. We develop a new programming methodology for distributed real-time systems. Our paradigm has a number of advantages. First, it allows concurrent object oriented programming languages to be used to code an application's functionality. Second, it allows the timing requirements to specified separately from the functional specifications. Such separation allows testing the consistency of timing requirements at the level of the source code. Finally, the abstract specification of the timing properties leaves the implementation free to use the best scheduling strategies based on the hardware and operating system behavior.

2 Separating Design Concerns

In distributed computing, individual components (objects) must exchange information and coordinate with each other to achieve integrated system goals. More specifically, in distributed real-time computing, individual components must not only interact with each other, but must also do so within given timing constraints. As pointed out by Hoogeboom and Halang [24], the problem of complex coordination between asynchronous components cannot be solved in its full generality by scheduling theory [22]. We argue that high level support for timing constraints on object synchronization should be provided to simplify the development of distributed real-time applications.

Consider an extension to the traditional producer/consumer problem — namely, the *time-bounded producer/consumer* problem. Assume that there is one producer and one consumer. The producer and the consumer have a common shared buffer. The producer put's products into the buffer, while the consumer get's products from the buffer. The shared buffer is bounded. In addition, each product must be kept inside the buffer for a minimum amount of time d1, and not longer than a maximum amount of time d2.

Thus the product should be in the buffer for an interval of time [d1, d2] after it is produced and before the consumer is allowed to consume it. This simple example involves two concerns, namely, the correctness of underlying computation for both the producer and the consumer, and the correctness of their timing behavior. We would like the timing specification not to require internal modification of either the producer's or the consumer's representation; in other words, it should be possible to reuse the original producer/consumer program in the real-time environment.

We separate the two different concerns — functional correctness and timing correctness — by specifying the timing requirements over a group of actors independently of the representation of the actors' behaviors. Figure 1 graphically illustrates the separation. Separation of timing constraints provides a basis for detecting inconsistent timing constraints at the source code level. It also allows schedulers to be specified independently of the application code; the schedulers can then be customized for specific processors and networks and changed to meet new application requirements.

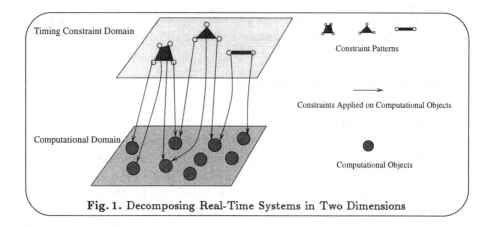

Fig. 1. Decomposing Real-Time Systems in Two Dimensions

2.1 Actor Model

The Actor model, developed by Hewitt [23] and Agha [2, 6, 7], provides a uniform abstract representation of distributed systems. Actors are encapsulated concurrent objects that interact with each other by sending buffered, asynchronous messages.

The Actor model is an abstract, language independent model of distributed computing based on partially ordered events. For our purposes, an event is discrete and instantaneous. An *actor* is a conceptual point in space on which events are 'localized'; corresponding to each actor is a set of linearly ordered events. We call this linear order the *arrival order* of events on that actor. The arrival order has an origin called the *creation event*. Intuitively, that is the point at which the actor is created. An event causes two types of effects: an internal change in the actor's behavior (which may affect how it responds to future events) and events at other actors. The latter represents events that change the behavior of other existing actors and/or creation events (corresponding to the creation of new actors).

Besides internal (sequential) operations, each actor has the following three primitive operations (as shown in Figure 2):

- **send** (a, v) sends a message to address a with contents v.
- **create** $b(v)$ creates a new actor with behavior b and initial parameter v; **create** returns a unique *aid* (actor id) of the newly created actor.
- **ready**(s) indicates that the actor has finished processing its current messages and is now ready to process another one with new behavior s.

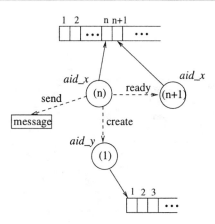

Fig. 2. Three Primitive Operations: An actor has a unique *aid*, and may perform 3 primitive operations upon receiving a message. Message processing is non-preemptive. $(n + 1)$ indicates the actor behavior when processing the $n + 1^{th}$ message

Actors extend the concept of objects to concurrent computation. Each actor potentially executes in parallel with other actors. Only the actor's own methods may operate on or change its local state. Actors communicate with each other by sending asynchronous messages. Graphically, an actor system may be illustrated as in Figure 3.

Each actor has a unique identification name (*aid*, actor id) which other actors can use to send it messages. Actors are reactive entities in that they start executing their methods only in response to messages received. Message passing in the Actor model is asynchronous and point-to-point. Specifically, the standard model of message passing in actors has the following characteristics:

1. an actor can send messages to only actors it knows the *aid* of; however, an actor's *aid* may be communicated in messages, hence allowing dynamic reconfiguration of interconnection topology;
2. sending a message is a non-blocking operation: the sender does not wait for a reply from the receiver, instead it immediately resumes its computation;
3. message processing at each actor is atomic and non-preemptive: once an actor begins executing a method, it continues non-preemptively until its completion;

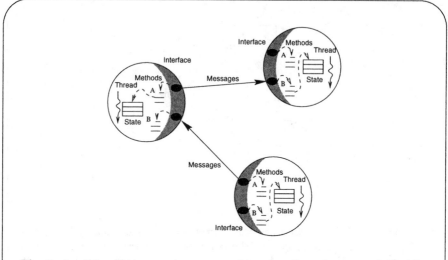

Fig. 3. An Actor System: actors encapsulate threads and states; the public methods that operate on the states comprise their interfaces.

4. messages sent but not yet processed by the receiver are (conceptually) buffered in the receiver's mailbox until they are picked up for processing by the receiver;

5. the system possesses a weak fairness property, i.e., messages sent out are guaranteed to eventually reach their destination and be processed but may be subject to arbitrary communication and scheduling delays. Thus message delivery order is nevertheless not guaranteed: messages may be received in some order that is different from the order in which they are sent;

6. message deliveries are the only observable events in actor systems.

Other forms of message passing are defined in terms of this basic mechanism (e.g. see [3, 5, 8]). Actor languages typically provide a wide variety of communication abstractions.

We will not be concerned with an actor's internal behavior. Of particular interest to us is the fact that events on different actors may be related by a partial order corresponding to a *causality relation*. It is important to observe that actors are asynchronous, thus there may be an arbitrary delay between causally connected events. A *pending event* is an event whose antecedent event has occurred but the consequent has not. In a completed computation, there are no pending events.

An actor computation unfolds as some pending events are nondeterministically realized. As a concrete representation, we identify events with the acceptance of a message at an actor. Thus, all interaction in this concrete representation is through sending and receiving messages. Other types of events are possible but they do not affect the formalism as long as causality and arrival orders are obeyed.

Figure 4 illustrates an event diagram which provides a pictorial representation of an actor computation. Figure 5 shows two possible unfoldings of the same computation.

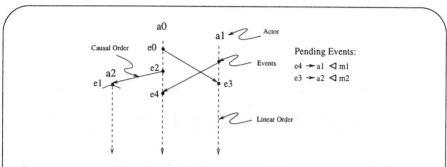

Fig. 4. Events, Orderings and Pending Events. Message $m1$ to actor $a1$ caused by event $e4$ ($e4 : a1 \Leftarrow m1$), and message $m2$ to actor $a2$ caused by $e3$ ($e3 : a2 \Leftarrow m2$) are pending.

The transitive closure of the causality relation and all the arrival orders is called the *combined order*. It is possible to map events to a global time (possibly corresponding to the real numbers) so that the mapping preserves the combined order. Of course, such a global time mapping is not unique — there could be many possible linear representations which would be consistent with the combined order of events since the combined order is only a partial order [14]. We will discuss the relation between the notion of realizability in global time and the concept of a global clock in more detail below (section 2.2).

The advantage of the Actor model is that it not only provides a uniform view of distributed computation units, but also provides scalability as a by-product of allowing only message passing as the inter-object interaction mechanisms. In addition, the asynchronous communication model does not infringe upon the concurrency inherent in applications.

In the Actor model, the function of each actor is to carry out a computation. We will call such actors *base actors*. It may be observed that the notions of time and timing constraints between a group of base actors

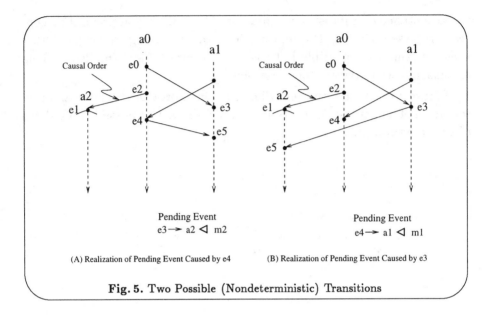

(A) Realization of Pending Event Caused by e4   (B) Realization of Pending Event Caused by e3

Fig. 5. Two Possible (Nondeterministic) Transitions

is not captured in actor systems. We extend the base Actor model by introducing a notion of real-time into the model.

2.2 Global Time and Timing Constraints

In distributed asynchronous systems, a wide range of temporal properties of a system can be interpreted in terms of a relation "$\prec$" (*precedes* or *happens before*) over the events of the system. Such a relation should be a strict (i.e. irreflexive) partial order. A complement relation to the *precedence* relation is *concurrency*, or simultaneity ($\sim$), which is defined as:

$$e \sim e' \Leftrightarrow \neg(e \prec e') \wedge \neg(e' \prec e).$$

Lamport's [29] causality effects is one way of viewing the *precedes* relation. That is, $e \prec e'$ means that it is possible for event e to causally affect event e'; two events are concurrent if neither can causally affect the other. However, the lack of a causal connection in the application level functionality is inadequate for describing some timing properties in hard real-time systems. To illustrate this inadequacy, consider two processes p_1 and p_2 running on different processors. When the processes finish, they will send out *finish* signals, s_1 and s_2, respectively. These two processes are not causally related. But in a real-time system we may want to constrain the generation of each signal to a specific order. However, according to the 'causality' view of the original computation, we can only conclude that

s_1 and s_2 finish in some indeterminate order, irrespective of the speeds of the processors.

Another way to obtain precedence relations over events is by using a global time domain to mark events as *instants* in the domain. The sufficient condition for $e \prec e'$ is that e happens before e' with respect to the mapping of the events in the global time domain. However, e *happens before* e' is not a necessary condition since the ordering in global time also depends on the granularity of the global time domain in which the timing observations are recorded. Nevertheless, explicit time using an appropriately chosen domain may be useful (as in the previous example, it may be possible to time s_1 and s_2 and determine which finishes first).

Since the precedence relation on a set of events may not be determinate in some time domains, is there a *universal* or global time domain such that any precedence relation on events can be given an *equivalent* characterization in terms of that domain? Clinger [14] has shown that a non-unique global time is realizable:

Axiom of Realizability *There exists a one-to-one mapping g from the events E into a set of real numbers, which preserves the combined ordering, such that the range of g does not contain any cluster points.*

Note that the absence of cluster points prevents an infinite number of events from happening in a finite amount of time.

We pick *real-time* as a unique global reference time, and extend the actor model to include a time dimension with the following assumptions. First, each actor a has its own local clock C_a with known bounded rate of drift $\rho \geq 0$ with respect to real-time. That is, for all a and all $t > t'$,

$$(1 + \rho)^{-1} \leq \frac{C_a(t) - C_a(t')}{t - t'} \leq (1 + \rho)$$

where $C_a(t)$ is the reading of C_a at real-time t. Additionally, each local clock is *approximately synchronized* with every other, i.e., there exists an ϵ such that for all t and any actors a and b, $|C_a(t) - C_b(t)| \leq \epsilon$. Second, method execution on each actor is atomic and non-preemptive. Finally, method execution time is insignificant compared to communication and scheduling overheads. Because the behavior of an actor in response to a given message is deterministic, the last assumption can in fact be relaxed.

To summarize, global clock time is one of the valid global time maps which preserves the partial combined ordering between events. A total global quantitative *precedence relation* ($\prec$) among events may be defined as follows:

Definition 1 (Precedence Relation ($\prec$))
For any two events e_1 and e_2 in a system with a global clock, if e_1 happens at time t_1, and e_2 happens at time t_2, with respect to the global clock, then $e_1 \prec e_2$ iff $t_2 = t_1 + d$, where t_1, t_2 and $d \in R^+$, R^+ is non-negative real numbers.

In distributed systems, the global quantitative precedence relation may be approximated by using a common clock, provided the granularity of observation is sufficiently coarse. For real-time applications, not only are the causal orders obeyed, but also some additional quantitative timing requirements between events must be met. Two types of real-time requirements are *relative time* and *absolute time* constraints. As defined in [24], a relative time constraint requires that an event or action must occur within a given interval of time relative to the occurrence of another event; whereas an absolute time constraint specifies the system behavior for given points in time, with accuracy relative to a chosen granularity. We extend the actor model to fix a unique global clock time called `real time`, and define a *timing constraint* (or just constraint) between events.

In order to capture the history of computation in an actor system that is significant for given real-time constraints, we encode the relevant history in the state of an object called *RTsynchronizer*. An RTsynchronizer also contains a set of constraints that are expressed in terms of its state. When triggered, these constraints constrain the scheduling of a group of actors. While different RTsynchronizers enforce their constraints conjunctively, different constraints may be conjunctively or disjunctively connected within an RTsynchronizer. Note that the actors affected by different RTsynchronizers may overlap. The next section discusses RTsynchronizers in detail.

2.3 RTsynchronizers

We first use a simple example to give an intuitive feeling about the underlying function of RTsynchronizers in real-time applications. Consider a pizza production line. A pizza maker puts an unbaked pizza into the baking line, which has a limited length; and a server takes it out within a certain amount of time: not too early nor too late!

The pizza maker and the pizza server can be modeled as two autonomous actors. Their functional behaviors are *to make a pizza and put it in the baking oven*, and *to take the pizza out and serve it to customers*, respectively. How long the baking line is and how long the pizza should be baked is a different concern than how the pizza is made, or how the pizza is taken out and served. By how we mean the sequence of actions required to make the pizza. Notice that the baking time may change with the oven temperature and conditions, independent of how the pizza is put together. Another characteristic of the problem is that the two actors work independently, but at the same time, because of the baking line length and baking time constraints, the maker and server must cooperate with each other to achieve a profitable pizza business. The cooperation is another aspect of the integrated system, which can be captured by a different abstraction. The role of RTsynchronizers is to specify such cooperation and ensure that the specified constraints are met by the independent actors.

This real life example is an instance of the *time-bounded producer/ consumer problem* mentioned earlier. In the example, the producer's put and the consumer's get behaviors need to be both qualitatively and quantitatively synchronized: qualitatively, if the buffer is full, put is not allowed and similarly, if the buffer is empty, get is not allowed; quantitatively, if put takes place at time t, get should take place in some time interval [t + d1, t + d2]. Constraints are in general orthogonal and external to objects' functionalities. They are based on the action names, or action *patterns*, but do not interfere with the details of the execution of actions. The constraints exist in a context furnished by RTsynchronizers. The buffer size, the time duration t, etc., comprise the context for the constraints in the time-bounded buffer example. Figure 6 illustrates the specification of the producer and the consumer, and the role of RTsynchronizers.

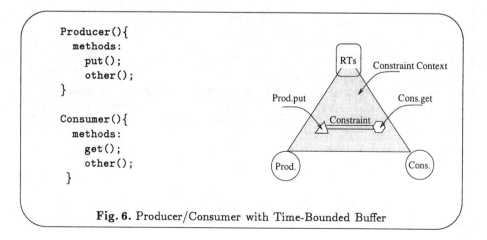

Fig. 6. Producer/Consumer with Time-Bounded Buffer

RTsynchronizers provide such a structure for expressing coordination constraints based on the interface of actors, but independent of how an actor's computation proceeds, and to ensure that such constraints among a group of individual actors are met. More generally, an RTsynchronizer provides an abstraction for programming an environmen. .n which computational objects operate. Within such an environment, computational objects must obey certain rules enforced by their environment. For real-time applications, computational objects carry out their computation in such an environment where timeliness is the key requirement.

Because RTsynchronizers affect how actors are scheduled, the behavior of an actor is affected by the existence of coordinating RTsynchronizers. The messages flowing to actors are observable by an RTsynchronizer that is coordinating the members of a group. An RTsynchronizer may change its own state upon observing certain messages. Figure 7 illustrates the relation between RTsynchronizers and the base actors they coordinate.

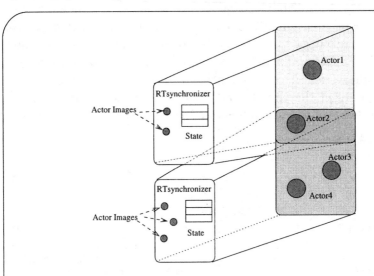

Fig. 7. Relation between Actors and RTsynchronizers: groups of actors are coordinated by RTsynchronizers; each RTsynchronizer has its coordinating actors' images, representing the actors' observable behavior; different RTsynchronizers may overlap over their coordinating actors.

Our programming methodology separates the specification of real-time systems as follows:

- represent the underlying functional computation (i.e. a computation with its timing requirements lifted) in terms of (base) actors.
- embed the base actors in an environment constrained by RTsynchronizers, to achieve the required timeliness.

A precondition for this approach to be correct is that the RTsynchronizers do not "destructively" interfere with a well-behaved underlying computation. Recall that base actors that carry out the logical computation are reactive objects: they act only upon receiving messages. In other words, no computation path is added by an RTsynchronizer. The implication of this property is that if RTsynchronizers do not send out messages to (base) actors, the underlying computation will retain its safety properties in the presence of RTsynchronizers; only the scheduling of when computational objects should act will be affected (some previously legal paths will be pruned from the nondeterministic computation tree).

To be more specific, let us consider the event diagram given in Figure 4 with its real-time extension, i.e. a global time is added into the diagram as shown in Figure 8.

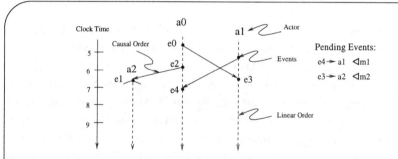

Fig. 8. Events, Orderings and Pending Events. Message $m1$ to actor $a1$ caused by event $e4$ ($e4 : a1 \Leftarrow m1$), and message $m2$ to actor $a2$ caused by $e3$ ($e3 : a2 \Leftarrow m2$) are pending.

Without the presence of RTsynchronizer, there are two possible (non-deterministic) transitions indicating whether message $m1$ or message $m2$ is delivered first. However, if there exists an RTsynchronizer which has two constraints, say, $5 \leq T(e5) \leq 10$ and $10 \leq T(e6) \leq 20$, where $e5 \equiv a1 \lhd m1$ and $e6 \equiv a2 \lhd m2$, the existence of the RTsynchronizer subsumes the non-deterministic choice between the two possible orders (as repeated in Figure 9) and only allows the one in which $e5$ precedes $e6$. Hence at a current global time of 7, only $e5$ is possible.

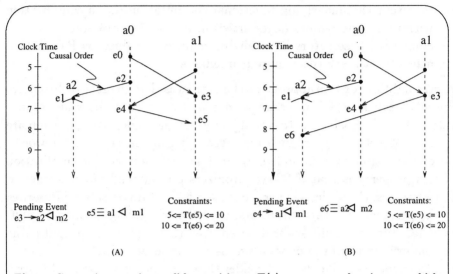

Fig. 9. Constraint restricts valid transitions. T(e) represents the time at which event e occurs. (A) Valid realization of event e5. (B) Constraint on e6 has been violated.

In accordance with this observation, we require that RTsynchronizers, as special actors, are not allowed to send messages. Moreover, since the existence of RTsynchronizers is transparent to base actors, no messages can be addressed to RTsynchronizers by such actors. Hence, RTsynchronizers do not receive messages either. However, they may change their states by observing certain messages being delivered at the (base) actors that they are coordinating. These restrictions on RTsynchronizers ensure that RTsynchronizers do not interfere with the safety properties of the underlying computations.

The design concerns can be divided into the three different views illustrated in Figure 7:

- The base actors' point of view.
- The RTsynchronizer's point of view.
- The integrated system's point of view.

From a base actor's point of view, the existence of RTsynchronizers should be *transparent*. In other words, RTsynchronizers should be able to enforce constraints without communicating with the constrained actors. Such transparency not only enables reuse of the base actors, but also allows separation of RTsynchronizers from constrained actors. Separating real-time constraints from the representation of actors provides a more clean and intuitive abstraction for reasoning about such constraints.

From the RTsynchronizer point of view, RTsynchronizers should rely only on actors' interfaces. As noted, the internal representation of actors is opaque to RTsynchronizers. Using actor interfaces as the connection boundary between base actors and RTsynchronizers, sustains object encapsulation and provides modularity and reusability of both RTsynchronizers and actors: changing the internal representation of the actors will not affect RTsynchronizers; the same RTsynchronizer can apply to different actors that have the same interfaces.

From the integrated system's point of view, the constraints specified by RTsynchronizers are *declarative* and independent of system architectures, such as processor speeds, node connections, etc. In addition, RTsynchronizers may overlap as shown in Figure 7 and should be composable. Composability enables decomposing complex constraints into simple and separately specified entities.

In order to ensure that timing constraints are met, RTsynchronizers need a reliable source of sufficiently accurate time signals. We assume that a global clock is part of an RTsynchronizer's state. In other words, real time is a parameter to each "observation" of an RTsynchronizer: an RTsynchronizer can read the global clock.

3   Representing RTsynchronizers

An RTsynchronizer is similar to an ordinary actor in that it has a mutable state and can be created dynamically. However, unlike ordinary actors, an RTsynchronizer does not send or receive messages. Rather, it provides a declarative constraint specification between certain message deliveries in a group of base actors. In addition, it changes its state by observing some events at the actors it constrains; in contrast, actors change their states upon receiving messages.

An RTsynchronizer is created by instantiating a *template* using constrained actors' unique names and other values for template variables. For example,

new MyRTS (**actor:**aid1, aid2, aid3; **int:** d1, d2)

creates a new RTsynchronizer whose behavior is given by MyRTS which constrains certain message deliveries at actors aid1, aid2, and aid3; d1 and d2 are values for the initial binding of local variables. The behaviors of RTsynchronizers (such as the one bound to the name MyRTS above) are specified by a template. The template variables, such as d1 and d2 in the above example, are mutable.

```
RTsynchronizer MyRTS(actor actor1, actor2, actor3; int v1, v2) {
  Declare
    /* declare and initialize local variables; */

  Constrain
    constraint_1;
    ...;
    constraint_n;

  Update
    pattern : state_variable = new_value;
    ...;
    pattern : state_variable = new_value;
    boolean_exp      : state_variable = new_value;
}
```

Fig. 10. RTsynchronizer Template

The internal structure of a template for RTsynchronizers has, in general, three sections: Declare, Constrain and Update, which abstract the three aspects of an RTsynchronizer: an RTsynchronizer has state; its functionality is to enforce a set of declaratively specified constraints on its base actors; and an RTsynchronizer changes its state upon observing certain events on controlled actors.

RTsynchronizer state variables are declared in the same manner as in ordinary objects: typeName varName [= iniValue], where the initial values are optional in the declaration. In other words, state variables may obtain initial values at a later time. However, uninitialized variables may not be used in expressions.

In the following subsection, we discuss the remaining two components of RTsynchronizers, namely, Constrain and Update, in detail.

3.1 Specifying Constraints

Constraints in RTsynchronizers are declarative assertions about the quantitative precedence relation among observable events at constrained objects. Recall that in the Actor model, an observable event is defined as a message delivery at the message target actor (see Section 2). Hence, events are independent of an actor's internal computation, and may be identified by the messages corresponding to an actor invocation. However, messages are dynamically created (and consumable) entities. Therefore, we need a syntactic category to express relations between types of messages. *Message patterns* may be used for this purpose [4, 19, 35].

Definition 2 (Message Patterns)
A message pattern is a 3-tuple

```
((sender, seqNo), receiver.c(parms)){where b_exp}
```

where (sender, seqNo) is message tag; c(parms) represents message: c is the method name, and parms are the values used for arguments in a message. The boolean expression b_exp is a side-effect free predicate over the parameters of the message and variables in the lexical scope.

Note that the synchronizer may not refer to the state variables in base actors. If the b_exp is not specified, it is assumed to be true. A message m is indicated by a pattern p if the following four conditions hold:

1. m's sender is the actor specified in the pattern-tuple as sender;
2. m is the seqNo message sent by the actor sender (seqNo is called the message's *sequence number*);
3. m's target is the actor specified in the pattern-quadruple as receiver;
4. the values transmitted in m, together with current enclosing RTsynchronizer state, satisfy the boolean expression b_exp.

Sender and seqNo are message tags, which we assume are supplied by the run time system. They may be transparent to an application programmer; actors implementing the functional behavior do not see this extra system level information. Sender and sequence numbers can be useful for specifying timing constraints on cyclic behavior. The b_exp may reference the state variables of the enclosing RTsynchronizer in which the pattern is specified, as well as values transmitted by the message.

A message may be uniquely specified by a pattern or it may contain certain wildcards. We use * to match *any sender*, or sequence number (seqNo), i.e. a * could occur in either or both of these positions. In this case, a pattern may identify more than one message. However, the target actor name is mandatory. When the sender and the message sequence number are not important, they need not be specified. Thus receiver.c(parms) is equivalent to:

```
((*,*), receiver.c(parms)) where True.
```

In the basic Actor model, messages are guaranteed to be delivered. When a message is delivered, it gets consumed. Thus, for each message there is one and only one corresponding event. Patterns identify messages, and hence identify events because of the 1-to-1 relationship between messages and events. The time when an event happens may be denoted by the pattern that identifies the specific message whose receipt triggers the event.

Conceptually, each constraint ties two different types of events into an observation pair: *triggering* event and *consequent* event. These two events need not have logical causal relations. But observationally, the occurrence of a triggering event *causes* the *consequent* event to be constrained to some time span. We express a constraint using the following syntax:

$$\{\texttt{pattern1} \rightarrow \} \texttt{ pattern2 in timeInterval}$$

The constraint asserts that upon the occurrence of an event e_1 satisfying `pattern1`, an event e_2 satisfying `pattern2` must happen in the time frame `timeInterval`, provided that `b_exp` evaluates to True. We say that an event e_1 creates the expectation of event e_2 satisfying `pattern2`. The `timeInterval` is a relative time duration: the starting point of such interval is relative to the time when `event1` occurred. A `timeInterval` [d1, d2] is a valid time interval if and only if d1, d2 $\in R^+$, and d1 $\leq$ d2. As usual [d1, d2] denotes a closed interval while (d1, d2) denotes an open interval. A consequent event that has been triggered is called an *expectation* since its realization is expected by the constraint. The same event may be used to satisfy two expectations triggered by different events satisfying the same pattern if a message satisfies the patterns instantiated by both. We do not write `pattern1` where unnecessary. Specifically, to specify absolute time, we assume a premieval event which occurs at time 0. However, we do not use a pattern to specify the premieval event; instead we simply skip the precondition.

Note that a message satisfying a triggering pattern may not be constrained in time; however, the consequence of delivering such a message is that another message is constrained in a time frame relative to the time when this message is delivered.

Definition 3 (Patterns)

A pattern is either a message pattern or a boolean expression over the local variables representing the state of a synchronizer.

Some constraints may be triggered by local state change. If we consider change in the clock time as a message, all state change in an RT-synchronizer is the result of observing either time change or some base level messages. Thus message patterns are logically sufficient to capture actions triggered by local state changes. However, it is convenient to use a state change pattern in atleast two cases:

- The state change pattern is triggered by incremental changes to the RTsynchronizer state, i.e., caused by more than one message.
- The same constraint may be generated by several message patterns. In this case, an RTsynchronizer state pattern can serve as a useful short hand.

3.2 Updating RTsynchronizer States

An RTsynchronizer encapsulates a local state which may be changed when the RTsynchronizer observes certain events. The Update section of an RTsynchronizer specifies when and how the RTsynchronizer mutates its local state. More specifically, for the update constraint:

$$\text{ptrn} \rightarrow \text{state\_var} = \text{new\_value}$$

the delivery of a message or entering a local state of the RTsynchronizer indicated by ptrn causes the state_var to assume the new value. Note that the state change and the delivery of the message of pattern ptrn happen atomically in the sense that no intermediate states between the delivery of the message and the state transformation are observable.

Since global clock time is part of an RTsynchronizer's implicit state, absolute time progression causes implicit state changes, and also may cause explicit state variables to assume new values. For example, with a constraint:

$$\text{cTime()} == 5 \rightarrow \text{timeUp} = \text{true},$$

the implicit RTsynchronizer state time change causes the explicit state variable timeUp to assume the value true. However, explicit state change caused by the progression of time does not happen until RTsynchronizer evaluates the validity of delivering constrained messages (to ensure state consistency through mutual exclusion).

To further understand the effects of an RTsynchronizer's implicit state change, namely clock variable change, consider an automatic home heating system in which the heater is turned on only after 6 O'clock in the morning. We use an actor Heater to model the heating system. When Heater is created, it is sent with an initial message start. One way to program the time setting is as follows:

```
RTsynchronizer RTheater(actor Heater; real t) {
  Declare
    Boolean canStart? = 0;
  Constrain
    (Heater.start() where canStart? == 0) in [0, inf);
  Update
    currentTime() >= t → canStart? = 1;
}
```

Fig. 11. A Heating System

Initially, `canStart?` is set to 0 (`false`) and the constraint disables the `start` message. When the global time (reflected by RTsynchronizer's implicit state `cTime()`) progresses silently to the point `t`, the explicit state variable `canStart?` is changed. An RTheater may be created by instantiating `t` to 0600.

This example demonstrates how clock time change may affect explicit state change and further affect system evolution.

In a complex system, there may be more than one RTsynchronizer. As Figure 7 illustrates, the control of RTsynchronizers may conjunctively overlap. Moreover, different RTsynchronizers may have overlapping constraint patterns. Thus, a message satisfying a pattern may be constrained by multiple RTsynchronizers and its delivery may cause multiple RTsynchronizers to change state. However, all the state changes and the delivery of the causal message are atomic and indivisible. It is worth noticing that within an RTsynchronizer, generating constraints on the consequent events and updating RTsynchronizers' state variables is serializable, and follows the static scoping rule and specification order.

4 Detecting Infeasible Timing Constraints

The consistency of timing constraints is a necessary condition for scheduling physical resources, such as processors and network, or logical resources, such as channels, threads, etc. An *infeasible timing constraint specification* is a specification that cannot be realized in a global time regardless of the physical and logical resources. In its full generality, the problem of finding a schedule to satisfy a given set of timing constraints is NP-hard [44]. However, if the constraint expression is in an appropriate form, distinguishing infeasible constraint sets can be done in polynomial time.

Schedulability analysis is traditionally done at a late stage; it is based on compiled code and is therefore machine dependent. On the other hand, for complex real-time systems which may have hundreds of constraints, it is useful to provide application programmers early feedback about the feasibility of the high-level timing requirements. We use pre-processing to detect infeasible timing constraint specifications; such detection allows software designers to make early corrections. An infeasible timing requirement implies that the specification cannot be met regardless of the scheduling strategy or architecture used.

It is important to emphasize the limitations of detecting such infeasibility. These include:

- there may be no schedule on a given architecture which satisfies the timing requirements, even if a timing specification is not infeasible.
- even if a schedule exists, one may not be found in real-time. Recall that the timing constraints may be dynamically triggered, The situation is similar to programs with a recursive construct: a program may be semantically correct, but fail at run-time because of insufficient memory on a given architecture.
- The fact that timing constraints are not infeasible does *not* guarantee that when such constraints are applied to a particular actors system, the actor system will in fact generate the messages that are needed to satisfy the constraints. While pre-processing checks to see the consistency of expectations, it cannot guarantee that a events satisfying a given pattern will be activated. In order to determine if such activation occurs, a message flow analysis of the actor program is required.

For the purposes of our analysis, we will assume that RTsynchronizers are not created dynamically. If RTsynchronizers were to be created dynamically, the current analysis technique would need to be extended to do incremental "pre-processing."

4.1 Mapping Constraints into Linear Inequalities

Recall that each constraint is of the form p1 $\rightarrow$ p2 in [d1, d2], where p1 and p2 are message patterns. The semantic meaning of A $\rightarrow$ B in [d1, d2] is that when a message of pattern A is delivered at the message's destination object, it requires a message of pattern B to be delivered (assuming such a message is in the system) in the time interval [d1, d2] relative to the time when A happened. Using t_a and t_b, respectively, to represent the time when A and B happen, the above constraint is denoted as two inequalities:

$$\begin{cases} t_a - t_b \leq -d1; \\ t_b - t_a \leq d2 \end{cases} \tag{1}$$

Theorem 1 *The assertion of p1 → p2 in [d1, d2] is equivalent to the linear inequalities system (1) in that the assertion is feasible if and only if the inequalities (1) have at least one set of solutions.*

Note that (1) is a canonical form of inequality we will use in later stages. The proof of the theorem is straightforward. But the conclusion serves as the basis for infeasibility detection: specifically, the methods used to solve linear inequality systems may be applied in deciding if a real-time constraint specification is feasible.

We use a simple example to show how pre-processing may help us detect inconsistent timing constraints. Once again, consider the time-bounded producer/consumer example. Assume that the Producer and the Consumer are started by another object Starter with the following constraints: the Producer must start its put 5 time units after the Starter sends out the start signal; the Consumer must start its get within 10 time units after the Starter sends out the start signal. In addition, every item the Producer puts in the buffer, must be kept in the buffer for at least 10 time units. These timing requirements are enforced by TBBuffer2 as shown in Figure 12.

```
RTsynchronizer TBBuffer2(int size; actor Starter, Producer,
                                            Consumer){
  Declare
    int count = 0;
  Constrain
    (Consumer.get() where count == 0) in [0, inf);
    (Producer.put() where count == size) in [0, inf);
    Starter.start() → Producer.put() in [5, inf);
    Starter.start() → Consumer.get() in [0, 10);
    Producer.put(x) → (Consumer.get(y) where x==y) in [10, inf)
  Update
    Producer.put() → count ++;
    Consumer.get() → : count --;
}
```

Fig. 12. Time Bounded Buffer

For simplicity, we use $x1$, $x2$ and $x3$, respectively to denote the time when Starter.start(), Producer.put(), and Consumer.get() occur.

The above constraints may be expressed in the set of linear inequalities as shown in Figure 13. The corresponding constraint graph indicates that there exists a negative-weight cycle, hence the timing constraint specification is not realizable on any architecture.

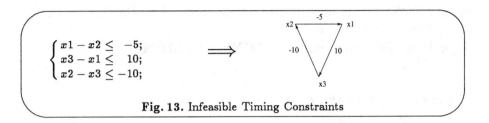

Fig. 13. Infeasible Timing Constraints

4.2 Transforming MCNF of Constraint Assertions into MDNF

Recall that different constraints in an RTsynchronizer, as well as different constraints in separate RTsynchronizers, work conjunctively. However, an individual constraint may itself be a disjunction of constraints. Hence the union of constraint assertions in a system is in monotone conjunctive normal form:

$$(C_{11} \vee \cdots \vee C_{1n}) \wedge \cdots \wedge (C_{m1} \vee \cdots \vee C_{mk}),$$

where the disjunct is within one constraint and the conjunct is between constraints in an RTsynchronizer (either on the same RTsynchronizer or on different RTsynchronizers).

To give a simple example, assume that we have two RTsynchronizers: rtsyn1 and rtsyn2 as follows:

```
rtsyn1(){                        rtsyn2(){
    ...;                             ...;
    Constraint:                      Constraint:
        p1 → p2 in [d1, d2] ||           p1 → p3 in [d1, d2]
        p3 → p4 in [d3, d4];             /* denoted as D */
        /* denoted as A || B */      }
        p5 → p6 in [d5, d6];
        /* denoted as C */
}
```

These constraint assertions may be specified as:

$$(A \vee B) \wedge (C) \wedge (D)$$

A polynomial algorithm exists to convert constraints in MCNF (such as the one above) into a monotone disjunctive normal form (MDNF), which can then be directly transformed into a system of linear inequalities. Given constraints in a monotone conjunctive normal form, we can use an approach similar to the naive polynomial multiplication method to expand MCNF into monotone disjunctive normal form (MDNF) as shown in the following algorithm:

Algorithm for transforming MCNF into MDNF

```
MCNF-to-MDNF(⋀ⁿᵢ₌₁ Cᵢ){
    if n > 1 then {
        C = expand(C₁, C₂);
        return MCNF-to-MDNF(C ∧ (⋀ⁿ⁻²ᵢ₌₁ Cᵢ₊₂))};
    else
        return Cₙ
}
```

Once it is in disjunctive normal form, each component in our context can be transformed into a linear inequality system. This allows the Bellman-Ford Algorithm to be used to decide if the linear inequality system has a solution. In the next subsection, we will first discuss how to build the inequality systems from the disjunctive normal form of constraint assertions written in our language specification constructs and then apply the Bellman-Ford algorithm. Finally, we will discuss the complexity of the pre-processing algorithm.

4.3 Generating Time Constraint Graphs and the Bellman-Ford Algorithm

Applying Theorem 1, each conjunction of constraint assertions may be mapped to a set of linear inequalities 2:

$$\begin{cases} x_1 - x_2 \le d_1; \\ x_i - x_j \le d_k; \\ \cdots \\ x_m - x_n \le d_p; \end{cases} \tag{2}$$

Given such a constraint system, we can construct a corresponding *constraint graph* $G = (V, E)$, where

$$V = \{v_0, v_1, \cdots, v_n\}$$

and

$$E = \{(v_i, v_j) : x_j - x_i \le d_k \text{ is a constraint}\} \cup \{(v_0, v_1), (v_0, v_2), \cdots, (v_0, v_n)\}$$

Each vertex v_i in the graph, for $i = 1, 2, \cdots, n$, corresponds to one of the n unknown variables x_i; each directed edge in the graph corresponds to one of the m inequalities involving two unknowns. The additional vertex v_0 is incorporated, to guarantee that every vertex is reachable from it. If $x_j - x_i \le d_k$ is a constraint, then the weight for edge (v_i, v_j) is $w(v_i, v_j) = d_k$, while the weight of each edge leaving v_0 is 0. Figure 14 shows an example of mapping a linear system into a constraint graph.

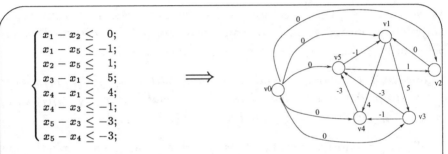

Fig. 14. Time Constraint Graph: An example of mapping a linear inequality system into a constraint graph

Theorem 2 *Given a system $Ax \le b$ of constraints, let $G = (V, E)$ be the corresponding constraint graph. It is feasible to satisfy the constraint specification only if G contains no negative-weight cycles.*

The theorem is directly derived from graph theory [15]. Given a constraint graph, the Bellman-Ford algorithm may be used to detect if the graph has negative-weight cycles. The algorithm is given in Figure 15.

When the conjunctive component indicates that the constraints are infeasible, we may continue to use the same algorithm to test the next conjunctive component until we either obtain a positive return or have tested the rest of the components and found that the constraints are infeasible to satisfy. In case of failure, the designers must reconsider the specification and make corrections.

```
Bellman-Ford(G, w, s)                    Initialize-Single-Source(G,s)
   Initialize-Single-Source(G, s)           for each vertex v in V[G]
   for i = 1 to |V[G]| - 1                      do d[v] = infinity
      do for each edge (u, v) in E[G]        d[s] = 0
         do Relax(u, v, w)
   for each edge (u, v) in E[G]
      do if d[v] > d[u] + w(u, v)          Relax(u, v, w)
         then return false                    if d[v] > d[u] + w(u, v)
   return true                                   then d[v] = d[u] + w(u, v)
```

Fig. 15. Bellman-Ford Algorithm

4.4 Complexity of the Infeasibility Detection

As we have seen, the detecting process has two steps: first, convert the conjunctive normal form into disjunctive normal form; second, apply Bellman-Ford Algorithm to each component of the DNF.

Theorem 3 *Given a conjunctive normal form* $f = \bigwedge_{I \in F}(\bigvee_{i \in I} x_i)$ *, it can be transformed into equivalent disjunctive normal form* $g = \bigvee_{J \in G}(\bigwedge_{j \in J} x_j)$ *in* $o(n^{C-1})$ *, where* $C = |F|$ *, and* $n = \max\{|I|, I \in F\}$ *.*

We skip the formal proof and instead give an simple example to show the rationale as follows:

$$\underbrace{\underbrace{(x_1 \vee x_2) \wedge (x_3 \vee x_4)}_{1} \wedge (x_5 \vee x_6)}_{2}$$

$=_1$ $((x_1 \wedge x_3) \vee (x_1 \wedge x_4) \vee (x_2 \wedge x_3) \vee (x_2 \wedge x_4)) \wedge (x_5 \vee x_6)$

$=_2$ $(x_1 \wedge x_3 \wedge x_5) \vee (x_1 \wedge x_3 \wedge x_6) \vee (x_1 \wedge x_4 \wedge x_5) \vee (x_1 \wedge x_4 \wedge x_6) \vee$
$(x_2 \wedge x_3 \wedge x_5) \vee (x_2 \wedge x_3 \wedge x_6) \vee (x_2 \wedge x_4 \wedge x_5) \vee (x_2 \wedge x_4 \wedge x_6)$

In this example, without losing generality, we assume that each term in CNF has the same number of literals, using a distribution law to expand the last two terms, as in ($=_1$). The result of the expansion has $n_1 \times n_2$ terms, and the process takes the $n_1 \times n_2$ amount of time, where n_1 and n_2 are the number of literals in each term, respectively. Repeating the process with the newly generated DNF of size $n_1 \times n_2$, as in ($=_2$), gives the final DNF of size $n_1 \times n_2 \times n_3$, and takes the $n_1 \times n_2 \times n_3$ amount of time. In our example $n_1 = n_2 = n_3 = 2$.

For any arbitrary CNF, we can repeatedly expend one term at a time, and the time it takes to expend any two terms is the product of the two terms' sizes, as shown in the above example. Therefore, the conclusion of theorem holds.

Theorem 4 *Bellman-Ford algorithm runs in time $O(VE)$.*

The rationale for the proof is as follows: the initialization takes $\Theta(V)$ time, each of the $|V| - 1$ passes over the edges takes $O(E)$ time, and the for loop takes $O(E)$ time, hence the algorithm takes $O(VE)$ time.

Our constraint specifications are transformed into a set of constraint graphs. In case the running result of the first constraint graph returns negative, that is, there is no feasible solution for it, we have to run the Bellman-Ford algorithm for the next constraint graph until we either check all the constraint graphs or get a positive result from an individual run of Bellman-Ford algorithm. Therefore, in the worst case, the Bellman-Ford algorithm is repeated D times, where D is the number of conjunctive terms in the transformed DNF. The entire procedure for detecting the feasibility of constraint specification can take exponential time in the worst case but may still be feasible in a real world system.

We have provided a simple polynomial time algorithm based on the derived constraint graph for early detection of inconsistent constraints at the source-code level, specified with our language constructs. Such infeasibility detection provides system designers early feedback about their specification at the source code level, and makes early adjustment on timing requirements possible. Since the timing specifications will eventually be combined with the computational specification to generate both functionally and timely correct executables, discarding inconsistent constraints at an early stage may significantly decrease the time taken by a scheduler to combine those two dimensions and generate a correct schedule. Moreover the tightness of constraints may also provide useful feedback.

5 Related Work

Real-time scheduling research is still mostly based on compiled code [17, 42] and the schedulability analysis is task (or process) oriented [39, 16]. One of the difficulties with these approaches is that the feedback based on the compiled code must be mapped back to *un-compiled* source code, which most of the time is not straightforward–although model checking on real-time specification languages has achieved promising results [27]. In some respects, our work is similar to that carried out independently by Al Mok who has studied infeasible timing constraints detection using heuristics. Al Mok assumes the constraints as specified in a real-time logic [32, 33]. Our work focuses on a programming language support for abstract specification.

Our general programming approach builds on the earlier work of Frølund and Agha [19, 20] who developed *synchronizers* to provide a declarative specification of coordination constraints on a group of actors. However, the semantics of RTsynchronizers are quite different, and are focused on *quantitative* constraints [38, 37, 34]. Moreover, synchronizers assume atomic (co-occurrence) constraints specified in different synchronizers are disjunctive rather than conjunctive.

A natural approach for providing high-level real-time languages is to augment existing programming languages with real-time constructs. Programming languages such as Flex [30], and RTC++ [26] are examples of such an approach. On the other hand, Ada [25] was specially designed for real-time applications. However, both Ada and augmented languages intermix real-time features with functional (or computational) aspects of the languages.

Akşit et al. [10, 9] proposed linguistic constructs called *real-time filters*, which lift the timing specification from the body of objects up to their interfaces. Structurally, it is cleaner. However, the potential difficulty of the filter approach is an inability to abstractly specify timing constraints among a group of distributed objects.

We discuss some of these high-level real-time programming languages in a little more detail below. A good survey of the historical development of real-time languages and a comparison of high-level real-time programming can be found in Halang [22].

Ada

Ada was designed for the U.S. Department of Defense as a general standardized programming language and a real-time programming language [25, 45]. The predefined library package CALENDAR in Ada provides programmers with wall-clock time. The only time-related language construct provided by Ada is *delay* which delays the executions of tasks by specified time periods. The specified time period is relative to the time when the *delay* statement is executed.

In Ada's semantics, atomic execution of statements is not enforced. Thus, execution of delay (p - t) can be interrupted after calculating (p - t) and before delay in a distributed real-time system. Moreover, the delay statement only guarantees that the process is not resumed before the delayed time; hence Ada does not provide a way to program precise periodic task execution [43].

Ada provides a rendezvous mechanism to synchronize tasks. Even though rendezvous may be set to be time bounded, the nondeterministic selection of an entry by the *select* statement introduces unpredictability. Moreover, rendezvous requires one task to call a named *entry* of another and does not take place until the called task decides to accept the call; in other words, it requires that each task be willing to wait for another. No asynchronous nonblocking inter-process communication is supported. Therefore, the rendezvous synchronization mechanism is not sufficient to specify arbitrary quantitative time dependencies among distributed asynchronous processes.

A later version of Ada (Ada 95), has enhanced the *delay* construct and provides a new *delay ... until* statement, which allows programmers to specify *absolute delayed* times. However, the semantics of both language constructs is that *delay* or *delay ... until* only guarantees the lower bound of the *delayed* time [1]. In addition, even though timing constraints can be specified based on the module's interface, the language itself does not prevent embedding the timing information inside the computational code.

In general, as a real-time programming language, Ada lacks adequate capabilities for expressing and enforcing temporal relations between and within different execution units in distributed systems.

FLEX

The programming language *Flex* [30, 28] is a derivative of C++. It provides a new language construct, *constraint block*, to describe constraints on time as well as other resources. A constraint block identifies restrictions that must apply while a section of code is in execution. It takes the form:

```
[label:] (constraint; constraint; ...) [~ {...}]{
    ...;
    statements;
    ...;
}
```

This block specifies a sequence of statements to be executed, and asserts that all of the constraints will be satisfied during the execution of the block.

In *Flex*, an event is defined as anything that may be identified with a specific instant such as the *start* and the *end* of some computation. Time is represented as a sequence of discrete, quantized instants. Control blocks can be nested. *Flex* supports absolute as well as relative timing constraints. It also defines a language construct *interval* to specify periodic tasks. Timing constraints are enforced on the control blocks which are at instruction level. In addition, *Flex* supports only sequential real-time computing–not parallel and distributed real-time computing.

Real-Time Mentat

The Real-Time Mentat programming language [21] is based on a combination of a macro data-driven computational model [18, 40] and an object-oriented programming paradigm.

In Mentat, a node in a program graph of a data-flow model is called an actor, which represents the computation at that point. Unlike other real-time programming languages which disallow recursion, dynamic memory allocation, dynamic process instantiation, etc., which are time unbounded and unpredictable actions, real-time Mentat provides the option of having timing constraints declared as either *hard* or *soft*. Only the actor which has *hard* timing constraints will be restricted to have bounded and predictable execution time and resource requirement. Furthermore, attributes: *start time, deadline, duration,* and *period* can be imposed on actors.

RTC++

RTC++[26] is another extension of C++. It provides two additional entities: (1) real-time objects which are based on multi-threaded object models; (2) timing constraints. Real-time objects are active objects with timing constraints. The language is designed based on the belief that "a real-time programming language should support (a) timing specification at each operation, (b) timing constraints for each statement, and (c) specifying a periodic task."

Hence, RTC++ provides *within, at*, and *before* statements to express statement-level timing constraints and provides a *cycle* statement to specify a periodic task. From our perspective, specific difficulties in using of RTC++ include:

1. Individual objects may be multi-threaded and need internal synchronization to maintain consistency of their internal state.
2. The multiple-threaded object model increases difficulty in analyzing temporal behavior in a distributed systems.
3. RTC++ separates objects into two different types: ordinary objects and active objects. Consider object A and object B have the same computational behaviors but A has timing constraints, while B does

not. In RTC++, A and B would belong to different classes and be unrelated. Furthermore, if timing constraints were added to object A, A would have to be redefined even though its computational behavior remained unchanged.

Other researchers have extended SmallTalk with real-time features, such as RealTimeTalk [13].

Composition Filters

Akşit et al. [10] noticed that in most current real-time object-oriented languages, changing application requirements or changing real-time specifications in a sub-class may require excessive redefinitions. They refer to this as *real-time specification inheritance anomaly* and propose the concept of *real-time composition filters* to resolve this anomaly.

One cause of real-time specification inheritance anomalies is mixing of real-time specification and computational code. Therefore, in order to avoid the real-time specification anomaly and to be able to reuse both application code and time specification, application code and real-time specification must be separated.

Composition filters add real-time "filters" on object interfaces. Timing constraints are specified in real-time filters, but the definition of member functions are time independent. These filters affect incoming and/or outgoing member function calls. The conceptual data structure of composition filters is illustrated in Figure 16.

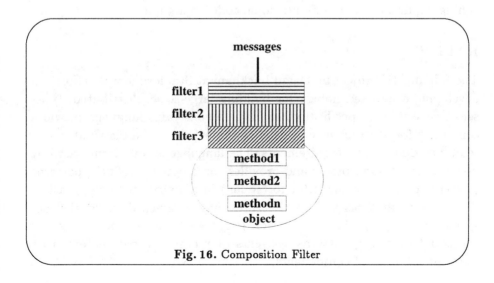

Fig. 16. Composition Filter

With composition filters, application code and timing constraint specifications can be separately reused, but a difficulty in using composition filters in distributed real-time systems is that they only provide mechanisms for specifying timing constraints for individual objects. Timing dependencies among a group of distributed objects are not addressed in composition filters. Furthermore, no formal semantics are given for composition filters.

Esterel

Esterel [12, 11] is a synchronous real-time programming language. It is based on the *strong synchrony hypothesis* that delay statement terminates *exactly* when its ending event occurs and all control transmission inside a program and all simple operations take no time. In Esterel, the only instruction which may take time are the ones *explicitly required* to do so. A program has no internal clock and it simply reacts instantaneously to external stimuli itself producing some stimuli to its output lines, and does nothing in absence of external stimuli. Furthermore, there is no dynamic creation of processes in an Esterel program. With such a framework, nondeterminism in the system is suppressed.

However, because real machines can not be infinitely fast and the communication latency in distributed systems cannot be ignored, the strong synchrony hypothesis that Esterel is based on is, in general, unrealistic. As is the case with other real-time programming languages we have discussed thus far, Esterel programs also embed timing requirements within the underlying computational code–making independent modification of timing requirements or computational code impossible.

RAPIDE

The Rapide [31] project by David Luckham at Stanford focuses efforts on developing a new technology for building large-scale, distributed, time-sensitive systems. Specifically the Rapide constraint language provides constructs for abstract specification of the behavior of a distributed system, including timing requirements. The language is constraint-based. It uses the timed poset model and provides constructs for defining patterns of events that are required (or forbidden) in a distributed computation. Component interfaces and architectures may be given detailed abstract specifications using the specification language. However, in the Rapide constraint language, patterns of events may based on parameters other than the interface of components.

6 Conclusion

We have observed that in distributed systems, the computational behavior of individual objects and the cooperation behavior among these objects are two different concerns. In a distributed real-time system, *how* an object performs its computation and *what* an object does are orthogonal to *when* the object does it. These three separate concerns should be captured by separate language constructs in order to achieve better modularity and code reusability. We have developed a new language concept and corresponding language construct RTsynchronizer to support such separation in distributed real-time computing.

The paradigm we have developed effort fits well with the future evolution of middleware. For example, in the current effort to develop real-time CORBA, scheduling is removed from the objects and provided through the middleware. Our implementation meta-architecture [38] provides a model for middleware.

RTsynchronizers express the timing constraints not as part of computational objects, but as independent entities. The entities provide an environment in which autonomous computational objects are constrained and forced to synchronize with each other in real time. Separating real-time aspects from computational aspects of a real-time system, both conceptually and 'physically', i.e. using distinct objects — RTsynchronizer, provides a high degree of modularity, and makes it easier and less error prone to design and maintain distributed real-time applications.

In addition, RTsynchronizers are transparent to computational objects, and their functionalities only depend on the interfaces, not the representations, of computational objects. Such properties make it possible to achieve code reusability in two ways: the same group of computational objects can be constrained by different RTsynchronizers in different applications — computational code reuse; the same RTsynchronizer can apply to different group of computational objects as long as they have the same interfaces — constraint specification reuse.

We have developed an operational semantics for the systems with both computation objects and RTsynchronizers. The operational semantics is represented by a set of transition rules extending traditional Actor semantics [34].

The transition rules separate *when* a transition is allowed to apply from *how* to choose a 'best' transition rule from a set of possible transitions. For example, when more than one message is available and satisfies the constraints, which message will be invoked first is indeterminate in our semantics. This further abstracts the semantics away from the scheduling mechanism and detailed implementation strategies.

We have developed an algorithm for detecting infeasible declarative timing specifications at the source code level. Such detection not only provides system designers early feedback about their specifications, but also decreases the time taken by a scheduler to combine computational code with timing requirements to generate a correct schedule.

A description of the implementation framework and the trade-offs in the implementation can be found in [36]. In summary, our approach is moderate in that it seeks to avoid conflict extremes. We assume the underlying architecture is an asynchronous distributed system, however, we assume the wall clock on each computation unit is synchronized. We use a pre-processing procedure to detect infeasible time constraints, but we do not explore the whole computation tree to statically generate a complete schedule off-line. Guided messages are checked for validation before they are invoked; however, the scheduler does not pick up an arbitrary message from the message queue and only takes RTsynchronizers as passive monitors; instead, the scheduler communicates with RTsynchronizers to do adaptive scheduling. Each individual RTsynchronizer is partially distributed (controlled objects share some of the RTsynchronizers state information) and is also centralized — it is single intact entity when communicating with schedulers.

Currently, we assume that for each system configuration, there is only one time which serves as the global time and we require that two different configurations must agree on the "current time" before they can be composed. The composition between ART configurations with different clocks needs to be further studied. Another important direction for future work is to build a complete programming environment for RTsynchronizers.

References

1. Ada95 6.0 reference manual. Technical report, Internet's Public Ada Library, 1995.
2. G. Agha. *Actors: A Model of Concurrent Computation in Distributed Systems.* MIT Press, 1986.
3. G. Agha. Concurrent object-oriented programming. *Communications of the ACM*, 33(9):125–141, September 1990.
4. G. Agha, S. Frølund, R. Panwar, and D. Sturman. A linguistic framework for dynamic composition of dependability protocols. In *Proceedings of the 3rd IFIP Working Conference on Dependable Computing for Critical Applications*, September 1992.
5. G. Agha, W. Kim, and R. Panwar. Actor languages for specification of parallel computations. In G. E. Blelloch, K. Mani Chandy, and S. Jagannathan, editors, *DIMACS. Series in Discrete Mathematics and Theoretical Computer Science. vol*

18. *Specification of Parallel Algorithms*, pages 239–258. American Mathematical Society, 1994.

6. G. Agha, I. A. Mason, S. F. Smith, and C. .L. Talcott. Towards a theory of actor computation. In *The Third International Conference on Concurrency Theory (CONCUR'92)*, pages 565–579. Springer Verlag, August 1992. LNCS 630.

7. G. Agha, I. A. Mason, S. F. Smith, and C. L. Talcott. A foundation for actor computation. *Journal of Functional Programming*, 7:1–72, 1997.

8. Gul A. Agha. Abstracting interaction patterns: A programming paradigm for open distributed systems. In Elie Najm and Jean-Bernard Stefani, editors, *Formal Methods for Open Object-based Distributed Systems*, pages 135–153. IFIP, Chapman & Hall, 1997.

9. M. Akşit and L. M. J. Bergmans. Composing and reusing synchronization and real-time specification. In *The Object-Oriented Real-Time Systems (OORTS) Workshop*, pages 13–22, San Antonio, Texas, October 1995. to appear in OOPS Messeuger, ACM SIGPLAN.

10. M. Akşit, J. Bosch, and W. Sterren. Real-time specification inheritance anomalies and real-time filters. In *Proceedings of ECOOP'94*, pages 386–407. Springer Verlag, July 1994. LNCS 821.

11. G. Berry, P.Couronné, and G. Gonithier. Synchronous programming of reactive systems: An introduction to esterel. In *Programming of Future Generation Computers*, pages 33–55. Elsivier Science Publishers, Amsterdam, 1988.

12. Gerard Berry and laurent Cosserat. The esterel synchronous programming language and its mathematical semantics. In *Seminar on Concurrency*, pages 389–448. Springer Verlag, 1984. LNCS 197.

13. E. Brorsson, C. Eriksson, and J. Gustafsson. Realtimetalk an object-oriented language for hard real-time systems.

14. W. Clinger. Foundation of actor semantics. Technical Report AI-TR-633, MIT, 1981.

15. Thomas H. Cormen, Charles E. Leiserson, and Ronald L. Rivest. *Introduction to Algorithms*, chapter 25, pages 515–550. MIT Press, 1990.

16. Z. Deng, J.W.-S Liu, and J. Sun. Dynamic scheduling of hard real-time applications in open system environment. Technical Report UIUCDCS-R-96-1981, University of Illinois at Urbana-Champaign, October 1996.

17. R. Gerber et al. Guaranteeing end-to-end timing constraints by calibrating intermediate processes. In *Real-Time Systems Symposium, 1994*, 1994.

18. Antony A. Faustini and Edgar B. Lewis. Toward a real-time dataflow language. *IEEE Software*, 3(1):139 — 145, January 1986.

19. S. Frølund and G. Agha. A language framework for multi-object coordination. In *Proceedings of ECOOP 1993*, volume 707 of *LNCS*. Springer Verlag, 1993.

20. Svend Frølund. *Coordinating Distributed Objects: An Actor-Based Approach to Synchronization*. MIT Press, 1996.

21. A. S. Grimshaw, A. Silberman, and J. .W. S. Liu. Real-time mentat at programming language and architecture. In *IEEE Globecom'89*, 1989.

22. W. A. Halang and K. Mangold. Real-time programming languages. In M. Schiebe and S. Pferrer, editors, *Real-Time Systems Engineering and Applications*, chapter 6, pages 141–200. Kluwer Academic, 1992.

23. C. Hewitt. Viewing control structures as patterns of passing messages. *Journal of Artificial Intelligence*, 8(3):323–364, 1977.

24. B. Hoogeboom and W. A. Halang. The concept of time in the specification of real-time systems. In M. Schiebe and S. Pferrer, editors, *Real-Time Systems Engineering and Applications*, chapter 2, pages 11–40. Kluwer Academic, 1992.

25. American National Standards Institute. The programming language Ada reference manual. In *The Programming Language Ada Reference Manual*. Springer Verlag, 1983.

26. Yutaka Ishikawa, Hideyuki Tokuda, and Clifford W. Mercer. Object-oriented real-time language design: Constructs for timing constraints. In *Proceedings OOPSLA/ECOOP '90*, pages 289–298, October 1990. Published as ACM SIGPLAN Notices, volume 25, number 10.

27. Farnam Jahanian, Aloysius K. Mok, and Douglas A. Stuart. Formal specification of real-time systems. Technical Report 25, The University of Texas at Austin, 1988.

28. Kevin B. Kenny and Kwei-Jay Lin. Building flexible real-time systems using the flex language. *IEEE Computer*, 24(5):70 — 78, 1991.

29. L. Lamport. Time, clocks, and the ordering of events in a distributed system. *Communications of the ACM*, 21(7):558–565, 1978.

30. K. Lin and J. W. Liu. Flex: A language for real-time systems programming. Technical Report 1634, UIUC, 1990.

31. David Luckhman. Guide to the rapide 1.0 langauage reference manuals. Technical report, Stanford University, http://anna.stanford.edu/rapide/rapide.html, 1996.

32. A. K. Mok. Real-time logic, programming and scheduling. In B. Randell, editor, *Real-Time Systems, Proceedings of the Joint University of Newcastle Upon Tyne/International computers Limited Semina*, Newcastle, September 1989.

33. A. K. Mok. Real-time scheduling and the boeing 777. In *European Educational Forum School on Embedded Systems 1996*, Veldhoven, NL, November 1996.

34. B. Nielsen and G. Agha. Semantics for an actor-based real-time language. In *Proceedings of the Fourth International Workshop on Parallel and Distributed Real-Time Systems*, Honolulu, April 1996.

35. O. Nierstrasz and M. Papathomas. Viewing Objects as Patterns of Communicating Agents. In *Proceedings OOPSLA/ECOOP '90*, pages 38–43, October 1990. Published as ACM SIGPLAN Notices, volume 25, number 10.

36. S. Ren. *An Actor-Based Framework for Real-Time Coordination*. PhD thesis, University of Illinois at Urbana-Champaign, 1997.

37. S. Ren and G. Agha. *RTsynchronizers*: Language support for real-time specifications in distributed systems. *ACM SIGPLAN Notices*, 30(11):50 – 59, November 1995.

38. S. Ren, G. Agha, and M. Saito. A Modular Approach for Programming Distributed Real-Time Systems. *Journal of Parallel and Distributed Computing*, 36(1):4–12, July 1996.

39. Karsten Schwan and Hongyi Zhou. Dynamic scheduling of hard real-time tasks and real-time threads. *IEEE Transactions on Software Engineering*, 18(8):736 – 747, 1992.

40. A. Silberman. Real-time mentat. Technical report, Department of Computer Science, UIUC, 1995.

41. J.A. Stankovic. A perspective on distributed computer systems. *IEEE Transactions on Computers*, C-33(12):1102 — 1115, 1984.

42. A. Stoyenko, V. Hamacher, and R. Holt. Analyzing hard-real-time programs for guaranteed schedulability. *IEEE Transactions on Software Engineering*, 17(8):737 – 750, August 1991.

43. S. Tucker Taft. Ada 9x: From abstraction-oriented to object-oriented. In *Proceedings OOPSLA '93, ACM SIGPLAN Notices*, pages 127–143, October 1993. Published as Proceedings OOPSLA '93, ACM SIGPLAN Notices, volume 28, number 10.

44. J.D. Ullman. Np-complete scheduling problems. *Journal of Computer System Science*, 10:384–393, 1975.

45. R.A. Volz and T.N. Mudge. Timing issues in the distributed execution of ada programs. *IEEE Transactions on Computers*, 36(4):449 — 459, April 1987.

Proof-Based System Engineering and Embedded Systems

Gérard Le Lann

INRIA, Projet REFLECS, BP 105
F-78153 Le Chesnay Cedex, France
E-mail: Gerard.Le_Lann@inria.fr

Abstract. We introduce basic principles that underlie proof-based system engineering, an engineering discipline aimed at computer-based systems. This discipline serves to avoid system engineering faults. It is based upon fulfilling proof obligations, notably establishing proofs that decisions regarding system design and system dimensioning are correct, before embarking on the implementation or the fielding of a computer-based system. We also introduce a proof-based system engineering method which has been applied to diverse projects involving embedded systems. These projects are presented and lessons learned are reported. An analysis of the Ariane 5 Flight 501 failure serves to illustrate how proof-based system engineering also helps in diagnosing causes of failures.

1 Introduction

Taurus (stock exchange), Relit (stock exchange), AAS (air traffic control), Confirm (on-line hotel and car reservation), Socrate (on-line railways seat reservation), Freedom (manned orbital station), P20 (nuclear power plants), Ariane 5 Flight 501 (satellite launcher). This is a small sample of projects that have been significantly delayed, or have been cancelled, or have entailed costs much higher than anticipated, or have resulted into operational failures, because of problems with "informatics". According to a study conducted over 8,380 computer-based system projects by the Standish Group in 1995, only 16% of these projects were found to be successful, i.e. completed in time, within their initial budget, and having produced systems that - as of 1995 - had not failed.

Industrialized countries are wasting huge amounts of time and money for the simple reason that our community is not very good at designing and building computer-based systems that match clients requirements at decent costs. Among those computer-based systems that function properly, how many are unjustifiably expensive, in terms of development and maintenance? Our community is not very good either at correctly identifying the real causes of project setbacks or operational failures. Too often, blame is inappropriately put on poor project management and/or poor software (S/W) engineering practice.

There is growing evidence that system engineering currently is the weakest (i.e., the least rigorous) of all those engineering disciplines covered by what the IEEE Computer Society refers to as the Engineering of Computer-Based

Systems. This view is not universally shared (yet). In certain circles, the motto is "S/W is all what matters". Interestingly enough, infatuation with S/W is manifest in some of those countries which have failed so far to develop a profit-making hardware (H/W) industry. That S/W is not a dominant cause of project setbacks or system failures is supported by a growing number of studies (see [10], [14], [16] for examples).

Asap, Better, Cheaper (ABC) now is the clients defined rule of the game. Meeting the ABC rule involves dramatic improvements in methods, processes and tools directed at systems engineering in general, at system engineering for computer-based systems in particular. This need has been acknowledged by the US industry and governmental bodies in the early 90's. As a result, the InterNational Council On Systems Engineering (originally called NCOSE) was created.

Let us now consider the body of knowledge that has been accumulated over the last 35 years by the research community in computer science. It is reasonably straightforward to conclude that a large fraction of those system engineering problems faced by the information industry and by the computing industry have solutions readily available. To be more specific, there are many architectural and algorithmic problems that have well documented optimal or correct solutions, notably in the areas of real-time computing, distributed computing, and fault-tolerant computing. These are the areas of relevance for embedded applications and systems. However, only a small subset of these solutions have so far translated into commercial, off-the-shelf (COTS) products or operational computer-based systems.

That time has come for major changes in system engineering (SE) methods, practices and tools directed at computer-based systems is no longer being questioned in professional circles. Which sorts of changes is the issue of interest. We believe - and we will attempt to convince the reader - that such changes should be aimed at introducing correctness proof obligations, as is (resp. is becoming) the case in the integrated circuits (resp. software) industry. We believe that proof-based system engineering for computer-based systems - referred to as proof-based SE in the sequel - is the privileged vehicle to successfully meet the ABC challenge. Many embedded applications being complex and/or critical, meeting correctness proof obligations seems even more appropriate in the case of embedded systems.

Proof-based SE is introduced in section 2. In section 3, we present a proof-based SE method - the TRDF method - and we show how to conduct the various phases of a computer-based system project according to this method. Some real projects addressed with the TRDF method are sketched out and lessons learned are reported in section 4. Section 5 serves to illustrate how proof-based SE, when applied a posteriori, helps in diagnosing the real causes of operational failures. The Ariane 5 Flight 501 failure is the case selected.

2 What is Proof-Based System Engineering

2.1 Introduction

With proof-based SE, one seeks to solve system engineering problems arising with computer-based systems in much the same way engineering problems are solved in such well established disciplines as, e.g., civil engineering or electrical engineering, that is by "exploiting" scientific results. Indeed, before they undertake the construction of a dam or the electrical cabling of a building, engineers draw plans first (design) and check that plans are correct (proofs). Of course, they do not have to re-establish theoretical results, such as theorems in hydrodynamics or the Kirchhoff laws. They apply well established engineering methods which build upon (and "encapsulate") fundamental scientific work. Why would it be different when it comes to computer-based systems?

The essential goal pursued with proof-based SE is as follows: starting from some initial description of an application problem, i.e. a description of end user/client requirements and assumptions (e.g., an invitation-to-tender), to produce a global and implementable specification of a computer-based system (denoted S in the sequel), along with proofs that system design and system dimensioning decisions made to arrive at that specification do satisfy the specification of the computer science problem "hidden" within the application problem.

With proofs, it is possible to ensure that future behavior of S is the desired behavior, before implementation or construction or fielding is undertaken. Proof-based SE aims at avoiding system engineering faults, in contrast with fault-tolerance approaches, such as those based on, e.g., "design diversity".

Any project involves a number of actors, namely a client, a prime contractor, co/sub-contractors. Roles taken on by actors are described wherever appropriate. Note that a client may not be a specific organization or company, but a team of marketing/business experts internal to a system vendor/integrator company that targets a certain market, in which case another team (of engineers) would take on the role of a prime contractor.

2.2 Three Essential Phases in a Project Lifecycle

Notation $<Y>$ (resp. [Z]) is used in the sequel to refer to a specification of a problem Y (resp. a solution Z). Notation $<y>$ (resp. [z]) is used to refer to a specification of a set of unvalued problem-centric (resp. solution-centric) variables. The term "specification" is used to refer to any complete set of unambiguous statements - in some human language, in some formalized notation, in some formal language.

Proof-based SE addresses those three essential phases that come first in a project lifecycle, namely the problem capture phase, the system design phase, and the system dimensioning phase. Proof-based SE also addresses phases concerned with changes that may impact a computer-based system after it has been fielded. For example, phases devoted to handling modifications in client-originated descriptions of application problems, coping with evolutions of COTS products, taking advantage of advances in state-of-the-art in computer science, and so on, are also covered by proof-based SE. Such phases simply consist in repeating some of the three phases introduced below, and which precede phases covered by other engineering disciplines (e.g., S/W engineering), which serve to implement system engineering decisions. The whole set of notations needed to describe these phases is summarized in figure 1.

$< A >$ ≡ specification of an invariant (i.e., generic) application problem A.
$< X >$ ≡ specification of the generic computer science problem that
matches $< A >$.
$< a >$ ≡ specification of the set of variables in $< A >$ that are left unvalued.
$< x >$ ≡ specification of the set of variables in $< X >$ that are left unvalued.
$[S]$ ≡ modular specification of a generic computer-based system S such
that $[S]$ satisfies $< X >$.
$[s]$ ≡ specification of the set of variables in $[S]$ that are left unvalued.
$[oracle.S]$ ≡ specification of a dimensioning oracle (obtained from correctness
proofs) for generic system S.
$V(< x >)$ ≡ some assignment of values to variables in $< x >$.
$V([s])$ ≡ an assignment of values to variables in $[s]$ that satisfies $V(< x >)$.

Notations

$$\{\text{description of an application problem}\} \Rightarrow < A > \left| \begin{array}{l} \Rightarrow < X > \\ \Rightarrow < a > \\ \Rightarrow < x > \end{array} \right.$$

Capture

$$< X > \left| \begin{array}{l} \Rightarrow [S] \\ \Rightarrow [s] \\ \Rightarrow [oracle.S] \end{array} \right.$$

Design

$$V(< x >) \Rightarrow oracle.S \Rightarrow V([s])$$

Dimensioning

Fig. 1. Organization of proof-based SE phases

The Problem Capture Phase

This phase has an application problem description as an input. Such a description, provided by a client, usually is expressed in some human language and is incomplete and/or ambiguous. The capture phase is concerned with, (i) the translation of an application problem description into $< A >$, which specifies the generic application problem under consideration and, (ii) the translation of

$< A >$ into $< X >$, a specification of the generic computer science problem that matches $< A >$. A generic problem is an invariant for the entire duration of a computer-based system project.

Specifications $< A >$ and $< X >$ are jointly produced by a client and a prime contractor. A client knows "what he/she wants", i.e. the semantics of the application problem of interest. A prime contractor is in charge of identifying which are the models and properties commonly used in computer science that have semantics that match those of the application problem. Consequently, a specification $< X >$ actually is a pair $\{< m.X >, < p.X >\}$, where m stands for models and p stands for properties.

For example, statement *"despite being read and updated possibly concurrently, files should never be inconsistent"* in $< A >$ would translate as *"serializability property (for operations on files)"* in $< X >$. Or statement *"workstations used by air traffic controllers should either work correctly or stop functioning"* in $< A >$ would translate as *"dependability property is observability = stop failure (for workstations)"* in $< X >$. Or statement *"how application-level service app will be invoked is unknown"* in $< A >$ could translate as *"unimodal arbitrary arrival model (for the event type that triggers app)"* in $< X >$ (see section 3.1 for an introduction to models and properties).

Besides making sure that a client fully understands what is implied with every model and property that appears in $< X >$, a prime contractor is in charge of helping a client decide which degree of genericity is appropriate. Inevitably, variables appear in specifications $< A >$ and $< X >$. Notation $< a >$ (resp. $< x >$) is used to refer to a specification of those variables in $< A >$ (resp. $< X >$) that are left unvalued. As for $< X >$ (resp. $< A >$), $< x >$ (resp. $< a >$) is a pair $\{< m.x >, < p.x >\}$ (resp. $\{< m.a >, < p.a >\}$.

The genericity degree of $< A >$ or $< X >$ may vary from 0 ($< a >$ and $< x >$ are empty) to ∞ (every variable in $< X >$ (resp. $< A >$) appears in $< x >$ (resp. $< a >$)).

Of course, any degree of genericity has an associated cost and a payoff. With a "high" degree of genericity, design work is "hard", but is valid for a very large number - say N - of problem quantifications and, therefore, releases of S, which entails possibly significant savings vis-à-vis design, dimensioning, implementation and testing activities. Conversely, with a "low" degree of genericity, design work is "easy", but it must be repeated "many" times in order to deliver these same N releases of S. Hence, design costs are higher. However, the cost of every single (specifically dimensioned) release of S is lower than that of any release resulting from a "highly" generic approach. (See also further, under the system dimensioning phase sub-section, and section 2.3).

Set $\{< A >, < X >, < a >, < x >\}$ is the contract established between a client and a prime contractor. Such a contract is essential for avoiding those misunderstandings or litigations that are commonplace with current system engineering practice. Any extra cost or delay incurred in a project due to changes in $< A >$ or $< a >$ is to be beared by a client. Similarly, any extra cost or delay due to erroneous $< X >$ or $< x >$ (i.e., any mistaken translation of $< A >$ or

$< a >$) is to be beared by a prime contractor. There are methods and tools (e.g., rapid prototyping) that may help a client produce a specification $< A >$ that correctly mirrors "what he/she has in mind". One of the purposes of proof-based SE methods is to help specify $< A >$ and $< a >$ as well as correctly derive a set $\{< X >, < x >\}$ from a given set $\{< A >, < a >\}$.

At present time, such derivations can be performed by experts, namely computer scientists and engineers who are aware of such methods. We foresee the existence of knowledge-based tools that will help automate these derivation processes.

The System Design Phase

This phase entirely is under the responsibility of a prime contractor. A design phase has a specification $< X >$ as an input. It covers all the design stages needed to arrive at $[S]$, a modular specification of a generic solution (a generic computer-based system), the completion of each design stage being conditioned on fulfilling correctness proof obligations. A design phase is conducted by exploiting state-of-the-art in various areas of computer science (e.g., computing system architectures, algorithms, models, properties), in various theories (e.g., serializability, scheduling, game, complexity), as well as by applying appropriate proof techniques, which techniques depend on the types of problems under consideration (examples are given in the sequel).

More precisely, one solves a problem $\{< m.X >, < p.X >\}$ raised at some design stage by going through the following three steps: specification of an architectural and an algorithmic solution designed for some modular decomposition, establishment of proofs of properties and verification that a design correctness proof obligation is satisfied, specification of a dimensioning oracle.

For example, let $\{<$ *distributed processes, some partially synchronous system model* $>$, $<$ *mutual exclusion* $>\}$ be a problem contemplated at some design stage. One cannot proceed further in the design phase unless, (i) one specifies a modular architecture that supports the distributed processes, (ii) one proves that the required safety property (mutual exclusion) is ensured with some to-be-specified distributed algorithm designed for a computational model "as strong as" - see section 3.1 - the specified partially synchronous model.

Similarly, if a real-time problem such as $\{<$ *distributed task models, multimodal arbitrary arrival model* $>$, $<$ *latest deadlines for completing task executions* $>\}$ is to be solved, one goes through that design stage by, (i) specifying a distributed modular architecture that supports the specified tasks, as well as a distributed scheduling algorithm, (ii) proving that the specified timeliness property holds for every task for feasibility conditions "as strong as" the specified arrival model.

The first stage of a design phase results into the breaking of the initial (possibly complex) generic problem $< X >$ into a number of independent generic subproblems. Fulfilling a design correctness proof obligation guarantees that if every subproblem is correctly solved, then the initial problem is correctly solved as well by "concatenating" the individual generic solutions. And so on. Consequently, a design phase has its stages organized as a tree structure (see fig. 2).

By the virtue of the uninterrupted tree of proofs (that every design decision is correct), the union of those specifications that sit at the leaves of a design tree is a modular specification of generic S that provably correctly satisfies $< X >$. This modular specification is denoted $[S]$. If $< X >$ is a correct translation of $< A >$, then, transitively, $< A >$ is provably correctly solved with $[S]$.

Clearly, this approach is based on compositionality principles very similar to those that underlie some formal methods in the S/W engineering field.

Every module of $[S]$ is deemed implementable, or is known (in a provable manner) to be implemented by some procurable product or is handed over to a co/sub-contractor. As will be seen in section 3, another output of a design phase is a specification of a system-wide dimensioning oracle - denoted $[oracle.S]$ - which includes, in particular, a set of constraints called (system-wide) feasibility conditions. Of course, $[oracle.S]$ must be implemented in order to conduct subsequent system dimensioning phases. From a practical viewpoint, $[oracle.S]$ is a specification of a $\{< X >, [S]\}$-dependent component of a more general system dimensioning tool.

The System Dimensioning Phase

The purpose of a dimensioning phase is to find an assignment $V([s])$, i.e. a quantification of system S unvalued variables, such as, e.g., sizes of memory buffers, sizes of data structures, processors speeds, databuses throughputs, number of databuses, processors redundancy degrees, total number of processors. $V([s])$ must satisfy a particular assignment $V(< x >)$, i.e. a particular quantification of the captured problem-centric models and properties. A dimensioning oracle, i.e. an implementation of $[oracle.S]$, is needed to run a dimensioning phase. Such an oracle may be owned by a client or a prime contractor, or both.

One or several dimensioning phases may have to be run until the dimensioning oracle declares that there is a quantified S that solves a proposed quantified problem $\{< X >, V(< x >)\}$. How many phases need be run directly depends on the genericity of $[S]$. Consider for example that $[s]$ is close to empty, for the reason that many (design and dimensioning) decisions were made prior to entering the design phase. This is typically the case whenever it is decided a priori that S must be based on specific COTS or proprietary products. The good news are that a small number of dimensioning phases need be run, given that many system variables are valued a priori. The bad news are that the oracle may find out (rapidly) that the proposed problem quantification is not feasible (e.g., some deadlines are always missed), no matter which $V([s])$ is considered.

Pair $\{[S], V([s])\}$ is a modular implementation specification of a system S that provably solves problem $\{< X >, V(< x >)\}$. Modules of $\{[S], V([s])\}$ are contracts between a prime contractor and those co/sub-contractors in charge of implementing S.

To summarize, a capture phase yields the specification of a generic problem in computer science that matches an invariant application problem. A design phase is the resolution of that generic problem, which yields a specification of a generic solution, exactly like in Mathematics where one demonstrates that some theorems hold - properties "as strong as" those stated in $< p.X >$ - for every

possible set of values taken by some set of variables *var*, for some axiomatics
- models "as strong as" those stated in $< m.X >$. After this is done, a client
or a prime contractor is free to quantify the generic problem, as many times as
desired. For each feasible quantification, there exists a matching dimensioning
of the generic solution (i.e., of S). To pursue the analogy with Mathematics,
theorems are applied for various assignments of values to set *var*.

If deemed implementable, set $\{[S], V([s])\}$ is the borderline between system
engineering on the one hand, S/W engineering, electrical engineering and other
engineering disciplines on the other hand.

S/W engineering serves the purpose of producing correct executable implementations of given specifications. Where do these specifications come from?
Obviously, they result from system engineering work. Hence, S/W engineering
necessarily follows system engineering in a project lifecycle. Why is it useless or,
at best, marginally productive to apply formal methods in the S/W engineering
field without applying proof-based methods in the system engineering field? For
the obvious reason that provably correct S/W implementations of specifications
that are flawed in the first place can only result into incorrect computer-based
systems. For example - as amply demonstrated by many failed projects and/or
operational failures - a faulty design decision results into specifying some inadequate algorithmic solution. No matter how correctly that specification ends up
being implemented, the resulting system can only fail to meet $< X >$. Specifications handed over to S/W engineers must first be proved correct w.r.t. some
client-originated problem.

2.3 Stochastic Versus Deterministic Approaches in Proof-Based System Engineering

System engineering for computer-based systems has been an area of concern
for almost half a century. Until recently, with few exceptions, design and/or dimensioning correctness proofs that have made inroads in industrial and business
circles are those based on stochastic approaches, namely probabilistic approaches
(e.g., analytical modeling, queueing theory) and statistical approaches (e.g., numerical simulation, event-driven simulation) [1].

We believe time has come for changes. We hope that the viewpoints presented
below will help to properly put current trends into historical perspective.

The major reason for changes is the clients defined ABC rule. Consider the
trends in the embedded applications area. Can we still "play with probabilities"
when, on the one hand, complexity and criticality go beyond certain thresholds
and, on the other hand, costs must go down, costs including losses incurred because of operational failures? With embedded applications, it is more and more
often the case that those computer science problems derived from client originated problems are of deterministic nature. Typically, clients want to be shown
that properties $< p.X >$, quantified as per $V(< p.x >)$, always hold under assumptions $< m.X >$, quantified as per $V(< m.x >)$, i.e. for possibly exceptional

---

[1] Proofs serve the purpose of predicting before constructing. Consequently, we do not
consider here such techniques as prototyping or testing.

or worst-case operational conditions. Most often, deterministic approaches are then mandatory.

For example, whenever initial $< X >$ indirectly raises a real-time, or a distribution, or a fault-tolerance issue, it is necessary to resort to such deterministic algorithms and "non probabilistic" proof techniques as those found in, e.g., [1], [5], [7], [15]. This is so for at least one reason: the set that includes all possible runs of a reasonably complex computer-based system cannot be built by, (i) resorting to models based on (independent) random variables, (ii) considering stochastic "adversaries".

Let us imagine we have to solve a distributed hard real-time problem. Any solution must include some distributed synchronization algorithm (e.g., concurrency control, consensus). Therefore, those variables that model individual processor states are related to each other in very specific ways. They cannot be seen as independent random variables. Furthermore, upper bounds on response times must be given for worst-case scenari such as, e.g., highest "load" densities (a deterministic "adversary"). This is radically different from expressing expected values and standard deviations of response times assuming, e.g., Poisson arrivals.

Composite algorithms built out of, e.g., concurrency control algorithms, fault-tolerant algorithms, distributed algorithms for fault-tolerance, real-time scheduling algorithms, on the one hand, reasoning techniques such as adversary arguments (game theory), proof techniques pertaining to mathematical logic, and such calculi as matrix calculus in (max, +) algebra, on the other hand, are needed to establish desired solutions and correctness proofs.

Of course, stochastic approaches have their own merits. Whenever appropriate, they should be followed. Nevertheless, we would like to dispel the following misconceived argument: "Given that "the world" is probabilistic, only stochastic approaches make sense". Firstly, it has never been proved that "the world" is probabilistic. Probabilities and coverage factors are one possible manner of modeling our inability to tell the future (of "the world"). Secondly, the fact that real future operational conditions may from time to time deviate from what has been assumed does not mean that it is impossible to prove properties "deterministically".

More to the point, we see three fundamental differences between deterministic and stochastic approaches.

The first one is related to the capture phase. As will be seen, in any of the classes of models that are considered under a deterministic approach, there is one model that is "extreme", in the sense that it reflects a fully unrestricted "adversary". Examples of such models are the asynchronous computational model, the byzantine failure model, the multimodal arbitrary event arrival model. Picking up these models has a price: one may run into impossibility results or one may end up with "demanding" feasibility conditions (which translates into costly computer-based systems). The beauty of such models is that they are "safe": no real future operational conditions can be worse than what is captured with these models. Therefore, the issue of estimating coverage factors is void with such models. Conversely, even with "extreme" stochastic models, the issue of estimating coverage factors must be addressed. Picking up models weaker than "extreme" ones involves a risk: operational conditions may be "stronger than" assumed during a capture phase. Again, this is unavoidable, given that we cannot "tell the future". However, it is fallacious to conclude from this (rather trivial) observation that only stochastic approaches make sense. "Deterministic" theorems are established under Euclidian or Riemannian axiomatics, without asking which matches best some given universe. The same is true with properties in computer science. Picking up the appropriate models for $< m.A >$ and $< m.X >$ boils down to making tradeoffs between having coverage factors sufficiently close to 1 and retaining models as weak as acceptable.

The second fundamental difference is related to the design phase. There is no probability or coverage factor involved with deterministic design approaches. Properties "as strong as" those stated in $< p.X >$ either hold or do not hold. For example, mutual exclusion or serializability or atomic broadcast or some timeliness property is either not ensured or it is (via some deterministic algorithm), under specific feasibility conditions. There are no probabilities or "proof coverage factors" or "proof confidence intervals" involved with proofs of properties or feasibility conditions.

Feasibility conditions are analytical expressions. For a given set of models, they define a set of scenari that, with certainty, includes all worst-case scenari that can be deployed by "adversary" $< m.X >$. (This set is exact, i.e., is not a ιperset, whenever feasibility conditions are necessary and sufficient). There are no probabilities or coverage factors involved with expressing computable lower bounds on a redundancy degree or on a number of modules, or computable upper bounds on response times. Conversely, there is inevitably some approximation involved with a stochastic modeling of those deterministic algorithms (probabilistic ones, in some instances) that constitute the inner mechanisms of computer-based systems.

Let us consider probabilistic approaches first. Even though the modeling of some deterministic arrivals models and algorithms is known to be tractable in queueing theory (e.g., ND/D/1), approximations cannot be avoided whenever queue servers model real processors that are actually synchronized. This raises the issue of estimating the level of error introduced with such approximations. Common practice consists in validating probabilistic analytical models via event-driven simulations. Hence the question: What can be expected from statistical approaches ?

Given that random number generators and limited numbers of input scenari are resorted to under such approaches, it is impossible to ascertain that every possible worst-case scenario has been explored. Coverage factors or confidence intervals depend on the sizes of the actual state spaces. In most real cases, these sizes are huge (see sections 3.4 and 3.5 for numerical examples). Which results into coverage factors or confidence intervals considered realistic or satisfactory when in the [95 % - 99 %] interval. This is problematic with critical applications. When highest accepted unavailability of critical services is set to 10^{-4} (resp. 10^{-7}) by a client (via $V(< p.x >)$) - as is the case with some airborne/spaceborne (resp. air traffic control) applications - we can no longer rely on stochastic proofs of properties, for the simple reason that levels of confidence reachable with probabilistic analytical modeling or statistical modeling have a distance to 1 which is orders of magnitude greater than 10^{-4} (resp. 10^{-7} a fortiori).

The third fundamental difference is related to the dimensioning phase. In both cases, quantifications of models (via $V(< m.x >)$) and properties (via $V(< p.x >)$) have some related coverage factors. However, in the deterministic case, there are exceptions. For example, quantification coverage factors need not be estimated when considering "extreme" models (e.g., the asynchronous computational model, the byzantine failure model) or such properties as serializability or timeliness. This being granted, it is important to see that, under a deterministic approach, physical dimensionings of computer-based systems have no coverage factors or confidence intervals or probabilities associated to them. Those numerical values that appear in $V([s])$ specify a "safe" physical dimensioning of a computer-based system. A "safe" dimensioning is a by-product of checking the feasibility of some problem-centric quantification $V(< x >)$. Consequently, such dimensionings are certainly sufficient (ideally, they should be necessary and sufficient), contrary to stochastic dimensionings, which are probabilistically or statistically correct.

We do not mean to dismiss the relevance of stochastic approaches. What is getting clearer is the existence of a strong trend in favor of resorting to deterministic approaches more often than has been the case in the past. Interestingly enough, besides embedded applications, such a trend is manifest in application domains that have traditionally been terra incognita for deterministic approaches such as, e.g., telecommunications [8]. In the sequel, we consider deterministic proof-based SE approaches and methods.

2.4 Current Status

As is the case with other engineering disciplines, various proof-based SE methods will emerge in the future. Work on proof-based SE which was started in 1993 [11], [12] has led to the development of a method named TRDF [2]. That name was retained for the reason that those application problems of interest to us raise real-time issues (R), or distribution issues (D), or fault-tolerance issues (F), or any combination of these issues. Embedded applications raise such issues. TRDF currently is the only proof-based SE method (based on a deterministic approach) we are aware of. Consequently, in what follows, we further explore proof-based SE as instantiated by the TRDF method.

---

[2] Temps Réel, Traitement Distribué, Tolérance aux Fautes (T is a common factor)

3 Proof-Based System Engineering and the TRDF Method

In this section, we provide a detailed description of what is involved with design and dimensioning phases. In order to do this rigorously, detailed notations are necessary. They are provided for the interested readers. However, these notations may be skipped by those who simply want to read this paper as an introduction to proof-based SE.

3.1 The Problem Capture Phase

Most often, properties (services to be provided to end users) and models (assumptions regarding future operational conditions) are not clearly separated in an application problem description. Furthermore, such descriptions inevitably contain many TBD (to-be-defined) quotations. This is felt to be a major cause of those difficulties faced by a prime contractor and, transitively, by co/subcontractors. It should not - and may not - be so. Too often, clients believe - or are told by prime contractors - that they must make early commitments on specific numerical values for variables appearing in the descriptions of their application problems.

Of course, this results into specific - hence, simpler - design problems. Conversely, this maximizes the likelihood that some of these values are changed by a client after a design phase has started or is completed. As a result, most often, existing design work is invalidated. This does not happen if invariants $< A >$ and $< a >$ are identified.

As explained in section 2, a capture phase involves a number of interactions between a client and a prime contractor. The identification of invariants $\{< A >, < a >\}$, as well as their translation into $\{< X >, < x >\}$, rest on combining knowledge of application-centric semantics and knowledge of those models and properties elaborated in computer science. For example, only a client can tell whether α-particles should be of concern. If such is the case, a prime contractor is responsible for translating this into appropriate failure models.

Let us now give a non exhaustive list of classes of models and properties (each class being non exhaustively described either). Every class has a hierarchical structure. In some cases, partial orders are known (see, e.g., [3], [17]). Of course, this is an area of on-going research. When element Y precedes element Z in the hierarchy or in the partial order considered, one says that Y dominates Z, or that Y is stronger than or equal to Z, which is written $Y \supseteq Z$. Notation $\supseteq$ correctly reflects the fact that Z is included in Y or that $Y = Z$ (see further for examples).

This definition of dominance or strength is consistent with the fact that work involved with a design phase is best described a la game theory, as follows. Set $< m.X >$ defines an "adversary". A designer is in charge of devising and specifying $[S]$, a set of architectural and algorithmic solutions, from which worst-case strategies that can be deployed by "adversary" $< m.X >$ can be inferred and proved. Computer-based system S should always "win against" $< m.X >$. One of the greatest difficulties is to identify and prove these worst-case strategies.

A model Y dominates another model Z if the "adversary" reflected by model Y is less restricted than that reflected by model Z (or is equally restricted). Similarly, this definition of dominance or strength applies to architectural and algorithmic solutions, as well as to properties.

Examples of Model Classes

- Architectural models
- Definition of which are the modules to be architected.
- Centralized shared memory, distributed clients-servers interconnecting sensors and actuators, meshed topology of point-to-point links, multiaccess broadcast bus, group of replicated processors.

- External event types models
- Arrival model (for every type):
  periodic (pr), sporadic (sr), aperiodic (apr), arbitrary (arr); the latter is based on the concept of bounded arrival density, which is defined via a pair of variables, namely a sliding time window of some constant size (w) and a maximum number (a) of arrivals within any such window; unimodal arbitrary ($uarr$) is the model such that only one pair is defined (per event type); multimodal arbitrary ($marr$) is the general case (i.e., ordered multiple pairs for an event type).

$$marr \supseteq uarr \supseteq apr$$
$$marr \supseteq uarr \supseteq sr \supseteq pr$$

- Collective attributes:
  sets of event types that are mutually dependent (causally, chronologically), constraints on arrivals (e.g., time gaps) between different event types.

- System or computational models
  They model advance knowledge relative to upper and lower bounds on computational delays (e.g., time taken by a processor module to make a computational step) as well as on communication delays (e.g., time taken by a network module to transmit a message). More than 30 models known, organized in three sub-classes:
- synchronous (sm): bounds exist, and their values are known,
- partially synchronous (psm): bounds exist, but their values are unknown; or, postulated values hold only after some unknown time; etc.,
- asynchronous (am): bounds do not exist (even if bounds exist, they cannot be reached, even with infinite runs).

$$am \supseteq psm \supseteq sm$$

- Models of shared persistent variables
- Consistency sets, i.e. sets of variables whose values are bound to meet specific sets of invariants.

- External variables, which are shared between tasks and the environment, as well as variables that depend upon these external variables. Examples: variables shared between tasks and sensors, between tasks and actuators.
- Internal variables, which are shared among tasks only, and which do not depend on external variables.

• Task models
- Individual structure: *sequence, star, tree, finite graph.*

$$finite\ graph \supseteq tree \supseteq star \supseteq sequence$$

- Individual attributes (per task): external variables accessed, conditions for (re)activation, suspension, abort (e.g., arrivals of external or internal events), shared internal variables, roll-backs allowed or prohibited.
- Collective attributes: sets of causally dependent tasks, of chronologically dependent tasks.

• Failure models (of architectural modules)
- Value domain: incorrect values.
- Time domain: crash $(crf) \equiv$ permanent halt without warning, omission $(omf) \equiv$ correct steps are not taken from time to time, timing $(tif) \equiv$ steps are taken, but too early or too late.

$$tif \supseteq omf \supseteq crf$$

Many models can be built by combining both domains. More than 20 models known. Most restricted model is *stop* (either correct behavior or crash). Most unrestricted model is *byzantine* (any behavior in the value domain, in the time domain).

• Failure occurrence models (for every module)
See external event arrival models. Most often, the aperiodic or the arbitrary models are considered.

Examples of Property Classes

• Safety: every possible system run (a collective execution of tasks) satisfies some set of invariants. Examples are *mutual exclusion, serializability, data consistency, causal ordering, linearizability.*

$$consensus \supseteq causal\ broadcast \supseteq reliable\ broadcast$$

• Liveness: for every possible system run, tasks that are invoked are activated and make progress. Examples are deadlock freedom, collision detection-and-resolution in bounded time.

• Timeliness: tasks are assigned timeliness constraints. For every possible system run, every timeliness constraint is met.

A timeliness constraint belongs to a category and has a type.
- Examples of categories: latest termination deadline (ld), bounded jitter (bj), earliest start time (st).

$$st \wedge bj \supseteq st \wedge ld \supseteq bj \supseteq ld$$

- Examples of types: constant (c), linear function (lf), or non linear function (nlf) of system or environment parameters. An example of type lf would be $deadline = \alpha/temperature$. An example of type nlf would be $deadline = \beta.(altitude)^2$.

$$nlf \supseteq lf \supseteq c$$

- Dependability: in the presence of partial failures, every possible system run satisfies some set of invariants. Examples are:
- observability (*module*): states which type of failure behavior is to be exhibited by *module*.
- total order: histories of steps (e.g., reads and writes over replicated data) in a group of modules are uniquely ordered.
- availability (*service* [3]): states that *service* can be activated whenever requested.
- reliability (*service*): states that *service* must be correctly delivered.

Note that our definitions of availability, of reliability, are "free from probabilities". This is consistent with the views presented in section 2.3. Under given models - e.g., an upper bound f on the number of module failures that can accumulate without repair, a computational model - and for some given architectural and algorithmic solution, one can establish feasibility conditions such as, e.g., a lower bound on the number of modules needed to cope with up to f failures. Under such conditions, desired dependability properties hold for sure.

With traditional "stochastic" approaches, the definition of a dependability property involves a "measure" - e.g., a probability, a coverage factor - of the smallest acceptable likelihood that this property does hold. In fact, such "measures" come into play for the reason that some of the models considered may be violated - by the environment of S - at run time [4]. If we were to follow this line of reasoning, then safety, or liveness, or timeliness properties should also always involve some "probabilistic measure". As we know, this is not the case at all.

Again, we see no benefits deriving from having probabilities or coverage factors appearing in specifications of properties, on the ground that specified models/assumptions may be violated. Conversely, what does matter is knowing how to compute probabilities or coverage factors for a set of models (such as, e.g., the

---

[3] A fault-tolerant *service* is obtained via replicated tasks and data.

[4] Faulty implementations are another popular motivation. Besides the fact that this is tantamount to assume that there is fundamentally no hope of achieving correct implementations, one may wonder how such "measures" can be used a priori by, e.g., S/W engineers, as ladders of acceptable "faultiness".

conventional "up to f failures without repair" assumption - a failure occurrence model).

Even without embarking on probabilistic or statistical calculations, clients may want to specify how properties should be "degraded" if it happens that some models are violated at run time. This is often achieved by specifying - in addition to the property attributes presented above - individual task or service "value" functions and by requiring that, for every possible system run, accumulated "value" be maximized. This leads to optimization problems akin to, e.g., minimum regret.

Regarding timeliness, constant "values" have been considered [9]. Results of interest in the presence of general "value" functions can be imported from game theory or decision theory. Feasibility conditions may not be satisfied transiently, because of spurious violations of an event arrival model. Thanks to some appropriate algorithmic solution, tasks that do not meet their timeliness constraints precisely are those being the least valuable whenever such violations occur. Similar comments and solutions apply to dependability properties.

• Complexity of [oracle.S]

A client may want to bound $C(oracle)$, the complexity of a dimensioning oracle, which is determined by the complexity of feasibility conditions.

3.2 The System Design Phase

Overview

Most often, real problems $< X >$ are of exponential complexity. Consequently, from a practical standpoint, algorithmic solutions - meant to be used on-line by S - are sub-optimal in most realistic cases. Therefore, a prime contractor has many ways of constructing a design tree, for any given $< X >$. From a practical standpoint again, it may be required (by a client) - or it makes sense - to have some of the modules of S based on COTS products (e.g., processors, operating systems, middleware). Early adoption of COTS products is tantamount to "freeze" a priori some of the intermediate nodes or some of the leaves of a design tree. This reduces the space of potential solutions to be explored, which is a good idea at first sight. However, correctness proof obligations have to be met at any design stage, regardless of the fact that COTS products are or are not being considered at that stage. There are potential difficulties involved with COTS products (see further).

The tree structure of a design phase is shown figure 2, where $[S] = \cup_{j \in [1,z]}[S_j]$ is the (modular) specification of S that "aggregates" all design decisions. A prime contractor stops designing along a branch whenever the specification arrived at is known to be implementable (e.g., via some COTS product, or as a customized H/W and/or S/W module), or when the to-be-continued design work is assigned to a co/sub-contractor (who is bound to apply a proof-based SE method as well). Indeed, in practice, a prime contractor may decide to end a design tree branch "prematurely", i.e. when arrived at some non implementable specification module $[S_u]$. Design work - to be continued - is contractually handed over to some

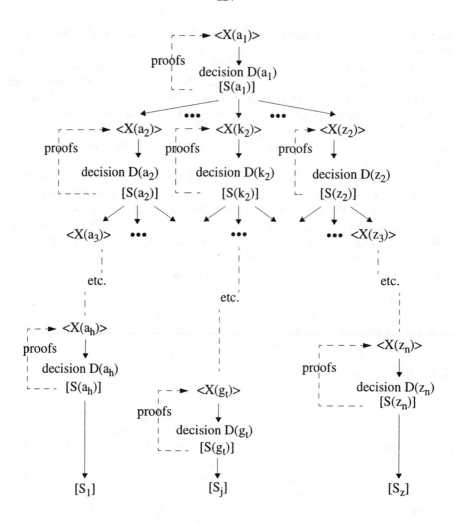

$$\text{modular specification of } S = [S] = \bigcup_{j \in [1,z]} [S_j]$$

Fig. 2. The tree structure of a design phase

co/sub-contractor. As explained further, the specification of problem $< X' >$, which is the contract handed over by the prime contractor, is directly extracted from $[m.S_u]$. To a co/sub-contractor, $< X' >$ is a design tree root.

Design Stages

Each stage has a unique reference r_i, i being a tree level and r being one element of the set of names needed to enumerate all stages of the same level. Problem considered at stage r_i is denoted $< X(r_i) >$. Initial problem $< X >$ is rewritten $< X(a_1) >$. Design decision/solution or design stage r_i is denoted $D(r_i)$.

<u>Generic solutions</u>

Design stage $D(r_i)$ consists in dividing $< X(r_i) >$ into a number - denoted $d(r_i)$ - of modules or subproblems, by specifying a modular decomposition. For every such module, one specifies a set of models, denoted $[m_k(ri)]$, $k \in [1, d(r_i)]$. Given a modular decomposition, one specifies a global architecture - denoted $[arch(r_i)]$ - as well as a global algorithmic solution (a composite algorithm, in most cases) - denoted $[alg(r_i)]$. Instantiation of $[alg(r_i)]$ (resp. $[arch(r_i)]$) local to module k is denoted $[alg_k(r_i)]$ (resp. $[arch_k(r_i)]$). Choice of models $m_k(r_i)$ is constrained by the obligation of fulfilling a design correctness proof (see further). Furthermore, for some modules, it may be that some associated models depend on $alg(r_i)$. This is often the case with event arrivals models (events triggered among modules).

The output of design stage $D(r_i)$ is a triple $\{[S(r_i)], \mathcal{P}.S(r_i), [oracle.S(r_i)]\}$, where :

- $[S(r_i)]$ comprises the $d(r_i)$ sets $\{[m_k(r_i)], [alg_k(r_i)], [arch_k(r_i)]$,
- $\mathcal{P}.S(r_i)$ is the set that describes those global properties - along with their proofs - that hold with $[S(r_i)]$,
- $[oracle.S(r_i)]$ specifies a dimensioning oracle (see further) which is derived from set $\mathcal{P}.S(r_i)$.

• Specification $[S(r_i)]$

For each of the specification sets in $[S(r_i)]$, there is one out of two possible outcomes. Consider $[S_k(r_i)]$. If deemed implementable or implemented by some procurable product, that specification terminates a design tree branch. In other words, $[S_k(r_i)]$ is a (level i) design tree leaf, i.e. a specification of a real (physical) module of S. If deemed non implementable or not implemented by some procurable product, then $[S_k(r_i)]$ - which then specifies an abstract module of S - translates into a (level $i + 1$) subproblem $\{< m.X(q_{i+1}) >, < p.X(q_{i+1} >\}$ trivially extracted from $[m_k(r_i)]$.

Let us illustrate the above with the following example drawn from our experience with project 1 (see section 4), where $< X(a_1) >$ is a distributed real-time fault-tolerant computer science problem and $[S(a_1)]$ is based - in particular - on a network module, node k of level 1 in the design tree. In $[m_k(a_1)]$, one finds the following :

- synchronous computational model : network delays range between min and max,
- failure model : bounded message omissions.

Furthermore, given the (external) event arrivals and the task models specified in $< m.X(a_1) >$ on the one hand, the algorithmic solution $alg(a_1)$ on the other hand, one derives time windows within which messages can be generated by tasks, i.e. the message arrivals model to be found in $[m_k(a_1)]$, e.g., the unimodal arbitrary model. Such derivations may raise non trivial issues, barely addressed so far in scientific publications.

Obviously, this postulated network module is not directly implementable with existing COTS products, or with other documented products. In fact, $[m_k(a_1)]$ raises the following level 2 subproblem (say, tree node c_2) :

- $< m.X(c_2) > = <$ unimodal arbitrary message arrivals model, message omission failure model $>$,
- $< p.X(c_2) > = <$ network delays $\in$ [min, max] $>$.

Solving this subproblem entails - in particular - designing a real-time communication protocol (an algorithmic solution) and establishing timeliness proofs, such as done in [4].

- Set $\mathcal{P}.S(r_i)$

This is the set describing properties and proofs that properties "as strong as" those specified in $< p.X(r_i) >$ do hold with $[S(r_i)]$. Establishing the existence of such properties is needed so as to meet a design correctness proof obligation, i.e. to prove that $[S(r_i)]$ is a correct solution. This is also essential for establishing $[f\_oracle.S]$ (see further). Proofs in $\mathcal{P}.S(r_i)$ may rest on establishing computable behavioral functions such as, e.g., upper (resp. lower) bounds on task response times (denoted B (resp. b)), lower bounds on redundancy degrees (denoted R).

- Specification $[oracle.S(r_i)]$

Most often, $[S(r_i)]$ contains unvalued variables, specified as per $[s(r_i)]$, such as, e.g., a boolean matrix reflecting how level i S/W modules are mapped onto the modules considered with $[S(r_i)]$, periods of invocation for task schedulers over every such module. $[s(r_i)]$ is decomposed as follows :

- $[!s(r_i)]$, which contains variables that may be valued (by a client or a prime contractor) prior to conducting a dimensioning phase; such valuations are performed via a tool component denoted $configurator.S(r_i)$; for example, some mappings being geographically constrained (for some particular release of S), corresponding variables have pre-determined values; some of the variables in $[!s(r_i)]$ may be left unvalued,
- $[?s(r_i)] = [s(r_i)] - [!s(r_i)]$, which contains variables to be valued by a tool component denoted $f\_oracle.S(r_i)$, i.e. by running (dimensioning) $oracle.S$ (see section 3.3).

In $[f\_oracle.S(r_i)]$, one finds generic feasibility conditions; such conditions are a set of constraints that, for pair $\{< X(r_i) >, [S(r_i)]\}$, bind together variables that appear in $< m.X(r_i) >, < p.X(r_i) >$, set $\mathcal{P}.S(r_i)$ and $[m.S(r_i)] = \bigcup_{k \in [1, d(r_i)]}[m_k(r_i)]$. Let $[oracle.S(r_i)]$ be the union of $[configurator.S(r_i)]$ and $[f\_oracle.S(r_i)]$.

Let us now take a broader view, and consider a complete design phase. As shown fig. 2, design tree leaves are relabelled consecutively. As for $[S]$, we have $[oracle.S] = \bigcup_{j \in [1, z]}[oracle.S_j]$, which is to be implemented as a tool component. Note that, rigorously speaking, $[S]$ is only partially implementable. For example, algorithms and protocols can be implemented in some language (or reused, if available), without having to know the outcome of a dimensioning phase. However, full implementation of S is conditioned on knowing $V([s])$.

Design correctness proof obligation: design_cpo($D(r_i)$)

A generic solution $D(r_i)$ provably solves problem $< X(r_i) >$ if the following two conditions are satisfied:

$$p.S(r_i) \supseteq p.X(r_i) \quad \text{and} \quad m.S(r_i) \supseteq m.X(r_i),$$

where $p.S(r_i)$ are properties enforced by $[S(r_i)]$, as given in $\mathcal{P}.S(r_i)$.

Obligation design_cpo($D(r_i)$) expresses the constraint that properties ensured with some $[S(r_i)]$ must dominate those stated in $< p.X(r_i) >$, under models that must dominate those stated in $< m.X(r_i) >$.

For example, with the real-time problem sketched out in section 2.2 (system design phase), picking up the periodic arrival model, which is central to the rate/deadline monotonic approach, would be invalid in our case. Indeed, proofs that the first condition of design_cpo(.) is met (no deadline is missed) would be irrelevant, as being non applicable to the problem under consideration (revealed by a violation of the second condition).

In fact, the periodic arrival model is quite inappropriate for modeling event arrival laws within distributed systems (i.e. its coverage factor is close to 0), even if one would assume periodic models for external event arrivals. This is essentially due to the fact that task durations, resource contention delays, sojourn times in waiting queues, are inevitably variable, even more so when failures are considered. Consequently - and contrary to widespread belief - results on periodic task scheduling have very limited usefulness in the case of distributed computer-based systems, even more so when established for sequential task models.

COTS Products and Current SE Practice

As stated earlier, one may have to conduct a design phase under the constraint that COTS products have been selected a priori. A COTS product has an architecture and contains inner mechanisms (algorithms) that ensure specific properties, for some environments. A vendor may not want to reveal which algorithms are used in a product that is considered for implementing some design tree leaf (say q), nor the proofs of properties. Keeping $\{[S_q], [s_q]\}$ undisclosed is acceptable provided that there is a commitment on a pair $\{< X >, < x >\}$ that specifies which is the problem solved by that product, and that there exists a matching dimensioning oracle. Under current industry/business practice, COTS products are not accompanied with (provably correct) specifications, neither with oracle-like tools. Consequently, there is no way of checking whether early adoption of a COTS product is or is not a correct design decision, or whether - if correct - that design decision is arbitrarily non optimal (hence, costly). Which explains many of the problems that bring clients and prime contractors, or prime contractors and co/sub-contractors, into conflict.

Yet, it is easy to eliminate such problems simply by requiring that design correctness proof obligations be fulfilled at every design stage, including those based on COTS products. Of course, it will take some time before we see S/W, computing or networking companies ship COTS products along with such specification sets as $\{[S_q], [s_q]\}$ or $\{< X >, < x >\}$. This simply mirrors the current immaturity of the (relatively young) computing and information industry. Is it not surprising that vendors of refrigerators make contractual commitments on specifications akin to $< A >$ or $< X >$, whereas vendors of such COTS products as "real-time" operating systems or middleware do not publish or do not make contractual commitments on similar specifications?

As explained earlier, fulfilling design correctness proof obligations yields feasibility conditions (FCs). One may establish FCs without expressing computable behavioral functions such as b, B or R. For example, for some {uniprocessor, periodic arrival model, timeliness} problems, it has been proved that Earliest-Deadline-First is an optimal algorithm, FCs being stated as $U \leq 1$, where U is a processor utilization ratio. Latencies (i.e., slack times before deadlines) of periodic tasks are unknown. One may also establish FCs by first expressing B (in $\mathcal{P}.S$), and then constrain it to match the timeliness property specified in $< p.X >$ by fulfilling a design_cpo. One would then know task latencies.

With realistic problems, the number of scenari that can be deployed by any given "adversary" $< m.X >$ is "high". "High" also is the number of states a computer-based system might enter whenever any of these scenari is instantiated. Consequently, set θ of pairs {adversary scenario, system state} may not even be enumerable (think of partial failures). FCs are generic computable constraints. They demarcate the boundary of a set of scenari that includes all worst-case scenari that can be instantiated by "adversary" $< m.X >$. This boundary determines a subset θ_f of set θ.

Under current SE practice, identification of set θ_f is ignored. A computer-based system S is accepted by a client provided that S has successfully gone through a finite number of tests that are supposed to represent real future operational conditions. Definition of these tests usually is based on past experience and on the identification of specific pairs {adversary scenario, system state} that are considered to be "of particular concern". This is tantamount to invite a client - who should not be involved at all in such decisions - to make early commitments on a limited number of elements in set θ, without knowing whether one is testing for worst-case scenari nor how many of worst-case scenari are left untested.

This explains why simulation and integration testing, as performed under current SE practice, do not allow for verifying whether or not a specification

$\{[S], V([s])\}$ is satisfied, even less a specification $\{< X >, V(< x >)\}$. Which explains many operational failures and project cancellations.

Conversely, it is reasonably obvious that FCs bring along the following benefits: (i) FCs yield a dimensioning of S such that problem-centric properties quantified as per $V(< p.x >)$ certainly hold for all possible worst-case quantified scenari "hidden" within $V(< m.x >)$, (ii) time needed to compute a set of constraints along the boundary of θ_f is vastly smaller than checking whether some invariants are satisfied for every element in θ_f, which is what must be done if one would resort to event-driven simulation or model checking (assuming furthermore that θ_f has been identified under these approaches). See sections 3.4 and 3.5 for more on this issue.

Final Comments

Experience shows that early design stages - design stage 1 in particular - are conducted more or less empirically under current SE practice. This explains many of the setbacks and operational failures experienced over the last 10 years with projects involving complex and/or critical embedded systems.

An appropriate illustration of this reality is the US FAA AAS project (air traffic control). The Center for Naval Analyses, which was asked to audit the project, diagnosed, in particular, the following problems and oversights:

- "There is no evidence that any in-depth analysis of the design architecture or the contractor methodology was conducted."
- "Major system and architectural engineering, so desperately needed early in the program, was not evident."
- "In addition to the S/W problems, the system lacked overall system engineering. The S/W and the H/W were broken into pieces without looking at the overall system requirements."

Another appropriate illustration of this reality is the failed maiden flight of the Ariane 5 European satellite launcher (see section 5).

See section 4 for an example of how to conduct design stage 1 in the case of a (complex and critical) modular avionics problem.

3.3 The System Dimensioning Phase

This phase can be conducted by a client, a prime contractor, or both. Before an implementation or some specific release of S can be undertaken, the physical dimensioning of every module of S need be specified. Such a dimensioning $V([s])$ depends upon a quantification specification $V(< x >)$. Recall that one cannot proceed with fully implementing or releasing S without knowing $\{[S], V([s])\}$.

Specification $[s]$ is the union of those subsets that contain unvalued system variables accumulated throughout design stages, i.e. from the root of a design tree. Hence, as for $[S]$, $[s] = \cup_{j \in [1,z]}[s_j]$ is a modular specification. As seen before, $[s]$ is decomposed as follows:

- $[!s_j]$, which contains variables that may be valued prior to conducting a dimensioning phase,

- $[?s_j] = [s_j]$ - $[!s_j]$; values to be assigned to variables in $[?s_j]$ are obtained as a by-product of verifying that specified feasibility conditions are satisfied.

Consequently, dimensioning oracle *oracle.S* for pair $\{< X >, [S]\}$ includes the following:

- a configuration component, denoted *configurator.S*; its input is some valuation of some of the variables in $[!s]$; its output is $V([!s])$,
- a feasibility oracle, denoted *f_oracle.S*, a component which implements feasibility conditions established for pair $\{< X >, [S]\}$; its inputs are $V([!s])$ and $V(< x >)$; its output is $V([?s])$.

For example, some valuation is assigned to a boolean matrix in $[!s]$ that reflects how application-level (i.e. level 1) S/W modules are to be mapped onto (real) modules of S. Values of other variables in $[!s]$, e.g. matrices that give mappings of low-level S/W modules, are computed by *configurator.S*.

Examples of variables that are valued by *f_oracle.S* are as follows in the case of a processor module: exact invocation period of a task scheduler, maximum execution time of this scheduler, exact or sufficient memory capacity needed to store the data structures used by application S/W modules mapped onto that module, exact or sufficient size of every buffer needed to store shared external variables and related variables, exact or sufficient size of every waiting queue, exact values of timers used to detect failures, lower bound of the group size that module belongs to. For a communication bus module, one would have: number of access ports, number of independent physical channels, exact or sufficient sizes of waiting outqueues and inqueues (one of each kind per access port), and so on.

Component *f_oracle.S* works as follows. For every variable in $[?s]$, it selects a potential value within a given range (ranges are specified in the feasibility conditions) and iterate in this range until, either quantification $V(< x >)$ of problem $< X >$ is declared non feasible, or a value that meets the dimensioning_cpo is found.

Let $V([s])$ be some proposed dimensioning of $[S]$. How do we know whether $V([s])$ is correct w.r.t. problem quantification $V(< x >)$?

Dimensioning correctness proof obligation: dimensioning_cpo($V([s])$)

A system dimensioning $V([s])$ provably satisfies a quantification $V(< x >)$ of problem $< X >$ if the following two conditions are satisfied:

$$V([p.s]) \supseteq V(< p.x >) \text{ and } V([m.s]) \supseteq V(< m.x >).$$

An illustration of the first condition for a real-time problem stating *bounded jitters* as a timeliness property would be that values of behavioral functions b and B, computed considering some processors speeds and processors storage capacity, match the values of bounded jitters set via $V(< p.x >)$. An illustration of the second condition would be: these values have been computed for values of upper bounds on arrival densities at least equal to those stated via $V(< m.x >)$.

It is reasonably obvious that whenever a proof-based SE method is resorted to, meeting a dimensioning_cpo with some $V([s])$ is automatically enforced by a dimensioning oracle, given that values of variables in [?s] are computed by the oracle. Nevertheless, it may be that meeting such a cpo is not possible, in which case the oracle returns a negative output. This may happen essentially for two reasons. One is that $V(< x >)$ is too "ambitious" (e.g., very small deadlines under very high arrival densities and for a widely dispersed architecture). Another (practical) reason is that acceptable $V([s])$'s are constrained, either technology-wise (there is no processor running at the speed required to meet $V(< s >)$) or budget-wise (their is a limit on what a client is willing to spend on S).

Another motivation behind the concept of a dimensioning_cpo is linked with the fact that proof-based SE is not very much practiced yet. Hence, especially when COTS products are considered, system engineers should be aware of what is involved with correctly dimensioning a computer-based system. Whenever COTS or proprietary products are targeted for the implementation of S, values of some variables in [!s] and [?s] are "frozen" a priori, i.e. prior to entering a design phase, which increases the likelihood of delivering a system S that will fail when being used. This can be avoided by showing system engineers how to check whether a computer-based system is correctly dimensioned. Quite often, approximate over-dimensioning - which is commonly practiced, to clients' expenses - may be shown to violate dimensioning_cpo's.

Correct $V([s])$ is optimal for the solution specified in [S] if, by choosing a dimensioning "weaker" than $V([s])$, at least one of the conditions of the dimensioning_cpo is not satisfied. Physical dimensionings translate into costs. In other words, with optimal $V([s])$, one knows what is the cheapest correct S that satisfies $\{< X >, V(< x >)\}$, with the solution considered.

Many different problem quantifications $V(< x >)$ may be contemplated by a client or a prime contractor, before a decision is made, e.g. before the fielding of a particular instantiation of S, or each time a new mission is set up. The latter would apply, for example, with embedded systems used for defense applications. Depending on the application considered, a client may or may not be willing to restrict complexity $C(oracle)$ - see section 3.1. Most real problems being of exponential complexity, an optimal oracle is hardly usable in practice. Small (resp. big) values of $C(oracle)$ translate into fast (resp. slow) oracles, but also into pessimistic (resp. more accurate) oracles. A pessimistic oracle may return a negative output despite the fact that problem $\{< X >, V(< x >)\}$ is feasible.

Note that the dimensioning of every variable that is shared by S and its environment (i.e., every external variable) is provably correctly specified, rather than being left undefined or to be decided upon by implementors of system engineering decisions (e.g., S/W engineers). Finding a correct dimensioning of a variable internal to some application S/W module is under the sole responsibility of the S/W engineer(s) in charge of that module. Conversely, finding a correct dimensioning of an external variable that is used by some application S/W module is not a S/W engineering issue.

Failure to understand or to acknowledge this distinction usually leads to disasters, as illustrated by the unsuccessful maiden flight of the European Ariane 5 launcher (see section 5).

Final Comments

As discussed in section 2.3, with deterministic proof-based SE, one may have to estimate coverage factors for some of the models specified in $< m.x >$, as well as for some of the quantifications specified via $V(< m.x >)$ and $V(< p.x >)$. By the virtue of the design_cpo's and dimensioning_cpo's, coverage factors related to $\{[S], V([s])\}$ can only be greater than those estimated for problem-centric set $\{< m.X >, V(< x >)\}$. Consequently, the capacity for a provably correct S to satisfactorily cope with violations of $\{< m.X >, V(< x >)\}$ is higher than mirrored by the problem-centric coverage factors, this being obviously true whenever feasibility conditions are sufficient rather than necessary and sufficient.

3.4 Benefits achieved with Proof-Based System Engineering

In addition to avoiding system engineering faults, a number of advantages derive from proof-based SE. Some of them are briefly reviewed below.

Technical Benefits

- Design reusability. Various generic application problems $\{< A >, < a >\}$ may translate into the same set $\{< X >, < x >\}$. Whenever a generic problem $< X >$ has been provably solved in the past, matching generic solution $[S]$ comes for free for any of these application problems. (Potentially huge savings in projects durations and costs).
- High and cheap system configurability. The fact that system design and system dimensioning are distinct phases makes it possible for a client to select at will any combination of application S/W modules, some quantification of the application problem of interest, and to be delivered a correctly dimensioned system S, without having to incur any of those delays and costs that are induced by the need to re-design S.
- Elimination of artificial dependencies between the capture, the design and the dimensioning phases has the effect of suppressing time and budget consuming inefficient work, such as looping back and forth between different design stages or between different phases of a project lifecycle.
- Rigorous assessment of COTS technology, via design and dimensioning correctness proof obligations.
- Simplification of final integration testing. Verification that a set of concatenated modules "behaves correctly" - the "system integration phase" - runs into combinatorial problems. Under current practice, such a verification is done via testing, within imposed bounded time and budget, which means that testing is necessarily incomplete, even with computer-based systems of modest complexity. Let us consider conservative figures. Imagine that 10 modules, each having 100 visible states (reduction to such a small number being achieved via unitary testing), go through integration testing. Complete testing involves checking 10^{20} global states, which is beyond feasibility. (Even if a global state could be checked in 1 millisecond, complete testing would take in the order of 3.10^9 years). Under a proof-based SE approach, it is proved beforehand that the union of modules is a global solution. If it would

be the case that every specification pair $\{[S_j], V([s_j])\}$ is correctly implemented, there would be no need for system S integration testing (theoretical viewpoint). Unitary tests, i.e. on a per module basis, being incomplete in general, system S integration testing still is necessary (practical viewpoint). However, the beneficial effect of proof-based SE is to bring the complexity of system integration testing down to acceptable figures, such as, e.g., pseudo-linear complexity in the number of modules' visible states.

Legal Benefits

Would a problem arise during the implementation, construction, fielding or utilization of a system, it is easy to find out which of the actors involved is/are to be held responsible. Contrary to usual practice - actors involved share the penalties - it is possible to discriminate without any ambiguity between client's fault (faulty specification set $\{< A >, < a >\}$), prime contractor's fault (faulty specification sets $\{< X >, < x >\}$, $\{[S], [s]\}$, or $[oracle.S]$), co/sub-contractors' fault (faulty implementation of set $\{[S], [s]\}$), prime contractor's or some co/sub-contractor's or some tool vendor's fault (faulty implementation of $[oracle.S]$).

Strategic Benefits

It is common practice to assign different pieces of a project to different contractors. It is possible for a client or a prime contractor (say M) to take full responsibility w.r.t. a complex application problem, to "break" it into simpler subproblems, either in one design stage or until some appropriate level of problem granularity has been reached. Subproblems can then be contracted, each having a precise specification $\{< X(.) >, < x(.) >\}$. M may ask contractors to show proofs of design and dimensioning correctness. Furthermore, note that M only has complete knowledge of the overall technical decisions. Therefore, M may subcontract work to its competitors, without giving away its technical know-how.

Of course, there are also many new (strategic) opportunities for tool vendors as well. Knowledge-based tools needed to support the various phases of proof-based SE are yet to be developed.

3.5 Proof-Based System Engineering and the Software Crisis

Our main thesis is that one of the major causes of the so-called S/W problems or "S/W crisis" is lack of proper identification of the real nature of those problems that the S/W industry has been faced with for years, without succeeding in solving them. Complexity is an archetypal example. In many instances, these problems are system engineering issues. It is not surprising at all that SE issues do not fade away when addressed as S/W engineering issues. Trying to resolve them by improving the quality of S/W implemented modules is like trying to successfully build a dam by improving the quality of blocks of reinforced concrete, without realizing that the problems are due to incorrect dam blueprints.

Whenever an operational computer-based system fails, S/W is being run at time of failure. It is then all the more tempting to believe that S/W is to be held responsible for a failure. Unfortunately, just because a problem is observed in S/W behavior does not mean that it is a S/W problem per se. Many such problems, especially the more difficult and subtle ones, are rooted into SE decisions (problems originate in SE faults), and propagate to the S/W levels through deficient specifications. Audits of a number of failed projects have indeed revealed that causes of failures were not due to latent faults in application S/W, as was believed by clients and/or contractors.

Planned or delivered systems did not operate properly simply because they did not include appropriate "system-level" (e.g., scheduling, synchronization) algorithms. As a result, application S/W modules (programs) could be interrupted at random and/or could run interleaved in arbitrary fashion. Even with perfectly correct application S/W modules, behavior of such computer-based systems could only be incorrect.

One pre-requisite for solving the "S/W crisis" is to move away from monolithic application S/W. Modularization and S/W modules reuse are sound principles. However, in order to reap the benefits of such principles, one must show that quasi or truly parallel asynchronous executions of S/W modules cannot jeopardize the integrity of any of these modules (a property commonly found in $< A >$). Which translates into showing that a set of invariants (I) is always satisfied, i.e. into specifying a safety property in $< X >$, such as, e.g., linearizability or serializability [1], which raises problems that have numerous and well documented solutions.

One approach - which is at the core of some formal methods popular in the S/W engineering field - consists in exploring every global state that can be entered by a given set of application S/W modules, and to verify for each global state that (I) is not violated. Let us make some rough calculations. Consider a set comprising 100 S/W modules (a conservative figure) and assume that, in average, every single module can enter 10 different intermediate states that are visible from other modules (again, a conservative figure).

This entails searching 10^{100} global states, which is beyond tractability, even if one would reduce this complexity by a few orders of magnitude via, e.g., binary decision diagrams. Verification methods directed at parallel synchronous or asynchronous computations in the presence of failures - the correct paradigms with embedded systems - and which are based on exhaustive searches of global state spaces, are doomed to fail even with modestly complex systems. Furthermore, their usage is hardly justifiable, given that there exists an impressive gamut of fault-tolerant and/or concurrency control algorithms. Companion proofs establish that a system equipped with any of these algorithms guarantees that (I) cannot be violated, whatever the set of application S/W modules considered. Proofs do away with the need for verification. Algorithms (SE originated solutions) serve the purpose of "breaking complexity", in a very cost effective manner.

The above is a simple illustration of the fact that oversight of SE issues inevitably complicates S/W design and S/W development. Proof-based SE promotes S/W reuse, S/W evolution and facilitates S/W management.

4 Lessons Learned with Proof-Based System Engineering

In this section, we give examples of projects where the TRDF method has been applied. As indicated in section 2.4, the TRDF method is aimed at application problems that raise any combination of real-time, distributed, fault-tolerant computing issues. It can be demonstrated that whenever either one of these issues is raised in $< A >$, this translates into a problem $< X >$ where at least one of the other two issues is raised as well.

In projects 1 and 2, INRIA's REFLECS team took on the role of a prime contractor. For the sake of conciseness, presentations of projects will mainly consist in summarizing lessons learned, to the exception of two projects that will be more detailed, namely project 1 (see below) and project 4 (see section 5). Work conducted during these projects has not been published, to the exception of project 4. Reports, in French, are available upon request.

4.1 Project 1

Clients: French DARPA (DGA/DSP) and Dassault Aviation. Modular avionics was the application problem considered. Objectives were to check the feasibility of decoupling fully the capture, design and dimensioning phases, as well as to deliver specifications $[S]$ and $[oracle.S]$, that were subsequently implemented by Dassault Aviation. Practical constraints were that COTS products had to be taken into account (e.g., specific processors, "real-time" monitors, object-based middleware), and that one design stage only was to be undertaken.

Sketch of application invariant $< m.A >$

- Application S/W is modular; dates of creation of application S/W modules (set M of modules) span over many years. Modules can be suppressed or created at will. That is, set M is unbounded.
- Application S/W modules should not depend on any existing or future COTS products.
- External events are pilot commands, sensors data, etc. They trigger application S/W modules which, when executed, produce outputs, such as responses displayed to pilot, commands applied to actuators.
- Numbers of sensors, actuators, are finite but unknown.
- Persistent variables that represent current global plane, environment, and system states, are read and written when application S/W modules are run.
- Any such variable may be shared among some unknown number of S/W application modules, as well as among modules and the environment.
- There should be no restrictions on the programming models used to develop application S/W modules; no restrictions either on which variables can be accessed by a S/W module.
- Distribution of application S/W modules and shared persistent variables (over future embedded system S) should be unrestricted.
- Some external event types are periodic sensor readings, arrival laws for other event types (a majority) are unknown.

- Failures internal to (future) S should be anticipated (environment is "aggressive").
- Failures occur at unpredictable times.

Sketch of application invariant $< p.A >$

- Many different releases of M, involving any combination of application S/W modules, can be fielded; this should not entail re-designing or re-proving S.
- At all times, any application S/W module should run as expected (no side-effect).
- At all times, values taken by shared persistent variables should consistently mirror the current plane and plane's environment states.
- Outputs generated by application S/W modules are non recoverable.
- Application S/W modules must meet "hard" real-time constraints.
- Some of the persistent variables are critical. In case such a variable is lost, pilot should be informed "rapidly".
- One should be able to generate any particular release of S (proved correct) "rapidly".

Sketch of problem invariant $< m.X >$

- The executable counterpart of an application S/W module is a task.
- Any task t, if run alone, has an upperly bounded execution time.
- Any set T of tasks t can be considered; size of T is unknown.
- Architectural model: a distributed system of modules, no shared memory; number of modules is unknown.
- External event type models: Set EV of event types (ev). Mapping of EV onto T to be specified via a boolean matrix. Subset EV1: periodic arrival model (values of periods: unknown). Subset EV2: unimodal arbitrary arrival model (values of densities: unknown).
- Computational model: synchronous.
- Models of shared persistent variables:
- Consistency sets in set DATA, i.e. subsets of variables whose values are bound to satisfy client defined invariants (I). Any task, if run alone, satisfies (I). There are no restrictions on which invariants (I) can be considered.
- Set c.DATA = subset of DATA; defines the set of "critical" variables.
- Type "internal" or "external" assigned to every shared persistent variable.
- Mapping of DATA onto T to be specified via a boolean matrix.
- Task models: finite graphs.
- Failure Models:
- Processor modules: stop.
- Network module: omission.
- Failure occurrence model: aperiodic and unimodal arbitrary arrival model.

Sketch of problem invariant $< p.X >$

- Safety:
- Exactly-once semantics for tasks. No task roll-backs.

- Invariants (I)
- Serializability: every possible run for any pair {T, DATA} satisfies (I).

- Timeliness:
  Task timeliness constraints: latest termination deadlines. Values of individual deadlines are unknown.

- Dependability:
- Very high availability and reliability for network services.
- Finite failure detection latency for computer modules that host c.DATA.

- Complexity $C(oracle)$: pseudo-linear in the number of tasks in T.

It turns out that $< X >$ specifies a generic computer science problem that is at the core of such drastically diverse application problems as stock markets, currency trading, defense ($C^3 I$, space), air traffic control, nuclear power plants.

Problem $< X >$ is NP-hard. The algorithmic solution alg, specified in delivered [S], includes a hybrid algorithm that is a combination of periodic distributed agreement, idling and non-idling, preemptive and non-preemptive First-In-First-Out, Earliest-Deadline-First, and template-based schedulers.

Sketch of $oracle.S$: precomputed schedule templates (not precomputed schedules) and particular constructs on graphs helped reduce $C(oracle)$ to what was specified. Note that the combination of arbitrary arrival models with finite graph task models yields a reasonably unrestricted "adversary". It turns out that, under such models, those proof techniques traditionally used to establish timeliness properties for weaker models (e.g, sequential tasks and periodic/sporadic arrival models) simply do not apply. Examples of techniques and results that were used are: optimal scheduling algorithms, analytical calculus, time based agreement algorithms, adversary arguments, matrix calculus in (max,+) algebra [2].

Lessons learned

The genericity of the TRDF method has been validated. It has been verified that it is possible to decouple fully the capture, design, and dimensioning phases. It was confirmed that the capture phase is essential and that having a contract such as $\{< A >, < X >\}$ is instrumental in clarifying responsibilities. At one point, Dassault Aviation felt that solution alg "had a problem". It did not take us long to agree that alg was correct vis-à-vis the contrat specified. What this client had in mind was in fact a variation of $< A >$. It turned out that the variation could be accomodated by alg, by restricting potential choices w.r.t. the schedule templates. However, the feasibility oracle (in [$oracle.S$]) had to be partially revisited.

What has also been clearly verified is how fast a dimensioning oracle can be compared to an event-driven simulator. For the task sets considered, run times never exceeded one hour with our dimensioning oracle, whereas run times could be as long as one day for the event-driven simulator developed by Dassault Aviation.

4.2 Project 2

Client: Institut de Protection et de Sûreté Nucléaire, French Atomic Energy Authority. The problem we had to examine was whether some COTS command-and-control system could be considered for automated safety related control operations in nuclear power plants.

We applied the TRDF method twice, in parallel. One thread of work was concerned with the capture phase only. Upon completion, the client was delivered specifications $< A >$ and $< X >$.

The other thread of work consisted in doing what can be called reverse proof-based system engineering. The COTS system considered had no such specification as $\{[m.S], [p.S]\}$ or $[alg]$. Consequently, we had to inspect the technical documentation and get information from engineers who were familiar with this system. The TRDF method was applied bottom-up. By analyzing the modules of the COTS system, we could reconstruct $[m.S]$ and algorithmic solutions of interest alg, which led us to specification $[p.S]$.

We could then establish that none of the conditions of a design-cpo was fulfilled (i.e., $[S] \supseteq < X >$ did not hold true). Our recommendation has been to disregard the command-and-control system under study.

Lessons learned

Here too, it was verified that, when conducted rigorously, a capture phase is time consuming. One difficulty we ran into during the first iterations was to have the client's engineers "forget" about the technical documentation of the COTS system they were familiar with, and to concentrate on their real application problem. The other lesson is that it is indeed possible to rigorously assess COTS products.

4.3 Project 3

Clients: French Ministry of Research and Dassault Aviation. We had to identify what were the dependability properties actually enforced by a simple embedded system considered for commanding and controlling essential actuators in future planes. Different teams of S/W engineers and scientists from various French research laboratories had applied formal (proof-based) methods to specify, develop and engineer S/W needed to command and control the actuators. When our work was started, proofs of S/W correctness had been established. Our work in this project was a bit similar to that of project 2. The TRDF method allowed to show that, despite redundant S/W and a redundant architecture, the embedded system could fail under certain circumstances. Essentially, that was due to the fact that physical time is heavily relied upon in order to achieve necessary synchronizations, and that physical time may not be properly maintained in the presence of partial failures.

Lessons learned

What was revealed by applying the TRDF method was the exact "gap" existing between those models (e.g., system model, failure models, event arrivals models) assumed in order to establish S/W correctness proofs and those models that correctly reflect the real embedded system and its environment. S/W correctness proofs were developed assuming models much weaker (in the $\supseteq$ sense) than the correct ones.

This is an illustration of the fact that it is not a good idea to apply formal S/W engineering methods without applying proof-based system engineering methods as well. This is due to the fact that those models that can be accomodated with existing formal S/W engineering methods are ideal representations of physical reality and of real computer-based systems. Hence the following choices: (i) either ignore such limitations, which inevitably leads to operational failures, (ii) or acknowledge these limitations and conclude - erroneously - that S/W correctness proofs are useless, (iii) or acknowledge the need for proof-based SE, whose role is to "bridge the gap" between both worlds. In other words, one of the benefits of proof-based SE is to emulate over real systems those "simple" models that can be currently accommodated with formal S/W engineering methods.

Project 4 - described in section 5 - is concerned with how the TRDF method was applied to diagnose the causes of the failure of Ariane 5 Flight 501.

5 A Case Study in Proof-Based System Engineering: The Ariane 5 Flight 501 Failure

5.1 Introduction

On 4 June 1996, the maiden flight of the European Ariane 5 satellite launcher ended in a failure, entailing a total loss (satellites included) in the order of 0.5 Billion US dollars and a delay for the Ariane 5 program, which was initially estimated to be in the order of 1 year. An Inquiry Board which was formed by the European Space Agency (ESA) - the client - and the French Space Agency (CNES) - the prime contractor - was asked to identify the causes of the failure. Conclusions of the Inquiry Board were issued on 19 July 1996, as a public report [6]. The failure analysis presented in the sequel is based upon the Inquiry Board findings.

Our conclusions deviate significantly from the Inquiry Board findings. Basically, the Inquiry Board concludes that poor S/W engineering practice is the culprit, whereas we argue that the 501 failure results from poor system engineering decisions. Most of what is labelled as S/W errors are in fact manifestations of system engineering faults.

Had a proof-based SE method been applied by the prime contractor and by the industrial architect (Aérospatiale), faults that led to the 501 failure would have been avoided. This analysis is meant to - hopefully - help those partners in charge of and involved in projects similar to the Ariane 5 program. Neither the prime contractor's system engineers nor the industrial architect's system engineers should be "blamed" for not having followed a proof-based SE approach, given that proof-based SE methods did not exist at the time the Ariane 5 onboard embedded system was ordered and designed.

Conversely, it would be hardly understandable to keep "taking chances" with such grandiose projects now that the basics of proof-based SE have emerged. No changes in system engineering methods or exclusive focus on S/W engineering issues is what we mean by "taking chances". Hopefully, this analysis may also serve to demonstrate that it is inappropriate to "blame" the S/W engineers involved, i.e. engineers with the industrial architect and with sub-contractors Matra Marconi Space and Sextant Avionique.

An initial version of this analysis appeared in [13].

5.2 The Failure Scenario

The Ariane 5 flight control system (FCS) has a redundant architecture. Two identical computers (SRI1 and SRI2), running identical S/W, are responsible for extracting inertial reference data (launcher attitude) and for periodically sending two other identical flight contol computers (OBC1 and OBC2) messages that contain flight data. A redundant MIL-1553-B bus interconnects the SRIs and the OBCs. The OBC computers, which run identical S/W, are in charge of maintaining the launcher on its nominal trajectory, by commanding the nozzle deflections of the solid boosters and the main engine. The FCS redundancy management is of type passive: in the SRI logical module, in the OBC logical module, only one physical module is active at any time, the other one - if not failed - being the backup.

The 501 failure scenario described in the Inquiry Board report is as follows. The launcher started to disintegrate 39 seconds after lift-off, because of an angle of attack of more than 20 degrees, which was caused by full nozzle deflections of the boosters and the main engine. These deflections were con,manded by the S/W of the OBC active at that time, whose input was data transmitted by the SRI active at that time, that is SRI2.

Part of these data did not contain proper flight data, but showed a diagnostic bit pattern of SRI2, which was interpreted as regular flight data by the OBC. Diagnostic was issued by SRI2 as a result of a S/W exception. The OBC could not switch to the backup SRI1 because that computer had ceased functioning 72 ms earlier, for the same reason as SRI2.

The SRI S/W exception was raised during a conversion from a 64-bit floating point number N to a 16-bit signed integer number. N had a value greater than what can be represented by a 16-bit signed integer, which caused an operand error (data conversion – in Ada code – was not protected, for the reason that a maximum workload target of 80% had been set for the SRI computers).

More precisely, the operand error was due to a high value of an alignment function result called BH (horizontal bias), related to the horizontal velocity of the launcher. The value of BH was much higher than expected because the early part of the trajectory of Ariane 5 differs from that of Ariane 4, which results in considerably higher horizontal velocity values.

The operand error occurred while running the alignment task. This task serves a particular purpose after lift-off with Ariane 4 but is useless after lift-off in the case of Ariane 5.

5.3 Conclusions and Recommendations from the Inquiry Board

According to the Inquiry Board, causes of the 501 failure are S/W specification and S/W design errors. Below are a few excerpts from the Board report:

Page 5: "Although the failure was due to a systematic S/W design error..."

Page 6: "... presumably based on the view that ... not wise to make changes in S/W which worked well with Ariane 4".

Page 6: "... S/W is flexible ... thus encourages highly demanding requirements ... complex implementations difficult to assess."

Page 9 : "... it is evident that the limitations of the SRI S/W were not fully analysed..."

Page 12: "This loss of information was due to specification and design errors in the S/W of the inertial reference system."

Hence, the following recommendations from the Inquiry Board (excerpts):

"Prepare a test facility ... and perform complete, closed-loop, system testing. Complete simulations must take place before any mission."

"Review all flight S/W...".

"Set up a team that will prepare the procedure for qualifying S/W,..., and ascertain that specification, verification and testing of S/W are of a consistently high quality..."

Of course, improving the quality of the on-board S/W cannot do any harm. However, doing just that misses the real target.

What caught our attention in the first place was the following sentence (page 3 of the report):

"... In order to improve reliability, there is considerable redundancy at the equipment level. There are two SRIs operating in parallel with identical H/W and S/W."

This is really puzzling. Simple (i.e., degree 2) non diversified redundancy is the weakest kind of redundancy that can exist. How can this be deemed "considerable"? Furthermore, this is the only sentence of the report that addresses system design issues. Very likely, the Board quickly concluded that, given this "considerable" redundancy, system design issues deserved no additional attention.

There is some irony with the fact that a minor improvement w.r.t. redundancy, that is considering degree 2 diversified redundancy in the encoding of some variables, could have helped avoid the 501 failure.

More fundamentally, it is somewhat disturbing to observe that, once again, S/W is held to be "all what matters" a priori. We refer the reader back to section 3.5 for more on this topic.

This case study helps showing how proof-based SE can be useful a posteriori, to diagnose the causes of a failure. We present those system engineering faults which, in our view, are the real causes of the 501 failure. In the sequel, we use the term "module" rather than "computer" to refer to SRIs and OBCs. A module is a set comprising application S/W tasks, system level S/W tasks (e.g., algorithms), related data and variables, a computer. When a probability of failure is estimated for a module, not just the computer (the H/W) should be taken into consideration.

5.4 Problem Capture Faults

Let $< X' >$ denote the actual specification established by the prime contractor and the industrial architect. Some of the necessary models (see section 3.1) were not specified in $< X' >$.

- Fault C_1 (models of shared persistent variables, SRIs): horizontal velocity, which is an external variable shared by the environment of the FCS and some of the SRI module tasks, had not been listed in $< m.X' >$. Neither N nor BH, which depend on horizontal velocity, had been listed either.

Fault C_1 led to system dimensioning fault Dim_1.

- Fault C_2 (task models, SRIs): Condition "must be aborted after lift-off" had not been specified as an attribute for the alignment task in $< m.X' >$.

The alignment task was running after lift-off. The "exception condition" (BH overflow) was raised while running this task. It was later acknowledged that there is no need to keep this task running after lift-off in the case of Ariane 5. This has resulted into system design fault Des_3.

- Fault C_3 (failure models, SRIs): It was implicitly assumed that SRI modules would fail according to the *stop* model.

Firstly, assumptions must be explicitly specified. Implicit assumptions can be violated, which happened. Secondly, this assumption was flawed in the first place. SRI computers, not SRI modules, were taken into consideration. This led to system design faults Des_1 and Des_4.

- Fault C_4 (failure occurrence models, SRIs): It was implicitly assumed that 1 SRI module at most would fail during a flight.

Again, assumptions must be explicitly specified. This implicit assumption also was violated. SRI computers, not SRI modules, were considered. Specification $< m.X' >$ should have included the following statement: "up to f SRI modules can fail during a flight". Recall that the dimensioning of f is conditioned on fulfilling a proof obligation which, itself, depends on design decisions (see further). This led to system design fault Des_4 and to system dimensioning fault Dim_2.

Some of the properties were not properly specified in $< p.X' >$. Serializability is an example. Some internal variables shared among SRI module tasks had not been listed in $< m.X' >$. For these variables, appropriate invariants were not specified. (Note, though, that this was not a cause of the 501 failure).

Continuous correct SRI inertial data service provided to the OBCs is essential to a correct functioning of the launcher. Availability, in particular, is an essential property. Availability was correctly specified, as follows: access to SRI inertial data service must be continuously ensured for the entire duration of a flight, with a probability at least equal to $1 - p$, $p \approx 10^{-4}$. (It was implicitly assumed that reliability - the SRI inertial data service delivered is correct - was ensured, as "demonstrated" by the many successful flights of Ariane 4).

Had proof-based SE been applied, the prime contractor and the industrial architect would have developed a specification $< X >$ that would have been a correct translation of the real application problem specification $< A >$, i.e. free from faults C_1 to C_4. A first obvious conclusion is as follows: given that $< X' >$ is weaker than $< X >$ (in the $\supseteq$ sense), no FCS that (possibly provably correctly) solves $< X' >$ can be a correct solution to the real application problem considered.

5.5 System Design Faults

Redundancy of the SRIs is managed by the OBCs via a detection-and-recovery algorithm, denoted F_1 (passive redundancy). A correct detection-and-recovery algorithm must ensure that no OBC module behaves incorrectly because of failing SRI modules, which means that such an algorithm must be proved correct for the failure models that correctly reflect actual failure behaviors (see fault C_3). Such has not been the case. F_1 does not insulate the OBC modules from failed SRI modules behavior.

- Fault Des_1 (SRIs, OBCs): The detection-and-recovery algorithm run by the OBC modules to manage the redundant SRI modules is inconsistent with the actual failure behavior of SRI modules (or vice-versa).

This is an example of a fault that results from not having designed the FCS "in-the-large". Such faults can be avoided by fulfilling a design correctness proof obligation. That would have resulted into having system engineers select a consistent pair {failure model, algorithm F}. Consequently, the respective specifications of SRI and OBC modules would have been globally consistent. Let us give examples.

One possibility is to retain the current design, i.e. to choose {$stop, F_1$}. Choice $F = F_1$ is valid only if the $stop$ assumption is shown to be actually instantiated vis-à-vis the OBC flight program (which commands the nozzle deflectors). It was believed that this assumption could not be enforced locally, at the SRIs, because of the 80% workload target. Therefore, the SRI $stop$ assumption had to be enforced by the OBCs. That involves two requirements: (i) F_1 had to include a "filtering" mechanism that would discriminate between "flight data" and "exception condition reporting" messages issued by the SRI modules, (ii) two separate OBC tasks should have been specified, one in charge of executing the flight program, the other one in charge of handling exception conditions (error messages). Had this been done, $stop$ behavior would have been correctly implemented vis-à-vis the OBC flight program. (This in fact should have been done - see fault Des_2).

One could also consider designs based on pairs {any failure model, masking algorithm F}. Recall that models stronger than *stop* have a higher coverage factor. For any such model, there are known solutions (e.g., algorithms F based on majority voting) for a synchronous computational model - which was retained for the FCS - as well as optimal feasibility conditions. In the presence of up to f failures, n modules are necessary and sufficient, with $n = 2f + 1$ (resp. $3f + 1$) if byzantine models are not (resp. are) considered. The latter is the design choice made for the US Space Shuttle on-board FCS. (Note that n is the behavioral function R introduced in section 3.2).

Given that other faults have also been made, doing the above would not have sufficed to avoid the 501 failure. Nevertheless, fault Des_1 is a latent fault that may lead to a future flight failure.

- Fault Des_2 (event models, task models, OBCs): Type of events "flight data" and type of events "error condition reporting" were not mapped onto two different OBC tasks.

Every event type that can be posted to a module must be listed. Similarly, tasks that can be activated over a module must be listed. A {task, event type} mapping must be specified. Had this been done, event type "overflow reporting" would not have been an input to the OBC flight program.

- Fault Des_3 (task models, SRIs): A task scheduling algorithm should have aborted the alignment task right after lift-off.

Given fault C_2, it was simply impossible for those system engineers in charge of designing/selecting the SRI task scheduler, as well as eligibility scheduling rules, to "guess" that the alignment task should have been aborted right after lift-off.

- Fault Des_4 (SRIs, OBCs): No proof was established that the probability of experiencing more than $f = 1$ SRI module failure during a flight is p at most.

Probabilistic computations that have been performed apply to SRI computers, rather than to SRI modules. This would have been revealed by attempting a proof that the stated availability property does hold. In doing so, system engineers would have run into the obligation of proving that the "up-to-f-out-of-n" assumption has a coverage factor greater than $1 - p$. Which would have led them to prove that f cannot be equal to n, which is tantamount to proving that there is no common cause of failure for the SRI modules.

- Fault Des_5 (SRIs, OBCs): Given the system engineering approach followed, diversified redundancy should have been specified.

Indeed, making such deterministic assumptions as "up-to-f-out-of-n" (up-to-1-out-of-2 for the FCS), or any similar assumptions of probabilistic nature, does not make sense unless these assumptions are validated. Quite clearly, any capture, design, or dimensioning fault is a common cause of failure, which invalidates such assumptions. Whenever a non proof-based SE method is applied, it is safer - if not mandatory - to specify diversified redundancy, in order to eliminate potential common causes of failure, with a sufficiently "high" probability. This is well understood vis-à-vis implementation phases (H/W engineering, S/W engineering). This seems not to be so well acknowledged (yet) vis-à-vis system engineering phases.

System dimensioning fault Dim_1 (see below) would have been avoided had proof-based SE been resorted to. Conversely, under the existing approach, had diversified redundancy been specified, a large enough size could have been picked up (with a bit of luck) for the memory buffer used to implement BH on one of the two SRI modules.

Other space missions have failed for the same reason (Mars Observer is an example).

5.6 System Dimensioning Faults

No rigorous capture having been conducted, and system design faults having been made, some of the variables that should have appeared in $\{[S], [s]\}$, the generic FCS implementation specification, were missing (the case for BH), or had been valued a priori (the case for f). Given that no dimensioning correctness proof obligation was fulfilled, this was not detected at the time the actual FCS specifications were handed over to S/W engineers.

This resulted into assigning an incorrectly sized memory buffer to variable BH. This resulted also into an empirical dimensioning of the SRI logical modules group.

- Fault Dim_1: Range of values taken by variable BH was assumed to be in the $]-2^{15}, +2^{15}[$ interval.

Had proof-based SE been resorted to, fault C_1 would have been avoided. Consequently, $< m.x >$ would have included variables horizontal velocity, N and BH. In order to run the dimensioning phase, the prime contractor and/or the industrial architect would have then been forced to ask Ariane 5 program space flight engineers to decide upon some $V(< x >)$. That is how the correct value range of external variable horizontal velocity would have been explicitly specified, i.e. the range that is valid for Ariane 5, not for Ariane 4.

This would have translated automatically into a correct quantification of the value ranges for N and BH, variables that depend on that external variable. As a result, with a very simple oracle at hands, a correct dimensioning of the memory buffer assigned to BH - specified via $V([s])$ - would have been obtained.

It may be that, for Ariane 4, the issue of how to dimension the BH buffer was raised and solved. Problem is that the SE method applied for Ariane 5 led the prime contractor and the industrial architect to ignore that issue.

- Fault Dim_2: It was implicitly assumed that f's value would be 1 and that simple redundancy ($n = 2$) would suffice.

The intrinsic reliability of a SRI module (H/ W + S/W + data), and related confidence interval, can be derived from statistics computed over accumulated experimental data and simulation results, or via probabilistic modeling. Intrinsic reliability, combined with launch duration, is used to compute a value for f. Obviously, the smallest acceptable value for f is such that the probability of experiencing more than f SRI module failures is smaller than p.

It appears that system engineers took SRI computers (i.e., H/W) only into consideration. Had SRI modules been considered rather, related confidence intervals on modules reliability could have led to choose $f = 2$ (for example).

Given that other faults have been made, picking up a value of f (resp. n) greater than 1 (resp. 2) would not have helped avoid the 501 failure. Nevertheless, this is a latent fault that may lead to a future flight failure.

The dual architecture of the FCS reflects the following widespread SE practice for many embedded systems : design for a "single-copy" architecture (1 SRI, 1 OBC in the FCS case) and duplicate.

From a more general perspective, if we compare the costs involved with applying a proof-based SE method and implementing a rigorously designed and dimensioned embedded system on the one hand, costs incurred with operational failures - such as that of the 501 failure - on the other hand, it seems there are good reasons to consider switching to proof-based SE.

5.7 Summary

It is now possible to understand what led to the failure of Flight 501. If we were to stick to internationally accepted terminology, we should write the following:

Faults have been made while capturing the Ariane 5 application problem. Faults have also been made in the course of designing and dimensioning the Ariane 5 FCS. These faults have been activated during launch, which has caused errors at the FCS modules level. Neither algorithmic nor architectural solutions could cope with such errors. Flight 501 failure ensued.

Flight 501 also is an example showing that integration testing phases - as conducted under current SE practice - are not satisfactory, for they are unavoidably incomplete. Flight 501 can be viewed as a (costly) continuation of an incomplete integration testing phase.

This case study also helps showing that S/W reuse - a very sound objective - has far reaching implications, which promote reliance on proof-based SE. Reuse of S/W modules - those which work fine w.r.t. the Ariane 4 application problem - is possible provided that those conditions under which they are to operate are kept unchanged. Which is not the case when considering the Ariane 5 application problem, or its quantification to the very least. As shown above, proof-based SE, which permits to address these issues rigorously, favors S/W reuse.

Let us now go back to the conclusions of the Inquiry Board and ask ourselves the following questions:

- Had all the modules as specified by system engineers been implemented in H/W, would Flight 501 have failed the way it did?
- Had the implementation - in S/W and/or in H/W - of every module as specified by system engineers been proved correct, would Flight 501 have failed the way it did?

Obviously, answers are "yes" in both cases. Specifications of the S/W modules as established by system engineers were incomplete/incorrect w.r.t. real problem $< X >$. There is no "S/W error" involved with that. Why should the concept of horizontal velocity be viewed as a S/W engineering concept rather than a H/W engineering concept? (It is neither). What if the conversion procedure which computes values of BH had been implemented in H/W? Flight 501 would have failed as well. However, the Inquiry Board would have then diagnosed a "H/W design error". Clearly, causes of the failure belong neither to the "S/W world" nor to the "H/W world". Issues at stake are system engineering issues.

The S/W implemented N-to-BH conversion procedure is absolutely correct. For any input value N, it computes a correct value BH. Not enough bits (15 instead of 18) were allocated for storing these correct values. Calling a faulty dimensioning of a memory buffer a "S/W error" is as misleading as calling the choice of too slow a processor a "S/W error".

Confusion between S/W engineering and system engineering should come to an end.

As for the recommendations of the Inquiry Board that system testing and system simulation must be complete, we refer the reader to sections 3.4 and 3.5. As we know, completeness - without resorting to proof-based SE - is beyond reachability. Such recommendations are not very useful for the simple reason that they cannot be implemented, if one believes that S/W is the only area of concern.

6   Conclusions

The principles presented in this paper are believed to be useful in helping set the foundations of proof-based system engineering for computer-based systems. These principles have been illustrated with a presentation of a proof-based SE method which has been applied to various problems, in cooperation with a number of companies and agencies. This has permitted to validate and to refine these principles.

The essential feature of the methodological revolution embodied in proof-based system engineering is that it has the effect of converting system engineering into a bona fide scientific discipline. Every technical or methodological field goes through this transition. When it does, advances occur at an unimaginable pace.

Times of changes are upon us when an area goes from trial-and-error to prediction based on knowledge of the inner mechanisms and principles at work. We are now on that threshold in the field of system engineering for computer-based systems.

References

1. Bernstein, P. A., Hadzilacos, V., Goodman, N.: Concurrency Control and Recovery in Database Systems. Addison-Wesley Pub., ISBN 0-201-10715-5 (1987) 370 p.
2. Gaubert S., Max Plus: Methods and Applications of $(max, +)$ Linear Algebra, IN-RIA Research Report 3088 (Jan. 1997) 24 p.
3. Hadzilacos, V., Toueg, S.: A Modular Approach to Fault-Tolerant Broadcasts and Related Problems, Technical Report, TR 94-1425, Cornell University (May 1994).
4. Hermant, J.F., Le Lann, G.: A Protocol and Correctness Proofs for Real-Time High-Performance Broadcast Networks, 18th IEEE Intl. Conference on Distributed Computing Systems, Amsterdam, NL (May 1998) 10 p.
5. Hermant, J.F., Leboucher, L., Rivierre, N.: Real-Time Fixed and Dynamic Priority Driven Scheduling Algorithms: Theory and Experience. INRIA Research Report 3081 (Dec. 1996) 139 p.
6. Inquiry Board Report: Ariane 5 - Flight 501 Failure, Paris (19 July 1996) 18 p. [http://www.inria.fr/actualites-fra.html].
7. Joseph, M., et al.: Real-Time Systems - Specification, Verification and Analysis. Prentice Hall UK Pub., ISBN 0-13-455297-0 (1996) 278 p.
8. Knightly E.W., Zhang Hui: D-BIND: An Accurate Traffic Model for Providing QoS Guarantees to VBR Traffic. IEEE/ACM Transactions on Networking, vol. 5, n°2 (April 1997) 219 - 231.
9. Koren, G., Shasha, D.: D-Over: An Optimal On-Line Scheduling Algorithm for Overloaded Real-Time Systems, INRIA Technical Report 138 (Feb. 1992) 45 p.
10. Kuhn, D.R.: Sources of Failure in the Public Switched Telephone Network, IEEE Computer (April 1997) 31 - 36.
11. Le Lann, G.: Certifiable Critical Complex Computing Systems. 13th IFIP World Computer Congress, Duncan K. and Krueger K. Eds, Elsevier Science Pub., vol. 3, Hamburg, D (Aug. 1994) 287 - 294.
12. Le Lann, G.: Proof-Based System Engineering for Computing Systems, ESA-INCOSE Conference on Systems Engineering, Noordwijk, NL (Nov. 1997) IEE/ESA Pub., vol. WPP-130, 5a.4.1 - 5a.4.8.
13. Le Lann, G.: An Analysis of the Ariane 5 Flight 501 Failure - A System Engineering Perspective. IEEE Intl. Conference on the Engineering of Computer-Based Systems, Monterey, USA (March 1997) 339 - 346.
14. Leveson, N.G., Turner, C.: An Investigation of the Therac-25 Accidents, IEEE Computer (July 1993) 18 - 41.
15. Lynch, N.A.: Distributed Algorithms. Morgan Kaufmann Pub., ISBN 1-55860-348-4 (1996) 872 p.
16. Neumann, P.G.: Computer Related Risks, Addison-Wesley Pub., ISBN 0-201-55805-X (1995) 367 p.
17. Powell, D.: Failure Mode Assumptions and Assumption Coverage, 22nd IEEE Intl. Symposium on Fault-Tolerant Computing, Boston, USA (July 1992) 386-395.

A Design Notation and Toolset for High-Performance Embedded Systems Development

Devesh Bhatt and John Shackleton

Honeywell Technology Center
3660 Technology Drive
Minneapolis, MN 55418. USA

Abstract. In traditional design methodologies, the system designer typically develops the application in a sequential paradigm almost to completion before addressing issues of parallelism and mapping to a heterogeneous architecture. As the architectural complexity of these applications increase, however, this process becomes too costly since implementation must be started anew after the design. The quality of the design also often suffers as a result. This is especially true for embedded applications, where the complexity lies within the system software and hardware architecture. We present a new methodology and toolset aimed at improving the system development process for high-performance embedded applications. The toolset provides a unified design representation from early design specification to integration—allowing for parallelism and synchronization specification in domain specific styles, and automating many process steps such as partitioning/mapping, simulation, glue-code generation, and performance analysis.

1 Introduction

The increased availability of relatively inexpensive embedded architectures has made it feasible to implement more and more high-performance applications. The potential benefit of parallel architectures, however, is often offset by the effort needed to develop and port applications on these architectures. This effort is further increased for embedded systems due to their real-time requirements and due to the complexity of integrating interacting application functions that may use different styles of parallelization and synchronization. This is unlike typical scientific applications that implement a single central algorithm. In addition, interactions between components must be understandable and verifiable for mission-critical applications.

In spite of recent progress in object-oriented design methods, parallel languages, communication libraries, and real-time operating systems, substantial manual effort is needed in developing an application using these often diverse technology components. The system designer typically develops the application in a sequential paradigm almost to completion before addressing issues of parallelism and mapping to a multilevel heterogeneous architecture, and using the communication and operating system services. Thus, the implementation becomes disjoint from the design— resulting in duplication of effort and inconsistencies.

The Multi-Domain Embedded System Architect (MESA) is a methodology and toolset that bridges this gap and addresses many issues facing the developers of complex embedded systems. MESA provides the following capabilities:

- an end-to-end development process driven by a unified design notation

- a design notation for specification of parallelism, synchronization, and scheduling properties within domain-specific programming styles.

- automated partitioning, mapping, analysis, and simulation of the complete software and hardware design.

- automated glue-code generation to specific target communication and operating system services on the hardware architecture, with performance monitoring

This paper is divided into five sections. Section 2 discusses the current design methods and languages and the need for domain-specific approaches. Section 3 presents an overview of the MESA methodology, focusing on the design notation. Section 4 presents some features of the MESA toolset in the context of an application. Finally, Section 5 presents the current MESA status and future plans.

2 Background and Motivation

2.1 Object-Oriented Methodologies

Much progress has been made recently in object-oriented (OO) design methods and tools for applications on sequential platforms. Published OO methodologies, such as Coad Yourdon [2], Shlaer-Mellor [3], and OMT [4], and their implementation in commercial Computer Aided Software Engineering (CASE) tools is gaining widespread acceptance in many application domains; typically those domains that do not require high-performance architectures and real-time operation.

Information Complexity vs. Architectural Complexity. In a typical system development today, one encounters two kinds of complexities:

1. *Information Complexity*. This is due to the different types of data, objects, inheritance, and relationships. The class diagrams in OO methodologies allow specification of these aspects for information-intensive applications such as databases.

2. *Architectural Complexity*. This is due to the parallelization/distribution of software functions, data striping, data buffering and pipelining, mapping of functions onto hardware, scheduling to meet real-time requirements. Embedded applications such as radar signal processing, tracking, automatic target recognition, avionics mission management, industrial process control have this kind of architectural complexity.

For example, a typical PC database application might exhibit 95% information complexity and 5% architectural complexity. On the other end, a typical embedded signal processing application might exhibit 5% information complexity and 95% architectural complexity. While the OO methodologies do a good job of analyzing and designing information-intensive applications, they are inadequate for a large class of embedded applications, especially those utilizing complex architectures to achieve high performance. We have indeed found this to be the case in our development of signal processing and tracking applications.

2.2 Parallel Languages and Models

To address certain issues of architectural complexity for parallel and distributed architectures, much progress has been made lately in languages, middleware, and operating systems. This includes: programming models such as Actors; programming languages such as Synchronizing Resources (SR), Compositional C++ (CC++), High Performance Fortran (HPF); communication systems such as Message Passing Interface (MPI); and micro-kernels such as Real-Time Mach. While these capabilities have greatly helped application developers, they still leave several issues unanswered:

- They do not address early phases in system development; i.e., a user must be ready to write code in order to use these capabilities. Activities such as design analysis, architecture trades, partitioning/mapping trades, and simulation—important for embedded system development—are not addressed.

- The parallel language compilers and message-passing systems support limited nesting of task and data-level parallelism, provide limited control over buffering, pipelining, and sequencing of functions over multi-level control-flow paradigms of the underlying architecture.

- They place too much flexibility, and thus responsibility, in the hands of the programmers. It is too easy to write programs with a myriad of interactions that are difficult to understand and are not easily configurable for different functions, problem sizes, degree of parallelism, and architectural heterogeneity. Even with parallel language or message-passing support, the applications take too long to implement and debug. The Actor model actually addresses some of these problems through methods of program transformation [8].

Most of the complexity mentioned here arises from the generality of the abstractions supported by these languages and communication systems. To provide the breadth of coverage for these general abstractions, specific customization and optimizations for the domain and architectures cannot be practically supported, since the general solutions are too complex. Furthermore, the general abstractions do not provide any guidelines to the programmer for structuring and constraining the application to suit the domain. This brings us to the need for domain-specific approaches, which attempt to overcome complexity by constraining the generality.

2.3 Domain-Specific Approaches

In many embedded application domains such as radar signal processing, flight control, and automated target recognition, developers have found that certain styles and structures for parallelization, communication, and scheduling are common across many different applications. In other words, only a small subset of the generic parallelization, partitioning/mapping, and scheduling capabilities are needed in a particular domain—hence the need for domain specific approaches that can make the aforementioned problems tractable by constraining the generality.

Several domain-specific tools have come in use, such as Ptolemy [7] for signal processing, MATLAB for a variety of domains, Khoros for image processing, and Matrix-X for control. A significant feature of these tools is that they provide application engineers and analysts with a graphical specification, simulation, and data visualization environment in the lexicons and idioms of their domains. One serious shortcoming of these tools has been that they have ignored the issues of parallelization and code generation for parallel embedded architectures supporting specific communication and library services. Recently, however, some efforts have started in these areas [10].

In contrast to these graphical specification and simulation environments, there are some domain-specific programming support libraries such as Scalable Programming Environment (SPE) [6, 9] and Data Flow Shell (DFS) [5] for signal processing; and Concurrent Program Archetypes [11] for many domains. The advantage of these library-based environments is that they are ready for programmers to start developing the applications using the domain-specific idioms, supported by the libraries. The libraries handle parallelization over a parallel architecture. The Concurrent Program Archetype work of Caltech is notable in this regard: it provides archetypes (templates) for parallel programs in many domains.

The gap between the design/simulation environment provided by tools and the parallel programming support provided by the libraries is quite wide. Neither provides the complete capability to move from conceptual design to parallel/distributed implementation. The former lack the design notations needed to specify architectures and parallelism. The latter have the parallelism specification idioms for a message-passing architecture, but lack the design specification and successive refinement necessary in system development.

System Engineering Concerns. None of the above approaches addresses the issues of system engineering; e.g., providing capabilities to perform architecture trades, partitioning/mapping, and integrated modeling and simulation of both hardware and software architectures. These capabilities are essential in embedded systems development where the system size, weight, power, and recurring/non-recurring costs must be carefully estimated and optimized as part of the system engineering process. There are several commercial tools (e.g., SES Workbench, PMW) available for modeling and simulation, but then these tools lack the domain-specific parallelism specification and parallel programming support. Thus, the system developer must enter different aspects of the systems design in different forms in different tools, without any automated interfaces among these tools—generally an error-prone and expensive process.

In the next section, we present a methodology and toolset that overcomes some of these limitations, while providing a domain-specific program composition style. The toolset is called Multi-Domain Embedded System Architect (MESA).

3 MESA Methodology and Notation Overview

The MESA toolset has been developed at the Honeywell Technology Center as an integration of many years of experience in embedded applications, systems engineering, parallel processing, software design techniques, and tool implementation. MESA is currently being used in embedded application areas such as radar signal processing, cockpit digital map/graphics, and image processing.

This section presents an overview of the MESA methodology, the system engineering process supported, the tool capabilities to capture system design, and specification of parallelism, synchronization, and function scheduling properties. The discussion of other aspects of system design and MESA capabilities is beyond the scope of this paper.

3.1 MESA System Development Process

Figure 1 presents a simplified version of the system development process supported by MESA. Rectangles denote a process step; ovals or rounded rectangles denote data and/

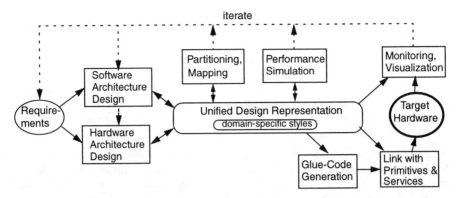

Figure 1. MESA System Development Process (simplified)

or a physical entity. The process flows from left to right through several stages of system development: requirements definition, software and hardware architecture design, protecting and mapping of software onto hardware, performance simulation, function primitives implementation, glue-code generation, and real-time monitoring/visualization. At the center of this process is a single *unified design representation* that all process steps read from and write to. For example, the partitioning and mapping step reads the hardware and software design and mapping preferences; it writes back the specific software to hardware mapping into the design representation. The architecture design and specific mapping information is then used by all the subsequent steps: performance simulation, glue-code generation, monitoring/visualization etc. The glue-code generation step uses this information to generate tables and code that provides the data flow and synchronization among the function, using underlying communication and operating system services. The steps links the tables and glue code with these services and function primitives that are either taken from libraries or are user implemented.

An important aspect of the design representation is the notion of a *domain-specific style* that consists of rules and constraints for hardware/software design capture, partitioning/mapping, and glue-code generation. The developer selects a style out of the available ones, that matches her domain, and that style guides the entire development process.

Iteration is an important part of the process. The feedback from the partitioning/mapping, simulation, and monitoring/visualization steps is used to modify the design (and sometimes requirements also) and perform the necessary trade-offs.

The following subsections describe the system design capture (hardware, software, mapping) and then parallelism and synchronization specification within the software design.

3.2 System Design Capture

Three *views* compose the major parts of system design under the MESA methodology: the software view, the hardware view, and the mapping view. In building the system design, very often these three views are set apart, and are described at different levels of abstraction. For example, the software functions defined in the software view may be described at a very coarse-grained level with very little detail, while the hardware view is described in great detail. The mapping view may not be described at all for certain phases of a particular design. Thus, the MESA methodology maintain a high degree of flexibility, so that the implementation details can be deferred until the design team has sufficiently verified the different views of the system separately. The single design environment of the MESA methodology then guarantees the design team the opportunity to test and verify the impact and interaction of the different views within a single design notation. Very often, this approach to system design is referred to as hardware/software codesign.

The *software view* describes the software architecture of the system design, which itself has two main parts. First, the system functionality (or behavior) must be defined and partitioned into distinct functional units. In the beginning, the partitioned units may be broad, describing only general categories (or classes) of functions that will later be refined as the system design progresses. Software partitioning will be constrained by the size of the application, the complexity of the application, the underlying hardware (defined in the hardware view), and the availability of existing software support, such as commercial off-the-shelf (COTS) source code libraries and legacy code. The MESA methodology encourages system designers to refine the functions down to their simplest, smallest units, so that their implementation and linkage to existing software source code is facilitated.

Once the functional units are set, the software view can describe how the functions communicate with each other. Function communication will depend on the type of information that is shared between functions, the required size/buffering of the data transmissions, and the scheduling requirements of the functions (e.g., whether the functions are periodic or event-driven, etc.). These aspects are described further in Section 3.3.

The *hardware view* includes any physical hardware resource, such as networks, memories and caches, devices such as sensors, disk drives, or any other type of I/O, processor components, and composite components such as boards or cards. Processors in this case is a very general term, and covers any component that can perform some computation, e.g. ASIC, FPGA, and traditional COTS processors. From a systems perspective, the hardware view is often more predictable than the software view, given the current trend towards COTS-based designs. This does not mean that hardware design decisions are not important. Great care must be taken when building the hardware view, since the practice of over-engineering, or designing more hardware than is necessary to cover any unanticipated problems, is not at all cost effective, and is no longer a viable approach. The hardware view allows system designers to perform trade-offs on the hardware components, and verify a hardware configuration with respect to a variety of criteria, in a manner that is apart from the software view, but not completely divorced from the software.

The final view, the *mapping view*, brings the other two views together. The mapping view describes how the functional units are mapped onto the hardware components of the system. A crucial step in the MESA methodology is performing trade-offs on the different mapping options. The system designer must decide which criteria weighs the heaviest when resolving mapping issues. Some common factors that effect the mapping view are software communication requirements, system latency requirements, the size and complexity of the software, and the overall hardware costs.

3.3 Parallelism and Synchronization Specification

An integral aspect of the *software view* is the specification of parallelism and inter-function synchronization (data/control flow) in the application, within a domain-specific *style*. The *style* essentially constrains the choices of parallelism and synchronization, and imposes composition rules. This approach essentially forces the application designer to create a design that is automatically parallelizable and partitionable using the rules of the domain-specific style. In this subsection, we describe the various aspects of parallelism and synchronization implemented in MESA, along with partitioning/mapping and code-generation techniques.

Specification of Task-Level and Data-Level Parallelism. Task-level parallelism refers to the concurrent execution of independent threads of control that communicate with other threads using data flows with specific synchronization associated with each flow. Each thread is represented as an *active function* in the system design, with a rounded rectangle, as illustrated in Figure 2a. The traditional concepts of "control flow" are captured by a combination of inter-function synchronization and scheduling properties of the threads on the sending and receiving ends of an arc.

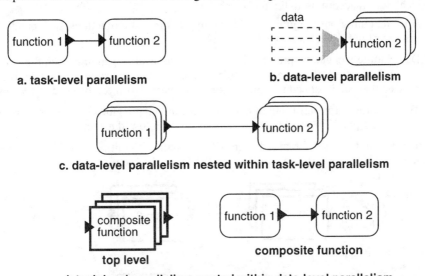

Figure 2. Different Types of Parallelism and their Nesting

Data-level parallelism, on the other hand, refers to multiple parallel threads that operate on individual slices of multi-dimensional data and are driven by a single control flow. It is shown as overlapping rectangles as illustrated in Figure 2b. In many applications such as signal processing, data-parallel threads are independent. In certain other applications, there may be some specific communication among the data-parallel threads similar to single-instruction multiple data (SIMD) style of programming. The current version of toolset support the specification of SIMD ports for such intra-function communication—leaving the programming task to the application programmer who writes the function.

Graphical Notation: In our notation, a thick-lined rectangle denotes a *composite function* which has a subdiagram; a rounded rectangle denotes an *active function* (thread); a small filled triangle denotes a *port*. Input data at a port are drawn graphically here to help the explanation; they are actually specified as *properties* of ports in the design.

Figure 2c illustrates the nesting of data-level parallelism within task-level parallelism. At the top level *function 1* and *function 2* are two task-parallel functions. At the next level, each function has multiple data-parallel threads. Note that each of the two functions can have different number of threads and the input data could be sliced in different dimensions for the two functions. Figure 2d illustrates the nesting of task-level parallelism within task-level parallelism. Here, at the top level, we have a data-parallel *composite function*. At the next level, *composite function* consists of *function 1* and *function 2* that are task parallel. In this example of nesting, some restrictions may apply—e.g., the data dimensions and the number of threads for both *function 1* and *function 2* are the same (the number of threads can be different in Figure 2c).

In general, data parallelism and task parallelism can be nested in a hierarchical graphical design according to the following rules:

1. After flattening out the graphical hierarchy of composite functions, task parallel-ism can only be present at one level.

2. Data parallelism can be present at more than one level, depending upon the num-ber of dimensions of the data—each level slicing one dimension of the data. E.g., for data that can be sliced in n dimensions, data parallelism can be used at n levels.

3. The techniques for partitioning, mapping, and automatic glue code generation for a particular platform would put restrictions on the allowed nesting.

Figure 3 illustrates an example design which contains multiple levels of nested parallelism. The design, at the top level of the hierarchy, consists of two composite

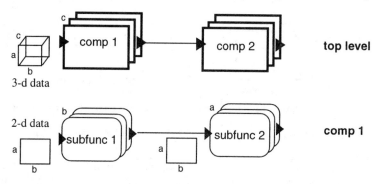

Figure 3. An Example Design with Multiple Levels of Nesting

functions. Function *comp 1* takes in 3-dimensional data and is data parallel in the dimension *c*. At the next level of hierarchy, *comp 1* consists of *subfunc 1* and *subfunc 2* which are themselves data parallel in dimensions *b* and *a* respectively.

Invocation Specification. An important aspect of the design of systems with multiple concurrent/distributed functions is the specification of data flows among functions and the specific synchronization associated with each flow. In MESA, the term *invocation* is used to describe this data flow and synchronization; it is specified as a property of each arc in the design diagram. Figure 4 shows the invocation alternatives provided by the design tool in the *invocation view* of the design. This view is broken up into two sub-trees, one describing the sender side and the other describing the receiver side of an invocation. The nodes in the graph represent types of senders or receivers; unidirectional vertical arcs represent specialization; and a bidirectional arc connecting a specific sender and a receiver node represents an *invocation*. Senders may be synchronous, i.e. they block until the invocation completes; they may be asynchronous, i.e. they do not wait for the invocation to complete; or they may be periodic. On the receiver side, there may be a thread blocked waiting for a message; a new thread may be created in response to the receipt of the message; or the receiver could be periodic. A new thread may be a transient thread created for the sole purpose of handling the message or it might be a thread that lives beyond the handling the message and performs other functions.

The invocation specifications are general enough to describe a variety of data/control flows, as described in one of our earlier papers [1]. For example, an asynchronous message passing interface of a communication system can be described as an invocation from an asynchronous sender to an existing receiver thread that explicitly executes an message receive statement. Similarly, remote procedure call (RPC) semantics can be described as an invocation from a synchronous sender to a receiver that creates a new temporary thread to handle the message. An Ada rendezvous may be described as

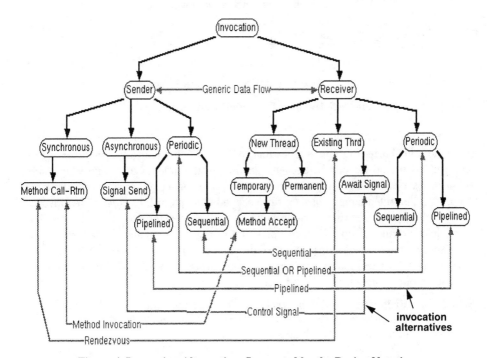

Figure 4. Invocation Alternatives Supported by the Design Notation

an invocation from a synchronous sender to an existing thread. In this case both the sender and the receiver threads block till the message is sent and explicitly received by the receiving thread. An important point to note here is that the invocation specification is editable in the design tool, so it can be modified and/or extended to represent the interface provided by a particular communication service.

For further discussion, let us use the invocations under the *Periodic* class of sender and receiver, namely: *Sequential* and *Pipelined*. These are the dominant types of invocations in many signal processing applications. Associated with each of these invocation is the number of buffers and buffer-sharing properties. When the user selects the invocation type for a particular arc, the properties of the invocation are automatically applied to that arc. Figure 5 illustrates different invocation and buffering options applied to a subsystem consisting of three functions (the buffer annotations are drawn here for explanation only).

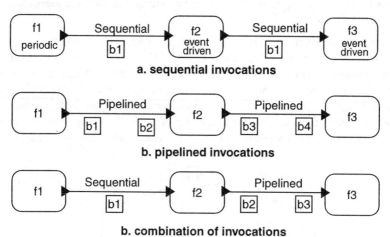

Figure 5. Different Invocations and Buffering Options

In the first example (a), the type of invocation for both arcs is *sequential* and they also share the same buffer *b1*. This implies that *f1*, *f2*, and *f3* are not fully concurrent—i.e., the user has traded off concurrency for savings in the amount of memory. In many applications, each function typically has ample nested data parallelism so this tradeoff is appropriate, given large data sizes. The second example (b), uses *pipelined* invocation which implies that two separate buffers are allocated for each arc. The realized parallelism in this example is three times that of the previous one, at the expense of four times memory. A combination of the two types of invocation is shown in example c, which is in between the first two examples in terms of amount of realized parallelism and amount of memory.

Scheduling Properties and Constraints. The designer must set the scheduling property of each function. We allow the following three top-level options (with more detailed specification within each option:

- *Continuous:* This represents a function thread that lives indefinitely and communicates with other threads using explicit message passing or rendezvous types of invocations.

- *Event Driven:* The function thread is scheduled when messages on the input ports are available according to some specified boolean guard condition. The function thread runs, produces messages on output ports, and exits—blocked for the next scheduling.

- *Periodic:* The function thread is scheduled repetitively, based upon a time period and/or output port synchronization conditions. The behavior is same as an event driven function.

The *scheduling* property of a function is actually closely intertwined with the *invocation* types on the arcs—i.e., only certain combinations are allowable. For example, only *event driven* scheduling is allowed for a function with an input arc of type *sequential* or *pipelined*; and only *periodic* scheduling is allowed if a function has no input arcs but has an output arc of these types. These constraint are captured as node attributes in the invocation view of Figure 4 such that they are automatically enforced by the design tool.

Real-Time Requirements: The software view also allows the specification of latency across points in software graph and the periodicity of input devices to be supported for required throughput. These requirements are automatically passed along to the partitioning and mapping tool as constraints to be satisfied. We also plan to explore the specification of other types of real-time requirements. Further discussion of these capabilities, however, is beyond the scope of this paper.

Control Flow and Program Composition. The invocation and scheduling properties together essentially fulfil the traditional role of control flow, as illustrated in the example of Figure 5a. This simple graphical example is actually equivalent to the following sequential program:

```
loop
    f1(b1);
    f2(b1,b1);
    f3(b1);
end;
```

Obviously, for more complex design graphs, equivalent sequential program notations are not possible. In many application domains such as signal processing and automated target recognition, we have observed that it is best to use event driven or periodic functions—each implementing a well-encapsulated primitive operation in the application. This allows for the best exploitation of concurrency and for a flexible mapping of the design onto the hardware architecture, as also suggested by Agha et al. in [8].

Domain-Specific Styles. As we have discussed in Section 2.3, it is essential to provide a domain-specific approach for the design activity in order to address the complexity of the problem. For each supported domain, MESA provides a domain-specific *style* which consists of rules and constraints. These form the basis of the design specification (especially parallelism), partitioning/mapping, glue-code generation, and integration with primitives' libraries. Chandy et al. have proposed a similar notion called concurrent program archetypes [11]. For every application or sub-application, the user must first select the style. The following are examples of some of the rules and constraints embodied by a style:

- A style allows only a specific subset of the invocation types. For example, the *data-parallel pipelined* style used for signal and image processing applications only allows the invocations *sequential* and *pipelined*. The designer can also specify *sequential or pipelined* invocation to be resolved later by the partitioning and mapping stage.

- A style can constrain the graphical composition in terms of specifying minimum and maximum limits on input/output ports of functions and fan-in and fan-out at these ports. Cyclic feedback may also be disallowed in a style.

- A style can constrain the specification of data striping for data parallelism and can also constrain the nesting of task and data parallelisms.

- A style can put constraints on the mapping of functions to hardware and on buffer allocation. It can specify limits such as maximum number of functions and/or threads per processor, and maximum number of threads per function. An example of a mapping constraint in our current implementation of *data-parallel pipelined* style is that two functions connected by *pipelined* invocation cannot be mapped within the same SHARC Board (ref. Figure 6)—i.e., pipelining is only supported across multiple SHARC Boards.

The MESA design tool provides a graphical editor for the specification of *styles* that can be used by tool smiths and system architects. Once a style is defined, an application engineer can apply it to a design without a need to know the details of it. The style's rules and constraints are automatically enforced by the design tool.

4   System Design using the MESA Toolset

In this section, we describe the usage of MESA toolset in system design, using an application example. Keeping within the scope of this paper, we will focus on the use of the MESA design tool which is the centerpiece of the toolset.

Subsection 4.1 summarizes the various activities in system development that can be performed using the MESA toolset. Subsection 4.2 describes the use of the design tool for the design capture of an example application.

4.1 Activities in System Development

A system design at the various stages of the MESA methodology is never static. Additional verification, testing, refinement can always be achieved and the design process can be iterated as shown in Figure 1. Listed here briefly is a set of activities that can be performed on a developing design using the MESA toolset.

System Design Capture. Before any subsequent activities are done, the designer must capture the software and hardware architecture design with the design tool, using the notation described in Sections 3.2 and 3.3. This design can subsequently be refined and/or modified based upon feedback from the other activities.

Partitioning and mapping. Although the system designer may have a good idea how the software architecture will look based on the system requirements, both partitioning and mapping can be very complex for large applications. Whenever possible, the system designers can take advantage of automated partitioning and mapping tool, so that their time may be devoted to other design decisions that require human interaction. Ideally, the automating tools will narrow the design space given a set of system requirements and designer's mapping preferences, so that the designer can pick from a reasonable set of options.

Analysis and Optimization. Similar to partitioning and mapping, other aspects of the system design can be automated, particularly the analysis of the design. For example, a design can be analyzed to see if system latency requirements are met. The hardware design can be optimized for cost or reliability. Essentially a system design can be optimized over any static characteristic.

Performance Simulation. System simulation in this case is different than analysis. While analysis is essentially static, like a spreadsheet program, simulation is dynamic and will give a closer estimation of system behavior. Simulation can be very abstract and high level, testing just the *performance* aspects of the system. In addition, simulation can be *functional* in nature, investigating how the actual software behaves on simulated hardware. System simulation can show if functional activity is fluid and consistent, or if the processing peaks are sporadic and bursty. Such simulation allows the system design team to model the design quickly, without the costly step of actually implementing the system design. The MESA toolset automatically generates a simulation model that reflects the captured hardware and software architecture design, using the VHDL performance modeling abstractions described in [12].

Testing, Monitoring, and Visualization. When a design has been refined to a sufficiently detailed level, one of the final activities to perform is the testing of a software implementation mapped onto the actual target hardware. Typically, the implementation of the software architecture is automated—e.g., auto-generated glue code links automatically to COTS function primitive libraries and services—so that debugging is kept to a minimum. The system designer can investigate how the "real" system will perform, running tests with real-world data. Our earlier-developed Scalable Parallel Instrumentation (SPI) [13] has been integrated into MESA to provide a real-time monitoring, analysis, and visualization capability. It allows the designer to visualize the following types of information directly in terms of the hardware and software design: resource usage, activity (application, I/O, overhead) profiling, timelines, and latency requirements checking.

4.2 Using MESA Design Tool in an Application

We now present some specific features of the MESA design tool and walk through a real example. The important features of the design tool to remember are:

- All aspects of the specification/modeling of system software and hardware is contained within a single unified design representation maintained by the design tool.

- Automatic generation of parallel distributed source code on the specific target platform.

- Seamless integration with partitioning/mapping optimization, analysis, and simulation tools

- Capability to develop the system design at varying levels of abstraction within the same notation, from the top level requirements capture, all the way down to application implementation.

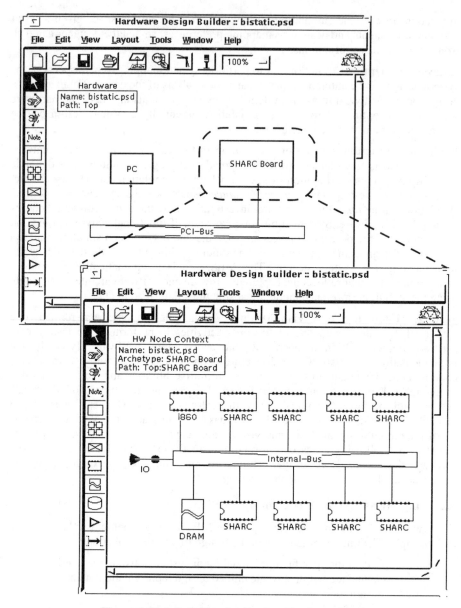

Figure 6. Bistatic Radar Application Hardware View

The application we have chosen is a bistatic radar example, a DSP-type application for monitoring weather conditions. The application itself will perform a series of FFT's and matrix multiplications to filter the sets of raw data, called dwells, into an acceptable output format.

Let us begin with the hardware view shown in Figure 6. We will design the system to use specialized DSP accelerator board, containing eight SHARC DSP processors, an

Intel I860 for a control processor, and some DRAM memory, all connected on an internal bus backplane. See Figure 6 for the representation of the hardware architecture in the MESA design tool. Accelerator boards of this nature, which can be plugged into the back of any standard Pentium based computer, are becoming popular (and cost-effective) solutions to complex, embedded applications.

In this example, the hardware design is fixed, so there is no need for elaborate analysis or simulation. However, a useful exercise would be to analyze how many of the SHARC processors on the accelerator board are required for the application, given an estimate for typical processing loads.

Next, we will examine the software view. Figure 7 shows the MESA display of the architecture of the bistatic application. Input data is read and the application performs a series of matrix operations before writing the results to a file.

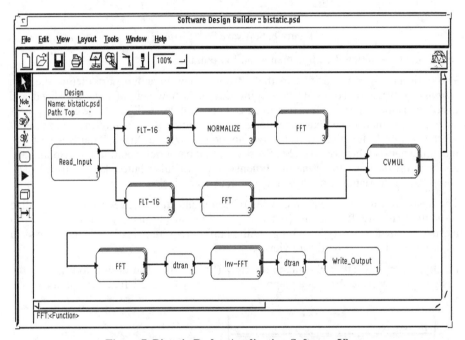

Figure 7. Bistatic Radar Application Software View

Each "bubble" in the display represents an indivisible, executable function that can be scheduled and run concurrently with other functions on a processing resource. Function nodes with the shadowed appearance indicate that the function can be parallelized. The numbers in the bottom-right corner of each function node represents the number of separate parallel threads required by the function. For the bistatic application, this number also indicates to the auto-code generator of the design tool the number of processors to apply to each particular function. For example, the *CVMUL* function above will eventually employ three SHARC processors to accomplish its subtasks. From the analysis we have done on this example, we have discovered that using only three SHARC processors on the accelerator board is optimal for bistatic, since increasing the number of SHARC's will also increase the communication

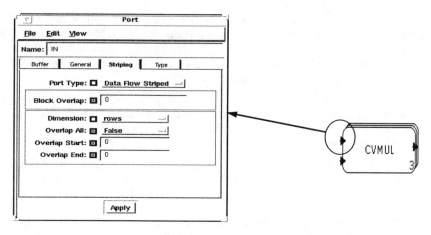

Figure 8. Software Port Striping

requirements, making the implementation I/O bound.

Ports are an important artifact in the software view. Function ports define the data *striping* between functions. Data striping describes how sets of data are sliced and distributed among parallel function threads. For example, in Figure 8 the circled port is striping a 3-dimensional data cube along its *rows* dimension. Each of the three threads of the *CVMUL* function will receive an equal sized 2-dimensional slice of the incoming data on that port. The MESA design tool has a rich notation for striping data, allowing the designer to define the dimension that the distributed data is striped over, and possible overlapping of striped, contiguous data blocks.

The designer can also define the types of communication between functions, called *invocation* (Figure 9). The arcs between functions in the display can be assigned a particular invocation type, along with buffer requirements, and any physical requirements from the hardware view.

Finally, we can examine the mapping view (Figure 10). The design tool allows the designer to describe different mapping preferences for each function thread in the

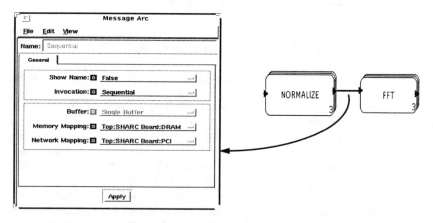

Figure 9. Invocation Arc Properties

system. A function can be assigned to a physical resource, meaning the function will map to a specific processing component from the hardware view. In addition, a function can map to a resource type, meaning the function threads will be applied to a collection of processors. In the MESA design tool, color can be used to denote function mapping.

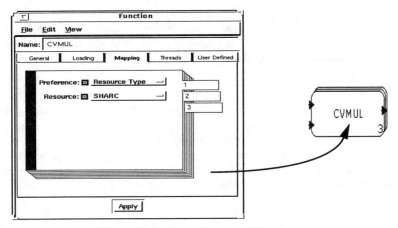

Figure 10. Software Function Mapping

In the example in Figure 10, the parallel function *CVMUL* has three threads that are mapped to the processor type SHARC.

Once the details of the bistatic requirements have been entered, the auto-code generator can be invoked, and the MESA design tool will build and compile the application on the target hardware (assuming the accelerator board is available). This approach has definite advantages, since the designer can run through a set of candidate system architectures very quickly, and investigate their resulting performance, without spending their time and resources debugging low-level source code.

5 Status and Future Work

We have presented here an overview of the MESA application development methodology, the design notation, and the design tool. Most of the tools in the integrated MESA toolset are now operational and have been applied in the development of signal and image processing application using heterogeneous architectures. The following is a summary of the current MESA toolset capabilities:

- end-to-end development process driven by a single unified design specification.

- a design notation and tool that allows comprehensive specification of parallelism, synchronization, and scheduling properties within domain-specific programming styles.

- automated partitioning and mapping of the software design onto the hardware architecture, optimizing for performance requirements, size, weight, power and cost.

- automated generation of VHDL simulation models.

- automated generation of glue code that provides data/control flow and scheduling of functions on multi-level architectures.

- real-time monitoring, analysis, and visualization of system performance and behavior in terms of the design notation.

Our future plans are to extend and apply the design notation to other domains such as avionics mission management and automated target recognition and extend the capabilities for real-time requirements specification. We also plan to extend the automated partitioning and mapping capabilities to meet the needs of these new domains and more complex heterogeneous architectures.

Acknowledgments

The authors are grateful for the contributions of the other members of MESA development team: Todd Steeves, Bill Wren, Mustafa Muhammad, and Subbu Ponnuswamy. We also thank Walt Heimerdinger for many suggestions and a critical review of the concepts presented here. Finally, we acknowledge the applications focus and development support provided by Joseph Philipose and his team at Honeywell Space and Strategic Systems Operation.

References

1. Devesh Bhatt, Vicraj Thomas, and John Shackleton, "A Methodology and Toolset for the Design of Parallel Embedded Systems," ACM OOPS Messenger, January 1996.

2. Peter Coad and Edward Yourdon, *Object-Oriented Analysis*, Second Edition, Yourdon Press, Prentice Hall Building.

3. S. Shlaer, S. J. Miller, "Object Lifecycles: Modeling the World in States," Yourdon Press, Prentice Hall Building, 1992.

4. J. Rumbaugh, M. Blaha, W. Premerlani, F. Eddy, and W. Loresnsen, *Object-Oriented Modeling and Design*, Prentice Hall, Englewodd Cliffs, NJ 07632.

5. David Grimm and John Samson, "Data Flow Shell Environment for Deterministic Signal Processing Applications," Technical Report, Space Systems Division, Honeywell, Inc., April 1995.

6. D. Cottel and P. Partow, "Experience Building a Scalable Programming Environment," Intel Supercomputer Users Group Conference (ISUG-94), June 1994.

7. J. T. Buck, S. Ha, E. A. Lee, and D. G. Messerschmitt, "Ptolemy: A Framework for Simulating and Prototyping Heterogeneous Systems," Int. Journal of Computer Simulation, special issue on "Simulation Software Development," vol. 4, pp. 155-182, April 1994.

8. Gul Agha, Svend Frolund, WooYoung Kim, Rajendra Panwar, Anna Patterson, and Daniel Sturman, "Abstractions and Modularity Mechanisms for Concurrent Computing," IEEE Parallel and Distributed Technology, vol. 1, no. 2, May 1993.

9. D. Cottel and P. Partow, "Scalable Programming Environment". Technical Report 1672 Rev. 1, September 1995.

10. A. Kalavade and E. A. Lee, "The Extended Partitioning Problem: Hardware/Software Mapping and Implementation-Bin Selection," Journal of Design Automation for Embedded Systems, March 1997.

11. K. Mani Chandy, Rajit Manohar, Berna L. Massingill, Daniel I. Meiron, "Integrating Task and Data Parallelism with the Group Communication Archetype", Proceedings of the 9th International Parallel Processing Symposium, April 1995.

12. Fred Rose, John Shackleton, and Carl Hein, "Performance Modeling of System Architectures," Journal of VLSI Signal Processing 15, 97-109, 1997.

13. Devesh Bhatt, Rashmi Bhatt, Rakesh Jha, Todd Steeves, and David Wills, "SPI: an Instrumentation Development Environment for Parallel/Distributed Systems," Proceedings of the 9th International Parallel Processing Symposium, April 1995.

The Maturity of Object-Oriented Methodologies

André van den Hoogenhof

Philips Research Laboratories
Information and Software Technology
Eindhoven,
Computing Science Institute
University of Nijmegen

Abstract. Methodologies within software engineering are introduced with the speed of improved soap-powders. One of the major movements is object-orientedness. It already started at language level long ago, with Simula 67 and Smalltalk, and nowadays many methodologies are labelled as object-oriented. And it is ongoing: unifications of object-oriented methods are introduced to get the maximum benefit of all involved. This article examines some important techniques and constructions used in the mainstream object-oriented methodologies, and elaborates on their common properties and weaknesses in practical use.

1 Introduction

"Software engineering" is the application of scientific principles to (a) the orderly transformation of a problem into a working software solution and (b) the subsequent maintenance of that software until the end of its useful life.

Software engineering is more than just programming, it also includes all documentation which is necessary to install, use, develop and maintain these programs. People and projects following an engineering approach generally pass through series of phases, as defined in the process model that is used. Furthermore, additional characteristics of applied software engineering are: software systems are built in teams rather than by individuals and they are made up by technical as non-technical aspects as well. Not only a thorough knowledge of computing science, also the ability to communicate, to plan and to manage are critical success factors in the field of software engineers.

A methodology is an explicit prescription for an activity, or set of activities, as required by the selected approach. A methodology, when applied to the right type of project and used by capable people, will with a high degree of probability, with a predictable amount of resources, lead to a solution of the problem.

The availability of (good) software development methodologies may be an indication for the maturity of the software engineering discipline.

The Capability Maturity Model [1] defines five levels of process maturity of which the lowest level is, euphemistically, called "Initial". The description, however, is less disguising: The Initial Process Level could properly be called ad hoc, and it is often even chaotic. At this stage the organisation typically operates without formalised procedures, cost estimates and project plans. Tools are neither well integrated with the process nor uniformly applied. Change control is lax, and there is little senior management exposure or understanding of the problems and issues. Since many problems are deferred or even forgotten, software installation and maintenance often present serious problems.

The past ten years the Software Engineering Institute (SEI) measured the level of organisations that are active in a "software process improvement" process. Of those organisations that have reported the assessment results the figures are presented [2]. In April 1997 over 60% of the reported organisations were assessed at level one (in '87 this percentage was over 80%). Totalling the percentages of the organisations that were assessed in one of the first three levels gets close to 100%. The naming of the successive levels are: Initial, Repeatable, Defined, *Managed*, and Optimising. The naming of the fourth level is the first one that suggests a certain 'maturity'.

Within the software engineering discipline there is certainly no lack of methodologies but their contribution to the maturity of the discipline seems limited. Not only the process quality is under discussion, remarks with respect to the content of methodologies can be made as well. The scientific principles, as mentioned in the characterisation of "Software Engineering", are hardly recognised in any software methodology. Strangely enough, this is quite accepted. Especially the lack of formalism is all too often regarded as an advantage instead of a handicap.

The use of formal methodologies is unfortunately the subject of extreme hyperbole or deep criticism in many 'popular press' science journals. From the claims that the authors of such articles make, it is quite clear that they have little or no feeling of what formal methodologies could contribute in industrial application. The aversion to formal methodologies is that high, that discussion exceeds the rational level and has become a religious debate a long time ago. The preconceived opinions as discussed in Hall's "Seven Myths of Formal Methods" [3] or in the article "Seven More Myths of Formal Methods" [4] are still the main belief of many. Introducing a formal method will probably not contribute to one's popularity.

In this article some important techniques and constructions, as used in the mainstream object-oriented methodologies, are examined. This article will focus on how the object modelling techniques of mainstream object-oriented methodologies are used, and the effect of these techniques on the object models that are made.

Chapter 2 contains a contemplation on the subject object-orientation. In section 2.1 the most common properties of mainstream object-oriented methodologies and the products that result from it, are summarised. Section 2.2 treats the fundamentals of the object-oriented methodologies. In section 2.3 the subject "orientation" is contrasted with "decomposition". Decomposition is about the model itself, the components that are used and their architecture. Orientation has much more to deal with the attitude one takes during the creation of the model. Section 2.4 provides an overview of the 'object-oriented' constructions.

Chapter 3 views on the 'practical' part of object-orientation. Along with some examples and/or cases some consequences of object-oriented modelling are considered. The fact that object-oriented is relatively new makes it a good candidate for over-enthusiasm and euphoric behaviour. Methodologies in general, and new methodologies often even more, suggest that, if followed, excellent results are guaranteed. In reality, however, every time and again one must conclude that the engineer is always responsible for the job done. A method may be of help, but never does the job.

Chapter 4 contains some observations.

2 Object-orientation

Problem analysis is the activity that encompasses learning about the problem to be solved (often through brainstorming and/or questioning), understanding the needs of the users and considering the constraints on the solution. Normally one can expect requirements ranging over a wide variety of system properties. Requirements may concern performance, interfaces, functionality, and data, the use of a specific platform or language and so on. Although it is important to fully understand all aspects of the problem, most methodologies emphasize just one aspect in their analysis model. The view taken during the first analysis steps are normally determined by the approach of the methodology that is applied. Examples of well known approaches are data-flow analysis, stepwise refinement, data-structure analysis, entity-relation diagramming (information modelling), state-transition diagramming, syntax driven program design and, of course, object-oriented analysis.

Object-orientation is one of the techniques for system modelling. The object-oriented technology originates from simulation applications. The language Simula 67 offers a number of concepts which are well suited for this purpose. Through the introduction of Smalltalk and its programming environment, the applicability of object-oriented languages were demonstrated. For some time object-orientation was seen as a technique used at implementation level; a methodology at the level of programming languages. For some it is still at that level, especially those who identify object-orientation by the programming language in use (e.g. C++, Eiffel, Ada, not Ada, Objective C, Smalltalk and not to forget Java). Others confuse object-orientation with a graphical user interface a system could have, a misunderstanding probably caused by the user interface provided in the Smalltalk environment. Nowadays, object-orientation is seen as a technique by which the system is modelled as a number of objects that interact.

2.1 Advantages of object-oriented methodologies

Unfortunately, the terminology of object-oriented methodologies is not well standardised, and there is not even agreement as to what object-oriented analysis, design or programming really is. There is no general consensus on what characterises an object-oriented method or language. But with respect to the advantages it seems that everyone agrees: "object-oriented software holds up better as requirements evolve". And the disadvantages of the 'old-fashioned' methodologies are clear too: "if requirements change, a system based on decomposing functionality may require massive restructuring. Although functional decomposition seems the most direct way of implementing, the resulting system can be fragile". An object-oriented approach will lead to a more stable system because its model is based on the underlying framework of the application domain.

In his dissertation [29] Paul Frederiks summarises the advantages of object-orientation that are encountered:

- A better integration of data and processes. In many analysis and design methodologies there is no satisfactory connection between the data models and process models. Object-oriented modelling techniques have *natural integration* of data and processes as a result of the encapsulation of attributes and operations in an object.
- Object-oriented systems are loosely coupled. A consequence of encapsulation of data and operations into an object is a *well defined interface* without side-effects.
- *Reuse* of classes. Objects, due the excellent cohesion and coupling properties, can be treated as stand-alone modules. Classes can be put into libraries, thus stimulating the reuse of classes.
- *Cheaper maintenance.* Encapsulation of data and processes makes it possible to change a class without changing other classes. Furthermore, before a class has to be changed the object library can be consulted for similar classes (generalisation/specialisation).
- *Better maintenance.* Conventionally developed systems are implemented to fit as good as possible for the available hardware, whereas object-oriented systems try to capture the reality as naturally as possible. The point of view in object-orientation fits better to changes that can be expected: 60% of the changes during maintenance are about changes in user requirements and data formats, only 6% are about changes in hardware [12].
- *Better communication* between analyst and user. Object-oriented methodologies try to describe the reality by objects which represent abstract and concrete notions of the problem area. The object model provides a better overview of the problem domain.
- *Better process model.* In contrast with conventional modelling techniques, models of object-oriented techniques for the different stages of the process have better connections. The products of the different stages of conventional modelling techniques often need an extra translation for their interfacing.

2.2 Fundamentals of object-orientation

Superficially the term "object-oriented" means that we organise software as a collection of discrete objects that incorporate both data and behaviour. This is in contrast to conventional programming in which data structure and behaviour are loosely connected. There is some dispute about exactly what characteristics are required by an object-oriented approach, but they generally include four aspects, or fundamentals: identity, classification, polymorphism, and inheritance [7].

In an object-oriented decomposition reality is reflected into a set of quantified discrete objects. An object is called concrete if it represents a concrete thing in reality, such as a ball, a vacuum cleaner, a light button, and so on. Objects characterising a notion are conceptual objects. Some examples of conceptual objects are the amount 3, a war strategy, or a ball. Each object has its own inherent identity. In other words, two objects are distinct even if all their attribute values are equal. Objects can be compared to variables in an imperative programming language: it is quite normal to have two variables (objects) of the type (class) integer both having the value 3. Identity is in many methodologies assumed, and not made explicit.

Object-orientation is poor naming: the most interesting part of object modelling is finding the classes. Classes are groups of objects that have the same data structure (instance variables) and the same behaviour (operations). This concept, classification, in its turn is very close to that of a type. Maybe a small difference can be argued since classes offer (most of the time implicit) 'create' and 'dispose' operations whereas types leave the object life to the declaration statements and the scope-rules of the programming language.

Polymorphism, often considered as one of the basic concepts, is treated most of the time only partially in documents on object-orientation. In the article "On Understanding Types, Data Abstraction, and Polymorphism" [8], a unifying framework for polymorphic type systems is presented. Distinction is made between *universal polymorphism* and *ad-hoc polymorphism*. Ad-hoc polymorphism is obtained when a function works, or appears to work, on several different types. There are two major kinds of ad-hoc polymorphism, overloading and coercion.

In *overloading*, the same function identifier is used to denote different functions and the context is used to decide which function is denoted by a particular instance of the identifier. The compiler can resolve the ambiguity at compile time by giving different names to the different functions; so in a sense overloading is just a convenient syntactic abbreviation.

Coercion allows the users to omit semantically necessary type conversions. The required type conversions must be determined by the system, inserted in the program, and used by the compiler to generate required type conversion code. Coercions are essentially a form of abbreviation that improves the programs readability, but may also cause subtle and sometimes dangerous system errors. Coercion is allowed in most programming languages; automatic conversion from integer to real is perhaps a well know example.

Whereas ad-hoc polymorphic functions will only work on a finite set of different and potentially unrelated types, *universally* polymorphic functions will normally work on an infinite number of types (all the types having a given common structure).

In the case of universal polymorphism, one can assert with confidence that some values (i.e. polymorphic functions) have many types, whereas in ad-hoc polymorphism this is more difficult to maintain, as one may take the position that an ad-hoc polymorphic function is really a set of monomorphic functions. In terms of implementation, a universally polymorphic function will execute the *same* code for arguments of any admissible type, whereas an ad-hoc polymorphic function may execute *different* code for each type of argument.

There are two major kinds of *universal* polymorphism, that is, two major ways in which a value can have many types. In *parametric polymorphism* a polymorphic function has an implicit or explicit type parameter which determines the type of the argument for each application of that function. In *inclusion polymorphism* an object can be viewed as belonging to many different classes that need not to be disjoint; that is, there may be inclusion of classes. A well-known example of parametric polymorphism is the use of structures (generic types). Inclusion polymorphism is used to model subtypes and inheritance.

The fourth aspect of object-orientation, inheritance, is imbedded in the third aspect (polymorphism). The reason to mention 'inheritance' as an object-oriented fundament explicitly, may be found in the fact that promoting a more extensive use of a construction at least needs the naming of it. And with respect to this construction (inheritance) one can expect a major change in the characteristics programs will have in which inheritance is used.

Polymorphism, and especially inheritance, is often implemented by dynamic or late binding. In practice leads the extensive use of polymorphism also to an extensive use of referencing (pointers) within the implementation. Which, in its turn, stresses the need for a garbage collector. For this reason some people regard dynamic binding and the availability of a garbage collector as fundamentals of object-orientation too.

2.3 Object-orientation versus object-decomposition

Object-orientation is introduced as *the* new way of decomposing systems. The object-oriented methodologies claim to use quite different decomposition criteria than those applied in other (old or old-fashioned) methodologies. A closer look reveals that this is not the case. Many of the techniques used in object-oriented methodologies can be found in existing (non object-oriented) methods or seem to be just small adaptations of existing techniques. However, all object-oriented methodologies will agree on the above stated: the system is modelled as a collection of interacting objects. In this view only the type of component that is used in a system description determines its object-orientedness, and any decomposition into object-components would deserve the label 'object-oriented'. So, along with the introduction of object-oriented methods many of the existing methods became 'object-oriented' too. All they did is some change in notation, to get an 'object' image, and added a few empirical rules to project the original decomposition onto object components. "Grouping by data" has been a good alternative. At the moment the discussion, whether such methods were object-oriented or not, got too heavy one ended in the compromise that it was 'object-oriented structured'.

In fact, the 'orientation' part of object-orientation is crucial and rarely recognised: it is the way of working, the use of dedicated decomposing criteria, the philosophical part of the method. It is easy to create a method that is functional-oriented and leads to an object-decomposition. As an example:

- take the set of functions describing the system found by a function-oriented method
- look at the parameters of these functions and for each type that occurs in the parameter lists, create an object type
- distribute the functions over the object types, based on the type of their most significant parameter.

The main challenge in transferring a method is to give insight in the way of thinking of that method. Many developers of methods must have hesitated, seeing the many faces their method got in and through the literature treating their method. This discrepancy between idea and its image is not reserved for object-oriented methodologies only, also in a book on a 'structured-analysis' one can find data-flow diagrams based on a function-oriented decomposition. The necessary data flows seemed to be added later, in stead of a decomposition as the result of an investigation of the data flows that can be recognised in the system.

Every mainstream method has a number of dialects, sometimes due to the evolution of the method, and often the consequence of the alternative books on the subject matter.

Abstraction is one of the major principles of object-orientation [5], as it is should be for every methodology. The Oxford Dictionary of Computing presents three definitions concerning abstraction:

Abstraction: The principle of ignoring those aspects of a subject that are not relevant to the current purpose in order to concentrate more fully on those that are.

Procedural abstraction: The principle that any operation that achieves a well-defined effect can be treated by its users as a single entity, despite the fact that the operation may actually be achieved by some sequence of lower-level operations.

Data abstraction: The principle of defining a data type in terms of the operations that apply to objects of the type, with the constraint that values of such objects can be modified and observed only by the use of operations.

It needs little imagination to map data-abstraction onto object-orientation, the similarities between the descriptions of both are obvious, and likewise holds the mapping of procedural abstraction onto functional-orientation.

New methods, new ideas, are normally introduced with enthusiasm, which is of course a necessary requirement to gain a field of existence. Never was the software community as enthusiastic as for object-orientation; for every activity in the software process there is an object-oriented version: object-oriented programming, object-oriented design, object-oriented analysis, object-oriented management, and object-oriented testing.

Not only every activity needs to be object-oriented, every module in the decomposition should be an object too; sometimes there is the need for a 'control' object, or a 'abstract' object, or a 'whatever' object, but every module, anywhere in the decomposition, is an object.

The same focusing can be recognised with respect to the use of inheritance, like in the early days of "structured programming" it was strictly forbidden to use the goto-statement, nowadays the use of inheritance is a must.

Under the guidance of slogans like "the integrated process approach" (every activity is 'object-oriented'), "horizontal and vertical uniformity" (every component at any level of abstraction is an object), and "the ultimate construction for reusability" (use inheritance!!), the herd of software-lemmingineers follow the object-oriented gurus [6]. That new methods lead to enthusiasm is understandable, but sometimes this enthusiasm is resulting in overkill.

In conclusion, object-orientation should be used to find objects (classes), function-orientation to find functions, etc. The same holds for components; to capture a function, make use of a functional module, for a control abstraction a control module, etc. It is very unlikely that trying to describe a system, that reflects the real world in a natural way, will be possible with the use of one type of component. The existence of the other types of orientation, others types of abstraction, is a proof this is not the case.

In every object-oriented methodology, apart from some object model, at least a functional, dynamic or behavioural model is found. The descriptions of the techniques, that are used to create these models, contain exactly those orientations that are not object-oriented at all: they reveal the use of control and functional-orientation. Object-orientation seems to be reserved for the object model only, the other models needed to complete the system description are found by non object-oriented techniques.

In a process model the software process is made up of a number of stages such as requirements engineering, design, implementation and so on. During requirements engineering, or analysis, abstraction is used to find a model of reality in such a way that the resulting model is recognisable by the customer. The customer will be the prime reviewer of this specification and therefore, amongst other reasons, it has to be stated in the problem domain language.

In the design and implementation phase, however, abstraction is used in quite a different way. These phases are about the construction of, and finding a solution for, the system to be build in the artificial world of computing. Whereas during analysis 'orientations' support in capturing the requirements in a clearly structured manner; during the design and implementation the only 'orientation' is towards the model that has to be constructed. The nature of design and implementation is one of transforming models into design models, finally ending in code (and showing that this is correctly done). Object-orientation is reserved for the analysis phase, and moreover, it is only a part of the analysis phase: it is one of the needed 'orientations' for full requirements.

2.4 Constructions in object-oriented

To support object modelling, the mainstream object-oriented methodologies describe a number of investigation techniques together with a notation in which the object model is to be described. A 'new' type of module is provided; the object module which is normally called a class.

To make a distinction between the components used within the system description and the investigation techniques used to find them helps in getting a better grip on the term 'object-orientation'. In section 2.3 "object-orientation versus object-decomposition" the conclusion was made that dynamic and functional modelling are not regarded as "object-oriented" modelling techniques, this despite the fact they are needed to obtain full requirements,.

2.4.1 The object model

An object model captures the static structure of a system by showing the classes in that system, the associations between the classes, and the attributes and operations that characterises each class. In object-oriented methodologies the object model plays a dominant role, systems are built around objects rather than around functionality.

Classes and Objects

A *Class* is a set of objects exhibiting common attributes and/or functions and/or states and/or common relationships with other objects. Object that are members of a class inherit the attributes, functions, states and relationships associated with that class [9].

Brad Cox [10] is very short on describing a class: the concept of class and instance will already be familiar. In programming languages the same concept is often called type. For example, *int LeftEdge*; just says "allocate an instance called LeftEdge of class int.".

In Object-Oriented Design [11], Grady Booch also maps the notion of a class onto the type construct but in a footnote he points out that there is a small difference in concept. Finally he ends with the conclusion that for most mortals separating the concepts of type and class is utterly confusing and adds very little value.

An *object class* describes a group of objects with similar properties (attributes), common behaviour (operations), common relationships to other objects, and common semantics [7].

As the diversity of the definitions above indicate, it is hard to give one meaning to the notion of class. "A class is a template for objects, describing their common behaviour" suggests that a class is at least close to the idea of an abstract data type. Based on the claims that objects hide their internal state for the outside world, one could come to the conclusion that a class and an abstract data type definition are the same (1). Brad Cox and Grady Booch seem to be in favour for this viewpoint.

Others point out that classes and types are not the same, types do not have operations for creation and deletion of objects (variables) of that type (class). Furthermore the class concept emphasizes the importance of hierarchies of classes. For some is the implicit definition of a number of operations (create, delete, the queries on instance variables) a reason to distinct between classes and types: classes need less specification texts. In these cases a precise meaning is not given, but classes are accepted to be 'type-like' (2).

A definition proclaiming a more concrete view can be found in "Object-oriented Software Construction" [12]. A certain hurry to start coding or the difficulty of building compilers that support separation of the definition and the implementation of a data type justifies the idea of 'specification by representation' principle. Although the instance variables can only be addressed by invoking the methods of the class, classes are specified in terms of their implementation. This leads to the opinion that a class is an abstract data type implementation (3).

Taken Rumbaugh's definition and considering " ... describes a group of objects with similar properties ..." the 'type'-vision does not hold any longer. Besides, being a description of a type, a class is also a collection of instances, a population (4).

It is interesting to see that the definitions sometimes lead to some strange observation. An abstract class is quite commonly used, abstract classes can be found in many inheritance trees in the role of superclass. The definition of an abstract class that is found in [11] starts with: a class that has no instances. An abstract class is written with the expectation that its subclasses will add to its structure and behaviour, usually by completing the implementation of its (typically) incomplete methods. Confronting this description of an abstract class with the definition taken from Rumbaugh, we must conclude that an abstract class describes what no (none) objects have in common.

It is quite normal to support the brainstorm sessions of the analysis phase in a software development project by a notation based on diagrams. A diagram provides a quick oversight, and is therefore well suited for brainstorming. The diagrams can also be used as input for the requirements specification.

Object modelling is obviously the main modelling activity of the mainstream object-oriented methodologies. Most notations contain the same type of information. In this article an OMT/UML-like notation is used.

The basic notation for a class consists of four parts; the class-name, the attributes, the operations and the constraints. The elements that serve as input for the (formal) specification are:

(a) the class-name, uniquely identifying the class

(b) the attributes and constraints determining the state-space of the objects belonging to that class

(c) the names of the operations, sometimes with their signature, offered by the class.

Class-name
Type1 Attr1 Type2 Attr2 ... [State space: $\{ (a,b) \mid a \in$ Type1 $\wedge$ $b \in$ Type 2 $\wedge$ $Pa \wedge Pc \}$]
Opr1 Opr2 (arg-list) : Return-type ...
Pa : Attr1 > 0 Pc : Attr2 < Attr1

Ad (b), the state space is the set of values an object can obtain. The state space, also called the valueset, consists of those elements of the cartesian product of the state spaces of its instance variables, that fulfil the constraints. Within the set of constraints two types can be recognised: attribute-constraints (Pa) a restriction on the admissible values of precisely one attribute, and a class-constraint (Pc), a further limitation based on the forbidden value combination of two or more attributes of that class.

Ad (c), the operations specify the behaviour of the class. It has become a custom to assume a number of operations to be implicitly specified: the creation and deletion of an object of that class, query operations on each of the attributes, and equality. Sometimes ordering operations ($<, >, \geq, ..$) are assumed available also. In the object model the meaning of the operations is suggested by the operation name, and, if available, the signature of the operation.

In 'advanced' notations it is possible to declare class-attributes and class-operations, recognised by a prefix (i.e. "$"). Whereas instance variables are instantiated for each and every object of that class, a class-attribute is instantiated once for the whole class, even when the class contains zero objects. This induces the fifth meaning of class: a class is an instance of an aggregation of its class attributes together with an instance of a group (the objects of that class) (5).

Associations

A class is not a stand-alone entity, that is, its definition depends on more than the attributes that are declared within the class alone. The definition of a class is also dependent on the associations it has to other classes. Any dependency between two or more classes is an association. However, only those associations that describe a structural property of the application domain will appear in the object model as an association. Associations indicating a transient event, or the functionality that serves such an event, will be modelled in the dynamic model (in a state transition diagram) and as operations within a class.

Attributes can be seen as the association of precisely one object (the attribute itself) with the class it belongs to. An attribute is a part of an instance of its class.. The types of these objects (attributes) are simple, normally offered by the imperative programming language that is used. At the moment there is a need for an attribute of a higher order abstraction level, the attribute could be typed by a class. This is the first reason to introduce the *aggregation* association. As the example shows: Heading and Section are 'higher-order attributes' of the class Document.

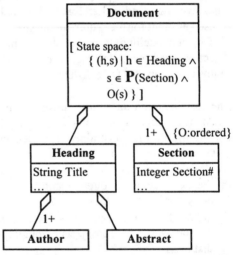

The existence of the classes Heading and Section have the same dependency to the class Document as attributes would have. Heading and Section are part of the class Document. A second reason to use the aggregation association is demonstrated by the class Section: whereas each Document had precisely one Heading, it can have multiple Sections. Attributes within a class normally define a single instance.

The state space of a class will be: those elements of the cartesian product of attributes and aggregations that fulfil all the constraints (the association constraints too). As the example already shows within the cartesian product one element, s, is a non-empty group (1+), described as an element of the powerset of the state space of the class Section. Due to the association constraint, O, the section numbers used in the possible values of "s" must be a closed interval in a linear ordered domain (Integer).

In the introduction of the aggregation association, some possible multiplicities were used. Within a Document the multiplicity of Heading was 'exactly one', the multiplicity of Section was 'one or more'.

Multiplicities, however, are used in all association types that denote a relation between instances (objects). In a generalisation association, a relation between classes rather than between objects, multiplicity is not meaningful.

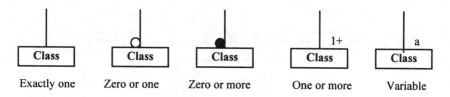

| Exactly one | Zero or one | Zero or more | One or more | Variable |

Above the drawing conventions that will be use in this article are presented: 'exactly one', 'zero or one', 'zero or more', 'one or more', and the name of a variable of which the possible values are specified in a constraint .

Suppose that a Catalogue should be made by putting all the Headings of the Documents together. A consequence of that decision is that the existence of an object of the class Heading is no longer solely dependent on the existence of its Document. The lifetime of Heading is now depending on the Document as well as the Catalogue, it has become a self-supporting entity. [26] .

Semantically there is not much difference with an association and a aggregation association. Associations have the same contribution to the state space as if they were aggregation associations. To denote the difference, Bertrand Meyer [12] introduced the notions of *reference* semantics and *value* semantics. Associations lead to references semantics, aggregation associations leave a choice: value semantics or reference semantics. Translated into implementation level terminology: an association forces to use pointers (reference) whereas an aggregation association leaves the choice between embedding the object into the object it is part of, or switch to an implementation using a reference (pointer).

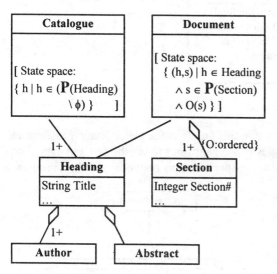

Having classes, associations and aggregation associations only, the actual information is found in the attributes of the classes that are present in the model. The information is structured by the associations and limited to meaningful values by the use of constraints. Sometimes it is more appropriate to add attributes to an association, e.g. if the information is fully dependent on an instance of the association. Such an instance of an association is called a link (compare: an object is an instance of a class).

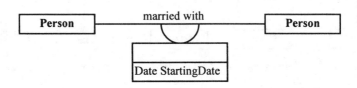

The notation for link-attributes is presented above. The StartingDate in the example is a link-attribute, its lifecycle is fully dependent on the instance of the association 'married with'. Link-attributes are presented in a class-style manner. It may be the case, however, that the information belonging to the link is recognised as a semantical unit: leading to the introduction of an association class. (See below).

The final association type treated within this article is the generalisation association. Within object-oriented methodologies it is conspicuous to see the fast and easy short-cut that is made between generalisation-specialisation relations and the inheritance construction.

A lot of literature is found on inheritance, little though on the abstraction mechanism behind it. A further elaboration on the subject matter can be found in section 3.4

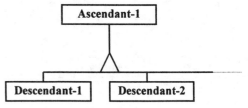

2.4.2. The dynamic model

Those aspects of a system that are concerned with time and changes (control), are the dynamic model, in contrast with the static, or object model. Control is that aspect of a system that describes the sequences of operations that occur in response to external stimuli, without consideration what the operations do, what they operate on, or how they are implemented.

Event-trace diagrams

An event is something that happens at a point in time and, if detected by the system, a reason to act. The 'use-case' technique makes use of this notion to explore the systems behaviour. For each initiator of events and for any type of event the services the system should offer as a reaction on such an event, are described in a use-case. Use-cases are written in the early stages of building the requirements (they are still vague descriptions). During design the use-cases are refined in more concrete descriptions: the scenarios. A scenario is a sequence of events that occurs during one particular execution of the system.

The most detailed descriptions of the dynamic aspects of the system are found in the event-trace diagrams, showing a thread of execution. Events transmit information from one object to another, the arrow (see figure) indicates who is the sender and who is the receiver object. Objects are represented by vertical lines. In an event-trace diagram time increases from top to bottom, but the spacing is irrelevant, it shows the sequence of events. Events can happens at the same moment (Event-etc and Event-5), and may be parameterised.

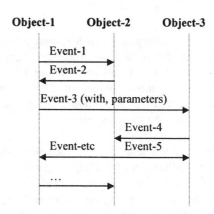

State transition diagrams

A state is a stable situation of an object in which an object resides for some time [23]. A state is denoted as a rounded-rectangle. This description refers to the same notion as is used in the Mealy machine. But it must be said that this notion does not hold throughout the use of states in the diverse methodologies. Actions are assigned to states as well as assigned to state transitions.

To denote a state two representations were found: the rounded-rectangle, which is normally used, containing the name of the state and the possible activities that are performed in that state, and a bulls-eye for an final-state.

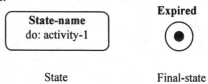

The final-state is possibly labelled to indicate the ending condition but it is not able to perform an activity. A final state implies the destruction of an object.

The initial states are indicated by an arrow starting in a solid circle, the circle may be labelled to indicate the initial condition. Switching of states is described by state transitions.

A state transition has a starting state and ending state which is possibly the same state as the starting state. State transitions are initiated by an event and during the transition an action may be performed.

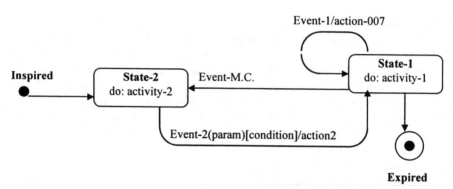

Above a summary of an unstructured state transitions diagram is presented. "State-2" is the only initial state. The final state "Expired" can only be reached from "State-1". With respect to the transition "Event-1" such a transition (start state is equal to the end state) has only meaning if it is labelled with a non-empty action. A condition may be used as a guard on the transition. A guarded transition is executed when its event occurs while the guard is true.

State transition diagrams are used to model object life-cycles to get insight in the dynamic behaviour of the object. In this technique one focuses on "all the things that could happen with an object" of a class. As a spin-off one obtains a better view on the pre-condition of operations: in those states in which an operation is permitted its precondition should be true. Modelling the object life-cycle also checks the expressive power of the state space of the object: is the state space supporting in determining all the different states that should be recognised?

State transition diagrams are also used to model the dynamic behaviour of the system. This technique may be called an event driven technique. Based on the event traces found a state transition diagram is built of the system.

2.4.3 The functional model

The functional model describes computations (the operations) within a system. The functional model is the third leg of the modelling tripod, in addition to the object model and the dynamic model. The functional model specifies what happens, the dynamic model when it happens and the object model what it happens to.

The functional model shows which values depend on which other values and the functions that relate them. The diagramming technique that is used to model functionality is mainly data flow diagramming. This modelling technique, however, is only used in a limited set of all object-oriented methodologies.

Some methodologies proclaim that the needed operations are found during object modelling and dynamic modelling already. The operations typically belonging to a class are modelled during object modelling, some of those even implicitly. Modelling the object life-cycles give rise to the definition of boolean operations that support robustness, and the set of operations, which are perhaps more dedicated to the application at this time, can be extended. The set of operations that completes the needed functionality of the system are found in the activities that are performed in the states of the system's dynamic model and in the actions defined at the state transitions. Data flow diagramming is seen as the dominant model in the 'structured' methodologies. More on data flow diagramming can be found in [7,9,27,28].

3 Now practical, O.O.

3.1 Mainstream methods and techniques

In the past twenty years, a large number of methodologies have been introduced. Up to the late eighties most methodologies were "structured", a nearby synonym for "data-flow oriented". In the past ten years, however, at least 20 object-oriented methods were proposed in book form and many more in papers. In this article the 'mainstream' object-oriented methodologies are subject of discussion. To provide an idea, which and what type of methodologies are meant to be 'mainstream' a short overview is given.

Shlaer and Mellor partition systems into domains, where a domain is defined as a part of the world with its own conceptual space of rules and behaviour. Example domains are the implementation domain (programming languages, operating systems, etc.), the service domain (containing utility functions for user interfaces, mathematical libraries, etc.) , and the problem domain (also called: application area, application domain, subject domain or problem space). Large domains will be partitioned into sub-systems that are loosely coupled but have close cohesion. This partitioning is an explicit step in for instance the Octopus method. Each subsystem is modelled as a collection of communicating objects. Shlaer and Mellor wrote "Modelling the word in data"[14] in 1988. It contains an object-oriented variant of information modelling. In 1992 "Modelling the world in states"[15] was written. It describes a pragmatic approach to model the dynamic behaviour of a system in terms of state and process models.

In 1990 Coad and Yourdon [5] published their book on object-oriented analysis. The conceptual decomposition of the system is described in an object model, consisting of the relevant classes. The structure layer adds the containment relations and inheritance trees. In the subject layer one can recognise a 'role' investigation, one of the investigations defined in OMT. The object model is refined with attributes, after which the functionality is explored in a service layer. Services are described in natural language, but the idea of state transition diagrams scenarios and event traces can be recognised in the specifications as a source of inspiration.

Booch [16] introduced his method for software design in 1986 with "software engineering in Ada". This work has been one of the inspirations of many object-oriented methodologies. In 1991 Booch published "Object Oriented Design" [17], and a successor (second edition) in 1994. Booch represents the structure of a software system by means of a class diagram and the behaviour of the objects by means of state diagrams. The rather simple state diagrams introduced in 1991, are replaced by a statechart-like notation in 1994. As were communications represented by timing diagrams in 1991, in 1994 these timing diagrams are sequence diagrams turned on their sides.

The Object Modelling Technique (OMT) was introduced by Loomis et al [18] and popularised by Rumbaugh et al [7]. A significant update, OMT95, was published in 1995. The decomposition of the system into objects is represented by the object model, again an object-oriented variant of information modelling. The behaviour of objects is described in the dynamic model; the notation is based on a statechart variant. Object operations are defined in the functional model. In OMT95 use cases (adopted from Objectory) are used to complement the problem statement. In the OMT-dialects that exist nowadays one can encounter techniques as: Data-Flow diagrams, scenarios, event traces, event-flow diagrams, state-transition diagrams and object life-cycles to be of support during the analysis and design phase.

Behaviour-based methodologies have been developed as alternatives to the methodologies based on conceptual models, e.g. information modelling. The underlying idea behind these methodologies is simple: communication aspects are analysed first, because in the final stage the system will be composed of a collection of communicating objects. Among the behaviour-based methodologies, Class-Responsibility-Collaboration cards, introduced by Wirfs-Brock [19,30], is well known. Objectory is the commercialised version of Object-Oriented Software Engineering [13]. The external functionality is explored in a use case driven approach, the preparation of the conceptual decomposition which in its turn is represented by a domain object model. Objectory can also be seen as one of the major behaviour-based methods.

Fusion, also an evoluting method, defines a decomposition of a system by first specifying a domain model, which is again a variant of an information model, of the application area. The system decomposition is found after that by outlining the systems boundary in the domain model. Everything inside the boundary is seen as part of the system, everything outside the boundary is assumed to be part of the environment.

CODARTS [20] has its roots in structured analysis and design. Recently, it has been complemented by a domain model which adds some more object-oriented flavour. The domain model defines several viewpoints for the analysis of the system. In one of these views, the data flow diagram notation is used to develop object communication diagrams. This shows the flow and control between nodes that are called concurrent objects.

In "Object-Oriented Technology" Awad et al. [21] describe their method as follows: the OMT and Fusion methods are the basis for the development of Octopus. The object model notation of OMT enables compact expression of all the necessary details, and the separation of structural, functional and dynamic aspects makes the models easier to build and understand. Basic separation between the analysis phase, concentrating on describing the external behaviour, and the design phase, concentrating on the internal behaviour of the application is borrowed from the Fusion method. The Octopus method is extended with techniques to cope with the characteristic problems of software development for real-time embedded systems.

The Unified Modelling Language (UML) [22] arose as a joint effort of Booch, Jacobson and Rumbaugh to unify the existing notations for object-oriented software specification. It combines the notations used in the 'Booch" method, Objectory and OMT, applies some simplifications, and extends this with new features in diagrams. However, the basic structure of the notations used in these methods remain recognisable. The intention is that it will be used as a diagram convention in those methods and probably in other methods as well. UML can therefore not be seen as a method but only as a notation, as the name suggests.

Reviewing the mainstream object-oriented methodologies one can argue that the differences are cosmetic. And with respect to the notations that is certainly true: in every methodology one can find syntactical support to express any type of abstraction and any type of component. Differences at notational level are mainly found in the shapes they use.

Already in the 'structured' decade three models were recognised: the functional model, the control model and the data model. In 'structured' methodologies normally the functional model acted as the main model, in 'real-time' versions heavily supported by the control model. In hardly any 'structured' methodology the data model was taken into account.

Object-oriented methodologies still recognise these three models, however, slightly modified. The main model of object-oriented methodologies is the object model, an enhanced data model. The elements of the object model are classes in which data and operations are integrated. The dynamic model has become the new name of the control model. The functional model is not renamed. Object-oriented methodologies perform their analysis with an 'object-vision' (object-orientation) thus leading to an object model (object decomposition). In that distinguish object-oriented methodologies themselves amongst other methodologies.

To determine the feasibility of a software project, a project will start with the construction of a draft version of the problem statement. Usually, such draft version is made through brainstorming and/or questioning. This is a starting point for every methodology. Within the mainstream object-oriented methodologies two strategies can be recognised. Some start to refine the problem statement first, for example through further investigation using use-cases. Others start object modelling right away using the problem statement and likely supported by a domain expert.

Further investigation on the problem statement has often a functional nature, and as such it is endangering the 'object-vision' needed to be object-oriented. The disadvantage of not doing further investigation on the problem, is that the draft problem statement is too vague and lacking important aspects of the problem. As a compromise some methodologies propose to complete the problem statement first, to get a better view on the problem, but neglect the 'functional' supplement during the construction of the object model. The functional nature of the supplement would diminish the object-orientation. Nevertheless, the 'functional' supplement can be used to validate the expressive power of the object model. Nowadays, problem investigation with use-cases is regarded as the most popular technique to complement the problem statement.

To support the recognition of objects (in fact classes) three techniques seem to be in favour: modelling 'nouns and verbs', responsibility driven modelling and information modelling. The 'noun and verbs' technique is simple: given a text, normally the problem statement, nouns are seen class indicators, the verbs are candidates for operations to be defined. Section 3.2 will treat the 'nouns and verbs' technique in more detail. Of the responsibility-driven technique CRC-charting [30] (Classes, Responsibilities and Collaborations) should be mentioned. Information modelling is probably the technique that most extensively used. That is, most object modelling techniques are derivatives from information modelling. Information modelling has its roots in data base design, data structures (attributes, records, tables, and the data base itself) were analysed using the technique of entity relationship diagramming. Focusing, therefore, is on the data of the system, or as expressed by Rumbaugh: the object model specifies what it happens to.

Methodologies, in general, start their analysis at an informal and vague level and tend to add detail in the successive phases (The program code is normally the first document that is completely formal). "From vague to concrete" would appropriately describe the nature of most development cycles. Usually, object models are represented in diagram form, leaving lots of aspects unspecified. (state space, pre & post conditions of operation, etc.) During design, however, one can recognise techniques to correct the previous mentioned omissions. Object life-cycle modelling is a broadly accepted technique within the construction of the dynamic model. Representing the object's life in a state transition diagram gives insight in; the operations needed (they are found as activities in the states or as actions on the state transitions) and on the pre and post conditions as well. Investigating in which states an operation is available, and in which states it is unauthorised, gives insight in the pre and post-condition of the operation. Furthermore is the state space checked against its expressive power.

Another part of analysis, contained in the dynamic model is the control of the system. Normally the use-cases, or the functional descriptions that where made in order to complete the problem statement, are refined into scenarios. In a next step the scenarios are translated into event-traces, the lowest level of control specifications. In these steps new operations are encountered, operations specifically needed in the application. These application dependent operations are added to the object model. The overall control of the system is reflected in state transition diagrams.

3.2 Finding the classes

One of the main difficulties in object-orientation is finding the relevant classes and objects. One of the most popular ways of finding objects, classes and their methods is by giving short problem statements and/or use cases, sometimes also called scenarios, and investigating the nouns and verbs used. In the literature one can find many discussions on the "nouns and verbs" technique, some claiming that it would lead to too many classes and, if applied to use-cases, to a functional decomposition.

In his book "Object-Oriented Software Construction" [12] Bertrand Meyer gives a warning with respect to this way of finding classes. He classifies it as a 'simple-minded' technique, which can give only rough results. Whereas Bertrand Meyer gives this technique the disclaimer "finding far too many candidate classes", others [23] explicitly demand an unrestricted selection of classes. Within the set of candidate classes further selection is carried out, based on findings such as:
- Does a class have a clear responsibility?,
- Does it have a self-supporting role in the problem domain?
- Or, is explicit information needed about this class, or can it serve me?
The 'real' classes and objects will be those for which the above questions are answered with a clear "yes".

With respect to the appliance of this analysis technique to use cases, one tends to be sceptical: it would lead too much to the same functional decomposition one would have found with the old-fashioned technique. The explanation for this is the functional-oriented way of describing a system when using use cases. An entry point for more detailed discussion is to be found in the article: "Be careful with Use Cases" [24].

But there is even more to it: the texts used during this investigation are biased by the problem on hand, thereby influencing the model that follows from it.

Object-oriented decompositions are said to be the natural way of specifying systems: the real world is reflected in an abstraction in a very recognisable way. Besides the remarks above, there is more to be said on the analysis technique based on the investigation of nouns and verbs. Even the careful application of such an investigation will lead to a decomposition which is highly dependent on the view that the writer of the problem statement or use case had. To illustrate the idea, three versions of the same (small) system are presented and models that may result from these texts are described.

The intercom system (1)
In order to improve communication in an office building, an intercom system is installed. With such a system it is possible to request a connection from one office to another. Each office has a room number which will be used in the request for a connection. However, requesting a connection is only confirmed under the following conditions;
- Both offices are free (are not involved in any connection)
- Both offices are in normal mode
- No 'self-requesting' is done
To avoid unwanted disturbance, an office can be shielded from possible connections by putting itself in private mode.

Following this problem statement we could easily conclude that an Intercom system consists of a group of Connections. A Connection relates a calling Office with a called one. Each Office is identified by its room number (qualified attribute) and has a mode (normal, private).*Request, EndOfRequest* and *SetMode* are methods (or operations) that can be expected to be defined and their behaviour is probably described in more detail in a use-case for each one of them.

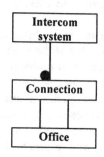

The intercom system (2)

In order to improve communication in an office building, an intercom system is installed. Such an intercom system implements the requests for communication made by people in the building. One can make a request by giving the number of the office one would like to connect to. A request is granted in case :

- neither one of the offices is connected in an pending request
- neither one of the offices is in private mode
- no attempt is made for connecting to oneself

To avoid unwanted disturbance, an office can be placed in private mode, so it can not be connected to.

In this specification the usage of the most important noun and verb are interchanged, the class *Connection* becoming the class *Request*. But still the same Intercom system is described. Now an *Intercom system* has become a set of *Request*s, and the *Request* is the object that characterises the link between two *Offices*, in the same way as *Connection* did in the previous example. Operations (or methods) that can be expected are: *Connect, DisConnect* and *SetMode*.

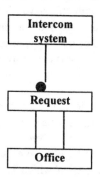

Perhaps in this case, due to the statement that a request may be pending, it will get an attribute called status with two possible values (pending, disconnected). In that case the Intercom system is characterised by the history of requests.

The only commonality left is the structure we found: The Intercom system is a set of tuples (pairs) in which a tuple characterises the link between two Offices. In our first example the tuple was called a Connection, in the second one request.

If we take in mind the statement "the natural decomposition", the first questions will arise. It is not that clear that a Request and a Connection are the same, nevertheless they are both describing the same notion, the link between two Offices. Things become even worse, however, if a more radical approach is taken than just changing the nouns and verbs. To illustrate this idea a third problem statement:

The intercom system (3)

In order to improve communication in an office building, an intercom system is installed. Therefore, each office gets an intercom. An intercom is addressed by its unique number, which is of course the same as the number of the office in which it is installed. An intercom has two modes: normal and private. An intercom is set to private if no disturbance through calls is allowed.

Another intercom can only be contacted if it is free and not in private mode.

This problem statement will lead to a totally different naming and structure as well. The *Intercom system* will become a set of *Intercoms*, identified by a number, being in a mode and may be contacting another Intercom.

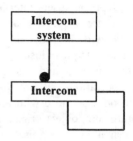

Given the high level of non-determinism, as the previous examples showed, it still occurs to be the "natural" decomposition? Or is object-oriented analysis not so easy, natural or straightforward as it is said to be?

Viewing the examples the correspondence between the Intercom system and a graph structure is evident. Examples 1 and 2 lay emphasis on the edges of the graph whereas in example 3 the nodes play the central role. Such imbalances in models are often not recognised, which is understandable if we take the focusing on the problem into account. As long as the models supports the system description, there is hardly any need to correct the model.

3.3 Application driven modelling

One of the conspicuous properties of all methodologies is their starting point for analysis: they use some description of the problem itself. Whether the problem is defined in a problem statement, a set of use-cases, a user-requirements specification or a functional specification, they all are directly inspired by the problem. After choosing the problem as a source of inspiration it is likely one is invited to focus on the problem and the resulting model will become problem dependent: a setback for the claim that it is reusable.

An attempt to construct less problem-dependent models is made by those who try to introduce 'domain knowledge' as a source of inspiration. The domain knowledge is not problem-specific but can be used for the class of problems belonging to that domain, just like mathematical science is not dedicated to one specific mathematical problem but to a large collection of mathematical problems. In order to deal with such problems, a mathematician uses his own language, his own abstractions of reality and his own logic.

Finding the reusable and natural model becomes a question of analysing and defining the language of the problem domain, not the problem itself. Given such a 'language' model, all ingredients needed for an arbitrary problem statement are available.

In the previous section, finding the classes, the possible effects of the 'nouns and verbs' strategy on the structure of, and the names found in the model were discussed. In this section a further elaboration is presented on some properties of the model that can be expected, if the problem statement is chosen as a start for requirements engineering.

In a graphical user interface, a number of windows are displayed on screen. The class Window will be one of the classes to be recognised. Typical instance variables will be: Length, Height, and its position. Likewise, typical operations will be: *Display*, *Move*, *Resize* and so on. For those who are familiar with the literature on object-orientation the presented model should be recognisable.

Window
Integer Xpos, Ypos Integer Length, Height ...
... Move ... ... Resize ... ... Display ...

This model of the class Window works fine until a change request introduces the idea of work spaces, or virtual screens. Windows are displayed on one or more work spaces, on possibly different positions. One of the Work spaces is displayed on the physical screen.

To be able to support this new functionality, the previous model has to be revised. The window position is no longer a characterisation of the Window itself. A better model would be one in which the Window position has become a association-class.

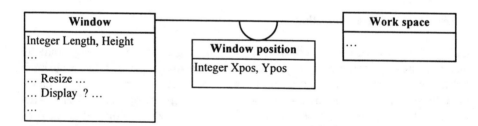

The operation *Move* is moved to another class and the operation *Display* is at least redefined to one with a parameter (the position) or defined elsewhere as well. The question, whether the first model of the class Window was good, bad or ugly, will rise. Answering the question is not easy; the model was sufficient at the time it was made. The reason the first model was chosen is obvious; it was made within one context, the problem on hand, and within that context the notion of Work spaces was not recognised.

Closely related to the methodologies of object-oriented analysis are those of domain analysis. Whereas object-oriented analysis typically focuses upon one specific problem at a time, domain analysis seeks to identify the classes and objects that are common to all applications within a given domain. If you are in the midst of a design and stuck for ideas as to the key abstractions that exist, domain analysis can help by pointing you to the key abstractions that have proven useful in other related systems. Domain analysis works well because, except for special situations, there are very few truly unique kinds of software systems [11].

The conclusion that is left to the reader is that object models as a result of domain analysis are more reusable than problem-oriented object models. Domain models are generally applicable. In a reverse direction one could state that, the more problem specific an object model gets, the less reusable it will be.

Object-oriented methodologies use the problem statement, or the set of use-cases describing the application, as the source of inspiration, thus constructing a quite problem specific model. And, moreover, in many of these methodologies the object model found during analysis is adjusted (down-sized) to the application that has to be build. So it ends up being even more specific.

Suppose, that the class Date, a commonly used class, is taken from the class library and the interface looks like:

Date	
Integer Day# Integer Month# Integer Year#	
Date CurrentDate () Boolean Today (Date checkdate) Date Tomorrow () Boolean Future (Date checkdate) Date Yesterday () Boolean Past (Date checkdate) Integer Daydifference (Date first,last) . . Boolean LeapYear (Date checkdate) Date NextLeapYear () . . Integer Age (Date birthdate) . .	. . Boolean Baby (Date birthdate) Boolean Toddler (Date birthdate) Boolean Adolescent (Date birthdate) Boolean Senior (Date birthdate) Boolean Aged (Date birthdate) Boolean Old (Date birthdate) . . . Boolean Marriageable (Boolean Gender, Date birthdate) . .

After such an impressive interface it is imaginable that one decides not to use this class. The operations may have been, and probably still are, very useful in an application, but there are too many operations available that are never needed in 'normal' applications. Adding operations specific for one application to the interface of the class makes the class less reusable. In the majority of object-oriented methodologies, however, it is normal to define the application dependent operations within the class definition.

3.4 Modelling inheritance trees

The inheritance principle forms the basis for a powerful technique of explicit expression of commonality. Inheritance allows us to specify common attributes and operations once, as well as specialise and extend those attributes and operations into specific classes. Object-oriented analysis uses inheritance to explicitly express commonality, beginning with the early activities of requirements analysis [5].

The ability to factor out common properties of several classes into a common superclass and to inherit the properties from the superclass can greatly reduce repetition within designs and programs and is one of the main advantages of an object-oriented system [7].

A class is a descendant of one or more other ones if it is designed as an extension or specialisation of these classes. This is the powerful notion of (multiple) inheritance [12].

Generalisation, specialisation, inheritance trees, without these no object-orientation is possible. An object model without some inheritance tree is at least suspicious. In this section is discussed whether inheritance fulfils the promises that are made. Are inheritance trees the ultimate solution to reusability? Is reality truthfully reflected in the model and thereby the 'natural' decomposition?

A requirements specification of a small case is modelled using an inheritance tree. Within this case, however, are all the elements that play a role in the discussion are present. It must be said that these elements seem of minor importance but that is due to the 'condensation' of the case itself. So will the sharing of attributes and operations of two types stand for a number of significant commonalities of these types, and the differences stand for significant differences.

In this case the class Person plays the central role. Each person is either a man or a woman. The classes Person, Woman and Man are needed in an application where simulation is done of the behaviour of waiting queues. Given a number of counters, a queue of persons is waiting for each counter. A counter will served the persons from its queue one by one. Depending on the gender of the person, male or female, service is adjusted. In this case is the required functionality as follows:

- Given a person, a man or a woman: the physical age.
- Given a person, a woman or a man: her or his name.
- Given a person: whether it is a man or a woman.
- Given a woman, or a person that is a woman: the number of children.
- Given a man, or a person that is a man: his secret.
- Given a person, a woman or a man: whether the marriageable age is reached. This function differs for a man and a woman, because the marriageable age of a man is 18 and the marriageable age of a woman is 16.

Within this application domain each man is characterised by his name, birthdate and his secret. Each woman is characterised by her name, birthdate and the number of children. The types String, Boolean, Date and Integer are assumed to be pre-defined types.

In object-orientation, the commonalities are located in supertypes (the generalisations) and the subtypes or descendants describe the specialisations. This is done by adding information to the already inherited information of its supertype. The following model is proposed:

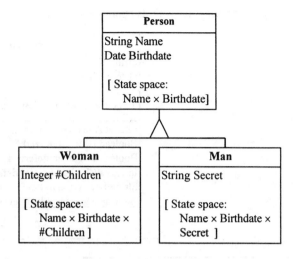

Locating the common instance variables in the superclass Person is no problem. To allocate the operations is less straightforward, some operations can not be defined within the class itself. For those cases, the solution within object-orientation is found in the declaration of "deferred" or "virtual" operations. The definition is postponed to the subclasses.

In this discussion an operation may have the keyword "specified", as a shorthand for the specification of the operation itself.

The operations are that simple, that it should not lead to any inconvenience. Furthermore, operations that are direct queries on instance variables and operations dealing with the object life-cycle (*Create, Delete*) are implicitly defined, as it is a custom in mainstream object-oriented methodologies. In case an operation can not be specified in the superclass nor in all of its subclasses a "partial deferred" is accepted, provided that the condition for which classes the operation holds is testable.

The model together with its operations becomes:

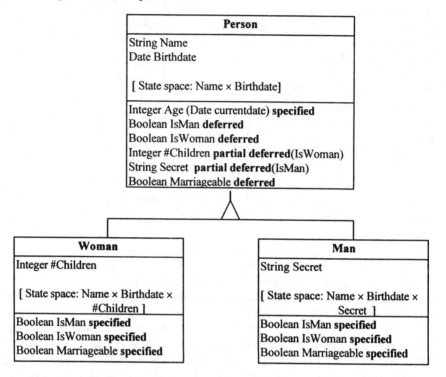

And this is the typical model we could expect, it follows the 'object-oriented methods' nicely. Looking at this model a number of drawbacks can be observed.

People regard their environment in terms of objects. Therefore it is simple to think in the same way when it comes to designing a model. A model which is designed using an object-oriented technology is often easy to understand, as it can be directly related to reality. Thus, only a small semantic gap will exist between reality and the model. The abstractions made from reality should be those that eliminate uninteresting details only. The model should comply with reality, not only containing the needed information but also reflecting the structure of reality truthfully.

Models that are not fulfilling the need for information will easily be classified as being incorrect. Nevertheless, models can still significantly deviate in structure and naming: The resulting model is depending on the orientation (functional, data, ...) the analyst has used, or the structure and naming of the model may be imposed by a view on a possible implementation. Deviations, due to the different 'orientations' will be inspected with the notion of compliance. Implementation bias will be recognised as "overspecification", one of the seven sins of the specifier. [25]. These specification sins will be the second metric to judge a model, followed by a short elaboration of its cohesion and coupling characteristics.

As a discussion aid, the state space of a class was introduced in the section on constructions in object-oriented. With the use of the state space, the compliance of the model is checked: is every man person? (and likewise for woman) and is every person either a man or a woman? These propositions hold in reality but not in the model. The so-called 'population' view is not reflected in the model.

The functions *Marriageable, IsWoman* and *IsMan* are specified in the class Woman as well as in the class Man. This has been done in order to fulfil the deferred declaration made in the class Person. Besides, that the postponement of function definitions is in fact forward referencing (one of the seven sins of the specifier [25]), it also creates a strong coupling between the classes involved. This strong coupling is well demonstrated by the, for the classes Man and Woman unnatural, specifications of the operations *IsMan* and *IsWoman*. This type of coupling, introduced by the use of deferred operations, is typical in specifications with commonalities located in a superclass. The commonalities, simply and solely, are not sufficient to specify all operations, which will in its turn unavoidably lead to the use of the deferred clause.

In the next model the previously mentioned disadvantages are solved. The class Person consists of either a Man or a Woman. The instance variable Gender will have the value True in case the Person is a Woman, False otherwise. The Gender will also be used as a discriminator in the constraint on Person.

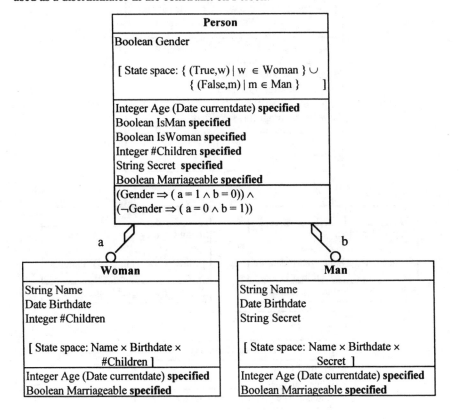

To show the relation between Person, Man and Woman an instance, I, of the class Person, and according to the definition of the state space I = (G,P), should be interpreted as P. In this model, the 'compliance' rule is not violated. Every element of Man, and every element of Woman is element of Person. No deferred operations are declared so neither unwanted forward referencing nor unwanted coupling.

But, from the point of view of the implementor, the first model has some qualities that can be used advantageously during implementation. The specifications of the classes Man and Woman have clearly much in common. Localising these commonalities will support the efficiency of the solution.

It is time to recall the software process models in which a clear distinction is made between analysis and design and their goals. It seems that the practical situation often blurs these phases. The first signs of 'rush to code' can be recognised in the need for 'efficient' specifications (which is in practice always a synonym for overspecification).

The second model is, because of the better fit to the customer, preferred to be placed in the requirements specification, leaving the idea of the inheritance tree as the result of a first design step:

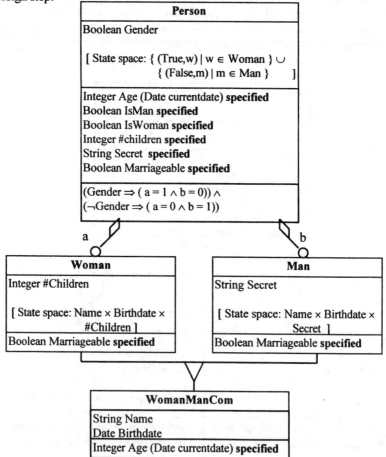

In this model the contradictory views on a superclass, being a union of populations and only containing the commonality of these populations, are separated. The class Person contains the 'union' view, whereas the commonalities are located in the abstract class WomanManCom. This class is introduced for implementation purposes during design as an aid for an efficient solution. In this final model all advantages, without having the disadvantages, are realised.

3.5 Specification by representation

Separation of concerns of specification (definition) and implementation is a very important issue in software engineering, on all levels. During system specification one concentrates on the out-side of the system, not on the internal details (implementation) of the system. Furthermore, during implementation, considerations about efficiency are important. Implementation details in a specification are often disrupting the clarity of that specification. In this section will be shown that in object-oriented methodologies the separation of concern is often neglected.

In the example of the previous section the class Woman was diagrammed. Within that class the instance variable "Integer #Children" was declared. In fact the attribute constraint expressing that one can not have a negative number of children should be stated. Attributes are not recognised as classes. So at every point where the #Children is needed, all aspects belonging to #Children have to be specified again. It is very unlikely that the

Woman
String Name Date Birthdate Integer #Children [State space: $\{ (n,b,c) \mid n \in$ Name $\qquad b \in$ Birthdate $\wedge$ $\qquad c \in$ #Children $\wedge$ C $\}$]
Integer Age (Date currentdate) **specified** Boolean Marriageable **specified**
C : #Children ≥ 0

#Children can be negative for any species on our world. In fact, the constraint C, is a class-constraint in a class #Children and has nothing to do with the class Woman. Besides that "Integer" and "#Children" differ in valueset, their behaviour is different too. It is quite normal to multiply integers resulting in integers, but multiplying #Children with #Children makes no sense (it would result in square #Children???). #Children and Integer can not be interchanged, Integer is a possible implementation for the class #Children. The function that projects the implementation values, integers, onto the values of #Children is a partial function with all the non-negative integers in its domain and the projection of the elements is their identity.

In retrospect, the conclusion must be made that all the leaves in an object model, classes that can be specified with a known (program language) type as universe, are not recognised as class at all. So typically, Length, Height, Salary, Room numbers, Age, etc., are never recognised as a semantic unit. A small semantic gap.

At the level of classes, which are specified as abstract data type implementations, the semantic gap becomes bigger.

Consider the classes Rectangle and Square, both classes in a large inheritance tree specifying all kinds of quadrangles. In order to be memory-space efficient the attributes of a Square are position and Width. The shape of a Rectangle is less straightforward, for the size of the edges may differ. Now is the question, who is inheriting who? Based on the consideration: a specialisation inherits from its generalisation, the Square should inherit from the Rectangle. A Square is always a Rectangle but not vice versa.

Square
Integer Xpos
Integer Ypos
Integer Width
Integer Colour

Rectangle
Integer Xpos
Integer Ypos
Integer Width
Integer Height
Integer Colour

Therefore Square is a subclass of the superclass Rectangle. The instance variables suggest, however, that the class Rectangle should inherit from the class Square. All attributes are inherited and one attribute, Height, has to be added.

The confusion is caused by the difference in the chosen implementations and the abstractions they described. The latter, the abstractions, are not described at all but are the source of the 'generalisation-specialisation' consideration. If Square and Rectangle were specified in the same universe, the 'generalisation-specialisation' could be recognised. Suppose, as a universe two diagonally opposed positions were chosen, a universe suitable for both shapes. The comparison between the two classes becomes a lot easier. The constraint stated in the class Square is stronger than the

Square
Integer Xpos1, Xpos2
Integer Ypos1, Ypos2
Integer Colour
$|Xpos2-Xpos1| = |Ypos2-Ypos1|$

Rectangle
Integer Xpos1, Xpos2
Integer Ypos1, Ypos2
Integer Colour
True

constraint of the class Rectangle, the weakest constraint possible (True) and normally omitted from the diagram.

Initially, the definitions of Square and Rectangle were inspired by a space efficient choice of attributes, and thereby each class had its own universe. The chosen implementation confused the designers of inheritance trees. In the second specification, however, the same universe was chosen but it violated the efficiency of the implementation.

Another cause of discussion on inheritance trees is the relation between generic types. Give some thoughts on the structures Set(type t) and Bag(type t). Which class should inherit from which class? Is the class Bag(type t), having an extra characteristic, namely, an operation to determine the frequency of an element, a specialisation of the Set? Or is the class Set(type t) a specialisation of the class Bag(type t), because as stated before, every element of Set(type t) is also an element of Bag(type t)? The Set(type t) would have a frequency of one for all its elements if seen as a Bag(type t).

4 Observations

The mainstream object-oriented methodologies reveal similarities with the ironically described 'life-cycle of a methodology':
- A methodology starts in a project that is successful and an *alternative procedure* is used to reached the project goals.
- A *buzzword* is introduced to denote the alternative procedure.
- An impressive *methodology*, recognised by the buzzword in its name, is designed. Probably, it has some links to the original idea behind the alternative procedure.
- Many seminars, courses and lectures are given on the methodology, meanwhile evolving.
- The methodology is described in *books*: an 'original' version, enhanced versions as a result of method evolution, 'super' versions as a result of unification with methodologies having the same buzzword in their name, a 'practical' version, a 'real-time' version and so on.
- Lots of projects later, the software engineering community is aware that projects still fail, and is seeking for the next generation of methodologies that, this time, really will solve their problems. The buzzwords are already waiting.

It will be clear that the requirements for the next methodology are:
(a) Informal, for reasons as discussed in "...Myths on Formal Methods" [3,4]
(b) No documentation other than code, for documentation slows down the development process. And, secondly, maintenance is done on code and not on documentation, so documentation is useless after the system is implemented.
(c) The result of the methodology has excellent properties, the product will satisfy the eleven quality factors as described in REliability and QUality of European Software Technology [31] fully .
(d) Everyone can use the methodology.
(e) The methodology is learned (at level of application) within a period of two weeks.
(f) The methodology can be applied in every type of software system.

Many experts believe that the object-oriented methodologies are a step forward in solving the software crisis, even though they lack:
(1) a formal foundation, (in general the syntax of graphical representations is explained by an enormous number of pictures, whereas the semantics is not defined at all)
(2) common terminology (e.g. five different meanings of a class were found) .
(3) a common view on what object-orientation is (using a object-oriented language, graphical user interfaces, or a decomposition into interacting objects).

Within the world of 'object-oriented' there are methodologies found that, though these methodologies result in an object decomposition, can not be seen as 'object-oriented' cause they lack the 'object-vision'. Furthermore, within the class of object-oriented methodologies some extreme implementations can be found: trying to describe everything as an object, over-emphasizing the use of inheritance, declare every activity to be object-oriented.

Within industrial environments a certain 'rush to code' can be observed and methodologies seem to adapt themselves to that:
• specification by representation
The first example to mention in this context are the attributes, directly declared as an instance of a type that is offered by the programming language. In section 3.6 is shown that attributes are just classes.

It needs no explanation that the class definitions are the second example, it is found in one of the meanings of the class: a class is an abstract data type implementation.
• implicit definitions
The state space of a class is normally not specified. The reader must get a feeling for the valid values of an object, based on the attributes and associations of that class and of course the constraints.

Within methodologies it becomes a custom not to specify a set of 'standard' operations but, they are assumed to be available. Whether this is convenient or not depends on the 'predictability' of those operations. Are all equality operations over all classes the same so they do not need to be specified?

For example: consider a class, Fraction, having two instance variables named nominator and denominator both of type integer. What is the state space? Is there a constraint needed? How are the 'standard' operations defined?

Leaving out specifications that seem to be trivial, are especially endangering the correct functioning of the system, the moment there is an anomaly.
• incomplete specifications
Special warnings are found in the prescriptions that methodologies offer with respect to the level of detail. "At most 50 uses-cases", "Seven, plus or minus two", "No user interface aspects" are examples of heuristics that lead to incomplete specifications. Indeed, all too often the user interface is not specified at all (such a detail, often more than 50% of the total code, is left for the designer and implementor of the system). Also the definitions that are made are refined during design and implementation, which means in practice, that significant details have to be added. Already in section 3.1 the conclusion was made that 'from vague to concrete' characterises the development cycle appropriately.
• overspecification
All examples of "specification by representation" are in fact examples of overspecification. Moreover, it is shown in section 3.4 that the early introduction of inheritance trees leads to overspecification. Another example of overspecification can be recognised in the algorithmically specified operations.

In section 2.1 the advantages of object-oriented methodologies were summarised. Some remarks upon these advantages could be made.

Natural integration and better communication
In section 3.2 is shown that the object models easily differ in their class-names and structure.
In section 3.4 the inheritance tree introduced a model that did not comply to reality. Not specifying attributes as classes limits the vocabulary of the object model to a subset of the vocabulary that is used in the problem domain.
Due to 'specification by representation' the vocabulary is expressed in a possible implementation, in contrast to the abstraction it encompasses.
Omitting relevant details during analysis makes the specifications vague.
Well defined interface
Interfaces contain only a subset of the operations (there is a set implicitly available) and operations are not formally specified.
The state space is usually not defined.
Classes are coupled through the inheritance tree(s) they are part.
Reuse
In the previous paragraph the 'well defined interfaces' of classes were discussed, ending in the conclusion that the proposition 'well defined' did not hold.
Section 3.3 "application driven modelling" discusses the measure of reusability in further detail. Besides that, in the object-oriented literature the problem of configuration management is rarely addressed.
Cheaper & better maintenance
The level of reusability will directly influence the cost of maintenance.
Whether the advantages hold in practice or not, given the remarks made above, there must be room for improvement.

After seeing the list of observations, the maturity of methodologies is only partially reflected by the properties of these methodologies. Perhaps the main problem is the attitude of software engineers. As long as the software community reflects their failures on the methodologies they use, and do not take full responsibility for their failures, it is unlikely that articles titled "...inheritance...considered harmful" will change anything. A discussion on the maturity of software methodologies will be marginal in effect as long as the software community is not prepared to adopt the scientific engineering principles as mentioned in the definition of software engineering.

References

1. W.S. Humphrey: Managing the Software Process. (1989) Addison Wesley.
2. SEI: Process Maturity Profile of the Software Community 1996 Year End Update. (1997) http://www.sei.cmu.edu/technology/measurement/profile.html.
3. J.A. Hall: Seven Myths of Formal Methods. (1990) IEEE Software, pag. 11-19 September.
4. J.P. Bowen, M.G. Hinchey: Seven More Myths of Formal Methods: Dispelling Industrial Prejudices. (1995) IEEE Software, pag. 34-41 July.

5. P. Coad, E. Yourdon: Object-Oriented Analysis. (1990) Yourdon Press
6. A. Davis: Software lemmingineering. (1993) IEEE Software pag. 79-84 September.
7. J. Rumbaugh, M. Blaha, W.Premerlani, F. Eddy, W. Lorensen: Object-Oriented Modeling and Design. (1991) Prentice-Hall, Inc.
8. L. Cardelli, P. Wegner: On Understanding Types, Data Abstraction, and Polymorphism. (1985) Computing Surveys, Vol. 17, No 4.
9. A.M. Daves: Software Requirements, objects, functions, and states. (1993) Prentice-Hall, Inc.
10. B.J. Cox: Object-Oriented Programming, an evolutionary approach. (1986) Addison Wesley.
11. G. Booch: Object-Oriented design, with applications [Second edition]. (1994) The Benjamin/Cummings Publishing Company, Inc.
12. B. Meyer: Object-Oriented Software Construction. (1988) Prentice Hall International (UK) Ltd.
13. I. Jacobson: Object-Oriented Software Engineering, a use case driven approach. (1992) Addison Wesley.
14. S. Shlaer, S.J. Mellor: Object-Oriented Systems Analysis, modeling the world in data. (1988) Yourdon Press.
15. S. Shlaer, S.J. Mellor: Object Lifecycles, modeling the world in states. (1992) Yourdon Press.
16. G. Booch: Software Engineering with Ada. (1986) The Benjamin/Cummings Publishing Company, Inc.
17. G. Booch: Object-Oriented design, with applications. (1991) The Benjamin/Cummings Publishing Company, Inc.
18. M. Loomis, A. Shah, J. Rumbaugh: An object modeling technique for conceptual design. In: Lecture Notes in Computing Science: European Conference on Object-Oriented Programming. pag. 192-202. Springer Paris.
19. R. Wirfs-Brock, B. Wilkerson, L. Weiner: Designing object-oriented software. (1990) Prentice-Hall.
20. H. Gomaa: Software Design Methods for Concurrent and Real-Time Systems. [reprint with corrections] (1993) Addison Wesley.
21. M. Awad, J. Kuusela, J. Ziegler: Object-Oriented Technology, for Real-Time Systems. (1996) Prentice-Hall, Inc.
22. UML: Notation Guide, Version 1.0. (1997) http://www.rational.com/ot/uml.html.
23. J. Warmer, A. Kleppe: Praktisch OMT. (1996) Addison Wesley.
24. E.V. Berard: Be Careful With "Use Cases". (1996) The Object Agency, Inc., http://www.toa.com/pub/html/use_case.html.
25. B. Meyer: On Formalism in Specifications. (1985) IEEE software pag. 6-26 January.
26. S. Cook, J. Daniels: Designing object systems - syntropy. (1994) Prentice-Hall.
27. I. Sommerville: Software engineering. (1989 third edition) Addison Wesley.
28. D. Hatley, I. Phirbai: Strategies for Real-Time Systems Specification. (1987) Dorset House.
29. P. Frederiks: Object-Oriented Modelling based on Information Grammars. (1997) University of Nijmegen.

30. K. Beck, W. Cunningham: A laboratory for teaching object-oriented thinking. (1989) OOPSLA'90 ACM conference, Addison Wesley.
31. ESPRIT project: REQUEST (REliability and QUality of European Software Technology) (1985) Doc. Id. REQUEST/STC-gdf/001/S1/QL-RP/00.7.

Object Oriented Development of Embedded Systems with the Octopus Method

Juha Kuusela
Nokia Research Center
P. O. Box 45
FIN-00211 Helsinki, Finland

juha.kuusela@research.nokia.com

Abstract. An overview of a software development method for embedded real-time systems and some experiences in using it is given. Description is limited to the main models used in different software development phases. Models are only partially described but they are all based on same example.

1. Introduction

This article describes a software development method for embedded real-time systems and some experiences in using it. In a short overview it is not possible to describe every detail of a complex method. Instead I try to limit the description to the main models used in different phases and use a single example to link partial models together. More detailed description can be found in [1].

OCTOPUS method was based on OMT [7] and Fusion [2]. We are also trying to keep it UML [8] compliant. However our case tool has not yet been updated and thus the models in this document do not yet follow the latest standard.

OCTOPUS method development at the Nokia Research Center started 1993 and continues. Development is based on the feedback from real practical work at the Nokia business units.

2. Example

As an example I will use the "Data Collection" problem from OOPSLA'96 DesignLab prepared by Bjorn Freeman-Benson and Brian Paisley.

> A local forest technology company, Forests ʼRʼ Us, wants to build and sell a system for gathering and analyzing weather information to predict forest fires and help with water table management. The Arbor2000 will be sold to National Forests, Environment Canada, the U.S. Forest Service, and large private land owners. It will consist of hardware and software both locally in the owner's office building and remotely in the forests.

The data sensors in the forest report at various intervals to the central computer via satellite, packet radio, cell phone, dial-up phone, or dedicated line. The central computer stores and analyzes the information. The users run a wide variety of reports, browsers, historical trend analysis, and future prediction algorithms over the data. Furthermore, given the inherently geographic nature of the data, many of the reports incorporate maps.

The sensors, such as temperature, sunlight intensity, wind speed and direction, rainfall, and so on, come in three basic types: those that report on a regular basis, those that only report when a significant event occurs and those that must be queried.

The sensors are produced by different manufacturers and return numeric values in a wide variety of units and at widely varying intervals and tolerances. Additionally, the data links are not necessarily reliable, and yet the system must deal with all these issues while presenting both a uniform and a detailed view of the data to the user and his or her agent/analysis programs.

3. Assumptions on problem and solution structure

In the early phases of requirement specification and analysis problem structure drives the process. In order to know how to approach an problem it has to be familiar at least from some perspective. Octopus is a special purpose method for development of embedded real-time systems. It places emphasis of issues that are irrelevant in the development of many other systems such as concurrency, synchronization, communication, handling of interrupts, ASIC, hardware interfaces and end-to-end response times.

As design decisions accumulate they soon restrict solution possibilities more than constraints imposed by requirements. A special purpose method can have a preset solution architecture and thus the constraints it imposes are also known. Preset architecture increases the efficiency of a method at cost of applicability.

Octopus method assumes that system is divided into subsystems. These subsystems have functional responsibilities and interface to each other through interface objects. The methods of these interface objects may then be invoked either synchronously or asynchronously. One of the subsystems is always hardware wrapper abstracting away from the specific details of a given hardware. On a more detailed level Octopus method assumes that the architecture of the software will:

- Base modularization on concepts of the domain
- Use objects as a mechanism for structuring the software
- Use explicit concurrency in terms of light-weight processes
- Base the process structure on the time requirements of the external events
- Base control mechanism between processes on messages
- Base data sharing on the use of single address space
- Separate the hardware layer from the application.

This architecture allows the method to provide strong guidance to the designer. In particular it makes the design of concurrency almost procedural.

4. Development Sequence

Octopus development sequence has separate system and subsystem levels. System level development divides the system into subsystems which then are developed concurrently. System level sequence has only two phases: system requirements specification, system before the concurrent subsystem development starts. At the subsystem level, the development sequence consists of analysis, design and implementation phases (see Figure 1).

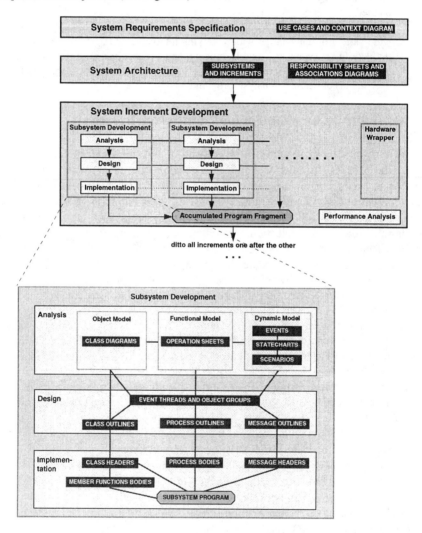

Figure 1. OCTOPUS development sequence.

Following chapters give a short overview of each phase.

5. Requirements Specification

Requirements specification has the following steps:
1. Rephrase the problem statement.
2. Develop and record use cases.
3. Capture requirements.
4. Organize use cases into a use case diagram.
5. Collect actors and develop a context diagram.

Each use case is recorded into a Use Case Sheet, the relations between these use cases are shown in a Use Case Diagram and the relation between the system and different external actors is visualized in a Context Diagram.

Use cases [6] describe what is the role of each actor in the system scenario and how the actors behave in it. A recommended practice for finding the use cases of a system is to consider all external agents that interact with it. Start by finding all external agents and try to distinguish their roles. Then consider their roles one by one:
1. What are the main tasks they want to perform?
2. When are these tasks applicable?
3. What are the exceptions?
4. What is the desired effect of the task?
5. What are the timing requirements?

This information is recorded on a use case sheet. The precondition should explain when the use case is applicable. If the precondition is satisfied, the system will eventually fulfill the postcondition, unless some of the exceptions occur. Following gives an example of a use case.

Use Case	(U2) Add a sensor array
Actors	Operators
Preconditions	New sensor array is in place and communication link works
Description	New sensor array is placed to its location, powered on and calibrated
Sub Use Cases	
Exceptions	
Activities	
Postconditions	Information from the new sensors is logged together with their identity until their correct position and other configuration data is entered.

Use cases have structure and this structure can be utilized to make specifications shorter. Structure is visualized as a *use case diagram* using the notation of object diagram. Use cases force the analyst to define what actors are using the system. This information is used to construct the *system context diagram* which gives a structural overview of the system's environment. For Arbor2000 I have determined to draw the system boundary between the sensors and the sensor array (see Figure 2).

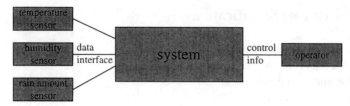

Figure 2. Arbor2000 context diagram

6. Software Architecture

Software architecture is the design at the level of abstraction that focuses on the patterns of system organization that describe how functionality is partitioned and how the parts are interconnected [4]. Octopus uses three models to capture the architecture:

1. The relations between different subsystems can be shown in a *subsystem diagram*.
2. Use cases help to understand the responsibilities of each subsystem. The responsibilities should be recorded into a *responsibility sheet*.
3. Once we understand the roles of independent subsystems we can start to sketch *subsystem interactions*.

Figure 3 shows one possible subsystem division for Arbor2000. This division is based on a data pipeline architecture as demonstrated by the subsystem interaction diagram (Figure 4). This architecture has the property that all the subsystems on the pipeline become rather generic and simple. The downside naturally is the complexity of the "intelligent" end.

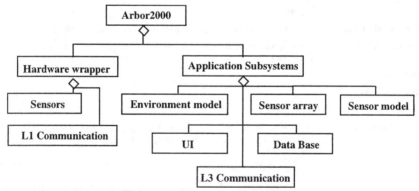

Figure 3. Subsystems of Arbor2000

Before the subsystems can interact the system must have an overall control and data flow mechanism. Several alternative mechanisms exist and different mechanisms can be combined. For different architectural alternatives you may refer to [4]. The description of the interfaces should be tuned according to the control mechanism. In Arbor2000 the hardware wrapper subsystems abstracts the various communication mechanisms used to communicate with sensors and model each sensor value so that the interface provided by sensor array subsystem is based on polling. Sensor array subsystem sends the group of sensor values periodically. These values are classified and stored into data base with sensor ids and time stamps. All the 'intelligent' subsystems operate on this data base.

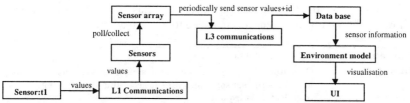

Figure 4. Subsystem interaction diagram for Arbor2000

Subsystem interfaces are defined during the subsystem analysis phase. Since the subsystem division is determined before analysis there is a need to iterate between architectural design and analysis.

7. Subsystem Analysis

Each subsystem is viewed from three different viewpoints producing the structural, functional and dynamic model. The structural model is also called object model. These three models complement each other. The relationship between the models is expressed by using the same name for any component wherever it appears. Each model uses a set of appropriate notations.

The *object model* defines the structure of the subsystem by describing the objects of the problem domain and their relationships. Object model for sensor array subsystem is built around the message to be sent to the central system. Rest of the object model shows connections to other subsystems. Note that we have already drawn a subsystem boundary line. Objects outside that boundary represent interfaces to other subsystems (like Sensor or Connection in Figure 5).

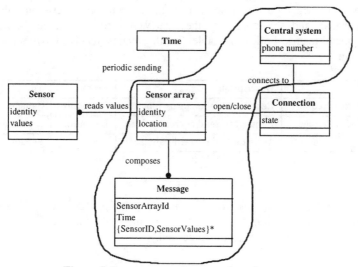

Figure 5. Sensor array subsystem class diagram.

The *functional model* describes the interface of each subsystem. This interface consists of a set of named services provided by the subsystem to other subsystems and external agents. Services are described using operation. Operation sheets are informal and may rely on natural language, although we tend to make operation definitions semi-formal based on the changes in class diagram attribute values. Following shows how new sensors are added to the sensor array.

Operation	(O1) Plug in a new sensor
Description	Operator adds a new sensor to the sensor array, sensor array identifies the sensor, configures it according to its type and starts to collect data from it
Associations	Sensor, Sensor array
Preconditions	Sensor is of a know type
Inputs	sensor_id
Modifies	new sensor
Outputs	
Postconditions	(new sensor).identity = sensor_id, and sensor_array reads_values_from (new sensor)

The *dynamic model* describes the events received by the subsystem It defines under what conditions a particular event triggers operations, how different events affect each other and how long the end-to-end response is allowed to take. The model shows how event sequences depend on the state of the subsystem and its environment. It specifies the order in which the response to multiple events is produced. The dynamic model includes the event list, a set of event sheets, a set of statecharts, a set of message sequence charts.

Hardware wrapper is the only subsystem to receive physical events. All other subsystems receive logical events. Need for these logical events can be determined either by examining the class diagram and paying special attention to the associations crossing the subsystem boundary or by considering operations and how they are triggered. Since logical events communicate between subsystems their purpose and the data that they carry has to be agreed between the development teams. Following table list the events received by Sensor array subsystem.

Event	Description	From	To
(E1) StatusRequest	Request to send status report	L3 comm.	Sensor array
(E2) ValueRequest	Request to send current values	L3 comm.	Sensor array
(E3) TimeToSend	Time to send current values	Timer	Sensor array

Table 1. Sensor array event List

The complexity resulting from a large number of distinct events can be managed by classification. Each event is described by an event sheet and all the properties of its super event will be inherited.

Event	TimeToSend
Response	A connection to central system is opened, message made and send.
Associations	Connection, Message, Sensor, Central system
Source	Timer
Contents	Time
Response Time	5 s
Rate	Periodical, period > 300 s

Statechart notion is used to describe state-dependent behavior [5]. Statecharts extend conventional state-transition diagrams. They allow building a hierarchy of states by nesting substates inside superstates and splitting off concurrent components at any level. A state in which other states are not nested is called elementary state. A transition can leave or enter an elementary state, as well as a superstate at any level (example in Figure 6).

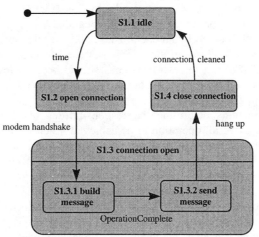

Figure 6. Main states of the sensor array

Analysis of state-dependent behavior according to OCTOPUS produces a model consisting of a collection of a statecharts. Statecharts should be complemented by an *actions table* to show the actions and activities.

All independent statecharts are assumed to be concurrent. State analysis is based on the assumption of the *collective other state* (Sx). The existence of Sx expands the state model in such a way that all events not shown on any statechart cause a transition from Sx to Sx. Event significance analysis is based on the compound state of a subsystem. A compound state is a valid combination of the elementary states from all statecharts describing the modality of the subsystem. Analysis of the criticality of an event in a compound state can be based on the criticality of the event in the elementary states.

8. Subsystem Design

Design transforms the abstract definition produced during analysis into a description that explains how to achieve the required features and functions. Design phase has following major steps:

1. Based on analysis models design the object interaction threads. Combine and expand them until you reach the triggering event. Continue until all events have been addressed. In parallel develop the class outlines.
2. Consider each interaction and decide whether a synchronous or asynchronous interaction mechanism is to be used.
3. Design the concurrency by grouping objects and by developing the outlines of the processes associated with the object groups.
4. Iterate over steps 1-3 and balance the design decisions. Determine how to synchronize access to shared objects.

An object interaction thread is a sequence of object interactions which has one trigger and can be traversed completely by one thread of execution. Object interaction thread can be initiated by any invocation. An event thread is an object interaction thread initiated by an event. Build all event threads. Object interaction graph notation [2] (colloboration in UML) is used to express the interaction of objects. Note that object interaction graphs should be completed to include each possible path of execution. If this is not done class outlines will be incomplete and some concurrency need can be missed.

Object interactions determine the responsibilities of each class. Operation sheets define the overall operation to be achieved. Each object that changes state in the operation description should participate in the interaction. Responsibility of each object is determined based on our intuition of the concept represented by this object, its data content and functional coherence. Class definitions are the primary abstraction mechanism and each responsibility added to a class is shown as an operation in the class definition. New classes can be introduced if needed.

Systems face some degree of accidental complexity. It stems from various interfaces to older systems, hardware variations in mechanics and timing, and spurious but practical requirements. Accidental complexity is not easily managed by abstraction. It is possible to classify along multiple dimensions and use composition to create actual classes, but the result is seldom worth all the effort needed. First your classifications are bound to be sparse - since "accidentally" only few cases are present in the software. Second each class in going to be far from complete as an abstraction, since only few of the responsibilities intuitively associated with the complex concept represented by the class is actually used in the program and finally since your abstractions are based on the peculiarities of the world found so far they tend to break as new peculiarities are uncovered.

Other way to treat accidental complexity is to represent it as is in the system. If this approach is selected it is important to limit its affect on the system. Use separate control objects to encapsulate complexity and treat them differently than other objects. You should also study different design patterns [3] created to alleviate the coupling created by accidental complexity.

In analysis models complexity is visible in the modality of subsystems. This modality can either be encapsulated within existing concepts or not. If it cannot be naturally presented within existing objects a new object encapsulating the corresponding statechart should be created.

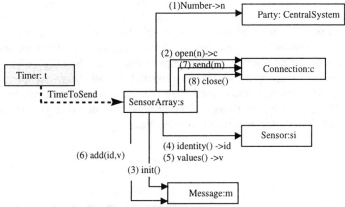

Figure 7. Example event thread.

Figure 7 is an example of an event thread. It shows how Sensorarray subsystem reacts to the TimetToSend request. The purpose of the event thread is to give a high-level overview of the control flow between objects. Details can be recorded in the class outlines. In these we use pseudo C++. We develop class outlines in parallel with the development of object interaction threads. Figure 8 shows a class outline based on the event thread in Figure 7.

```
class Message
    function init() return message
    function add(identity, values) return message
endclass;
```

Figure 8. Class outline for Message derived from the example event thread.

The event threads are the first step towards the explicit concurrency model. After that, each interaction between two objects is investigated and a decision is made about the *interaction mechanism*: synchronous (nested member function call) or asynchronous (implemented using operating system inter-process messages). The resulting event threads are called qualified event threads. The decision about the interaction mechanism is based on concurrency requirements, significance and time requirements of the events, the expected duration of the requested service and the communication with other subsystems.

A synchronous interaction is visualized in the object interaction graph by using a solid line whereas any asynchronous interaction is visualized by using a dashed arrow. When an interaction that has a return value is converted to asynchronous, a new additional asynchronous interaction is required to carry the return values from the server object to the client object. In our example we could change opening connection into asynchronous. Connection building takes time and we could use that time to build the message. Symmetrically we should then make also send and close asynchronous. Do we need to know that connection is open before we send the message? Answer depends on many issues - in particular we have to decide how to and where we handle errors in connection setup. Simplest design seems to be one where connection errors are handled in the connection subsystem.

Once all event threads have been qualified, design is continued by mapping the objects into *object groups*. Grouping is based on the interaction mechanism between the objects; all objects in an event thread which interact synchronously with each other are grouped into a single object group. Grouping starts from an event or an asynchronous interaction. Thus, adding asynchronous interaction would increase the number of object groups in the system (see Figure 9).

The process of grouping objects is repeated for all the event threads in the subsystem. As a result, some objects may belong to more than one object group. Because the execution of these object groups is concurrent (interleaved), the access to the shared objects must be synchronized.

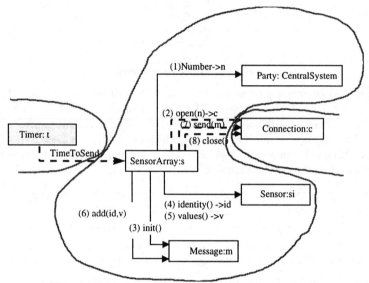

Figure 9. The object groups of the example event thread.

The execution threads of object groups are implemented using operating system processes. Class outlines are modified to reflect the decisions on interaction mechanism. Wherever asynchronous communication has been introduced instead of a synchronous one, the original member function invocation is changed into a message to the target process

Implementation follows the outlines of classes, processes, inter-process messages and member functions.

9. User experience

In general our experience in using Octopus has been positive. However there are still many problematic issues.

Octopus is a heavy method with lot of paper work before coding takes place. We tried to make Octopus a light weight method with lot of optional documents.

However in real life designers are asked to provide documents with given contents and they cannot decide what option to take.

Lot of duplicate work. Early division the system to subsystems increases the work. Subsystems do not partition the conceptual space of requirements. The same requirements will be analyzed several times. Common concepts in different subsystems will result in multiple classes having similar names but different definitions. There implementation leads to extra runtime consistency management and memory waste.

Difficult to design subsystem interfaces. Subsystem responsibilities are difficult to assign. However if the responsibilities are not clear lot of negotiation is needed to define subsystem interfaces.

Subsystems object level communication problem. It is hard to verify object level interface between the subsystems. The problem can be compared with the problem of using common variables by several concurrent tasks.

Tendency to reverse the order of design consideration and build the task structure first. This is cheated into Octopus method by using excessive number of subsystems. Large number of subsystems multiplies the problem of independent analysis of same conceptual space and resulting design wastes everything.

Analysis paralysis. The early phases of architectural design and analysis are added to the traditional life cycle and their importance is often not understood by the management. Since the results of those early phases are rather abstract they are never finished and it is difficult for an inexperience designer to move forward into the following phases. Only experience can cure analysis paralysis.

On the positive side we can report that designers seem to like our method. Based on our limited experience we can also claim that fears regarding excessive memory consumption or low performance of object oriented implementations have not materialised.

10. References

[1] Maher Awad, Juha Kuusela and Jurgen Ziegler: Object-Oriented Technology for Real-Time System: A Practical Approach Using OMT and Fusion, Prentice Hall, 1996.

[2] Derek Coleman, Patric Arnold, Stephanie Bodoff, Chris Dollin, Helena Gilchrist, Fiona Hayes, Paul Jeremaes: Object-Oriented Development: The Fusion Method, Prentice Hall, 1993

[3] E.Gamma, R.Helm, R.Johnson, and J.Vlissides. Design Patterns: Elements of Reusable Object-Oriented Software Addison-Wesley, 1994.

[4] David Garlan and Mary Shaw, "An introduction to software architecture", in Advances in Software Engineering and Knowledge Engineering, V. Ambriola and G. Tortora, Eds. New York, World Scientific, 1993, vol. 2 ACM Press 95.

[5] David Harel: Statecharts: a visual formalism for complex systems in Science of Computer Programming, vol. 8, pp. 231-274, 1987

[6] Ivar Jacobson et al. Object-Oriented Software Engineering - A Use Case Driven Approach, Addison-Wesley, 1992

[7] James Rumbaugh, Michael Blaha, William Premerlani, Frederick Eddy, William Lorensen: *Object-Oriented Modeling and Design* by Prentice-Hall, inc. 1991

[8] Unified Modeling Language: Notation Guide, version 1.0, 13. January 1997, Rational Software Corporation

Engineering of Real-Time Systems with an Experiment in Hybrid Control

Anders P. Ravn, Thomas J. Eriksen, Michael Holdgaard and Hans Rischel

Computer Systems Section
Department of Information Technology
Technical University of Denmark
DK-2800, Lyngby, Denmark
E-mail: `apr@it.dtu.dk`

Abstract. The core of this paper reports on development of a multi-threaded, multiprocessor program for an embedded system. It covers all phases of the development from requirements through successively refined designs with formal verification to implementation. The program controls an experimental hydraulically powered manipulator with two links. The architecture uses local control for each of the links, and has a mode switched control algorithm which detects and reacts on changes in model parameters due to variations in the forces acting on the link.
The result shows that it is feasible to check a design against realistic top level requirements with specific assumptions about th control and mode detection algorithms. The design is detailed to an architecture that isolate these and other algorithms supplied by control engineers, thus providing a precise interface description with a potential for reuse. Specifications of requirements and designs are expressed in duration calculus, a real-time interval logic, which is also used in verification. The implementation is done in occam for a network of four transputer's. Low level timing constraints are checked manually by calculating path lengths.

Keywords: Embedded system, hybrid system, real-time, requirements, design, formal specification, architecture, implementation, duration calculus.

1 Introduction

The use of computer programs to monitor and control physical systems is gaining a firm foothold as a technology. This leads to some concerns about the safety of engineering methods for developing such digital systems, in particular the software. Certification agencies must be concerned that there are no generally accepted procedures for producing and documenting embedded systems. Some standards, e.g. [40] demand formal methods and rigorous reasoning, but how shall they be applied in the overall development process?

The objective of the research reported here has been to shed some light on such questions, and in particular to investigate one formal method and its interplay with control engineering when developing embedded, real-time systems.

For that purpose we have completed a non-trivial and complete engineering case study. The questions that we ask ourselves are: How do we

- formalize properties (objectives) of systems?
- organize a collection of automata?
- verify a design?
- (re)use CE techniques for controller synthesis?
- implement the program?

In order to place these questions in context, we summarize our understanding of the term embedded real-time system, and we describe the physical plant that forms the basis for our study.

1.1 Embedded real-time systems

We have been engaged in research aiming at sound and practical methods for developing embedded systems for little over a decade [32], and we and co-workers have successfully completed many case studies that illustrates what we mean by an embedded computing system: On-off gas burner [33], Railway level crossing [27], Tracking device [30], Water Level Monitor [5], Air traffic Monitoring [14], Production Cell [4], Steam Boiler [34,35].

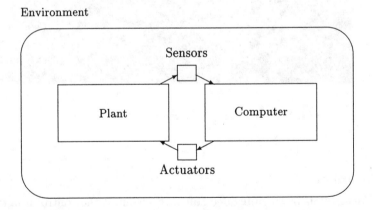

Fig. 1. Structure of Embedded System

These case studies have used the framework of duration calculus [42]. It is a real-time interval logic with a basic model similar to the one used in conventional dynamical (hybrid) systems: A collection of state variables that are functions of time modelled by the non-negative reals. A state variable is sectionally continuous which in the discrete case means that it is a step function. A discrete variable may model a program variable or a discrete component of the physical system or *plant*; a continuous variable models a component of the plant, or perhaps, analog interfacing electronics. The structure of an embedded system is shown in Fig. 1. The symmetry between plant and computer explains our choice of a common model.

Properties at the requirements level include the usual bounded response and bounded invariance [9] constraints of real-time systems, but also more abstract bounded presence of certain states, corresponding to a threshold on accumulated duration of a state. Some of the specifications also include integral equations corresponding to conventional control engineering descriptions.

Fig. 2. Hydraulically powered experimental robot

1.2 The robot

A concrete example of an embedded software system is the control program for the robot shown in Fig. 2. Technically speaking, it is a hydraulically powered two linked manipulator. It contains two hydraulic cylinders which can be independently controlled through interfaces to separate transputer processors, which again are linked to two central transputers through channels. The assembly was built in 1991 by the mechanical engineering control department as an experimental platform; mainly to gain insight into the characteristics of fluid power components in heavy duty robots. It may be worth noting that the International Federation of Automatic Control (IFAC) includes both Hydraulic Positioning and Robotic Systems among their 13 benchmark problems [13] - these are combined in the robot assembly.

Experiments with the robot are focused on tracking, i.e. letting a tool center point on the upper link follow a given trajectory with reasonably high speed (moving about 3 meters in under 2 seconds) and high precision (maximal deviation less than 1 cm).

In early 1994 we came into touch with the mechanical engineering department and decided to try out hybrid systems ideas and architectures. The results were promising [31,1], and in a second round ending in 1996 we produced a more general, parameterized software system [6] which has been used to investigate several advanced control algorithms. The resulting system is presented in the body of this paper.

1.3 Related Work

The approach we use is closely related to the development phases of the ProCoS project [8]. We have, however, been less formal in the implementation phases, because experimentation with the assembly was a main goal; hence development of compilation and transformation techniques would lead us astray.

Among the many experiments going on within the rapidly expanding field of hybrid systems, we might point to two which we find similar in spirit although with different methods.

One experiment has recently been undertaken at Linköping University. The system considered here was a landing gear for an aircraft [26]. The identification of the physical system was here done using bond graph techniques and resulted in a hybrid control model. The experiment has concurrently investigated the use of hybrid automata based techniques for design and verification [10] and use of DC for verification of more complex properties.

Another project at MIT investigates development of automated rail systems [21]. It uses the IO automata framework with hybrid extensions [22]. It is characteristic by considering the overall safety features of the moving vehicles without going into details of the low level control mechanisms.

1.4 Overview

Before we proceed to the case study, we must introduce the mathematical universe for hybrid systems in Section 2 and our specification language in Sect. 3. Section 4 commences with an overview of the architecture for the system and continues with a specification of top level requirements which are then successively refined. Experience from implementation and experiments is summarized in Sect. 5. The paper ends in Sect. 6 with a discussion of the issues that we have encountered and which are topics for further research:

- specification and simulation languages for hybrid systems;
- links to implementation languages and scheduling theory and techniques.

2 Mathematical Universe

A basic premiss in engineering is that systems are modelled by a state changing over continuous time. This allows the use of conventional mathematics of dynamic systems, where a vector of state variables defines the application specific state. Each state variable denotes a total function from time to a value domain. In classical dynamic systems the value domain is the continuum of reals [20]. Complex systems will, however, be *hybrid*, that is have states that are best modelled with discrete changes in their evolution. Thus, the conventional mathematics of continuous, differentiable functions is not sufficient to describe such plants. Simple examples are bouncing balls, gear boxes, or cruise controls. A formulation with a minimal extension is found in a hybrid system model [2] with a family of ordinary differential equations, e.g.:

$$\dot{\boldsymbol{x}}(t) = F_i(\boldsymbol{x}(t), \boldsymbol{u}(t)) \, , i \in S$$

where the plant state is given by the vector $\boldsymbol{x}$, the continuous control input is the vector $\boldsymbol{u}$, and the actual models are specified by the functionals F_i, indexed by a discrete index set S. The index changes based on conditions on the current value of $\boldsymbol{x}$ or the current state of an underlying automaton, that models the program of the embedded computer system.

Example: A hydraulic actuator Figure 3 illustrates a hydraulic actuator as found in the robot. The two main components are the piston and the servo valve regulating the flow of hydraulic oil. The position of the piston is denoted x, while the control input (u) determines the valve position.

Mathematical models of such an actuator are complex and cannot be described accurately by a single linear relationship. Therefore a set of linear submodels are developed, each describing the actuator in a subset of the state space [1]. The submodels are derived through linearization of a complex non-linear model around an operating point in each subset of the state space resulting in 6 submodels or modes:

$$\dot{x}(t) = A_i x(t) + B_i u(t) \, ,$$

where we call the solution $x_i(t)$. For each mode, a control algorithm is developed:

$$u_i(t) = K_{p_i} \cdot (r(t) - x(t)) + K_{ff_i} \cdot \dot{r}(t) \, ,$$

where $r(t)$, $\dot{r}(t)$ and $x(t)$ are the reference position, the reference velocity and the measured position of the actuator, respectively.

The general structure of the 6 control algorithms consists of a proportional feedback part, parametrized by K_{p_i} (the proportional gain), and a reference velocity feedforward part, parametrized by K_{ff_i} (the feed-forward gain). (K_{p_i}, K_{ff_i}) are the applicable parameters for the control algorithm when the plant is in mode i.

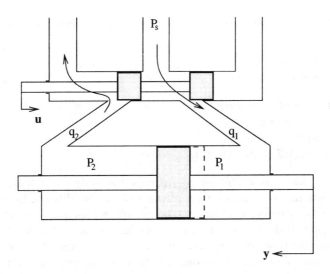

Fig. 3. A hydraulic actuator

The modes are represented by overlapping subspaces of the plant state space. An autonomous switch of the vector field is detected by evaluating the model error e_i over a period T:

$$e_i = \int_t^{t+T} (x(\tau) - x_i(\tau))^2 \, d\tau \ ,$$

where i ranges over the six modes and x_i denotes the model state. The model always chooses a mode i with a minimal error, and a transition is hence done when the index of the minimal e_i changes. The autonomous switching set S_i is thus defined implicitly.

When an autonomous switch is detected (by evaluation of the e_i's) the parameters of the control algorithm are changed to match the new plant mode. That is, in response to a detected autonomous switch a controlled switch of control algorithm is performed.

Remarks The framework presented above is somewhat biased towards a description of the plant, which comes out in the subsidiary role of the index i. Actually, the embedded system is modelled by

$$\dot{x}(t) = F(i, x(t), u(t))$$
$$i(t^+) = P(i(t^-), x(t^-)) \ ,$$

where $i(t^+)$ denotes the limit from the right at time t, and $i(t^-)$ $(x(t^-))$ the limit from the left. The functional P describes the steps of the control program. Note that the control input u may change with i through the functional F, and that i may be an aggregate of variables. In order to have reasonable properties of the program model, the discrete valued state variables i have to be step functions.

Another approach to hybrid systems [15] focuses on the program, which is conveniently modelled by a transition system $\langle \Pi, \Sigma, \Theta, \mathcal{T} \rangle$, where

1. Π, the set of *state variables*.
2. Σ state values or *states*.
3. An *initial condition* Θ.
4. A finite set $\mathcal{T} \subseteq \Sigma \times \Sigma$ of *transitions*.

It is clear that i is in Π, but it extends smoothly to include x and u, and the transitions may then be supplemented by the differential equations that determines continuous evolutions. The system is thus modelled by infinite traces of successive state transitions and evolutions with *real* time stamps marking the transition time or the start time of an evolution. It is evident that the two frameworks essentially encompass the same phenomena, and that the main challenge is to express and evaluate model properties.

In summary, a system model is a collection of state variables which range either over discrete domains or over the continuum of reals. Real valued states are used to model physical quantities that do not have particular stable values. Discrete valued states are used when only stable values are considered important, and intermediate values are considered irrelevant, as is the case for digital components.

The state variables are assumed to be well behaved, i.e. at least sectionally continuous and bounded on bounded intervals. Further smoothness properties may be imposed on state variables that occur in differential equations, For discrete states, we shall ignore isolated discontinuities.

3   Specification Language

A specification constrains the state functions of a system and thus defines the possible system *behaviours*. In conventional control theory , constraints are given by differential equations, algebraic equations, and boundary conditions. Implementations of control systems are almost exclusively based on digital systems, where the continuous states are observed and changed through discrete sampling with equidistant and rather close sampling points. Since sampling is a well researched area, we shall not consider sampling part of the hybrid system design. We consider it a low level technology, and abstract from it in the same way that we abstract from the analog transistors implementing the digital computer.

Control theory has been remarkably useful, perhaps because it expresses constraints in terms of tractable differential equations only. However, such equations cannot in practice express any but the most trivial program behaviours. Cf. Ljung's remark about a program behaviour: "it may not be feasible to summarise it analytically" [19], p. 6. Another limitation of differential equations is that they are deterministic, they do not easily allow decomposition of systems into loosely coupled parts. With the few state variables (less than 20) usually considered in conventional control theory, this is not a major problem. However, computer control increases the state. With program variables, there are in the order of thousands of elementary state names, compositionality and its dual — abstraction — become crucial for practical design.

Generalising equations to weaker predicates on states makes it obvious to consider temporal logics as a specification language[23]. A conventional temporal logic introduces the notion of an assertion on the state holding for a current time point, or for some past or future time points. The time domain can either be branching or linear, corresponding to either a partial or total ordering of time points. Time is usually discrete; but continuous time has been investigated [28,16]. Another logic of time replaces time points by intervals. Interval logics [37,24,41] have a more symmetric view of time, and introduce the notion of a state assertion holding for a given interval of time. This view gives a neighbourhood interpretation of predicates, similar to the use of a differential equation to constrain a function within an interval.

Interval logics contain the usual logic operators of conjunction (tightening constraints), disjunction (loosening constraints), and negation (absence of certain states as a constraint). Furthermore, the interval logic by Moszkowski [24] includes a "chop" operator which is analogous to relational composition when intervals are seen as pairs of time points. This operator gives the means to glue phases of behaviours together.

The remaining issue is the form of atomic formulas for observations. The duration calculus [42] measure the set of time points where a state assertion P holds within an observation interval. This measure, denoted $\int P$, is the *duration* of P; it is a real number for any given bounded interval. A constraint is a relation among durations and real numbers. E.g. the constraint that a state assertion P shall hold almost everywhere is that the duration $\int P$ is equal to the length of the interval. Introducing the symbol ℓ for the length of an interval, the constraint is written: $\int P = \ell$. Conversely, an illegal set of states specified by an assertion P' should have a duration of zero: $\int P' = 0$ or equivalently $\int(\neg P') = \ell$. Durations between zero for an illegal state and ℓ for an invariant state limit the time spent in critical states. Durations thus gives a sliding transition between real-time constraints and logical constraints, and abstracts from time points. A consequence of the duration concept is that one do not describe observations of a a state in isolated points.

Durations are easily generalised to *integrals* of real valued state expressions. Together with notation for the value of a state expression at the beginning (**b.**) and the end (**e.**) of an interval, this gives a link to mathematical analysis [30,44]. An equation $\dot{x} = F(x)$ is interpreted as the predicate $\mathbf{e}.x = \mathbf{b}.x + \int F(x)$.

In the following, we define the syntax, semantics and calculus.

3.1 Syntax

The syntax for state expressions includes basic symbols for state names (symbols for state functions), rigid variables (time independent variables), and operators including predicate symbols. The basic symbols are used to form terms and propositions in the usual fashion.

State names x_i, $i = 0, \ldots$, with a typical element x. Each state name x has an associated type. The type system includes at least the types **R** and **Bool**.

Rigid variable symbols v_i, $i = 0, \ldots$, with typical element v.

Operator symbols F_i, $i = 0, \ldots$, with typical element F. We assume the usual constants and arithmetic operator symbols for the type **R**.

A subset of the operator symbols are the **Predicate symbols** R_i, $i = 0, \ldots$, with typical element R. Each R has a result type **Bool**. The predicate symbols include at least the boolean constants and the propositional connectives. Furthermore, we assume equality is a predicate for the different types and inequality for the type **R**.

State terms f_i, $i = 0, \ldots$, are built from state names, rigid variables and operator symbols by the usual rules.

$$f ::= x \mid v \mid F(f_1, \ldots, f_n)$$

State assertions P_i, $i = 0, \ldots$, are state terms of Boolean type. A *state expression* se_i, $i = 0, \ldots$, is a state term of type **R**.

Durations or integrals are formed from state expressions or assertions:

$$d ::= \int se \mid \int P$$

where the integral of a state assertion uses the encoding: *false* $= 0$ and *true* $= 1$. A "length of interval" symbol is thus defined by the abbreviation $\ell \stackrel{\text{def}}{=} \int true$.

Duration terms are built from durations, real valued rigid variables, and initial (**b**.se) and final values (**e**.se) for state expressions, using real valued operators.

$$dt ::= d \mid v \mid \mathbf{b}.se \mid \mathbf{e}.se \mid F(dt_1, \ldots, dt_n)$$

Duration formulas Atomic formulas are built by appying predicates over reals to duration terms. Propositional formulas are formed with the propositional connectives and a "chop" connective. Finally, quantifiers bind rigid variables.

$$
\begin{aligned}
D ::= \ & R(dt_1, \ldots, dt_n) \\
& \mid \ \neg D \mid D_1 \wedge D_2 \\
& \mid \ D_1 \ ; \ D_2 \\
& \mid \ \forall v : T \bullet D
\end{aligned}
$$

Remark: The same symbols are used as propositional connectives (arithmetic and relational operators) in state assertions and in formulas. This does not lead to ambiguity as the meaning can be inferred from context.

A *closed formula* is one, where every rigid variable is bound by a quantifier. In the semantics below, we consider only closed formulas. When we write concrete formulas with free rigid variables, universal closure is assumed, i.e., any free rigid variable v is bound by universal quantification ($\forall v$) on the outermost level.

Abbreviations The abbreviations ($\vee$, $\Rightarrow$, $\Leftrightarrow$, $\exists$) are defined as usual. We omit the type specifier for rigid variables of non-negative real type: $\forall v \bullet D$ means $\forall v : \mathbf{R}^+ \bullet D$, and introduce abbreviations to denote interval properties:

$$\lceil\rceil \;\stackrel{\text{def}}{=}\; \ell = 0 \qquad\qquad \text{the point interval}$$
$$\lceil P \rceil \;\stackrel{\text{def}}{=}\; \textstyle\int P = \ell \wedge \ell > 0 \quad P \text{ holds (essentially) everywhere}$$
$$\lceil P \rceil^r \;\stackrel{\text{def}}{=}\; \textstyle\int P = \ell \wedge \ell = r \quad P \text{ holds for } r \text{ time units}$$

Further abbreviations similar to temporal logic operators "eventually" and "always" are defined.

$$\Diamond D == true \;;\; D \;;\; true \quad D \text{ holds somewhere}$$
$$\Box D == \neg \Diamond \neg D \qquad\qquad D \quad \text{holds everywhere}$$

Precedence rules In order to avoid excessive use of parentheses the following precedence rules are used:

first:	$\int$, **b.**, **e.**
second:	real operators
third:	real predicates
fourth:	$\neg$, $\Box$, $\Diamond$,
fifth:	;
sixth:	$\vee$, $\wedge$
seventh:	$\Rightarrow$
eight:	$\forall r \bullet$, $\exists r \bullet$, $\forall v : T \bullet$, $\exists v : T \bullet$

3.2 Semantics

The meaning of duration formulas is given by an *interpretation* that assigns a fixed meaning to each state name, type, and operator symbol of the language. In order to distinguish the interpretation from language symbols x, T, F, P, we dash corresponding interpretations x', T', F', P'. The interpretation thus defines a structure that contains:

1. Sorts: The sorts include truth values $\mathbf{Bool}'$, real numbers $\mathbf{R}'$ and a subset hereof, the non-negative reals $\mathbf{R}'^{\geq 0}$.
2. State functions as delimited in Sect. 2.
3. Values of the given sorts.
4. Operators which satisfy the conditions for forming state functions.
5. Predicates which satisfy the conditions for forming state assertions.
6. An integration operator $\int'$, mapping a state function and an interval of $\mathbf{R}'$ to a value in $\mathbf{R}'$ and satisfying properties of the Riemann integral.

Valuations A *valuation* $\mathcal{V}_{\mathcal{I}}$ in a given interpretation $\mathcal{I}$ is now an assignment of values to all duration formulas. A valuation for an interpretation is a family of valuations, giving a valuation for each closed interval $I = [b, e]$ of *Time*, which here is taken to be a copy of R'^{+}.

For a fixed interpretation $\mathcal{I}$ we write $\mathcal{V}$ for $\mathcal{V}_{\mathcal{I}}$. This valuation is now defined inductively for any interval I:

1. Values of the proper kind and sorts are assigned for every rigid variable $\mathcal{V}[I](v_i) = v_i'$. The value v_i' is the same for all intervals I. A rigid variable thus has a common valuation for all intervals.

2. The value of a state term f is already defined for simple terms x and v. For a composite term $f = F(f_1, \ldots, f_n)$ the value is the state function defined by valuating the arguments and interpreting the operator symbol.

$$\mathcal{V}[I](f) = \lambda t : I \bullet F'(\mathcal{V}[I](f_1)(t), \ldots, \mathcal{V}[I](f_n)(t)) \ .$$

3. The value of a state assertion $P = R(f_1, \ldots, f_n)$ is the indicator function.

$$\mathcal{V}[I](P) = \lambda t : I \bullet \textbf{if } (\mathcal{V}[I](f_1)(t), \ldots, \mathcal{V}[I](f_n)(t)) \in R'$$
$$\textbf{then } 1 \textbf{ else } 0 \ .$$

4. Durations are valuated by $\mathcal{V}[I](\int d) = \int_I' \mathcal{V}[I](d)$.

5. Initial values take the limit from the right on the interval and final values take the limit from the left on the interval of a state expression.

$$\mathcal{V}[I](\mathbf{b}.se) = \mathcal{V}[I](se)(b+)$$
$$\mathcal{V}[I](\mathbf{e}.se) = \mathcal{V}[I](se)(e-) \ ,$$

where $I = [b, e]$. The final value in $0-$ for the point interval $[0, 0]$ is defined to be the value in 0.

6. Duration terms dt are valuated as terms.

7. Formulas are valuated as follows:

    (a) Atomic duration formulas $R(dt_1, \ldots, dt_m)$ are valuated as as relations on reals.

    (b) $\mathcal{V}[I](\neg D) = true'$ iff $\mathcal{V}[I](D) = false'$.

    (c) $\mathcal{V}[I](D_1 \wedge D_2) = true'$ iff $\mathcal{V}[I](D_1) = true'$ and $\mathcal{V}[I](D_2) = true'$.

    (d) $\mathcal{V}[I](D_1 \ ; \ D_2) = true'$, iff there exists m such that $I_1 = [b, m]$ and $I_2 = [m.e]$, for $I = [b, e]$; and $\mathcal{V}[I_1](D_1) = true'$ and $\mathcal{V}[I_2](D_2) = true'$.

    (e) $\mathcal{V}[I](\forall v_i : T \bullet D) = true'$ iff $\mathcal{V}^i[I](D) = true'$ for all valuations $\mathcal{V}^i$ that are *i*-equivalent with $\mathcal{V}$. (Two valuations $\mathcal{V}$ and $\mathcal{V}^i$ are *i-equivalent* if $\mathcal{V}(v_k) = \mathcal{V}^i(v_k)$ for all $k \neq i$. Note that the interval I is not mentioned, because rigid variables have the same valuation for all intervals.)

Satisfaction, models and validity Given an interpretation $\mathcal{I}$, a valuation $\mathcal{V}_{\mathcal{I}}$ and an interval I, every duration formula D will evaluate to one of the two truth values *true'* or *false'*. The valuation $\mathcal{V}_{\mathcal{I}}[I]$ *satisfies* the formula D if the value is *true'*. A formula D is said to *hold* for the interpretation $\mathcal{I}$ and interval I (written

$I \models_{\mathcal{I}} D$) when every valuation $\mathcal{V}_{\mathcal{I}}[I]$ satisfies D. If the interpretation is fixed by context, we shall often drop it and write $I \models D$ for D holds on I.

A closed formula is satisfied if and only if it holds for a given interpretation and interval.

A formula may characterise the behaviours or trajectories of a system. A given behaviour corresponds to an interpretation $\mathcal{I}$, and is characterised by the formula D just when D holds for $\mathcal{I}$ for all *prefix intervals*, $[0, e]$ with $e \in$ *Time*. We shall write this as $\models_{\mathcal{I}} D$.

It is easy to see that there are formulas which do not model behaviours, e.g. $\ell = 1$ which cannot hold for an arbitrary prefix interval. When the set of interpretations B for which a formula D holds. is non-empty, we say that the formula is *feasible* [29].

A special class of formulas are those that holds for all interpretations, such formulas are said to be *valid*.

3.3 Calculus

The behaviours of a system are modelled at a given level of detail by a formula. A design step is checked by proving logical entailment between formulas. A verification is thus a mathematical argument that one formula entails another. It can use mathematical analysis on the underlying model, but in most cases it is done by calculation, using the proof system of the logic. The duration calculus provides a number of equivalence laws, refinement laws, and induction principles.

The language of duration formulas is evidently an extension of a many sorted first order theory *Mat* that includes real analysis and thereby real arithmetic. We shall assume that *Mat* can be used to derive properties of state terms, and that operator and predicate symbols have their standard meanings. The notation $Mat \vdash R$ is used to signify that R is provable in *Mat*.

In the following, the calculus is presented in a conventional style, with axiom schemes and inference rules.

Duration properties The duration calculus has the following special axioms, axiom schemes and rules for durations. The first three formalises that durations are measures.

Zero	$\int false = 0.$
Positive	$\int P \geq 0.$
Measure	$\int P_1 + \int P_2 = \int (P_1 \vee P_2) + \int (P_1 \wedge P_2).$

The following rules allows substitution of assertions that are provably equivalent,and use of real arithmetic on durations.

Assertion If $Mat \vdash P_1 \Leftrightarrow P_2$ then $\int P_1 = \int P_2$.

Reals If $Mat \vdash \forall r_1, \dots, r_n \in \mathbf{R}^+ \bullet R(r_1, \dots, r_n)$ then
$R(\int P_1, \dots, \int P_n)$.

Some useful consequences are:

Dur-Range $0 \leq \int P \leq \ell.$
P-monotone   If $Mat \vdash P_1 \Rightarrow P_2$ then $\lceil P_1 \rceil \Rightarrow \lceil P_2 \rceil.$
P-And $\lceil P_1 \wedge P_2 \rceil \Leftrightarrow \lceil P_1 \rceil \wedge \lceil P_2 \rceil.$

Interval laws The following elementary laws from interval logic are useful.

Monotone   If $D_1 \Rightarrow D_1'$ and $D_2 \Rightarrow D_2'$ then $D_1 \; ; \; D_2 \Rightarrow D_1' \; ; \; D_2'.$
Associative $(D_1 \; ; \; D_2) \; ; \; D_3 \Leftrightarrow D_1 \; ; \; (D_2 \; ; \; D_3).$
Chop-Or $(D_1 \vee D_2) \; ; \; D_3 \Leftrightarrow (D_1 \; ; \; D_3) \vee (D_2 \; ; \; D_3)$
         and a mirrored version
         $D_1 \; ; \; (D_2 \vee D_3) \Leftrightarrow (D_1 \; ; \; D_2) \vee (D_1 \; ; \; D_3).$
Chop-false $D \; ; \; false \Rightarrow false$ and $false \; ; \; D \Rightarrow false.$

A point is a unit of chop. This reflects the definition of the ℓ operator.

Chop-Point $D \Leftrightarrow D \; ; \; \lceil \rceil \Leftrightarrow \lceil \rceil \; ; \; D.$

Chop-And $D_1 \; ; \; (D_3 \wedge \ell = r) \; \wedge \; D_2 \; ; \; (D_4 \wedge \ell = r)$
        $\Leftrightarrow (D_1 \wedge D_2) \; ; \; (D_3 \wedge D_4 \wedge \ell = r)$
        and the mirrored version
        $(D_1 \wedge \ell = r) \; ; \; D_2 \; \wedge \; (D_3 \wedge \ell = r) \; ; \; D_4$
        $\Leftrightarrow (D_1 \wedge D_3 \wedge \ell = r) \; ; \; (D_2 \wedge D_4).$

Notice that $D_1 \; ; \; D_3 \; \wedge \; D_2 \; ; \; D_3$ does not in general imply $(D_1 \wedge D_2) \; ; \; D_3.$ A counter-example is $D_1 = (\ell = 1)$, $D_2 = (\ell < 1)$ and $D_3 = true.$

Chop-Neg $\neg(D_1 \; ; \; D_2)$
         $\Leftrightarrow \ell < r \; \vee \; (\neg D_1) \; ; \; \ell = r \; \vee \; true \; ; \; (\ell = r \wedge \neg D_2)$
         and its mirrored version.
Chop-Exists $(\exists v : T \bullet D_1) \; ; \; D_2 \Leftrightarrow \exists v : T \bullet D_1 \; ; \; D_2,$
         provided v does not occur free in $D_2.$
         There is also a mirrored version.

Summation laws The following axiom link durations and intervals.

Sum $(\int P = r_1) \; ; \; (\int P = r_2) \Leftrightarrow \int P = r_1 + r_2, \; r_1, r_2$ in $\mathbf{R}^+.$

Some consequences are:

Chop-part $r \leq \int P \Rightarrow (\int P = r) \; ; \; true.$

Chop-Add
     A predicate over non-negative reals $R(r_1, \ldots, r_m)$, which is preserved under addition, is preserved over durations in a chopped formula.

$$\frac{Mat \vdash R(r_1, \ldots, r_m) \wedge R(r_1', \ldots, r_m') \Rightarrow R(r_1 + r_1', \ldots, r_m + r_m')}{R(\int p_1, \ldots, \int p_m) \; ; \; R(\int p_1, \ldots, \int p_m) \Rightarrow R(\int p_1, \ldots, \int p_m)}$$

E.g.: $\int p_1 \leq \int p_2 \; ; \; \int p_1 \leq \int p_2 \Rightarrow \int p_1 \leq \int p_2.$

Chop-true	*true* ; *true* $\Leftrightarrow$ *true.*
Chop-P	$\lceil P \rceil$; $\lceil P \rceil \Leftrightarrow \lceil P \rceil$.
Chop-P-And	$\lceil P_1 \rceil$; *true* $\wedge$ $\lceil P_2 \rceil$; *true* $\Leftrightarrow$ $\lceil P_1 \wedge P_2 \rceil$; *true,*
	true ; $\lceil P_1 \rceil$ $\wedge$ *true* ; $\lceil P_2 \rceil \Leftrightarrow$ *true* ; $\lceil P_1 \wedge P_2 \rceil$.
Neg-P	$\neg \lceil P \rceil \Leftrightarrow \lceil \rceil \vee \Diamond \lceil \neg P \rceil$.
P-Always	$\lceil P \rceil \Rightarrow \Box (\lceil P \rceil \vee \lceil \rceil)$.

The following laws define properties of the conventional modal operators.

Somewhere-Or	$\Diamond (D_1 \vee D_2) \Leftrightarrow \Diamond D_1 \vee \Diamond D_2$.
Chop-Always	$\Box D \wedge \ell \geq r_1 + r_2 \Leftrightarrow \ell = r_1$; D ; $\ell = r_2$.
Always-idem	$\Box \Box D \Leftrightarrow \Box D$.
Always-And	$\Box (D_1 \wedge D_2) \Leftrightarrow \Box D_1 \wedge \Box D_2$.
Always-Chop	$\Box D_1 \wedge \Box D_2 \Rightarrow \Box (D_1 ; D_2)$,
	$\Box D \wedge \Box D_1 ; D_2 \Rightarrow (\Box D \wedge D_1) ; (\Box D \wedge D_2)$.

Always-Once-Somewhere	$\Box D \Rightarrow D$ and $D \Rightarrow \Diamond D$.

Finite Variability is the basis for the following laws.

P-Cover	$\lceil P \rceil$; *true* $\vee$ $\lceil \neg P \rceil$; *true* $\vee$ $\lceil \rceil$,
	true ; $\lceil P \rceil \vee$ *true* ; $\lceil \neg P \rceil \vee \lceil \rceil$.
Chop-P-Neg	$\neg (\lceil P \rceil ; true) \Leftrightarrow \lceil \rceil \vee \lceil \neg P \rceil$; *true,*
	$\neg (true ; \lceil P \rceil) \Leftrightarrow \lceil \rceil \vee true$; $\lceil \neg P \rceil$.
Chop-P-Or	$\lceil P_1 \vee P_2 \rceil$; *true* $\Leftrightarrow \lceil P_1 \rceil$; *true* $\vee \lceil P_2 \rceil$; *true,*
	true ; $\lceil P_1 \vee P_2 \rceil \Leftrightarrow$ *true* ; $\lceil P_1 \rceil \vee true$; $\lceil P_2 \rceil$.

Integrals Systems with differentiable, continuous states have been studied intensively in control theory by means of mathematical analysis. The duration calculus is neither suggested as a replacement for these theories nor for the conventional mathematical techniques they use. The purpose of the following axioms and laws is to interface results from such theories to the duration calculus.

Analysis

If a relation among initial value, final value, integral and length of interval is proven using mathematical analysis, it is a law.

$$\frac{Mat \vdash \forall [b, e] \in Intv \bullet R(f(b+), f(e-), \int_b^e f(t)\,dt, e - b)}{R(\mathbf{b}.f, \mathbf{e}.f, \int f, \ell)}$$

Since durations are special cases of integrals, this scheme can be used to lift results about combinations of discrete and continuous states to formulas.

We also need to combine values across a "chop". Here a weaker form of the *Sum* law will always hold.

Integration	$\int se = v_1$; $\int se = v_2 \Rightarrow \int se = v_1 + v_2$.

Initial and final values are consistent for subintervals.

Values $\mathbf{b}.se = v \Leftrightarrow \mathbf{b}.se = v$; *true* and $\mathbf{e}.se = v \Leftrightarrow true$; $\mathbf{e}.se = v.$

If we only assume piecewise continuity, it is hard to develop very useful rules for the initial and final values in "chopped" formulas, because the values may jump at arbitrary points. In most control systems, the states are totally continuous, and we have some laws for real valued, *continuous* terms. The laws do not in general apply ' ' piecewise continuous terms.

Continuity $\mathbf{e}.se = v_1$; $\mathbf{b}.se = v_2 \Rightarrow v_1 = v_2.$

A partial inverse to the Integration rule is the mean-value rule.

Mean   For a continuous state expression *se*:
$$\mathbf{b}.se = v_1 \wedge \mathbf{e}.se = v_2 \wedge v_1 \leq v \leq v_2 \Rightarrow \mathbf{e}.se = v \; ; \; true.$$

For a differential equation $\dot{x} = se$, we assume that mathematical analysis has been applied to prove that there are solutions to the equation, such that x denote a continuous state. The Mean value theorem of analysis can then be used to justify the interpretation: $(\dot{x} = se) \overset{\text{def}}{=} \Box\,(\mathbf{e}.x = \mathbf{b}.x + \int se).$

3.4 Modules

In mathematics and generally in engineering, quantities are introduced informally by phrases like 'let x denote ...' and 'let A be a set ...'. This works very well for a small set of quantities used in a single development; but in development of a larger system with a modular structure and going through several stages of refinement, declarations must correspond to the composition of subsystems. In this case study, we have used the Raise Specification Language [7] to give a module structure to the state variables, miscellaneous constants (parameters), and auxilliary functions.

3.5 Refinement

In system design, a useful refinement concept is model inclusion. A system Sys_2 refines a system Sys_1 just when the models for Sys_2 are included in those for Sys_1. If the two systems have the same universe, it is clear that refinement corresponds to $Sys_2 \Rightarrow Sys_1$. In practice, this can be demonstrated by proving that the specification formula D_2 of Sys_2 implies D_1 of Sys_1. Soundness of the proof system for duration calculus means that $\vdash_{DC} D_2 \Rightarrow D_1$ entails validity $\models D_2 \Rightarrow D_1$ which is the desired result.

Sometimes a system Sys_2 with states $x_1, \ldots, x_m$ in a universe $Univ_2$ implements another system Sys_1 with states $y_1, \ldots, y_n$ in a universe $Univ_1$, without a simple refinement relation between the two systems. The two universes might for instance be totally different, but related by a transformation relation $\hat{\phi} : Univ_2 \leftrightarrow Univ_1$, with characteristic predicate ϕ. A suitable refinement relation between the two systems would then be proven by $\phi \wedge D_2 \Rightarrow D_1$ The simple notion of a transformation as an arbitrary relation may, however, endanger feasibility. The formula ϕ may not define a model for D_1 given a model for D_2. Semantically, we want a transformation to define at least one abstract state for each implementation state, i.e., an *upward simulation* [12]. In an extended refinement notion, we shall only use the properties of an upward simulation which ensures feasibility under refinement.

3.6 Special operators

This section introduce derived operators, which are used in specifications.

It is often useful to express that a system which is in some *current* region of its state space changes to a *goal state*. The characterisation of a current region may involve previous history and is therefore specified by a general formula, while the goal is taken to be a state assertion (or in general a prefix closed non-point formula) in the "followed-by" operator.

Definition [*Followed-by*] For a given formula D and state assertion P, the construct $D \longrightarrow \lceil P \rceil$ (D followed by P) is defined by

$$D \longrightarrow \lceil P \rceil \stackrel{\text{def}}{=} \Box((D \land \ell = r) \,;\, \ell > 0 \Rightarrow \ell = r \,;\, \lceil P \rceil \,;\, true) \;.$$

The followed-by operator ($\longrightarrow$) has the priority of implication.

Progress from a point $\lceil \rceil \longrightarrow \lceil P \rceil$ is equivalent to $\Box(\lceil \rceil \lor \lceil P \rceil)$, i.e., that P holds for any proper interval. Other simple cases are: $D \longrightarrow \lceil true \rceil$ which is trivially true, and $D \longrightarrow \lceil false \rceil$ which is equivalent to $\Box \neg D$.

Followed-by is monotone like an implication.

Fb-monotone If $D' \Rightarrow (true \,;\, D)$ and $Mat \vdash P \Rightarrow P'$ then
$$(D \longrightarrow \lceil P \rceil) \Rightarrow (D' \longrightarrow \lceil P' \rceil).$$

There are the following distributive laws.

Fb-Or1 $(D_1 \lor D_2 \longrightarrow \lceil P \rceil) \Leftrightarrow (D_1 \longrightarrow \lceil P \rceil) \land (D_2 \longrightarrow \lceil P \rceil).$
Fb-And2 $(D \longrightarrow \lceil P \land P' \rceil) \Leftrightarrow (D \longrightarrow \lceil P \rceil) \land (D \longrightarrow \lceil P' \rceil).$

A final law illustrates that D followed by P can be interpreted as the absence of $D \,;\, \lceil \neg P \rceil$. This is a specification by counterexample.

Fb-Neg $\neg(D \longrightarrow \lceil P \rceil) \Leftrightarrow \Diamond(D \,;\, \lceil \neg P \rceil).$

State transitions occur when a system moves from a current region specified by a state assertion P_1 to a state given by the assertion P_2 or stays in P_1. The possibility of a transition is specified by $\lceil P_1 \rceil \longrightarrow \lceil P_1 \lor P_2 \rceil$.

Progress A most useful property of a system is that it is guaranteed to move from an current region to a goal state within a certain time.

Definition [*Progress*] For a given formula D, state assertion P and positive real number t, the construct $D \xrightarrow{t} \lceil P \rceil$ (D for t progresses to P) is defined by

$$D \xrightarrow{t} \lceil P \rceil \overset{\text{def}}{=} (D \wedge \ell = t) \longrightarrow \lceil P \rceil \ .$$

It is easy to check that $(\ell < t) \xrightarrow{t} \lceil P \rceil$ is trivially valid, thus we must expect the current region D to be potentially of length t to be interesting.

When the current region is a lifted state assertion, a propagation law characterises progress.

Propagation $\lceil P_1 \rceil \xrightarrow{t} \lceil P_2 \rceil$
$$\Leftrightarrow$$
$$\Box (\lceil P_1 \rceil^r \ ; \ \ell > 0$$
$$\Rightarrow r < t \vee \ell = t \ ; \ \lceil P_1 \wedge P_2 \rceil^{r-t} \ ; \ \lceil P_2 \rceil \ ; \ true).$$

If the goal state excludes the current state ($P_1 \Rightarrow \neg P_2$) then the duration of the current state is bounded.

Bounded stability $\qquad \lceil P \rceil \xrightarrow{t} \lceil \neg P \rceil \Leftrightarrow \Box(\lceil P \rceil \Rightarrow \ell \le t)$.

When t approaches zero, we get $\lceil P \rceil \longrightarrow \lceil \neg P \rceil \Leftrightarrow \Box \neg \lceil P \rceil$ as expected.

Another consequence is

$$\lceil P_1 \rceil \xrightarrow{t} \lceil P_2 \rceil \Rightarrow \Box (\lceil P_1 \rceil \Rightarrow \ell \le t \vee \ell = t \ ; \ \lceil P_1 \wedge P_2 \rceil) \ .$$

When t approaches zero, we get $\lceil P_1 \rceil \longrightarrow \lceil P_2 \rceil \Rightarrow \Box (\lceil P_1 \rceil \Rightarrow \lceil P_2 \rceil)$ as expected. The converse, does not hold because there is progress of time built into "followed-by".

Progress is monotone with respect to time for state assertions.

Progress-time-monotone $\quad (\lceil P_1 \rceil \xrightarrow{t} \lceil P_2 \rceil) \wedge t \le t' \Rightarrow \lceil P_1 \rceil \xrightarrow{t'} \lceil P_2 \rceil$.

Progress is transitive in the following sense.

Progress-transitive $\qquad (\lceil P_1 \rceil \xrightarrow{t_1} \lceil P_2 \rceil) \wedge (\lceil P_1 \wedge P_2 \rceil \xrightarrow{t_2} \lceil P_3 \rceil)$
$$\Rightarrow \lceil P_1 \rceil \xrightarrow{t_1 + t_2} \lceil P_2 \wedge P_3 \rceil.$$

In many applications, monotonicity is used to eliminate the intermediate P_2, giving: $(\lceil P_1 \rceil \xrightarrow{t_1} \lceil P_2 \rceil) \wedge (\lceil P_2 \rceil \xrightarrow{t_2} \lceil P_3 \rceil) \Rightarrow \lceil P_1 \rceil \xrightarrow{t_1 + t_2} \lceil P_3 \rceil$.

Up-to Progress forces a transition at some moment, but it does not and should not say anything about the possible transitions while the system moves to this moment. The changes enabled up to that moment are expressed by "up-to" constraints. These are often time bounded, as expressed in the abbreviation.

Definition [*Bounded time invariance*] For a given formula D, state assertion P and positive real number t, the construct $D \stackrel{\leq t}{\Longrightarrow} \lceil P \rceil$ (D upto t may P) is defined by

$$D \stackrel{\leq t}{\Longrightarrow} \lceil P \rceil \stackrel{\text{def}}{=} (D \wedge \ell \leq t) \longrightarrow \lceil P \rceil \ .$$

3.7 Summary

With this section we have all the notations ready for demonstrating specification techniques for embedded systems. The RSL modules give a notation for introducing common functions, constants, predicates etc. in a conventional manner.

The development of an extended refinement concept and transformations is part of the preparations for refinement of modular specifications. Transformations are used when a system with an abstract state space is implemented by a component with a different concrete state space.

The "followed-by" operator can be seen as a dense time equivalent of an implication and a "next" operator.

One aspect which has not been covered is the precautions that must be taken to preserve feasibility when modules are refined separately. Essentially, a sufficient condition is to separate the state names, such that *controlled* variables, occurring in a goal state of a "followed-by" are contained in one module. Other state names are *inputs*. A fuller discussion is found in [29].

4 Design

A system, i.e. a plant for use in a given environment, has usually to achieve something in a safe manner. The planned functional and safety properties constitute the *expectations*. In practice, expectations are not a mathematical formula because the plant is constructed of components from different technologies (chemistry, mechanics, electronics, etc.), each with separate theoretical underpinnings. What we expect, is that it is possible to define states which define the *plant state space*. We also expect that the required functional and safety properties can be formulated as a collection of formulas on the plant state, called *commitments*.

The plant may already constrain the behaviours of the system. Some of these constraints are based on science and engineering knowledge, and they constitute the *assumptions*. Under all circumstances we assume that such knowledge can be described in formulas, such that there is a collection of assumptions $A_1, \ldots, A_m$.

The system *requirements* R are now given by a conjunction of commitments relative to assumptions $R = \bigwedge_{i=1}^{m}(A_i \Rightarrow C_i)$, where A_i is the assumption relevant for the commitment[1] C_i.

---

[1] In some of the literature, the terms rely and guarantee are used instead of assume and commit.

The obligation of a designer is to clarify the assumptions, and come up with a suitable specification of a *design Des* such that $Des \Rightarrow R$. The design may be refined to an *architecture*, with component specifications.

4.1 System model

We model a tracking control system by the following states:

```
1.0     context: DC
 .1
 .2     scheme
 .3       Model =
 .4         extend DC with
 .5           class
 .6             type
 .7               Coord = Real,
 .8               Ref = (R_plus → Coord) × (R_plus → R_plus)
 .9
 .10            value
 .11              X : Time → Coord,
 .12              halt : Time → Bool,
 .13              R : Time → Ref
 .14          end
```

Here X is the state of the plant and has the range *Coord*, which is the reals. The Boolean state halt models whether or not the system faces a safety-critical situation.

The last state of our most abstract system model is the state R which is the reference input for the tracking control system. The range of R, *Ref*, calls for further explanation:

The main input to a tracking control system is a reference path which X is supposed to trace, and it is essentially a mapping from time-points to values of the range of X. The implicit expectation following the trajectory is for the system to control the plant state along a realized path close to the reference. This being a formal approach we need to formalize this expectation and in particular what is meant by "close". Fixing the allowed error in the requirements would not be a very interesting approach. For instance in a robot, one often requires a more precise control at low velocity than at high velocity. We therefore model a reference band as an element of the type, *Ref*, that is, a pair of total functions on the non-negative reals (i.e. time-points). The first function (we shall refer to it as r) is the reference-path and the second function (we shall refer to it as ϵ) gives the allowed distance between the plant state and the reference for each point in time.

4.2 Top-level commitments

We now present the commitments we have chosen as basis for the design. We extend our system model with the following definitions of parameters and a state:

```
2.0    context: Model
 .1
 .2    scheme
 .3      Toplevel =
 .4        extend Model with
 .5          class
 .6            value
 .7              /* Parameters */
 .8              K : R_plus,
 .9              S : R_plus,
.10              D : R_plus,
.11              P : Ref → R_plus,
.12              acc : Ref → Bool,
.13              /* state */
.14              t : Time → Bool,
.15              /* skolem function */
.16              φ : Ref → {| t : R_plus • t ≤ D |}
.17          end
```

The parameter K enables us to formalize the expectation of a halt in case of a safety-critical situation:

Halting. $(\lceil \text{halt} \rceil \land \mathbf{b}.X = x) \longrightarrow \|\mathbf{b}.X - x\| < K$

We have chosen to model the reference input as a "band" (the state R). This does not, however, ensure that X can be controlled according to arbitrary values of R. We call a reference, which the system will be able to realize, an *acceptable* reference. This is codified in the function *acc*. During the design we will go into details about *acc* and its role in a real system.

The Boolean state, t (*trace*), is true when the system is tracing the current (acceptable) reference:

Starting. $\lceil \neg \text{halt} \land R = R \land acc(R) \rceil \xrightarrow{P(R)} \lceil t \rceil$

The system must control X according to the (stable) value of R no later than time D after the *trace* phase is entered:

Tracing. $(R = (r, \epsilon) \land \lceil \neg t \rceil^{S} \; ; \; \lceil t \rceil^{v+D} \land \lceil R = R \land \neg \text{halt} \rceil) \longrightarrow$
$\qquad \|\mathbf{b}.X - r(v + \phi(R))\| < \epsilon(v + \phi(R))$

In Tracing, v models a timer. The stability parameter, S, is necessary to prove some of the forthcoming design steps as components are introduced for the monitoring of halt and R.

4.3 System architecture

We have adopted the layered system architecture proposed by Najdm-Tehrani in [25]. The architecture provides separation between high level planning and control mechanisms and low level control algorithm components. The layered architecture is shown in Fig. 4 with the three layers: Analysis, Rule and Process layer, each layer consisting of one or more function blocks.

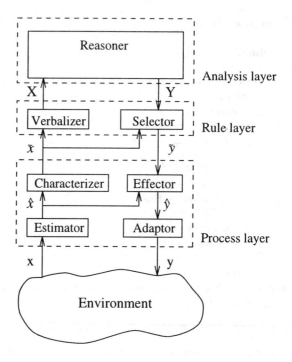

Fig. 4. The layered system architecture.

Analysis layer The Analysis layer is provided with relevant information about the environment from the lower layers (and from a "user"), and on this basis, it performs a dynamic selection of control tasks. Examples of different control tasks in a tracking control system are: halting due to a safety-critical situation, a change of reference or a stable reference, the latter being the most interesting. The Analysis layer executes in an aperiodic manner, and the layer consists of one block.

Reasoner performs dynamic selection and long term optimization of selected control algorithms. Reasoner maintains information about the available control algorithms located in Process layer. When a new reference is input from the user, Reasoner determines a priori whether the reference is acceptable by trying to plan a schedule of switches between control algorithms. A job Y which is the control task selected by Reasoner is sent to the Rule layer for execution. Reasoner receives information X from the Rule layer about the execution of a job. It can on that basis acquire more knowledge about the control algorithms and possibly generate a modified job.

Rule layer The Verbalizer and Selector blocks constitute the Rule layer. The layer executes in an aperiodic manner and facilitates execution of a job received from the Analysis layer and provides support for achieving more accurate information about the control algorithms.

Verbalizer performs classification of sequences of important events $\bar{x}$ received from the Process layer to obtain higher level descriptions to be used in Reasoner. Verbalizer furthermore monitors safety-critical conditions.

Selector determines the control algorithms to be used in the Effector on basis of the job received from Reasoner. If a job requires switching between several control algorithms, Selector performs the switching by sending dispatching events $\bar{y}$ to the Effector at the appropriate points in time. In order to perform a dynamic improvement of the schedule, Selector receives information about the current status (i.e. important events).

Process layer The Process layer consists of the Estimator, Effector, Adaptor and Characterizer blocks. The Process layer executes the control algorithms as dispatched by the Rule layer, and since we are using a digital system it operates in a periodic manner (according to a sampling frequency). In addition, characterization of information about the control algorithms and the environment is provided.

Characterizer classifies the current situation and detects important events on basis of the sampled values $\hat{x}$ received from Estimator.

Effector contains the control algorithms provided by the system and executes the control algorithm selected by Selector. The result $\hat{y}$ is given to Adaptor.

Estimator converts the analog values x measured by the sensors to the representation used by Characterizer $\hat{x}$.

Adaptor converts the outputs $\hat{y}$ received from Effector to a form y suitable for the actuators, for instance through a DA converter.

4.4 Design$_1$

The aim of the first design is to introduce a *Verbalizer* component that monitors the halt state. In an implementation the halt state will most likely be refined to a more general state assertion and observed in an intricate manner. Introducing a halt sensor allows the refinement of halt and its sensor and of the remaining part of the system to take place independently.

The first design step introduces the following extensions of the parameter and state space and the following assumptions:

```
3.0     context: Toplevel
 .1
 .2     scheme
 .3       Design1 =
 .4         extend Toplevel with
 .5           class
 .6             value
 .7               /* Parameters */
 .8               ρ : R_plus,
 .9               K' : R_plus,
.10               P' : Ref → R_plus,
.11               S' : R_plus,
.12               v_max : R_plus,
.13               /* Controlled state */
.14               c : Time → Bool
.15
.16             axiom
.17               forall R : Ref •
.18                 /* Assumption A2 */
.19                 K > K' + 2.0 * v_max * ρ,
.20
.21                 /* Assumption A3 */
.22                 P(R) > P'(R) + 2.0 * ρ,
.23
.24                 /* Assumption A4 */
.25                 S > S' + 2.0 * ρ
.26           end
```

Here v_{max} is the maximum speed[2] of the plant state X. The parameter is used to make the assumption A1, a Lipschitz condition:

A1. $\ell > 0 \Rightarrow \lceil |\dot{X}| \le v_{max} \rceil$

The parameters K', P' and S' together with the assumptions A2, A3 and A4 are consequences of the fact that Halt-sensor and its control state c, introduces a delay which is upper bounded by the parameter ρ.

A specification of Halt-sensor is given by the following five formulas:

H1. $\lceil \rceil \vee \lceil c \rceil^{2\rho}$; *true*   Initialization
     Progress

H2. $\lceil halt \rceil \xrightarrow{2\rho} \lceil c \rceil$ Progress

H3. $\lceil \neg\, halt \rceil \xrightarrow{2\rho} \lceil \neg c \rceil$

H4. $\lceil \neg c \rceil$; $\lceil c \rceil \xrightarrow{\le 2\rho} \lceil c \rceil$ Stability

H5. $\lceil c \rceil$; $\lceil \neg c \rceil \xrightarrow{\le 2\rho} \lceil \neg c \rceil$

H1 says that initially the system is in a safety-critical situation. The purpose of the sensor is to react upon a change in the value of halt "as quickly as possible". This is specified in a feasible way by H2 and H3.

---

[2] It is not possible to write subscripted names like v_{max} in RSL, it is thus written as v_max.

The *Reasoner* component is the *Coordinator*. It basically takes over the top-level commitments. However, every instance of halt is replaced with a corresponding c which reflects the purpose of Halt-sensor. The commitments together with assumptions A2-A4 illustrates how one at the top-level must allow room (in time and - due to A1 - space) for refinements.

C1.1. $(\lceil c \rceil \wedge b.X = x) \longrightarrow \|b.X - x\| < K'$

C1.2. $\lceil \neg c \wedge R = R \wedge acc(R) \rceil \xrightarrow{P'(R)} \lceil t \rceil$

C1.3. $(R = (r, \epsilon) \wedge \lceil \neg t \rceil^{S'} ; \lceil t \rceil^{v+D} \wedge \lceil R = R \wedge \neg c \rceil) \longrightarrow$
$\qquad \|b.X - r(v + \phi(R))\| < \epsilon(v + \phi(R))$

Verification The verification that the design refines the requirements (commitments under the assumptions) is done in the follwing proof outlines. In all cases, the *Fb-Neg* is used to convert the proof to a proof by contradiction. (*Asm* $\wedge$ *Des* $\wedge$ $\neg Reg$ $\Rightarrow$ *false*). This style has been found useful, because $\neg Req$ describes an instance of an illegal "pattern" of behaviour.

The Halting commitment is verified hereafter.

$\qquad \exists r, x \bullet true ; (\lceil halt \rceil \wedge b.X = x \wedge \ell = r) ; \|b.X - x\| \geq K$

$\Rightarrow \{$First case $r > 2\rho$, H2$\}$
$\qquad \exists x \bullet true ; (b.X = x \wedge \ell = 2\rho ; \lceil c \rceil) ; \|b.X - x\| \geq K$
$\Rightarrow \{$A1$\}$
$\qquad \exists x \bullet true ; (b.X = x \wedge \ell = 2\rho ; (\lceil c \rceil \wedge \|b.X - x\| \leq 2v_{max} * \rho))$
$\qquad ; \|b.X - x\| \geq K$
$\Rightarrow \{$Chop-And, C1.1, Mat$\}$
$\qquad \exists x \bullet true ; (K \leq \|b.X - x\| \leq K' + 2v_{max} * \rho$
$\Rightarrow \{$A2, Chop-False$\}$
$\qquad$ *false*

$\Rightarrow \{$Second case $r \leq 2\rho$, A1$\}$
$\qquad \exists x \bullet true ; (b.X = x \wedge \ell \leq 2\rho ; (K \leq \|b.X - x\| \leq 2v_{max} * \rho$
$\Rightarrow \{$A2, Chop-False$\}$
$\qquad$ *false*

The Starting commitment is verified hereafter.

$\qquad \exists R \bullet true ; \lceil \neg halt \wedge R = R \wedge acc(R) \rceil^{P(R)} ; \lceil \neg t \rceil$
$\Rightarrow \{$A3, H3$\}$
$\qquad \exists R \bullet true ; (\lceil R = R \wedge acc(R) \rceil^{P(R)} \wedge \ell = 2\rho ; \lceil \neg c \rceil) ; \lceil \neg t \rceil$
$\Rightarrow \{$Chop-And$\}$
$\qquad \exists R \bullet true ; \lceil \neg c \wedge R = R \wedge acc(R) \rceil^{P(R)-2\rho} ; \lceil \neg t \rceil$
$\Rightarrow \{$C1.2$\}$
$\qquad true ; (\lceil t \rceil \wedge \lceil \neg t \rceil) ; true$
$\Rightarrow \{$Chop-False$\}$
$\qquad$ *false*

The Tracing commitment is verified hereafter. We assume $v \geq 0$.

$$\exists R, v, r, \epsilon \bullet R = (r, \epsilon) \wedge true \; ; \; (\lceil \neg t \rceil^S \; ; \; \lceil t \rceil^{v+D} \wedge \lceil R = R \wedge \neg \, \mathsf{halt} \rceil) \; ;$$
$$\|\mathbf{b}.\mathsf{X} - r(v + \phi(R))\| \geq \epsilon(v + \phi(R))$$
$$\Rightarrow \{\text{A4, H3}\}$$
$$\exists R, v, r, \epsilon \bullet R = (r, \epsilon) \wedge true \; ; \; (\lceil \neg t \rceil^{S-2\rho} \; ; \; \lceil t \rceil^{v+D} \wedge \lceil R = R \wedge \neg \, \mathsf{c} \rceil) \; ;$$
$$\|\mathbf{b}.\mathsf{X} - r(v + \phi(R))\| \geq \epsilon(v + \phi(R))$$
$$\Rightarrow \{\text{C1.3, } \textit{Chop-False}\}$$
$$\textit{false}$$

The proofs of the subsequent refinements have a similar style, and since they are more engineering calculations than intersting mathematical proofs, we shall elide them (although we are willing to mail them to any ardent reader!).

4.5 Design$_2$

The concept of acceptability of a band means that we must determine it for a given band. Thus we introduce a *Planner* component into the *Reasoner*. It determines whether or not the current input band (i.e. the current value of R) is acceptable or not. Design$_2$ introduces the following definitions, assumptions and extensions of the state and parameter space.

```
4.0      context: Design1
 .1
 .2      scheme
 .3        Design2 =
 .4          extend Design1 with
 .5            class
 .6              type
 .7                ControlAlg,
 .8                Switch == switch(T : R_plus, C : ControlAlg),
 .9                SwitchL = {| s : Switch^ω • iswf(s) |},
 .10               Job' == Undef | Stop | job(SwitchL, Ref),
 .11               Plan == Null | job(SwitchL, Ref),
 .12               Plannerphases == planning | unacceptable(Ref) | scheduled(Ref)
 .13
 .14             value
 .15               /* Parameters */
 .16               T_m : R_plus,
 .17               plan : Ref → Plan,
 .18               P'' : Ref → R_plus,
 .19               iswf : Switch^ω → Bool,
 .20               /* d is the mathematical norm in its general sense */
 .21               d : Coord × Coord → Real,
 .22               /* Controlled states */
 .23               sched : Time → Job',
 .24               π_p : Time → Plannerphases,
```

```
.25                    /* Shorthand states */
.26                    p : Time → Bool,
.27                    s : Time → (Ref → Bool),
.28                    u : Time → (Ref → Bool)
.29
.30              axiom
.31                forall R : Ref, s : Switchω •
.32                    /* Assumption A5 */
.33                    P'(R) > ρ + P''(R) + T_m ∧ P''(R) > 2.0 * ρ,
.34
.35                    /* Assumption A6 */
.36                    acc(R) ≡
.37                      (
.38                        ∃ r : R_plus → Coord, ε : R_plus → R_plus •
.39                        R = (r, ε) ∧
.40                        (
.41                           ∃
.42                             sl : SwitchL,
.43                             R' : Ref,
.44                             r' : R_plus → Coord,
.45                             ε' : R_plus → R_plus
.46                           •
.47                             plan(R) = job(sl, R') ∧
.48                             R' = (r', ε') ∧
.49                             (
.50                               ∀ t : R_plus, x : Coord •
.51                                 d(x, r'(t)) < ε'(t) ⇒ d(x, r(t)) < ε(t)
.52                             )
.53                        )
.54                      ),
.55
.56                    /* Assumption A7 */
.57                    S' > 2.0 * ρ
.58              end
```

Among the types introduced is ControlAlg which is left under-specified. This is our very abstract view of the control algorithms of the system; a set of indices.

The function *plan* determines whether a band is acceptable or not as expressed in assumption A6. The type SwitchL is the data model of a plan produced by *plan* given an acceptable band. The predicate *iswf* will be specified later in the design process. Given an unacceptable band *plan* returns a void value, Null (cf. the type Plan).

The state sched is a shared state between Planner and Coordinator and holds the value of the current schedule, thus reflecting the decision taken by *plan* about the current band (cf. the type Job'). The phases of Planner correspond to the values of sched as shown in the following definitions:

$\lceil p \rceil \equiv \lceil \pi_p = planning \rceil$
$\lceil u(R) \rceil \equiv \lceil \pi_p = unacceptable(R) \rceil$
$\lceil s(R) \rceil \equiv \lceil \pi_p = scheduled(R) \rceil$

$\lceil \text{sched} = Undef \rceil \equiv \lceil p \rceil$
$\lceil \text{sched} = Stop \rceil \equiv \lceil \bigvee_{R:Ref} u(R) \rceil$
$\lceil \text{sched} = job(sl, R') \rceil \equiv \lceil s(R) \wedge plan(R) = job(sl, R') \rceil.$

The planner specification is:

Initialization
P1. $\exists R \bullet \lceil \rceil \vee (plan(R) = Null \wedge \lceil R = R \wedge u(R) \rceil)$
$\quad \vee \lceil R = R \rceil$; $\lceil R \neq R \wedge u(R) \rceil$; $true$
Sequencing
P2. $\lceil u(R) \rceil \longrightarrow \lceil u(R) \vee p \rceil \wedge \lceil s(R) \rceil \longrightarrow \lceil s(R) \vee p \rceil$
$planning$ stability
P3. $\lceil \neg p \rceil$; $\lceil p \rceil \overset{\leq 2\rho}{\longrightarrow} \lceil p \rceil$
$planning$ progress
P4. $plan(R) = Null \wedge \lceil p \wedge R = R \rceil \overset{P''(R)}{\longrightarrow} \lceil u(R) \rceil$
P5. $plan(R) = job(sl, R') \wedge \lceil p \wedge R = R \rceil \overset{P''(R)}{\longrightarrow} \lceil s(R) \rceil$
$planning$ selection
P6. $plan(R) = Null \wedge \lceil \neg p \rceil$; $\lceil p \wedge R = R \rceil \longrightarrow \lceil p \vee u(R) \rceil$
P7. $plan(R) = job(sl, R') \wedge \lceil \neg p \rceil$; $\lceil p \wedge R = R \rceil \longrightarrow \lceil p \vee s(R) \rceil$
$unacceptable$ stability
P8. $\lceil \neg u(R) \rceil$; $\lceil u(R) \wedge R = R \rceil \longrightarrow \lceil u(R) \rceil$
$unacceptable$ progress
P9. $\lceil u(R) \wedge R \neq R \rceil \overset{\rho}{\longrightarrow} \lceil p \rceil$
$scheduled$ stability
P10. $\lceil \neg s(R) \rceil$; $\lceil s(R) \wedge R = R \rceil \longrightarrow \lceil s(R) \rceil$
$scheduled$ progress
P11. $\lceil s(R) \wedge R \neq R \rceil \overset{\rho}{\longrightarrow} \lceil p \rceil$

The initial R value is "unacceptable" as Planner is initially in the *unacceptable* phase and remains there until R changes. This is stated in P1. P2 defines the possible (un-timed) phase transitions. P3 states stability of the *planning* phase for at least 2ρ time-units. P4 and P5 state that it takes at most $P''(R)$ time-units in the *planning* phase to determine the value, $plan(R)$, and assign this value to sched. P6 and P7 frame the value of sched. P8 and P10 are stability of the *unacceptable* and *scheduled* phases, respectively. P9 and P11 are progress from these phases.

The introduction of Planner encapsulates the monitoring of R. The intention is that the remaining part of the system monitors sched (or, equally, the phase of Planner) instead of R. This entails a reformulation of the Coordinator commitments:

C2.1. $(\lceil c \rceil \wedge \mathbf{b}.X = x) \longrightarrow \|\mathbf{b}.X - x\| < K'$
$tracing$ stability
C2.2. $\lceil \neg t \rceil$; $\lceil t \wedge s(R) \wedge \neg c \wedge R = R \rceil \longrightarrow \lceil t \rceil$
$tracing$ progress
C2.3. $\lceil t \wedge \neg (\bigvee_{R:Ref} s(R)) \rceil \overset{\rho}{\longrightarrow} \lceil \neg t \rceil$

C2.4. $\lceil t \wedge c \rceil \xrightarrow{\rho} \lceil \neg t \rceil$
    $\neg$ *tracing* stability
C2.5. $\lceil t \rceil \; ; \; \lceil \neg t \wedge \neg (\bigvee_{R:Ref} s(R)) \rceil \longrightarrow \lceil \neg t \rceil$
  C2.6. $\lceil t \rceil \; ; \; \lceil \neg t \wedge c \rceil \longrightarrow \lceil \neg t \rceil$
    $\neg$ *tracing* progress
   C2.7. $\lceil \neg t \wedge \neg (\bigvee_{R:Ref} s(R)) \rceil \xrightarrow{\rho} \lceil \neg t \rceil$
   C2.8. $\lceil \neg t \wedge s(R) \wedge \neg c \wedge R = R \rceil \xrightarrow{2T_m} \lceil t \rceil$
   C2.9. $\lceil \neg t \wedge c \rceil \xrightarrow{\rho} \lceil \neg t \rceil$
   C2.10. $(R = (r, \epsilon) \wedge \lceil \neg t \rceil \; ; \; \lceil t \rceil^{v+D} \wedge \lceil \neg c \wedge \text{sched} = job(sl, R) \rceil) \longrightarrow$
      $\| \mathbf{b}.\mathsf{X} - r(v + \phi(R)) \| < \epsilon(v + \phi(R))$

Each reference, R, is assumed stable for at least $P''(R) + \rho$ time-units as stated in assumption A8: $\lceil R \neq R \rceil \; ; \; \lceil R = R \rceil \xrightarrow{\leq P''(R)+\rho} \lceil R = R \rceil$.

4.6 Design₃

At the abstraction level of Design₂ the system faces two major control tasks in which it is required to control the plant state X accordingly. This is reflected by commitments C2.1 and C2.10. The purpose of the following refinements is to decide *how* this control will be carried out. With the architecture in mind this means that we shall be introducing components of the Rule and Process layer. Prior to this, however, we need to have a well-structured interface to the lower layers. It is the purpose of Design₃ to introduce such an interface.

The definitions, assumptions and extensions of the parameter and state space introduced by Design₃ are presented in the following:

```
5.0      context: Design2
 .1
 .2      scheme
 .3        Design3 =
 .4          extend Design2 with
 .5            class
 .6              type Job == Stop | job(SwitchL, Ref)
 .7
 .8              value
 .9                /* Parameters */
.10                K" : R_plus,
.11                /* Controlled state */
.12                J : Time → Job
.13
.14              axiom
.15                /* Assumption A9 */
.16                K' > K" + 2.0 * v_max * ρ ∧ K" > v_max * D,
.17
.18                /* Assumption A10 */
.19                T_m > 2.0 * ρ
.20          end
```

The introduction of the state, J, is the means to provide the interface to the lower layers. The type of J is Job^3 and values of J are referred to as *jobs*. With the introduction of J we are able to give a precise definition of the state t and thus of the concept of tracing. The system is tracing just when the current schedule is the current job: $\lceil t \rceil \equiv \lceil J = job(sl, R) \wedge \text{sched} = job(sl, R) \rceil$.

Using these definitions the commitments of Design$_3$ for Coordinator become:

Initializations

C3.1. $\lceil \rceil \vee \lceil J = Stop \rceil \vee \ell > \rho$

Stability of J

C3.2. $\lceil J \neq j \rceil \; ; \; \lceil J = j \rceil \xrightarrow{\leq \rho} \lceil J = j \rceil$

Progress of J

C3.3. $\lceil J = j \wedge c \rceil \xrightarrow{\rho} \lceil J = Stop \rceil$

C3.4. $\lceil J = j \wedge \neg (\bigvee_{R:Ref} s(R)) \rceil \xrightarrow{\rho} \lceil \bigwedge_{R:Ref} (s(R) \Rightarrow J \neq \text{sched}) \rceil$

C3.5. $\lceil J = j \wedge s(R) \wedge \neg c \rceil \xrightarrow{T_m} \lceil \bigwedge_{R:Ref} (s(R) \Rightarrow J = \text{sched}) \rceil$

Selection of J

C3.6. $\lceil J \neq j \rceil \; ; \; \lceil J = j \wedge c \rceil \longrightarrow \lceil J = j \vee J = Stop \rceil$

C3.7. $\lceil J \neq j \rceil \; ; \; \lceil J = j \wedge \neg (\bigvee_{R:Ref} s(R)) \rceil$

$\quad \longrightarrow \lceil J = j \vee \bigwedge_{R:Ref} (s(R) \Rightarrow J \neq \text{sched}) \rceil$

C3.8. $\lceil J \neq j \rceil \; ; \; \lceil J = j \wedge s(R) \wedge \neg c \rceil$

$\quad \longrightarrow \lceil J = j \vee \bigwedge_{R:Ref} (s(R) \Rightarrow J = \text{sched}) \rceil$

As reflected by commitment C3.3 the unique job value, Stop, is dedicated for use in the presence of a safety-critical situation, thus modeling the reaction upon such as an exception. The ideal would be to model it as "just another job" but this has a disadvantage. The required behaviour in a safety-critical situation is to keep the plant (almost) in a fixed state, namely the state which the system was in when the safety-critical situation occurred. In order to obtain this behaviour through an "ordinary" job, Coordinator needs to monitor X (this follows from the type of J). However, as Coordinator is placed in the Analysis layer of the chosen architecture (cf. section 4.3) we expect it to operate on high level descriptions of the plant behaviour. As X is definitely not a *high level* description of the plant behaviour we do not want Coordinator to monitor X. C3.1 takes the consequence of H1 of the Halt-sensor specification.

Control of X is from now on taken care of by Selector and its commitments are as follows.

S3.1. $(\lceil J = Stop \rceil \wedge b.X = x) \xrightarrow{D} \|b.X - x\| < K''$

S3.2. $(R = (r, \epsilon) \wedge \lceil J \neq job(sl, R) \rceil \; ; \; \lceil J = job(sl, R') \rceil^{v+D}) \longrightarrow$
$\|b.X - r(v + \phi(R))\| < \epsilon(v + \phi(R))$

The two commitments reflect quite well the fact that, at this level of abstraction, Selector monitors J only. The refinement of Coordinator has now come to an end

---

[3] Note that since sched is of type Job' and J is of type Job, it is not strictly correct to write $\lceil J = \text{sched} \rceil$ as a part of a commitment. As the only reason for having both types Job' and Job is to eliminate the value $Undef$ as a possibility for J, we will abstract from this in order to obtain readable formulas.

and we have succeeded in eliminating R from the commitments. Furthermore a neat interface to the lower layers of the architecture has been introduced by means of J. The different control tasks are "merged" into J.

4.7 Design₄ to Design₆

The description above has given an idea of the design process. In this paper we shall not continue by adding the details of the last three refinements. Their purpose is to get specific about the execution of jobs, wher the Selector is seen as a job sensor.

Design$_4$ introduces the definitions, assumptions and extensions of the state and parameter space for that purpose.

Design$_5$ handles a given job. The Selector commitments of Design$_5$ are based on a different phase automaton than the one used in Design$_4$. The transformation between the automaton used in Design$_4$ and the present one is an upward simulation. The purpose of the transformation is to get more specific about the *fixjob(job(sl,R))* phases but at the same time remain abstract about the *fixjob(Stop)*.

Design$_6$ introduces a new state IE (short for Important Event) which is to be controlled by a new automaton, Characterizer, and observed by the Selector automaton. The Selector commitments are thus reformulated to cope with important events.

4.8 Summary

This section has illustrated the steps in a design and the calculations which we done in order to check the designs. The full design consists of about 20 pages, and the full proof outlines are another 42 pages.

5 Implementation

The translation of the design into a collection of communicating occam processes involves coding of the data structures and translation of the input and output duration formulas to communications, cf. [35]. The resulting program architecture is shown in Fig. 5. This activity did not give many problems, so we shall focus on the interface to the control engineer. We illustrate the parameters of the interface as pieces of occam code taken from the actual program.

Recall from Sect. 4 the four major parameters of the interface:

1. A planning algorithm for á priori planning of switches.
2. An algorithm for the detection of important events.
3. A selection algorithm to react upon important events.
4. A set of control algorithms.

Starting with the last parameter, a control algorithm is implemented as a separate process. This gives the advantage of a possible internal state which is often used in control algorithms, e.g. when numerical integration is used.

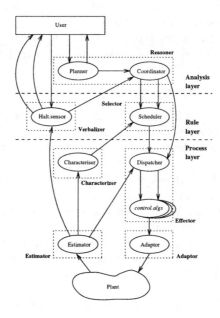

Fig. 5. Program architecture

```
PROC Control.alg
  (CHAN OF PARAMETERS parameters,
   CHAN OF CA.INPUT ca.input,
   CHAN OF CA.OUTPUT ca.output)
WHILE TRUE
  ALT
    parameters ? param.l::param  -- start up
      ...
    ca.input ? r; m
      ...
      ca.output ! f(r, m)
```

The control algorithm processes are each identified as an *index*, and the specific algorithm is parametrized with a set of parameters. The selection of a control algorithm thus consists of choosing a process index and sending a suitable set of parameters on its `param` channel. A control algorithm process receives its parameters as it is selected and will from then on and until another is selected receive measurements and reference values from *Dispatcher* on the channel `ca.input` and produce outputs on the channel `ca.output`.

A switch of control algorithm is either pre-planned or provoked by an important event. The pre-planning activity resides in the *Planner* process, and the concrete interface is the subroutine, `plan`:

```
PROC plan ([Max.ref.size]REAL32 xref, [2][Max.no.switches]INT sl,
           [Max.ref.size]REAL32 R,    [Infosize]INT info)
```

Input is the reference (xref) and output is a list of pre-planned switches (sl), a possibly modified reference (R) and some auxiliary information (info). Pre-planning uses static knowledge about the control algorithm characteristics. The process index and the set of parameters of a pre-planned switch are thus selected from a fixed range of possible values. This is organized in two tables that are part of the interface as well:

```
VAL [][]INT Index.no.param IS
   [[0,1], [1,2], [2,4]] :


VAL [][]REAL32 Params IS
   [[100.0, Dummy, Dummy, Dummy],
    [ 50.0,  20.0, Dummy, Dummy],
    [ 45.0,  10.0,   5.0,   0.5]] :
```

An element in sl now consists of the time for a planned switch and a key to the table, An element of the table consists of an index of a control algorithm process and the number of applicable parameters. These parameters are fetched from Params using the key.

The *Characterizer* process instantiates a detection algorithm. This makes it possible to maintain an internal state.

```
PROC Characterizer(CHAN OF C c.input,
                   CHAN OF I.E important.event)
   WHILE TRUE
     c.input ? r; m
     ...
     IF ...                 -- if event detected
        important.event ! ie.r; ie.i
:
```

The *Characterizer* must be ready to accept input in every sampling period in order not to block the control loop. An important event is output on the channel, important.event, and consists of a variable length list of floating point numbers and integers.

The last major parameter of the interface is the mechanism for reacting upon important events. The reaction is a selection of a (possibly) different control algorithm and the parameter subroutine, idsyn (*identify and synthesize*), is instantiated with the concrete selection algorithm:

```
PROC idsyn ([Ie.r]REAL32 ie.r,
            [Ie.i]INT ie.i,
            INT ca.i,
            [Max.no.param]REAL32 param)
```

The input to idsyn is the information received from *Characterizer* in an important event (ie.r and ie.i). The output is an index ca.i of a control algorithm and a suitable set of parameters param for the algorithm. These parameters can either be selected from the tables, or be generated on basis of the information given in the important event.

5.1 Timing aspects

With a sampling rate of 1 milliseconds, computation and communication time cannot be ignored in the implementation. In order to minimize external communication, the system of Fig. 5 is placed on the transputer's as follows: The Analysis layer is located in the processor that comes with the occam development system. It has the largest space requirements and is not time-critical. The Rule and Process layers with an instance for each link are placed on the main processor. The Estimater and Adaptor are placed in two copies on separate processors that contain the hardware AD and DA adapters.

The concrete programs in the sampling loop are then analyzed, and a computation and communication overhead is estimated to be around 170 microseconds. The blocks between communications are all relatively short, so it is not unreasonable to assume an even distribution among the high priority processes of the two sampling loops. The lower priority of the processor is used for the Schedulers. This means that the control algorithm and event detector has about 200 microseconds per sample. It is sufficient for the purpose; but might become critical if synthesised control algorithms are implemented.

6 Discussion

The robot experiment is completed, and the previous sections have given an account of the theories and techniques that have been used in the development, in particular during the stepwise design. The experiment has been successful in creating an architecture which the control engineering group appreciates, and which they intend to reuse for other experimental platforms. However, with some reprogramming ahead, because we must move away from occam and the transputer for commercial reasons.

During the work, we have often discussed whether it was really necessary to use that many tools and theories:

- mathematical analysis and Matlab for development and simulation of the control laws for the plant;
- duration calculus and RSL for program design;
- occam and c for the actual implementation and experiments.

Overall, our conclusion is that these levels are unavoidable. It is hard to imagine a single framework that encompasses all of the necessary details. Yet, there is room for improvement in linking the pieces of the puzzle.

Hybrid Systems engineering

A major improvement for the control engineering task would be use of a hybrid systems development platform like OMOLA or HyTech [10,11]. Such a platform would improve the confidence in the simulations used in estimating parameters of the concrete system. It would also give a precise specification of the lower levels of the design in the Process layer of our architecture. It would probably not be suitable for design of the Planning and Rule layers, because they manipulate complex data structures.

Hybrid Systems may become terribly complex if one tries to identify the global behaviour of a plant. The transition from viewing the robot as a single entity to a view of it as two independent links gave a much simpler model. In this particular case, the experiments showed only a slight decrease in performance, because the "disturbance" from the other component was absorbed in the mode switching. If there is greater interaction, one might consider communication between the controllers. Such communications corresponds to the planned switches in our architecture. With communication, one must be careful with an automata framework, because ad-hoc communication may lead either to time-lock or deadlock, or rather complex communication protocols. A marriage between hybrid automata and either IO-automata [22] or process algebra [43] may improve the chances of success.

Specification Languages

Let us for a moment assume that the robot system was designed using a hybrid process algebra to give the upper layers with a hybrid simulation tool to develop the concrete control. Would there then be any need for duration calculus? Could the reasoning not be done in the other frameworks? In principle, yes, as shown in [17] and [36]. However, requirements may look nicer and be easier to manipulate in duration calculus than expanded into explicit time dependent history variables. Needless to say, tool support will help to make the calculations easier. Recently, we have ported the verification assistant [39,38] to a new PVS platform and extended it with constructs for analysing real valued state variables.

At the low level of design where automata dominates, matured proof methodologies [9] are attractive, and there is some indication that the structural proof methodologies for timed transition systems may be reused to prove duration formulas in standard forms [18].

Other development issues

An issue which is often ignored in formal methods is the link from the design to the actual code. There seems to be quite some room for improvement. Low level designs could, it seems, without many problems be translated directly into a machine program. The most difficult part might be to accept standard treatment of composite data structures.

At this level it is also annoying that scheduling had to be checked with manual count of operations in the distributed control loop. There are working solutions in Ada95 [3], but it is not a widespread language in control applications.

The design and development of a hybrid system involves both control engineers and programmers. We have observed the differences in culture during the project, and it might be worthwhile for the two groups to learn a bit more about each others frameworks. However, this is a question of engineering education, and a prerequisite is that the common framework is crystallized from the many research projects and written up as textbooks and in tools. This may yet be a while, in the meantime it may be most fruitful to experiment with a view to linking up the components of the framework.

Acknowledgements We thank Zhiming Liu for his comments that clarified some points.

References

1. T. O. Andersen, F. Conrad, A. P. Ravn, T. J. Eriksen, and M. Holdgaard. Mode-switching in hydraulic actuator systems - an experiment. In *Proceedings of Eigth Bath International Fluid Power Workshop*. Research Studies Press, 1995. Bath, United Kingdom, September 1995.
2. Michael S. Branicky, Vivek S. Borkar, and Sanjoy K. Mitter. A unified framework for hybrid control. In *Proceedings of the 33rd Conference on Decision and Control. Lake Buena Vista, FL*, 1994.
3. A. Burns and A. Wellings. Advanced fixed priority scheduling. In M. Joseph, editor, *Real-Time Systems: Specification, Verification and and Analysis*, Prentice-Hall Internaltional series in computer science, pages 32–65. Prentice-Hall, 1996.
4. H. Dierks. The production cell: A verified real-time system. In B. Jonsson and J. Parrow, editors, *FTRTFTS'96*, volume 1135 of *LNCS*, pages 208–227. Springer-Verlag, 1996.
5. M. Engel, M. Kubica, J. Madey, D. L. Parnas, A. P. Ravn, and A. J. van Schouwen. A formal approach to computer systems requirements documentation. In R. L. Grossman, A. Nerode, A. P. Ravn, and H. Rischel, editors, *Hybrid Systems*, volume 736 of *LNCS*, pages 452–474, 1993.
6. T. J. Eriksen, S. Heilmann, M. Holdgaard, and A. P. Ravn. Hybrid systems: A real-time interface to control engineering. In *Proceedings of 8th Euromicro Workshop on Real-Time Systems*, pages 114–120. IEEE Computer Society Press, 1996.
7. The RAISE Language Group. *The RAISE Specification Language*. The BCS Practitioner Series, Prentice-Hall, 1992.
8. Jifeng He, C. A. R. Hoare, M. Fränzle, M. Müller-Olm, E-R. Olderog, M. Schenke, M. R. Hansen, A. P. Ravn, and H. Rischel. Provably correct systems. In H. Langmaack, W.-P. de Roever, and Jan Vytopil, editors, *Formal Techniques in Real-Time and Fault-Tolerant Systems*, volume 863 of *LNCS*, pages 288–335. Springer-Verlag, 1994.
9. T. Henzinger, Z. Manna, and A. Pnueli. Temporal proof methodologies for timed transition systems. *Information and Computation*, 112(2):273–337, 1994.
10. T. A. Henzinger and P.-H. Ho. HyTECH: The cornell hybrid technology tool. In P. Antsaklis, W. Kohn, A. Nerode, and S. Sastry, editors, *Hybrid Systems II*, volume 999 of *LNCS*, pages 265–293, 1995.
11. T. A. Henzinger and H. Wong-Toi. Linear phase-portrait approximations for non-linear hybrid systems. In R. Alur, T. A. Henzinger, and E. D. Sontag, editors, *Hybrid Systems III*, volume 1066 of *LNCS*, pages 377–388, 1996.
12. C. A. R. Hoare, He, Jifeng, and J. W. Sanders. Specification in data refinement. *Inf. Proc. Letters*, 25:71–76, 1987.

13. E. J. Davison (Ed.) IFAC Theory Committee. Benchmark problems for control system design. Technical report, International Federation of Automatic Control, May 1990.

14. R. Inal. Modular specification of real-time systems. In *Proceedings of 1994 Euromicro Workshop on Real-Time Systems*. IEEE Computer Society Press, 1994.

15. Y. Kesten, Z. Manna, and A. Pnueli. Verifying clocked transition systems. In R. Alur, T. A. Henzinger, and E. D. Sontag, editors, *Hybrid Systems III*, volume 1066 of *LNCS*, pages 13–40, 1996.

16. R. Koymans. Specifying real-time properties with metric temporal logic. *Real-Time Systems*, 2(4):255–299, November 1990.

17. L. Lamport. Hybrid systems in TLA$^+$. In R. L. Grossman, A. Nerode, A. P. Ravn, and H. Rischel, editors, *Hybrid Systems*, volume 736 of *LNCS*, pages 77–102, 1993.

18. Z. Liu, A. P. Ravn, and X. Li. Duration properties of timed transition systems. Technical Report 1997/12, Math. and Comp. Sc., Leicester University, GB, May 1997.

19. L. Ljung. *System Identification. Theory for the User*. Prentice-Hall Information and System Sciences Series. Prentice-Hall, 1987.

20. D. G. Luenberger. *Introduction to Dynamic Systems. Theory, Models & Applications*. Wiley, 1979.

21. N. Lynch. Modeling and verification of automated transit systems, using timed automata, invariants and simulations. In R. Alur, T. A. Henzinger, and E. D. Sontag, editors, *Hybrid Systems III*, volume 1066 of *LNCS*, pages 449–463, 1996.

22. N. Lynch, R. Segala, F. Vaandrager, and H. B. Weinberg. Hybrid i/o automata. In R. Alur, T. A. Henzinger, and E. D. Sontag, editors, *Hybrid Systems III*, volume 1066 of *LNCS*, pages 496–510, 1996.

23. Z. Manna and A. Pnueli. *The Temporal Logic of Reactive and Concurrent Systems*. Springer-Verlag, 1992.

24. B. Moszkowski. A temporal logic for multi-level reasoning about hardware. *IEEE Computer*, 18(2):10–19, 1985.

25. Simin Nadjm-Tehrani. *Reactive Systems in Physical Environments*. PhD thesis, Dept. Comp. and Inf. Science, Linköping University, Sweden, May 1994. Linköping Studies in Science and Technology, Dissertation no. 338.

26. Simin Nadjm-Tehrani and Jan-Erik Strömberg. Jas-95 lite: Modelling and formal analysis of dynamic properties. Technical Report LITH-IDA-R-96-41, Dept. Comp. and Inf. Science, Linköping University, Sweden, 1996.

27. E-R. Olderog, A. P. Ravn, and J. U. Skakkebæk. Refining system requirements to program specifications. In C. Heitmeyer and D. Mandrioli, editors, *Formal Methods in Real-Time Systems*, Trends in Software-Engineering, chapter 5, pages 107–134. Wiley, 1996.

28. A. Pnueli and E. Harel. Applications of temporal logic to the specification of real-time systems (extended abstract). In M. Joseph, editor, *Proceedings of a Symposium on Formal Techniques in Real-Time and Fault-Tolerant Systems*, volume 331 of *LNCS*, pages 84–98. Springer-Verlag, 1988.

29. A. P. Ravn. Design of embedded real-time computing systems. Technical Report ID-TR 1995-170, ID/DTU, Lyngby, Denmark, October 1995. dr. techn. dissertation.

30. A. P. Ravn and H. Rischel. Requirements capture for embedded real-time systems. In *Proceedings of IMACS-MCTS'91 Symposium on Modelling and Control of Technological Systems*, volume 2, pages 147–152. IMACS, 1991. Villeneuve d'Ascq, France, May 7-10.

31. A. P. Ravn, H. Rischel, M. Holdgaard, T. J. Eriksen, F. Conrad, and T. O. Andersen. Hybrid control of a robot - a case study. In P. Antsaklis, W. Cohn, A. Nerode, and S. Sastry, editors, *Hybrid Systems II*, volume 999 of *LNCS*, pages 391–404. Springer-Verlag, 1995.

32. A. P. Ravn, H. Rischel, and H. H. Løvengreen. A design method for embedded software systems. *BIT*, 28:427–438, 1988.

33. A.P. Ravn, H. Rischel, and K. M. Hansen. Specifying and verifying requirements of real-time systems. *IEEE Trans. Softw. Eng.*, 19(1):41–55, 1993.

34. H. Rischel, J. Cuellar, S. Mørk, A. P. Ravn, and I. Wildgruber. Development of safety-critical real-time systems. In M. Bartošek, J. Staudek, and J. Wiedermann, editors, *SOFSEM'95: Theory and Practice of Informatics*, volume 1012 of *LNCS*, pages 206–235. Springer-Verlag, 1995.

35. M. Schenke and A. P. Ravn. Refinement from a control problem to programs. In J. R. Abrial, E. Börger, and H. Langmaack, editors, *Formal Methods for Industrial Applications: Specifying and Programming the Steam Boiler Control*, volume 1165 of *LNCS*, pages 403–427. Springer-Verlag, 1996.

36. S. Schneider. Specification and verification in timed CSP. In M. Joseph, editor, *Real-Time Systems: Specification, Verification and and Analysis*, Prentice-Hall Internaltional series in computer science, pages 147–181. Prentice-Hall, 1996.

37. R. L. Schwartz, P. M. Melliar-Schmith, and F. H. Vogt. An interval logic for higher-level temporal reasoning. In *Proceedings of the 2nd. Annual ACM Symposium on Principles of Distributed Computing*, pages 173–186, 1983.

38. J. U. Skakkebæk. *A Verification Assistant for a Real-Time Logic*. PhD thesis, Dept. Comp. Science, Technical University of Denmark, November 1994. ID-TR 1994-150.

39. J. U. Skakkebæk and N. Shankar. Towards a duration calculus proof assistant in PVS. In H. Langmaack, W.-P. de Roever, and J. Vytopil, editors, *Formal Techniques in Real-Time and Fault-Tolerant Systems*, volume 863 of *LNCS*, pages 660–679. Springer-Verlag, 1994.

40. *The procurement of safety critical software in defence equipment, Part 1: Requirements*. Kentigern House, 65 Brown St., Glasgow G2 8EX, April 1991.

41. Y. Venema. A modal logic for chopping intervals. *J. Logic of Computation*, 1(4):453–476, 1991.

42. Chaochen Zhou, C. A. R. Hoare, and A. P. Ravn. A calculus of durations. *Information Proc. Letters*, 40(5), Dec. 1991.

43. Chaochen Zhou, Wang Ji, and A. P. Ravn. A formal description of hybrid systems. In R. Alur, T. Henzinger, and E. Sontag, editors, *Hybrid Systems III*, volume 1066 of *LNCS*, pages 511–530. Springer-Verlag, 1996.

44. Chaochen Zhou, A. P. Ravn, and M. R. Hansen. An extended duration calculus for hybrid real-time systems. In R. L. Grossman, A. Nerode, A. P. Ravn, and H. Rischel, editors, *Hybrid Systems*, volume 736 of *LNCS*, pages 36–59, 1993.

Formal Methods in the Design of a Storm Surge Barrier Control System

Pim Kars[*]

Tele-Informatics and Open Systems Group,
Department of Computer Science, University of Twente,
P.O. Box 217, 7500 AE Enschede, The Netherlands.
kars@cs.utwente.nl

Abstract. The BOS project concerns the design and implementation of a storm surge barrier control system. Formal methods are used to improve the quality of the design, providing a firm basis for the building and testing phases. Notably, the SPIN tool set (SPIN and XSPIN) is used to validate crucial parts of the design, in particular the communication interfaces with the outside world. Furthermore, PROMELA (the modelling language of SPIN) combined with Z is used to formally specify the design.

After an introduction to the BOS project in section 1, we discuss the "why, what and how" of the use of formal methods in the project in section 2. Section 3 outlines the experience in the areas of validation, specification and testing. Finally we present some conclusions in section 4. Our emphasis will lie more on the practical issues of this endeavour; some technicalities are discussed in the appendices.

1 The BOS Project

After the last major storm flood of the low, western part of the Netherlands in 1953, a project was launched by the Dutch Ministery of Public Works to prevent such disasters from happening in the future. The keystone of this 40-year project is the construction of a movable storm surge barrier near the Hook of Holland in the Nieuwe Waterweg, the canal connecting the harbour of Rotterdam to the North Sea. In other cases in this project a fixed barrier was installed as a protection against the devastating forces of the sea. But in this case the barrier has to be movable, because the Nieuwe Waterweg is the vital link between Rotterdam harbour and the sea.

The construction of the barrier is unique. It consists of two hollow semi-circular steel walls. Each wall is connected to a ball joint by a steel arm the size of an Eiffel tower. The ball joints themselves rest in sockets supported by a large slab of concrete covered with tons of sand.

---

[*] Current affiliation: Utopics BV, Kastanjelaan 4, NL-3833 AN, Leusden, The Netherlands. PKars@utopics.nl.

When opened, the walls of the barrier rest in dry-docks at both sides of the canal. Closing the barrier means pumping water into the dry-docks, opening the doors of the dry-docks, moving the floating walls to the centre of the canal, and sinking them to the bottom of the canal by pumping water into them. In this position it closes off most of the water coming from the sea. Opening the barrier is just the reverse of this procedure.

In closed position the barrier is able to sustain the pressures of the sea; that is what it is built for in the first place. Too much pressure from the land side, however, could result in lifting the whole construction from its sockets. Since the Nieuwe Waterweg is one of the outlets of the Rhine, leaving the barrier in a closed position too long may be hazardous to its health. This makes the operation of the barrier quite an intricate affair.

The barrier will operate fully automatically because human intervention was deemed too error prone. BOS, an acronym for "Beslis- en Ondersteunend Systeem" (Decision and Support System), is the central system that decides when and how the barrier has to move, and that controls its movements. In order to perform these tasks, the BOS system collects measurements of water levels, tidal information, weather data and predictions from several sensors and networks. Furthermore, it includes a software module (provided by a third party) that predicts water levels based on the various measurements.

BOS Functionality. Figure 1 shows a simplified picture of the software architecture of the BOS system. The BOS system continuously gathers data from the various sources and predicts the water level in the near future at a few locations. Should the predicted water level be too high, it starts the procedure to close the barrier by sending commands to BESW, the system that operates the valves, pumps and motors of the barrier. As soon as the circumstances are favourable again, it reverts this procedure and opens the barrier. The basic cycles are: water levels are measured every 10 seconds, and the predictor is run every 10 minutes. The barrier is expected to close once every 5–10 years and its lifetime is 100 years.

At the heart of BOS is a state machine that embodies the precise procedure to follow. This procedure is not fixed, however, but programmable in order to be flexible. A special language called *script language* has been designed to encode the procedure, called a *script*. This script is interpreted by the script interpreter.

Reliability. The main incentive to apply formal methods in the BOS project was the very high reliability requirements the BOS system has to satisfy. These reliability requirements are expressed as failure rates of undesirable events. For example, the probability of failure to close the barrier when called for should be less than $3 * 10^{-4}$. The probability of failure to open the barrier in time after a closure should be less than $5 * 10^{-5}$. Not closing in time could result in the flooding of cities like Rotterdam. As explained above, if the barrier is not opened in time after a closure, it could be severely damaged since its design only caters for sustaining pressure from the sea side. Even if the barrier stays in place, the continuous inflow of water from the Rhine might cause flooding from the land

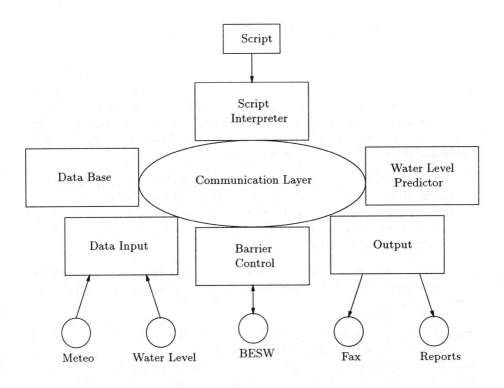

Fig. 1. Software architecture of the BOS system.

side. Moreover, while the barrier is closed, the important harbour of Rotterdam is cut off from the North Sea, leading to great economic loss.

Computer Management Group (CMG) — a company providing a wide range of information technology services with branches in the United Kingdom, The Netherlands and Germany — was awarded the contract from the Ministery of Public Works to build BOS. It was clear from the outset to project management at CMG that extra measures were needed in this project given the high reliability requirements. Reliability at the hardware level is covered by using a fault-tolerant Stratus system. However, it is infeasible to quantify the reliability of software with such precision [1]. The IEC 65A draft standard for highly reliable systems (and its successor, the IEC 1508 standard) strongly recommends the use of formal methods. Therefore, CMG set up a close collaboration with the Formal Methods group at the University of Twente to transfer knowledge and provide consultancy on the application of formal methods to system design. (As an aside, the use of "we" in this paper generally includes both the BOS project team at CMG and the Formal Methods group at the University of Twente.)

2 Formal Methods in the BOS Project

2.1 Formal Methods

Formal methods are methods that allow to unambiguously describe the behaviour of systems (specification) and to reason about and analyse properties of the behaviour (verification/validation). They are used to improve the quality of a system, ideally showing their correctness beyond doubt. Other potential benefits of the use of formal methods include:

- a formal specification of the design eliminates the ambiguity of informal specifications or pseudo-code, which is a common source of errors.
- the process of formalizing a design in itself already requires a more careful analysis than usually done at this stage and reveals many errors or prevents them from being introduced.

The earlier formal methods are used in a project, the larger the benefits will be, since errors can be detected earlier and hence do not propagate to a point where they are costlier to repair.

The field of formal methods has grown in the past decade to the extent that languages and tools have become available which allow to specify various kinds of systems and check for various properties. However, in practice it is still not feasible to completely formally specify a large system, fully validate it, and use for example refinement techniques to get to an implementation within a short time span. Therefore careful consideration should be given to the purpose and use of formal methods in a project.

2.2 Approach

We started with explaining to the people at CMG what formal methods are, what can be expected of them and, more importantly, what cannot be expected, i.e. temper their expectations.

Next we made an inventory of opportunities to use formal methods in the project, which included:

1. Formalization of the functional specification, the main input document to the project. In about 700 pages it describes the required behaviour in terms of
   - Data Flow Diagrams (DFDs), a hierarchical graph of functions, buffers and stores, linked by streams;
   - informal descriptions of the (normal and error) behaviour of each function;
   - a Data Dictionary (DD) describing data elements and composite data.
2. Formal specification of the design.
3. Validation of the design against the specification.
4. Test derivation from the specification, or manual test specification and validation against the specification.

5. Code generation from the specification or code validation.

6. Formalization of the script language semantics.

7. Compiler/interpreter correctness.

8. Script validation.

In any case it was clear that any formal activity would presume some sort of formal specification; be it of the functional specification or the design.

Ideally, we would have liked to do all of the above. But, as mentioned above, this is not feasible in practice.

The options are constrained by many factors such as

- our own background: we had knowledge of and experience with several methods and tools such as LOTOS, CSP, Z, SPIN, CWB, ...
- man power: since our own involvement is limited we needed the involvement of the whole BOS project team (to some degree). This pertains particularly to the design: the people at CMG have the skills to design and build the system; we add the formal methods. This may be contrasted with e.g. an approach where validation is performed off-line by specialists.
- knowledge within the project team: there was no prior experience with formal methods, hence a learning curve has to be taken into account.
- time: the project has a fixed deadline.
- tool support: preferably the methods selected should be supported by adequate software tools. There is an obvious trade-off here between expressivity of a specification language and the availability of tools; in general, the more expressive a language is, the more undecidable interesting properties will be.
- money: time is money, tools cost money. The project was accepted on a fixed price basis, which incidentally was only a small fraction of the cost of the "concrete and iron" part of the barrier.
- risk reducement: introducing too many new techniques into a project can be a risky affair.

Given these constraints, choices had to be made. As part of an effort to integrate formal methods within CMG's design trajectory, the decision was made to concentrate on two tasks:

1. Validation of crucial parts of the design to get more confidence in the correctness of the mechanisms chosen in the design. In particular, this included the communication interfaces with the outside world: their functional specification was not above suspicion and problems may be expected when part of an interface cannot be controlled.

2. Formal specification of the design to get an unambiguous and complete interface to both the building and testing phases. Since the functional specification contained many ambiguities, especially related to data handling, these would have to be resolved.

2.3 Choice of Methods

The methods selected were PROMELA/SPIN [7] and Z [14]. See appendix A for a short description of these methods.

The choice to use PROMELA/SPIN for validation was a natural choice: we already had experience using SPIN, it is able to handle large state spaces, and the language and tool are relatively easy to learn and use. The last factor was particularly important since the desire to integrate formal methods meant that engineers at CMG would do most of the actual work. The choice of a specification language for the design was harder. Z is very expressive as far as the definition of data and operations on data is concerned, but it lacks features to specify control. The solution was to use two languages: PROMELA (which already had to be learnt for the validation) for the control part and Z, embedded in PROMELA, for the data part. This embedding of Z into PROMELA is briefly described in appendix B.

2.4 Integration

Formal methods are only one means to enhance the quality of the system. As such they should be integrated with other measures. Starting from the functional specification, the strategy to get to an implementation was set up roughly as follows:

1. Basic design: decomposition of the functionality into subsystems,
2. Function Failure Analysis to determine critical functionality,
3. Detailed design per subsystem:
   - specification in Z and PROMELA
   - validation of critical parts with SPIN
   - selective prototyping
   - review of the design
4. Implementation in C++ and extensive testing by separate teams.

The detailed design is described in a set of documents, one per subsystem, containing

- Dutch text for descriptions and explanations,
- PROMELA for specifying I/O and control structure,
- Z for specifying data and operations on data, and
- Data Flow Diagrams for documenting the overall structure.

The case tool SDW [3] is used to link the elements in order to maintain consistency and the relation to the functional specification on which the design is based. One of the reasons to choose SDW as case tool is that it was also used for the functional specification.

Also measures were taken to reduce the complexity of the design, e.g. functionality common to the various interfaces was extracted and put into a separate subsystem, giving a clearer separation of concerns and a simpler design. Finally, several measures were taken related to good software engineering practice, such as the use of C++ coding rules that use only safe language constructs [6].

3 Experience

3.1 Validation

SPIN was used to validate most of the communication interfaces with the outside world and parts of the internal process control layer. Our experience with SPIN and PROMELA was positive:

- SPIN/PROMELA is very easy to learn and use, even for an engineer with no previous exposure to formal methods. This was important since most of the actual work was done by engineers of CMG. Most of the language elements are simple and intuitive (the only language construct that caused some confusion is the nondeterministic choice). There is a fine tutorial, and many of the validation requirements can be expressed in a simple way without having to learn temporal logic.
- SPIN was useful to expose errors in the proposed communication interfaces and in getting confidence in the final design.
- Message Sequence Charts were a valuable aid, not only to trace the sources of errors, but also in convincing management of problems in the protocols and the need to repair them.

It is interesting to note that in one case, the validation of the crucial interface between BOS and BESW (the system that actually operates the barrier), most errors were found during formalization, i.e. specification of the model in PROMELA, not during the validation itself. This confirms the idea that the analysis required for formalization can be extremely useful in itself.

Some of the errors found were quite severe. One of them was a race condition between a command from BOS to stop an operation of the barrier and a signal from the barrier indicating that it completed part of the operation. This resulted in a live-lock where both systems were waiting for each other. This interface has been redesigned and is currently being revalidated at the University of Twente.

One of the things that PROMELA/SPIN misses is the ability to model and validate *timed* systems. This would have been particularly useful in the validation of the BOS-BESW interface.

3.2 Specification

Before embarking on the specification of the design, a few of the more data intensive functions were chosen as a pilot for formal specification. After getting experience in this way, the BOS project team was given a short course in Z, leaving out those constructs that were not expected to be needed. Besides the communication interfaces, most parts of the design were subsequently specified using the combination of PROMELA and Z. Z schemas are used to model data (in particular the state of a subsystem), and also to specify operations on the state. Many practical problems had to be solved such as setting up a naming convention and finding "Z idioms" to concisely express frequently occurring constructs e.g. the modelling of data base access.

The use of Z turned out to be less simple than expected. On the positive side, its expressiveness allowed to specify everything that was needed. Ambiguities that were present in the functional specification have been detected and resolved the design. The Z style that is used is largely constructive and deterministic, with a clear split between pre- and postconditions. Completeness (in the sense that all cases have been covered) can be checked by calculating the preconditions of operations. This was done manually, but tool support would have been welcome. Z type checkers, notably ZTC [9] and *f*UZZ [15], were very useful to check the static consistency of the Z parts of the specification.

On the negative side, some "simple" things cannot be expressed clearly and concisely, e.g. specifying an operation that changes one state component while leaving the other components unchanged (an instance of the "frame problem"). There is only tool support for type checking and proof assistance (the latter was not used); but not for test derivation, precondition expansion, animation/simulation (at least not for the full language).

Learning to use Z, especially to write specifications, took more time than expected. Fortunately the number of people writing specfications, i.e. the designers, was much less than the number of people reading the specifications, i.e. the implementers and testers, and reading Z is obviously simpler than writing Z.

3.3 Testing

The real pay-off of investing in the formal specification of the design came at the testing phase [4]. Functional testing was done by (manually) deriving test cases from the specifications and instrumenting the code under test (using a tool) to measure the coverage. The procedure to derive test cases for a particular operation is to look at the Promela part for the right stimuli (inputs), stepping through all the disjuncts ("cases") of the Z part and finding appropriate data values to exercise the particular disjunct. It turned out that this procedure provided an excellent coverage and, moreover, hardly any severe errors were found. On this basis, test planning was also greatly simplified. Furthermore, due to their preciseness the specifications were an ideal reference point to settle disputes between implementers and testers.

4 Conclusions

The use of formal methods has undoubtedly improved the design of the BOS system. It is hard to substantiate this claim, since we cannot compare the quality of the current design to what the result would have been without using formal methods. However, one of the signs of succes is that the testing phase turned out to be easier and it revealed less errors than "usual" in this kind of project. CMG is sufficiently impressed by the experience with formal methods that it has extended our collaboration and started applying formal methods in other projects. The other main accomplishments of the use of formal methods can be summarized as:

- early fault detection in external interfaces,
- more careful analysis during the design stage, preventing errors from being introduced,
- better, i.e. less ambiguous and more complete, specification of the design, and
- the formal specification served as a good basis for the building and testing phase.

Among the obstacles encountered, we should mention that a lot of work went into learning the new languages and setting up the structure, style, idiom, etc. for the design. As a result the design phase took longer than usual, and even though project management was prepared that this would happen, it was sometimes difficult to suppress the urge to start writing instead of thinking. As explained, this problem was balanced by the testing phase.

Looking back at the inventory of opportunities for formal methods in the project in section 2.2, we can identify some items where more work needs to be done before they can be accomplished.

- Support for test derivation.
  Test derivation algorithms, in particular for (non-deterministic) finite-state machines or labelled transition systems, could be used to derive tests from PROMELA models. Currently work is in progress at the University of Twente to implement an algorithm for test derivation adapted to PROMELA [16]. To support fast random testing, derivation of so-called test oracles from Z specifications might be used. Some work in this area is reported in [12]. The fact that the Z specifications of BOS are largely constructive and deterministic should make it easier to apply the results of these developments.
- Support for getting from design to code.
  Code generation from PROMELA might be useful here. Some work has been done in this area, see for instance [11]. Code generation from Z specifications is hard in general. Note that preconditions of Z schemas can be used as assertions in the code to check input data in data operations.

Finally, validation of the script is of utmost importance since that is where the real decisions are taken. Translation of a script to PROMELA seems feasible, making it amenable to validation. One of the problems here is modelling the environment of the script interpreter, which is basically the whole BOS system.

For more information the reader is referred to [10, 17]. The Ministery of Public Works provides some information on the project including pictures at http://www.minvenw.nl/rws/dzh/svk.

Acknowledgements. The work reported here was carried out in collaboration with the BOS project team at CMG's Advanced Technology Division in The Hague, in particular the chief designer Klaas Wijbrans and Eric Burgers, and the other members of the "BOS team" at the University of Twente: Ed Brinksma, Wil Janssen and Job Zwiers. Jan Tretmans did a great job scrutinizing a draft version of this paper.

A Features of Selected Formal Methods

A.1 Promela and Spin

SPIN [7] is a tool for simulation and validation of models described in PROMELA, a language loosely based on Dijkstra's guarded command language and Hoare's CSP('78). A PROMELA model is a (dynamic) collection of processes communicating through channels and global variables; this allows the modelling of both shared memory systems and message-passing systems. The model is asynchronous/interleaved, i.e. at every step one process executes a statement that is enabled in the current state.

Simulation comes in three flavours: random, interactive and guided. Interactive simulation of a model is similar to what a debugger of an implementation language does and for similar reasons: to gain confidence that the model correctly describes what was intended. In interactive simulation, the user steps through enabled actions of the model and is offered a choice when more than one action is enabled. Random simulation is similar to interactive simulation, but at every point where more than one action is enabled, one of them is chosen randomly. In guided simulation the choises are taken from a trace that has been recorded, typically from a violation detected during validation.

Validation means that the model is explored to detect the violation of properties. Validation can be done at several levels. At the simplest level, SPIN runs through the full state space and reports deadlock states, assertion violations and unreached code. Non-progress cycles can be detected if the user indicates in the model which states are considered to be progress states. At a more advanced level, general properties of the model, expressed as linear-time temporal formulae, can be checked. Errors are reported by saving a trace of the actions leading to a violating state/cycle. This trace can be replayed by guided simulation.

XSPIN is a user interface on top of SPIN that allows easy control of all of SPIN's features. During simulation, the behaviour and current state of the system can be displayed in various ways, among which as Message Sequence Charts.

To be able to validate models with large state spaces, SPIN uses a number of techniques: compression of the state vector, partial order reduction (based on the fact that some paths through the state space are equivalent and therefore only one of them needs to be checked), and bit state hashing. Bit state hashing is a technique that —from a user point of view— allows one to validate very large state spaces, without a guarantee that all states have been explored, but usually with a good coverage [8].

A.2 Z

Z [14] is based on a typed version of first-order logic with equality. On top of this Z uses so-called schemas for structuring. A schema is a set of named components (cf. records in Pascal or structs in C) together with a predicate that restricts the allowed values of the components. Schemas are neatly integrated in the logical language; there are specialized operators on schemas and reuse of schemas is encouraged.

The "established strategy" [2] of using Z to specify the behaviour of systems is to model the state of the system by a schema; the components are just the state components and the predicate is an invariant of the state. Operations on the state are also modelled by schemas: the components of an operation schema are the state components before and after the operation, inputs and outputs; the predicate describes/prescribes the relation between these four items. The state components after the operation are indicated by a prime: ′. A feature notably lacking in this strategy is "control": there is no indication which operation is executed when.

Z specifications should always be accompanied by "informal" explanations to aid the human reader in interpreting them. The benefit of this approach is that it provides redundancy: the informal and formal descriptions can be checked against each other, reducing the risk of small errors with large semantic consequences such as inadvertently leaving out a prime.

Z can be used at various levels:

1. It can be used to specify the behaviour of a system.
2. As a logical language, it allows to derive and check properties of the system.
3. There is a theory of refinement to support the transition from specification to implementation.

In the BOS project emphasis is on the first use. An interesting variant of the second use is that a formal specification may be manipulated using the laws of logic, resulting in a simpler specification. This simpler specification may then be used to rephrase the informal specification in a clearer and more concise way. There were a few occassions in the BOS project where such a simplification was applied successfully.

B Promela + Z

We assume some basic familiarity with Promela and in particular Z.

Embedding Z into Promela. Conceptually, the embedding of Z into PROMELA may be described as

- All Z data types occurring in the specification are added to the PROMELA data types.
- Z schemas denoting operations are considered to be *atomic* PROMELA operations. Such an operation is enabled when its precondition holds.
- Z state schemas are considered to be declared as local variables within the corresponding PROMELA process declaration.

A Promela + Z Example. We present a simplified example of the specification of a function in Promela + Z to give an impression of what the resulting structure of the design looks like. The function F reads data from a stream S; every 10 seconds it stores the timestamped mean of the values received in the buffer B. The relevant part of the DFD in the functional specification is shown in Fig. 2.

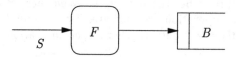

Fig. 2. Functional specification of F.

'We will assume that in the design phase F is split into two operations:

- $FGet$ to read the data values from S and store them in the data store $FState$, and
- $FStore$ the stores the mean in buffer B and clears $FState$.

The DFD of F in the design is shown in Fig. 3.

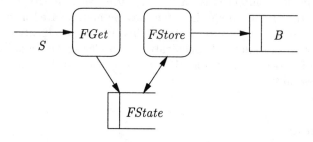

Fig. 3. Design of F.

The PROMELA part of the specification becomes:

```
proctype F (chan S)
{
  InitFState ;
  do
  :: S ? d -> FGet
  :: FStore
  od
}
```

(To keep things simple, we have used the convention to leave out the declarations of *FState* and *d* and the parameters of *FGet* and *FStore*; they can be deduced from the context.)

This specifies a process *F* that behaves as follows:

- *F* initializes *FState*, then loops and nondeterministically chooses between *FGet* and *FStore* whenever one of them is enabled.
- *FGet* is enabled when data arrives on stream *S*, i.e. it is data-triggered.
- *FStore* is enabled when its precondition holds (see below), it is time-triggered.

The relevant part of the Data Dictionary in Z is shown in Fig. 4. Note the way in which the buffer *B* is specified. The contents of a record in *B* are specifed in an auxiliary schema *DB*. The main definition is the schema *SB*; operations on *B* include this schema. It defines *B* as a partial function from a key of type *Time* to the full contents of a record, i.e. including the key. The predicate in *SB* specifies that the key is indeed the first component of *DB*. The advantage of this approach is that all components of a record can be accessed in a uniform way.

Data element types:

$$Tdata == \ldots$$
$$Time == \mathbb{N}$$

Streams:

$$S == Tdata$$

Buffers:

```
┌─ FState ──────────────────────────────────────────────
│  data : Tdata
│
└───────────────────────────────────────────────────────
```

```
┌─ DB ──────────────────────────────────────────────────
│  time : Time
│  data : Tdata
│
└───────────────────────────────────────────────────────
```

```
┌─ SB ──────────────────────────────────────────────────
│  B : Time ⇸ DB
├───────────────────────────────────────────────────────
│  ∀ key : dom B • key = (B key).time
└───────────────────────────────────────────────────────
```

Fig. 4. Data dictionary in Z.

The operations defined in Z are shown in Fig. 5. Note that *FStore* uses an input *now?* of type *Time*, the time trigger, and it has a constraint on this time as a precondition.

$$\begin{array}{l}\_\mathit{InitFState}_____ \\ \mathit{FState}' \\ \Xi\, SB \\ \hline \dots data\ initialization \dots \end{array}$$

$$\begin{array}{l}\_\mathit{FGet}_____ \\ d?:S \\ \Delta\mathit{FState} \\ \Xi\, SB \\ \hline \dots update\ of\ data\dots \end{array}$$

$$\begin{array}{l}\_\mathit{FStore}_____ \\ now?:Time \\ \Delta\mathit{FState} \\ \Delta SB \\ \hline now?\ mod\ 10=0 \\ \dots update\ of\ SB\dots \\ \dots clear\ data\dots \end{array}$$

Fig. 5. Operations in Z.

References

1. Ricky W. Butler and George B. Finelli. The infeasibility of quantifying the reliability of life-critical real-time software. *IEEE Transactions on Software Engineering*, 19(1):3–12, 1993.
2. Rosalind Barden, Susan Stepney, and David Cooper. *Z in Practice*. Prentice Hall, 1994.
3. Cap Gemini, Utrecht, The Netherlands. *SDW — System Development Workbench*, 1993.
4. Wouter Geurts. Validation of the BOS system. In A. G. Engels and L. M. G. Feijs, editors, *Derde Landelijke Testdag*, Technische Universiteit Eindhoven, The Netherlands, 1997.
5. Jean-Charles Grégoire, Gerard J. Holzmann, and Doron A. Peled, editors. *The SPIN Verification System. Proc. of the Second Workshop on the SPIN Verification System*, volume 32 of *DIMACS Series in Discrete Mathematics and Theoretical Computer Science*. American Mathematical Society, 1997.
6. Les Hatton. *SAFER C: Developing Software for High-Integrity and Safety-Critical Systems*. McGraw-Hill, 1995.
7. Gerard J. Holzmann. *Design and Validation of Computer Protocols*. Prentice-Hall, 1991. See also: http://netlib.bell-labs.com/netlib/spin/whatispin.html.
8. Gerard J. Holzmann. An analysis of bitstate hashing. In P. Dembiński and

M. Sredniawa, editors, *Proc. IFIP/WG6.1 Symp. on Protocol Specification, Testing and Verification: PSTV'95*. Chapman and Hall, 1995.

9. Xiaoping Jia. *ZTC: A Type Checker for Z Notation — User's Guide*, 1995. Available from `ftp://ise.cs.depaul.edu`.

10. Pim Kars. The application of PROMELA and SPIN in the BOS project. In Grégoire et al. [5], pages 51–63.

11. Siegfried Löffler and Ahmed Serhrouchni. Creating implementations from PROMELA models. In Grégoire et al. [5], pages 91–100.

12. Erich Mikk. Compilation of Z specifications into C for automatic test result evaluation. In Jonathan P. Bowen and Michael G. Hinchey, editors, *ZUM'95*, pages 167–180, 1995. LNCS 967, Springer.

13. John Nicholls, editor. *Z Notation*, 1995. Version 1.1 of the Draft Z Standard. See: `http://www.comlab.ox.ac.uk/oucl/groups/zstandards/index.html`.

14. J. M. Spivey. *The Z Notation: A Reference Manual*. Prentice Hall, 2nd edition, 1992. See also: `http://www.comlab.ox.ac.uk/archive/z.html`.

15. Mike Spivey. *The ƒUZZ Manual*, 1995. Included in the ƒUZZ distribution.

16. Jan Tretmans. Test generation with inputs, outputs and repetitive quiescence. *Software—Concepts and Tools*, 17:103–120, 1996.

17. K. C. J. Wijbrans. Practical experiences with formal methods in the BOS project. In Rom Langerak, editor, *Proceedings of the Third Dutch Specification Day*, University of Twente, The Netherlands, 1996.

Statecharts in Use: Structured Analysis and Object-Orientation

Bruce Powel Douglass[1]

David Harel[2]

Mark Trakhtenbrot[3]

Abstract

We describe how statecharts are used to model the behavior of complex reactive systems. The paper is divided into two parts, according to the two main ways that have been suggested for modeling the structure of such systems: structured analysis (SA) and object-orientation (OO). It uses a cardiac pacemaker example for illustration.

1 Introduction

Computerized systems have been steadily increasing in complexity since their inception. Many of these systems operate autonomously or semi-autonomously and must react in complex ways to incoming events in extremely diverse environments. Frequently, these systems have significant impact on safety and so must be rigorously specified despite their elaborate behavior. Many complex systems are *reactive* [HPn], in that their primary behavioral focus is on monitoring incoming events and reacting appropriately.

Often these systems exhibit complex modal behavior as well, changing their behavior depending upon operational conditions. A patient ventilator in normal operation, for example, flows respiratory gas and shapes the breath envelope based on user-set respiration rate and tidal volume, monitors a patient's natural breaths, monitors inspired and expired gas concentrations, and alarms when the patient is at risk. The system must dynamically react and respond appropriately to the occurrence of expected and unexpected events including patient pathologies, breathing circuit disconnects, and equipment faults. Ventilators also often have service, demonstration or training modes in which they simulate incoming events and simulate resulting actions.

Taken as a whole, the entire behavioral space for even such a relatively simple system is extremely complex yet has high requirements for both reliability and safety. In order to manage systems of this and higher-level complexity, the designer must make a number of simplifying assumptions about the system's environment and behavior. Finite state models are a common and effective means for managing the complexity of such reactive systems.

Finite state models assume that the system may be approximated as existing in an operational condition, called a *state,* for some period of time. While in a particular state, the system behaves in the same fashion in terms of the events it accepts and the actions it performs. Events can cause the system to change to another state by triggering a transition. As a result of taking a transition, entering a state, or leaving a state, a set of *actions* can be executed. Both transitions and actions are assumed to take an insignificant amount of time so that the system spends all of its time in states.

These simplifying assumptions make complex reactive systems much more approachable because it is easier to make rigorous statements about the behavior of these idealized models. If the systems are implemented in a manner that approximates these models, these conclusions are transferable to their physical implementation.

---

[1] i-Logix inc., Andover, MA; bpd@ilogix.com
[2] The Weizmann Institute, Rehovot, Israel, and i-Logix inc.; harel@wisdom.weizmann.ac.il
[3] i-Logix Israel Ltd., Rehovot, Israel; mark@ilogix.co.il

While finite state models have proven to be enormously successful, their application to increasingly complex systems has highlighted their limitations. Most notable is the well-documented problem of state explosion. Traditional state models have no notion of decomposition of states into hierarchies so that all states are considered at the same level of abstraction and all exist within the same scope. Traditional state models have no ability to break down the complete set of states into independent components, unless these are a reflection of the physical components in the final implementation. Often, then, one must model the system by enumerating the entire state space.

Statecharts were proposed in [H1] as a means for describing "raw" reactive behavior, in a way that is supposed to overcome these drawbacks. In the 15 years since their inception, statecharts have progressively increased in popularity. They have been used successfully in many demanding real-time environments and have been the subject of considerable research. One of the most interesting issues around them involves embedding statechart descriptions of behavior into a model that captures system structure. The two the main approaches to high-level modeling of structure have been *structured analysis* (SA) and *object-orientation* (OO). The two are about a decade apart in initial conception and evolution.

SA started out in the late 1970's by DeMarco, Yourdon and others (see, e.g.,[De]), and is based on "lifting" classical procedural programming concepts up to the modeling level. The result calls for modeling system structure by functional decomposition and flow of information, depicted by data-flow diagrams. As to system behavior, the early and mid 1980's saw several methodology teams (such as Ward/Mellor [WM], Hatley/Pirbhai [HPi] and the STATEMATE team from i-Logix [H+]) making detailed recommendations, which enriched the basic SA model with means for capturing behavior based on state diagrams (in the case of [WM, HPi]) or the richer language of statecharts (in the case of [H+]).

OO modeling started in the late 1980's, and in a way its history is very similar. The basic idea for system structure was to "lift" concepts from object-oriented programming up to the modeling level. Thus, the basic structural model for objects in Booch's method [B], in OMT [R+] or ROOM [SGW], and in the recent unified modeling language UML [UML], deals with classes and instances, relationships and roles, operations and events, and aggregation and inheritance. Visuality is achieved by object models that are an enriched form of entity-relationship diagrams, and behavior is described using statecharts.

In this paper we first give a brief description of basic statecharts, detached from any kind of structural embedding, and we then describe the way statecharts have been adapted to fit into the SA and OO paradigms. For the first of these we follow the work on the languages of STATEMATE in [H+], more fully described in [HPo], and for the second we follow the executable object modeling (XOM) work of [HG], which has become the heart of the UML language set [UML]. The two approaches have been implemented in the STATEMATE and Rhapsody tools, respectively, available from i-Logix. We provide brief discussions of these tools too.

1.1 Basic Statecharts

Statecharts are a visual formalism that describes reactive behavior. The nature of the entity whose behavior is thus described differs depending on the approach taken for system decomposition. In structured analysis (SA) methods, systems are decomposed into functional subunits using data flow diagrams, or what we call *activity-charts*. These subunits are called *processes* or *activities*, and they are rather loosely mapped onto programmatic primitives of functions, procedures, and data stores (variables) so that the statechart ultimately represents the collaborative behavior of this group of programmatic subunits designed to meet the requirements of the process. In this way, the process serves as the applicable entity for statecharts in traditional functional decomposition.

The fundamental unit of decomposition in object-orientation (OO) is the *object*. An object, within the scope of this paper, is a cohesive collection of data and related operations (functions) that act on them. Objects always have crisp boundaries since they are an explicitly represented entity in object-oriented approaches. Objects are the unit to which statecharts apply using this manner of decomposition.

A *state* is often taken to mean a ontological condition that persists for some period of time, that is distinguishable from other such conditions by the events it accepts, the actions it performs, and the reachable set of subsequent states.

An *event* is often taken to mean an occurrence of some significance that occurs at a specific point in time. For example, turning a trim knob to the right might result in the event *KnobTurnRight*. Events may be due to an external occurrence, a condition becoming true, or the completion of an activity.

Events may cause a *transition* to occur. A transition is the changing of an entity's state. Transitions are typically labeled with the events that cause them, and may have associated lists of *actions*, which are operations or functions executed when the transition is taken.

These notions are applicable to traditional Mealy-Moore state models as well as to statecharts. However, as argued in [H1], traditional finite state models have trouble handling such reasonable statements as:

- "in all airborne states, when the yellow handle is pulled the seat will be ejected"
- "gearbox change of state is independent of braking system state"
- "when selection button is pressed, enter selected mode"
- "display mode consists of time display, date display, and stopwatch display"

The inability to parsimoniously and clearly represent such simple and useful descriptions was a motivating factor in the development of statecharts. In addition, traditional state models lack modularity and hierarchy, which leads to a host of problems. Further, lack of useful support for independent components leads to the phenomenon of state-space explosion, thus limiting the scalability of the approach. Statecharts were proposed as a solution to these limitations, and they may be thought of as an extension to traditional state models, including:

- OR decomposition of states into hierarchies of states
- AND decomposition of states into orthogonal components which (may) execute concurrently and independently.
- Inter-level state transitions that can originate from or lead to nested states on any level of the hierarchy.
- Event propagation and broadcasting for communication and synchronization of concurrent state behavior.
- Default and history entrances.
- Timing and delay constraints.

We describe some of these extensions in some detail below.

A statechart is a *higraph* (see [H2]) consisting of rounded rectilinear blobs representing states, linked together with transitions. A simple statechart is shown in Figure 1. The arrow emanating from the black dot signifies an initial or default state. The T connector indicates a termination of the entity.

Actions may be associated with transitions or states. Actions on transitions are specified in an action list, separated from the transition's trigger by a slash, as shown in Figure 1. The transition labeled with the event name α has two actions associated with it, $f(x)$ and $g(y,z)$. State actions may be executed either on entry into the state or upon exit from the state. Additionally, states may have *activities* associated with them in a *throughout* manner: These are actions that are executed as long as the state is active. For example, it is conceivable that a state named *Flowing_Gas* might have an entry action *OpenValve(aperture)*, an exit action *CloseValue*, and activities *FlowGas* and *MonitorFlow*. State *C* in the figure illustrates the syntax for inclusion of these features in the diagram. (However, it is not required that they be shown in the diagram; they can be represented within the entity's data dictionary entry if desired.) States may also have reactions, that is, pairs consisting of triggering events and actions that constitute responses, but which do not cause state transitions.

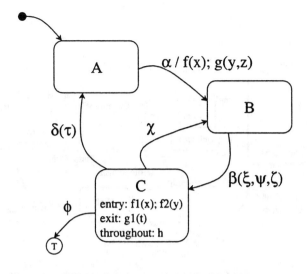

Figure 1: Simple Statechart

Additionally, transitions may have guarding conditions. A *guarding condition*, or more simply, a *guard*, is a boolean expression that evaluates to TRUE or FALSE. For a transition to be taken, the entity must be in the correct starting state, the corresponding event must occur, and the guard must evaluate to TRUE. Guards are written within square brackets following the event name.

A transition is fully specified by its source and target states, and its label that includes the *trigger* (composed of event name and guarding condition) and associated action list. All elements of the transition label are optional. All of the following are syntactically correct transition labels:

	No name: transition is always enabled
A	Event name only
A[g]	Trigger composed of event name and guard
A[g] / f1; f2	Event name, guard and action list

In order to support modularity and hierarchical decomposition, statecharts are based on higraphs rather than graphs, and hence they provide nesting of states. The enclosing state is called the *superstate* and the enclosed states are called *substates*.

Nesting of states is a vital facility within statecharts because it allows different levels of abstraction to be represented in a single diagram. A microwave heating element may be *On* or *Off*, and these states are arguably at the same level of abstraction. A heating element in the *On* state may be operating at intensities of *Low*, *Medium*, or *High*, which are nested substates at a different level of detail than *On* or *Off*. Within the *Medium* intensity substate, the system may rapidly transition from *Emitting* and *Quiescent* as a means to run at less than full intensity with the amount of time spent in the *Emitting* substate constituting the duty cycle of the emitter.

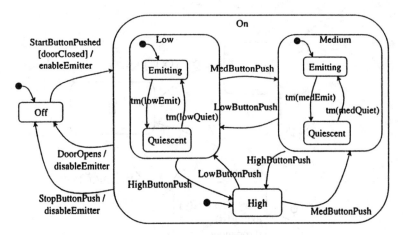

Figure 2: Microwave Oven

Figure 2 shows a simple statechart for a microwave oven. It is turned on by pressing the start button (note the [*doorClosed*] guard) and then the user can set the intensity by pressing an intensity button (*Low, Medium,* or *High*). Each level in the hierarchy has its own default state. A single transition to the *On* state labeled *StartButtonPush* is drawn, and because it is drawn to the *On* superstate, the default substate (*High*) is entered. Transitions can be drawn to directly enter a substate, in which case the default substate is ignored. Similarly the transition exiting the *On* superstate applies to all substates, however deeply they are nested. In a flat state model both the *StopButtonPush* and the *DoorOpens* transitions would have to be drawn from every On substate.

Figure 3 shows examples of default entries. It also shows a *history* entrance, depicted by the H connector. History captures an additional way to enter a group of states -- by the system's history in that group. The meaning is to enter the most recently visited substate of this group. This feature is very convenient for modeling interrupt handling. This connector indicates that when the enclosing superstate is exited and reentered, the last active substate will be entered. Note the default state within state *G*, which is the one entered in the absence of history, e.g., when *G* is first visited.

Statecharts provide a conditional connector (depicted by C), which allows the selection of one transition from many possible paths, based on a single event. The selection is made via the guarding conditions on the transition exiting the conditional connector. If none of the guards evaluate to TRUE, then the transition is not taken and the entity remains in its previous state. If more than one guard evaluates to TRUE then one of the relevant branches is taken non-deterministically.

Entities exhibiting state behavior are often composed of independent or almost independent components, each of which exhibits state behavior. Of course, one can construct a flat state model in which the set of states is the cross product of the sets of the components. A flight control computer, for example, might have 1000 states to control its behavior. If the system can independently be in autopilot mode or not, then this results in 2000 states. If the avionics system can also be in radar, GPS or inertial guidance modes, the number of states grows to 6000 states. This is relevant not only when the system can be decompsed into tangible components, but also when the state space can be naturally decomposed into conceptual components.

The statechart solution is to represent these by so-called *orthogonal components* of the statechart which are modeled by the Cartesian product notation of higraphs [H2]. In the above model, rather than having to draw 6000 states, it is sufficient to explicitly draw only 1005. The statechart notation for orthogonal components is to place them within an enclosing state scope and separate with dashed lines. Figure 4 illustrates the syntax. The enclosing superstate *Y* has two orthogonal components, labeled *A* and B, and each of the two components *A* and *B* has its own default state.

Superstate *Y* may be thought of as AND-state, because when an entity is in state *Y* it must be in exactly one state of component *A* **and** one state of component *B*. This is in contrast to a superstate such as On in Figure

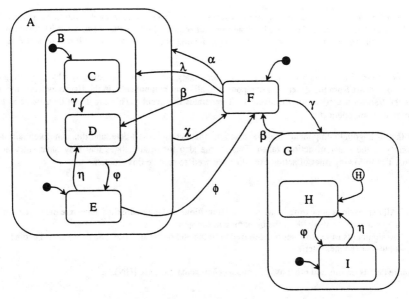

Figure 3: Default Substates

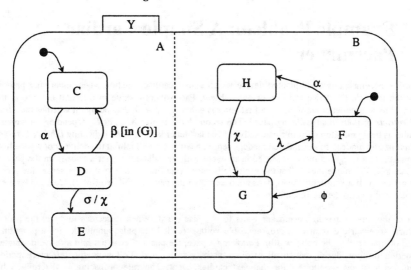

Figure 4: Orthogonal Components

2, which can be thought as an OR-state (more properly, exclusive-or). Being in *On* means being in exactly one of its substates: *Low, Medium,* or *High.*

OR-states and AND-states can appear at any level of the state hierarchy; in particular, an AND-state may appear within an orthogonal component of another AND-state. But typically, all states within a single component are OR-states.

The entity accepts events which may affect zero or more components. For example, both components in Figure 4 accept event α, which may or may not cause a transition to be taken in each component, depending on its current state.

Orthogonal components can communicate in a several ways. The first is through conditional guards. Such a guard is shown in Figure 4. The *in*( ) boolean operator requires that another component be currently in that state. In the figure, the transition caused by event β in component *A* is taken only if component *B* is in state *G*.

Another means to pass synchronization information among orthogonal components is by generating events that are broadcast from the generating component to all other components. In the figure, when component *A* takes the transition associated with event σ, it generates the event χ.This event can then be accepted and acted on by component *B*.

Note that orthogonal components may have actions that act on shared data, and this can potentially lead to ambiguity in the order of actions taken. This is true also for nested states that may have entry and exit actions. The following rules of action execution are used to resolve this problem:

- All expressions appearing in all executed transitions and entered/exited states are evaluated with the data values available at the beginning of the step;
- Assignments of new values are deferred until the end of the step (i.e., the new values become inputs for the next step).

For more details on this and other aspects of statechart semantics, see [HN].

2   Example Problem: A Simple Cardiac Pacemaker

A cardiac pacemaker is an implanted device which assists cardiac function when underlying pathologies make the intrinsic heart rate too low or even absent. Pacemakers operate in different behavioral modes, indicated by a three-letter acronym. The first letter is either *A*, *V*, or *D*, depending on whether the *Atrium* or the *Ventricle* or both (dual) is being paced. The second letter is also *A*, *V*, or *D*, depending on which heart chamber is being monitored for intrinsic activity. The last letter is *I*, *T*, or *D*, indicating *Inhibited, Triggered,* or *Dual* pacing modes. In an inhibited mode, a sensed heart event will inhibit the delivery of a pace from the pacemaker. In a triggered mode, a sensed heart event will immediately trigger a pace from the pacemaker. For example, *VVI* mode means that the ventricle is paced (the first *V*) if a ventricular sense (the second *V*) does not occur. If a ventricular sense does not occur, then the pace is inhibited (the *I*). Dual modes are more complex and will not be discussed here.

Most of the time, a pacing pacemaker waits for a sense event. When it decides to pace, the pacemaker conducts an electric current of a programmable voltage (called the pulse amplitude) for a programmable period of time (called the pulse width). Following a pace, the pacemaker is put into a refractory state for a set period of time during which all cardiac activity is ignored. Following the refractory period the pacemaker resumes monitoring for the next cardiac event. The rate of pacing is determined by the programmable pacing rate. The period of time the pacemaker will wait in the waiting state is computed based on the pacing rate and the pulse width. The refractory period is fixed. This particular pacemaker operates in *VVI, AAI, VVT, AAT,* and *AVI* pacing modes as programmed by the physician.

Pacemaker parameters are programmed via a telemetric interface to an external programmer. Telemetry is sent by pulsing an electromagnetic coil a certain number of times to indicate a "0" bit and a different number of times to indicate a "1" bit. To avoid inadvertent programming by electrical noise, a magnetically-activated reed switch must be closed before programming is enabled. The commands constructed from the bits must be checked prior to acting on them. The programmer can set or request any of the following pacing parameters: *Pacing Mode, Pacing Rate, Pulse Width,* or *Pulse Amplitude*. The programmer may also inquire as to the battery voltage determine if the pacemaker must be replaced in the near future.

Later we will see how this example system can be modeled in both the SA and OO paradigms.

3 Statecharts in Structured Analysis

3.1 The Embedding

Structured analysis and design use the *function*, often called *activity*, as the fundamental unit of decomposition. Overall system functionality is comprised of a collection of activities, interconnected by data and control flows. Activities can be repeatedly broken down into subactivities, and the ones on the bottom level of this hierarchy are termed *basic*.

Non-basic activities will typically exhibit state behavior and be modeled as statecharts. Basic activities can also be implemented as statecharts, but they often be implemented by functions and procedures operating on shared data. This implementation can be represented by module charts (similar to structure diagrams) or PDL.We describe our structured analysis language-set very briefly here; see [HPo] for a full account.

The functional view of the system is depicted by an *activity-chart*. Activities are shown as rectangles. Subactivities are shown either physically nested within their parent activity or in a separate activity-chart.

A special form of activity-chart used to show the interaction of the system with its external environment is the context diagram. This diagram shows the entire system as a single activity with the control and data flows coming from and going to the environment. Figure 5 shows the primary elements of a context diagram. The system is shown as an activity using the usual notation. External entities use activity rectangles with dashed lines to distinguish them from the system under development. External entities may be anything in the external context of the system, with which it communicates by sending or receiving events or information, such as sensors or actuators, and humans. External entities are not decomposed in the model, as they are beyond the scope of the system analysis.

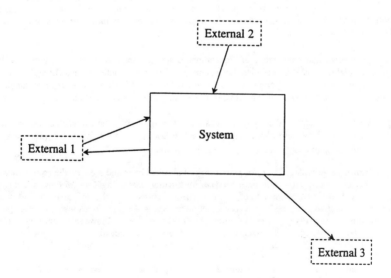

Figure 5: Activity Context Diagram

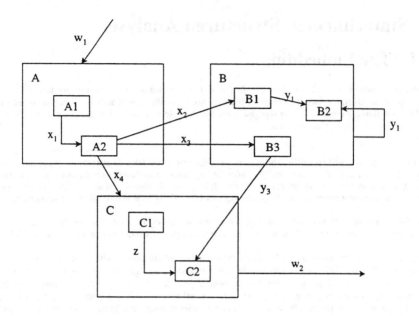

Figure 6: Activity Decomposition

The system is decomposed into sub-activities in subsequent diagrams. Figure 6 shows an example decomposition. Flows *w1* and *w2* have an unattached end, indicating that the end is attached outside the enclosing activity scope. If the activity scope is the entire system, then these flows must connect with external entities. If the enclosing scope is an activity within the system, then they connect to other system activities or external entities.

When a flow connects to an outer scope of a decomposed activity, such as *w1* or *x4*, it indicates that the information is available to all sub-activities. For example, *w1* is sent to both *A1* and *A2* and *x4* is sent to both *C1* and *C2*. If the activity is decomposed in another diagram and is shown as a single rectangle in the current diagram, then the flow endpoints must be resolved into more detail on the subsequent diagram.

Outgoing flows from a decomposed activity, such as *w2* in the figure, indicate that each of the decomposed activities may affect it. In the case of *w2*, it is possible that both *C1* and *C2* update the value of a shared variable used in the outgoing flow.

Two types of flows are provided. *Data flows* are drawn with solid lines and indicate the communication of information required for computation or other kinds of information processing. *Control flows* are drawn with dashed lines and indicate the transmission of event signals, conditions, or other information used to control the system activity, such as commands or synchronization messages. The data items may be simple primitive values, or structures recursively composed of primitives or other structures. Flows in an activity-chart do not provide temporal information, such as sequencing. They simply indicate that one process may provide information to another. The processes themselves may be sequential or concurrent.

Data can be stored within an activity in a *data store*. A data store is depcited by rectangles with dashed vertical edges, and is used to hold information.

Activities may have at most one *control activity*, depicted by a rounded rectangle, and described by a statechart. A control activity within an enclosing activity controls its sibling activities.

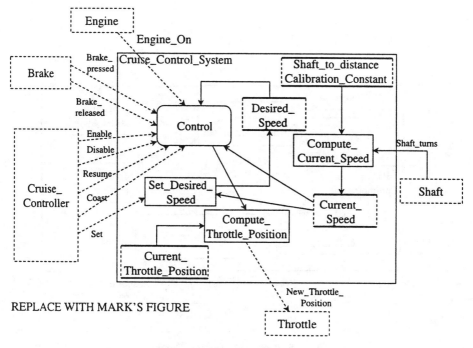

Figure 7: Sample Activity-Chart

Figure 7 shows a sample activity-chart for a simple, well-known example, the automobile cruise control. This example shows all the basic elements of activity-chart that we have presented. In this simple system we only show three sub-activities: *Compute_Current_Speed*, *Set_Desired_Speed*, and *Compute_Throttle_Position*. The external incoming flows are primarily control inputs from the brake, the engine, and the user-activated cruise controller. The output is the throttle position.

The flows to and from the data stores are not labeled. This is common when the flows have the same names as the appropriate data stores. The control activity, here labeled simply *Control*, represents the statechart that machine controls the system activities.

3.2 The Example

Let us now proceed with the structured analysis and decomposition of the pacemaker example of Section 2. The context diagram for this hypothetical pacemaker is given in Figure 8. We can see how the requirements from the problem statement are represented in the system context. The data store *Pacing_Parameters* holds a set of primitive values. The bi-directional flows connecting the data store to the *Communicate_with_Programmer* activity indicate that the activity can both set and read these values. The *Pace_Heart* activity can only read them and is not permitted to write them. These two primary activities can be decomposed into more primitive activities, as shown in the next three figures.

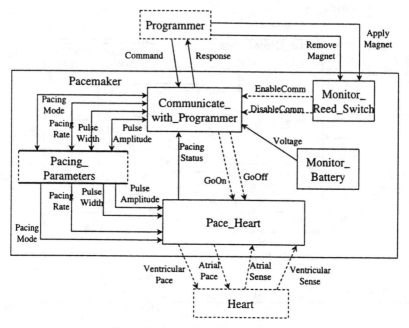

Figure 8: Pacemaker Context Diagram

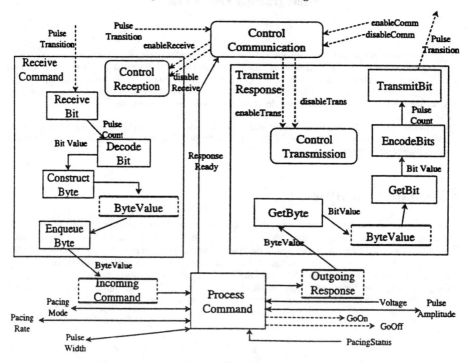

Figure 9: Communicate_With_Programmer Activity-Chart

Flows need to be balanced as one descends or ascends within the hierarchy of activities. This means that the flows entering or leaving an activity must correspond to the flows entering or leaving the activity when it is decomposed. Much of the time, this balancing is obvious, as the flows at different hierarchical levels have identical labels. However, Figure 9 shows cases in which there is no correspondence. The incoming flow *Command* on the context diagram corresponds to an incoming flow of *Pulse_Transition* on the decomposed *Communicate_With_Programmer* activity-chart. This is because the high-level concept of *Command* is composed of more primitive parts, bytes and bits, which are ultimately manifested as telemetric pulse transitions. This correspondence is normally maintained in the data dictionary where the data flow *Command* is decomposed into its composite parts, and is commonly done using a *data definition language*. The data dictionary declaration for *command* might be:

Command = (1..n)[Byte]
Byte = (8)[Bit]
Bit = (8 | 15)[Pulse_Transition]

The data decomposition is read: a command is composed of 1 to n Bytes; a byte is composed of 8 bits; a bit is composed of either 8 or 15 Pulse Transitions.

Other decomposed data flows include:

IncomingCommand = [CmdByte] (0..n)[Byte] [CRC]
CmdByte = [SetParameterCmd | GetStatusCmd |
GetBatteryLevelCmd | EnablePacingCmd]
OutgoingResponse = [ResponseByte] (0..n)[Byte] [CRC]
ResponseByte = [NAKResponse | ACKResponse | StatusResponse |
BatteryLevelResponse]

The data flows consist of two units, the data unit and a cyclic redundancy check (CRC) unit. The data unit specifies the message type and any parameters required for the message. For example, *Set_Parameter_Cmd* has a leading command byte, a series of data bytes, and a CRC. The leading command bytes may be any of set of bytes. The range values in parentheses specify the iteration count for the field that follows. *(1..n)[A]* states that there is a repeated set of A fields: at least one and no more than n. *(0,1)[A]* states that the A field is an optional single field.

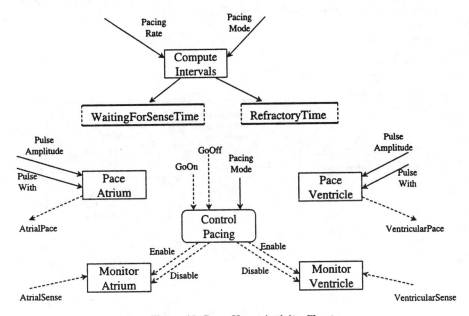

Figure 10: Pace_Heart Activity-Chart

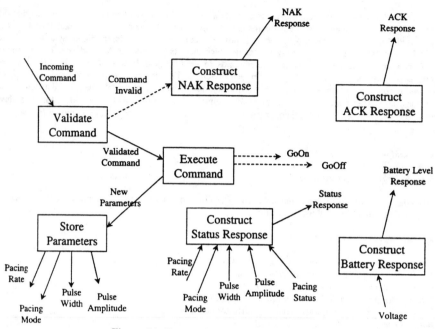

Figure 11: Process_Command Activity-Chart

These three activity charts describe the data flow and the process steps that must occur within the pacemaker. Nothing is said about the sequence of steps. That level of behavior is captured by the statecharts associated with the control activities, which are given in Figures 12 through 21.

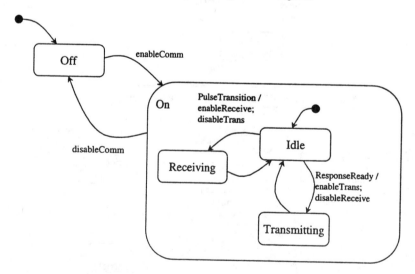

Figure 12: Communicate_With_Programmer Statechart

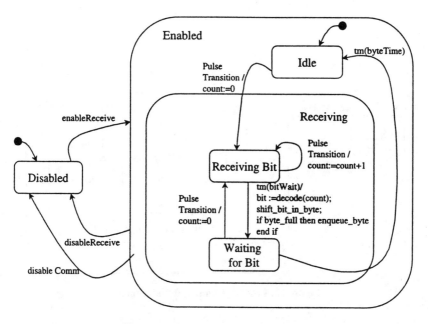

Figure 13: Receive_Command Statechart

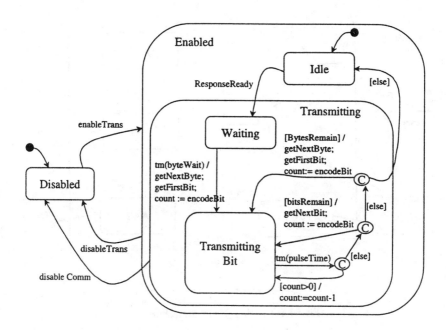

Figure 14: Transmit_Response Statechart

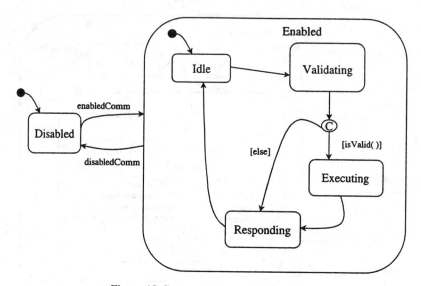

Figure 15: Process_Command Statechart

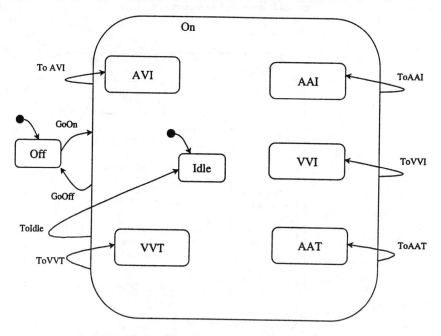

Figure 16: Pacing_Heart Statechart

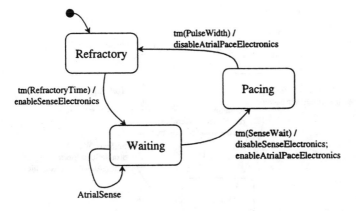

Figure 17: AAI Statechart

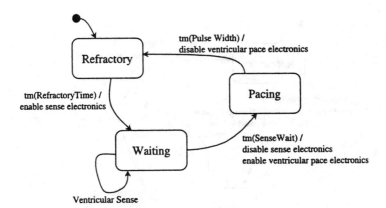

Figure 18: VVI Statechart

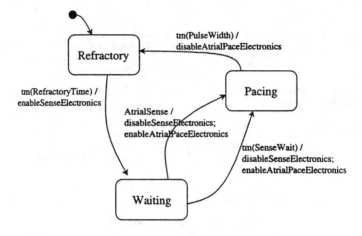

Figure 19: AAT Statechart

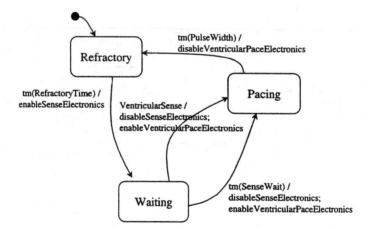

Figure 20: VVT Statechart

3.3 Statemate

The structured analysis language set based on statecharts is implemented in Statemate, which is a system design automation tool for the development of complex reactive systems. Statemate allows for graphical modeling of a system's functional and behavioral aspects, static and dynamic analysis, and code generation for embedded and workstation based environments. This section gives a brief summary of Statemate's central features. More can be found in the documentation from i-Logix.

System modeling (details in [HPo]):

- Activity-charts are used for functional description, and statecharts for behavioral descriptions. Behavior of basic activities can also be described textually, by either mini-specs (that utilize the trigger[guard]/action syntax), or by routines written in C or Ada.

- Design is captured by a hierarchy of charts. At any level of description, the decomposition can be continued in the same chart or in a separate one. Each chart in a design may define a new set of visible elements and its descendants. Such separation and scoping is the basis for the building of large-scale systems.

- Generic activity-charts and statecharts are allowed, which can be instantiated multiple times. This way, reuse of functional and behavioral components is supported.

- Rich data modeling capabilities are provided. Starting with basic types (such as *bit, integer, real, string*), it is possible to build complex types using appropriate type constructors: *enumeration, arrays, records, unions,* and *queues.*

- The action language includes basic programmatic constructs, such as assignment, conditional *if-then-else, for* and *while* loops, procedure and function calls, and a variety of operations for all supported types.

- Procedures and functions can be described textually (using either the action language or C or Ada), or graphically. In the latter case, statecharts are used again, this time in a restricted, flow-chart-style, way.

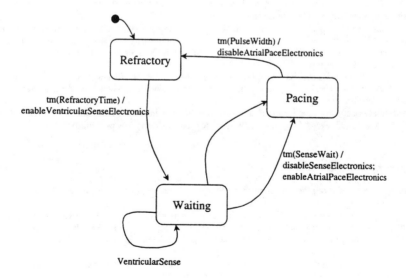

Figure 21: AVI Statechart

User interface modeling:

Along with the system functional and behavioral model, Statemate allows also for creation of graphical panels (mock-ups) that capture system's user or internal interface. A variety of input/output interactors can be used for this purpose (such as push/pull levers, switches, radio-buttons, knobs, sliders, etc.), as well as shapes that can be combined to form objects to be animated. Animation is based on binding panel objects to elements in the system model. When used in simulation and execution of generated code, such panels allow the designer to drive and monitor system behavior in terms of the problem domain. Hence, this front-end to system model provides a basis for communication between the various people involved in the system's development.

Static analysis:

Syntactic and semantic checks of the model are used to verify completeness and correctness. Completeness identifies missing and excess interfaces of system components, elements that are not fully defined, etc. Correctness checks, such as type checking, reveal contradictions between the way elements are defined and then used in the model.

Simulation:

Statemate allows for dynamic analysis of the system's behavior through simulation (interpretive execution) of its model. Dynamic analysis enables early detection of logical faults, and aims at obtaining a correct and reliable specification. This core ability is based on the fact that the language set of Statemate, and especially the statecharts language, is formal and rigorously defined, both syntax and semantics (see [HN,HPo]). The semantics defines system reaction in terms of a step, given its current status (which includes state configuration, values of internal data conditions, etc.) and external stimuli (i.e. values of external data and generated events).

Simulation in Statemate allows the designer to address the following issues:

- "What if" checks: to check alternative decisions, to perform tuning of various system parameters, to examine various "impossible" scenarios.
- Performance and timing analysis: to check that system reactions satisfy the required timing constraints.
- Analysis of situations when several events occur simultaneously, or when there is an attempt to simultaneously access/modify certain resource. Such analysis is essential to resolve scheduling and priorities issues in the system.
- Analysis of the system sensitivity to values of certain data, and its stability with respect to changes of the data. This includes checks of system behavior in extreme situations when certain parameters get their maximum/minimum values.
- Check rarely occurring situations that are difficult to achieve in reality. For example, the reaction of the system when certain events happen in some specific order with very low probability.

Simulation can be performed in two modes:

- In interactive simulation, the user represents the system's environment. He/she can change values and statuses of elements, and observe system reactions, usually on a step- by-step basis.
- In batch (programmable) simulation, a special script language (SCL - Simulation Control Language) is used to describe scenarios under which the system is to be examined. This allows running massive simulations unattended, and the desired information can be collected in files for post-run analysis.

The designer may simulate the system on any level of detail, according to choice. This can be either the entire system model, or any part of it that includes statecharts, mini-specs, or C code.

Analysis features in Statemate simulation include:

- Animation of charts and mock-up panels to drive the execution and to observe the latest changes in the system
- Graphical waveforms that show how elements change as time passes.
- Simulation of time that allows to "look into" fast processes, and, on the other hand, to quickly check processes that in reality take lengthy periods of time.
- Notification in cases of non-determinism, and the ability to explore the various possible continuations.
- Notification about read-write or write-write conflicts (racing).
- Use of random generators of data to simulate the system's environment, and various uncontrolled and unpredictable factors.
- Generation of execution traces for post-run analysis (textual reports and graphical waveforms).
- Playback scripts recorded for repeated runs of same scenario. This may be used to reproduce a discovered problem, or to see that a modified model now behaves as expected.
- Saving a snapshot of system status, to allow simulation continuation from any point.
- Breakpoint mechanisms to suspend the normal run of simulation when designer-defined conditions are fulfilled.
- Use of statecharts to describe test scenarios and to monitor system behavior. Such statecharts (also called watchdogs, or testbenches) are not a part of the system model. A designer may add them in order to describe and check various temporal properties of the system; for example, "when the system gets a request on accessing a certain resource, it allocates this resource before the next such request arrives".

Code Generation:

- Fully functional code in C or Ada is generated; automatic generation of system prototype.
- Can be run in a realistic environment, either workstation based or embedded (such as VxWorks). Can generate, compile and link on a host workstation, then download and execute on a target system.
- Graphical back animation of statecharts during code execution.
- Panel animation.
- Model-level tracing and debugging during code execution.
- User-guided modularization, customization and optimization.
- Hooks to incorporate hand-written extensions.
- Generation of reusable modules that can be plugged into software developed outside of Statemate.

4 Statecharts in Object-Oriented Analysis

4.1 The Embedding

The object-oriented approach is somewhat different and a lot more elaborate than the traditional structured analysis approach. Rather than decompose the system into functions, object-oriented approaches decompose the system into objects. Objects collaborate using associations with other objects, and the associations are typically implemented by pointers or references. Communication is achieved by sending messages between associated objects. This message passing is an abstraction of the communication that will be part of the final design. The two means for implementing message passing are the direct invocation of an object's member function, and the sending of an event, to be later read off the event queue by the target object.

The kinds of associations between objects identified in the XOM method and the UML [HG,UML] are *simple association, aggregation*, and *composition* (which is a strong form of aggregation), arranged from least-to-most tightly coupled. A simple association means that one object may use the facilities of another, but that is all. There is no implied ownership or lifecycle dependency between them. A client-server association is a common example in which possibly multiple clients associate with an object (the server) providing a set of services. Aggregation indicates a more tightly coupled association in which one object (the whole) contains the other (the part). Part objects may be passed among multiple owners and can be shared. One of the whole objects will be responsible for the creation of the part object and one (possibly the same) will be responsible for its destruction. Composition is the strongest form of association: the part object (known as a component) can only have a single owner, who is responsible for both its creation and destruction. And there are other implications of compositionality, such as the fact that destroying the composite destroys its components too.

The structure of a system is given in an *object model diagram*, where a class is depicted by a rectangle, possibly with a multiplicity indication. Associations may also have multiplicities specified. Ranges and lists of valid multiplicities may also be specified. Associations are shown as edges, directed or undirected, connecting the objects. Aggregation is indicated by a diamond at the whole end of the association. Composition is indicated by physical inclusion.

Another special relationship between classes and their instances is *inheritance*, representing generalization/specialization, and which is depicted by an edge with a triangular icon. The meaning of inheritance at this time in mainly structural: a subclass inherits all of the structural characteristics of its parents, such as interface, and data and function members. There are some behavioral implications of inheritance, but more research on this is needed.

Figure 22 shows an example of an object model diagram for a graphical user interface, in which a *Window* is a composite that may contain other objects, aggregates other windows, and receives input from input devices. The *Window* class is specialized into different kinds of inhereting windows including *Multiple Document Interface (MDI)* windows, *Single Document Interface (SDI)* windows, dialog windows, and window controls.

A statechart will typically be attached to a class, specifying the behavior of all instances thereof. These statecharts capture the state of the object in terms of its willingness, as a server, to respond to events or requests for services, and also the dynamics of its internal behavior in carrying out those responses, and in maintaining its relationships as a client (or aggregate) with other objects. More details can be found in [HG], in the i-Logix documents on Rhapsody, and in [D].

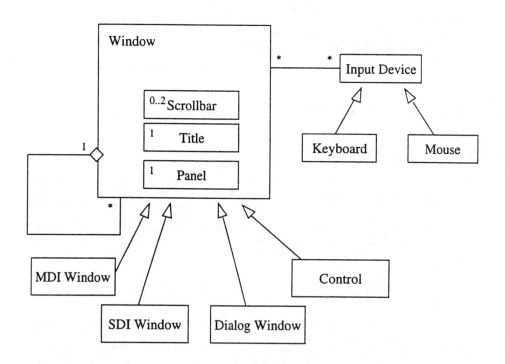

Figure 22: An Object Model Diagram

4.2 The Example

Figure 23 shows the pacemaker as a composite object, which contains its various components and communicates with its environment. The subclasses are divided into communications and pacing.

This simple example is composed mostly of singletons, i.e. classes that have only a single instance. The statecharts for these are shown in the next several figures, and they are, for the most part, very similar to the statecharts for the structured analysis model. There are a few interesting differences. First of all, the communication model is decomposed differently (objects versus activities) and so the statecharts are reorganized. The most interesting difference comes in the pacing engine.

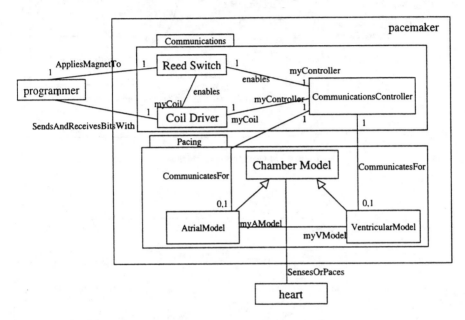

Figure 23: Pacemaker Object Model Diagram

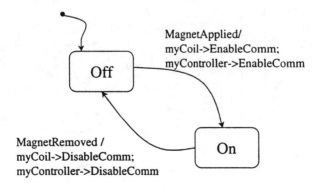

Figure 24: ReedSwitch Statechart

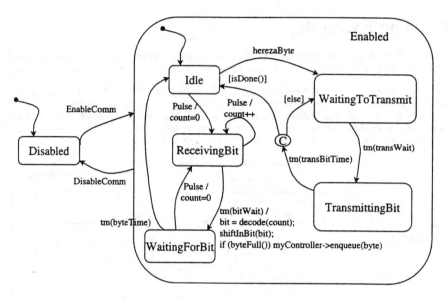

Figure 25: CoilDriver Statechart

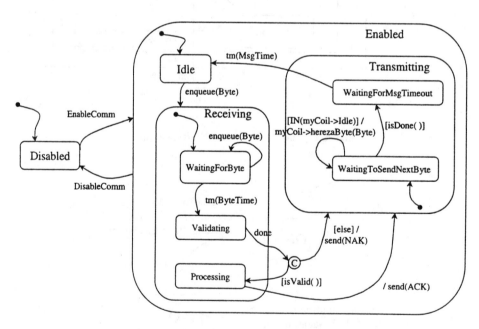

Figure 26: CommunicationsController Statechart

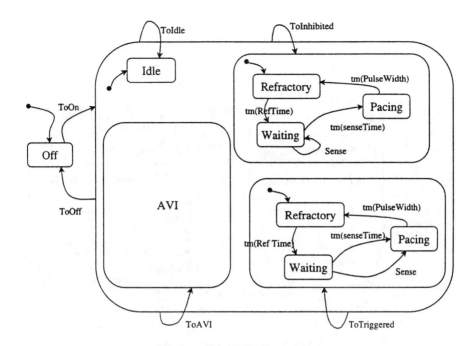

Figure 27: ChamberModel Statechart

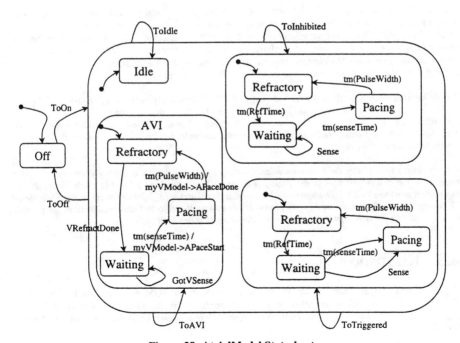

Figure 28: AtrialModel Statechart

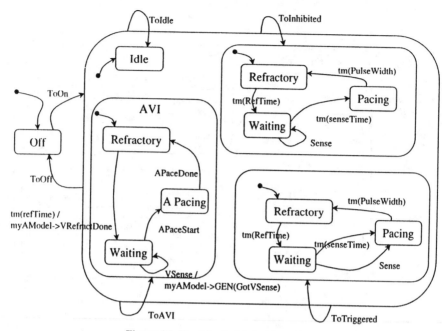

Figure 29: VentricularModel Statechart

The *AtrialModel* and *VentricularModel* classes are (almost) identical. Their common elements are abstracted away and put into the *ChamberModel* superclass from which both these classes inherit. The *AtrialModel* behaves in a certain way in *AAI* mode, for example, in terms of its statechart. The *VentricularModel* behaves identically when it is in *VVI* mode; - the difference is only one of context. The *AtrialModel* connects to the *Atrium* and the *VentricularModel* connects to the ventricle, but they behave the same way.
Similarly, the two classes behave the same in *AAT* and *VVT* modes, respectively.

The difference between the *AtrialModel* and *VentricularModel* lies solely in how they behave in *AVI* pacing mode. Since they differ in this mode but are the same elsewhere, the statecharts of the subclasses are specialized for this mode. The *ChamberModel* statechart shows *AVI* state as undifferentiated. The *AtrialModel* and *VentricularModel* subclasses elaborate this behavior by adding substates and events to realize the desired behavior.

It is interesting to note that the *CommunicationsController* adopts a slightly by different role in this system because of the object structure of the pacing package. When it receives a *To_AAI* mode command, for example, it must send a *To_Idle* event to the *VentricularModel* and a *To_Inhibited* event to the *AtrialModel*. The controller coordinates the mode setting between the two pacing objects. Other architectures are possible, including having the two objects themselves coordinate all their behavior.

4.3 Rhapsody

Object-oriented analysis based on the statecharts approach, as in XOM and UML, is implemented in Rhapsody, which is similar in many ways to Statemate. It is intended for software design and implementation of complex real-time embedded systems. Here are some items that differentiate Rhapsody from Statemate.

System modeling:

- Object model diagrams are used for structural description, and statecharts and sequence diagrams for behavioral descriptions.

- Inheritance of statecharts is allowed, and several restrictions are placed on the way the inheriting statechart can be constructed from the inherited one (for example, new states and transitions may be added but not deleted). This helps support reuse of behavioral specifications.

- Behavior can be coded as member functions that can be called from the statecharts.

- The data modeling capabilities of the "native language" (C++ in Rhapsody's first versions) are used, and the action language included is that of the "native" implementation language.

Code Generation:

- User tunable code generation: the generated code, such as the containers used to implement a group of values, can be tuned by the user using pretences, e.g., using STL containers.
- Different schemes can be used when generating code. One is the reuse-scheme, which emphasizes reuse of code. Another is a flat scheme, that results in more efficient production code.
- Single event processing.
- Run-to-completion semantics (see [HG]).
- Event delegation.

Design level debugging during execution:

Rhapsody allows for dynamic analysis (debugging) of the system behavior through instrumented execution of the generated code. This is somewhat different from Statemate in that the graphical animation is carried out via the generated code and not via a separate algorithm. As in Statemate, animation shows the current states and transitions. Also, an animated sequence diagram (an MSC) can be usded to see object collaboration during execution.

More details about Rhapsody can be found in the i-Logix documentation.

5 Acknowledgements

The second-listed author owes much thanks to Jonah Lavi for initiating his involvement in these topics in 1983, and to Eran Gery for prodding him to renew that involvement in the context of object-orientation in 1995. The specialization of statecharts to the SA paradigm and the SA embedding were carried out jointly with several people, predominantly Michal Politi, Rivi Sherman and Amir Pnueli. The specialization of statecharts to the OO paradigm and the OO embedding were carried out jointly with Eran Gery, with much help from Michael Hirsch. We are grateful to the many extremely talented and dedicated people at i-Logix Israel, Ltd., for their great help in conceptualizing, designing, and building the Statemate and Rhapsody tools over the years. We would like to thank Beery Holstein for his help on the Rhapsody parts of the paper.

6 References

[B] Booch, G., *Object-Oriented Analysis and Design, with Applications* (2nd edn.), Benjamin/Cummings, 1994.

[De] DeMarco, T., *Structured Analysis and System Specification*, Yourdon Press, New York, 1978.

[D] B. P. Douglass, *Real-Time UML: Developing Efficient Objects for Embedded Systems*, Addison-Wesley, Reading MA, 1997.

[H1] D. Harel, "Statecharts: A Visual Formalism for Complex Systems", *Science of Computer Programming* **8** (1987), 231--274. (Preliminary version: Tech. Report CS84-05, The Weizmann Institute of Science, Rehovot, Israel, February 1984.)

[H2] D. Harel, "On Visual Formalisms", *Comm. Assoc. Comput. Mach.* **31:5** (1988), 514--530.

[HG] D. Harel and E. Gery, "Executable Object Modeling with Statecharts", *Computer* (July 1997), 31--42. (Also, *it Proc. 18th Int. Conf. Soft. Eng.*, Berlin, IEEE Press, March, 1996, pp. 246--257.)

[H+] D. Harel, H. Lachover, A. Naamad, A. Pnueli, M. Politi, R. Sherman, A. Shtull-Trauring and M. Trakhtenbrot, "STATEMATE: A Working Environment for the Development of Complex Reactive Systems", *IEEE Transactions on Software Engineering* **16** (1990), 403--414. (Early version in *Proc. 10th Int. Conf. Soft. Eng.*, Singapore, April 1988, pp. 396--406.)

[HN] D. Harel and A. Naamad, "The STATEMATE Semantics of Statecharts", *ACM Trans. Soft. Eng. Method.* **5:4** (Oct. 1996), 293--333. (Preliminary version appeared as Technical Report, i-Logix, Inc., 1989.)

[HPn] D. Harel and A. Pnueli, "On the Development of Reactive Systems", in *Logics and Models of Concurrent Systems*, (K. R. Apt, ed.), NATO ASI Series, Vol. F-13, Springer-Verlag, New York, 1985, pp. 477-498.

[HPo] D. Harel and M. Politi, *Modeling Reactive Systems with Statecharts: The STATEMATE Approach*, McGraw-Hill, to appear. (Early version titled *The Languages of STATEMATE*, Technical Report, i-Logix, Inc., Andover, MA (250 pp.), 1991.)

[HPi] D. J Hatley and I. Pirbhai, *Strategies for Real-Time System Specification*, Dorset House, New York, 1987.

[R+] Rumbaugh, J., M. Blaha, W. Premerlani, F. Eddy and W. Lorensen, *Object-Oriented Modeling and Design*, Prentice Hall, 1991.

[SGW] Selic, B., G. Gullekson and P. T. Ward, *Real-Time Object-Oriented Modeling*, John Wiley & Sons, New York, 1994.

[UML] Unified Modeling Language, Semantics Document, Version 1.1, Rational Corporation, 1997.

[WM] P. Ward and S. Mellor, *Structured Development for Real-Time Systems* (Vols. 1, 2, 3), Yourdon Press, New York, 1985.

Embedded Systems in Consumer Products

R.H. Bourgonjon
Philips Sound & Vision

Consumer products

Since decades, almost every individual and almost any household in the modern world is confronted with and using electronic consumer products. Traditionally there was a kind of distinction between real electronic products such as radios and televisions, and more mechanical products such as vacuum cleaners, electric shavers, washing machines and alike. However, in the last 50 years, where both electronics and mechanics very much evolved through mass production, the distinction became fuzzier. Products such as camcorders or portable CD players are in fact a sophisticated combination of tightly coupled electronical and mechanical solutions.

One of the most striking observations for most electronic consumer products is that the price for a certain functionality, especially when taking inflation into account, came down by a factor of between 50 and 100. A radio was costing in the Netherlands in 1935 roughly Dfl. 150,- at that time. Correcting for inflation that would mean certainly Dfl. 2000,- now. A radio with the same functionality or more would actually now cost no more than Dfl. 25,-.

Until recently, consumer products such as televisions or telephones had little in common with computers. With digital signal processors and general purpose micro-processors also becoming in the "consumer " price range, this is dramatically changing.

The remainder of this paper will be devoted to show how the influence of software in consumer products not only drastically changes the characteristics of these products and the way they are developed but also how the whole consumer business is affected by software and in the longer term human behaviour and the society we live in.

Embedded software in consumer products

Computers traditionally were made and used for computing (40's and 50's) and later for administrative applications (60's and 70's). The professional electronic products were the first that could afford the price of computers in so-called "real-time control" applications. In the late 60's and 70's many products such as computer controlled telephone switching systems, aircraft control systems or manufacturing control systems saw the light. A whole new range of technical concepts emerged like real-time operating systems, data communication protocols or real-time programming languages. It was the invention of the micro processor in the 70's that finally made it feasible to use such techniques in consumer products as well.

In the mid 80's, 4 and 8 bits micro controllers were applied in many televisions and audio sets; in the beginning only having a few kilobytes of ROM. Later, micro controllers crept in in almost every electronic product. One indication on how quickly this evolution is taking place is a kind of "folk" statistics indicating how many micro controllers are in products that one uses daily.
The statistics collected in 1996 were as shown on the right.

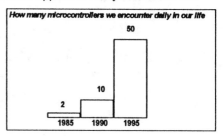

Not only the number of computer controlled consumer products is rapidly increasing, also the amount of control software per product is doubling roughly every 2 years.
Below are given some figures whereby the amount of software is measured in ROM size rather than Lines Of Code (LOC), in order to have comparable numbers for different programming languages.

	1985	1990	1995	1998 (exp.)
High-end Television	10K	100K	800K	1.4M
Standard TV	-	5K	64K	265K
Hifi Audio Set	-	10K	100K	256K
VCR	10K	100K	800K	1.2M
GSM phone	-	-	1M	2M
Set-top box	-	2K	128K	1M
Shaver	-	2K	16K	16K

Of course, ROM size normally is not a very exact way to measure software effort. However, it turns out for these kind of products that ROM size indeed is almost proportional to software development effort, ignoring reuse between different product lines. In other words : software development effort per product has grown in a similar way.

Moore's law

Early 60's, Gordon Moore, one of the founders of Intel, stated his famous law that IC technology (chip density, speed, etc.) would double it's performance every 18 months. Ever since, this estimate has been shown extremely accurate and it is expected to remain accurate for the coming 10 years. A similar performance increase is observed in mass storage (magnetic and optic) and transmission. Sometimes new standards are needed to enable the possibilities for newer applications, which appears as a step function in performance.

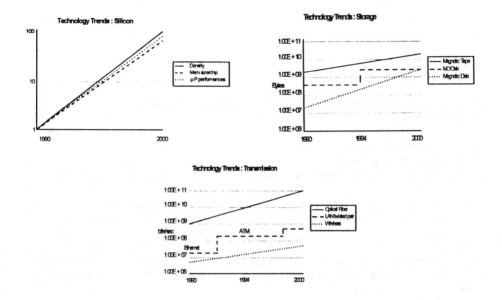

It is therefore expected by the semi-conductor industry that early in the next century, it will be quite feasible to integrate on one 100 square mm chip a complete mixed analogue/digital system. Examples could be a cellular phone, TV, ATM switch, Global Positioning System, Digital Video decoder, digital camera etc. together with a 32 bits micro controller and 1 M byte ROM/RAM. This for a selling price of about $15 per chip.
This would imply that the consumer industry would be able to create an almost infinite number of products for a reasonable price, provided that they can develop the software in time. And there lies the current and future challenge. Filling about 1M memory with high quality and documented code still requires between 20-50 manyears of effort.

Moore's law and software development

One could argue whether or not the consumer products would follow Moore's law. In other words, will consumer products use all this improved IC capability or will it stabilise for a set of "normal" or "standard" features.
There is all the evidence that this will not be the case and that indeed there will be a rapidly increasing number of familiar and new consumer products using al the capabilities provided by the IC technology when it comes in the consumer price range.

There are two additional reasons why software contents is rapidly increasing :

On the one hand, economic mass production requires standardisation of components and minimising variety. On the other hand embedded software can be used to create easily (from a manufacturing point of view) different versions or variants focused on specific applications. This implies that the consumer product companies are more and more trying to solve the needed diversity by software rather than by hardware.
The second reason is the need for improved user interfaces.
The introduction of embedded software in consumer products caused an explosion of new features in products. Many of these features merely stemmed from a "technology push" rather than a real consumer need. Moreover, the introduced product complexity

caused that a lot of products were difficult to use by the average consumer. Currently much emphasis is placed in improving the user interfaces and e.g. for televisions a user interface management system is a major part of the product software

Software productivity

Basically there are three ways to cater for the enormous growths of embedded software in consumer products :

- Increase productivity per engineer
- Employ more engineers
- Re-use software components over different products (i.e. write less new code)

Software productivity can be measured in the number of (non-commentary) lines of tested and released code that a software engineer is capable to develop in a year. Although this is a far from precise definition, it can be used within a certain range of applications to measure whether the productivity goes up. One might hope that, similar to IC technology, also software technology would improve according to some kind of "Moore's law" . And indeed, some automatic software generation tools do have that effect in some specific cases.

Unfortunately, overall it is not the case. Some sources (Applied Software Improvement, Capers Jones) claim a 15% compound annual improvement in software productivity in some applications. However, some other statistics show that software productivity per person is heavily dependant upon overall program and team size. The productivity of a team of 2-3 people writing 100K LOC of software, can be 20 times higher than a team of 200 people writing 10M LOC of software. The latter kinds of projects were up until now only done in the military or telecommunication domain but they become less unusual also for some consumer product developments.

As indicated above, productivity increase as realised now is by far not sufficient to meet the growing demands. There are no signs that a breakthrough in software engineering technology will quickly change the situation.

It is also clear that the exponential growth of embedded software cannot be met with a similar growth in software personnel. Still all electronic consumer companies are confronted with quickly growing software staff. The growing need for embedded software engineers is a world-wide phenomenon. Embedded software is the fastest increasing area of information technology, with the exception of the sometimes called "intermittent programming" (which are those non-software professionals that still perform a kind of programming task for their work).

The estimate made by a group of experts in 1994 for the people employed
in software in the coming 10 years show this clearly :

Software categories	People employed 1994	People employed 2004
Software business	400 000	1 M
Embedded Software	2 M	10M
Automation (IT)	2M	1M ?
Intermittent Programming	20M	200M

It is therefore evident that the real demand for embedded software in consumer products can only be met by reusing standard software components within one or more standard software platforms.

How the consumer products evolve slowly in that direction is the subject of the next chapters.

The evolution from embedded software to embedded systems

As indicated before, software contents of consumer products has dramatically increased over the last decade and will continue to do so for many years to come. The reason is simply that Moore's law allows to put ever more functionality in consumer products for roughly the same (hardware!) cost.

This rapid growth also requires an evolution in the internal software and system architecture of the products which, in its turn, is causing an evolution (or revolution) in the business characteristics of those products.

To clarify the point, this evolution is subdivided into four phases :

1. Implementing existing functionality (hardware-bound software)
2. Adding new features (monolithic closed software)
3. Mastering size and complexity (proprietary architecture)
4. Increased "system" aspects (open architecture)

In the first phase, a micro-controller with embedded software is merely introduced to implement the traditional functionality of the product in a simpler and more cost effective way. Often the software is restricted to control mechanical or electrical devices and some sensors or buttons. The software in this phase is usually small and programmed to optimise speed and memory requirements. Usually little or no attention is paid to software structure, readability, upgradability or reuse.

The software is made by small teams (1-3 people) and because indepth knowledge of the hardware is important, the people often have a hardware background.

In the "adding new features" phase, the possibilities offered by software are further exploited. Features that are almost un-implementable by electro-mechanical means are added to the product. Typical examples are found in audio equipment.

Micro-controllers were introduced for e.g. motor, tuner and button control : later all kind of features such as synchronised copying between CD and Tape, random playback, optimising tape layout etc. were added. The software is rapidly growing but its structure and development methodology are not yet adapted. Often the resulting software structure is rather monolithic (i.e. without clear and specified interfaces between sub-modules).

After a certain point in time, the size of the software reaches a point where much attention has to be paid to structuring and architecture.

Teams become so large that they subdivided and often located at different sites. This requires a clear division of the software in subsystems and modules with well defined interfaces.

Also the number of non-product related supporting activities such as a software development environment, quality systems, project management and change management is quickly increasing.

It is often in this phase that organisations are confronted with software problems and that much attention has to be paid to sound and reliable software engineering processes and proper software architectures that meet business needs. Current day televisions, which require between 50-100 person year of software development, are definitively in this phase.

It is in this phase that a strong business drive for organising reuse emerges. A proper implementation is affecting not only software architecture and tools but also organisation and business processes. Much experience in this area has been gained over the last years in the consumer industry also building upon the know-how of the professional field.

Often in the three previous phases, the consumer product (e.g. television) has still its traditional physical borderlines with some standard interfaces to the outside world (cable, scart plug , audio plug etc.). However, more and more the consumer products are interconnected and the <u>system</u> aspects of the interconnected products become of greater importance than the individual component characteristics.

Typical systems add several aspects of complexity to consumer products. To mention a few :

- system lifetime exceeds individual product lifetime
- networking, distributed control, distributed user interface
- modularity; global system architecture

Another aspect of such systems is that it becomes rather arbitrary in what physical box a certain system function is implemented. In other words, the software borderline between different consumer products becomes fuzzier.

For example, an Electronic Programme Guide (EPG) may be implemented in a TV, a VCR or a set-top box. When TV's will be connected to Internet, the number of possibilities for implementing such a feature will become even larger.

This phenomenon causes that the role of (defacto) standards will be increasing in the consumer domain.

Standards not only between physical boxes as in the past, but standard API's between software components of a larger system architecture.

Digital TV systems and set-top boxes are already architectured as a kind of "open" system, using commercially available operating sytems, protocol stacks and browsers.

The four phases sketched above are of course not mathematically defined nor do they have any scientific significance. They are merely an illustration of a continuous process whereby the characteristics of consumer products is changing by the introduction of more and more embedded software.

One can observe is that almost all consumer products go, because of Moore's law, through phases 1 → 4.

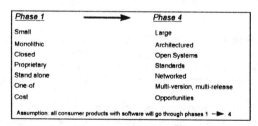

Phase 1	→	Phase 4
Small		Large
Monolithic		Architectured
Closed		Open Systems
Proprietary		Standards
Stand alone		Networked
One-of		Multi-version, multi-release
Cost		Opportunities

Assumption: all consumer products with software will go through phases 1 → 4

Consumer products versus computer products

One might argue that consumer products and PC's converge to the same kind of systems. From a technology point of view, this is certainly the case. Especially the new digital products such as set-top boxes (digital decoder/receiver) are implemented by all kinds of computer technology such as RISC processors, operating systems, user interface management systems, Java VM's, TCP/ IP protocol stacks, etc. But there are still some important differences that may last for many years to come :

– Consumer products are "virtually" error free.
When someone buys a consumer product, one expects it always to work properly (unlike PC's). No maintenance is done on the product when sold, no new software versions can be loaded into it (although this is changing for networked products).
Software development organisations in consumer companies are paying much attention to remain at this high quality level even in the case of much larger software contents.
– Consumers do not want to be trained in using the product.
– Consumer products are much lower priced.
The fact that customers expect a certain price level for consumer products causes that still much emphasis has to be put upon cost effective and therefore potentially dedicated hardware and software solutions.
– The PC business is governed by open platforms where software and hardware providers form different business categories. In the consumer product world software is (still) not unbundled and forms for the user an invisible part of the product. This means that the software as such does not form a business in its own right.

The above sketched differences indicate that despite large technological similarities, the business characteristics are quite different. The speed in which the business will come together currently differ from the speed in which the technology converges.
The conflicts arising from this are the subject of violent debates, especially in the USA. The question to what it boils down is : who will be in control in the consumer product market. Nobody knows the answer yet.

Consumer products and multi-media

Multi-media is one of the most ill-defined, still one the most frequently used terms when speaking about the future of electronic consumer products. Also I will not try to give a precise definition.

Four aspects are in my view essential to call some product, system of function "multi-media".
Firstly, it deals with digital information sources (e.g. audio, video, text, graphics, etc.). Secondly, there are more than one of them, thirdly there is some form of intelligent processing done on the digital data, either per source or in combination and fourthly there is some interactive behaviour of the user..

It is again Moore's law that allows for efficient and inexpensive digitization of all kind of information. Traditionally computers handled text, later graphics and pictures digitally. All kind of standards emerged in this domain, e.g. ASCII, PostScript, SGML, GIF, JPEG, AVI.

In the consumer world, digital audio recording started in the early 80's. Later digital video compression (MPEG) was introduced, HTML became a defacto standard on Internet. For consumer products, MHEG is aiming at similar applications.

The crucial point here is that, if all information is provided in <u>digital</u> form, a computer with software may start manipulating and combining these information sources for new applications. An example could be a car navigation system were static digital maps on video disc are combined with real-time updated traffic information and advertisements from the nearest Pizza restaurant. All this information may come from different sources but form one consumer function. An interesting and fun-to-read book on the potential of multi-media applications is : "Being digital, Nicholas Negroponte, 1995" .

In the previous chapters, it was explained how in software intensive embedded systems, the borderlines between physical equipment become fuzzier. The introduction of multi-media makes that the borderline between traditional information sources and even information providers become fuzzy. It will certainly come in the next decade that most of the traditional information sources (TV, video tape, radio, telephone lines, etc.) become digital and that digital consumer products, which can handle the information, are connected to several digital sources and are interconnected via communication networks.

In other words : the traditionally separated worlds of entertainment (TV, video, audio), communication (Telephone, mail) and computing become unseparable.

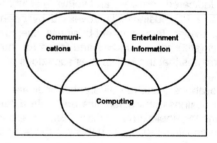

How such a "universal" digital consumer products will look like is still uncertain. Also it is uncertain who will make a profitable business from it. It may be the consumer companies, software vendors, PC makers, service providers, IC vendors or some completely new kind of business. Hopefully there will be room for everybody.

Standardisation

The role of standardisation in the consumer product world is changing. Traditionally standards were agreed between different suppliers or organisations when there boxes or services had to cooperate.

With some simplification, one can say that standards were agreed at an "input/output" level.
Currently, because borderlines between equipment and even between services and functions become fuzzy, standards are needed that cover all kinds of interfaces in a (global) system architecture.

One can see defacto standards arising, which are set by one or more large companies (e.g. Windows for PC's), standards that emerge because of easy availability (e.g. JAVA or in the past UNIX) or standards that are set by committees (e.g. CORBA, MPEG).

Another way to look at standards is to consider their functional domain. One can recognise :

- Computing platforms
  - general purpose (WINCE, POSIX, Java)
  - domain specific (DAVIC)
- Data
  - formats (MPEG2-video, AC3, MHEG-5, GIF, JPEG)
  - dynamic objects (Java beans)
- Communication
  - distributed computing (CORBA, OLE)
  - data communication (SDH, ATM, MPEG2-TS, TCP/IP)
  - management & control (TAPI, SNMP, DSMCC)

Any standards expert will look in disgust to my classification above. However, one of the problems is that since that are so many stake-holders in the standardisation arena, standards tend to be grouped per application domain (e.g. DAVIC, which is the Digital Audio and Video Council) and different groups start to overlap.

There are two main reasons why standards become so important in the consumer product world.
The first is the obvious one : because products, functions, data, etc. from different manufacturers, providers etc. have to smoothly cooperate.
The second reason is more subtle. Since all future electronic consumer products are filled with large amounts of embedded software, it will be a sheer impossibility that the individual manufacturers can create all this themselves as propriatory software.
As a consequence future consumer systems (which is a better word than products) will have to be made by integrating software from different providers. Standard interfaces are then a must.

Conclusions

I have sketched the evolution of electronic consumer products.
The main observations are that they will contain more and more embedded software, that as a consequence they will evolve to architectured embedded systems, similar to computer products and that, due to Moore's law, they can stay in a consumer price range and thus become quite ubiquitous.
Furthermore that the traditional functional borderlines between products is changing and that, especially caused by digitalisation (multi-media) also the borderlines between traditional businesses are changing.

Nobody knows yet what the outcome will look like.

The Long Road from Research to Telecommunication Applications

Hans F. van Rietschote

Origin International BV.
Vonderweg 11,
5611 BK Eindhoven
The Netherlands
+31-653-990855
Hans.van.Rietschote@iname.com

Abstract. This paper presents Telecommunication Applications as the largest, most complex embedded software applications in the world today. By presenting a simple example of a GSM voice call it is shown how large and complex this embedded software application is. After listing the characteristics of telecom applications it is shown what this type of application needs from software engineering research. It will become clear that there is still a real big gap between the two. Finally this paper will discuss what Research could do for enabling programming LARGE and COMPLEX embedded systems.

1. Introduction

This paper is based on my experiences while helping to develop embedded software for public telephony switching systems for more than ten years at both Philips Telecommunication Industry and AT&T (now Lucent). After this I spent two years working at Philips Research in the Information and Software Technology sector. All statements made in this paper are my own and can not be contributed to any of my former or current employers. Also my statements are based on my personal experiences with Software Engineering Research mainly in the Netherlands, whether they apply to other parts of the world is left as an exercise to the reader.

2. Characteristics of Telecommunication Applications

Telecommunication applications are usually very big, they have been around for a long time, they are still changing, they are critical, they are used by everyone, everyday, everywhere and they apply everything known in software engineering research and more. Let's look in detail to these aspects:

2.1 They Are Big

A typical public telephony switching program contains more than ten millions lines of code and has over 50 identifiable sub systems. This software is spread over more than 10,000 files. Back in 1980 (more than 15 years ago), the off-line version of the software that I was working on took a tera-byte of storage.

This amount of software also takes an enormous amount of human effort to create: it is known that one programmer can only deliver ten lines of fully designed, written, tested and documented code PER DAY. With 200 working days a year this gives us 2000 lines per programmer year. So ten million lines of code takes more than 5000 programmer years. In order to get this work done, multiple distributed teams with a total size of 1000 people were employed. The architecture design of the total system employed dozens of system architects.

2.2 They Are Old

The first version of the software that I worked on was created more than 25 years ago. This first version was designed to take advantage of the most modern chip technology at that time: the 8086. Because of this, available main memory was limited and a one megahertz clock was considered very fast. All the software of the first version was created BEFORE software-engineering research was even started!

2.3 They Are Changing

For more than 25 years 500 programmers created ten lines of code per day, which means that we made more than 25 million lines of code. But only ten million are used in the actual product. This means that on the average the same line of code was changed 2.5 times. All these changes were needed in order to adapt to new standards created over the past 25 years (i.e. digitalisation, ISDN, GSM).

Another reason for the changes was the switch in hardware. After starting with hardware based on the 8086 chip-set, it was decided to switch to the more modern 68000, then to the 68010, the 68020 and finally the power PC. These changes in hardware meant large changes in the software architecture: memory limits were drastically changed and processing speeds went up with a factor of 100.

On the support side: at the beginning of the development all software was created on a single mainframe (running UNIX), then we moved to a cluster of mainframes, then again we moved to minis and currently single user workstations are used. The only change we did not make: we always kept things running on UNIX. (although this was a very special, dedicated version).

2.4 They Are Critical

Telecommunication applications are critical for today's world. Some obvious examples where telecom is used and things plainly would not work without are:
- logistics: using the telephone to order goods

- banking: electronic fund transfers, and even getting your money "out-of-the-wall" requires telecom access to check the validity of your bank account
- transportation: airline scheduling is done via telecom
- personal safety: being able to call the doctor, the fire brigade, or the police: all require telecom

It is quite simply true that without the ability to communicate via telecom the world as we know it would be VERY different.

2.5 They are Used by Everyone, Everyday, Everywhere

Telecommunication applications are used by everyone, everyday. The normal telephone is obvious but also all data traffic between computers (i.e. Internet) is just another telecom application. We have all heard how big the Internet is becoming, still the total telecom network is bigger.

2.6 They Apply Everything Known in Software Engineering Research and more

If we have a look at the "Unified Classification Scheme for Informatics Education"[1], then is becomes clear that a telecom application is involved with every aspect that is mentioned: hardware, software, systems, information systems and even the context of Informatics is covered.

```
Unified Classification Scheme for Informatics Education
1. Computer Systems
1.1 Hardware structures and digital systems
1.2 Computer architecture
1.3 Interfacing and peripherals
1.4 Communications and networks
1.5 Operating systems and system software


2. Software Systems
2.1 Programming languages
2.2 Software architecture
2.3 Software engineering
2.4 Artificial intelligence (AI)
2.5 Theory of computing

3. Information Systems
3.1 Databases, knowledge bases
3.2 Information systems architecture
3.3 Information systems engineering
3.4 Human computer interaction
```

3. A Simple Telecommunication Application: GSM Voice call

In order to show that all aspects of software engineering research & education are being applied in a typical telecom application I will describe a simple GSM voice call. We will use the following picture.

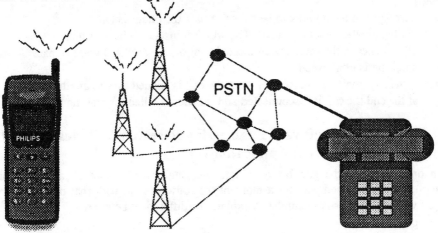

In the picture we have three essential parts: the mobile GSM phone on the left, the Public Switched Telephony Network (PSTN) in the middle and a normal phone on the right. Let's look at the steps needed to make a voice connection between the GSM phone on the left and the phone on the right.

3.1   Turning on the GSM Phone

After the user pushes the "ON" button, the hardware is initialised, the operating system is started and user identification is done by having the user type in a pin-code. The GSM will then announce itself to the network and will first look to find the network it is a member of and if this one is not found will try to locate another network, from all available networks it will pick the one with the strongest signal. Then the GSM phone will try to lower its own transmitting power to the lowest possible level (so it can still be received by the network), this saves the batteries. Once connected it will download all SMS text messages waiting for the user.

3.2   Off-line Functionality

Even without making a phone call there are quite some things the user can do with the GSM phone:
•   use the built-in database for storing the frequently dialled numbers

- edit/read/delete/send SMS text messages
- set/unset alarms
- calculator
- watch
- PCMCIA interface with laptop computer
- some even have built-in PDA functionality

3.3   Connecting the Voice call

To make a voice call connection the telecom application needs to take the following steps:
- user types in the number to be called or uses the phone book
- dialled number is sent to the PSTN, which translates it into a route
- all switches in the route are connected to allow the digitised voice to pass
- charging is established
- if the user moves from location then the call is handed over to another network
- at the end the call is disconnected and the user is billed for making the call

4. Gap Between Software Engineering Research & Education and Telecommunication Applications

In order to show the gap between Software Engineering Research and Telecom applications I will compare for a moment the software field with that of Chemistry. So I will use Chemistry examples to explain the differences between:
- pure research
- programming in the small
- programming in the large

4.1   Pure Research

In order to make gold in pure chemistry research we only need to know the formulae that defines gold:

```
A + U -> AU (gold)
```

This can be compared by the software research that shows that it is possible to write error-free programs by using correctness proofs on them. It works (in theory).

4.2   Programming in the Small

Of course if we really want to produce physical gold then we need to get out our chemistry set:

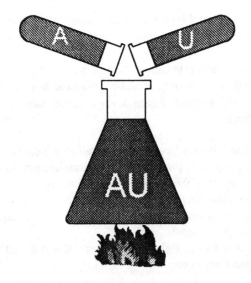

This approach will demonstrate in a laboratory that small amounts of gold can be made by adding substances A and U, mix them well and heat until the reaction is complete.

In software this would mean that we will show on a ten line program that correctness proofs can indeed be done. (although it takes 30 minutes and a whole blackboard full of mathematical scribbles).

4.3   Programming in the LARGE

Now that we have proven in the laboratory that we can indeed make gold we would like to start a company that produces gold at large amounts which we can then sell to our customers. The picture now becomes somewhat more complicated:

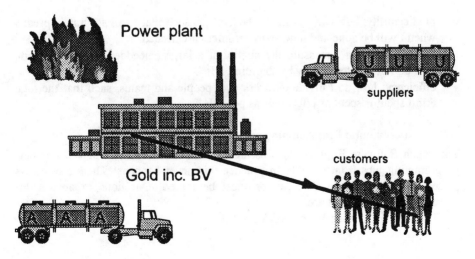

We now need to worry about things, which are totally outside the scope of research:
- logistics on how to obtain the right amount of A and U at the right time for processing
- will the power plant generate enough heat 24 hours a day?
- how do we ship these gigantic amounts of gold (which is very heavy)
- how do we size the amount of gold down to pieces that customers can afford? (gold is expensive).

In programming in the large we have the same scaling problems:
- how do you do correctness proof for a ten million line program?
- how do you manage the 10,000 files it is contained in?
- how do you find something in these 10,000 files?
- how do you check that one change made by a programmer does not affect any of the other 1000 programmers?
- if something does not work right: how do you test it and find the location of the bug in ten million lines of code?

5. What Software Engineering Research & Education Should Focus on

In order to close the gap between what Software Engineering Research & Education is working on and what is needed by the large telecom applications (and for that matter ALL large software products), I would like to propose the following areas for study:

5.1 Programming in the LARGE

The Chemistry example above has made it clear that much more study needs to be done into all aspects that appear as soon as you start developing large embedded software products. What is needed by every project manager for such large projects is:
- predictability: how can I estimate the total job such that I can accurately predict when I will be done and how many resources are needed
- quality: how can I measure the quality of a large embedded software system, how do I guarantee quality by "building it in".
- efficiency: how do I divide the work over people and teams, such that the total effort spent is spent as effectively as possible.

5.2 Incremental Programming

Too much Software Engineering Research & Education focuses on starting new programming jobs from scratch. In practice this never happens! There are always pieces of software code that can or must be reused. Questions to answer for incremental development are:
- how do I build re-usable code efficiently?

- how do I know exactly what the software does that I re-use/re-cycle?
- how can I re-architecture my old system to make it work under the new requirements such that I can leave the walls so the roof does not collapse?

5.3 Personal Software Process

Students of software engineering disciples should be trained to work in teams. Today too much of the Education process is focused on grading individual student. During the whole education system, students are trained to do things alone, not in groups. In real life however, all work in software engineering is done as part of a team. Software Education should spend more effort on training students to accept and even demand peer reviews of everything they design, code and test.

6. Conclusion

All though it seems clear that major Gaps exist between Software Engineering Research and the Industry that needs to create large scale embedded software products, all is not lost. Just like we have next to Chemistry as a research topic something called Chemical Engineering, I propose that we concentrate in the software discipline on **Software Engineering Application.**

We already have plenty of theoretical models, what we need now is making these work in large-scale applications. However I realise that there is a long road between the two, too often we rush a new method or programming language from research into industry use, this is clearly dangerous. Just imagine what would happen if the same quick approach was taken by aeroplane builders:
- on day one research will discover a new metal that is lighter, stronger and cheaper
- on day two we rush this metal to the factories and start producing all planes with it
- on day three all passenger will fly in these new planes
- on day four we find out that ..... (We did not take enough time to prove that methods developed in Research are scaleable to real life, large scale embedded products).

7. Acronyms

GSM	Group Special Mobile
	Global System for Mobile telecommunication
ISDN	Integrated Services Digital Network
PC	Personal Computer
PCMCIA	PC Media Connection Interface Adapter
PDA	Personal Digital Assistant
PSTN	Public Switched Telephone Network
SMS	Short Message System

8. References

1. Fred Mulder: Identiteit van Informatica-onderwijs, Inaugurale rede Open Universiteit Heerlen. Open Universiteit, Heerlen, 1972

Development of Embedded Software at ICT

Freddie T.G. Veltmaat

Program Manager at ICT Automatisering,
Keulenstraat 7, 7418 ET Deventer, The Netherlands,
E-mail: Freddie.Veltmaat@home.ict.nl

The realistic side of embedded software development at ICT Automatisering is presented. Included are an introduction of ICT Automatisering and an overview of the big mean world of embedded software.
To give insight in the big mean world of doing embedded software projects, a real life example of an embedded software product is discussed: the development of the embedded control software for a Colour TV product range for the combined North and South American market. This example is used to demonstrate the impact of the various factors that contribute to an embedded software project. Via this example the link to the necessary future cooperation between the software industry and the scientific community is made. Included are some philosophical thoughts about rules of conduct and possible way to improve the cooperation between the different forces.

1 Introduction to ICT and the Big Mean World

1.1 Who is ICT

ICT Automatisering is one of the largest embedded software development companies in the Netherlands. ICT currently employs about 500 professionals who are active in the area of consultancy, development and maintenance. In our daily practice we face many challenges in the following industry segments:

- Consumer Systems (e.g. Colour TV's, Video Recorders, Set-top Boxes)
- Multi-Media (e.g. CD-ROM Players, DVD Players, CD Recordable)
- Distributed Systems (e.g. X-Ray Scanners, Digital Imaging Equipment)
- Mechatronics (e.g. Integrated Circuit Processing Equipment)
- Professional Systems (e.g. Remote Sensing Equipment)
- Telecom (e.g. Large Telephone Switches, Network Management Tools)

Although from the technical and market point of view large differences can be seen between these industry segments, from the embedded software point of view there are many similarities. Similarities that make it possible for ICT to successfully service such a broad range of industry segments.

1.2 Big Mean World of Embedded Software

Over the years, by doing and analysing, we have developed a view about what we refer to as the 'Big Mean World of Embedded Software'. We realize that our view on embedded software is far from complete and for sure not unique. We also realize that compared to other areas of engineering, the engineering of embedded software is a relative young and immature science. But, for ICT, our view has proven to be very instrumental to achieve a better understanding of and to get a better grip on embedded software. Our view can best be expressed by the following statements:

Embedded Software content is still growing. Some five years ago, for example a typical Colour TV embedded software application occupied about 16 Kbyte of executable code. Currently, a typical Colour TV application occupies about 128/256 Kbyte of executable code (a high-end Colour TV contains about 1 Mbyte of executable code). In other words more than a 10-fold increase in embedded software content in five years. We have noticed similar increases in other embedded software applications like video recorders, digital media players (CD, CD-I, DVD), mobile telephones, etc.

Simply trying harder doesn't help. While in the midst of the daily hectic of a full-blown project, a human reaction one often sees is to start working long hours. Indeed working long hours can have a short term positive effect on the progress of the project. But already after a few weeks the people on the project will get tired, quickly irritated and tend to make more errors. Your people will start losing their motivation. Sometimes even their health if stress levels remain too high for a prolonged period of time.

Can't handle increase complexity, do it smarter. The technical challenges that we face in our daily practice are still increasing. A few years ago it was quite normal that a single software designer understood most of the mechanics of a software system. Nowadays you need the combined intelligence and insight of a complete team of software architects and software system engineers to even understand a medium-scale software system. No single one of them understands the complete software system anymore.

Organizational limits are within view, do it smarter. In particular due to the growing embedded software content and the increasing complexity and functionality, large software development teams are required (larger than what we were used to a few years ago). When teams become larger, the 'good old buddy' approach doesn't work anymore. Although team-building sessions help to build stable and cooperative teams, additional (formal) ways of communication and cooperation have to be established within the project team.

Past entrepreneurial stages, we must mature. Forced by the software failures of the past and forced by the increasing impact of software systems on the business performance of many companies, software is more and more becoming an industry segment where the normal rules of doing business apply. Where in the past the 'sky was the limit', nowadays our clients consider metrics like *return on investment* and *payback period* before they decide to subcontract a software project. As a result, not only at our clients but also at

ICT, the software business has matured from 'skunk work' and 'technology nerds' to 'viable projects' and 'professional team members'.

Software development capacity limits are within view. The trend for more software content and larger development teams is pushing the available software development capacity beyond its limit. Even with the application of professional, competent and well-managed development teams, there remains a need for more software development capacity. More capacity within a given time frame leads to a demand for more software professionals. Right now software professionals are already scarce. But when looking at the rate software content is growing and the rate at which software engineers are graduating with a relevant bachelor or master degree, the situation in the near future will very likely get worse.

Understand the Push/Pull situation. There exists a push/pull situation within the software industry. The force that appears to push the software industry to higher levels of achievement and competence is the ongoing grow in *software size* and *complexity*.

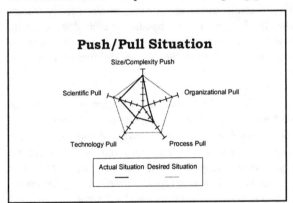

Figure 1 Push/Pull Situation

This size and complexity push within the software industry results in a *science pull*, a *technology pull*, a *process pull* and an *organizational pull*. These profound pulling forces stimulate other parties to move into the direction of the software industry.

The scientific pull stimulates universities and research centres to perform essential scientific studies. For example advanced dedicated programming languages, new validation and verification methods and improved formal specification languages.

The technology pull stimulates progress in hardware technology, like faster computers, larger memory and more network bandwidth, but also encourages the development of optimizing (cross-)compilers, intelligent symbolic debuggers, advanced emulators and even complete integrated software development environments.

The process pull enables the development and application of process models like the Capability Maturity Model [1]. These models used to be software specific, but tend to move in the direction of generic process models (including non-software disciplines).

The organizational pull creates awareness within software organizations about the maturity of the organization. Resulting in activities like organizational (self-)assessments, followed by organization wide improvement plans.

These push/pull forces are shown in figure 1. In this figure the dashed line is the desired situation, i.e. all forces are in balance and optimal overall performance exists. The solid line is a possible actual situation, i.e. balance is absent and the overall performance is below the wanted level. One should always strive for balance between the forces.

2 A Practical Example

2.1 Introduction

To give insight in the Big Mean World of Embedded Software a real life example will be described. The example will show the characteristics of a typical embedded software project. Also it is demonstrated how such a project, by applying the above described view, can be executed in a predictable and successful way.

2.2 Colour TV software for the Americas

Introduction. ICT was asked, in 1995 by a large international consumer electronics company, to develop the embedded software for a Colour TV that was intended for the combined North and South American market (the Americas).

The embedded software, in this particular case referred to as the control system, drives the TV chassis. The TV chassis is the printed circuit board in the TV that contains all involved hardware (e.g. audio processing, video processing, power supply, safety circuitry, picture tube drivers). Besides driving the TV chassis, the embedded software controls the required user functionality including the semi-graphical user interface. To facilitate the manufacturing and service handling of the TV, special functionality was included to streamline these two processes.

Characteristics of the Project. The Colour TV embedded software project had the following characteristics. Some 64 Kbyte of embedded software, to be mask programmed in a *dedicated micro controller* for TV applications, a *multi-team and multi-site* project organisation where project members spoke different languages and lived in different time-zones around the globe, use of assembly language for memory saving reasons, use of a *generic software architecture* for possible future re-use, a *fixed-date* situation for reaching the exact market introduction window of the product and a *development process* that had to be equal or better than level 2 of the Capability Maturity Model as defined by the Software Engineering Institute [1]. Some of these characteristics will be discussed in more detail to give a better understanding of the project.

Dedicated Micro Controller. Since a Colour TV is a typical large quantity consumer system, the product will be sold millionfold. This makes it economically possible to develop and apply a dedicated micro controller. In this real life example, a dedicated Colour TV micro controller was used with the following characteristics:

- 64 Kbyte ROM
- 384 Bytes RAM
- 34 columns by 16 lines On Screen Display, various character sets
- 16 general Input/Output lines
- 2 serial interfaces
- 2 sixteen-bit timers
- 4 four-bit Analog Digital Converter inputs
- 10 seven-bit Pulse Width Modulation outputs

- 13 source 10 vectored interrupt handling
- Integrated Closed Captioning circuitry (analog to simple TeleText)
- 640 by 9 bit display RAM
- 12 MHZ clock

Since this micro controller is dedicated for Colour TV applications, the micro controller architecture supports many typical Colour TV embedded software requirements. This enables an efficient and elegant implementation of the required functionality. The down side of a dedicated micro controller is often the lack of professional software development tools. The micro controller is still 'wet', so one has to cope with all kind of child diseases in the development tools. Since it is quite impossible to find a secondary supplier for the development tools (too dedicated) one has to life with the flaws.

Multi-Team Multi-Site approach. Given the availability of embedded software engineers with relevant experience and given the geographical situation within the project ICT installed, in cooperation with the client, three development teams in three different locations on the globe. The largest software development team was located in the Netherlands (Deventer). The software development team specialized in North-American product requirements was located in the USA and the software development team specialized in South-American product requirements was located in Brazil (Sao Paulo).

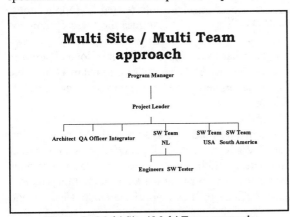

Figure 2 Multi Site / Multi Team approach

The overall coordination of the software project between ICT and the client is done by the Program Manager, who is primarily responsible for assuring the proper level of mutual cooperation and communication, including the handling of the agreements. The daily management of the software teams is done by the Project Leader. All three software development teams had access to the services of the software architect, the software quality assurance officer and the software integrator. The only exception is the software tester. All test activities were performed within the software development team in the Netherlands.

Generic Software Architecture.
In the Colour TV embedded software project we applied a generic software architecture that is fairly common for this kind of applications. In a real-time Colour TV application, a large amount of external events (e.g. a certain key on the remote control has been pressed) and internal events (e.g. timeout of displaying of the TV channel name has expired) have to be processed within strict time limits. So the event scheduling approach is of major importance within the architecture. In this project the event handling is based

418

on a cooperative multitasking approach, which is a compromise between cyclic execution and pre-emptive multitasking. This is flexible, yet easy on RAM usage. The events were handled via a single table, with fixed priorities. Starvation of tasks is avoided via the lowest task in the table. This lowest task resets the starvation timer. If due to real-time circumstances the starvation timer should expire, a single round robin scheduling is performed to be sure that all tasks are handled. If the performance requirements of the Colour TV application are correctly handled within the architectural framework, the occurrence of starvation and thus potential performance hiccups is unlikely to happen.

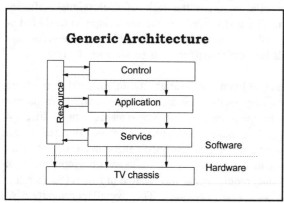

Figure 3 Generic Architecture

Within the architecture, four layers can be distinguished: The *control* layer maintains the proper state of the TV, defines the relationship between events and associated actions; defines the state-dependant availability of end-user functionality. The *application* layer combines the functionalities of several services into macroscopic and interrelated applications; defines the logical functions as can be seen by the end-user. The *service* layer models the bare hardware functionality into logical services (maximal abstraction of the under laying hardware); behaves like a software TV chassis. The *resource* layer provides to all other layers services like: memory management, IO-handling, initialization and scheduling.

Fixed Date. Timely delivery of the software product was very critical for this client, since consumer systems like Colour TV's have very small manufacturing and market introduction windows. Delivery too late would be costly. Due to a delay in revenues because one has to wait for the next manufacturing and/or market introduction window, but also due to a decrease in revenues because the ongoing price erosion decreases the price of the product.

Development Process. To be able to deal with a multi-team and multi-site approach, the use of a generic software architecture and a fixed date delivery of the software product, a serious amount of attention has been given to the software development process, in particular to the following process areas:

Requirements Management. Specification in natural language with a semi-formal layout, use of Structured Analyses for real-time Systems based on Yourdon with events, states, responses and details.

Project Management. Ongoing planning and tracking of the project planning, computer assisted, use of bench marking with other project to check validity of assumptions.

Configuration Management. Identification of items like input documents, source code etc. to be controlled, base lining of items to define common status quo, use of promotion model to handle fluid status of items under development, computer assisted.

Quality Management. Use of a project specific quality assurance workshop at the beginning of the project for all involved project members, a quality assurance officer within the project who supports the project members with all quality related issues and supervision by our project independent corporate quality assurance group.

Process Management. Watch and safeguard the impact of process models like CMM [1] on the development process. Improve the ongoing process step-wise while consolidating achieved improvements.

People Management. Make sure that the individual project members are sufficiently trained in generic and project specific software issues. Be sure to maintain as project management a sufficient level of job satisfaction among the project members, while keeping the 'ego's' under control in a positive way.

Only by carefully nurturing and managing of the above-mentioned process areas, both within the project team but also in the surrounding business environment, an excellent project and thus product results can be achieved.

Results. Besides a satisfied client and a pleased development team, the quantitative measurements done within the project reflect a more objective status quo:

Relative effort overrun (actual effort versus planned effort)   = 15%
> Overall the project required 15% more effort than originally planned. This 15% consists of 9% extra activities not foreseen at the beginning of the project and 6% effort adjustment due to activities that were estimated too low in effort. Compared to a typical software project 15% effort overrun is quite low.

Relative schedule overrun (actual delivery versus planned delivery)   = 0%
> During the overall project, no major software deliverable (e.g. hardware test software, manufacturing test software, final software) was delivered too late compared to the agreed planning.

Detected major errors after release (errors per 1.000 KLOC)   = 100 ppm
> Detected major errors after release of the final software product are expressed in ppm (are errors per 1.000.000 Lines of Code or 1.000 KLOC). So far the final product is about 1 year in production already and has suffered 1 major software error. Since the final product contains some 20.000 lines of source code, this translates to 100 ppm.

Again, by using the lessons learned from the past (see the paragraph 'Big Mean World of Embedded Software'), by applying a well organized multi-team and multi-site approach and by using a proper development process, excellent results for an embedded software project can be achieved.

3 How to Bake a better Cake

How will the scientific and engineering future of embedded software look like? Many people have expressed their visions about it already. I don't have the pretension to argue with their point of view. I leave that up to you. But I sincerely believe in the following rules of 'How to Bake a better Cake' or how to improve our global embedded software development situation:

Use the right mix between Science, Technology, Process and Organization. Never forget that it is all about people, behind each ingredient that is part of the right mix are people, people and people. So investing in your people is of key importance.

Focus on process is okay, but the product counts. For sure one has to invest in the development and application of process models like CMM, SPICE, Bootstrap, TickIT, etc. Remember that in the end the end-customer buys the product and not your process. A process is only instrumental with respect to the product. Overemphasis on process typically leads to poor products.

Focus on science is okay, but the product still counts. Again one has to invest in fundamental and applied science. In the area of (semi-)formal specification understandable by engineers and clients, conversion of specification to executable code, verification and validation, etc. many opportunities exit. But remember that in the end the product still counts for the end-customer and not the science applied in the product.

Improve the 'Science' awareness at the business level. Within the industry there is a tendency to 'do it yourself' without even thinking about a proper 'literature scan' or asking a specialized group within the scientific community. The motive is often the required implementation speed, argumentation like 'we have to be pragmatic' or even a surfacing 'not invented here syndrome'. Besides the normal xenophobic reaction between engineers and scientists, the deeper reason is very likely lack of understanding the benefits of cooperation with the scientific community.

Improve the 'Business' awareness at the science level. For sure the scientific community is looking for what is going on in the software industry. If not for input for own research programs then for financial and logistic backup for joined research programs. In my recent contacts with the scientific community I noticed that still too many applied research is done isolated from the industry (of course fundamental research is beyond the scope of this statement). An Isolated research program leads to shelf-ware and only feeds the bias of the industry towards the scientific community.

It is all about mutual understanding and respect between Science and Business. So are we, the software industry and the scientific community, back to square one? Looking back at the ongoing improvements between the business and science levels, the answer has to be negative. There are many examples of excellent cooperation between the industry and the scientific community. The common denominator in these cases of cooperations is mutual understanding and respect. Mutual understanding leads to finding each other and initiating a joined research program. Mutual respect makes it possible to have trust in each others contribution and keeping the joined research program on track.

With the insight given in embedded software development, by means of a real life Colour TV example, the scientific community should have a better understanding of the needs of the software industry. On the other hand, the software industry should find it easier to make the step towards the scientific community. Personally I realise that there is more needed than just reading an article to understand embedded software development, both from the industry and scientific point of view. I also think that my views on this subject are for from complete and perfect. Since I consider this subject to be of great importance, the reader is invited to express their personal point of view to me since I always try to keep my mind open.

References

1. Capability Maturity Model, Carnegie Mellon University, Pittsburgh Pennsylvania, USA.

Author Index

Springer
and the
environment

At Springer we firmly believe that an international science publisher has a special obligation to the environment, and our corporate policies consistently reflect this conviction.
We also expect our business partners – paper mills, printers, packaging manufacturers, etc. – to commit themselves to using materials and production processes that do not harm the environment. The paper in this book is made from low- or no-chlorine pulp and is acid free, in conformance with international standards for paper permanency.

Springer

Lecture Notes in Computer Science

For information about Vols. 1–1439

please contact your bookseller or Springer-Verlag